MONEY-WISE

Richard J. Stillman

MONEY-WISE

The Prentice-Hall Book of Personal Money Management

PRENTICE-HALL, INC. □ *Englewood Cliffs, New Jersey*

For my family

Darlene Ellen • Richard Joseph, II • Kathleen McKinley • Thomas Slater • Ellen Darlene • Helen Fisher • Roy Fisher • Grace Joseph • Philip Joseph •

Material in Chapters 12, 13, 14, 15 and 16 has been reprinted by permission of Chilton Book Company from *Do-It-Yourself Contracting to Build Your Own Home: A Managerial Approach* by Richard J. Stillman, © 1974.

Moneywise: The Prentice-Hall Book of Personal Money Management
by Richard J. Stillman

Prentice-Hall International, Inc., London
Prentice-Hall of Australia, Pty. Ltd., Sydney
Prentice-Hall of Canada, Ltd., Toronto
Prentice-Hall of India Private Ltd., New Delhi
Prentice-Hall of Japan, Inc., Tokyo
Prentice-Hall of Southeast Asia Pte. Ltd., Singapore
Whitehall Books Limited, Wellington, New Zealand
10 9 8 7 6 5 4 3 2 1

Library of Congress Cataloging in Publication Data
Stillman, Richard Joseph, Date
Moneywise.

Includes bibliographies and index.
1. Finance, Personal.   2. Consumer education.
I. Title.
HG179.S8417   332'.024   77-25493
ISBN 0-13-600734-1

Preface

During my twenty-eight years of teaching, writing and research in the field of money management, I have often been called upon to help individuals in dire financial straits. Recently I met with a couple who were over $79,000 in debt to a total of nineteen different firms. The husband, a physician, had had no training in financial management and his well-established medical practice made it all too easy to borrow funds. Although his salary approximated $85,000 a year, his annual expenses had exceeded his income over the last five years.

In contrast to such cases, I have talked with people who have accumulated several million dollars. Their secret? An analysis of the financially successful almost inevitably reveals a sound money-management program with well-planned goals. After years of observing the successful and those less so, I am convinced that it is relatively easy to establish a personal finance plan that helps eliminate money worries and frees one to devote more time to family, work and the good life that abounds in the United States. My objective in writing this book is to provide the reader with the information that will enable him or her to achieve this goal.

Moneywise has its roots in my writings on this subject over more than two decades. In 1968 I developed a total approach to personal finance and portrayed this concept in two models, which I further tested and developed in my management and finance classes for four years. The outgrowth of this research resulted in the publication of _Guide to Personal Finance_ (1972), written primarily for the college-textbook market. This book depicted the reader as a business manager, with the models highlighting this idea. The two editions of _Guide_ (1972 and 1975) went into ten printings and were adopted by over two hundred colleges in forty-five states.

Moneywise is essentially an adaptation of _Guide_ meant for the general reader. It was written in order to make the views contained in my textbook available to a wider audience. The field of personal finance is fast changing and the material in this book is three years newer than that in my current text. In addition to new and revised material, my two models have been modified to highlight the interrelationship of all aspects of personal finance. A comprehension of this interrelationship can help you become a better money manager and achieve your financial goal.

During the four years spent in researching and writing _Moneywise_, I became increasingly aware of the extent to which money management is linked to virtually every phase of living—and dying. I found the size and scope of my project increasing with each passing day until I had compiled a veritable encyclopedia of money management whose twenty-eight chapters cover topics ranging from budgeting, taxes, food, clothing, borrowing and major appliances to investing wisely in bonds, stocks, hobbies and mutual funds, and, finally, to retirement and estate planning.

My basic program for successful money managment is twofold: the *careful consideration of all legitimate sources of investing* in order to arrive at the best program for you and your family, and the *establishment of a sound spending program*. After all, at least 90 percent of the average budget consists of funds that are utilized to buy goods and services, with 10 percent or less going to savings.[1] Therefore, expenditures on such items as cars, health care, housing rentals and insurance are studied here with the same attention that is given to various investment sources.

The necessity for effective money management is greater than ever today due to the eroding effects of inflation and the energy crisis. As William Simon said on national television during his term as Federal Energy Administrator, "We must learn to change our life-style." He went on to point out that the energy shortage facing the United States will have an impact on the lives of all Americans in the coming decade. Furthermore, President Carter recently informed the nation that the energy shortage "is the great challenge that our country will face during our lifetime." We have already felt that shortage in numerous areas that affect our pocketbooks. A look at our utility bills is sufficient indication of the sharp rise in gas and heating-oil prices since 1973. Housing has priced itself out of reach for some people. Mortgage money is expensive and often difficult to obtain. Food, clothing and medical costs continue to climb. Social Security deductions for workers have been increased. Tax loopholes have been tightened. Industry layoffs in some areas have increased unemployment.

In addition to problems relating to the energy shortage, we find ourselves confronted with inflation. The recent marked loss in the purchasing power of the dollar is an inevitable corollary of the rapid rise in the Consumer Price Index. This in turn adds to the terrible beating being suffered by those whose money is tied up in low-paying, fixed-income investments. My text both questions the old investment formulas and suggests new means by which to keep pace with our fast-changing society, offering the latest available information in the vital areas of budgeting, consumer spending, investing, housing, insurance, taxes, retirement and estate planning.

Moneywise is designed as both a quick reference source for immediate information on a specific topic and a tool for those who wish to establish a sound "lifetime" money-management program. Chapter 1 explains my concept of money management and each succeeding chapter examines a specific aspect of

---

[1]This figure of less than 10 percent assumes that housing is an expense as a result of renting just as during the early years of a heavily mortgaged home, the majority of each monthly payment goes to meeting interest costs.

personal finance, pointing out how it fits into a complete money-management plan. In this manner, every aspect of personal finance is given appropriate consideration. I hope that the reader will make frequent reference to my personal-finance charts (Chapter 1, Figures 1-1 and 1-2), which present my total money-management approach in graphic form. Figure 1-1 is a diagrammatical overview of my concept broken down into its five major components: objective, personal-finance areas, resources or educational tools, functions and key. Figure 1-2 lists the seven major areas of personal finance[2] and the twenty-eight topics covered in this book. The Appendix also includes a list of financial periodicals and services, and a glossary of financial terms.

Through proper money management, you should achieve financial health at an early date. Then you can concentrate on building up an investment program containing cash reserves, bonds, stocks and perhaps such elements as real estate, profitable hobbies and commodities. Concurrently you can satisfy your insurance and housing requirements, and over the years attempt to minimize tax payments in accordance with existing state and federal laws.

From the start, you will be keeping orderly financial records that will help to guide you down the road to long-range financial health (effective record keeping will be discussed in Chapter 2). These computations will assess your yearly net worth as well as the value of your estate—and will prove invaluable in retirement and estate planning.

The closer one looks, the clearer it becomes that effective money-management principles are essential to monetary health in every area of personal finance. I therefore trust that you will find this book a profitable reading experience. I look forward to receiving any suggestions you might have for improving future editions and promise to answer your letters within a reasonable time.

---

[2]The Achievement of Financial Health; Major Expenditures; Housing; Insurance and Social Security; Fixed-Income Investments; Growth Investments; Retirement and Estate Planning.

Contents

HOW TO ACHIEVE FINANCIAL HEALTH

This opening section of *Moneywise* points out the steps necessary for the achievement and maintenance of financial health, a topic of vital importance to us all. Chapter 1 presents a scientific approach to the establishment of a successful personal financial program, portraying the reader as a business manager responsible for all his financial affairs. It goes on to chart the parameters of the field of personal finance, stressing the inter-relationship of the various areas of money management. For easy reference, all of the components and areas that comprise the field of personal finance are summarized in two models, Figures 1-1 and 1-2, featured in Chapter 1.

Chapter 2 emphasizes the importance of a good budgeting system and how to design one. Chapter 3 discusses the merits of consumer-protection agencies and how they may help you. Chapter 4 cautions the reader to use consumer credit wisely, and the fifth and final chapter in Part One concludes our discussion of credit by urging the reader to "Get out of debt and stay out," citing three exceptions to the rule.

1
SUCCESSFUL MONEY MANAGEMENT IN AN ERA OF INFLATION & ENERGY SHORTAGE

What is money management? In my view, it is the development and implementation of a sound personal-finance program tailored to meet your particular objectives. Achievement of these objectives requires an understanding of *all* investment sources and their interrelationship. It also calls for knowledge of a sound spending program, since 90 percent or more of today's average budget goes toward the purchase of goods and services.

The knowledge needed for effective financial planning can best be acquired by utilizing a management approach. The old approaches to personal finance are clearly obsolete in view of the current dynamic changes in our society—social, political, military, economic and technological. We need only look at the negative effects of inflation and the energy crunch on our hard-earned dollars to see how times have changed.

THE IMPACT OF INFLATION

During the depression thirties, a prominent advertisement spoke of "How to Retire on $100 a Month." In the intervening years, this sum increased to $200, $300, and now $800 per month. What might it be in the year 2000?

It is obvious that inflation is eroding the value of the dollar, so that each year it takes more to buy the same items. At this writing, the erosion amounts to over 7 percent a year. People who placed the bulk of their savings in insurance annuities during the period 1930–77 found that their dollars had shrunk in value as much as 75 percent. And it does little good today to invest the majority of your earnings in a savings institution at 5 percent, because when taxes are taken into consideration on top of the current percent erosion, you stand to lose significant sums yearly. Although rampant inflation is being curbed, we face a continued long-term erosion in the dollar.

The marked loss in the purchasing power of the dollar is apparent from a look at the Consumer Price Index (CPI) for the period 1951–77 (Table 1-1). This monthly index, prepared by the Department of Labor, can be helpful in keeping track of inflation. The CPI "is a statistical measure of change, overtime, in the prices of goods and services in major expenditure groups—such as food, housing, apparel, transportation, and health and recreation—typically purchased by urban consumers."[1] Each of the five major groups shall be examined in detail in the course of this book with emphasis on how to get the most from every dollar spent in these areas.

---

[1]U.S. Department of Labor. *The Consumer Price Index*. Revised 1978, p. 1. The CPI was revised effective with the January 1978 index. Reason: to reflect substantial changes in what Americans buy and the way they live. The Bureau of Labor Statistics (BLS), Department of Labor, now publishes 1) a revised CPI for Urban Wage Earners and Clerical Workers, and 2) a new CPI for All Urban Consumers.

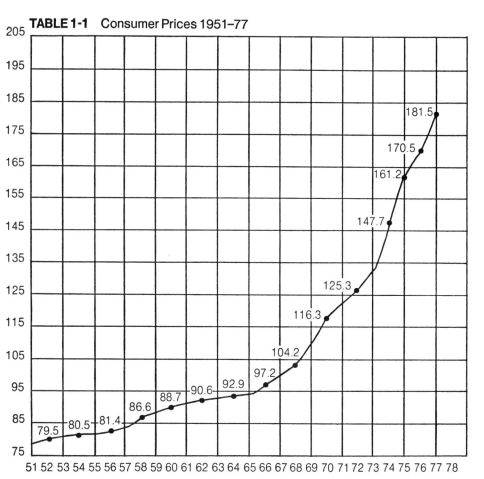

TABLE 1-1   Consumer Prices 1951–77

Consumer prices for 1977 rose to 181.5 percent of the 1967 average. Note the sharp rise since 1967 in contrast to earlier years. From 1951 to 1967, the CPI rose 22.2 percent. But between 1967 and 1977 it rose 81.5 percent. This recent sharp climb is apparent from a look at Table 1-1. The yearly CPI used in this chart is based upon the average for each year and not the year-end CPI.

Source: *Monthly Labor Review,* U.S. Department of Labor, Bureau of Statistics.

Consumer prices for 1977 rose to 181.5 percent of the 1967 average. The 1977 CPI was 6.5 percent higher than in 1976. Three years earlier the rise was 11 percent—the largest annual increase in twenty-nine years. A high of 14.4 percent occurred shortly after World War II. The first months of 1978 found a substantial consumer price increase. This was apparent from the fact that the CPI went up at an annual rate of nearly ten percent.

During World War II, many people bought twenty-five-year U.S. Treasury bonds at 2½ percent interest per annum. Due to inflation, these bond holders took a terrible beating in terms of low interest received over the years and, if the bonds were sold prior to maturity, often suffered considerable loss of principal. Yet, in terms of so-called safety, Treasury bonds had been given the highest rating.

5

THE ENERGY SHORTAGE

The energy shortage has already taken its toll on our tempers and pocketbooks. We can all remember the rising cost and frustration involved in obtaining gas in 1974, when the Arabs reduced their supplies and increased prices fourfold. The result has been a change in our transportation habits. Consumers have turned to smaller cars that provide better mileage. Manufacturers, too, have begun to look at means of increasing mileage, as well as at alternative forms of power such as electricity, diesel and steam. The U.S. Government reduced the speed limit to 55 mph and increased its efforts to improve mass transportation, while encouraging citizens to form driver pools and make greater use of presently available public transportation. It is also providing the public with helpful information in the conservation field. An example of this trend is the Environmental Protection Agency's report on gas mileage for a variety of cars.

Inflation and the energy shortage are two primary reasons for questioning old standards. We clearly need new guidelines to help us keep pace with our fast-changing society, and providing them is one of the most important functions of this book. It is essential to remember, for example, that most of your money should be placed where it has the potential to increase at a faster rate than the loss in the purchasing power of the dollar. This means investing a good share of your funds in areas in which your principal has a chance to grow—areas such as subcontracting your own home, investing in stocks, land and housing and taking up a profitable hobby. To acquire adequate funds for this purpose, it is wise to use successful money-management concepts.

Successful money management requires a certain amount of work. There is no magic formula for turning your income into a sizable nest egg while you lie in a hammock. Of course, there is always the element of luck—but it pays to court the lady.

PERSONAL-FINANCE MODELS AS MANAGEMENT TOOLS[2]

Familiarity with the personal-finance model shown in Figure 1-1 is essential to an understanding of my approach to money management. Visualize yourself as a manager responsible for all your personal financial affairs. As your own

---

[2]Personal-finance models, as defined here, are schematic diagrams portraying factors to consider in arriving at sound decisions for managing your money.

Figure 1-1 A graphic overview of the five major components of personal finance from a managerial perspective.

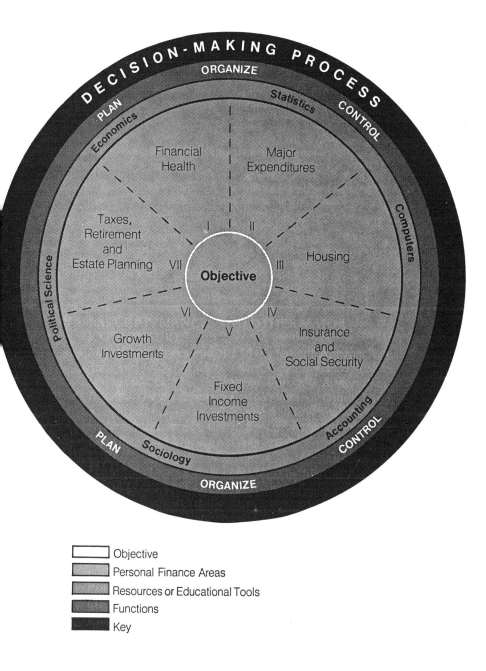

Objective

Personal Finance Areas

Resources or Educational Tools

Functions

Key

money manager, you must consider the five major components (rings) of the model: objective, personal-finance areas, resources or educational tools, functions to be performed, and the decision-making process. Let us examine each of these areas more closely.

ESTABLISHING OBJECTIVES

Only you can determine your personal-finance goal. Perhaps it is to become a millionaire and enjoy good living in the process. This has been a popular American dream. Table 1-2 indicates how time can work to the advantage of the young in achieving this goal. It is possible, however, to plug into the program at any age and improve your financial position.

Let us assume that you have entered the work force at age twenty-two and would like to work until age sixty-five. Your financial objective is to have a

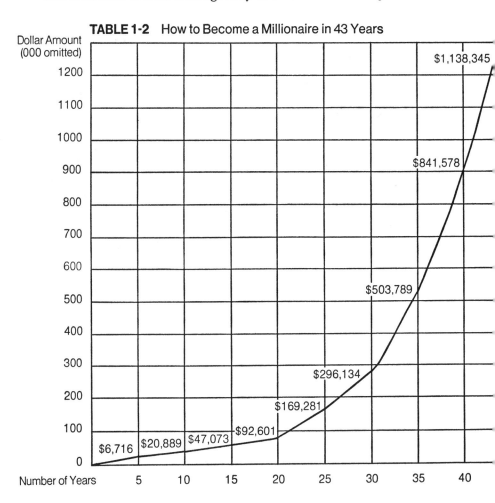

TABLE 1-2 How to Become a Millionaire in 43 Years

nest egg of over $1 million. How would you go about accumulating that amount? One approach would be to invest the following sums at a return of 10 percent compounded annually:

TABLE 1-3 Investment Program

Years	Dollars Invested Each Year*	Cumulative Dollars Invested Each 5-Year Period †
1–5	$1000	$ 5,000
6–10	1500	7,500
11–15	2000	10,000
16–20	2500	12,500
21–25	3000	15,000
26–30	3500	17,500
31–35	4000	20,000
36–40	4500	22,500
41–43	5000	15,000
	Grand Total	$125,000

*It is assumed that all dividends and interest are reinvested and payment of income taxes is made from other earnings.
† Only three years included in the 41–43 period in this program.

In this concept you would set aside $1,000 in each of the first five years. This amount would be increased by $500 in each succeeding five-year increment. Thus, in the second five years (6–10) you would put aside $1,500 annually, and in the final years (41–43) you would be setting aside $5,000 annually.

The assumption in this program is that the higher your salary through the years, the more you will save. Another assumption is that you can obtain a 10 percent annual return. The *super* magic of 10 percent compounded interest, increasing savings and the importance of time in obtaining a sizable retirement nest egg of over $1 million is portrayed in this table.

Rather than making a sizable fortune, you may wish to set a modest financial goal and devote your life to public service. Perhaps you desire only enough savings to educate your children and leave a charitable contribution behind you. Whatever your goal might be, it is essential to determine your objective and decide how best to achieve it. Otherwise, you may spend much unnecessary time on your personal money problems.

Your objective should provide answers to the questions of what, when, where, how and why. If your goal, for example, is to become a millionaire, you might state your prime objective as follows: "I want to become a millionaire, by age sixty-five, through the establishment of my own financial services company in Chicago and eventually leave my money to aid research in mental health." Establishing a primary objective also necessitates the development of subobjectives, or intermediate goals. One subobjective might be "to build a residence in Morgan Park, utilizing subcontractors and completing the project

Figure 1-2 A schematic presentation of the seven major areas of personal finance.

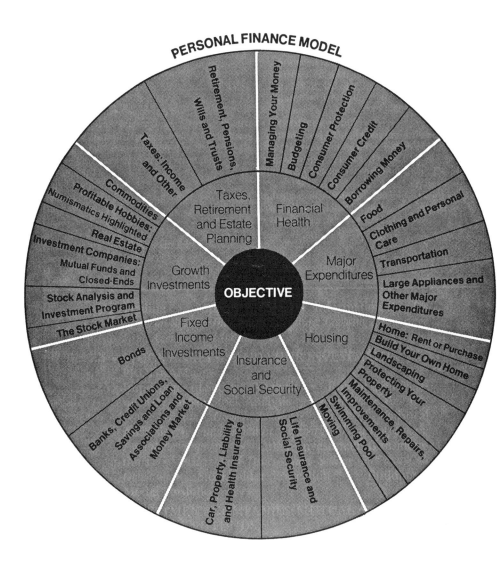

within four months at a 25 percent savings in total cost." Intermediate goals will be discussed further in Chapter 2.

PERSONAL-FINANCE AREAS

Once your personal-finance goal is established, it is necessary to determine what areas of endeavor are available to help you achieve it. The twenty-eight presented in this book (see Figure 1-2) are classified into seven major groups. Each of these major areas and their components are discussed at length in the text in an attempt both to shed light on the nature of personal finance and to show you how you can operate within these categories to your best monetary advantage.

Achieving Financial Health

As shown in Figure 1-2, one deals with establishing a program for achieving *financial health* (Chapters 1–5). The big question is always, "How do I begin?" As a start, you must find out where you stand today and prepare a long-range projection for tomorrow. If you are in debt, you need to determine the amount and how to pay it off. Remember, too, that financial health requires the effective utilization of available resources, such as credit purchases, interest costs, credit cards, quality of merchandise and consumer protection. Once you have your house in order, it is easier to fulfill your other needs.

The tragedy of financial illness is highlighted in Dr. David Caplovitz's book *The Poor Pay More*. In the introduction, Esther Peterson, former Special Assistant to the President for Consumer Affairs, states:

> The dilemma of the low-income family is stated clearly and succinctly: Their need to possess major durable items is frustrated by a lack of cash and information that the wise shopper must have in our technological society. But, curiously, the poor have a marketable item—their own untenable credit position, which too often makes them good business for the salesman who sells a television set or washing machine at inflated prices and on inflated credit terms.[3]

Major Expenditures

Spending your money wisely is essential to the achievement of financial health. Chapters 6–9 therefore feature information on cars, food, clothing, personal care, large appliances and other major expenditures—all subdivisions of Group Two.

[3]David Caplovitz, *The Poor Pay More*. New York: The Macmillan Company, 1967, p. vii.

Housing

That place of your own is important; thus, Group Three concerns *housing* (Chapters 10–16). What type of dwelling appeals to you—a mobile home, an apartment or a house? Or perhaps you are considering building a home of your own. Whatever the case may be, knowledge of construction techniques can help you tackle a new home with greater confidence. The chapters in Group Three also examine the financial aspects of maintenance and repairs, landscaping, swimming pools, protecting your property and moving.

Insurance and Fixed Investments

Group Four of Figure 1-2 relates to insurance. Chapters 17–18 present a comprehensive insurance program that gives consideration to death insurance, Social Security, pensions and annuities, as well as car, theft, health and other coverage. Group Five (Chapters 19–20) is the fixed-investment area. This includes cash reserves, the money market, notes and bonds.

Growth Investments and Ultimate Planning

Group Six, the area of growth investments (Chapters 21–26), includes information on the stock market, investment companies, real estate, profitable hobbies and commodities. Finally, Group Seven is comprised of taxes, retirement and estate planning (Chapters 27–28).

RESOURCES OR EDUCATIONAL TOOLS

Once you have established your objective and listed your personal-finance topics, it is time to turn to the third ring shown in Figure 1-1. The field of personal finance draws heavily upon your educational experience. The turbulence of today's world, with the promise of more upheavals to come, makes an understanding of political and social ramifications a helpful tool in arriving at financial decisions. Likewise, accounting and statistical skills can facilitate the analysis of various investment media and the preparation of that yearly income-tax return.

In terms of resources available to the money manager, the ever-increasing role of computers should be stressed. These mechanisms permit the analysis of a far greater amount of statistical data than would otherwise have been possible, because of their speed and accuracy. You may find a low-cost minicomputer helpful in implementing your own financial program in tomorrow's world. Time is money, and the less time you need to devote to personal finance, the more you will have available for other activities. The feasibility of home computers was recently presented in an article on the evolution of microscopic electronic circuits. This "miniaturization," coupled with "large-scale integration" (LSI), will permit the development of increasingly accessible supercomputers and pocket-sized calculators. The writer states, "Within a few years [miniaturization] may make possible such products as an inexpensive home computer to pay the bills and help with the children's homework, trouble-free mechanisms on dish and clothes washers, flat television sets, and telephones with built-in memories."[4]

An example of how various educational tools can be used to your advantage is provided by the following message distributed by the manager of a successful mutual fund to its shareholders. It clearly takes a practiced money manager to interpret this document correctly:

> The early months of 1977 have been an unsettling period for investors. Worries about the economy have run the gamut from the fear of renewed recession on the one hand to the fear of runaway boom and escalating inflation on the other. Opinions as to the consequences of the severe winter freeze which engulfed much of the country are an indication of these divergent points of view. One school of thought believes the cold weather will have long-lasting, depressing impact on consumer confidence and will materially retard consumer and business spending. Others contend that higher food and energy prices arising from the combined impact of the freeze and Western drought will lead to a rapid reacceleration of inflation.
>
> The probable outcome is neither of these extremes. The economy is already rebounding at a fairly healthy pace, so the current quarter should be a strong one in terms of real economic growth. At the same time, rising food and fuel prices will mean somewhat higher inflation than would have been the case in the absence of adverse weather but should not lead to an inflationary blowoff. In fact, the inflation rate by the end of the year is likely to be significantly lower than now.
>
> Opinions are likewise mixed on the Carter Administration's proposed stimulus program. Some argue that it is unnecessary, given the clear evidence of renewed economic activity, and will only serve to reignite inflation. Others consider the package inadequate and consequently advocate even greater stimulation (which would also be inflationary). Congress, although it is altering the overall shape of the Administration's program, is not increasing the size to any measurable extent. Hence, the final outcome will probably be legislation which neither helps nor harms the economy in any meaningful way.
>
> Given this array of crosscurrents and uncertainties, it is understandable that the securities markets have been declining since the beginning of the year. Although some of the weakness is undoubtedly a

[4]David Brand, "Little Giants," *The Wall Street Journal,* June 22, 1970, p. 1.

reaction to the exuberance that prevailed in late 1976, the more fundamental reason relates to changed perceptions on the outlook for inflation and economic growth.

Therefore, some perspective is appropriate. It is possible to construct a negative economic forecast, but to do so entails overlooking many of the positive elements at work. The financial condition of the corporate sector has improved significantly in the past two years. Corporate earnings and dividends are continuing to grow at above-average rates. Finally, and most importantly, the caution of consumers and businessmen alike and the conspicuous absence of economic and financial excesses auger well for a continued moderation of inflation and a sustained economic advance.

Reflecting the diverse trends at work in the securities markets, the net asset value of your Fund declined 8.7% from $13.96 per share on December 31, 1976, to $12.75 per share on March 31, 1977. More detailed long-term figures are provided under "Investment Performance."

On April 20, 1977, the Board of Directors of your Fund declared a dividend of $0.11 per share from the first quarter's net investment income which compares with $0.10 per share for the first quarter of 1976.

Transactions in the fixed-income portion of your Fund's portfolio during the first quarter were designed to maintain high quality standards and good income levels while holding the average maturity within the 10–15 year range. Activity in the common stock section resulted in an increase in your Fund's exposure to the consumer durable and aerospace sectors, but decreased participation in the computer and industrial machinery industries. At the close of the quarter your Fund remained invested in a portfolio of fixed-income securities and common stocks offering a combination of attractive current income and opportunities for capital appreciation.[5]

FUNCTIONS

Managing your personal finances effectively requires the performance of functions comparable to those in the managing of any other activity, be it a small business, a school or a large government agency. As presented in Figure 1-1 (ring four), the three major functions are 1) planning your actions, 2) implementing your plan and 3) checking (controlling) what you have done. These steps are essential to successful money management in the areas discussed in this book and we will refer to them constantly. In Chapter 11, for example, where we discuss building your own home, a project that can save you a bundle of money, the importance of using a budget to serve both as a

[5]Message from Robert B. Kittredge, president of Loomis-Sayles, to shareholders, dated April 26, 1977.

planning document and as a means of control to determine if the actual expenditures come within the planned estimate will be stressed. In Chapter 2, we will see how the three managerial functions are utilized along the road to financial health.

DECISION-MAKING PROCESS

The final ring portrayed in Figure 1-1 represents the decision-making process.[6] This is the key to successful money management. In arriving at your major personal-finance decisions, keep these questions in mind:

1. What is your objective?
2. Do you have the necessary facts to make a sound decision?
3. What are the alternatives?
4. Have you chosen the most profitable alternative?

The personal-finance model can assist you in arriving at your decision. Assume, for example, that your objective is to buy the cheapest form of transportation—a reliable vehicle for travel to and from your job. You should give appropriate attention to prepurchase planning including such considerations as costs, service, condition, compact or standard, foreign or domestic, where to buy, testing and impact of the energy crisis. This planning effort will require the use of certain educational tools—thoughtful weighing of economic factors, compiling of statistical data and basic accounting. The end result should be the selection of adequate transportation at a fair price. (See Chapter 8 for a more detailed discussion of car buying.)

General Guidelines in Decision Making

The following guidelines may help you arrive at personal-finance decisions. They will be emphasized throughout the book:

1. It helps to be in good physical and mental condition / Taking care of yourself permits better management and greater enjoyment from the monetary rewards you will achieve. Furthermore, human parts are difficult to replace. There are many fine organizations that provide the opportunity to stay in shape. The YM/YWCA, for example, has splendid facilities at very reasonable prices. *This could be your soundest investment.* I find that jogging at the Y is a great way to stay in shape. It also permits exchanging views with a lot of interesting people. "Jog talk" makes a mile or two pass all too rapidly.

---

[6]For further information on the decision-making process, consult in Jerome E. Schnee, E. Kirby Warren, and Harold Lazarus, *The Progress of Management,* Third Edition (Englewood Cliffs, N.J.: Prentice-Hall, Inc., 1977), Part Three, "Planning Elements of Decision Making," and Part Four, "Planning Decision Making in an Enterprise."

2. Time is a valuable commodity; use it to your advantage! / A management approach to personal finance also minimizes time spent on money matters.

3. Be flexible and imaginative / Key your financial program to the times. Do not sacrifice vision and bold decisions for the rigidity often characteristic of an "organization man." The energy crisis and inflation necessitate a dynamic new approach to money management. For example, President Ford pointed out the importance of making "economizing fashionable. Shop wisely, look for bargains, . . . recycle scrap materials, and organize citizens' groups to collect cans, glass, and newspaper."[7] This innovative and flexible approach will be important in car buying during the years ahead. We can look forward to sizable gas savings in future models and the possibility of a major breakthrough in the development of electrical or diesel-powered vehicles. Therefore, the astute buyer must be alert to change and ready to modify his car requirements. This could include adjustments in his ideas concerning the number of vehicles needed for the family as well as about size, design, type and the amount to be invested in automobile purchase. When investing in a car, both initial cost and maintenance expense should be considered.

4. Develop a long-term, flexible plan, then check and implement it regularly to keep it workable / Have a cradle-to-grave approach with adequate provisions for after your departure. Chapter 2 will discuss how to go about long-range planning.

5. Make your personal-finance program a family affair / Both husband and wife should be thoroughly familiar with all its details and children should be brought into such a program at an early age. Participation could begin through sharing a profitable hobby (see Chapter 25). A coin collection, for example, can be a delightful family affair. Likewise, all family members can cooperate in conservative measures such as turning off unnecessary lights! A review of the monthly budget can also be a rewarding family project.

6. Go first class / If the higher-priced item is of better quality, it will cost you less in the long run and give greater satisfaction. Good-quality shoes, for instance, may cost 50 percent more than a poorly constructed pair but could last more than twice as long and will look and feel better.

7. Make it a general practice to get out of debt and stay out / Why pay credit charges of 18–42 percent or higher? You can normally earn only 5–15 percent on your money, so why make the other guy rich by paying him such a high return? Freedom from debt should normally be part of your long-term program. The subject of borrowing and credit will be presented in Chapters 4 and 5.

[7]*The New York Times,* October 16, 1974, p. 20.

8. Minimize your costs and maximize your returns / Eliminate the middleman wherever possible. If you can buy through a reputable discount house at 20 to 40 percent off list prices, why not do so? Likewise, you may wish to participate in a successful food cooperative (see Chapter 6) and reduce your grocery expenditures.

9. Deal only with reputable people who have good track records / Patronize only those companies that stand behind their products. This includes the buying and selling of stocks or bonds as well as money spent for various goods and services. Dealing with questionable firms can mean disaster.

10. Keep your money working for you at all times / You worked hard to earn it! Consider how banks employ your money. What would happen to a bank manager who failed to invest his excess funds daily?

11. Place the majority of your funds in growth situations / Growth opportunities may present themselves in strange packages. For example, 9–11 percent bond offerings in 1974 provided both a high yield and capital-gains potential. An individual who bought $10,000 of the 9 percent U.S. Treasury Notes, due in 1980, would receive $900 a year. If he were to sell the issue at this writing, he would have a $450 appreciation. Thus, his $10,000 investment would increase to $10,450 and he would have received a 9 percent return until the sale was made. Gold futures could have been purchased in 1977 for resale a few weeks later at a sizable profit.

12. Develop a profitable hobby / Leisure-time activities can be lucrative as well as fun. You might explore such areas as coins, stamps, antiques, painting and sewing. Again, try to make this a family affair.

13. Capitalize on your experience / This has worked for people like Billie Jean King, Mark Spitz, Bill Russell, Bobby Riggs, John Glenn, Joe Namath and Jim Bouton, who have channeled their know-how into such areas as writing, politics and business. You may not achieve their prominence, but you can make the most of your own special knowledge. As you go through life, there will be ample opportunity to acquire expertise—don't be afraid to try.

14. Maximize your after-tax dollars / If you are in the 40 percent federal-tax bracket, it may be better for you to buy a 6½ percent prime municipal bond in lieu of a comparably rated 10 percent corporate bond. A $1,000 municipal, for example, would provide an annual return of $65, whereas the corporate bond would leave you with only $60 after payment of your federal income tax.

15. Focus on timing / Choosing when to act is an important factor in such areas as grocery-store shopping, buying and selling securities and purchasing a car. For example, food should be bought during weekend specials, cars when sizable discounts are being offered and stocks in periods of recession.

16. Think American! / An understanding of the American way of life is a cornerstone of the personal-finance program. Our democratic environment with its free-enterprise system provides a fertile climate for financial success, and this is the framework within which you will be working. In this era we hear much negative talk about the economy and the future of our country. Yet with all our faults, we have achieved the most successful political, economic, social and military system in the world. It is important that we believe in our country and invest in it.

17. Have faith in yourself / Be willing to work your way to financial success. The American way of life provides the opportunity but *you* must supply the determination. Dr. Christiaan Barnard, the distinguished South African heart surgeon, gave appropriate credit for his success to the following anonymous lines he read as a young man:

IT'S ALL IN THE STATE OF MIND

If you think you are beaten, you are,
If you think you dare not, you don't;
If you like to win, but you think you can't
It's almost a cinch you won't.
If you think you'll lose, you've lost,
For out in the world you find
Success begins with a fellow's will;
It's all in the state of mind.
Full many a race is lost
Ere ever a step is run;
And many a coward fails
Ere ever his work's begun.
Think big and your deeds will grow,
Think small and you'll fall behind,
Think that you can and you will;
It's all in the state of mind.
If you think you're outclassed, you are;
You've got to think high to rise;
You've got to be sure of yourself before
You can ever win a prize.
Life's battles don't always go
To the stronger or faster man,
But sooner or later the man who wins
IS THE FELLOW WHO THINKS HE CAN.

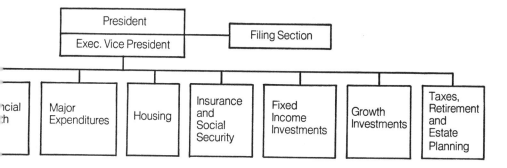

Figure 1-3 A hypothetical organization for managing a personal-finance program.

ORGANIZING YOUR FINANCES

What is the most effective way to manage your financial matters? One approach is to view yourself as your own personal business manager. Figure 1-3 demonstrates this approach in chart form. Let's take a look at the various blocks in the organization, beginning with those at the top. If you are single, there isn't any question of who will be boss. If you are married, you might establish a co-presidency in accordance with the guideline that makes personal finance a family affair. Next you will want to set up a working file system. This can prove invaluable as you face up to the annual income tax demands from your state and the federal government; it can also help avoid unhealthy interest charges on overdue monthly bills. In addition to the leadership and filing sections, the organization chart portrays the seven major areas of personal finance–financial health: major expenditures; insurance and social security; housing; fixed-income investments; growth investments; taxes; retirement and estate planning.

SUGGESTED EQUIPMENT

Three items useful to money managers are typewriters, adding machines and electronic calculators. Typing your letters and other materials can save time and add a professional touch. An adding machine with printed tape can be a real timesaver in budget keeping and the preparation of income taxes. It becomes a necessity as your financial assets become sizable. The pocket-sized electronic calculator is valuable in shopping for food and clothing and has innumerable other uses.

A number of companies manufacture quality calculators. Shop around to find the one best suited to your needs. It is foolish, for example, to spend the extra money for such features as scientific notations or log functions if you or your family do not intend to use them.

A fourth noteworthy aid to successful money management is up-to-the-minute information. I therefore highly recommend that you subscribe to *The Wall Street Journal.* It provides splendid financial and business news as well as an excellent resumé of world affairs. Excerpts of statistical data culled from the *Journal* appear throughout this book.

In addition, I suggest the purchase of *Consumer Reports.* This monthly publication furnishes helpful ratings on a variety of consumer items, including cars, auto insurance, radios, stereo receivers and outboard motors.

2
BUDGETING

In Chapter 1, I explained my approach to the establishment and maintenance of a successful lifetime money-management program. We will now turn to the consideration of a tool essential to the achievement of financial health: the budget process.

Effective budgeting can be of invaluable assistance in getting out of debt—and staying out. I see it as a five-phase process, consisting of:

1. Determining where you stand today (your net worth).
2. Estimating income and expenses for the current year.
3. Developing a long-range program based on your primary objective and intermediate goals.
4. Maintaining records that indicate actual income and expenditures.
5. Comparing your plan with reality and modifying your estimates when appropriate.

This chapter will examine each of these phases in detail, with emphasis on how to set up the best program for your personal needs. We will then go on to examine the resources available to achieve your budget objectives.

WHY BUDGET?

The problem today is not so much how to *make* money as how to manage it, once it is acquired, to serve your needs best. Madison Avenue can have its hands in your pockets before you realize it. Sophisticated marketing techniques make it difficult to say no. And the clever pitches by loan companies make them sound as if they're your best pals:

"We have you in mind."
"Money in minutes."
"Let us eliminate your financial worries by consolidating all your loans."
"We are not a loan company, but a money-management service established to help you."

Thanks to "kindhearted" businesses willing to give you merchandise with nothing down, and loan companies that make it all so simple, there are many people who suddenly find themselves in dire financial straits. Regardless of their income levels, these unfortunates all display the same symptoms—too many bills and too little cash. Their dollars have simply been drained away faster than they could be replenished. One way to cope with such business and financial institutions is to join them—if they are so profitable, after all, it may be desirable to invest money here or even to enter the field yourself. In terms of a sound personal-finance program, however, it is best to remember that despite what the ads may say, instant store credit and "happiness loans" can result in a bucketful of headaches.

Thanks to a logical long-range plan—that is, a carefully devised budget—you can stay out of the red. By keeping out of current debt, you will find that you and your family will have more "goodies" for tomorrow. After all, spending is delayed saving and saving is delayed spending. Saving today means more funds for the future. And if you don't think that companies expect you to save to meet your installments, try skipping a payment!

An article in *The Wall Street Journal* points out the pressures businesses exert to collect even small sums:

> Elvira Pachon's dream of a high-school diploma rapidly became a financial nightmare.
>
> In late 1970, the 26-year-old New Yorker signed up for a $465 high-school equivalency course offered by LaSalle Extension University of Chicago, a Macmillan, Inc. subsidiary that, with 100,000 students around the world, is one of the largest correspondence schools in the country. Because of work and family commitments, Mrs. Pachon fell behind in her studies, but the company didn't fall behind in its bills. After more than two years, Mrs. Pachon had finished only two of the 16 subjects in the course but had paid more than $400.
>
> Financially strapped, Mrs. Pachon finally told the school she was dropping out and wouldn't pay the last $48.50 she owed. Then, she says, things got rough: "I got notes from the school. Then I started getting calls from the collection agency. They told me I would be sued and said they would find out where I worked and garnishee my paycheck. It got worse and worse and they got nastier and nastier."[1]

SAVINGS

The incentive for saving a portion of one's earnings for tomorrow instead of spending it all (and more) today springs from the desire to achieve certain goals. You might want a nest egg to use for periodic ski vacations, a second car, the purchase of a boat, the meeting of emergencies, an education for the children and/or ownership of a home.

Or perhaps you want to provide funds with which to augment your retirement income. Consider those senior citizens trying to live off meager Social Security benefits. It's tough going, and you can't count on a utopian government to provide a cornucopia for those twilight years.

In addition, money is power; throughout life you can use it to help attain

[1]Rich Jaroslovsky. "Live and Learn." *The Wall Street Journal,* December 31, 1974, p. 1.

your ends—political, social or otherwise. There may also be the satisfaction of giving or leaving a sizable sum for what you deem to be a worthy cause.

Finally, peace of mind is difficult to come by these days. Freedom from financial worry saves a lot of headaches. As one of my colleagues put it: "When I got out of debt, it was great to be able to tell my ex-creditors where to go!"

Only you can be the judge of your personal-finance needs. In determining what should be set aside to meet your requirements, it is important to keep in mind that the long-term trend has been inflationary; therefore, ample amounts should be projected to meet each need. For example, in the last twenty years, the cost of attending college has tripled, and in a number of areas, housing has quadrupled in value. Most of us can expect a retirement income after having worked for a corporation or government agency, and Social Security payments should follow soon behind. However, those with such commitments as children requiring a college education after their parents' retirement will normally need a substantial amount of additional funds. And, of course, professional and self-employed people will have to set up adequate long-range savings programs. Your retirement program should normally include establishing an Individual Retirement Account (IRA) because of the tax-deductible feature. Both the IRA and the Keogh Plan will be discussed in Chapter 28.

ESTABLISHING YOUR BUDGETING PROGRAM

Let us now examine each of the five phases of a successful budgeting program in detail.

DETERMINING NET WORTH

Acquiring and conserving capital in order to reach your objectives involves saving a percentage of income and using dollars effectively. This is so simple to state and yet so difficult to achieve. In order to save a percentage of what you earn, it is helpful to know what you are worth and what you will receive (income) in relation to expenses for the current year. A good way to begin the budget process is to find out where you stand today (Table 2-1). Fortunately, this process doesn't require a degree in accounting, nor need you try to itemize every minute expenditure, a hopeless waste of time and effort.

It *is* necessary, however, for you to determine what you own (assets) and to estimate their current value. List such items as cash, bonds, furniture, car, value of home and cash value of life insurance. Prices should be based on the current market value of these items should they be converted into dollars. Against these assets, list all the amounts owed (liabilities). These might include

TABLE 2-1 My Worldly Possessions on
December 31, 1977

What I Own:

Cash on hand	$ 100	
Cash in checking account	2,300	
Cash in bank	5,100	
Cash in S & L association	5,100	
U.S. Savings bonds	1,100	
U.S. Treasury note	11,000	
Corporate stocks:		
One hundred shares, ABC Co.	3,400	
One hundred shares, DEF Co.	3,300	
Car	5,500	
Furniture	2,200	
Clothing	1,100	
Home	55,000	
		$95,200
What I Owe:		
Notes payable	$26,000	
Car payments	1,700	
Furniture payments	1,500	
Home mortgage	35,000	
		$64,200
My True Worth		$31,000

installment purchases, funds borrowed from banks and money due on home and car, as well as outstanding obligations to hospital, doctors or dentists. The amount owed is then subtracted from that owned, and the result indicates your dollar ownership (net worth) as of that date.

The terms *assets, liabilities* and *net worth* are common parlance in the accounting field, and a listing of them is known as a balance sheet, or statement of financial condition. Assets minus liabilities equals net worth. Once you know your net worth, you can establish a course of action. In some cases, you may be chagrined to find that you are currently in debt. Conversely, you may be pleasantly surprised to find that you *have* a positive net worth. Table 2-1 indicates that "My" has $95,200 in assets and $64,200 in liabilities, for a net worth of $31,000, on December 31, 1977.

INCOME AND EXPENSES

The second phase of the budget process is to estimate your income and expenses for the year. Table 2-2 points out that "My" will have an income of $31,700 and expenses of $31,000, with only $600 saved, by December 31, 1978.

The preparation of your annual income-and-expense statement requires keeping adequate records. The income portion would include salary

TABLE 2-2 My Estimated Income and Expenses,
January 1–December 31, 1978

Income:		
Earnings (salary)	$31,000	
Interest	600	
Dividends	100	
		$31,700
Expenses:		
Home	$ 6,000	
Food	4,500	
Car	2,800	
Clothing	2,900	
Vacation and recreation	3,200	
Medical	1,700	
Insurance	2,400	
Taxes	7,600	
		$31,100
Savings		$ 600

paid by your employer, plus moonlighting work or additional funds earned by your mate, and other sources of income such as bonds, bank interest and gifts. Against this income, all expenses for the year should be itemized. These should include the repetitive expenses like food and clothing, such budgeted costs as insurance, automobile payments and mortgage, and a myriad of other possible outlays. Subtracting expenses from income gives you the savings or deficit estimated for the one-year period.

It is essential that income exceed expenditures, or it will be impossible to pay up debts or amass funds for investment purposes. If expenses exceed income, husband and wife had better sit down together and determine how expenses can be reduced or income increased. Additional revenue might be brought in by an unemployed spouse going to work or by other family members taking on added employment. If this is not feasible, then certain expenses must be reduced or eliminated in order to improve one's financial condition.

The income and expense statement for the year ahead may be modified in format to reflect what is popularly referred to as the cash-flow statement.[2] Such a report enables you to determine your total cash inflow from such items as salary, dividends, interest, rents and royalties. From this money income, you would deduct items normally taken from your salary by your company. This would include federal, state and local income taxes as well as Social Security. The difference would be money *actually received* by you. From this amount cash payments for fixed and variable expenditures are deducted. These might include monthly payments on a car, loan, insurance premiums, mortgage,

---

[2]A cash-flow statement is a financial report that indicates the number of dollars available (cash inflow) for spending and investing (cash outflow). This statement, in contrast to an income and expense report, would not include depreciation. Reason: depreciation does not require an expenditure of cash.

TABLE 2-3 Annual Cost of an Intermediate Budget
for a 4-Person Family[1] Autumn 1976

AREA	FAMILY CONSUMPTION ⟱ Total Budget[2]	Total Consumption	Food Total	Food at Home	Food Away From Home
URBAN UNITED STATES	16236	12370	3859	3237	622
Metropolitan Areas[11]	16596	12621	3917	3263	654
Nonmetropolitan areas[12]	14625	11254	3598	3121	477
NORTHEAST					
Boston, Mass	19384	14447	4224	3576	648
Buffalo, N.Y.	17175	12892	3958	3299	659
Hartford, Conn.	17238	13610	4194	3494	700
Lancaster, Pa.	15685	11923	3992	3383	609
New York-Northeastern N.J.	18866	13994	4436	3649	787
Philadelphia, Pa.-N.J.	16836	12604	4268	3548	720
Pittsburgh, Pa.	15515	11754	3966	3295	671
Portland, Maine	16633	12964	4184	3601	583
Nonmetropolitan Areas[12]	16040	12226	3903	3393	510
NORTH CENTRAL:					
Cedar Rapids, Iowa	15976	12027	3431	2850	581
Champaign-Urbana, Ill.	16578	12775	3820	3276	544
Chicago, Ill.-Northwestern Ind.	16561	12763	3903	3304	599
Cincinnati, Ohio-Ky.-Ind.	15708	12023	3859	3291	568
Cleveland, Ohio	16412	12730	3893	3206	687
Dayton, Ohio	15101	11687	3795	3236	559
Detroit, Mich.	16514	12502	3756	3236	659
Green Bay, Wis.	16008	11765	3482	2963	519
Indianapolis, Ind.	15911	12301	3767	3191	576
Kansas City, Mo.-Kans.	15628	12000	3798	3211	587
Milwaukee, Wis.	17307	12645	3675	3063	612
Minneapolis-St. Paul, Minn.	16810	12071	3776	3149	627
St. Louis, Mo.-Ill.	15623	12005	3957	3322	635
Wichita, Kans.	15102	11683	3606	3060	546
Nonmetropolitan Areas[12]	14926	11366	3587	3138	449
SOUTH:					
Atlanta, Ga.	14830	11489	3767	3176	591
Austin, Tex.	14209	11279	3427	2860	567
Baltimore, Md.	16195	11962	3720	3046	674
Baton Rouge, La.	14472	11367	3827	3263	564
Dallas, Tex.	14699	11637	3498	2838	660
Durham, N.C.	15525	11673	3650	3098	552
Houston, Tex.	14978	11836	3790	3105	685
Nashville, Tenn.	14821	11731	3593	3046	547
Orlando, Fla.	14378	11398	3479	2896	583
Washington, D.C.-Md.-Va.	16950	12647	3949	3298	651
Nonmetropolitan Areas[12]	13855	10794	3506	3027	479
WEST:					
Bakersfield, Calif.	15004	11547	3571	3019	552
Denver, Colo.	15906	12081	3689	3105	584
Los Angeles-Long Beach, Calif.	16016	12281	3639	2962	677
San Diego, Calif.	15989	12255	3582	2889	693
San Francisco-Oakland, Calif.	17200	13154	3795	3164	681
Seattle-Everett, Wash.	16204	12789	3948	2266	682
Honolulu	19633	14375	4627	3261	666
Nonmetropolitan Areas[12]	14627	11149	3477	3015	462
ANCHORAGE, ALASKA	23071	17070	4614	4001	613

[1]The family consists of an employed husband, age 38, a wife not employed outside the home, an 8-year-old girl, and a 13-year-old boy.
[2]Total budget costs include personal income taxes, social security, other items and total consumption.

AREA	FAMILY CONSUMPTION ⇨ Housing[3]				
		Shelter			House-Furnishing & Operat
	Total	Total[4]	Renter[5]	Homeowner[6]	
URBAN UNITED STATES	3843	2996	1901	3362	847
Metropolitan Areas[11]	3952	3119	1974	3500	833
Nonmetropolitan Areas[12]	3357	2451	1573	2743	906
NORTHEAST:					
Boston, Mass.	5193	4333	2225	5036	860
Buffalo, N.Y.	4042	3155	2058	3520	887
Hartford, Conn.	4401	3583	2140	4064	818
Lancaster, Pa.	3533	2735	1917	3008	798
New York-Northeastern N.J.	4774	3923	2231	4487	851
Philadelphia, Pa.-N.J.	3818	3001	1722	3427	817
Pittsburgh, Pa.	3336	2517	1583	2828	819
Portland, Maine	4023	3149	2046	3517	874
Nonmetropolitan Areas[12]	3979	3175	1766	3644	804
NORTH CENTRAL:					
Cedar Rapids, Iowa	3803	3004	2006	3336	799
Champaign-Urbana, Ill.	4068	3210	2467	3457	858
Chicago, Ill.-Northwestern Ind.	4058	3246	2096	3629	812
Cincinnati, Ohio-Ky.-Ind.	3578	2806	1481	3248	772
Cleveland, Ohio	3966	3119	1670	3602	847
Dayton, Ohio	3349	2509	1566	2823	840
Detroit, Mich.	3991	3217	1751	3706	774
Green Bay, Wis.	3775	2861	1812	3211	914
Indianapolis, Ind.	3675	2872	1791	3232	803
Kansas City, Mo.-Kans.	3459	2617	1683	2928	842
Milwaukee, Wis.	4186	3373	1980	3837	813
Minneapolis-St. Paul., Minn.	3692	2895	1895	3228	797
St. Louis, Mo.-Ill.	3490	2648	1547	3015	842
Wichita, Kans.	3340	2492	1914	2684	848
Nonmetropolitan Areas[12]	3472	2608	1840	2864	864
SOUTH:					
Atlanta, Ga.	3169	2343	1531	2613	826
Austin, Tex.	3118	2270	1506	2524	848
Baltimore, Md.	3578	2628	2141	2790	950
Baton Rouge, La.	3055	2263	1364	2563	792
Dallas, Tex.	3335	2548	1678	2838	787
Durham, N.C.	3468	2649	1905	2897	819
Houston, Tex.	3280	2434	1652	2694	846
Nashville, Tenn.	3474	2609	1584	2950	865
Orlando, Fla.	3368	2522	1821	2756	846
Washington, D.C.-Md.-Va.	4045	3174	2148	3516	871
Nonmetropolitan Areas[12]	3050	2095	1335	2348	955
WEST:					
Bakersfield, Calif.	3299	2490	1824	2712	809
Denver, Colo.	3594	2688	1554	3066	906
Los Angeles-Long Beach, Calif.	3726	2923	2066	3209	803
San Diego, Calif.	3835	3089	1875	3493	746
San Francisco-Oakland, Calif.	4349	3470	2721	3719	879
Seattle-Everett, Wash.	3909	3025	2261	3279	884
Honolulu	4774	3832	2767	4187	942
Nonmetropolitan Areas[12]	3290	2366	1656	2603	924
ANCHORAGE, ALASKA	6459	4940	4251	5169	1519

TABLE 2-3 (Cont.)

[3]Housing includes shelter, housefurnishings and household operations. The higher budget also includ allowance for lodging away from home city.
[4]The average costs of shelter were weighted by the following propositions: Lower budget, 100 perce families living in rented dwellings; intermediate budget, 25 percent for renters, 75 percent for homeov higher budget, 15 percent for renters, 85 percent for homeowners.
[5]Renter costs include average contract rent plus the costs of required amounts of heating fuel, electricity, water, specified equipment, and insurance on household contents.
[6]Homeowner costs include interest and principal payments plus taxes; insurance on house and con water, refuse disposal, heating fuel, gas, electricity, and specified equipment; and home repai maintenance costs.

AREA	FAMILY CONSUMPTION ⇨ Transportation Total	Automobile Owners	Clothing	Personal Care	Medical Care[8]
URBAN UNITED STATES	1403	1474	1141	355	900
Metropolitan Areas[11]	1411	1500	1150	362	929
Nonmetropolitan Areas[12]	1369	1369	1103	328	771
NORTHEAST:					
Boston, Mass.	1715	2059	1167	358	837
Buffalo, N. Y.	1519	1519	1341	358	767
Hartford, Conn.	1559	1559	1190	454	833
Lancaster, Pa.	1347	1347	1157	335	713
New York-Northeastern N.J.	1331	1573	1113	375	995
Philadelphia, Pa.-N.J.	1309	1561	1057	349	914
Pittsburgh, Pa.	1348	1398	1079	347	786
Portland, Maine	1412	1412	1285	326	839
Nonmetropolitan Areas[12]	1436	1436	1083	305	781
NORTH CENTRAL:					
Cedar Rapids, Iowa	1424	1424	1316	373	797
Champaign-Urbana, Ill.	1410	1410	1367	366	884
Chicago, Ill.-Northwestern Ind.	1463	1736	1099	364	968
Cincinnati, Ohio-Ky.-Ind.	1411	1411	1191	313	797
Cleveland, Ohio	1421	1481	1196	431	889
Dayton, Ohio	1352	1352	1152	333	811
Detroit, Mich.	1344	1398	1166	380	971
Green Bay, Wis.	1373	1373	1145	361	739
Indianapolis, Ind.	1524	1524	1220	333	875
Kansas City, Mo.-Kans.	1450	1450	1192	395	828
Milwaukee, Wis.	1387	1387	1286	357	862
Minneapolis-St. Paul, Minn.	1360	1360	1154	375	816
St. Louis, Mo.-Ill.	1467	1533	1092	360	776
Wichita, Kans.	1434	1434	1184	370	859
Nonmetropolitan Areas[12]	1349	1349	1157	337	726
SOUTH:					
Atlanta, Ga.	1338	1338	1138	356	847
Austin, Tex.	1431	1431	1212	347	839
Baltimore, Md.	1347	1402	1146	350	938
Baton Rouge, La.	1345	1345	1118	366	774
Dallas, Tex.	1470	1470	1049	362	1023
Durham, N.C.	1306	1306	1098	367	890
Houston, Tex.	1422	1422	1146	364	986
Nashville, Tenn.	1431	1431	1265	328	766
Orlando, Fla.	1366	1366	1074	319	902
Washington, D.C.-Md.-Va.	1401	1454	1037	353	936
Nonmetropolitan Areas[12]	1357	1357	1067	328	767
WEST:					
Bakersfield, Calif.	1498	1498	995	329	1031
Denver, Colo.	1383	1383	1390	333	836
Los Angeles-Long Beach, Calif.	1469	1529	1125	344	1132
San Diego, Calif.	1453	1453	1126	339	1079
San Francisco-Oakland, Calif.	1475	1539	1213	409	1026
Seattle-Everett, Wash.	1405	1405	1274	390	971
Honolulu	1492	1492	1159	408	960
Nonmetropolitan Areas[12]	1331	1331	1165	338	820
ANCHORAGE, ALASKA	1741	1741	1427	502	1439

[7]The average costs of automobile owners and nonowners in the lower budget were weighted by the following proportions of families: Boston, Chicago, New York and Philadelphia, 50 percent for both automobile owners and nonowners; all other metropolitan areas, 65 percent for automobile owners, 35 percent for nonowners; nonmetropolitan areas, 100 percent for automobile owners. The intermediate budget proportions are: Boston, New York, Chicago and Philadelphia, 80 percent for owners, 20 percent for nonowners; Baltimore, Cleveland, Detroit, Los Angeles, Pittsburgh, San Francisco, St. Louis, and Washington, D.C. with populations of 1.4 million or more in 1960, 95 percent for automobile owners and 5 percent for nonowners; all other areas, 100 percent for automobile owners. The higher budget weight is 100 percent for owners in all areas.
[8]In total medical care, the average costs of medical insurance were weighted by the following proportions: 30 percent for families paying full cost of insurance; 26 percent for families paying half cost; 44 percent for families covered by noncontributory insurance plans (paid by employer).

TABLE 2-3 (Cont.) AREA	Other Family Consumption[9]	Other Items[10]	Social Security & Disability Payments	Personal Income Taxes
URBAN UNITED STATES	869	731	898	2236
Metropolitan Areas[11]	900	740	908	2328
Nonmetropolitan Areas[12]	729	692	852	1828
NORTHEAST:				
Boston, Mass.	953	804	895	3238
Buffalo, N.Y.	907	749	911	2623
Hartford, Conn.	979	774	895	1959
Lancaster, Pa.	846	715	895	2152
New York-Northeastern N.J.	970	788	922	3162
Philadelphia, Pa.-N.J.	889	739	904	2589
Pittsburgh, Pa.	892	709	895	2157
Portland, Maine	896	752	895	2022
Nonmetropolitan Areas[12]	739	726	920	2168
NORTH CENTRAL:				
Cedar Rapids, Iowa	883	719	895	2335
Champaign-Urbana, Ill.	860	745	895	2163
Chicago, Ill.-Northwestern Ind.	908	745	895	2158
Cincinnati, Ohio-Ky.-Ind.	874	719	895	2071
Cleveland, Ohio	934	744	895	2043
Dayton, Ohio	895	707	883	1824
Detroit, Mich.	894	736	895	2381
Green Bay, Wis.	890	710	895	2638
Indianapolis, Ind.	907	729	895	1986
Kansas City, Mo.-Kans.	878	718	895	2015
Milwaukee, Wis.	892	741	895	3026
Minneapolis-St. Paul, Minn.	898	720	895	3124
St. Louis, Mo.-Ill.	863	718	895	2005
Wichita, Kans.	890	707	883	1829
Nonmetropolitan Areas[12]	738	696	868	1996
SOUTH:				
Atlanta, Ga.	874	700	866	1775
Austin, Tex.	905	693	831	1406
Baltimore, Md.	883	717	895	2621
Baton Rouge, La.	882	696	848	1561
Dallas, Tex.	900	705	860	1497
Durham, N.C.	894	707	895	2250
Houston, Tex.	848	712	878	1552
Nashville, Tenn.	874	709	866	1515
Orlando, Fla.	890	697	842	1441
Washington, D.C.-Md.-Va.	926	741	895	2667
Nonmetropolitan Areas[12]	719	676	815	1570
WEST:				
Bakersfield, Calif.	824	702	968	1787
Denver, Colo.	856	721	895	2209
Los Angeles-Long Beach, Calif.	846	728	985	2022
San Diego, Calif.	841	727	985	2022
San Francisco-Oakland, Calif.	887	758	985	2303
Seattle-Everett, Wash.	892	746	895	1774
Honolulu	955	801	895	3562
Nonmetropolitan Areas[12]	728	688	857	1933
ANCHORAGE, ALASKA	888	895	960	4146

[9]Other family consumption includes the average costs for reading, recreation, tobacco products, alcohol beverages, education and miscellaneous expenditures.

[10]Other items include allowances for gifts and contributions, life insurance and occupational expenses.

[11]As defined in 1960–61. For a detailed description of these and previous geographical boundaries, see th 1967 edition of *Standard Metropolitan Statistical Areas,* prepared by the Office of Management an Budget.

[12]Places with population of 2,500 to 50,000.

Source: *News,* U. S. Department of Labor, Bureau of Labor Statistics, Washington, D.C., Aprii 27, 1977.

property taxes, savings, utility bills, school education, food, clothing and medical care. The remainder, spendable income, is money available for buying a variety of goods and services in the next twelve months.

It may also be helpful to look at Table 2-3 in estimating your expenditures.[3] This table lists the dollars allocated yearly by a family of four for food, housing, transportation, clothing, personal care, medical care, other items of family consumption, Social Security and disability payments, and personal income taxes. Table 2-3 also points up the considerable variation in expenses between different locations. The total budget figure for Anchorage, Alaska, is $23,071 in contrast to that for nonmetropolitan areas in the South, amounting to $13,855. On a percentage basis, the amount expended for each budgeted item would be as follows:

TABLE 2-4 Intermediate Budgets for 4-Person Families, Autumn 1976 (Percentage Basis)

	Urban U.S.	Anchorage, Alaska	Nonmetropolitan South
Food	24%	20%	25%
Housing	24	28	22
Transportation	9	8	10
Clothing	7	6	8
Personal care	2	2	2
Medical care	5	6	6
Other family consumption	5	4	5
Other items	4	4	5
Social Security and disability payments	6	4	6
Personal income taxes	14	18	11
Total	100%	100%	100%

Source: *News,* U.S. Department of Labor, Bureau of Labor Statistics, Washington, D.C., April 27, 1977.

In order to chart your monthly progress you must take your annual income and expenditures and break them down into monthly amounts. For example, if $210 of the monthly income is to be spent on food, you must stay within this budget. The same approach can be applied to rental costs, entertainment, clothing and furniture. The important point to remember is the necessity to remain within the guidelines established, yet to stay away from minute details. Each month, a review can be made of how effective the planning has been to date.

[3]This is an intermediate budget. The Bureau of Labor Statistics provides estimates for three hypothetical annual family budgets—lower, intermediate, higher. The U.S. average cost of the lower budget was $10,041 a year for an urban family of four; the intermediate budget was $16,236; and the higher budget was $23,759.

TABLE 2-5 A Long-Range Financial-Health Program
(Prepared December 31, 1977)

	Dec, 31. 1978	Dec. 31, 1979	Dec. 31, 1983	Dec. 31, 1993	Dec. 31, 2007
My worldly possessions:					
Cash					
Notes and bonds					
Stocks					
Car					
Furniture and household equipment					
Clothing					
Home					
My debts:					
Notes payable					
Car payments					
Installments due on furniture					
Home mortgage					
My true worth					
My estate:					
Insurance protection (term)					
Total estate					
My income for the year:					
Earnings (salary)					
Interest					
Dividends					
My expenses for the year:					
Home					
Food					
Car					
Clothing					
Vacation and recreation					
Medical					
Insurance premiums					
Taxes					
My savings for the year					

LONG-RANGE PLANNING

The third phase of the budget process is to develop a long-range plan based upon your primary objective. Let us assume that your objective is to accumulate a million dollars, with a retirement date of 2007. Table 2-5 presents a format for recording the necessary data.

This kind of projection begins with the current year and makes an initial estimate for one year hence. It then proceeds forward in time, to five, fifteen, and twenty-nine years ahead. These projections are obviously only "guesstimates"; but such planning forces you to come to grips with answers to the questions, "Where am I today? Where do I want to be tomorrow?" By revising your long-range plan annually, you may be pleasantly surprised at how effective this document can be in assisting you to reach both your ultimate objective and various intermediate goals.

TABLE 2-6 Actual Daily Expenses, January 1–31, 19–

Date	Food	Housing	Transpor-tation	Clothing	Personal Care	Medical Care	Other Family Consump-tion	Other Items	Social Security and Disability Payments	Prsonal Income Taxes
1/1										
1/2										
1/3										
1/4										
1/5										
.										
.										
.										
1/31										
Total										

TABLE 2-7 Actual Income and Expenses (by Months), January 1–December 31, 19—

	Jan.	Feb.	Mar.	Apr.	May	June	July	Aug.	Sept.	Oct.	Nov.	Dec.	Year's Total
Income:													
Salary													
Interest													
Dividends													
Other													
Total													
Expenses:													
Food													
Housing													
Transportation													
Clothing													
Personal care													
Medical care													
Other family consumption													
Other items													
Social Security and disability payments													
Personal income taxes													
Total													
Savings													

MAINTAINING PROPER RECORDS

An important step in ensuring the success of your budget program is the careful recording of actual income and expenditures. You may wish to make a daily record utilizing the format shown in Table 2-6. Each month, expenditures should be totaled and posted to a monthly income-and-expense statement (see Table 2-7 for a sample format). We will discuss proper record keeping in detail later in this chapter.

REALISTIC PROGRAM EVALUATION

The final phase of the budget process involves comparing your planned income and expenses with what is actually occurring; this should be done on a monthly basis. For example, if you find at the end of February that your actual expenses have exceeded the estimate by 10 percent, you must take steps to reduce expenditures, or perhaps secure additional income, during the next ten months to make up for this overspending. Another way to portray your monthly income and expenditures in visual terms is presented in Figure 2-1, which indicates how much of your income is going to each particular expense. Preparing a chart of this kind may help you decide if you are making the appropriate allocation. Alternatively, instead of a single chart to portray all this information you can make a master chart with two overlays (Figures 2-2a, 2-2b, 2-2c, and 2-2d). The chart itself would list permanent information. The first overlay, on a sheet of acetate, would include estimated expenditures written in with a grease pencil. The second overlay would list actual figures. This would permit a rapid comparison of how you are really expending funds in relation to the estimate.

In addition to the monthly analysis, it is essential to evaluate your long-range plan yearly, reviewing your goals and making adjustments where appropriate. Likewise, more current information on your future salary projections could change your estimates. It is important to make these corrections in order for your long-range program to be of real assistance to you.

Figure 2-1 A graphic portrayal of my estimated income and expenditures for the period January 1–December 31, 1977.

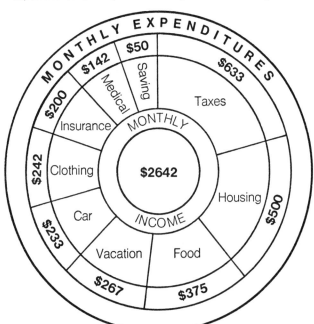

Figure 2-2a Master chart listing permanent information.

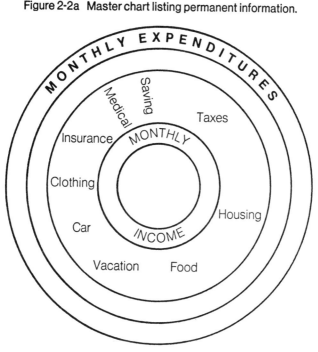

Figure 2-2b First overlay on acetate. The figures written with a grease pencil itemize "My estimated income and expenses."

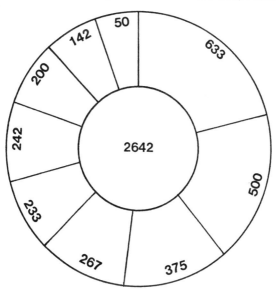

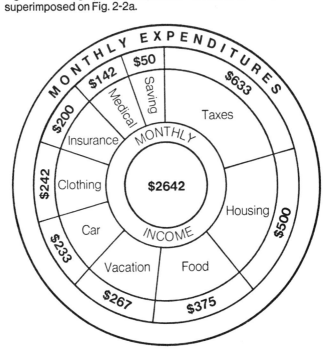

Figure 2-2c   A graphic portrayal after overlay (Fig. 2-2b) has been superimposed on Fig. 2-2a.

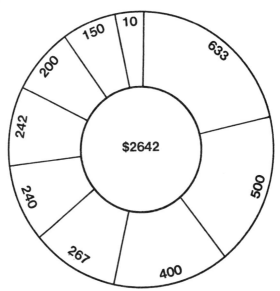

Figure 2-2d   Second overlay on acetate. The figures written with a grease pencil itemize "My actual income and expenses." This overlay would be superimposed on Fig. 2-2c.

TABLE 2-8   Rhoda's Balance Sheet, December 31, 1977

Assets:		
Cash	$ 25.00	
Notes and bonds		
Stock		
Car		
Furniture		
Clothing	300.00	
Home		
		$325.00
Liabilities:		
Charge accounts	$ 66.75	
Notes payable		
Car payments		
Furniture installments		
Home mortgage		
		$ 66.75
Net worth		$258.25

CASE: RIK AND RHODA RICHTUN

The following case is an example of long-range planning utilizing the format found in Table 2-4.

Rhoda Richtun, a graduate of my personal-finance course, was forced through necessity to become budget-minded at an early age. Hers is an example of the budget process beginning during school days and developing through her marriage to Rik, a young businessman with whom I jog at the Y. This is how Mr. and Mrs. Richtun went about developing their budget. "During college," said Rhoda, "I had to live on limited means. Out of the money I made each summer, I had to pay for my tuition, sorority dues, clothes, contact lenses, insurance and miscellaneous expenses. My parents had to be thrifty, having five children, two of college age. Accordingly, we had much firsthand experience with keeping a budget. I kept my own from freshman days; it was a necessity. By my senior year, my total net worth was a meager $258.25 (Table 2-8). My actual income and expenses for 1977 permitted a net saving of $66.00 (Table 2-9). So when I married Rik, shortly after graduation, there was precious little in the bank account. Fortunately, he was in better shape financially.

"After our marriage, it was time to plan a budget for two and then for a family. We were careful to work out our long-range objective, as well as the intermediate goals (Table 2-10). We want that million dollars, but we have objectives along the way that are more important. Being together, being able to sleep peacefully—that's our idea of happiness.

"As for income, in 1978 we will both be working. Rik has a job with an accounting firm and should be making $12,000. My part-time teaching should earn $7,200 and I have asked that my salary be paid on a twelve-month basis. Our income estimate for 1978 amounts to $19,245 and will permit us to live

TABLE 2-9   Rhoda's Actual Income and Expenses,
January 1–December 31, 1977

Income:		
Earnings (salary)	$ 800	
Interest	2	
Dividends		
Money from my parents	390	
		$1,192
Expenses:		
Rent ($400 less $370 scholarship)	$ 30	
Tuition ($600 less $400 scholarship)	200	
Food ($700 paid direct from parents)		
Sorority dues	135	
Laundry	30	
Insurance	15	
Taxes	36	
Vacation	40	
Medical expenses		
Spending money	390	
Clothing	150	
Gifts	100	
		$1,126
Saving		$ 66

TABLE 2-10   Rik and Rhoda's Objectives,
January 1, 1978–December 31, 2007

Second year:
    Pay off all debts
    Save money for furniture
    Start investment portfolio
    Start a family
Fourth year:
    Start purchasing antique furniture
    Build up investment portfolio
    Purchase a subcompact car
    Have a second child
Sixth year:
    Build our own home
    Rhoda starts teaching again
Eighth year:
    Purchase two cars (one sub-compact used car and one new
        compact sedan), and trade in every three years
    Increase size of investment portfolio
    Reduce debt on home

TABLE 2-10 (Cont.)

Twelfth year:
  Purchase boat and trailer
Sixteenth year:
  Install swimming pool
  Trade in boat
Twentieth year:
  Pay off debt on home
  Finance children in college
  Travel to Europe
  Have net worth of $480,000
  Trade in boat
Twenty-fifth year:
  Terminate our payment of children's education
  Take extended vacation
  Trade in boat
  Rhoda stops teaching in order to devote more time to her art hobby.
Longest term (thirty years):
  A million-dollar nest egg for children and charity

TABLE 2-11 Rik and Rhoda's Estimated Income and Expenses, January 1–December 31, 1978

Our income:		
Rik's earnings	$12,000	
Rhoda's earnings	7,200	
Interest	25	
Dividends	20	
		$19,245
Our expenses:		
Home and insurance	$ 2,000	
Food	1,560	
Car	825	
Clothing	630	
Vacation and recreation	625	
Medical	500	
Insurance premiums	160	
School		
Furniture	100	
Taxes	3,410	
		$ 9,810
Savings		$ 9,435

TABLE 2-12 Rik and Rhoda's Estimated Income and Expenses (by Month), January 1–December 31, 1978

	Jan.	Feb.	Mar.	Apr.	May	June	July	Aug.	Sept.	Oct.	Nov.	Dec.	Year's Total
Our income:													
Rik's earnings	$1000	$1000	$1000	$1000	$1000	$1000	$1000	$1000	$1000	$1000	$1000	$1000	$12,000
Rhoda's earnings	600	600	600	600	600	600	600	600	600	600	600	600	7,200
Interest												25	25
Dividends			5			5			5			5	20
Total	$1600	$1600	$1605	$1600	$1600	$1605	$1600	$1600	$1605	$1600	$1600	$1630	$19,245
Our expenses:													
Home and Insurance	$ 167	$ 167	$ 167	$ 167	$ 167	$ 167	$ 167	$ 167	$ 166	$ 166	$ 166	$ 166	$ 2,000
Food	130	130	130	130	130	130	130	130	130	130	130	130	1,560
Car	69	69	69	69	69	69	69	69	69	68	68	68	825
Clothing	53	53	53	53	53	53	52	52	52	52	52	52	630
Vacation and Recreation	53	52	52	52	52	52	52	52	52	52	52	52	625
Medical	42	42	42	42	42	42	42	42	41	41	41	41	500
Insurance premiums	40			40			40			40			160
School													
Furniture	9	9	9	9	8	8	8	8	8	8	8	8	100
Taxes	285	285	284	284	284	284	284	284	284	284	284	284	3,410
Total	$ 848	$ 807	$ 806	$ 846	$ 805	$ 805	$ 844	$ 804	$ 802	$ 841	$ 801	$ 801	$9,810
Savings	$ (752)	(793)	(799)	(754)	(795)	(800)	(756)	(796)	(803)	(759)	(799)	(829)	(9,435)

TABLE 2-13 The Richtun's Long-Range Financial-Health Program
(as of December 31, each year)

	1978	1979	1983	1985	1989	1992	1997	2002	2007
Our worldly possessions:									
Cash	$ 546	$ 601	$ 662	$ 730	$ 886	$ 1,075	$ 1,305	$ 1,665	$ 2,163
Notes and bonds	1,500	3,600	6,200	11,200	24,200	47,000	75,000	132,000	220,000
Stocks	6,740	14,490	25,795	45,400	93,000	174,000	296,000	532,000	880,000
Car	1,200	2,500	1,600	3,500	3,000	3,500	5,500	4,000	8,000
Furniture and household equipment	880	1,100	2,300	3,000	4,300	6,000	8,200	12,000	16,000
Clothing and jewelry	660	800	970	1,177	1,723	2,600	4,400	7,090	11,200
Home			40,000	44,100	53,500	72,000	85,500	102,000	122,000
Boat					4,500	5,000	5,000	5,500	3,200
Total	$11,526	$23,091	$77,527	$109,107	$185,109	$311,175	$480,905	$796,255	$1,262,563
Our debts:									
Notes payable	500								
Car payments									
Installments due on furniture									
Installments due on home			$24,000	$ 22,600	$ 19,400	$ 9,600			
Total	$ 500		$24,000	$ 22,600	19,400	9,600			
Our true worth	$11,026	$23,091	$53,527	$ 86,507	$165,709	$301,575	$480,905	$796,255	$1,262,563
Our estate:									
Insurance protection	$10,000	$15,000	$15,000	$ 20,000	$ 25,000	$ 35,000	$ 50,000	$ 70,000	$ 90,000
Total estate	$21,026	$38,091	$68,527	$106,527	$190,709	$336,575	$530,905	$866,255	$1,352,563

TABLE 2-13 (Cont.)

Our income:									
Rik's earnings	$12,000	$15,000	$17,000	$19,000	$26,000	$36,000	$46,000	$59,000	73,000
Rhoda's earnings	7,200		9,000	9,730	11,370	13,300	15,500	18,400	
Interest	25	125	250	410	1,000	2,000	3,400	5,900	9,600
Dividends	20	113	200	362	800	1,550	2,650	4,750	7,980
Total	$19,245	$15,238	$26,450	$29,502	$39,170	$52,850	$67,550	$88,050	$90,580
Our expenses:									
Home and insurance	$2,000	$2,200	$8,000	$4,300	$4,700	$12,100	$4,800	$3,900	$4,400
Food	1,560	1,770	2,000	2,160	2,500	2,900	2,800	2,900	3,400
Car	825	2,500	1,040	3,500	2,050	2,300	4,000	2,700	3,600
Clothing	630	700	770	840	1,050	1,250	2,500	1,950	2,500
Vacation and recreation	625	675	725	825	5,425	2,580	8,000	5,000	1,600
Medical	500	500	400	440	520	600	1,000	850	975
Insurance premiums	160	200	200	250	300	400	750	750	950
School		200	300	1,250	1,450	1,650	4,000	4,300	
Furniture	100	500	2,400	400	800	1,000	1,300	1,550	1,800
Taxes	3,410	2,780	5,920	7,150	11,240	17,460	25,900	37,500	38,180
Total	$9,810	$12,015	$21,755	$21,115	$30,035	$42,240	$55,050	$61,400	$57,405
Savings	$9,435	$3,213	$4,695	$8,387	$9,135	$10,610	$12,500	$26,650	$33,175

satisfactorily and save, I hope, a substantial amount (Table 2-11). We both like to economize. To permit a frequent comparison of actual income and expenses against our estimate, we have prepared a monthly statement for the period January 1–December 31, 1978 (Table 2-12).

"We are fortunate to start out with so little debt and to both be working. Rik hopes to advance rapidly in an accounting firm, becoming a partner some day or perhaps a treasurer or controller in a corporation. As for me, I will probably stop working for a few years to have children, but I plan to teach thereafter. My art hobby is fascinating and may eventually contribute to our income. I was offered $100 for a recent painting but gave it to my parents. A final review of our long-range plan (Table 2-13) convinces us we can reach our objectives. We have high hopes for the future."

EFFECTIVE RECORD KEEPING

We have already spoken of the importance of keeping adequate records. I would suggest that you obtain a file cabinet and appropriate folders in which to arrange your financial material for easy reference. Your budget data may be divided into three sections: Balance Sheet; Income and Expenses; and Long-Range Financial Health Plan. Instead of keeping this data in folders, you may wish to keep all your budget material in a large three-ring loose-leaf notebook, using dividers to separate it into the five following categories:

1. Primary objective and intermediate goals.
2. Net worth.
3. Estimated income and expenses for the current year (this information should be presented on a daily, monthly and yearly basis).
4. Long-range plan.
5. Actual income and expenditures for the current year. (Documentation of actual income and expenses should follow the same format used for estimated income and expenses in order to permit ready comparison.)

Acetate overlay sheets are helpful in documenting your long-range plan. They permit easy erasure and adjustments with each annual budget review. These overlays are also useful in comparing actual income and expenses with estimates (see Figures 2-3a and 2-3b for sample format).

All records dealing with financial material should be kept in your file cabinet. An ideal time to begin such record keeping is when you first acquire

Figure 2-3a Master chart listing permanent information on
long-range plans.

Long-range Plan

	1977	1978
Our worldly possessions:		
Cash		
Notes and bonds		
Stocks		
Car		
Furniture & household equipment		
Clothing & jewelry		
Home		
Boat		
Total		
Our debts:		
Our estate:		
Our income:		
Our expenses:		
Savings		

Figure 2-3b Overlay acetate that will be superimposed on
master chart (Fig. 2-3a). Dollar amounts on overlay should be
written with a grease pencil to permit ease in correcting them
with each annual review.

	1977	1978
	$ 546	$ 601
	1,500	3,600
	6,740	14,490
	1,200	2,500
	880	1,100
	660	800
	$11,526	$23,091

worldly possessions. However, you can begin anytime; the sooner, the better. Well-organized records can save you much time. And time is a valuable commodity. The more efficient your records, the less hours you must devote to your finances.

SAMPLE RECORDS

How do you set up an effective system of record keeping? Let us assume that you have acquired a variety of possessions. Begin by attempting to group them into major categories like the seven listed below. Place dividers between each major category, then prepare appropriately labeled manila folders to insert in each category. Most important, tailor your system to your specific needs. One successful money manager used the following sequence and labeling for his records:

    I. Financial Health (Divider)
       A. Budget (Objective and Subobjectives)
          1. Balance sheet
          2. Income and expense statement
          3. Long-range financial-health plan
       B. Consumer credit
       C. Loans
   II. Major Expenditures (Divider)
        1. Food
        2. Clothing
        3. Personal Care
        4. Transportation
        5. Large Appliances
        6. Other Major Expenditures
        7. Taxes
          a. Federal
          b. State
          c. Other
  III. Housing (Divider)
        1. Building Our Own House
        2. Protecting Our Property
        3. Landscaping
        4. Maintenance, Repairs, Improvements
        5. Swimming Pool
        6. Moving
  IV. Insurance and Social Security (Divider)
        1. Life Insurance
        2. Car, Property and Liability Insurance

      3. Health Insurance and Medicare
      4. Social Security
      5. Annuity and Pensions
  V. Fixed-Income Investments (Divider)
      1. Banks, Credit Unions, Savings and Loan Associations
      2. Money Market
      3. Bonds
  VI. Growth-Potential Investments (Divider)
      1. Stocks
      2. Investment Companies
      3. Real Estate
      4. Profitable Hobbies
      5. Commodities
  VII. Retirement and Estate Planning (Divider)
      1. Retirement
      2. Wills and Trusts

Additional formulas for record keeping in specific areas will be presented throughout this book under the appropriate chapter headings. Let me stress here, however, the importance of keeping *a master list of all possessions.* Copies should be kept in three separate places: your bank safety-deposit box, your attorney's office and your personal file. Your most valuable financial records, such as stock and bond certificates, should be kept in a safety deposit box.

THE ROLE OF BUDGETING IN PERSONAL-FINANCE MANAGEMENT

The value of the budget process is that it forces you to devise a plan to meet your various objectives. It can be a valuable servant or a Frankenstein's monster. Make sure not to get caught up in a morass of petty details. Furthermore, as earnings increase, you need be less exact in meeting your budgeted expenses in each category. Keep in mind that they are guidelines only.

    The most important point in implementing your program is to deduct your savings allotment first. Either have an automatic deduction for investment purposes or do it yourself on receipt of each salary check. Second, be sure to make an annual review of your long-range plan and a monthly check on your yearly projection. Remember that the budget process is useful in areas other than planning. As we saw in Figure 1-1, personal-finance management draws on the functions of planning, organizing, implementing and controlling. In terms of budget keeping, these functions may be translated into the following steps:

1. *Planning* what you are going to save and spend in relation to your income.
2. *Implementing* your plan.
3. *Checking* to see that what you spent and saved were in accordance with your budget.

The importance of item three cannot be overemphasized. Effective control of your finances involves frequent verification of actual expenditures in terms of your overall plan. Where appropriate, make the necessary modifications to face the realities of the current situation. For example, assume that you have allotted fifty dollars a month for rent in 1980, because your company plans to send you to Paris and will subsidize most of your living expenses. It is essential that you revise your budget if you quit your job in June 1980 to accept a government post in New York City.

It is also desirable to provide an adequate cash reserve in your budget for unexpected emergencies. Along with death and taxes, they are certain to occur!

3
CONSUMER PROTECTION

Consumer-protection legislation is a reality today, thanks to increasing public demand for a fair deal in buying goods and services.

Under the leadership of Ralph Nader, Esther Peterson, Bess Myerson and others, the American consumer has learned to speak out against inferior products and workmanship. He is also beginning to seek a voice in the management decision-making process. As a result of this rising protest, Congress and the government agencies concerned are taking additional action to protect the consumer in a variety of areas.

President Carter recommended to Congress in 1977 that it create an Agency for Consumer Protection (ACP). He said, "I'm in favor of the establishment of the consumer protection agency. . . . [This measure] will enhance the consumer's influence within the government without creating another unwieldy bureaucracy. I believe [it] will increase confidence in government by demonstrating that government is considering the people's needs in a sensitive and responsible way."

The proposed agency would have had no regulatory or other legal powers. Its primary function would have been to represent consumer interests before federal agencies and courts. Another agency responsibility would have been to supply unbiased information to consumers concerning products and business practices. It would also have collected consumer complaints, analyzed them for patterns of abuse and forwarded them to the appropriate governmental organizations for resolution.

The President appointed Esther Peterson as his Special Assistant for Consumer Affairs and instructed her to work with Congress to assist in passage of the ACP. However, lobbying by the U.S. Chamber of Commerce and some large corporations were factors in defeating this proposed legislation. In my view, it is important to have a separate agency in order to adequately represent the consumer. Such an agency should be given cabinet rank comparable to the Department of Commerce, which represents business.

But the finest laws and best of agencies are of little value unless the individual consumer understands how to utilize existing legislation and regulations to his advantage. Such knowledge is particularly important in the field of credit.

This chapter will review existing legislation, organizations and materials available to protect the consumer today, stressing the importance of collective as well as individual consumer action and suggesting ways of wielding greater leverage in years to come. "The squeaky wheel gets the grease" and a lot more squeaking will have to be done to ensure the American consumer a fair deal.

ORIGINS OF CONSUMER LEGISLATION AND THE ROLE OF THE FTC

President Kennedy proclaimed the Consumer Bill of Rights in 1962, indicating that the consumer should:

1. Be informed about the merchandise.
2. Be able to utilize products with safety.
3. Be given a choice based upon appropriate facts as to contents, ingredients, and so on.
4. Be heard in the decision-making process of management.

Kennedy's initial concept was expanded by Presidents Johnson, Nixon and Ford. A major result of this presidential impetus was the increased emphasis given to consumer interests by the Federal Trade Commission (FTC). In 1968, the FTC held a series of open hearings on the subject of national consumer protection. Appearing before the commission were interested parties, including consumer organizations; professors; federal, state and local officials; Better Business Bureau representatives; and businessmen. It is interesting to note the admission of the FTC chairman, Paul Dixon, who stated in the opening session:

> We are particularly gratified by the responses of numerous consumer organizations, and we hope that the holding of this hearing will mark the beginning of increased cooperation between the commission and such groups. We believe that the commission can and will benefit greatly from frequent contacts with the organizations who know the consumers' problems firsthand and see such problems through the eyes of the consuming public.[1]

Betty Furness, then Special Assistant to the President for Consumer Affairs, stated that "these hearings will prove to be an important landmark in this country's continuing consumer revolution." She went on to emphasize the key problems facing the consumer:

> The consumer deserves to be satisfied in products and services. The consumer deserves to be served by the producer—and not vice versa. The consumer deserves equal rights in the marketplace. The consumer, as a customer, deserves an effective voice in government.
>
> The textbook concept of the free-enterprise system assumes an open, competitive marketplace of informed buyers and sellers. But we

[1]*National Consumer Protection Hearings* (Washington, D.C.: Federal Trade Commission, November 1968), p. 2.

know today that in our fast-changing, complex, and impersonal market-place, the consumer is not the equal of the seller. He does not enjoy a genuine bargaining position.

Too often he is dissatisfied with the quality. Too often he is misinformed, or not fully informed about product characteristics. In other words, these marketplace malfunctions prevent the consumer from fulfilling his proper role in the free-enterprise system.

And to add insult to injury, the consumer is too often denied redress. We have yet to provide adequate means for the voicing and arbitration of grievances. Needless to add, the system which poses such problems for the more affluent works much greater hardship on the poor.[2]

The hearings were chock-full of descriptions of the mistreatment meted out to the consumer over the years. A number of constructive recommendations were made by people who appeared before the commission. The most comprehensive list of proposals was presented by Wilbur Cohen, Secretary of Health, Education and Welfare. Speaking from thirty-four years of experience in the federal government, he made the following recommendations:

1. Authorize a central or agency publication to provide consumers with information relevant to consumer choice, developed through government-sponsored research paid for by the taxpayer.
2. Provide federal financial aid to states to improve their consumer-service programs, providing service and protection through representation, education, information, mediation, and litigation.
3. Initiate, in cooperation with interested state and local groups, a study of the antiquated, inconsistent, inequitable federal and state laws relating to sales practices, contracts, and credit, including recommendations for action.
4. Continue to expand the Bureau of Federal Credit Union programs to enable them to work with more low-income groups to encourage savings, and to provide credit at reasonable rates. In addition, encourage the establishment of other cooperatives, such as bookstore and housing co-ops, to help college students and their parents meet the rising cost of a college education.
5. Provide for the coverage of certain prescription drugs under the Medicare Program.
6. Authorize payments for drugs under Medicare and Medicaid on the basis of reasonable price range. The cost should not exceed the amount at which the drug is generally available for sale to establishments dispensing drugs in a given strength or dosage form by its established name, or, if lower, by proprietary designation. In the

[2]Ibid., p. 4.

case of a prescription-legend drug a reasonable fee, or in the case of a prescribed non-legend drug a reasonable billing allowance; or if lower, usual or customary charge at which the dispenser sells or offers such drug to the public.

7. Authorize the Secretary of HEW to publish and disseminate an up-to-date U. S. Drug Compendium of prescription drugs listed by their generic names, with pertinent information on each drug.

8. Require that all prescription drugs in tablet or capsule form bear an identification which would reveal the manufacturer and identify the drug. We should also require that the manufacturer's name and the generic or established name appear on the label of prescription-drug containers.

9. Provide for pre-market clearance of cosmetics, as we now do with drugs, to protect American women from the many hazards to their health and beauty.

10. Require pre-market clearance of medical devices and establish sufficient standards to assure safety and efficiency.

11. Extend coverage of the Hazardous Substances Act to toys that may be injurious to children because of a mechanical hazard.

12. Require firms and consulting laboratories which produce food and color additives, pesticide chemicals, cosmetics and over-the-counter drugs to submit records and reports of product performances.[3]

FTC LITERATURE

The 1968 FTC hearings proved beneficial in airing consumer complaints, offering solutions and providing commission members with greater insight into consumer problems. Increased consumer interest in recent years has also spurred the FTC to issue pertinent pamphlets, such as *Color Television and the X-Ray Problem; Protection for the Elderly; Advice for Persons Who Are Considering an Investment in a Franchise Business; Pitfalls to Watch For in Mail-Order Insurance Policies; Investigate, Stop, Look Says the Federal Trade Commission; Look for That Label; Unordered Merchandise; Don't Be Gypped;* and *Guard Against Phony Ads.*

A complete list of FTC literature can be found in the *List of Publications, Federal Trade Commission.* Any of the priced FTC Documents (the fee is very small) may be obtained by writing to: Superintendent of Documents, U. S. Government Printing Office, Washington, D. C. 20402. The FTC also has a number of free pamphlets, single copies of which are available without charge while the supply lasts. Address your requests to: Division of Legal and Public

[3]Ibid., pp. 223, 224.

Figure 3-1   Federal Trade Commission—Regional Offices.*

Atlanta Regional Office: Federal Trade Commission, Room 1000, 1718 Peachtree St., N.W. Atlanta, Georgia 30309.

Boston Regional Office: Federal Trade Commission, Room 1301, 150 Causeway St., Boston, Massachusetts 02114.

Chicago Regional Office: Federal Trade Commission, Suite 1437, 55 East Monroe Street, Chicago, Illinois 60603.

Cleveland Regional Office: Federal Trade Commission, Room 1339, Anthony J. Celebrezze Federal Office Building, 1240 East 9th Street, Cleveland, Ohio 44199.

Dallas Regional Office: Federal Trade Commission, Suite 2665, 2001 Bryan Street, Dallas, Texas 75201.

Denver Regional Office: Federal Trade Commission, Suite 2900, 1405 Curtis Street, Denver, Colorado 80202.

Los Angeles Regional Office: Federal Trade Commission, Room 13209, Federal Building, 11000 Wilshire Boulevard, Los Angeles, California 90024.

New York Regional Office: Federal Trade Commission, 2243-EB, Federal Building, 26 Federal Plaza, New York, New York 10007.

San Francisco Regional Office: Federal Trade Commission, 450 Golden Gate Avenue, Box 36005, San Francisco, California 94102.

Field Station:

Federal Trade Commission, Room 605, Melim Building, 333 Queen Street, Honolulu, Hawaii 98613.

Seattle Regional Office: Federal Trade Commission, 28th Floor, Federal Building, 915 Second Avenue, Seattle, Washington 98174.

Washington, D.C. Regional Office: Federal Trade Commission, 6th Floor, Gelman Building, 2120 L Street, N.W., Washington, D.C. 20037.

---

*Each of the regional offices is supervised by a Regional Director, who is available for conferences with attorneys, consumers, and other members of the public on matters relating to the Commission's activities.

Source: *Your FTC: What It Is and What It Does,* 1977, U.S. Government Printing Office, Washington, D.C., 20402

Records, Federal Trade Commission, Washington, D. C. 20580. Your local library may also have FTC publications.

It is well worth your time to read the pamphlets dealing with subjects of interest to you. There is much good information, for example, in *Bargain? Freezer Meats,* a twelve-page document that presents hard facts and concludes with the advice, "If you do get cheated, don't take it lying down. Write a letter, giving all the facts, to your local public prosecutor, state Attorney General, or the Federal Trade Commission." A list of the FTC offices appears in Figure 3-1. If you live in one of the areas cited, a phone call may provide you with desired pamphlets and other information.

PROTECTION IN BUYING FROM DOOR-TO-DOOR SALESMEN

A recent Federal Trade Commission ruling illustrates the commission's positive efforts to help the consumer. This rule gives you the right to cancel, within three days, any purchase on door-to-door sales of twenty-five dollars or more. The salesman must inform you of this cancellation right and give you a written contract as well as two copies of your notice-of-cancellation form. The contract must: 1) be in the same language he used when talking to you; 2) be dated, showing name and address of seller; 3) contain the following statement near your signature: "You the buyer, may cancel this transaction at any time prior to midnight of the third business day after the date of this transaction. See the attached notice of cancellation form for an explanation of this right."

If you wish to cancel the contract, read the Notice of Cancellation, detach, sign and date one copy and send it to the seller within three business days; keep one copy and your contract for your records.

If you cancel, the seller must, within ten days: refund your money; return any goods or property traded in; cancel and return any documents that you've signed; tell you if he plans to pick up any merchandise he may have left with you.

Within twenty days of cancellation, if he *has* left goods with you, you must: have the article available for pickup in the same condition that you received it; or, if you agree, you must ship the item to him (the seller must pay any return shipping expenses). The notice of cancellation must: be in the same language used by the seller when making the sale; 2) be easy to detach from the contract; 3) be completed by the seller including such information as date of sale, name and address of seller, date by which notice must be sent to the seller.

If the seller fails to meet any of the above requirements he has violated the FTC rule and you should write to your nearest FTC office (see Figure 3-1).

The FTC can act only in the broad public interest, not on behalf of individual consumers. But in order to fulfill its responsibilities to the public at large, the FTC relies on individual complaints, which will be studied and recorded.

If you fail to fulfill your half of the contract and the seller fulfills his, you are responsible for all agreements in the contract.

Certain "door-to-door" sales are not covered by this rule, including sales of under twenty-five dollars; orders placed at the seller's address; telephone orders; sales made entirely by mail; some "emergency repairs" sales and real estate, insurance or securities sales.

CONSUMER CLAIMS AND DEFENSES

The FTC, on May 14, 1976, enacted a new regulation titled "Preservation of Consumer Claims and Defenses." It was directed to sellers and creditors who together participated in unfair and deceptive practices in regard to consumer credit.

The new rule gives the consumer some important rights. When a firm extends credit to you or assists in arranging credit for you, your responsibility to pay for the services or goods is directly connected to the seller's responsibility to deliver the services or goods and to perform related duties such as warranty repairs. Misconduct on the seller's part, such as fraud, misrepresentation, delivery of faulty goods or breach of warranty, may give you the right to withhold credit payments until the seller meets his obligations. If the obligations are not met, you may have the right to recover amounts you have already paid. There must be, however, an existing business arrangement between the creditor and the seller.

A firm that makes you a loan or helps to arrange one for you must see to it that the following notice is in the credit contract you sign:

> Any holder of this consumer credit contract is subject to all claims and defenses which the debtor could assert against the seller of goods or services obtained with the proceeds hereof. Recovery hereunder by the debtor shall not exceed amounts paid by the debtor hereunder.

CONSUMER PRODUCT SAFETY COMMISSION[4]

Another federal agency created to help the consumer is a commission on

---

[4]The source for the information on this topic is a pamphlet titled, *Towards an Equal Opportunity in Consumer Safety,* by Constance B. Newman, Commissioner, CPSC, February 1974, Washington, D. C.

product safety. The Consumer Product Safety Act, passed in 1972, called for the creation of the Consumer Product Safety Commission (CPSC). This commission was activated on May 14, 1973, to fulfill the following purposes:

1. Protection of the public against unreasonable risks of injury associated with consumer products.
2. Assistance to consumers in evaluating the comparative safety of consumer products.
3. Development of uniform safety standards for consumer products and to minimize conflicting state and local regulations.
4. Promotion of research and investigation into causes and prevention of product-related deaths, illnesses and injuries.

In order to fulfill its purposes the CPSC is required to collect data on injuries. Through the National Electronic Injury Surveillance System (NEISS), it gets input from 119 hospital emergency rooms nationwide. This surveillance data is recorded by computer daily and tabulated to show which products are associated with injuries.

The following hypothetical case illustrates the part the Consumer Product Safety Commission might play in settling a grievance.

Assume the following:

A product was designed with minimal concern about safety.

There was no reference to safety in the advertising of the product.

The retailer was not sufficiently concerned about safety in the selection of products and hence sold a defective product.

The product was purchased by a consumer unaware of the product's defect.

The consumer was injured.

The injured consumer may do none, one, some or all of the below:

Complain to the Manufacturer, Retailer or Distributor

Many consumers complain directly to the manufacturer or the retailer about products that do not work, that cause injury or disintegrate. Sometimes the consumer's expectation is a refund. At other times the consumer's expectation is that the manufacturer will note the complaint and redesign the product for the benefit of future consumers.

Sue the Manufacturer, Retailer, Distributor

Injured consumers frequently want and need more than a refund of the purchase price of the product. Hospital bills, lost wages, pain and suffering may incite them to sue.

Complain to the Consumer Product Safety Commission

Since the new regulatory agency is dedicated to reducing injuries associated with consumer products, many consumers write letters, call or petition the commission regarding their experiences with unsafe products. The commission shares existing product information with the consumer and uses consumer input to help determine how it can best protect the public.

Go to the Hospital

The injury to the consumer may be serious enough to require hospitalization or outpatient care, thus triggering Consumer Product Safety Commission attention.

ROLE OF THE FOOD AND DRUG ADMINISTRATION[5]

The Food and Drug Administration is a division of the U. S. Department of Health, Education and Welfare. It employs 6,500 people and has an annual budget of $160 million. There are more than 100 offices in communities throughout the United States.

The FDA carries out the responsibilities assigned to it by the Congress. The majority of its activities are authorized by four laws:

1. The Federal Food, Drug and Cosmetic Act requires that foods be safe and wholesome, that drugs be safe and effective, and that cosmetics and medical devices be safe. All of the above products must be properly labeled.

2. The Fair Packaging and Labeling Act requires that labeling be honest and informative, so that shoppers may easily determine the best value.

3. The Radiation Control for Health and Safety Act protects consumers from unnecessary exposure to radiation from X-ray machines and consumer products such as microwave ovens and color TVs.

4. The Public Health Service Act establishes the FDA's authority over vaccines, serums and other biological products. It also provides the basis for the FDA's programs on milk and shellfish sanitation, restaurant operations and interstate travel facilities.

FUNCTIONS OF THE FDA

In accordance with the authority granted by Congress, the FDA performs

---

[5]Source: Food and Drug Administration pamphlet *We Want You to Know About Today's FDA,* DHEW Publication No. (FDA) 74-1021, Washington, D.C.: U.S. Government Printing Office.

many functions designed to help the public and to protect consumers. These include:

1. Inspection of plants where foods, drugs, cosmetics or other products are made or stored to assure that good practices are being observed.

2. Review and approval of new drug applications and food-additive petitions before new drugs or new food additives may be used.

3. Approval of every batch of insulin and antibiotics, and most color additives before they may be used.

4. Establishment of standards for consumer products, as in foods like peanut butter that are made according to a set recipe; testing of products to assure that they meet government standards.

5. Review of all prescription and nonprescription medicines, biological drugs and veterinary drugs now on the market to assure that they are safe, effective and properly labeled.

6. Development of regulations for proper labeling—for instance, recent ingredient labeling of cosmetics and compulsory nutrition labeling on many foods.

7. Working with the industries it regulates to help them develop better quality-control procedures.

8. Regular testing of approved drugs to make sure they continue to meet standards of potency, purity and quality.

9. Issuance of public warnings when hazardous products have been identified.

SCOPE OF THE FDA'S LEGAL AUTHORITY

What is the FDA empowered to do?

1. It can prevent certain products, including new drugs and new food additives, from being sold until they are proved safe.

2. It can initiate removal of a product from the market when new scientific evidence reveals unacceptable or unexpected risks—for instance, the FDA ban on hexachlorophene as an active ingredient.

3. It can go to court to seize illegal products and to prosecute the manufacturer, packer or shipper of adulterated or mislabeled products.

4. It can take action against false and misleading labeling on the products it regulates.

5. It *generally* can act only against products sold in interstate commerce. A product made and sold solely within a state is usually subject to regulation by that state only.

6. It *cannot* prevent an unscrupulous person from selling certain products, such as worthless medical devices or harmful cosmetics, until after they are actually marketed. The burden is on the FDA to prove that such products are worthless or harmful.

7. It *cannot* recall a product. It can, however, ask a manufacturer to do so, under the threat of legal action.

8. It *cannot* control the price of any product.

9. It *cannot* directly regulate the advertising of any product except prescription drugs.

10. It *cannot* regulate cigarettes.

The FDA points out the consumer's responsibility as follows: "To get the maximum benefits from the products you buy, you should read labels, observe directions and precautions, and use common sense. If you find a product regulated by FDA that you believe is mislabeled, insanitary, harmful, or in violation of the law, you will be performing a public service by reporting it to FDA. Just call the nearest FDA office, or write to FDA. Many actions taken by FDA originate from complaints made by consumers."

The FDA prepares a variety of helpful publications including: *Food Safety in the Kitchen; Nutrition Labels on Food; Labels on Medicines; Medicines Without Prescriptions; Adverse Reactions to Medicines.*

Single free copies of these publications are available from your local Consumer Affairs Officer or from the Food and Drug Administration, HFI-10, 5600 Fishers Lane, Rockville, Maryland 20952.

In addition to its other consumer-information materials, the FDA publishes a magazine called *FDA Consumer,* written especially for the public. Topics in a recent issue included: "The Changing Food Supply"; "Food Shoppers' Beliefs—Myths and Realities"; and "What About Vitamin C?" To subscribe for a year, send $8.55 to the Superintendent of Documents, Government Printing Office, Washington, D. C. 20402.

OTHER SOURCES OF CONSUMER INFORMATION

In addition to FTC and FDA literature, there is valuable consumer information to be gained from other sources.

CONSUMER INFORMATION CENTER

In 1970, President Nixon established the Consumer Information Center in the General Services Administration. This center is responsible for encouraging "Federal agencies to develop and release information of interest to consumers. It is also responsible for increasing public awareness of existing Federal publications."[6] In order to further public awareness, the center has published a very

[6]*Consumer Information Catalog* (Summer 1977) Consumer Information Center, General Services Administration, Pueblo, Colorado 81009.

helpful index of more than 200 selected federal consumer publications on how to buy, use and take care of consumer products. Titled *Consumer Information Catalog,* it is available at no charge from the Consumer Information Center. Among the topics covered are automobiles; children; employment; education; food; diet and nutrition; health; housing; gardening; money management; and retirement years. The U. S. government has spent much time and money researching these areas. It pays to take advantage of their efforts.

GUIDE TO FEDERAL CONSUMER SERVICES

The myriad of consumer services provided by thirty-five government departments and agencies has been summarized in a pamphlet titled *Guide to Federal Consumer Services.* It gives addresses and phone numbers for registering views and complaints, and also provides the phone numbers of Federal Information Centers that you can call when you have questions about any program or agency of the federal government (see Figure 3-2). You can obtain a free copy of this publication from the Consumer Information Center, Pueblo, Colorado 81009.

Virginia H. Knauer, then Special Assistant to the President for Consumer Affairs and Director, Office of Consumer Affairs, Department of Health, Education and Welfare, pointed out the value of this booklet in her introduction to the 1976 edition:

> This ... edition of the *Guide to Federal Consumer Services* has the answers to such questions as: What are the Federal Government's benefits and services for consumers? Which Federal Department or Agency can help me? How can I obtain service?
>
> The right to information, to choice, to safety, to redress and to education does exist. It exists for consumers at all levels—the marketplace and local, State and Federal Governments. However, while consumers are entitled to these rights, some may not know where and how to exercise these rights in dealing with the Federal Departments and Agencies. They need a guide.
>
> This publication reflects the Federal Government's response to this need and the President's continuing reaffirmation of these rights. *Guide to Federal Consumer Services* has been updated and revised to list the consumer services of Federal Departments and Agencies that are directly concerned with these issues.[7]

BETTER BUSINESS BUREAUS

The 140 Better Business Bureaus (BBBs) in the United States have a variety of

[7]Office of Consumer Affairs, *Guide to Federal Consumer Services,* Department of Health, Education and Welfare, Washington, D.C., p. 2.

Figure 3-2   Federal Information Centers.

ALABAMA		**MISSOURI**	
Birmingham	205/322-8591	Kansas City	816/374-2466
Mobile	205/438-1421	St. Joseph	816/233-8206
ARIZONA		St. Louis	314/425-4106
Tucson	602/622-1511	**NEBRASKA**	
Phoenix	602/261-3313	Omaha	402/221-3353
ARKANSAS		**NEW JERSEY**	
Little Rock	501/378-6177	Newark	201/645-3600
		Trenton	609/396-4400
CALIFORNIA		**NEW MEXICO**	
Los Angeles	213/688-3800	Albuquerque	505/766-3091
Sacramento	916/449-3344	Santa Fe	505/983-7743
San Diego	714/293-6030	**NEW YORK**	
San Francisco	415/556-6600	Albany	518/463-4421
San Jose	408/275-7422	Buffalo	716/842-5770
COLORADO		New York	212/264-4464
Colorado Springs	303/471-9491	Rochester	716/546-5075
Denver	303/837-3602	Syracuse	315/476-8545
Pueblo	303/544-9523	**NORTH CAROLINA**	
CONNECTICUT		Charlotte	704/376-3600
Hartford	203/527-2617	**OHIO**	
New Haven	203/624-4720	Akron	216/375-5475
DISTRICT OF COLUMBIA		Cincinnati	513/684-2801
Washington	202/755-8660	Cleveland	216/522-4040
FLORIDA		Columbus	614/221-1014
Fort Lauderdale	305/522-8531	Dayton	513/223-7377
Miami	305/350-4155	Toledo	419/244-8625
Jacksonville	904/354-4756	**OKLAHOMA**	
St. Petersburg	813/893-3495	Oklahoma City	405/231-4868
Tampa	813/229-7911	Tulsa	918/548-4193
West Palm Beach	305/833-7566	**OREGON**	
GEORGIA		Portland	503/221-2222
Atlanta	404/526-6891	**PENNSYLVANIA**	
HAWAII		Philadelphia	215/597-7042
Honolulu	808/546-8620	Pittsburgh	412/644-3456
ILLINOIS		Scranton	717/346-7081
Chicago	312/353-4242	**RHODE ISLAND**	
INDIANA		Providence	401/331-5565
Indianapolis	317/269-7373	**TENNESSEE**	
IOWA		Chattanooga	615/265-8231
Des Moines	515/282-9091	Memphis	901/534-3285
KANSAS		**TEXAS**	
Topeka	913/232-7229	Austin	512/472-5494
Wichita	316/263-6931	Dallas	214/749-2131
KENTUCKY		Fort Worth	817/334-3624
Louisville	502/582-6261	Houston	713/226-5711
LOUISIANA		San Antonio	512/224-4471
New Orleans	504/589-6696	**UTAH**	
MARYLAND		Ogden	801/399-1347
Baltimore	301/962-4980	Salt Lake City	801/524-5353
MASSACHUSETTS		**WASHINGTON**	
Boston	617/223-7121	Tacoma	206/383-5230
MICHIGAN		Seattle	206/442-0570
Detroit	313/226-7016	**WISCONSIN**	
MINNESOTA		Milwaukee	414/271-2273
Minneapolis	612/725-2073		

booklets available that can be helpful to the consumer. These pamphlets currently cover such subjects as:

Appliance Service	Guarantees and Warranties
Audio Products	Home Study Schools
Bait and Switch	Mail Order Profit Mirages
Buying By Mail	Multi-Level Selling Plans
Buying Encyclopedias	Refunds and Exchanges
Buying On Time	Sales Contracts
Car Care On the Road	Television Sets
Computer Careers	Water Conditioners
Drycleaning	Work-At-Home Schemes

The Role of the BBB

The Better Business Bureau works to maintain ethical practices in the advertising and selling of products and services by business, and to combat consumer fraud. Its operating funds come from membership dues paid by its business and professional members. In general, it issues reports, handles complaints, checks advertising, reports on solicitations, and informs consumers.[8]

Local BBBs may issue bulletins discussing local problems. In one community, such a report is issued monthly to BBB members and their employees. Only businesses may join the BBB, but individuals can become subscribers to BBB reports. The annual subscription rate is seven dollars.

Your local BBB can also be helpful in providing information on companies whose products you plan to buy or whose services you want to use. You need only call their office. Although the BBB does not endorse or recommend any product, company or service, it can supply you with facts that will assist you in making a sound decision.

Council of Better Business Bureaus

The BBB has made progress from a consumer standpoint, since it established the Council of Better Business Bureaus (CBBB) in 1970. This national organization has a mandate "to re-establish communication with the consumer and bridge the gap between the consumer and business at every level."[9]

The former president of the CBBB, H. Bruce Palmer, proposed a Code of Consumer Obligation (Figure 3-3) to its members in 1971. At that time he asked, "If business had lived by this Code for the last twenty years, would it be faced with a consumer problem today?" In concluding his talk, Mr. Palmer said:

[8]Better Business Bureau of Greater New Orleans Area, Inc., 301 Camp Street, New Orleans, Louisiana 70130.
[9]Extract from the pamphlet *The Promise of the CBBB Program: A Vital Force for Consumer Protection*, address by H. Bruce Palmer, president of CBBB, May 16, 1971, p. 1.

Figure 3-3 Code of Consumer Obligation, as proposed by H. Bruce Palmer, president of the Council of Better Business Bureaus.

1. "To assume full, personal responsibility for the quality and performance of the product or service I sell. This responsibility extends to every phase of my business, from research and development through design and manufacture, to sales and service."

2. "To recognize that consumerism is not a passing fad or a figment of the politician's imagination, but a genuine rising tide of dissatisfaction, disillusionment and indignation by my customers."

3. "To build money's worth into my product."

4. "To be honest in my advertising. Not simply to stay within the Federal Trade Commission's tolerances, but to start with a sincere intention to inform rather than deceive. To charm, beguile and entertain the consumer with my advertising, to add beauty and gaiety to his life with my packaging and promotion—but not to fool him."

5. "To avoid—in sales contract, labels and promotion efforts—making promises that will not be delivered, or even creating expectations that are not likely to be fulfilled."

6. "To institute customer service depart-ments if none already exists. To open lines of communication with my customers and respond rapidly to their complaints."

7. "To cooperate with standards or practices established by my industry association."

8. "To devote more of my total Marketing Dollars to the consumer."

9. "To channel a proportionate share of those consumer-earmarked Marketing Dollars through the most effective mechanism for dealing directly with the consumer."

And the mechanism, we think, is the BBB's with the cohesion and reach of the Council. Put us to work. Employ us to interface with the consumer, to be your Consumer Consultant. We can do things for you that you cannot do for yourself—and at a lower cost than you would have to spend even if you could or would:

10. "To eliminate duplication and overlap and to prevent proliferation in the consumerism movement. To counter the hostile voices of consumer advocates with a single, powerful and positive voice speaking in behalf of business."

Source: *Guide to Federal Consumer Services* (1976), pp. 38–39, Department of Health, Education, and Welfare, Washington, D.C., 20402.

What we're doing is trying to save business from the looming threat of greater government regulation at the behest of the aroused consumer. What we're doing is educating and informing the consumer himself in ways no individual business can possibly do. We are doing it through revitalized and strengthened local Bureaus and through national programs that are at once practical and inspired.

We shall and must be successful for one reason if for no other: The consumer problem starts with business; so business can best solve the problem.

But not—as I told Ralph Nader at our Fort Wayne meeting—not in an atmosphere of hostility, mistrust, and mutual recrimination. Only in an atmosphere of trust, confidence, and open dialogue—which the CBBB uniquely can provide. And only, I might add—voluntarily.

In this spirit, our mission will succeed![10]

[10]Ibid., pp. 11–12.

The CBBB's approval of the code was a step forward in improving consumer-business relationships. And local BBBs have grown increasingly helpful since 1971. If you encounter problems with a business that you think is operating contrary to the CBBB code, I suggest you write to the present CBBB head, Mr. William Tankersley. His address is: Council of Better Business Bureaus, Inc., 1150 17th Street N.W., Washington, D. C. 20036.

STATE AND CONSUMER AGENCIES

Governor's Office of Consumer Protection

Fifty states now have consumer agencies in state government, eight of them having located such agencies directly in governors' offices. Of these eight, only the states of Louisiana and Hawaii have consumer offices in the executive branch empowered with the enforcement of laws pertaining to unfair and deceptive trade practices. In Louisiana, the Governor's Office of Consumer Protection (GOCP) was created in 1972.[11] The newly elected governor, Edwin Edwards, said his main concern was that the office do everything within the law to protect the consumer and the honest and legitimate business people of Louisiana. The major duties of the GOPC are: 1) to mediate and investigate consumer complaints; 2) to conduct public hearings into commercial and trade practices; 3) to advise the governor and legislature on consumer matters; 4) to promote consumer education; 5) to promulgate rules and regulations interpreting the act; 6) to advise the attorney general of any unfair methods of competition and unfair or deceptive acts or practices; 7) to suggest means of securing consumer representatives on public boards and commissions.

The GOPC act also created a permanent Advisory Board that meets four or more times annually. The seventeen members appointed by the governor represent diverse interests throughout the state. In addition, the GOCP has a working relationship with the Commercial Fraud Prosecution Unit of the attorney general's office and the local district attorneys.

The GOCP also publishes a helpful bimonthly newsletter that has three responsibilities:

1. Furthering the goal of integrity in the marketplace by continuing to inform Louisiana citizens of false, misleading policies that are practiced by those who seek to defraud the public and thus take unfair advantage of the legitimate merchant.

2. Keeping all Louisianians informed on what the GOCP can do in the area of legitimate complaints and in providing assistance through education programs.

---

[11]Source for information on the GOCP: *Report*. State of Louisiana, Office of the Governor, Office of Consumer Protection. P. O. Box 44091, Baton Rouge, Louisiana 70804.

3. Alerting Louisiana citizens to new state and federal legislation that directly affects their lives and pocketbooks.

The following case history appeared in a recent newsletter. It points out how a consumer can be assisted by the GOCP and serves as a warning to prospective investors:

"In the month of July, I answered an ad in a leading newspaper to become a representative for Best Buy Panty Hose. I received a telephone call from the American Dispensing Systems. They asked for some references and I gave them. They in turn sent a letter with their references.

"A salesman for American Dispensing came to my home on August 16, 1973. After listening to him and thinking about it for a day, my husband and I decided to purchase five dispensing (vending) machines from his company. He explained the contract and we signed it. A company locator, he said, would place the machines for us; our job was to keep them filled, and report to the company monthly. He also said that if we had any questions at any time, all we had to do was call him collect (he wrote the phone number in the upper left hand corner of the purchase agreement); he would gladly answer any questions. The machines and training bulletin were to arrive within 45 days.

"I wrote the company a check in the amount of $2,797.50, for five machines. By the end of September I had heard nothing from the company—no phone call, no training bulletins, no letters. I tried calling the company collect, at least four times that week. The secretary would tell me to leave my name and number and she'd have someone return my call. No one ever did. On October 6, I called the company on my own and talked to the secretary because everyone else was either in conference or out of the office and she told me to leave my name and number and someone would call me back.

"By November, I figured that I had been taken. I sent two telegrams and finally received my first communication from the company—some 105 days after they had cashed my check. The communication stated there was a delay in manufacture. On January 25, 1975, I flew to Garland, Texas, and confronted the salesman, Mr. Don Earp, and the President, Mr. Hewitt. They said the delay was due to (no fault of the company) the coin machines' mechanisms, but that my machines should arrive shortly. I told them I no longer wanted them, just my money back. Mr. Hewitt said he had two notes in my file saying that two phone calls from me had been answered. I told him that this was not true. He insisted that it was. When I asked who returned these calls, he had no answer. Before I left his office, Mr. Hewitt assured me that my money would be returned to me as soon as I signed a release form which his attorney would draw up. Mr. Hewitt called me the following Monday, January 28, and said he would put the release in the mail that evening. I was to sign it, and as soon as they received it back I would receive my full $2,797.50. It is now February 6, 1974, and I haven't received the release form or the money."

The foregoing comments are from an actual letter asking our help, received by Governor's Office of Consumer Protection February 11th of this year; it shows how some of these business-opportunity/investment operations work.

An investigator was assigned. Only after much diligent investigation, research, telephoning, and letter writing was the case resolved satisfactorily. The consumer received and cashed a check for $2,797.50 on May 2, 1974, from the American Dispensing Systems. She was lucky. Most others who invest money with such outfits get little or nothing back.[12]

Community Consumer Affairs Offices

In my view, all states should follow the examples of Hawaii and Louisiana and be empowered with the enforcement of laws concerning unfair and deceptive trade practices. You may wish to write your governor or state representative to encourage him to pass such regulations in your state. In addition to state consumer agencies, many communities have such organizations. In New Orleans, for example, the Mayor's Office of Consumer Affairs mediates consumer complaints, conducts consumer education programs, distributes consumer information and researches consumer education. The distribution of information includes advising the public in many areas. For example, an announcement pointed out what the Louisiana Consumer Credit Act does about harassment:

A number of persons have complained to this office about creditors who harass them for payment of debts.

There are defenses against these tactics. However, you should remember that your creditor still has the option of suing to collect the debt.

Your first defense is the Louisiana Consumer Credit Law, which limits your creditor to four (4) personal contacts once you notify him by certified mail to cease further contacts. Your creditor should not threaten action not otherwise permitted by law.

Contact your attorney or the Office of Consumer Affairs if your creditor contacts you at work or at school, or you feel you have been harassed in any way.

The telephone company will also assist you if the harassment is in the form of frequent or threatening telephone calls or calls at inconvenient hours. Notify your service representative at the telephone company business office of any such calls that you receive.

[12]*Report.* State of Louisiana, Office of the Governor, Office of Consumer Protection. P. O. Box 44091, Baton Rouge, Louisiana 70804.

Remember, the Consumer Credit Act does not exempt you from payment of any legitimate debt. It does protect you from undue harassment.[13]

Community Consumer Affairs offices also distribute helpful pamphlets. The following directions on how to avoid being taken comes from one such publication:

1. Avoid "unclaimed" or "repossessed" merchandise—unless you know the dealer—because you probably will be shown pieces that are damaged, seconds, or mismatched—then SWITCHED to a higher price tag.

2. Beware of "puzzle contests." Simple solutions are often lures to get you to sell magazines, cosmetics, or other goods—or your "prize" may be a "come-on" to get you to buy an overpriced item.

3. Forget the "freezer food plan" that promises: a "free freezer"; "wholesale food"; or to "pay for itself" out of savings. The chances are you'll be dissatisfied with the food and be stuck with freezer payments that are double what they should be.

4. And if you should "win a prize," it should never cost you money to collect. A store credit "GOOD FOR $50" is often "good for nothing"—because prices are usually raised to offset it!

5. Watch "selling-out" sales carefully—some stores have fake "selling-out" sales just to get you into the store. Be sure the merchant is really selling out before you buy.

6. Be wary of the "private-party sales." Such ads are often run by "residence dealers." They operate "stuffed flats" selling furs, jewelry, and furniture. Prices are actually high and goods often misrepresented.

7. Resist tempting "deals" for your car. The salesman's boss may deny the offer after you're hooked. The price of a used car is often inflated so that the dealer can appear to give you a "real good deal" on your car.

8. Don't fall for the "sympathy" approach. It's often a "line" to get you to sign up. Organized crews are trained to tell sob stories. Once you sign, they move on to the next town.

9. Widows—Beware of "obituary ghouls." Gypsters sometimes read obituary notices and send widows bills for nonexistent debts—such as a gift for you the "dear departed" ordered just before he died. Don't pay until you're sure!

10. Watch out for final big-payment financing. It's called "BALLOON NOTE" financing: small monthly payments, then a final, unexpected, big payment.

[13]Office of Consumer Affairs. Consumergram Number 25, City Hall, New Orleans, Louisiana, 1974.

11. Suspect those offers for "free inspections." Furnaces, chimneys, roof, trees—are all subject to gyp "free inspection" deals that cost you money. Better to do business with a reputable local dealer.

12. Don't pay for a neighbor's package unless you've been told to accept it. It may turn out to be unordered junk!

13. Would you believe you can cut your gasoline bills in half? Fuel-saving devices for your car are often fakes. The U.S. Attorney's office received 15,000 complaints about one fuel-saving gadget. There are others on the market.

14. There's no "easy way to earn money at home." Most schemes require you to buy something in order to earn. You find later there is no market for what you produce, or your efforts are "not up to standards."

15. Beware of leads to unexpected inheritances. Gypsters have collected millions of dollars in fake "expenses" by leading people to believe they can inherit money from estates of distant relatives.

16. You risk your life or your money on quick "cures." If you are worried about your health—see your doctor. Don't take chances on quack medicines or mail-order cures.

17. Watch out for high "interest" rates. Credit cost can more than double the total cost of things you buy. Compae the cash price and the total cost when all interest and finance charges are included. Know the true annual interest rate. Shop around for financing as you would for shoes.

18. Vanity can cost you money or health. No known product or service can: grow your hair; make you taller; remove or prevent wrinkles; develop your bust; reduce your weight by massages, creams, belts, girdles, sweat baths.

19. Avoid "bait and switch" ads. Such deals are often "come-ons" in which the salesman may try to get you to switch to overpriced items. Also watch fake measurements and "grades" of merchandise.

20. Read and understand everything before you sign a contract. Is the guarantee specific? Are all blank spaces filled in? Are all charges itemized? Are all promises in writing? Have you a copy? Beware of legal "double-talk." "As is" means no warranty. Read the small print. Have a question? See a lawyer.[14]

LIBRARIES

Your local library can be a splendid source of consumer information and assistance. Some libraries publish current reading lists on topics like automobiles, budget and finance, consumer education, environmental protection, health, medicine and drugs, food and nutrition. One such booklet closes with this helpful advice:

[14]Mayor's Office of Consumer Affairs. "20 Ways Not To Be Gypped." New Orleans, Louisiana, 1973.

Consumer information is available in many of the periodicals found in the library. The following indexes can help in locating articles: Applied Science and Technology index; Biological and Agricultural index; Business Periodicals index; Reader's Guide to Periodical Literature.

In addition, the library has the Consumer Index to Product Evaluations and Information Sources, which can help you find a particular article in minutes.

We'll also supply you with the answers to questions on: Consumer Complaint Agencies; product evaluations; used car prices; nutrition; company addresses; brand name manufacturers; repair information. . . . Just call us.[15]

Take advantage of your public library. After all, your taxes pay for this service. If you don't receive courtesy and prompt treatment, inform the head librarian or local authority responsible for the facility.

MEDIA PARTICIPATION

Public-service radio and TV stations offer splendid consumer advice. Relevant programs can be most helpful in saving you money and preventing serious mental anguish. Here is an example of one station's offerings:

1/06/76 See You in Court! How to Use Small Claims Courts
1/13   How's Your Bird? A Look at Pets
1/20   Don't Bank on It! A Look at Financial Institutions
1/27   Surelock Homes (Home Security Systems)
2/03   Paying Through the Teeth: A Brush-Up on Dental Care
2/10   Many Happy Returns: A Look at Income Tax
2/17   CONfounded: A Look at Investment Frauds
2/24   New! Improved! And Other Myths! A Look at Advertising
3/02   Oh Say Can You See: A Look at Glasses, Contacts, and Eye Doctors
3/09   You Bet Your Life! How to Buy Life Insurance
3/16   Ills, Pills and Bills: A Look at Prescription Drugs
3/23   Split Decision: A Look at Divorce
3/30   Auto Repairanoia II: Body Work
4/06   How's Your Fern? A Look at Plants
4/13   Pack Up Your Troubles: How To Plan Vacations
4/20   Hey Buddy, Can You Spare a Job? (Employment)
4/27   Stop, Look and Listen! (Home Entertainment Units)
5/04   Ears to Ya (Hearing)
5/11   The Last Resort: A Look at Nursing Homes

---

[15]A booklist prepared by the Business and Science Division, New Orleans Public Library, New Orleans, Louisiana.

TRUTH IN LENDING ACT

A landmark action in consumer assistance was Regulation Z, issued by the Board of Governors of the Federal Reserve System pursuant to Title I (Truth in Lending Act), Title V (General Provisions) of the Consumer Credit Protection Act (Public Law 90-321; 82 Stat. 146 et seq.).[17]

The Truth in Lending law went into effect on July 1, 1969. Its purpose was to let consumers know exactly what they were being charged for credit, thus facilitating comparisons between various credit sources. The law requires creditors to state their charges in a uniform way. It also makes it easier for borrowers to ascertain two of the most important things about the cost of credit. One is the finance charge—the amount of money paid to obtain credit. The other is the annual percentage rate, which provides a way of comparing credit costs regardless of the dollar amount of those costs or the length of time over which payments are made. Both the finance charge and the annual percentage rate must be displayed prominently on the forms and statements used by a creditor to make the required disclosures. The Truth in Lending law also gives a new look to credit-term advertising and has an important provision designed to protect you in case your home is used as collateral.[18]

---

[16]Mayor's Office of Consumer Affairs, Consumergram Number 26, New Orleans, Louisiana, 1974. Tapes of these presentations may be obtained by writing to *Consumer Survival Kits,* Owings Mills, Maryland 21117. The cost is $1 per tape. The entire series can be obtained for $26.

[17]For details on Federal Regulation Z, read "What You Ought To Know About Federal Regulation Z: Truth in Lending," Board of Governors of the FRS, Washington, D.C., 1969 and, as amended, 1974.

[18]Information on Truth in Lending was taken from the pamphlet "What Truth in Lending Means to You," prepared by the Board of Governors of the FRS, and obtainable by writing to them in Washington, D.C. 20551.

THE EQUAL CREDIT OPPORTUNITY ACT

The Consumer Credit Protection Act of 1968 had a significant amendment that was passed in 1974 (Public law 93-495 H.R. 11221). It was titled "Equal Credit Opportunity Act" and became effective in 1975—one year after the date of its enactment. The purpose of the act was to require financial institutions and other firms engaged in the extension of credit to make that credit equally available to *all* credit-worthy customers without regard to sex or marital status. The act prohibits credit discrimination and states: "It shall be unlawful for any creditor to discriminate against any applicant on the basis of sex or marital status with respect to any aspect of a credit transaction."

There are stiff penalties for failure of creditors to comply with the provisions of this Act. One provision states:

> Any creditor who fails to comply with any requirement imposed under this title shall be liable to the aggrieved applicant for punitive damages in an amount not greater than $10,000, as determined by the court, in addition to any actual damages provided in section 706(a): Provided, however, that in pursuing the recovery allowed under this subsection, the applicant may proceed only in an individual capacity and not as a representative of a class.

FAIR CREDIT REPORTING ACT

Another important piece of consumer legislation, the Fair Credit Reporting Act (FCRA), became law on April 25, 1971. The purpose of this act is to protect consumers against the circulation of inaccurate or obsolete information about them, and to ensure that consumer-reporting agencies exercise their responsibilities in a manner that is fair and equitable to consumers.

Under this law, you can now take steps to protect yourself if you have been denied credit, insurance or employment, or if you believe you have had difficulties because you have been the subject of an unfavorable consumer report. Here are your specific rights under the FCRA:

1. To be told the name and address of the consumer-reporting agency responsible for preparing a consumer report that was used to deny you credit, insurance or employment or to increase the cost of credit or insurance;
2. To be told by a consumer-reporting agency the nature, substance and sources (except investigative-type source) of the information (except medical) collected about you;

3. To take anyone of your choice with you when you visit the consumer-reporting agency to check on your file;
4. To obtain all information to which you are entitled, free of charge, when you have been denied credit, insurance or employment within 30 days of your interview. Otherwise, the reporting agency is permitted to charge a reasonable fee for giving you the information;
5. To be told who has received a consumer report on you within the preceding six months, or within the preceding two years if the report was furnished for employment purposes;
6. To have incomplete or incorrect information reinvestigated, unless the request is frivolous, and if the information is found to be inaccurate or cannot be verified, to have such information removed from your file;
7. To have the agency notify those you name (at no cost to you) who have previously received the incorrect or incomplete information that this information has been deleted from your file;
8. When a dispute between you and the reporting agency about information in your file cannot be resolved, you have the right to have your version of such dispute placed in the file and included in future consumer reports;
9. To request the reporting agency to send your version of the dispute to certain businesses for a reasonable fee;
10. To have a consumer report withheld from anyone who under the law does not have a legitimate business need for the information;
11. To sue a reporting agency for damages if it willfully or negligently violates the law and, if you are successful, to collect attorneys' fees and court costs;
12. Not to have adverse information reported after seven years. One major exception is bankruptcy, which may be reported for fourteen years;
13. To be notified by a business that it is seeking information about you which would constitute an "Investigative Consumer Report";
14. To request from the business that ordered an investigative report more information about the nature and scope of the investigation;
15. To discover the nature and substance (but not the sources) of the information that was collected for an "Investigative Consumer Report."[19]

If you desire to know what information a consumer-reporting agency has collected about you, either arrange for a personal interview at the agency's office during normal business hours or call in advance for an interview by telephone.

[19]Federal Trade Commission leaflet on the Fair Credit Reporting Act (FTC Buyers Guide No. 7). For more detailed information read: *Compliance With the Fair Credit Reporting Act,* 2d edition, January 1977, FTC, Washington, D.C. 20540.

The consumer-reporting agencies in your community can be located by consulting the Yellow Pages of your telephone book under such headings as "Credit" or "Credit Rating or Reporting Agencies."

RECENT TRENDS IN CONSUMER ACTION

Bitterly opposed by most lenders and retailers, it took six years for "truth in lending" to become a law. However, consumers are better organized today than ever before. Even though they recognize that they have a long way to go to ensure themselves of a really fair deal, recent efforts have produced results. Congress has passed three important bills. The first gave consumer groups the right to join together in "class-action" lawsuits in order to recover damages from companies allegedly engaged in unfair practices. The second bill established an independent consumer-protection agency within the federal government, with authority to represent consumer interests in cases before federal agencies and the courts. The third protects the consumer against the circulation of inaccurate or obsolete information. It also provides that consumer-reporting agencies exercise their responsibilities in a manner that is fair and equitable to consumers.

Ralph Nader and others are crusading for corporations to become more socially responsible. There are also many active consumer groups demanding a fair deal for the public. You can make your contribution by joining such groups and protesting to the appropriate authorities, rather than, as the FTC states, "taking it lying down."

The FTC advice is being followed by some people, as is apparent from a delightful article titled "Calling Mr. Big—Many Irate Consumers Phone Corporate Chiefs at Home to Complain." The story reports:

> . . . A goodly number of executives believe, like Mr. Heinz, that they should always be available to anyone who wants to talk to them. They have listed numbers, they answer their own phones, and they patiently and willingly talk to anyone—drunk or sober—who calls with an idea, a complaint, a threat. Sometimes, the calls are collect and the executives end up paying to hear themselves cursed out.
>
> Some callers have legitimate complaints and call only after being totally frustrated by corporate bureaucracies.[20]

The consumer should expect to participate in the corporate decision-making process. Ralph Nader put it well when he said the consumer needs to "toilet-train the corporations."[21]

---

[20] *The Wall Street Journal,* June 19, 1970, p. 1.
[21] Statement on the "David Frost Show," July 5, 1970.

THE CONSUMER'S FUTURE ROLE

The seventies have been referred to as the decade of the consumer. Perhaps it would be more realistic to look at the role of the consumer on a B.N. and A.N. (Before and After Nader) basis. Prior to Ralph Nader's confrontation with General Motors before a congressional committee in 1966, little real concern was shown for the consumer. The general attitude was "buyer beware." However, since Nader's courageous presentation, the consumer movement has come alive. There are currently more than two thousand local and national consumer agencies at work; Nader himself has a splendid organization. Yet, whereas there are powerful forces representing every segment of business, labor and the military, *there is no single voice in Washington, D. C., lobbying for the consumer.* Surely America's 220 million consumers merit a unified spokesman of their own who will carry their message effectively to Congress and the executive branch of the government. Furthermore, consumer representatives should be on the board of directors of every major corporation. It is impossible to have an equitable voice in our American capitalistic system without, as President Kennedy recommended, being heard in the decision-making process of management.

A major obligation of government agencies and consumer groups in the years ahead will be to get the word to people who need it the most. A recent study on "Consumer Awareness of Truth in Lending" highlighted the depth of public ignorance in this area and offered excellent suggestions to remedy the situation. The article concluded:

> Truth in Lending is not helping the low-income, less-educated, minority consumer who is usually in need of much help in financial matters. Special efforts should be made to reach this particular consumer. Neighborhood workshops on credit are a possibility. Credit education in the public schools may be a long-run solution. Required credit counseling for welfare recipients should be studied. Utilization of the mass media should be made to carry simple but sound credit practices to the consumer. An ad that tells the consumer to write for further information will not work. Repetition of simple credit rules will do more to reach the "underprivileged" consumer and "sell" that consumer. If Truth in Lending is going to enable the consumer to "avoid the uninformed use of credit" more direct effort will have to be made to present the Law to those consumers who will not or can not become informed about Truth in Lending through their own effort. Only with such special effort will the purpose of Truth in Lending become a reality for all consumers.[22]

[22]William H. Balen. *Consumer Awareness of Truth in Lending.* Eastern Michigan University, College of Business; Bureau of Business Services and Research, Vol. VII, No. 2, Fall, 1974, p. 41.

4
CONSUMER CREDIT

The American family is often pictured as living in a mortgaged house, driving an installment-plan car and utilizing credit cards for its purchases. It may be argued that credit has provided many people with opportunities to enjoy the advantages of modern life that would not otherwise have been available to them because of a shortage of cash. In 1976 alone, 8.7 million passenger cars were purchased, four out of five of which were obtained on credit. A majority of the 12.9 million television sets sold last year were installment sales.

However one feels about credit buying, it seems to be here to stay.

As noted in Chapter 3, an understanding of consumer protection is particularly important as it relates to the field of credit. Therefore, in this chapter and the next we will examine credit and its cost to the consumer, keeping in mind that the effective use of credit is essential to the achievement and maintenance of financial health.

TYPES OF CONSUMER CREDIT

Consumer credit is divided into two major categories: sales credit, which includes charge account and installment purchases; and cash credit, which involves loans.

SALES CREDIT

Charge accounts became popular when America moved from an agrarian to an industrial economy. As more goods became available in the latter part of the nineteenth century, stores enlarged their stocks, and soon the chain store came into being. At first, charge accounts were permitted to only the well-to-do customers, but over the years the "buy now, pay later" concept expanded and aggressive efforts were made to solicit all income categories. The prime requirement was that the applicant have a source of income. The development of credit bureaus and effective techniques for pressuring people to "pay up" minimized the risks for business and maximized the rewards. Credit sales not only permitted the merchant to sell more articles but also gained him interest that often exceeded markup profits.

The second form of sales credit is the installment plan. It came into being in the mid-nineteenth century with the increased production of such costly household items as sewing machines, furniture, elaborate baby buggies and pianos—whose purchase necessitated series payments. The primary impetus for installment buying, however, came shortly before World War I when Henry Ford and his colleagues in Detroit learned to mass-produce cars. In order to sell these expensive vehicles, dealers had to grant purchasers the opportunity to make partial payments, and the manufacturers were forced to provide the dealers with means of financing their inventories. This dealer-and-customer financing operation became so profitable that every major manufacturer established his own credit organization. Installment purchases have been the most consistently profitable source of income for car manufacturers.

CASH CREDIT

The second major category of consumer credit is known as cash credit—the lending of money. Banks have long had the reputation of being conservative lenders, concentrating on corporations and good income producers. Although this policy has changed somewhat over the years, the little guy has often had to look elsewhere for his money. Primarily to meet the needs of the lower-income groups, a massive growth of large and small loan companies evolved, accompanied by loan sharks—unscrupulous lenders who charge whatever the traffic will bear—and pawnshops with lower, but still elevated, finance charges. In contrast, credit unions came into being sixty-five years ago, providing lower rates and good service. (For further information on credit unions see Chapters 5 and 19.) Unfortunately, credit unions are not always available to prospective buyers and many people must rely on other sources. Chapter 5 will discuss various cash-credit sources in detail and investigate how to obtain money at a fair price. The topic of home financing will be discussed in Part Three.

SALES-CREDIT COST

Now let us turn to the penalty for sales-credit purchases—the charge paid for the pleasure of buying on time. An easy way to compute this cost is to multiply the monthly payment by the total number of months and then add the down payment. Subtract the advertised price, and you can see the heavy cost of installment buying. Thanks to the Truth in Lending regulation, each company must now spell out its interest charges. Sears, for example, permits you to pay in installments, with a minimum payment of five dollars per month. For this privilege, as each bill rendered states, "If the FINANCE CHARGE exceeds 50¢, the ANNUAL PERCENTAGE RATE is 18% of the average daily balance excluding any purchases added during the monthly billing period and excluding any unpaid FINANCE CHARGE." And here is what appears on the back of the statement:

> A Vendor's Lien and Privilege on the merchandise listed on the reverse side which has been identified on your sales slip is retained by Sears until paid for in full in accordance with your Sears Charge Agreement.
> FINANCE CHARGE is based upon the AVERAGE DAILY BALANCE which is determined by dividing the sum of the balances outstanding for

each day of the monthly billing period by the number of days in the monthly billing period. The balance outstanding for each day of the monthly billing period is determined by subtracting payments and credits from the previous day's ending balance excluding any purchases added to the account during the monthly billing period and excluding any unpaid FINANCE CHARGE. No FINANCE CHARGE will be assessed: (a) In a monthly billing period during which there was no previous balance; (b) in a monthly billing period during which payments and/or credits equal or exceed the previous balance; (c) on unpaid FINANCE CHARGE; or (d) on purchases during the monthly billing period in which they are added to the account. The FINANCE CHARGE will be an amount determined by applying a periodic rate of 1.5% per month (ANNUAL PERCENTAGE RATE of 18%) to the AVERAGE DAILY BALANCE. On average daily balances of $33.00 or less, the FINANCE CHARGE may be 50¢.

Note that the ownership of the merchandise remains with Sears; this permits the company to repossess it if full payment is not made.

If you are having trouble saving money, it could be due in part to the expenses involved in sales-credit purchases. Bear in mind that money management is based, to a great degree, upon the interest rate you can earn with your dollars. The person who is receiving, say, 2 percent per month from you has found a good way to invest *his* money. But what about *you?*

"COST-FREE" CREDIT

It is important that your dollars give you the maximum return—both those spent today for current requirements and those saved for investment purposes. To use current dollars more effectively, *you should make credit purchases only when there is no charge involved.* For example, if a charge purchase at Sears is fully paid for within thirty days after the billing date, there is no interest cost. This type of credit also has the advantage of facilitating return of unsatisfactory merchandise. Have you noticed how pleasantly you are treated in most stores at the time of sale, but how difficult things become when you want to return an item and receive your money back? A charge account helps here. Of course, charging merchandise has its drawbacks too, encouraging you to buy more than you might on a cash basis. And, should you be late with your payments, this can mean costs which, as mentioned earlier, can range from 18 percent up, on an annual basis.

These high interest charges for the privilege of buying on time support the theory that credit purchases should be made only when there is no extra cost. This is a broad statement in an era of liberal credit. A bank executive recently told a group of businessmen that potential borrowers visiting his firm were not concerned about the interest charges, but only about how to obtain minimum monthly payments, regardless of how long they had to continue paying them. I have found, in setting up long-term investment programs for some of the people who have come to me heavily in debt, that although a cash-payment plan at first appears improbable, in the long run their funds will buy several times as much by following such a plan. Available dollars permit purchases at local discount houses and other facilities where there may be considerable savings from list prices, possibly amounting to as much as 50 percent off list on certain luxury articles. In contrast, long-term credit on such items as furniture, including carrying charges, may double the retail price—in fact, some people may be paying up to *three times* what the price would be on a cash basis.

QUALITY MERCHANDISE AT BARGAIN PRICES

In accordance with the guidelines established in Chapter 1, anything you buy should be of good quality. In the long run, inferior merchandise will be less durable and give less satisfaction during its use. A number of fine discount houses carry name-brand merchandise with great savings from prices charged in retail outlets. Such publications as *Consumer Reports* will help you to determine the quality and value of merchandise and should be available at your local library.

Military service has its disadvantages, but it *does* offer healthy financial benefits, if you take full advantage of them. The armed forces have many excellent facilities that give you the most for your dollar. The local store (ship's service, base or post exchange), gas station, grocery store (commissary), hospital and military sales outlet, all provide merchandise or services at good savings. During tours overseas there are opportunities to purchase costly American items through the military, as the government is anxious to improve our balance of payments, or gold outflow, and one way to accomplish this is to keep servicemen from spending the bulk of their money in foreign countries. Accordingly, American-manufactured cars, appliances and other merchandise can be obtained at real bargains. It is important to demand the same quality of service from these establishments as you would expect from outstanding private sources. Complaints about lack of courtesy, inferior quality goods or unavailability of authorized items should be brought to the attention of the authorities.

Upon comparison I found that prices for nine items—razor blades, a camera, luggage, a lighter, an electric mixer, a pen, a necktie, a toothbrush and an electric razor—totaled $477.60 at retail, in contrast to $351.24 at the post exchange. This saving of $126.36, or approximately 26 percent, can also be achieved by shopping at quality discount houses or by taking advantage of sales advertised in the daily papers. Keep an eye peeled for bargains. The president of a local college fraternity recently told me, "With ample money in our bank account as a bargaining device, there is no difficulty in getting sizable discounts on all items required for our house." You should also check with the business firm you intend to work for, to see if it establishes special prices for its employees or provides a store comparable to the military for this purpose.

In summary, buy for cash from the place that will give you the best deal. Purchase only good-quality merchandise.

CREDIT CARDS

The credit card is a relatively new device for encouraging mass spending. This 2-by-3½-inch bit of plastic permits the owner to charge a multitude of items. In 1975 there were more than 67 million cardholders carrying approximately 500 million credit cards.[1] The annual business done via cards in 1950 came to less than $1 billion, in contrast to more than $120 billion in 1975. Credit cards are aggressively marketed by companies that specialize in this field, by banks and by large corporations.

COMPANIES SPECIALIZING IN CREDIT CARDS ONLY

The American Express Company, one of the leaders in this category, has two types of credit cards. The regular green card offers the following advantages, as stated in the company brochure:

1. Security and Convenience. The Card eliminates the need to carry large amounts of cash, giving you charge privileges almost everywhere—for virtually everything. This includes airline, steamship and railroad tickets, hotel/motel accommodations, dining and theater tickets, auto repairs, car rentals, shops and resorts.
2. Limited Loss Liability. If the Card is lost or stolen you're protected. Your liability is limited to $50. And there's no liability at all if you report the loss prior to fraudulent use.
3. Worldwide Recognition. The Card is the closest thing yet to international money. It is honored in most countries at thousands of service establishments.
4. Money Management. One American Express Card statement saves you the trouble of keeping complicated records, and also verifies all your deductible expenditures.
5. Family Membership Plan. For only $10 a year (in addition to your basic membership fee), you can obtain additional American Express Cards for all your qualified dependents.
6. Emergency Personal Check Cashing Worldwide. The Card guaran-

[1]There are about 3,400 different types of credit cards available.

80

tees your personal check for up to $50 at participating hotels and motels in the United States where you are a registered guest. During working hours you can, as always, obtain emergency cash (up to $50) worldwide at most American Express Company subsidiary and representative offices with your personal check and Card.

You can obtain up to $250 in Travelers Cheques in the United States in emergencies (up to $450 abroad) by presenting your personal check and the Card at most American Express Company offices in the United States and at subsidiary and representative offices in 120 other countries.

7. Cable Money Abroad. With only your personal check and the Card you can cable up to $300 in Travelers Cheques and/or cash to a relative or friend traveling abroad. This service is available at most American Express Company Travel Offices in the U.S. at the usual handling charges.

8. Your own "American Express Private Line." Six special lines are now available in San Francisco, Miami, Phoenix, Los Angeles, Chicago, and New York City on 24-hour service. When in these cities, you can call these numbers for restaurant information, sightseeing and shopping tips, and such emergency assistance as legal and medical referrals.

9. Expanded Automatic Flight Insurance. This unique plan was developed exclusively for American Express Cardmembers to provide automatic flight insurance on any scheduled airline flight anywhere in the world where tickets are charged on the American Express Card.

When enrolled, Cardmembers have available $150,000 automatic insurance coverage against accidental death or dismemberment at a cost of only $3 per trip.[2]

10. "Be My Guest" restaurant privileges. You can now play host—without a service charge—to dinner guests, even if you are separated by hundreds of miles. Select a restaurant that honors the American Express Card. Send your guests' names, maximum dollar amount of the charge, and desired restaurant. American Express will send along a handsome invitation to your guests. Only the actual amount of the dinner, tax and tip will be billed to your account.

11. Toll-Free Telephone Service. On your monthly statement is available a toll-free telephone number for you to call during business hours for information about your account. You will be able to speak directly with people who can answer all or most of your questions.

12. Emergency Card Replacement While Traveling. The Emergency American Express Card replacement program can provide this

[2]Because of current legal requirements, this plan is not presently available to residents of New York, Florida, Oklahoma or New Hampshire unless already enrolled in the existing Automatic Flight Insurance plan.

service from offices in Paris, Rome, New York, Frankfurt, Mexico City, Miami, Phoenix and Sydney. More offices are being added each month. Should your Card be lost or stolen while traveling, just check the telephone directory white pages and/or call the local American Express office for instructions and the address of the emergency issue office or near a city on your itinerary.

An Executive Card is also utilized by American Express. The annual cost in 1977 to the American Express member was twenty dollars. Other major companies prominent in the credit card field include Diners Club and Carte Blanche.

BANK CREDIT CARDS

Certain banks provide similar services to those furnished by the American Express type of card. One of the most widely used in this category is VISA (formerly BankAmericard).

The major advantage of a VISA card is that you pay no annual fee. It is sponsored by fifteen major banks and many of their correspondents throughout the United States. Businesses that sign up with VISA are normally charged 4 percent of the bills they submit. In turn, they receive their money immediately from the bank in their community. Companies are paid as soon as they present the sales draft to the local banks, instead of waiting until the customers pay their bills. The collection problem, if any, rests with the bank. This method gives the businessman his cash promptly, at a discount, whereas if he had his own credit system, there would be a delay of from thirty to forty-five days in receiving money, and he would also have to carry the loss from bad debts.

Any interest payments from customers who fail to pay their accounts on time accrue to the local bank. Each VISA affiliate establishes a monthly line of credit for an individual cardholder that usually amounts to $1,000, a ceiling designed to keep people from spending beyond their means. Nevertheless, some cardholders have gone on real sprees and spent tens of thousands of dollars. Although the terms of the issue are stringent, it is difficult to check on the $1,000 limit in time. It is also a problem to collect from the bankrupt, or from those with stolen cards.

Each new VISA cardholder receives a warm reception. The literature highlights the following advantages: The card replaces cash and entails one bill and one payment; there are no fees, no dues; the card enables you to charge cash, as well as shop by telephone and mail.

CARTE BLANCHE VS. BANK CARDS

In early 1975, Carte Blanche took a full-page ad in *The Wall Street Journal* to point out its advantages over bank cards. The heading read "Charging Lunch vs. Financing It." The ad stated in part:

> With a Carte Blanche card you pay a $20 membership fee. And that's it. You pay for exactly what you get.
>
> Unlike bank cards, Carte Blanche is in the business of offering services, not building up credit. So we present you with a bill each month for what you owe in total.
>
> Bank cards present you with a bill that encourages minimum payment on the balance due, and maximum interest on the rest.
>
> Over a period of a year that can cost you as much as 18% more than what you really intended to pay.

The ad went on to point out "things we do they don't," as follows:

> If business takes you to Europe, we'll be there waiting. In six major cities we have International Service Centers with office space, multilingual office staffs, interpreters and just about everything you'll need to get around a place you've never been around before.
>
> You even have access to the services of English-speaking doctors in 75 countries. Which is great if all you happen to speak is English.
>
> If you get sick in this country your Carte Blanche card guarantees you admission credit at hundreds of hospitals across the U. S.
>
> With Carte Blanche you can even shop at home because we have a service that lets you order a large number of selected prestige gifts through the mail.[3]

In my view, the Carte Blanche ad is a good marketing effort. But in no way does it refute the fact that you save twenty dollars with a VISA card. Interest charges are the same for *both* companies if payments are not made on time, and each provides services not offered by the other.

The information that Carte Blanche desires prior to issuing you a card appears in Figure 4-1. It is similar to that required by other credit card companies. Carte Blanche will know a great deal about your financial position, including your annual earnings, once you send them the application form. If you earn less than twelve thousand dollars yearly salary you must indicate the amount of your other income. Other questions include whether you rent or own your home, years at your present address, company name, years with the company, nature of the business, two bank references and other credit references. Note that Carte Blanche is interested in your other credit cards and asks you to list the card numbers. In my view the information asked by creditors is more extensive than is necessary to determine whether a person is a good risk. This could be another area of consumer complaint.

[3]*The Wall Street Journal,* January 10, 1975, p. 9.

Figure 4-1 Carte Blanche credit card application form.

𝒸ℬ Carte Blanche.
an Avco Financial Service

PLEASE PRINT. APPLICATION MUST BE COMPLETED AND SIGNED.

— FOR CARTE BLANCHE USE ONLY —

3460 Wilshire Blvd., Los Angeles, CA 900

LAST NAME	FIRST	MIDDLE	AGE	OPTIONAL: I would like correspondence addressed to me as

☐ Mr. ☐ Mrs. ☐ Ms.
☐ Miss ☐ Other_____

HOME ADDRESS	STREET	CITY	STATE	ZIP CODE

MAILING ADDRESS (If different from Home Address)	STREET	CITY	STATE	ZIP CODE

HOME PHONE and AREA CODE REQUIRED ( )	YEARS AT PRESENT ADDRESS	OWN HOME ☐ RENT ☐	NUMBER OF DEPENDENT CHILDREN	SOCIAL SECURITY NUMBER / /

PREVIOUS HOME ADDRESS	STREET	CITY	STATE	ZIP CODE	HOW L

NEAREST RELATIVE NOT LIVING WITH YOU NAME	ADDRESS	PHONE & AREA CODE ( )	RELATIONSHIP

EMPLOYER/COMPANY NAME	NATURE OF BUSINESS

ADDRESS	STREET	CITY	STATE	ZIP CODE

YEARS WITH FIRM	PHONE & AREA CODE ( )	POSITION	YOUR ANNUAL EARNINGS

IF YOUR ANNUAL EARNINGS ARE LESS THAN $12,000—INDICATE SOURCE AND AMOUNT OF OTHER INCOME. DISCLOSURE OF INCOME FROM ALIMONY, CHILD SUPPORT OR MAINTENANCE REQUIRED **ONLY** IF YOU WISH IT TO BE CONSIDERED FOR PURPOSE OF THIS APPLICATION.

OTHER INCOME.

TOTAL ANNUAL INCOME

PERSON TO CONFIRM OTHER INCOME	NAME	STREET	CITY	STATE	ZIP CODE

PREVIOUS EMPLOYER (if present employment is less than 3 years)	NATURE OF BUSINESS	YEARS WITH FIRM

ADDRESS	STREET	CITY	STATE	ZIP CODE

COMPLETE THIS SECTION IF YOU DESIRE A JOINT ACCOUNT WITH YOUR SPOUSE.
(Even if married, you may apply for a separate account.)

SPOUSE'S NAME — LAST	FIRST	MIDDLE

SPOUSE'S EMPLOYER	ADDRESS	PHONE & AREA CODE ( )

POSITION	YEARS WITH EMPLOYER	ANNUAL EARNINGS

BANK	STREET	CITY	STATE	ZIP CODE	☐ CHECKING ☐ SAVINGS ☐ LOAN ACCT. NO.

BANK	STREET	CITY	STATE	ZIP CODE	☐ CHECKING ☐ SAVINGS ☐ LOAN ACCT. NO.

CREDIT REFERENCES	ACCT. NO.
☐ American Express	List Oil Co., Dept. Store, Other Credit Cards
☐ Diners	
☐ BankAmericard ☐ Master Charge	
Former or present Carte Blanche member ☐ Yes ☐ No	

$20.00 fee covers 12 months' membership dues (includes six colorful issues of Carte Blanche Magazine valued at $2.50).

Do not enclose payment — We will bill you later.

If this application is accepted, I promise to pay all ch incurred by use of the Carte Blanche card, in accor with the terms and conditions accompanying the ca company account, cardholder and company assume joi several responsibility for all amounts charged by use Carte Blanche card. If personal account with additional holder (or joint account), both cardholders assume joi several responsibility for all amounts charged by use Carte Blanche card. I understand that I may receive p tional literature from time to time, subject to my requ the contrary. A renewal card will be issued automatic my account is in good standing.

TYPE OF ACCOUNT (Check One)
☐ Personal Account — bill me at home address
☐ Personal Account — bill me at office address
☐ Company Account — bill my company

SIGN HERE →

SIGNATURE OF APPLICANT	DAT

SIGNATURE OF ADDITIONAL CARDHOLDER (or joint applicant)	DAT

☐ Issue additional card as follows

RELATIONSHIP:

FIRST NAME	MIDDLE	LAST

Additional credit cards may be obtained for members of your family or your firm at $10.00 each.

IF COMPANY ACCOUNT — signature of officer, partner, or owner	
TITLE	DAT

Source: Courtesy of Carte Blanche Corporation.

84

SPECIALTY CREDIT CARDS

Gas companies, airlines, stores and hotels frequently offer specialty cards. These cards do not provide as broad a diversification of charges as those cards discussed above, but rather function as a service to be used for purchase of the individual company's products. In other respects they are similar to the VISA card.

USE OF CREDIT CARDS

Credit cards are a major business in the United States today. The card can be used to your advantage, and you should make full use of it. It not only reduces the amount of cash you need to carry but delays payment for up to forty-five days with no finance charges. It is a chance to use the other fellow's money free.

Remember, however, that credit cards should be used with care. They provide a sense of power that makes it easy to overspend. Their exclusive use may also preclude taking advantage of bargains offered by companies that do not honor them.

There is no annual charge for a VISA card or a Master Charge card. Since they both have wide acceptance, it would seem wiser to carry one of these, rather than a group of specialty cards which give you a bulging wallet and a greater risk of loss.

PAYMENT OF CREDIT-CARD BILLS

It is important to pay your credit-card bill within the specified time. VISA has an 18 percent finance charge, and if the company advances you money, the charge amounts to 24 percent. This charge policy appears on the VISA statement as follows:

EXTENDED PAYMENT SCHEDULE

If your New Balance is:	Minimum monthly payment
$10 to $200	$10
over $200	5% of New Balance

(Balances under $10 are payable in full)

FINANCE CHARGES are calculated at a PERIODIC RATE of 1½% (ANNUAL PERCENTAGE RATE 18%) on numbers 1 through 3 below.
1. Previous balance, less unpaid FINANCE CHARGE, less previous month's purchases.
2. Previous month's purchases, 2 days after billing date.
3. CASH ADVANCE from date of advance.
4. A fee of 2% of total amount of CASH ADVANCE is charged during the statement period when CASH ADVANCE is made (ANNUAL PERCENTAGE RATE 24%).

PROTECTION AGAINST CREDIT-CARD LOSS

There are organizations that will insure your credit card against loss, but this costs money. One company that specializes in card indemnification states, "Even if you have credit card insurance, you still need us. Your insurance company doesn't send out notification of your losses for you, nor does it remove that awful waiting period when charges can mount up." Realistically speaking, if you take care of your card and report its loss immediately, your chance of sustaining substantial loss is minimal.

5
IF IT'S MONEY YOU MUST BORROW

"Get out of debt and stay out" was a guideline listed in Chapter 1. If followed, this advice can be an important factor in achieving financial success. However, statistics show that over 50 percent of all families living in the United States are currently in debt. Therefore, this chapter will begin by examining and evaluating the various sources for borrowing money and will then suggest ways to break out of the debt cycle.

There should be only three situations that require you to ask for a loan: to obtain an education, to meet an emergency and to buy a home. When borrowing you must, deal only with reliable companies that have good reputations. And don't forget that your goal is to kick the loan habit for good.

DETERMINING BORROWING COSTS

It is important to determine the cost of renting money in order to obtain the best possible loan to suit your needs. The best deal from an interest standpoint can be computed with relative ease. Let us see how to compare loan costs.

The Truth in Lending law requires every firm to list its yearly charges on a percentage basis. In loan shopping, you may wish to make a list as follows:

Firm	Annual Finance Charge	Other Expenses	Total Cost	Name of Organization (person to contact, address, phone)
A				
B				
C				

If you desire to check on the annual percentage charged by the lending agency, you can use the following formula:

$$\frac{2AB}{C(D+1)} = E$$

where:

A = total finance charge in dollars
B = number of periods in one year (use 12 if monthly payments, or 52 if weekly, irrespective of the months or weeks specified in the loan agreement)
C = dollar amount of the loan
D = actual number of payments to be made
E = annual finance charge, in percent

Let us now apply the formula. Assume you obtain a $300 loan and agree to repay the lending agency $342 in 24 monthly payments. By utilizing the formula above, you obtain the answer of 13.44 percent as the annual finance charge:

$$\frac{2 \times 42 \times 12}{300\,(24+1)} = \frac{1008}{7500} = .1344, \text{ or } 13.44\%$$

Remember that when you are quoted an add-on rate of interest, it can be misleading. For example, if a loan officer states, "It's an eight percent add-on," this does not mean that you will be paying $8 on a one-year loan basis.[1] This type of loan requires the borrower to pay back the money in equal amounts during the life of the loan; so on a one-year loan, you are in possession of only 6/12ths of the principal ($50) at the end of six months. Therefore, to determine what you actually have to pay in interest, let us use the formula above, applying it on a $100 loan repayable monthly over a one-year period at a cost of $8.

$$\frac{2 \times 8 \times 12}{100\,(12+1)} = \frac{192}{1300} = .148, \text{ or } 14.8\%$$

Tables are available that calculate this interest for you. Ask your lending agency to let you see them. Note that the dollar cost for life, accident and health insurance is listed. Lending agencies like to sell these extras because it means added profit. The life coverage also protects the lender in the event of your death.

LOAN SOURCES

Let us now look at available sources from which to secure a loan.

FRIENDS AND RELATIVES

You may be able to obtain the necessary money at no interest from a relative or a dear friend. Perhaps that rich aunt may make the loan at a nominal rate. Personal sources can be particularly helpful if you are going to college and run into difficulty securing money elsewhere. But this type of borrowing can turn friends into enemies. It is extremely important to pay back such loans in accordance with a written agreement.

---

[1] There is such a thing as a single-payment loan, but this is normally the type made by lending agencies to corporations.

GOVERNMENT AGENCIES

This source is open to students who need financial assistance in order to secure an education. There are two major programs available.

Student Loan Program

The National Direct Student Loans (NDSL) program is authorized under the National Defense Education Act. It enables eligible persons to obtain up to $5,000 over a four-year period for the purpose of attending a college or university. Scholastic records are examined, in addition to family income.[2] There must be a demonstrated need for the money. No repayment of principal is required and no interest charged as long as the person is attending school at least half time. After leaving school, the borrower must begin repaying the loan within nine months in principal installments of not less than thirty dollars per month. There is an interest charge of 3 percent per year on the unpaid balance. Payments may be made over a ten-year period. An extension is granted if a recipient goes on to graduate school or enters the military.[3]

State Aid

State Guaranteed Loan (SGL) programs make it possible for needy students to borrow funds from participating loan agencies. The state will guarantee such loans and with federal assistance pay interest on the loan while the students are enrolled in school. The loan limits in one state are as follows:

> $1,500 per year for undergraduates and up to $2,000 annually for graduate students.[4] Family adjusted gross income must be less than $15,000 to qualify.

The above programs provide eligible students with an outstanding opportunity to obtain a college education. Further information on educational loans can be obtained at school Student Aid and Placement offices.

---

[2]People with exceptional financial need may be eligible to receive money under the Basic Educational Opportunity Grant program. This provides up to $1,400 per year in financial assistance for those who need it to attend post-high school educational institutions. Recipients of this grant obtain it free. Normally it is insufficient to meet all educational costs and requires other financial assistance, such as a scholarship, job or loan. There is also a plan for those with *very exceptional financial needs*. This Supplemental Educational Opportunity Grant program provides up to $1,500 per year.

[3]Those who desire a career in teaching receive an added inducement from the U.S. government. After graduation, they are required to pay back only the principal.

[4]Louisiana State Guaranteed Loan Program.

LIFE INSURANCE POLICIES

Life insurance policies with a cash-surrender value provide a good source of money, because the interest rate is reasonable—5 to 6 percent. You may borrow most of the policy's cash-surrender value.[5] The Veterans Administration, for example, permits you to borrow up to 94 percent on government life insurance. The loan statement in their policy reads as follows:

> At any time after the expiration of the first policy year, and before default in payment in any subsequent premium, and upon execution of the loan agreement satisfactory to the Administrator of Veterans Affairs, the United States will lend to the Insured on the sole security of this policy, any amount which shall not exceed ninety-four percentum of the cash value and any indebtedness shall be deducted from the amount advanced on such loan. The loan shall bear interest at the rate not to exceed six per centum per annum, payable annually, and at any time before default in payment of premium the loan may be repaid in full or in amounts of five dollars or any multiple thereof. Failure to pay either the amount of the loan or the interest thereon shall not void this policy unless the total indebtedness shall equal or exceed the cash value thereof. When the amount of indebtedness equals or exceeds the cash value, this policy shall cease and become void.

It is apparent from the above statement that you should understand the conditions outlined in the policy before making the loan. You buy life insurance for its protection. It is essential, if you borrow money on your policy, that you should not then be forced into a position of having the policy voided. You must also keep in mind that if death should occur during the time a person has borrowed on his policy, the money due the beneficiary will be reduced by the amount of the indebtedness.

Some insurance companies do not provide loan information in the policy itself. If this is the case, you should write the company or contact the local agent in order to obtain the necessary details. Here are the rules established by one company:

> After two years of membership a member may borrow up to 100 percent of the cash value of his insurance computed on the last preceding anniversary of the date he joined the Association.
>
> *Provisions*
>
> a. No loan may be granted if the loan plus interest for one year will exceed the loan value for the following year.

[5]Cash-surrender value is the dollar amount a policyholder would receive from his insurance company if he cancelled his policy.

b. Only one loan may be in existence at any one time. If a loan is requested, it will be automatically combined with the old loan.

c. Interest will be charged at the rate of 5 percent compounded annually. Interest is computed annually on the anniversary date of the loan unless the loan is to be paid in full or replaced by a new loan.

d. Payments may be made at any time.

e. Interest is due for the day a loan is granted but not for the day of repayment.

f. Notice of interest due will be mailed 30 days prior to the due date. Payments received after the close of the month in which interest is due are credited to loan principal account.

g. Unpaid interest will automatically be carried as principal for the following year.

Although loans are permitted and the Association will make every effort to facilitate payment of loan values, we caution each member that his life insurance coverage is reduced by the amount of the loan. Keep in mind that the primary function of insurance is to provide an adequate estate for a beneficiary and that any action reducing the level of coverage may affect this estate.[6]

It is relatively simply to borrow on your life insurance as compared with the other forms of borrowing we will be discussing in this chapter. All that is required by one company is to sign copies of the Loan Agreement and Certificate of Assignment (Figure 5-1), indicating the exact amount you wish to borrow.

In my view, insurance companies should not charge interest for letting you use your own money. This same money would be paid to you, at no charge, in the event that you desired to cancel your policy. But if it is borrowed, there is a 5 to 6 percent interest cost. Why not simply charge borrowers for the cost of the paperwork involved in making this kind of loan transaction?[7] (For further information on life insurance, see Chapter 17.)

CREDIT UNIONS

Credit unions should be given careful consideration as a source of loans. You must be a member in order to be eligible. The prime advantage of borrowing from a credit union is that the total cost is often lower than that of other lending institutions. One credit union points out its cost advantage over banks, dealer financing, finance and small-loan companies and department stores. It stresses the fact that interest is the *only* finance charge here, with no added-on

---

[6]Army Mutual Aid Association, Fort Myer, Arlington, Virginia 22211.

[7]Insurance companies may argue that this is money removed from their interest-earning investments.

Figure 5-1 Loan agreement and certificate assignment.

Army Mutual Aid Association

AMOUNT OF LOAN $ _____

AMOUNT OF INTEREST $ _____

FORT MYER

Arlington, Virginia 22211

LOAN AGREEMENT AND CERTIFICATE ASSIGNMENT

I, the undersigned, insured by the Army Mutual Aid Association under Certificate of Membership No. _____ , hereby certify that I have this day borrowed from the Association the above sum and hereby assign to said Association the Certificate of Membership to secure the repayment of said loan and the interest thereon. It is Understood and Agreed:

First: That said Loan shall bear the true interest rate of five per cent per annum on the unpaid balance, payable at the end of each loan year, and that the interest, unless duly paid, shall at the anniversary date of the loan be added to the loan principal account and bear interest at the same rate and be subject to the same conditions.

Second: That should membership be surrendered, forfeited in any manner, or allowed to lapse, the amount of the loan, including all unpaid interest, shall be deducted from any surrender value of the membership. Any indebtedness shall operate to reduce the amount of any paid-up or the terms of any extended term insurance that would otherwise be available.

Third: That if any membership certificate shall mature before the amount of any loan and interest indebtedness shall have been paid, said indebtedness shall be deducted from the amount otherwise payable by the Association.

Fourth: That if the loan plus interest shall at any time become equal to or exceed the loan value of my membership, the membership shall automatically be forfeited or void unless total indebtedness is reduced to said loan value within thirty days after notice to that effect has been mailed to the last known address of the person to whom the loan is made.

Fifth: The loan may be repaid in whole or in part at any time prior to maturity, provided the membership is not in default.

Sixth: I warrant and certify that no person, firm or corporation has any interest in or claim to my pecuniary interest in said Certificate of Membership and that I have the sole right to assign the same and am under no legal disability to assign said Certificate to the Association.

In Witness Whereof, I have hereunto set hand and seal this ____ day of _____ 19___

Please . . . bear in mind that you are paying interest from the date on the check. It is clearly to your advantage to negotiate the check as soon as possible after it is received.

SIGNATURE

NAME TYPED OR PRINTED

ADDRESS

Source: Army Mutual Aid Association, Arlington, Virginia 22211.

TABLE 5-1   Pentagon Federal Credit Union Loan Information*

Collateral	Amount Financed	% of Purchase Price Financed New	Used	Repayment Period New	Used	% Rate
Auto	Up to $4,000	90%	80%	36	36	10.8%
	$4,000–$15,000	90%	80%	48	36	10.8%
Motorcycle	Up to $15,000	85%	75%	36	36	10.8%
Truck	Up to $4,000	90%	80%	36	36	10.8%
	$4,000–$15,000	90%	80%	48	36	10.8%
Truck Camper (Slip On) purchased with Truck	Up to $6,000	90%	80%	48	36	10.8%
Truck Camper (Chassis Mount) Motor Home	$6,000–$15,000	90%	80%	60	48	10.8%
Airplane Boat Mobile Home Travel Trailer	Up to $6,000	85%	75%	60	48	10.8%
	$6,000–$15,000	85%	75%	84	72	10.8%
Truck Camper (Slip On) purchased separately	Up to $15,000	85%	75%	48	36	10.8%
Camping Trailer (Tent or Pop-Up)	Up to $15,000	85%	75%	36	24	10.8%
Share Loan	All amounts	N/A	N/A	Up to 118 months		9.0%
Signature Loan	Up to $2,500	N/A	N/A	Up to 36 months		12.0%
College Tuition Loan	Up to $15,000	N/A	N/A	Up to 118 mos.		10.8%
Home Improvements	Up to $10,000	N/A	N/A	Up to 118 mos.		10.8%

*Rates and terms listed by a credit union.
Source: Pentagon Federal Credit Union.

services or credit reports to raise the total cost. This credit union also pays the premium for credit life insurance and does not impose a finance charge on any amount you have already repaid. Finally, you can pay ahead of schedule without incurring penalties.

Credit unions may provide money to purchase many things, including a car, motorcycle, truck, truck camper, motor home, mobile home, travel trailer, camping trailer, boat or airplane. Table 5-1 lists the terms for these items. You may wish to use this information for comparison with charges elsewhere.

The loan application of a credit union asks for considerably more detail than is required if you borrow on your life insurance. However, such forms are less detailed than those required by other lending agencies. (For further information on credit unions, see Chapter 19.)

COMMERCIAL BANKS

Reputable commercial banks are another good source of needed funds. Their finance charges are more reasonable than those of small-loan companies. However, they require a stronger financial position. Banks generally offer two types of loans. The first is the unsecured loan—money granted on the basis of your signature alone. The second type of loan, the secured loan, is less expensive but requires the borrower to put up collateral. This collateral may be in the form of bonds, stock, or savings accounts. If the loan is made for the purchase of a car, refrigerator, TV set, or air conditioner, such items will normally serve as the collateral. If the borrower fails to meet his loan obligation, the lending agency may sell the merchandise to recover the amount due. The remainder, if any, is returned to the borrower.

Money borrowed against a savings account can usually be obtained at 2 percent above what the bank pays its savers in interest. For example, if a bank pays 5 percent on its savings accounts, it generally permits its savers to borrow up to the amount of their savings at 7 percent. In contrast, borrowers without savings accounts are charged twice that amount.

But why keep your money in a bank at 5 percent and pay 7 percent to borrow it? It is wiser to withdraw your savings, thus cutting your costs. This will save you the considerable time and effort required to fill out loan applications and personal financial statements. You will also be spared the frustration of awaiting approval, the need to make weekly or monthly repayments and worry should an emergency arise. There may, however, be a situation in which you can save a good deal of money with a loan against your savings account rather than a withdrawal. This could be true if you need a loan for only a short time and your bank or savings and loan association does not pay interest from date of deposit to date of withdrawal.

Banks, like other lending agencies, furnish the borrower a coupon book indicating the number of each payment, amount and date due. It should be noted that there is a late-charge penalty in the event that the regular monthly payment is ten or more days past due. This late fee is normally 5 percent. On an annual basis, this means a 60-percent extra expense, so it is important to make payments on time.

Prior to signing a loan agreement with a bank, *read it with care.* Have the loan officer explain any points that seem unclear. Thanks to the Truth in Lending law, a complete disclosure of all costs is required of the lending agency. Be sure you find out the amount of rebate for prepayment[8] and the specific default charge.[9] Credit insurance[10] is not required, *"nor is it a factor in the approval of the extension of credit."* If you find that pressure is exerted on you to

---

[8]Prepayment—payment of the loan prior to the maturity date.

[9]Default charge—extra money required from a lender if payment is not made on time.

[10]Credit insurance—life insurance issued through a lending agency to cover payment of a loan in case of death of borrower.

take out such insurance, report it promptly to the BBB and the appropriate consumer advisory agency in your area. Keep in mind that if your loan is secured by collateral, your failure to meet payments could result in the loss of *"all your household goods and appliances of every kind located in or about the premises."*

SAVINGS AND LOAN ASSOCIATIONS

These institutions make collateral loans comparable to those of commercial banks in such areas as home improvements and mobile homes. They will also make signature loans against the amount of money the borrower has saved in share accounts. One such association we investigated employs a differential of 2 percent. Thus, if your passbook account is paying you 5¾ percent, the association will charge you 7¾ percent. If, however, you have no savings account with them, their charge on a secured loan is currently 9½ percent. (For further information on savings and loan associations, see Chapter 19.)

PERSONAL-LOAN COMPANIES

Small-loan companies charge the highest rate of interest authorized within legal limits. Therefore this is an expensive way to obtain money. In every sizable community in the United States, there are small-loan companies actively seeking your business at the cost of up to 42 percent interest per year, a figure regulated by the individual states. Needless to say, such firms make large profits.

Who uses the services of personal-loan companies? *Barron's* reported:

> The typical customer is the skilled or semiskilled worker with an income of from $6,000 to $12,000 a year, who frequently owns his home. Almost 80% of personal loans are obtained to consolidate previously accumulated debt and to get an extension of time to put it off. In fact, the average borrower takes out a new loan three times before managing to liquidate his existing balance; he stays in debt to the finance company for 39 months. The widespread use of credit cards, instead of hampering the personal loan business, is boosting it. The easy-to-use credit cards are pushing more people deeper into debt. They can extricate themselves only by taking out personal loans.[11]

Personal loans totaled $40 billion in 1976. Of this total, over 40 percent, or $18 billion, was provided by small-loan companies. The remainder came from banks, savings and loan associations and credit unions. According to *Barron's,*

---

[11]"Personal Loan Companies." *Barron's*, September 17, 1973, p. 3.

the "prime target of money-lenders is the under-35 population; this is not only the fastest-growing segment but also is least willing to defer buying goods and services."[12]

PAWNBROKERS

The pawnbroker is available in many communities. He requires a borrower to leave him an item of value against which the broker lends a sum of money. Failure to repay the loan allows the pawnbroker to sell the collateral to recoup the loan plus interest.

In order to protect himself, the pawnbroker normally lends only a small portion of the retail value of the item pawned. A word of caution: You pay a high rate of interest (24 to 120 percent!) and risk losing an item of sentimental value if the loan cannot be repaid on time. One of my students told me the following tale of woe:

> I needed money and pawned a four-month-old automobile quad stereo tape player with an FM stereo radio. The player cost me $205 but I received only $25 in cash. I was to pay back the loan within 90 days at $2.50 per month interest. I couldn't do it, so the pawnbroker sold my equipment for only $38. I got back $5.50.

LOAN SHARKS

These are illegal lenders who charge whatever the market will bear. One of their games is to loan $10 for one week charging $2 interest. This amounts to an annual rate of 1040 percent! Loan sharks like to keep their clients barely able to meet their interest payments. Theirs is a dangerous game to play, and you should never use their services.

IMPACT OF INFLATION AND TAXES ON BORROWING

Inflation and taxes can reduce your borrowing costs—a factor that merits consideration. The annual erosion in the purchasing power of the dollar can be expected to continue. There are, however, two unknowns: the annual percentage increase, and which specific items will show price rises.

Let us assume that a dining-room set, which could be bought for $1,000 last year, now sells for $1,050. This means that in twelve months your dollar power has been reduced by nearly 5 percent ($1,000 ÷ $1,050). If you had

[12]Ibid.

borrowed the $1,000 last year to buy the furniture, you could pay the money back with cheaper dollars.

Let us further assume that your $1,000 loan is obtainable at 12 percent, with the entire interest and principal to be paid at the end of the twelfth month. In such a case, the impact of inflation would in theory result in your paying 7 percent interest ($1,120 − $1,050).

The actual interest savings will depend on the amount of inflation that may take place with respect to your particular purchase.

The second point to consider is the effect of borrowing on income-tax payment. Let us assume that you are in the 30 percent bracket. If you use the long form (Form 1040), the federal government permits you to deduct interest charges from taxable income (see Chapter 27). Using the furniture example, it would enable you to save $36 of the $120 interest charge. However, the majority of Americans do not itemize deductions. If you do not have sufficient expenses to exceed the zero bracket amount ($3,200 maximum) this furniture loan would not benefit you from a tax standpoint.

YOUR LOAN ELIGIBILITY

Whether or not you can borrow money when you please, and what the interest rate will be depends on your past record. What do lending agencies look for in determining eligibility and setting prices?

A senior bank official informed me that his officers carefully examine the loan application and the personal finance statement. They pay particular attention to the following points:

1. *Current employment*: The number of years on the job and present salary are important considerations. Past positions are also studied. The bank wants to be sure a borrower can keep a job and is earning enough money to make payments.
2. *Indebtedness*: A hard look is taken at the list of creditors, unpaid balances and monthly payments. The bank also looks at your response to an important question: "Have you been in bankruptcy or been the subject of any judgments, garnishments,[13] or other legal proceedings?"
3. *Home ownership*: If a person owns his home and has a reasonable down payment, this indicates a sense of responsibility. Likewise, renters that have lived in one place for a period of time are looked on with favor.

---

[13]Specified amounts of debtor's pay taken from wages, by legal action, to satisfy creditors.

Figure 5-2   Credit rating denoting the usual manner of payment.

USUAL MANNER OF PAYMENT	TYPE ACCOUNT		
	O	R	I
Too new to rate; approved but not used	0	0	0
Pays (or paid) within 30 days of billing; pays accounts as agreed	1	1	1
Pays (or paid) in more than 30 days, but not more than 60 days, or not more than one payment past due	2	2	2
Pays (or paid) in more than 60 days, but not more than 90 days, or two payments past due	3	3	3
Pays (or paid) in more than 90 days, but not more than 120 days, or three or more payments past due	4	4	4
Account is at least 120 days overdue but is not yet rated "9"	5	5	5
Paying or Paid Out under Wage Earner Plan or similar arrangements.........	7	7	7
Repossession. (Indicate if it is a voluntary return of merchandise by the customer.)	8	8	8
Bad debt; placed for collection skip	9	9	9

Source: Credit Bureau Services, Chilton Corporation

4. *Net worth*: The financial statement is reviewed to see that assets clearly exceed liabilities. Savings accounts, stock, bonds and such are all pluses. It is also advantageous to have an account at the bank from which you desire to borrow money.
5. *Other considerations*: Family size is taken into account since a large family requires a healthy income. Prompt payment of credit-card accounts, charge accounts and other bills is a favorable sign.
6. *Credit-bureau check*: It is the policy of the bank I questioned to lend only to applicants who have been checked out by a credit bureau and received number 1 or 2 ratings (see Figure 5-2 categorizing the manner of payment from 1 through 9).

LOAN SHOPPING

If you must borrow, be sure to shop around for the loan. In my city, for example, a local savings and loan association charges 9½ percent for a home-improvement loan. In contrast, a finance company advertised real-estate loans at 14.1 percent. The ad read, "Homeowners, now you can get $3,000 to

$30,000 when secured by a first or second mortgage."[14] The rates were spelled out (see Table 5-2) as follows:

TABLE 5-2   Real Estate Loan Costs

Amount Financed	Monthly Payment	Months to pay	Total of Payments	Annual Percentage Rate
$3,000	$ 70.00	60	$4,200.00	14.1%
$5,000	$116.66	60	$6,999.60	14.1%
$7,000	$163.33	60	$9,799.80	14.1%

If you select a finance company, your loan must normally be secured by a mortgage to obtain their lower rate. Otherwise, it could cost up to 42 percent. Length of payment is listed as five years. Note also how interest charges mount up; if you borrow $7,000 for 60 months, it costs you $2,799.80.[15]

KICKING THE LOAN HABIT

The loan habit is a series of bad trips. Once you are in its grip, it is difficult to break out. There is a real effort on the part of lenders to keep you trapped in a cycle of debt so you must work to get out of debt and stay there. Keep in mind that borrowing for emergencies can become a way of life. Unfortunately, if you borrow to the hilt, it may become virtually impossible to obtain money when it is of crucial importance. I recently heard the following story from a client:

> I never paid any real attention to money matters. If we had any extra expenses, I easily got a loan from our bank. But this changed when I lost my twenty-four-year job with Boeing. There was no work in Seattle, and I found meeting my bills costing me a frightful rate of interest from small-loan companies. My "good friend" at the bank cut me off when I couldn't find a job. Then one crisis happened after another. My wife became seriously ill. My son was in an auto accident, and we were hit with injuries and lawsuits. My mother had to move in with us. My need for money became a nightmare. I sold off everything, including pawning our most precious heirlooms. In desperation, I turned to loan

---

[14]"Associates Financial Services of America, Inc." New Orleans *Times Picayune,* May 22, 1973, p. 5.

[15]You may be asked to take out a life-insurance policy for $534 (if not, you will be required to assign a $7,000 portion of your present policy for the life of the loan). An accident and health policy is encouraged amounting to $602. Thus, your cost could be increased to $3,936.

sharks. This resulted in threats and unbelievable mental anguish. Thank God, I finally got a decent job, but it took me seven years of struggling to pay off my debts.

GETTING OUT OF DEBT

The question I am most frequently asked is "How can I get out of debt?"

One approach that has proved successful is to start by preparing a balance sheet, income statement and budget as presented in Chapter 2. An examination of your balance sheet will permit you to see how deeply in debt you are. Let us assume that you find your debts total $5,000, broken down as illustrated in Table 5-3:

TABLE 5-3 My Debts

Amount	Finance Charge	Source	Payment Due
$1,000	36%	X Loan Co.	Monthly, for 1 year
$3,000	6%	U.S. govt. policy	Monthly, for 10 years, beginning 4 years from now
$1,000	5%	Y Insurance Co.	Entire amount 2 years from today

Once you have determined the extent of your indebtedness, the next step is to examine your income statement and determine where savings can be made. You may also want to investigate ways to augment your salary. Your balance sheet and income statement will help you to prepare a budget for a one-year period. This document should be worked out so that your income will exceed your expenses by a reasonable amount, which should be applied to your loan. Any savings made during that first year should be utilized to reduce your most expensive debt—the 36-percent finance charge.

Your balance-sheet examination might indicate $500 in a bank that earns 5 percent. Some people like the security of a savings account for emergencies. But it is poor money management to earn 5 percent and pay up to 42 percent for a loan. If you have to obtain money in a hurry, as a result of paying off a debt, your improved credit rating should enable you to do so. Furthermore, instead of going to a small-loan company at 15 to 42 percent interest, you should be able to obtain funds from a bank at a lesser cost. You can also use a credit card (at no interest) to meet plane fare or other expenses connected with emergencies.

The key to getting out of debt is yourself. You alone can make the decision and summon up the necessary willpower to follow it through. The hazards of borrowing are apparent from the following experiences reported by two of my former students. Jim's story went like this:

> My worst financial experience at first seemed too good to be true.
>
> It all began when I went to X Loan Company and asked to borrow $2,735 to buy a car. The manager was such a nice person. He spelled out the interest on the loan and told me there would be small extra charges for other services. I signed the agreement and received my money a week later. Unfortunately, I didn't check the monthly payments until my first visit to the company. The three-year loan would cost me $4,178. I lost my job six months later, and the "nice" loan manager took my car and kept my payments.

Dave's experience was just as bad:

> Last summer, I got a good job, but it required furnishing transportation. I found a car for $800 but had to borrow $500 to buy it. I hurried to _____ and got ripped off in less than twenty minutes. An employee pointed out how their interest worked and handed me a pen. I signed and now own a little payment book. There are eighteen months' payments, each for $43, for a grand total of $774.

MAJOR EXPENDITURES

Part Two provides a course of action for spending your money wisely. As pointed out in Chapter 2, major budget expenditures include: food (20–25 percent); transportation (8–10 percent); clothing (6–8 percent); personal care (2 percent); medical care (5–6 percent); other items of family consumption (8–10 percent). Although rental of a home or apartment is a major expenditure (22–28 percent), this topic is dealt with in Part Three under housing, which looks at both renting (expenditure) and buying (investment). Social Security and Disability Payments (4–6 percent) are included in Part Four, which examines the field of insurance as a means of financial protection. Income tax (11–18 percent), which calls for another major outlay, is treated in the concluding section (Part Seven) because an understanding of all areas of personal finance is important prior to preparing your income tax.

Each chapter in Part Two emphasizes the importance of taking a management approach to buying expensive budgeted items. This means _planning_ what you intend to buy, _implementing_ your plan, then _checking_ on what you have done.

6
FOOD

Allocations for food comprise one-quarter of the budget of the average family living in the United States. Thus, in order to make funds available for savings and other budgeted expenditures, it is essential to spend your money wisely at the grocery store.

Here again, good management is the key.

This chapter will consider the techniques of good grocery management, for shopping carefully and well plays a vital role in ensuring your family's physical and mental well-being.

PLANNING YOUR FOOD PURCHASES

Your health is your most precious asset and nutritious meals can be an all-important factor in maintaining it. It is therefore essential to allocate sufficient funds to guarantee you and your family a proper diet.

In order to purchase food successfully, you should apply the concepts laid down in Chapter 1, remembering to *plan* wisely, *implement* your plans and *check* to see that your plans have been accomplished. Let us first examine the *planning* aspect of food purchases, keeping in mind three factors: facilities, budget and preshopping hints.

FACILITIES

Start off your planning by assessing your capacity for home storage of staples and frozen items. Do you have a freezer? How much storage space do you have in your refrigerator? How convenient are grocery stores? How often do you eat out?

BUDGET

Review your budget to determine the amount of money allocated for food. Table 2-4 shows that a four-person family in the urban United States, earning $16,236, spends $3,859[1] for food, or 24 percent of its total budget. On a weekly basis, this amounts to $74.21.

Once the weekly-expenditure ceiling has been established, you should develop nutritious menus for this time period. Itemize the food required, such as meats, poultry, fish, bakery products, nonalcoholic beverages, fruits, vegetables, eggs, fats and oils, prepared foods, sugar and sweets. Remember to allow for parties and visits by friends—including your children's.

After estimating the quantity of food required for your weekly meals, you should determine its cost. Prices can be determined on the basis of prior

---

[1]This total includes food costs at home ($3,237) and away from home ($622).

shopping experience. You may also call supermarkets and check ads in the local newspaper. The price of snacks at the malt shop and planned dining out must also be established. If your total exceeds the budget, modify your menus and away-from-home eating.

In making a yearly food budget, remember that grocery prices can be expected to increase. I would allow for a 10-percent rise annually. Food purchased for the family away from home—such as restaurant meals and snacks must also be included in the budget. The sharp rise in food costs over the past several years seems to concern everyone.

PRESHOPPING HINTS

Let us assume that your current week's food cost is estimated to be eighty dollars. Your grocery list is now completed, and the money required has been withdrawn from the bank. However, before you go shopping, it is wise to check out the following points:

1. Are you taking advantage of specials advertised on radio, on TV and in newspapers? Find out what stores have unadvertised specials. Some post announcements in their windows; others make loudspeaker announcements. *But don't automatically buy these items if they are not within your planned budget.* At the same time, be flexible. For example, if you have a freezer and an outstanding beef special is announced, you may wish to buy in sufficient quantity for the next three weeks' menus. Likewise, if you discover a vegetable selling at bargain prices when you get to the store, consider substituting it for your planned vegetable purchase.

Keep in mind that the store's objective is to sell you the maximum amount of food, and that it employs techniques such as unadvertised specials to lure you into spending, much of which is unwise and unnecessary.

2. Don't spend more than you save by driving long distances for a single bargain. It doesn't make sense to drive an extra ten miles to save twenty-five or thirty cents. The cost of gas and other car expenses will far exceed the food savings.

3. Try to do volume buying. Make it a point to shop weekly instead of daily. Your time is valuable and should be taken into consideration.

4. Patronize quality discount facilities. If you belong to an organization that has stores providing considerable savings, be sure to take advantage of this. The armed forces, for example, have commissary privileges that enable them to save up to 30 percent and recently, wholesalers in certain communities opened their doors on weekends to people making sizable purchases. In cases involving large grocery orders, it pays to drive a few extra miles.

5. Don't go grocery shopping when you are hungry. You are far more tempted to make extra purchases on an empty stomach. Perhaps you have noticed thirsty customers taking orange juice or other beverages from the

cooler and drinking a few sips enroute to the checkout counter. Others can be seen sampling cookies or tasting fruit while shopping.

6. Buy quality merchandise. It doesn't pay to buy food that the store wishes to dispose of owing to its inferior quality. How many times have you come home and found a packaged special on fruit to be overripe, or the berries under the top layer inedible?

7. Shop with a neighbor or friend. This not only cuts your transportation cost in half but provides you with an opportunity to exchange views on good buys and stores that give you a fair deal.

8. You may find it wise in this era of energy shortage to take a team approach and shop with two or three people. One group of four wrote me:

> Our group meets weekly to plan our food-shopping strategy. This involves determining the items to purchase, estimating costs and choosing the store with the best specials. We are so well organized that our time spent in the supermarket has been cut in half from when we first started a year ago, and we need to shop less often. One person has a calculator; two of us act as runners to obtain the merchandise—this includes a careful inspection of each item; the fourth member handles the money. The savings from this team approach, we found, approximate 10 percent as compared with when we shopped separately. More important, it gives us more time to do other things. It is desirable to have a compatible group to do this food shopping. We are truly a mini food cooperative without the headaches of such a formal organization.

9. Buy the house brand, where quality is comparable. In almost every instance, it is more reasonable. Major grocery chains obtain price savings due to quantity buying and no advertising costs. Some of these savings are passed on to you.

10. Buy meat, fish and poultry when prices are low and freeze them. It may pay to store other bargain specials as well if you have adequate space. You might also can or freeze fresh fruits and vegetables in season. A&P Director of Consumer Affairs, Barbara Sullivan, offers the following tips on storing meat in your home freezer:

1. Wrap meats in single-meal, or single-portion quantities.
2. Put two sheets of paper between pairs of shaped patties or steaks, so that they can easily be separated while still frozen.
3. Wrap the meat tightly in moisture and vapor-proof paper. Lay the meat in the center of the wrap, bring the long edges together, fold over and over, butcher's-style flat against the meat, fold ends of the wrap over and over to make a tight seal. Tie firmly or seal with freezer tape.
4. Label each package with contents and date of storage. Be sure to use meat before recommended storage time is up.

5. Freezer storage times are 6–8 months for beef and poultry, 6–7 months for lamb, 3–4 months for pork and veal, 1–3 months for ground meat and cooked meat and 1 month for sausage.

11. Price per serving should be taken into consideration when meat-buying. The A&P ran an ad recently pointing out "How to get more meat for your meat dollar." The ad stated in part:

No matter what cuts of meat you buy, here's an important rule to follow. It's the price per serving that counts, not the price per pound. If boneless round is $1.49 per pound it's a better buy than short ribs at 98¢ per pound, because you can get 4 servings out of the boneless round at about 38¢ apiece—whereas you might only get two servings out of the short ribs at about 49¢ apiece. Of course the size of a serving really depends on your family's individual needs. But three ounces of cooked lean meat is the most common definition of a serving. And two is a satisfactory amount for small children, or older people with small appetites. In planning your shopping list, the following guides to portions per pound can help.

Purchase	Yield:
1 lb. boneless low-fat meat, such as lean-meat cubes of roast.	3–4 portions
1 lb. boneless fatty meat	2–4 portions
1 lb. small-bone meat, such as blade roast or chops.	2 portions
3/4 to one pound bony meat, such as spareribs.	1 portion[2]

There is merit in the A&P recommendation. However, bones are not a total waste. They make an excellent ingredient for soups and gravies.

12. The health factor is paramount. Keep nutrition in mind at all times. Fresh vegetables and fruits in season are cheaper and may be more healthful than canned items.

13. Shop around and compare stores in your general area in terms of quality, service, location, cleanliness and price. Other things being equal, it pays to shop where you obtain the best financial deal.

In this respect, remember that the saving stamps offered by some grocery stores cost the owner money. He must pass this extra cost on to his customers. So don't let yourself be enticed by the stamps unless the food items you desire to buy are equal to, or less than, the price elsewhere.

There are important price differences among stores in every locality. A recent survey of 113 stores in the Greater New Orleans area emphasized this point. The Louisiana Consumers' League checked items considered to be part

[2]The New Orleans *Guide,* February 12, 1975, Sec. 2, p. 4.

of any well-rounded grocery list. More than 100 volunteers inspected groceries of similar size, weight and brand in every store. Prices ranged from $19.39 to $26.57, a difference of over 37 percent. A family that spends $3,000 a year on food could save as much as $1,110 a year by buying at a chain store instead of the convenience shops. Note, however, that even a single grocery chain has small price differentials among its various outlets. There are also major differences in prices charged by chain stores.

14. Familiarize yourself with unit pricing. It enables you to pick out which of a number of comparable items is the least expensive by providing a common unit of measurement.

You may, for example, believe that you have found the lowest price on an eighteen-ounce can of Del Monte peaches, as a result of checking newspaper ads from three stores. However, when you arrive at the store with the best deal, you find they have five different brands of peaches, in various-sized containers. A look at your shopping list will indicate the price for the Del Monte brand advertised in the paper. But in order to compare this brand with the four others, you must have a common denominator—in this case, it is the *price per pound.* This unit price should appear on the shelf under each brand and permits you to make a valid comparison. In this case you can quickly determine that Brand E sells for the least cost—17½ cents per pound.

It does not necessarily follow, however, that you should buy the cheapest brand. The can may be too large to store satisfactorily (Brand E is a twelve-pound item); the contents may not taste as good to you or your family as those of another make; there may be fewer peaches than in a competitor's brand. (The total weight is utilized in unit pricing and includes the liquid contents.) Still, in spite of its limitations, unit pricing can be a helpful device that should be considered in arriving at your buying decision.

15. Stay alert for unusual bargains. For example, water utilized in some communities has been suspected of being a health hazard. Bottled water from deep artesian wells has been suggested as an alternative. Some enterprising people in New Orleans buy their milk in one-gallon plastic containers (the cost for the nonreturnable carton is five cents) and when they have saved up a goodly number, three or four friends get together and drive one car thirty-five miles to Abita Springs to obtain bottled water free at the public well. The saving is sizable because a gallon of this water costs from twenty-nine to forty-nine cents in the supermarket.

16. Save your coupons. They provide anywhere from five to seventy-five cents off on the purchase of food items, resulting in savings of 5 to 25 percent. These coupons appear in newspapers, magazines, on boxed foods and are sent through the mail. When you have collected a good supply, take your coupons to the stores where you normally shop and receive the best prices. But don't fall into the same trap as one shopper I know, who told me: "I use all my coupons

but unfortunately I don't use many of the items. But they seem like such bargains, I can't refuse." Two final thoughts: Check the expiration dates of the coupons, if any, and consider swapping coupons with friends.

IMPLEMENTING YOUR PLAN AT THE GROCERY STORE

Once the planning aspect is complete, you are ready to tackle the shops with confidence. So let's turn to points you should consider in *implementing* your grocery-shopping plan.

1. Abiding by your shopping list is in the best interest of your health. The majority of Americans overeat and are overweight. Dr. Nathan Shock of the National Institute of Child Health and Human Development has stated, "If you could . . . eliminate all the obesity in the population, you'd be more likely to increase life span than by almost any other means."

Follow your marketing list. It is one thing to itemize your grocery needs, but *the real challenge is to abide by the list once you are in the store.* Why is this so difficult? Supermarkets are set up most attractively to encourage you to maximize your purchases. For example, the narrow checkout counters at which you may be forced to linger are loaded with all sorts of goodies that encourage you to do impulse buying. The longer the line, the greater the opportunity for the store to make such sales. Once forewarned, however, you can foil this game plan.

After all, what is the point of making a budget if you don't stick to it when you get to the store?

2. Look at each packaged item to be sure that it is undamaged and is what you are looking for, both in brand and quantity. It is disappointing to arrive home and find that you have an eleven-ounce package when you wanted fifteen ounces. Also see if the box contains a usage date such as: "Better if used before Jan 05, 1979." Be sure to select the freshest item with the longest life. And keep an eye out for coupons estimating the percentage savings.

3. Examine fruits and vegetables carefully for possible damage. It is better to do this at the store than to come home and find that your produce is spoiled. At the same time, be considerate of your grocer, respecting the attractive display and perishable merchandise.

4. Be systematic. Proceed in an orderly fashion from the time you enter the supermarket until your departure, noting the overhead signs that label the aisles. Your time is valuable—use it wisely.

5. Watch carefully while your purchases are being tallied. Be sure the cashier takes adequate time, and be alert as the prices are being rung up. Major

mistakes can be made; after all, supermarket cashiers are neither certified public accountants nor mathematics majors.

During the pricing of your groceries, you should be watching the register rather than talking with a neighbor or friend. Prior to leaving the checkout counter, make a point of examining your total bill, including tax. It should approximate the sum you had estimated. If there is a sizable difference, recheck every item. Also, keep an eye on how your groceries are packed. Don't hesitate to speak out if the bagger attempts to put fragile items on the bottom.

CHECKING ON YOUR PURCHASES

The final function in good grocery management is to *check* on what you have bought. This should be done as follows:

1. Return home promptly after shopping and unpack your groceries. Examine each item for possible damage. Any defect should be noted and the merchandise should be returned on the next visit. It is desirable to phone the store manager promptly and inform him of your intention to bring back the unsatisfactory merchandise. This inspection might include checking eggs and other perishables by opening a carton, as well as inspecting packaged meats, poultry, fruits and so on. Food is expensive and you have paid good money for it. You are entitled to good groceries! Don't be timid about returning unsatisfactory items.

2. Enter the amount of money spent on food in your account journal. Check it against what you had planned in your budget. If you have overspent, you will have to make up for it the following week. This can be painful but is essential in order to achieve your financial objectives.

FOOD AND HEALTH

Let me emphasize once more that your health is your most precious asset, and that proper diet is essential to its maintenance.

The U.S. Department of Agriculture (USDA) has prepared an excellent daily food guide, geared to ensure your family an adequate diet. The USDA categorizes food into four major groups—meat, milk, vegetable-fruit and bread-cereal—giving daily requirements for each. In accordance with management techniques established earlier in the chapter, you should proceed as follows:

1. Prepare meals for a one-week period that will give you a healthy diet. (Use Tables 6-1 and 6-2 as guidelines.)

TABLE 6-1 A Daily Food Guide

SERVINGS RECOMMENDED	WHAT COUNTS AS A SERVING*
Meat Group 2 OR MORE	2 TO 3 OUNCES OF LEAN COOKED MEAT, POULTRY, OR FISH. As alternates: 1 egg, ½ cup cooked dry beans or peas, or 2 tablespoons of peanut butter may replace ½ serving of meat.

Milk Group
CHILD, under 9 .... 2 TO 3
CHILD, 9 to 12.3 OR MORE
TEENAGER . . .4 OR MORE
ADULT.......2 OR MORE
PREGNANT
  WOMAN . . . . .3 OR MORE
NURSING
  WOMAN . . . . .4 OR MORE
	ONE 8-OUNCE CUP OF FLUID MILK—whole, skim, buttermilk—or evaporated or dry milk, reconstituted. As alternates: 1-inch cube cheddar-type cheese, or ¾ cup cottage cheese, ice milk, or ice cream may replace ½ cup of fluid milk.

Vegetable–Fruit Group 4 OR MORE, INCLUDING: 1 GOOD OR 2 FAIR ·SOURCES OF VITAMIN C 1 GOOD SOURCE OF VITAMIN A–AT LEAST EVERY OTHER DAY	½ CUP OF VEGETABLE OR FRUIT; OR A PORTION, for example, 1 medium apple, banana, or potato, half a medium grapefruit or cantaloupe. *Good sources:* Grapefruit or grapefruit juice, orange or orange juice, cantaloupe, guava, mango, papaya, raw strawberries, broccoli, brussel sprouts, green pepper, sweet red pepper. *Fair sources:* Honeydew melon, lemon, tangerine or tangerine juice, watermelon, asparagus, cabbage, cauliflower, collards, garden cress, kale, kohlrabi, mustard greens, potatoes and sweet potatoes cooked in the jacket, rutabagas, spinach, tomatoes or tomato juice, turnip greens. *Good sources:* Dark-green and deep-yellow vegetables and a few fruits, namely: Apricots, broccoli, cantaloupe, carrots, chard, collards, cress, kale, mango, persimmon, pumpkin, spinach, sweet potatoes, turnip greens and other dark-green leaves, winter squash.
Bread–Cereal Group 4 OR MORE	COUNT ONLY IF WHOLE-GRAIN OR ENRICHED: 1 slice of bread or similar serving of baked goods made with whole-grain or enriched flour, 1 ounce ready-to-eat cereal, ½ to ¾ cup cooked cereal, cornmeal, grits, spaghetti, macaroni, noodles, or rice.
Other Foods as Needed TO ROUND OUT MEALS AND MEET ENERGY REQUIREMENTS	Refined unenriched cereals and flours and products made from them; sugars; butter, margarine, other fats. Try to include some vegetable oil among the fats used.

*Amounts actually served may differ—small for young children, extra large (or seconds) for very active adults or teenagers.

Source: U.S. Department of Agriculture.

113

TABLE 6-2 Use of Food Groups—Some Ways to Use in Family Meals

Meat Group
Foods from meat group usually appear as the main dish, the "meat," at a meal; or as an ingredient in main dish—a soup, stew, salad, casserole, or sandwich. Small amounts of two or more foods from th group used during the day can add up to a serving. Egg used in custards and baked goods counts, too.

Milk Group
Milk may be served as a beverage at meals or snacks. Some may be included on cereals and in prepar tion of other foods—soups, main dishes, custards, puddings, baked goods. Cubed or sliced chee (plain, on crackers, or in sandwiches) and ice cream or ice milk (at meals or in between) may repla part of the milk.

Vegetable-Fruit Group
Vegetables or fruit are part of most meals. Serve some raw and some cooked, some with crisp textu and some with soft; and contrast strong flavor with mild, and sweet with sour for variety in mea Brighten meals with color—a slice of red tomato, a sprig of dark greens, or other colorful vegetable fruit. Both vegetables and fruit are used in salads and as side dishes; some vegetables in casserol stews, and soups; and some fruits raw, as juices, and in desserts, such as cobblers, pies, or sho cakes. Many families include their vitamin-C food as a citrus fruit or juice, as melon or strawberri (when in season) at breakfast.

Bread-Cereal Group
Foods from this group are served at breakfast as toast, muffins, pancakes, or grits; cereals, cooked ready-to-eat; at lunch and dinner as macaroni, spaghetti, noodles, or rice in a casserole or a side di as any kind of bread and as a baked dessert, such as cake, pastry, and cookies. Because breads a cereals are well liked, usually inexpensive, and can be served a number of ways, they are us more than four times a day in most households.

Other Foods as Needed
Some of these items, such as flour, sugar, and fats, are ingredients in recipes. Some may be added other foods at the table—sugar on cereals, dressing on salads, and spread on bread.

Source: U.S. Department of Agriculture.

2. Determine the cost of this menu. Check the cost against the money available in the budget for this purpose. Make appropriate modifications to stay within the budget—*but in no case should doing this mean sacrificing the health of your family.* If necessary, make a savings elsewhere in your budget.

3. Utilize the list you have prepared in doing your weekly shopping. Most families use similar foods each week. You may wish to make up a chart showing item, brand, unit price, estimated cost and actual cost to help you itemize your needs as to quantity and cost.

4. Check your purchases against the list when you arrive home.

Your doctor is the best person to advise you on a diet tailored to meet your needs. You, however, are the only person capable of implementing his recommendations. Doing so takes will power but pays off in a trimmer figure and greater zest for living. It should also reduce your grocery and medical bills.

HOME CANNING

Home canning can be a money saver but requires care. This fact is highlighted from time to time when people die from botulism, a type of food poisoning that results from improper canning. When canning, be sure to select appropriate foods, and sterilize and seal your material meticulously.

FOOD CO-OPS

You may wish to organize a consumer-owned and operated food co-op or join one already in existence. Food co-ops consist of groups of people who buy groceries collectively at wholesale for their own use, doing all the work necessary to purchase and distribute the food. In order to secure money to buy items, each member contributes a small amount that normally ranges from five to ten dollars.

CO-OPS IN ACTION

Co-op members may be organized into five working groups: buyers; weighers; storekeepers; transporters; and cleaners-up. By sharing duties, no single member ends up with too much to do. Willingness to work and cooperate are essential.

In a food co-op the following specific jobs must be done each time food is bought and distributed:

1. Collecting the orders of members;
2. Buying the food from wholesalers and bringing it to a convenient distribution point;
3. Separating the purchases into categories: potatoes, rice, beans, tomatoes and so on;
4. Weighing and pricing items sold by weight, and pricing items sold by the piece;
5. Opening the doors for business after the above tasks are completed, at which time members can come in and pick up their orders for the week (be sure to open promply at the time you had specified);
6. Assuring that the storekeeper is available to accept payment for goods

and record sales and has the financial records available for members to review;

7. Seeing that members turn in their orders for next week while making their pickups;

8. Cleaning up the distribution area after all members have picked up their orders, and storing co-op equipment until the following week.

ADVANTAGES OF CO-OPS

What benefits are there to members of a successful food co-op? A co-op can obtain food at a lesser price because purchases are made at wholesale and sold to the members at that price plus operating costs. Since members share the work, the primary costs are transportation, rent (if any) of a distribution site, paper for keeping records and an adding machine. There are no expenses for salaries and profits.

A co-op provides a limited number of items. It is neither a supermarket for one-stop shopping nor a grocery store, and often starts out selling only produce. As the membership increases, dairy products, eggs and some grains might be included. A large setup can offer canned goods, spices, fish and other items. The more conscientious the group members, the more money you can save. But a co-op may not always be able to sell every item at a lower cost than the chain store.

IMPORTANCE OF GOOD MANAGEMENT

Like any other successful business venture, a food co-op must be well managed. It should be run according to the same three principles emphasized throughout this book. Members must *plan what they are going to do, do it according to plan* and then *check to see that it has been done properly.* In regard to a food co-op, *planning* includes establishing money needs, necessary personnel, required space, wholesalers to contract, membership, items to buy and determining what kind of operating procedures are needed. The *implementation* of the plan calls for a good organization spelling out who does what. And *checking* includes keeping a close eye on the money, equipment and membership.

A GARDEN OF YOUR OWN

With the high cost of living, home growing of fruit and vegetables would appeal to those wishing to save money, as well as to the health-minded and environmentalists.

Attractive as it sounds in theory, however, home gardening can be demanding, discouraging and expensive. A neighbor of mine planted a small vegetable garden, specializing in tomatoes, only to find that before he could apply protective measures, insects had eaten the green fruit. Things went from bad to worse, and after six months, he gave up the project.

In contrast, another has kept a vegetable garden for years and spends much of his spare time with his hobby. If you are interested in trying your luck, I would suggest that you contact your local county agent. He can give you good advice on maintaining your soil and inform you of the crops that do well in your locality. For further information on gardening refer to Chapter 12.

COOKBOOKS AND OTHER GUIDES

In order to plan your menus wisely, you should buy a good cookbook. There are many general texts available as well as special-purpose books dealing with such topics as low-calorie, meatless, poultry and hamburger dishes. In spite of the flood of cookbooks written by "personalities," I recommend that old favorite, *Joy of Cooking.*[3] Well-written and featuring splendid recipes, chapters also discuss The Foods We Eat; Entertaining; Menus; Canning; Salting and Smoking; and Freezing. Another good seller is *Weight Watchers Cookbook,* with daily menus that enable you to reduce.[4] People who like to count their calories should also enjoy *The Low Calorie Diet.*[5]

How Sex Can Keep You Slim received much publicity when it appeared in 1972.[6] The author, Dr. Abraham Friedman, has treated metabolic diseases and obesity for over twenty-five years. His recommendations include, "Reach for your mate instead of your plate." He also prescribes essential foods that he calls R.S.V.P.:

Raw fruits—three servings per day. (Be sure to include at least one citrus fruit or juice daily.)

Salads—all you want. Use vegetable oil (1 tablespoon) and vinegar dressing.

Vegetables—three servings per day, especially the green or leafy vegetables.

Protein—three servings per day.[7]

[3]Irma S. Rombauer and Marion Rombauer Becker. Indianapolis: Bobbs Merrill Co., Inc., latest edition.
[4]Jean Nidetch. Great Neck, N.Y.: Hearthside Press, latest edition.
[5]Marvin Small. New York: Pocket Books, latest edition.
[6]Abraham Friedman. Englewood Cliffs, N.J.: Prentice-Hall, Inc., 1972.
[7]Ibid., p. 104.

Dr. Friedman states that "proper nutrition plays an important role in our general health and well-being. It is essential for proper performance of all our body functions and activities, including sexual activity. A proper diet will help keep you fit and slim, and even enhance your sexual potency."[8]

There is an abundance of current literature on cooking that can be obtained free. For example, most public utilities furnish their customers with pamphlets that contain menus, recipes and suggestions helpful to the home-maker. These are frequently available at public libraries as well as directly from the utilities.

Another potential source of information is the dietitian at your local hospital, who can offer good advice on menus and may have literature available. Public Health officials and librarians can also provide helpful material on cooking. Be on the alert for new recipes appearing in newspapers and magazines. TV also offers several good programs on food preparation.

[8]Ibid., p. 104.

7

CLOTHING &
PERSONAL CARE
(Including Health Maintenance)

Clothing and personal care comprise about 9 percent of the budget of the average family living in the United States. As in the case of food, it is essential to spend your money wisely in these areas so that adequate funds are available for savings and other expenditures.

Here again, good management is crucial.

Performing the management functions of wise *planning, implementing* these plans and *checking* to see that what you have planned has been carried through will help you meet your clothing and personal-health needs within the allotted budget. This chapter will investigate techniques for maximizing your clothes-buying power and keeping you as fit as possible. A word of caution: Don't skimp on health care—it is far less expensive to take preventive health measures than to pay for operations.

CLOTHING

PLANNING YOUR CLOTHING PURCHASES

Before considering specific purchases, sit down and reexamine your budget in terms of the *total sum* you have allotted to clothing and personal needs. The majority of such expenditures will not be made in equal amounts throughout the year. Therefore, you must itemize your specific requirements on a weekly basis. Certain personal-care expenses, such as visits to the barbershop, beauty parlor and drugstore for sundries, may occur regularly, each week or month. Such expenses should be easy to estimate accurately. In contrast, your expensive outer clothing may be bought on a seasonal basis. These expenditures will be rather difficult to determine, but do your best. It is helpful to develop a checklist itemizing the entire family's clothing needs from the skin out. Your estimated cost should allow for a 10-percent increase during the year.

Once you have decided upon the amount of money needed for clothing, you may wish to consider the following guidelines, which can help you stay within your budget.

1. Shop around. Before you buy, compare stores in your community as to quality, service, location, cleanliness and price. *Other things being equal,* it pays to shop where you can obtain the best price; but again, I stress, "other things being equal."
2. Consider reputation. Choose a store that is known for its quality merchandise and willingness to accept returns graciously. A number of stores have fair return policies and place competent people in their adjustment departments.

    Since many items of clothing are expensive, the possibility of returning unsatisfactory merchandise is important. A dollar saved on a costly item is meaningless if, upon examination at home, the garment turns out to be shoddy and unfit to wear. Return privileges should include receiving your money back, obtaining full credit, or being able to to exchange the article in question. The choice should be yours.

As noted earlier, it is surprising how pleasant some stores can be at the moment of purchase but how disagreeable at the time of return.

3. Take advantage of legitimate specials as advertised on radio, on TV and in the newspapers. Stores will often reduce prices on clothing before or after each season. But be sure that these specials won't soon be going out of style and are not faulty. Sales are not announced for your benefit; they permit stores to bring in business at slow times or unload merchandise that it is not to their advantage to retain.

4. Beware of buying from stores going out of business. There is no opportunity to return merchandise after the owners have liquidated their stock. Such "bargains" also permit some unscrupulous merchants to restock their shelves with inferior merchandise. A recent article stated:

> . . . Police Department detectives have padlocked a store and arrested two men for allegedly violating a rarely enforced state law prohibiting false advertising. . . . A department spokesmen said the store was sealed after detectives reported discovering two men unloading suits into the store during its advertised liquidation sales.
>
> The establishment currently is advertising a "going out of business sale" urging shoppers to hurry to make their purchases. The advertisements also declare, "Every item in the store reduced."
>
> Police allege, however, that on at least one occasion and possibly two others, the store's stock was replenished with additional suits drawn from an allotment of nearly 1,000, valued at more than $20,000, in a waiting van parked in an apartment complex. . . .
>
> The van, which was found to contain 846 suits, and a car used to transport the suits to the store, were seized after the arrests.[1]

5. Patronize quality discount facilities. Many communities have quality discount stores that offer sizable savings. Again, let me stress the importance of checking the return policies of any firm you deal with.

6. Don't buy garments that are too high-styled. Manufacturers and retailers realize that by changing styles frequently, they will increase sales. The higher-styled the item, the quicker it will be outdated. Try to purchase a dress or suit that can last for a reasonable period of time, so that it will wear out and not "style out."

7. Consider usefulness. Before buying a piece of expensive clothing, question its versatility. For example, the color of a jacket should permit it to be worn with more than one pair of slacks. And don't

[1]"Stock Reported Added to 'Out of Business Sale.' " New Orleans *Times Picayune,* October 7, 1973, Sec. 1, p. 3.

forget that basic black dress that can be used for morning, afternoon or formal wear with an appropriate choice of accessories.

8. Plan to make some of your clothes. It is surprising how much you can save by buying material and making your own garments. The earlier in life you learn to sew, the greater the savings. You should therefore allow for a sewing machine in your budget. This investment can pay for itself many times over, not only in terms of dress making but by permitting you to do your own repairs and alterations.

There is considerable satisfaction in creating your own fashions. Furthermore, the workmanship in most clothing today is not comparable to what you can do at home. Patterns are readily available in stores and by mail order. Sewing lessons can be obtained in most communities.

Over the years, my wife has made dresses for herself and our daughter at considerable savings. She has also designed drapes, curtains and bedspreads. Recently, she saw a dress that was selling for fifty-nine dollars in a prominent department store. Here is what it cost her to duplicate it:

Material (polyester knit)	
3 yards @ $3.95 per yard	$11.85
Buttons	1.50
Zipper	1.00
Pattern	2.00
Thread	.50
Trim and interfacing	2.10
	$18.95

This well-confected dress required ten hours to complete. Simpler patterns, such as sports clothes, take her only three to four hours. It is apparent that adequate time is needed to do a good job, but my wife says, "I love to sew. It's fun to design my drapes or improve on a dress I've seen in a store. The extra loving care of quality workmanship pays off in ample seams, regular topstiching, wide hems, quality materials and good fit. It's fun to wear my creations to parties and have friends guess where I bought them."

9. Know your fabrics. Whether you make your own clothes or buy them ready-made, beware of materials that are not washable, durable or easy to work with. Watch for fabric sales—particularly for good remnants: material that is flawless but has only a few yards remaining in the bolt. It is often available at half price because of its limited quantity.

10. Buy practical clothing. Garments should be wrinkle-resistant and ready to wear after coming out of the washer and dryer. There is no need to spend time ironing today. How delightful to pack all your clothing in one small bag that can be slipped under the seat of the airplane!

IMPLEMENTING YOUR PLAN AT THE SHOPS

What are the points you should keep in mind while shopping?

1. Abide by your list of planned clothing purchases. Bring along a list of the items you plan to buy and stick to it. When you walk into the store, go directly to the department where you intend to make your purchases. Stores will make every effort to induce you to buy additional goods. Their displays will be attractive, and their salespeople are trained to push their wares. When you buy shoes, for instance, you may be encouraged to select a matching bag or other coordinated accessories including scarves and hats. Don't waver from your planned list.

   Salespeople in some stores receive bonuses (often a 5–10 percent commission) for selling old merchandise—items that may have been in the store for several months or even years. Therefore, be suspicious of items that are not in style. Several of my students also work for department stores where they receive a splendid on-the-job education on how to encourage sales. One young woman who sells ladies' apparel told the class, "I have been taught to play to a person's vanity. This approach is highly successful. Sometimes it requires my calling the store manager to assist in closing a flattery sale. He's good-looking, and the customers love his approval."

2. Shop with someone whose judgment you respect in order to find out what really looks best on you. The salesman's advice may prove costly, as he may automatically favor the most expensive item.

3. Shop during a quiet time of day whenever possible. This permits you to examine the merchandise more carefully; and the salespeople are more helpful when they are not being harassed.

4. Check carefully on the alteration policy of the firm prior to making a purchase. Are alterations made free of charge? Do the tailors do first-class work? Faulty workmanship can ruin an expensive suit. If you have to return to the store several times for a proper fit, you may decide it isn't worth the effort. The garment then remains in your closet until you give it away or throw it out.

CHECKING ON YOUR PURCHASES

1. As soon as you get home, reexamine your merchandise for defects. If the color or style has lost its appeal in the light of day, you may decide to return your purchase. If so, do it promptly. Keep all your receipts and leave the tags on your garment so that there is no question as to where you bought them. The importance of a receipt and prompt return is illustrated in the following tale related to me by a client:

   I bought an $11 shirt as a gift for a friend. He wasn't satisfied with the color, so I offered to exchange it. I went back to the store with the shirt and explained the situation to the salesperson, and that's when the problem started. There were no more shirts like it, so she offered to give me a credit of $7. When I told her I had paid $11 for the shirt, she said that the shirts had been reduced to $7. I had no proof of purchase and had to accept the $7. I then went across the street and found the exact shirt at $16. After buying the desired color, I found myself paying almost double ($20) the cost of the original item. I learned the hard way to *always hang on to my receipts* for at least a couple of weeks, especially if the purchase is for a gift.

2. Maintain your clothes by keeping them neat and clean and making minor repairs. But once they go out of style or look worn, eliminate them from your wardrobe! It may not pay, for example, to have shabby shoes half-soled. The repair cost is too high as compared with the price of buying a new pair.

   You may be able to sell your old clothes to a thrift shop or want to include them in a garage sale. The Salvation Army or other charitable organizations will be happy to pick them up. Remember, if you give them away, there may be a tax benefit on their fair value at the time.

3. Keep your clothing needs to a minimum, reviewing your wardrobe frequently. If you have a limited amount of storage space, it is foolish to fill it with dust collectors. Don't overbuy and make yourself a storage center. Styles change too quickly, and more practical garments are being created each year. You don't need the stockpile your parents required, because it is so easy to "wash and wear" clothing today.

4. If you have received a bum deal, keep after the store until it makes a fair settlement. This may require going to the BBB, local consumer agency or small claims court. And tell your friends about your experience. Here is how one person won out:

   Last year, I bought a pair of tennis shoes. They had been used only eight times in three weeks, but both shoes wore out in the inside heel.

   I took the shoes back to the store in hopes of exchanging them for another pair. The manager of the shoe department kept me waiting for 45 minutes. He then told me the shoes would have to be returned to the manufacturer, who had to OK the exchange. A reply was promised within six weeks. The manager told me that I would be called when he received the word.

   After waiting eight weeks, I finally called the store and was informed that no answer had been received. I called several times in the next two months and was given the same story, "No word yet."

   Two more weeks passed, and I decided to visit the store with my roommate, who is an attorney. When I introduced my friend, the manager informed me that he had received authorization for me to select another pair of shoes. It took perseverance, but sometimes this seems to be the only way to get results.

PERSONAL CARE

Major personal-care items should include a yearly medical examination, dental checkups, health-club membership, beauty parlor and barbershop visits and sundries for good grooming. *Don't skimp* on these expenditures.

ANNUAL PHYSICAL EXAMINATION

An annual physical examination is your best single investment. It is surprising how many people will spend more on checkups of their car than of their own health.

A first-class medical examination can be obtained at reputable hospitals in your area. If you don't have a family doctor, contact the hospital director for the name of a physician who specializes in this type of work.

There are a number of hospitals in the United States that have obtained national recognition for the thoroughness of their physical examinations. Among them are the Mayo Clinic in Rochester, Minnesota; Ochsner Clinic, New Orleans, Louisiana; and Duke University Hospital, Durham, North Carolina. You normally spend one or two days in the hospital, with the cost ranging from $175 to $350 plus travel and accommodations. The advantage of going to a quality hospital is that it has specialists in many areas. Thus, a problem that might go undetected elsewhere could be diagnosed properly and corrective measures taken promptly.

The best time to have a physical examination is when you are well. A detailed health check can permit the physician to advise you of possible danger signals. He can then prescribe courses of action to improve your health, thus preventing costly and debilitating illness.

DENTAL CHECKUPS

Periodic dental checkups are also important. They permit problems to be detected before they become serious. At the same time, have your teeth cleaned. This enhances your personal appearance as well as preventing serious trouble.

HEALTH-CLUB MEMBERSHIP

The importance of physical fitness was emphasized in a *Newsweek* article titled "Tips On How To Stay Young."[2] It pointed out the advantages of keeping your weight down, avoiding alcohol and tobacco[3] and having a sound exercise

---

[2] *Newsweek,* April 16, 1973, p. 63.

[3] Over the years, I have found that a fitness and diet regime pays off financially as well as in terms of good health. A reformed two-pack-a-day smoker can save over three hundred dollars a year. Savings on liquor and drugs are likely to be even greater.

125

program, regular physical examinations and a healthy mental outlook which permits useful and satisfying activities. An enjoyable way to fulfill the exercise part of the bill is to join a health club.

Health-club memberships at the YMCAs throughout the country vary in price from $150 to $300. The facilities available for this fee normally include steam, sunlamp, sauna, massages, exercise room, indoor track, weight equipment, swimming pool, gymnastics, basketball, volleyball, handball, squash, fitness testing and counseling.

PHYSICAL-FITNESS PLANS

Today, the importance is recognized of having an exercise program that strengthens the heart and improves the cardiovascular system. An outstanding fitness program, currently being sponsored by the YMCA, is based on the Fitness Finders system of conditioning exercises. The pilot study was headed by Glen Suelymes, Director of Program Development for the President's Council on Physical Fitness and Sports. The significant results of the twelve-week program were lower pulse rates, decreased body weight and increased muscular strength and endurance. The program also proved to be fun.

PROPER DIET

In addition to new developments in exercise, diets prescribed by experts have been modified. The cardiovascular system, in particular, has received much attention recently, in view of the fact that heart attacks are a major killer. There have been studies with respect to the limits of saturated fats in the diet. Now doctors are talking about unsaturated and polyunsaturated fats.

Saturated fat has been cited as a possible cause of coronary heart disease. Foods rich in such fat include eggs, cheese, whole milk, butter, pork, chocolate and avocado. *The Prudent Diet* is a book written by Dr. Norman Jolliffe, head of New York City's Bureau of Nutrition, to help combat heart attacks. His diet reduces the consumption of saturated fats and increases the intake of unsaturated fats. He suggests limiting the number of eggs eaten to four per week and including fish frequently as part of the menu.

PERSONAL EXERCISE PROGRAM

Last year I did a TV commercial for the YMCA, describing the series of exercises that keeps me in shape. My three-times-a-week workout includes the following routine: 1) head stand: one minute; 2) rope skipping: two hundred times; 3) sit-ups: fifty; 4) pull-ups: six; 5) jogging: five miles.

A history of nutritious meals and appropriate exercise permitted me to establish a physical-fitness record in the military and made it easy to complete the paratrooper course as a senior officer. Today, exercise and proper diet help me to meet my commitments as a teacher and author. At times, I may be tempted to skip my exercise routine. But my friend and jogging companion, Dr. Martin Klein, will encourage me, saying, "Come on and run—you'll feel a helluva lot better afterwards!" Marty's medical advice always proves to be right.

TRACK CLUBS

In recent years there has been increased interest in competitive track events for people in their middle and senior years. Mr. Ted Haydon is presently coach at the University of Chicago Track Club. It has about 200 members ranging in ability from Olympic-level competitors to individuals in their sixties. Haydon was an assistant track coach of the U. S. Olympic track teams in 1968 and 1972. His specialty is developing long-distance runners.

A *Wall Street Journal* article featured Coach Haydon and quoted the views of a fifty-eight-year-old Chicago lawyer who began running at the club for exercise twelve years ago:

> "Ted let me go on my own for a while, but pretty soon he started asking me to get into one of his meets. He said I'd get more out of it if I had a competitive goal," says Mr. McLendon. "I told him that nobody wanted to see some old guy stagger in after everybody else had gone home. He said that no matter how slow I was, there'd be somebody out there slower. He was right."
>
> Mr. McLendon now enters about a dozen meets a year, competing in everything from the 220-yard dash to the marathon. "Every once in a while I catch some kid by surprise," he says with a laugh. "It does him a lot of good, you know? He figures that if a man my age can beat him, he'd better start working harder."
>
> Mr. Haydon, too, still competes in track despite his 62 years; he runs fairly regularly and holds several age-groups in his specialty, the hammer throw. For the ordinary middle-ager, however, he prescribes moderation in exercise. "It's better to do too little than too much, especially at first," he says.[4]

Please note Coach Haydon's advice: "Better to do too little than too much."[5] The cost of membership is unbelievably low. There are no dues. Entry fee for each meet is $1 if no medals are awarded. If medals are presented, the fee is $1 for each event entered.

[4]Frederick C. Klein. "To Be on This Team You Needn't Be Great to Enjoy Yourself." *The Wall Street Journal,* February 25, 1975, p. 1.
[5]I learned the hard way. I joined the New Orleans Track Club in 1975 and participated in a meet on the morning of June 5, 1976. My events and times: 100 yards—13:2; 440 yards—1:23; 1/2 mile—3:15; 1 mile—6:49; 2 miles—15:43. I won three firsts and two seconds in my age group and my Achilles tendons were sore for a month. Now it's back to jogging in moderation.

Most sizable communities have track clubs. New Orleans, for example, has the New Orleans Track Club, Inc. Last year it held twenty-two meets. Annual membership dues for adults are $5; for students high-school age or less: $2.50. Entry fees for adults are $1; 50¢ for students high-school age or less.

BARBERSHOPS AND BEAUTY PARLORS

What about barbershop or beauty parlor visits and sundries for good grooming? They can be good for your morale (mental health) and good for those who look at you if you are well-groomed.

It is important to select a hair stylist with a good reputation. Your friends and relatives can give you sound advice. Prices vary considerably so obtain charges *prior* to a visit (and don't forget to add the cost of a tip). Salons may offer such varied services as cutting, washing, blow drying, coloring, setting, conditioning, permanent waves (straight, body, curl), shampoo and sets, facial, manicure, pedicure, hairpieces (to include cleaning and styling), straightening, hair analysis and hair-care products.

In view of the many services available at hair salons it is easy to exceed your budget allotment for personal care. After a recent visit to a beauty shop my daughter, Ellen, remarked: "I intended to spend twenty dollars but my hair stylist was cute and said I needed a conditioner plus a number of hair-care products. His friendly persuasion resulted in my spending thirty-nine dollars."

If you are handy, you may decide on the do-it-yourself approach for much of your personal grooming. And many mothers have become proficient at hair styling for members of their family. It is important to shop wisely for hair-care products and other sundries in the manner suggested earlier in the chapter for clothing.

8

TRANSPORTATION— HIGHLIGHTING CARS

(continued on p. 130)

A car is a major investment. It is also a recurring purchase, made at frequent intervals.

If you buy twenty cars in your lifetime, you could easily spend $100,000 for this purpose. In addition, another $30,000 could be spent on finance charges. The primary purpose of this chapter is to present facts that will enable a car buyer to save up to $50,000 of a potential $130,000-outlay. We will also discuss how to maintain and sell a car most advantageously, then go on to examine such alternate forms of transportation as motorcycles, bicycles, public transportation and our own two feet.

A successful car buyer over the years once told me, "I have owned sixteen cars, including Fords, Cadillacs and Mercedes, keeping them from one to six years. Most were good buys, but one was a disaster. My first purchase was an emotional thing; I had to have that car, and it cost me a bundle. I gradually learned, however, that in order to obtain a good deal, I needed to take my time and examine all aspects of the transaction." A careful reading of this chapter should provide you with the information needed to follow his example.

CAR BUYING AND THE MANAGEMENT APPROACH

THE PLANNING PHASE: DETERMINING YOUR OBJECTIVE

Successful car purchasing not only requires time and study but profits from a management approach. As explained in Chapter 1, to arrive at a sound decision, you should first *determine your objective,* answering the questions what, when, where, how and why.

First, *what* type of car is best for you? Factors to consider include size of your family, purpose for which the car is to be used and availability of funds, for both the initial purchase and the upkeep. It can be helpful to prepare a checklist of points that you wish to consider in making your purchase. Table 8-1 presents a format that can be modified to meet your requirements.

If your checklist indicates that economy and ease of parking are of prime importance, a subcompact may be the answer. Contrariwise, if money is not a main concern and luxury is paramount, you may select one of the expensive models. A Cadillac, Continental or other large car will give you a comfortable ride. But you will pay for this privilege in such areas as greater initial cost, limited gas mileage, considerable annual depreciation, sizable maintenance charges and increased parking problems. Likewise, the number of service agencies available may be fewer than for the popular low-priced automobiles.

Given the current concern about energy shortages and pollution, manufacturers of luxury automobiles may be subjected to greater pressure in the

131

TABLE 8-1 Format to Help Determine Which Car Is Appropriate for You

Size of family	_1 _2	_3 _4	_5 _6	_over 6
Purpose	_business	_pleasure	_business and pleasure	
Yearly mileage	_less than 5,000	_5,000-15,000	_over 15,000	
Funds available:				
Initial purchase	_less than $1,000	_$1,000-2,999	_$3,000-4,999	_over $4,999
Annual upkeep	_less than $1,200	_$1,200-2,599	_$2,600-3,799	_over $3,799
Reputation of dealer	_outstanding	_good	_fair	_poor
Availability of service	_outstanding	_good	_fair	_poor
Resale potential	_outstanding	_good	_fair	_poor
Features desired	_ego satisfier _ease in parking _good mileage	_comfortable ride _fast acceleration _immediate delivery		
Accessories	1. 2. 3. 4.	5. 6. 7. 8.		

future to reduce their products' size. In Europe, the most expensive cars are considerably smaller than comparably priced vehicles built in the United States. This trend to smaller cars may influence your decision because of the reduced resale value of large luxury cars in the event that they are no longer manufactured.

This question of size recalls a conversation in 1966 between my wife and the president of a major automobile company. We had recently returned from living in Europe for three years.

Mrs. S.: Why don't you build a small car like the European models? We found them so practical and economical.

President: Well, you see, we make our largest profit per car on our biggest and most expensive vehicles. From an economic standpoint, it would be foolish to make a small car.

This large differential in profit between larger and smaller cars was pointed out in a quote in *Consumer Reports*:[1]

> The production cost difference between a Chevrolet Caprice and a Cadillac de Ville with comparable equipment is $275 to $300. But the selling price differs by $2,700 giving GM a $2,400 extra gross profit on the Cadillac.

Let us look at the next aspect of the objective. *When* is it desirable to buy your car? Do you want one of the first new models off the line? It may be fun to show off the latest thing to the neighbors, but new models can present real problems due to their very newness. This is particularly true if the model has been radically

---

[1] "Quote Without Comment." *Consumer Reports,* February 1975, p. 82. The quote was taken from *Business Week.*

altered. Regardless of tests, there are frequently bugs uncovered in the early production that are corrected later in the model year.

Suppose you buy a car at the end of the year, when the manufacturer is converting over to his new model. Your initial cost should be less, but you will have a car which—even though "new"—is in fact one year old. Thus, the depreciation factor will be greater than if you waited a short time and bought a current model. If you trade in such a buy within a couple of years, you may lose more than if you had bought the model shortly after it was introduced.

Where do you want to purchase your car? If you can obtain a fair price in your neighborhood, there is considerable advantage from a service standpoint in buying close to home. If you have traveled long distances to get the best financial deal, you will not normally go back to your place of purchase for service but will patronize a local agency for minor repairs and upkeep. Should major problems arise, it is aggravating and expensive to be forced to take a long trip. Therefore, it is wise to deal with a local agency from the start. Neighborhood dealers are likely to make a special effort to keep your business.

In deciding where to buy, you should also consider the reputation of the dealer. Has he been in business a long time? A respectable neighborhood dealer may charge you a few dollars more than another source, but it may be worth it.

How do you plan to purchase your car? With cash or on credit? By making a minimum down payment and borrowing the remainder? If you borrow, how long should it be for? Will you trade in your old car or try to sell it yourself? These and other questions will be discussed later in this chapter, under the heading, "That Car Loan."

Why do you need to buy a car? Is it really the most economical means of going to and from work? Perhaps it is a second car you are considering. Whatever your requirements, before purchasing weigh such alternatives as public transportation, taxi, bicycle, motorcycle. There is also the possibility of leasing a car instead of buying it.

You should not purchase an automobile until after you have clarified your objective by answering the questions what, when, where, how and why. Let us assume that you determine your objective as follows: I will buy a *subcompact,* upon *graduation,* for *cash,* from a *neighborhood dealer,* because it will be *essential for my job.*

NEGOTIATING FOR A NEW CAR

Once you have determined your objective, you are in a position to be a tough negotiator. Some people pay the sticker price without questioning it. This delights the salesman and the dealer because the latter buys the vehicle for about 75 to 85 percent of the manufacturer's suggested list price. Furthermore, the profit differential on accessories may run up to 40 or 50 percent. To obtain a good deal you may have to do some homework and resort to tough bargaining.

1. Obtain the facts about costs[2] on a used car from a current manual prepared by the National Automobile Dealers Association (NADA). Look at both wholesale and retail prices on cars that you would like to purchase. If you want to make a trade-in, be sure to have your car appraised. Facts about new-car dealer costs and retail prices can be obtained from current issues of two books, Edmund's *Car Prices* and Car/Puter's *Auto Facts*. Armed with this information and a knowledge of the markup, you are prepared to discuss a deal.

2. Visit several dealers to secure their prices. At times it may help to talk directly to the owner of a small firm. Keep in mind that when you come to the closing, the boss has the final word.

3. Buy at the time when dealers are hurting. In a period of economic recession and high inventories, you can get a much better bargain. And take your time closing the deal. The dealer will be anxious to complete the sale, so set your price and stick with it. Dealers have been schooled in salesmanship and have all the answers. They are not above playing on your sympathies. If you cave in, it is just that much more money in their pockets. One successful dealer told me, "I size up every customer. Over the years, I have found what gets to them. Selling is a game, and I love to win."

The dealer's need to win was pointed out by the following experience of one of my clients:

I recently went to a Dodge dealer to purchase a new Charger after determining that this was the car that best met my objective. The salesman was ready for me.

Salesman: Good evening, may I help you?
Me: I'm looking for a good deal on a Charger.
Salesman: We have just the thing!

He showed me a pretty black-on-red model which he was selling quickly for $3,685. I informed him that the daily paper had advertised it for $3,285. He told me that the price had been changed and then went into his act about what a great car I was buying, which aroused my suspicions. He concluded, "I need this sale. My wife is in the hospital." I then decided to do my own act, remarking, "I can get a much better deal from your competitor. My cousin lives in Detroit and when I visit her I may buy it through Nationwide."

After two weeks of negotiation with the salesman and the owner, I ended up buying the car for $2,995. Instead of being outsmarted, I came out with a fair deal. A check of the dealer's cost for the car and

---

[2]Further information on costs of used cars is given later in chapter.

equipment indicated he had made $185 on the sale. However, he does a high volume and may have received an additional discount.

How sad the salesman looked as I walked out the door with the keys to my new car! He proved to be an actor to the end.

4. Use friendships to help you get that special discount from a reliable dealer, or to save on such accessories as air conditioners.

5. Recheck all figures *prior* to closing. The importance of such a review cannot be emphasized too strongly. And be sure you receive the estimate *in writing*. A college student related the following story about his high-school graduation present.

My dad was friendly with the fleet manager at the Ford dealership in town. We made a visit to his office and were informed that the cost for my new Pinto would be $100 above wholesale. The car of my choice was quoted at $2,750.26. Without checking other agencies, or asking to look at the figures, my father accepted the deal and gave his friend a check for $100 deposit. Two days later I picked up my Pinto 3-Door Runabout after paying the remaining $2,650.26. The following week, Dad saw an ad in the paper announcing a new Runabout for $2,610 (plus tax and license). We decided to check it out and found precisely the same car (to include AM radio). Dad then proceeded to find out how his friend had arrived at his price and compared our price with the manufacturer's suggested retail price (Table 8-2).

TABLE 8-2 Comparative Prices for Ford Pinto

Our Price	Retail (Sticker) Price	Ad Price
$2226.21 Dealer Cost*	$2568.00 Base Price	$2610.00 (included
20.00 Preparation and	61.00 AM radio	freight, service,
Conditioning	2629.00	& AM radio)
25.00 Ford Dealers Ad-	105.00 Freight	157.80 Sales Tax
vertising Fund	2734.00	9.50 Actual cost of
2.40 Gas (There was so	50.00 Service and	Tag and Title
little gas in the	Handling	$2777.30
tank the car barely	$2784.00	
reached the station)	177.04 Sales Tax	
51.82 AM radio	15.00 Tag and Title	
2325.43	$2976.04	
105.00 Freight		
2430.43		
100.00 Mark Up		
50.00 Service and Handling		
2580.43		
154.83 Sales Tax		
15.00 Tag and Title		
$2750.26		

*Because the car was sold near the end of the month and the manufacturer was anxious to move cars in a slow month, he provided the dealer another 5% below this normal cost of $2226.21.

135

After reviewing the figures it was apparent that we hadn't received the $100 above wholesale. We did slightly better than the ad, although this might have been subject to negotiation. And we saved $226 over retail. But Dad's friend had added on a $50 service charge. Likewise, the tags and title cost $9.50 but friend charged $15.00. Dad was also informed that the Agency received a 5 percent rebate for this end-of-month sale. Next time, I'll check all figures prior to purchase because recently my cousin went to our dealer friend, armed with my facts, and saved the $50 service charge as well as $5.50 by buying his own tag and title.

BUYING A NEW CAR AT $125 OVER THE DEALER'S COST

After talking with dealers in your area, you should be able to determine how much you will have to pay over cost for a new car. You may wish to utilize a checklist to post your facts (see Table 8-3). As mentioned previously, the dealer cost and manufacturer's suggested retail price can be obtained from Car/Puter's *Auto Facts* or Edmund's *Car Prices*.

If the price you receive from a dealer exceeds his cost by $125 or more, you may wish to consider an alternative. Buy through an organization that will "deliver the car you want for $125 over dealer cost." This firm, the aforementioned Car/Puter, is located in Brooklyn, New York. For ten dollars it provides a printout of the retail prices and dealer costs for the car you are considering, as well as its various options. If you are unable to obtain a satisfactory price from your local dealer, "Car/Puter will arrange the purchase (and delivery to your city) [of the car of your choice] through our participating national network of authorized new car dealers. You pay only $125 over dealer cost, even on cars retailing for $6,000 or more. The only exceptions are foreign makes and a few limited-production, luxury and specialty models like Cadillac, Corvette and Mark IV. Some of these models, however, are available at a substantial discount through Car/Puter."[3]

Informing your dealer that you are aware of the conditions offered by Car/Puter should help you obtain the best possible price. If you post all initial costs on the price-comparison chart (Table 8-3), it becomes apparent where you can obtain the lowest price.

Once the dealer has established a selling price for his car, you can discuss a trade—but not before. To check on your car's present retail value you can consult a current NADA manual. If you don't obtain a fair offer for your used car, you may prefer to sell it yourself and utilize Car/Puter. However, for simplicity's sake, you may choose to sell to your local dealer.

[3]Car/Puter Auto Facts Department, 1603 Brunswick Avenue, Brooklyn, New York 11207. Extract of advertisement appeared in Car/Puter's *Auto Facts* (New York: Davis Publications, Inc., 1975), p. 145.

TABLE 8-3   Price Comparison Chart

	I Manufacturer's Suggested List	II Dealer's Cost	III Dealer's Best Price A B C	IV Car/Puter
Initial cost:				
Car X (base price)				
Accessories:				
Air conditioning				
Power disc brakes				
Power steering				
Radio, AM				
Destination charge				
Dealer preparation				
Gas and oil				
Dealer advertising				
Tax				
Total initial cost				
Annual cost:				
License				
Oil and gas				
Insurance				
Maintenance and repairs				
Depreciation				
Finance charges				
Total annual cost				

SELLING YOUR CAR

Let us assume that you decide to sell your car in the retail market. How do you go about it? The following points should be considered by prospective sellers:

1. See that your car is clean and neat. Take time to wash and wax it. Vacuum the interior. Clean under the hood.
2. Be sure the car is in satisfactory working condition. Check the paint, battery, brakes, tires and so on. Make minor repairs yourself when possible. Replace deteriorating items such as a failing battery or a smooth tire.
3. Set a fair dollar value on your car, based upon the current market price of a comparable model. Check several dealers to see what they are asking; in addition, consult the NADA.
4. Utilize free advertising facilities, such as school and business bulletin boards. Talk to your friends. Place a sign on your car. If this free advertising doesn't bring you a buyer, consider using a newspaper. Place your ad where it will be read by the largest audience—perhaps in the weekend editions of your local paper. Ask the paper to help devise an effective ad.
5. Try not to sell when the used-car market is depressed.
6. Be on time for appointments. Be honest about the good and bad features of your car. Make certain you have all the necessary papers,

including title and bill of sale. If the bill of sale must be notarized, know where this can be done. Accept only cash, a money order or a certified check.

BUYING A USED CAR

Buying a used car successfully requires the same management approach that has been presented for purchasing a new car. In addition, however, the car's condition must be carefully assessed. When you buy a new car from a reputable dealer, you can be sure that no one has used or abused it. But in purchasing a secondhand vehicle, you run the risk of choosing a lemon. I regret to report that normally, the less you pay, the greater the risk.

The major advantage in buying a quality used car is the considerable savings in price. Once you have driven a new car around the block, it becomes used and depreciates as much as 30 to 35 percent off the list price. If you can find a used vehicle in first-rate condition, it can be a good investment. People who cannot afford a new car because of the initial down payment and monthly finance charges may find the used auto a feasible alternative. There are two major sources for buying a used car: dealers and owners.

Dealer Buying

If you purchase a car through a dealer, be sure to check out his reputation! How long has he been in business? Verify his record with your Better Business Bureau and local bank. Is he a member of the National Automobile Dealers Association? And remember, there is no substitute for satisfied customers. Contact people who have bought his cars and ask for their views. This information can be very helpful. The advantage of buying through a reputable dealer is that he may provide some type of warranty. In contrast, if you make the purchase through a private individual, you cannot take the car back for free service once the factory-established warranty period has expired.

Private Sales

An established dealer normally makes some repairs on a vehicle that he takes in on a trade. But in purchasing from an individual, you take the car as is. There are, however, two advantages in buying from the private party: 1) you may well obtain a lower price because the middleman has been eliminated; 2) since you know the owner, you can probably ascertain whether he has given the car tender loving care. Such knowledge is extremely helpful.

In order to obtain a fair deal, you should check the current NADA *Official Used Car Guide*[4] to price the used car of interest to you. Your local bank

---

[4]Published by the National Automobile Dealers Used Car Guide Co., 2000 K Street, N.W., Washington, D.C. 20006.

loan officer should have a copy of this monthly publication. Three prices are shown for each domestic and imported car: average retail, average loan and average trade-in. The *Guide* also lists the additional charges for certain equipment, such as air conditioning, power steering, AM/FM stero and automatic transmission. Read this NADA pamphlet carefully. It includes tables on the effect of different mileages on the value of various cars. There is also information on the insurance designation of each vehicle: high performance, intermediate performance, sport, rear-engine.

NEGOTIATING FOR A USED CAR

When used-car shopping you should utilize the same bargaining procedures suggested for buying a new car. A Better Business Bureau pamphlet "offers several tips that will increase the odds that purchasing a used car can be as satisfying as buying a new one.[5] The above BBB publication includes the following six suggestions on which used car to buy:

1. The make of used car is not as important as its condition.
2. Forget the mileage shown on the odometer. It could have been altered or disconnected by the former owners.
3. Ask to see the car's service record. Be sure the car has received service as recommended by the manufacturer.
4. Try to talk with the former owner. Ask him about the mileage reading. Why did he trade the car? What problems did he have with the car?
5. Do not overlook the manufacturer's warranty. How much of the warranty is still in effect? Has it been kept up to date?
6. If you know little about automobiles, have a good mechanic check the car. It is well worth the investment.[6]

A final cautionary note on used-car buying is provided by this delightfully-written story from the pen of a colleague and friend:

> Some used-car dealers have cars which may look OK on the outside, but which are certain to break down quickly and need expensive repairs. They are sold on credit with a very small down payment. These cars are called Lassies because they always come home. The victim quickly finds out that the car is no good and stops making payments. The dealer repossesses the car. He then sells it at auction to satisfy the debt of the victim. The auction is poorly publicized and the dealer or a friend of his buys the car for a scrap-value price or even less. No one who knows what he is buying would pay more. The victim learns that he still owes his debt

---

[5]"How to Buy a Used Car," Better Business Bureau of Greater New Orleans Area, Inc., New Orleans, Louisiana 70130.
[6]Ibid.

on the car, less what the dealer got for it minus his selling costs. Often the debt has already been sold to a finance company or other holder in due course which claims no responsibility for the quality of the car. The courts will force the debtor to pay. Meanwhile the dealer sells his Lassie to his next victim and the process repeats itself. I am told that it is not uncommon to have eight or ten people paying off debts on the same Lassie at one time.[7]

ANNUAL COST OF A CAR

Prior to buying a car, you should give serious thought to its upkeep. What facilities do you have for storage, both at home and at work? If, for example, you will be keeping your car outdoors in extremes of weather, you don't want a model with a reputation as a temperamental starter.

Take the case of a friend of ours who bought a luxury foreign car to be used in North Dakota. He keeps it in a heated garage at home. When he is at work, however, it stays in the outdoor parking lot. In cold weather, the only way he can be sure it will bring him home at night is to leave the motor running all day. More than once, he has received a call over the loudspeaker system: "Will the owner of a car with license number 99999P report to the information desk immediately." Needless to say, our friend's extra fuel consumption adds up to a sizable bill on an annual basis, but despite the added cost and inconvenience, he refuses to sell the car because it fulfills a lifelong desire.

What are the annual costs that you should compute before purchasing an automobile? The lower segment of Table 8-3 can be helpful in estimating the various yearly expenses car owners face. Let us examine them in closer detail.

LICENSE FEES

You might begin by checking on the cost of the license and any additional state or city tax on the car. In some states, such taxes vary considerably based on the price of the vehicle.

FUEL

Gasoline has become a costly item, and the amount you spend on it each year will depend greatly upon the car you select. Fuel consumption on various makes of 1978 cars ranges from ten to twenty-nine miles per gallon for city driving. Carefully check the mileage differential in cars that interest you. The

[7]Joseph Horton, Chairman, Department of Economics and Finance, Slippery Rock State College, Slippery Rock, Pennsylvania.

most helpful guide I have found is a report by the U.S. Environmental and Protection Agency (EPA) listing miles per gallon for selected cars.

The EPA report also points out that the following factors influence gasoline consumption:

Vehicle weight and engine size are the most important items affecting overall fuel consumption. Generally speaking, in city driving, a 5,000 pound car will require twice as much gasoline to run as a 2,500 pound car. Optional equipment not only adds weight to the car but also requires power from the engine and thus requires fuel to operate. For example, using an air conditioner can reduce gas mileage by more than 10 percent in city driving.

An automatic transmission usually reduces gas mileage as compared with a manual transmission.

Rapid acceleration can reduce fuel economy by 15 percent over moderate acceleration

The best fuel economy occurs at speeds between 30 and 40 miles per hour with no stops and no rapid speed changes.

Using radial tires, instead of conventional or bias-ply tires, can result in a 3 percent improvement in gas mileage. Improper front-end alignment and tires inflated below the recommended pressure will reduce gas mileage.

An idling engine burns about a half-pint of gas every six minutes, so don't idle your engine needlessly.

A tuned car will average 6 percent better mileage than an untuned one. And a properly maintained car also helps reduce air pollution.

Unnecessary braking, excessive driving in low gears, dragging brakes and short trips all reduce fuel economy.

A copy of the EPA *Gas Mileage Guide for New Car Buyers* may be obtained by writing: Fuel Economy, Pueblo, Colorado 81009.

INSURANCE

Be sure to determine what the insurance will be on the car of your choice. Shop around for the best deal. Car insurance will be discussed in detail in Chapter 18.

MAINTENANCE AND REPAIRS

These, too, are expensive items today and can be expected to rise in cost. If you plan on buying a high-priced car available through only a handful of authorized dealers, you can expect to have costly charges for maintenance and repairs. Be sure to budget an adequate amount for this purpose. We will examine automobile maintenance more closely later in the chapter.

ANNUAL DEPRECIATION

This expense can be easily determined by finding out what your car is currently selling for in the marketplace. Then consult the NADA manual for the price of a car one year older. The difference between the prices for the current and the older model should provide a fair depreciation figure. Another approach is to use one of the depreciation methods suggested by the Internal Revenue Service (see Chapter 27). Normally, the higher the price, the greater the dollar depreciation.

YEARLY FINANCE CHARGES

These costs should be checked with care. Be sure you obtain the necessary information from the various lending agencies in your area.

It is important to estimate accurately your total annual cost (Table 8-3). Time and again, I have been told, "My car is being repossessed—I couldn't make my monthly payments." In each instance, the car owner had failed to consider what it would cost annually to maintain the car.

THAT CAR LOAN

If you must borrow money to buy a car, make the maximum down payment and pay off the loan in the shortest time. A typical credit union posted the following rate in the 1978 era of high interest:

> Annual Percentage Rate is 10.8%; the Periodic Rate is 9/10 of 1% per month on the unpaid balance: and the Finance Charge is $5.84 per $100 per year, provided equal monthly payments are received every 30 days from the date the loan is disbursed.

Other advantages listed by a credit union were:

1. Loan-protection insurance.
2. Financing of up to 90 percent of the actual purchase price (after discount) of a new car.
3. The right to select your automobile insurance carrier in order to secure the best rates on collision and comprehensive insurance.
4. Acceleration of your loan payments in any amount at any time in order to reduce the cost of financing.
5. The privilege of moving your car to a new assignment anywhere in the world.
6. No extra charges or fees of any kind.

Before accepting a credit-union loan, you should check with other sources, including your car dealer, local bank, insurance company and a loan company. You may wish to use a checklist that permits a valid comparison (Table 8-4).

TABLE 8-4 Format for Comparing Auto Loans

	Credit Union	Loan Company	Bank	Insurance Company	Auto Dealer
1. Finance charge per year					
2. Total finance charge					
3. Annual percentage rate					
4. Provides loan-protection insurance?	Yes __ No __	Yes __ No __	Yes __ No __	Yes __ No __	Yes __ No __
5. Will finance up to 90 percent of the actual purchase price (after discount) of a new car?	Yes __ No __	Yes __ No __	Yes __ No __	Yes __ No __	Yes __ No __
6. Permits you to select automobile insurance carrier, in order to secure the best rates on collision and comprehensive insurance?	Yes __ No __	Yes __ No __	Yes __ No __	Yes __ No __	Yes __ No __
7. Accelerates your loan payments in any amount at any time, in order to reduce the cost of financing?	Yes __ No __	Yes __ No __	Yes __ No __	Yes __ No __	Yes __ No __
8. Privilege of moving your car to a new assignment anywhere in the world?	Yes __ No __	Yes __ No __	Yes __ No __	Yes __ No __	Yes __ No __
9. Pay no extra charges or fees of any kind?	Yes __ No __	Yes __ No __	Yes __ No __	Yes __ No __	Yes __ No __
10. Reputation of the firm	Outstanding__ Good__ Fair__ Poor__	Outstanding__ Good__ Fair__ Poor__	Outstanding__ Good__ Fair__ Poor__	Outstanding__ Good__ Fair__ Poor__	Outstanding__ Good__ Fair__ Poor__

If the answer is Yes to item 9 in Table 8-4, determine exactly what these extra charges and fees include. Recently I obtained the following information from a bank loan officer:

RJS:	What is your current car-loan rate?
Loan Officer:	7½ percent, plus 1 percent for life coverage and another ½ percent for accident and health.
RJS:	Is this the annual rate?
Loan Officer:	No, this amounts to 13.69 percent on a three-year loan.
RJS:	What is the maximum length of time I can borrow this money, and what is the cost per $1,000?
Loan Officer:	We are presently making 36-month loans. The total payment on $1,000 for three years is only $296.45, and life $38.89.
RJS:	Are there any other facts I should know?
Loan Officer:	Yes, you must have an active account with us, and in view of the tight money market, we like you to carry a compensating balance of 20 percent. This means that for every $1,000 we lend you, you should have $200 in some type of account with us.

Let us assume that you have decided on car type and place of purchase, and have completed the loan arrangements. Once you have taken possession of the vehicle, it is essential to have necessary insurance protection. But don't wait until the last minute to buy car insurance. Its purchase requires the same careful study as any other sizable investment. Again, for details on car insurance, see Chapter 18.

AUTOMOBILE MAINTENANCE

It is important to keep your car in good condition from the moment you purchase it. Good maintenance will cut your costs, reduce your need for repairs and help your car run smoothly. If you have done a good job in choosing a car, maintaining it should not present an undue problem. If you have purchased a lemon, however, your repair costs can be unreasonable. So buy carefully.

How do you go about taking care of your car? The following pointers may help:

1. Read the warranty booklet provided by the manufacturer. Follow his recommendations for service checks, tire pressure and so on. Be sure you understand all important facts presented. If you have any questions, contact the dealer or his service manager.
2. Take your car to a respected authorized dealer for the recommended inspections within the mileage and times specified. His mechanics work exclusively on your make of car and should be factory-trained.

3. Use the proper gas and oil. Be sure to change your oil when it is dirty, and make sure it comes up to the required level. Engines can be—and have been—ruined by inadequate oil.

   Economize on your gasoline consumption; you will save money, reduce pollution and conserve our natural resources. Here are some tips on how this can be accomplished:

   a. Plan the day's errands so as to keep mileage to a minimum.
   b. Have your car's points, plugs, filters and automatic choke checked periodically.
   c. Buy premium fuel only if your car requires it.
   d. Keep tire pressure a few pounds above the lowest recommended pressure.
   e. Don't drive at excess speeds. About 10 percent more gas is used for each 10 mph over 50.
   f. Avoid "jackrabbit" starts. Steady acceleration and driving can cut gas consumption as much as 60 percent.
   g. Don't idle the engine excessively. Restarting burns less fuel than prolonged idling.
   h. Use air conditioning only when absolutely necessary.
   i. Use your phone for all it's worth to run errands, shop and make appointments.[8]

4. Make period preventive maintenance checks yourself. Your personal inspection is the best way to prevent costly repairs. You may wish to make up a reminder list of items to look at weekly. This might include the following points:

   a. Battery. Does it have sufficient water? If not, add distilled water to the desired level and don't spill it elsewhere. You should also see that the terminals are clean.
   b. Tires. Buy a good gauge. Check the pressure on all tires, including the spare. Examine each tire for wear; if it is uneven, take the car to the service manager and find out if the wheels need to be aligned and/or balanced. Also, look at your tires carefully to determine if any are worn enough to be replaced. It is false economy to drive with unsafe tires. Learn how to change a tire.
   c. Oil. Keep an extra quart on hand, so that you can add oil if necessary.
   d. Water. Check the water in the radiator. In cold climates, make certain you have adequate antifreeze for the lowest readings.
   e. Appearance. Wash and wax the car yourself whenever possible. It's a good form of exercise and saves money. More important, doing it yourself gives you an opportunity to examine your car and find problems before they can become serious. It is much

[8]South Central Bell Telephone Company. *Bell Notes,* September 1973.

easier and cheaper to tighten a loose screw than to replace a piece of equipment that has fallen off.

5. When repairs become necessary, take the car to that respected authorized dealer. Do it promptly, before the car can no longer be used. Obtain an estimate in writing before any work is done, and require the service manager to notify you if any increase is necessary after work begins. Finally, check out the repair work carefully with the service manager prior to payment. This may require a test drive. Owners become very unhappy when their cars break down shortly after being repaired. An on-the-spot inspection immediately after the work has been done can alleviate the problem.

6. What should you do if you encounter serious trouble with a dealer in regard to repairs? First, bring it to the attention of the service manager. If this fails, put it in writing to the owner. Next, write the car manufacturer and send copies to the local Better Business Bureau and appropriate consumer-affairs office. Finally, you may wish to take the matter to a small claims court yourself. If it is important enough, hire a lawyer. Stay with it until you get a fair deal.

FUTURE OF THE AUTOMOBILE

There are currently more than 130 million cars in use in the United States. Automobiles caused over 45,000 deaths in 1976 and more than 3 million injuries. By the year 2000, our population will increase by 50 percent, to 300 million. At that time, we can expect 210 million cars on our highways and in our cities.

The car problem is all too obvious today what with pollution, auto accidents, the gas shortage, acres of unsightly car cemeteries and cities glutted with vehicles. What will the situation be a quarter of a century from now? Much worse—unless we use smaller, more efficient cars and develop other forms of first-class transportation. Perhaps electrical motors will replace some of our gas-driven engines.

It behooves all of us to think in terms of what we can do to improve the situation in the years to come. If more forceful action is not taken, vehicular deaths will increase, the energy crisis will worsen, pollution will become unbearable and driving will become a nightmare. Surely American ingenuity can devise cars that are virtually pollution-free, safer, longer-lasting and more economical. The annual model changeover is ridiculous. It results in failure to eliminate deficiencies that could be worked out if cars remained pretty much unchanged for several years. The recall of large numbers of vehicles is due in considerable measure to the manufacturers' modification policies.

The time has come to focus on improving alternate means of transportation, thus lessening the need for automobiles. We must also demand more positive action by our political leaders.

TO READ BEFORE YOU BUY

Buying a car is an expensive investment. An astute person can save hundreds of dollars by having the facts prior to making such a purchase. In order to obtain the facts, it is essential to read the latest editions of certain publications. I particularly recommend that you read the following literature:

1. Edmund's *Car Prices.* This book, mentioned earlier in the chapter, is published by Dell and is available for $1.95. It lists new-car prices (foreign and domestic), showing the base cost to the dealer and the manufacturer's suggested list price. It also gives good advice on "choosing the right car for you." Other topics presented include questions and answers on importing a car, discount buying and vehicle-registration statistics.
2. Car/Puter's *Auto Facts* is published three times a year and provids information somewhat similar to Edmund's. It is a Davis publication and sells for $1.50. As noted earlier, it gives you dealer cost and manufacturer's suggested price. Car/Puter also includes information on insurance needs, discount buying, how to get the best financing deal and a coded freight chart.
3. Consumers Union frequently publishes valuable material on cars in their monthly *Consumer Reports.* These findings are based on their own tests of various vehicles. Current articles should be read with care before making a purchase.
4. The Ford Motor Company has prepared a helpful booklet titled *Car Buying Made Easier.* The first section gives you general information about cars; the second concentrates on vehicles produced by Ford. It can be obtained free of charge by writing to Ford's Customer Service Division, 19855 West Outer Drive, Dearborn, Michigan 48124.

ALTERNATE FORMS OF TRANSPORTATION AND THE MANAGEMENT APPROACH

Henry Ford II, chairman of the Ford Motor Company, in a recent interview pointed out the need for conservation, saying:

We're still living in a fool's paradise in this country. We have always thought that we could have an endless supply of cheap energy and we can't. We've got a major energy problem, but the American people don't believe it. We waste so much. We waste everything in this country. . . . I wonder, theoretically, if it's right that the auto industry should chew up as much raw material as it chews up.[9]

A good way to consume less of our raw materials is to turn to other means of transportation. Let us look briefly at some alternate approaches that could benefit our pocketbooks, society and health. The financial aspects of motorcycles, bicycles, mass transit and person power (jogging and walking) will be presented.

Once again, I suggest that you use a management approach to help you obtain the type of transportation best suited to your needs at the most reasonable price.

TABLE 8-5 Format to Help Determine Which Alternate Means of Transportation Is Best for You
(Assumption: A serviceable car is presently owned)

	Motorcycle	Bicycle	Mass Transit	Walk/Jog
What is the initial cost?	$ 4__3__2__1__	$ 4__3__2__1__	$ 4__3__2__1__	$ 4__3__2__1__
What is the annual upkeep (including insurance)?	$ 4__3__2__1__	$ 4__3__2__1__	$ 4__3__2__1__	$ 4__3__2__1__
What are clothing costs?	$ 4__3__2__1__	$ 4__3__2__1__	$ 4__3__2__1__	$ 4__3__2__1__
How well does it meet my objective?	4__3__2__1__	4__3__2__1__	4__3__2__1__	4__3__2__1__
Will it be available in all weather?	4__3__2__1__	4__3__2__1__	4__3__2__1__	4__3__2__1__
How safe is it?	4__3__2__1__	4__3__2__1__	4__3__2__1__	4__3__2__1__
Are outlets available nearby to provide parts and service?	4__3__2__1__	4__3__2__1__	4__3__2__1__	4__3__2__1__
Is it a convenient and comfortable service?	4__3__2__1__	4__3__2__1__	4__3__2__1__	4__3__2__1__
What are the risks of theft or mugging?	4__3__2__1__	4__3__2__1__	4__3__2__1__	4__3__2__1__
What does it do for my morale upon arriving at my destination?	4__3__2__1__	4__3__2__1__	4__3__2__1__	4__3__2__1__
Total				

Scoring: 4 Best rating
3 Second best
2 Third best
1 Fourth best

[9]*Time,* February 10, 1975, p. 71.

THE PLANNING PHASE: DETERMINING YOUR OBJECTIVE

In order to reach a sound decision about the appropriate form of alternate transportation for you, first determine your objective. What will best suit your needs? This requires providing answers to the questions what, when, where, how and why. First, what type of transportation should you utilize. Let us assume that you have already decided that your wife requires a subcompact for her work and shopping. Factors to consider in determining what further form of transportation you need include purpose for which it is to be used and availability of funds for the initial purchase as well as for upkeep. In determining your objective it can be helpful to use a formula similar to that discussed for car buying. Likewise, preparing a format similar to Table 8-5 can assist you in deciding what mode of transportation is best suited for you. Let us assume that your planning is completed and a motorcycle is your choice. You should then proceed to implement your plan (buy the motorcycle) and then check to see that the machine is in good working order by riding it.

MOTORCYCLES

Motorcycles are the most expensive form of alternate transportation. Nevertheless, registrations have increased nearly fourfold since 1965, and the continuing energy shortage and rising car prices should lead to even further increases in motorcycle sales.

TYPES OF MOTORCYCLES

There are three categories of bikes: street—for use strictly on the road; dirt—off the road and for use in competitive meets; and scrambler—which may be used for both the road and dirt. We will concentrate here on the street bike, which is the most suitable model for traveling to and from work. These street motorcycles, like cars, range from stripped-down economy models to luxury machines. Engines vary from one- to four-cylinder types. They may be two-stroke or four-stroke. A lightweight two-stroke, two-cylinder machine can be obtained for less than $500 and may travel over 100 miles on a gallon of gasoline. In contrast, a large four-stroke, four-cylinder motorcycle might cost over $4,000 and get only 40 miles to the gallon. Honda recently advertised a small bike that would get 98.7 miles to a gallon and a large machine that would get 50.1 miles per gallon.

ESTIMATING COSTS

In purchasing a bike you must be sure to determine the basic price and cost of extras like riding lights, special seat and chrome trim. Other expenses include insurance, license, helmet and appropriate clothing such as heavy shoes. The annual upkeep should also be estimated. Bike maintenance provides a great opportunity to save money by doing it yourself. The skills required are not nearly as great as those needed for work on a car. However, it is important to learn to tune your bike properly. If in doubt, take it to a skilled mechanic. You should also calculate what percent of the year you will be unable to ride your bike due to inclement weather. What will the price of substitute transportation be?

Another factor to consider is the cost aspect of accidents. The hard facts are that there were only 3½ deaths per 100 million miles of driving for autos, in 1975, in contrast to 18 for motorcycles. In addition to the death rate, there are more injuries to bike riders per miles traveled. This risk is reflected in insurance costs. Another element which jacks up insurance costs is a high risk of theft. In cities like New York, where theft is rampant, rates are sky-high.

THE SECONDHAND MOTORCYCLE MARKET

Good used motorcycles are frequently available for purchase. A look in most local newspapers will indicate the number and types on the market. My son, Richard, obtained a secondhand BMW, while a sophomore at Harvard, for $750. He used it for two years and prior to graduation sold it for $975. In spite of a number of close calls including falling in front of an oncoming car on an ice-covered highway, he was never injured, but he chalked up $200 worth of damage to the bike.

In selecting your motorcycle, service and parts replacement are impor-tant. The Japanese recently account for about 80 percent of all bikes sold in the United States. The big four include Honda, Kawasaki, Suzuki and Yamaha. Honda is by far the largest seller.

A student friend who is a motorcycle buff made this recommendation: "I suggest buying a Honda because they offer the best quality and service in the United States. They also sell the largest percentage of all motorcycles made. Their dealers seem to be more interested in the safety of the rider than trying to sell the biggest bike in stock to whomever comes in the store. As an experiment I went to Honda, and to other motorcycle outlets. At each store, I told the dealer that I wanted the biggest bike he had. Only at Honda was I told that a 175cc to 300cc motorcycle would be more suitable for both my needs and my size."

FUEL CONSERVATION

In order to take full advantage of cost savings in using a bike in place of a car it is important to conserve fuel by good riding habits. Honda offers seven excellent suggestions:

After starting your bike, perform a fast-idle warm-up for about a minute; this procedure completely lubricates all internal engine parts, and also protects against stalling as you move out (repeated stalling eats up fuel).

Accelerate slowly and smoothly as you begin to ride. Don't be a "heavy hand"—fast acceleration can consume up to 25% more fuel than an easy getaway. And you'll get where you're going just as fast!

Watch the traffic and traffic lights ahead of you; anticipate stops. The less idling, and less stopping and starting, means more gas savings—plus a smoother, more enjoyable ride!

Combine as many trips as possible into one. Stop for shopping on your way to or from work. Plan your shopping expeditions so you can do all your errands in one trip.

Keep your bike's tires inflated to the recommended pressure. Under-inflated tires really cut into fuel mileage—and the tires wear out faster, too.

Keep your engine in top-shape with a tune-up. That means an optimum carburetor adjustment, clean spark plugs, proper point setting and proper lubrication.

Hold your riding speed within reasonable and prudent limits. Observe speed limits or, when traffic allows, ride slower than posted limits. The faster you ride, the far faster you use up fuel. Just take it easy, ride safely and sanely, enjoy the fun of motorcycling.[10]

MOTORCYCLES VS. CARS

Are motorcycles a practical substitute for a car? That depends. According to one dealer: "Motorcycles are really recreational vehicles and are usually bought to ride for fun and only later may be used as transportation to and from work. The energy crisis has really helped us out because people rush out and spend a thousand dollars or more on a bike only to find that they still use their cars as the main mode of transportation. Bad weather and the personal safety factor make most people return to their cars."

A neighboring high-school senior who bought a motorcycle last year has regretted it ever since. He paid $1,950 for his motorcycle, helmet and other equipment. He chose a bike instead of his brother's used car, which he could have purchased for about the same price. He says of his misfortune: "It was my biggest mistake. My girl friend dropped me because her parents wouldn't let her ride round on the back of a motorcycle looking like a 'motorcycle mama.' I've ruined a lot of my favorite clothes by having to repair the bike when I wasn't dressed for the job, not to mention all the times I've been caught in the rain."

[10]Source is a pamphlet, prepared in 1975, by the American Honda Motor Company titled: *How Honda Helps You Get Around the Cost of Getting Around.*

BICYCLES

TYPES OF CYCLES

A bicycle may be defined as a two-wheeled vehicle with a rear-drive wheel that is solely human-powered. There are two main categories of bicycles—sidewalk and track. A sidewalk bicycle is a vehicle with a seat height of no more than 635 millimeters (25 inches); the seat height is measured with the seat adjusted to its highest position. Track models are designed and intended for sale as competitive machines and feature tubular tires, single crank to-wheel ratio, and no freewheeling feature between the rear wheel and the crank.[11]

We will deal only with sidewalk models here, focusing on costs. Sidewalk cycles vary from one gear speed to three, five, ten and even fifteen speeds. Prices range from $45 to $750 and up for the sophisticated models. A top-of-the-line Schwinn Deluxe Paramount, for example, has a suggested retail price of $575. (It has fifteen speeds and is an ideal touring bike.)

BICYCLE SAFETY

In recent years bicycles have surpassed automobiles in numbers purchased. Presently there are 87 million bicycles in use compared to 121 million cars. However, bicycles can be expected to overtake cars in the near future in view of the continuing energy shortage, increased interest in healthy exercise, the development of bicycle paths in many communities and improved safety measures.

Unfortunately, along with increased bicycle usage there has been an increase in accidents. According to the Consumer Product Safety Commission (CPSC), serious bicycle accidents exceeded 500,000 in 1976. Much has already been done to solve the accident problem, however, thanks in part, to the CPSC, which established major safety standards for bicycles. These standards appeared in the Federal Register. Some of the features the CPSC required on bicycles after January 1, 1975, included: brakes that must stop within fifteen feet at a test speed based upon gear ratio; a seat that cannot extend more than five inches; the marking of recommended tire pressure on sidewalls; the placing of reflectors on back and front fenders as well as on pedals; the passing of an obligatory stress test administered to the front fork of the frame.

Although the federal government has established good safety standards, bicycle owners must take their own appropriate precautions to protect their lives and pocketbooks. A neighbor related this sad experience: "Last week my son

---

[11]The source for the definitions in this chapter is a pamphlet prepared by the *Consumer Product Safety Commission* titled "Bicycles," appearing as part of the *Federal Register* series, Volume 38, No. 137, Part II, Washington, D.C., July 16, 1974, p. 26, 105.

failed to check his handlebars, which had become loose and needed tightening. In trying to make a sharp turn while on his newspaper route he fell off his bicycle and gave himself a nasty scrape. Fortunately, vehicular traffic was moving slowly and the car behind stopped in time. However, he was bleeding badly and his mother rushed him to the doctor. His recovery was rapid but the scars linger on." The costs were as follows:

Tetanus shot	$10.00
Doctor bill	25.00
Bike repair	23.71
Loss of paper-route job for 10 days	32.00
Clothing damage	26.50
Total	$117.21

In order to protect life and limb while riding your bicycle, as well as keeping costs to a minimum, it pays to heed the following safety measures when sharing the road with cars.

Keep to the right as close to the curb as practicable.
Ride in a straight line, single file.
Observe all traffic regulations, stop signs, red lights, etc. Always yield the right-of-way.
Watch for parked cars pulling into traffic and for car doors that open suddenly.
Use proper hand signals for turning, stopping, slowing. Always be aware of traffic behind as well as in front of you.
For night riding, equip your bike with a white headlight visible to 500 feet and a red reflector on the rear fender visible to 300 feet.
Look ahead for broken pavement, stones and wet spots to allow time to reduce speed to a safe level.[12]

IS CYCLING ECONOMICAL?

What can you save by bicycling to work instead of using your car? This will vary depending upon distance traveled, size of car and parking costs. For those with a subcompact and a free place to park, the cost differential may be minimal. But consider the case of this San Francisco doctor: "I used to drive from the proximity of the Presidio of San Francisco to my office three miles away. It took me thirty minutes from house to office. My parking and car expenses ran $1,045 a year. In contrast, my bicycle upkeep was only $28 last year and I made the trip in half the time—12 to 15 minutes. It has proved to be a great way to exercise. My only problem is a few nutty drivers!"

[12]South Central Bell Telephone Company. *Bell Notes.* June 1974.

IMPROVING THE CYCLIST'S LOT

Some communities have taken real steps to make bicycles a feasible substitute for cars. However, much can be done to improve the situation throughout the country. This should include providing safe bicycle paths and ensuring adequately protected parking areas adjacent to schools, businesses and so on. Group insurance for cyclists should be made available at reasonable rates. In some climates it may be desirable for organizations to provide dressing-room facilities where bicycle riders can shower and change their clothes.

PUBLIC TRANSPORTATION

Any decision regarding your total transportation requirements should take into account mass transit facilities. Perhaps one car is essential for a family's work and vacation needs. But what should your alternate choice be? A motorcycle? A bicycle, perhaps? You may find that current and planned bus and subway facilities will provide the best service.

Some communities offer good public conveyances at reasonable prices. In New Orleans, for example, it is possible to travel throughout the city for only thirty cents. The buses are clean, air-conditioned, on schedule and closely spaced. During rush hours express buses charging thirty-five cents facilitate transport. There are also pleasant 30-cent streetcar rides through much of the older section of the city.

Washington, D.C.'s new subway system promises to provide an efficient means of travel within the city. California's Bay Area transit system has the potential for fine service for the long-distance commuters, and the San Francisco cable cars can often be a delightful way to reach a destination. New York's subways leave much to be desired in cleanliness but they are strong on speed.

The energy shortage of tomorrow will place greater demands on mass transportation. Responsible citizens should contribute their views and support to improving existing facilities.

PERSON POWER—WALKING AND/OR JOGGING

The cost of walking or jogging to work and back is minimal. The only expenses involved are additional wear and tear on shoes and clothing. Such expenditures are more than likely to be countered by health benefits—good exercise and the elimination of driver stress. Factors to consider, however, are the distance involved, possibility of changing clothes at work, personal safety in the area traveled and alternate forms of transportation available in the event of inclement weather.

A special assistant to the Attorney General reported the following reasons for walking from his Georgetown residence to the Justice Department building:

> My first month in Washington I drove the three miles to work. It cost me $3.45 per day when I added up fuel cost, maintenance and parking. The traffic was frustrating and it took me about twenty-five minutes from the time I left my house until I arrived at the office. The second month I used the bus. This, too, proved to be an unpleasant experience. The cost was 80 cents per day and the trip took me about forty-five minutes. Somehow I always seemed to miss the bus and had to wait ten to fifteen minutes at the bus stop. When a bus finally came, all the seats would be taken so I'd have to stand. We were packed in like sardines and Washington gets hot! Traffic resulted in our stopping every couple of minutes. On my last trip the driver refused to pull out of one stop, saying: "Look, if you people don't all crowd to the back to let more passengers on I won't move. I'm paid by the hour and I can wait here all day."
>
> For over a year I've walked to and from work and find it a delightfully pleasant experience. Each day I take a somewhat different route. I find the variety of architectural styles in the area fascinating. Walking also gets me closer to nature and other people. During the hottest weather I simply keep a change of clothes in my office. My sturdy rain gear has enabled me to walk even in the worst weather. A good umbrella, rubbers and raincoat are a must. Even walking in the rain or snow is fun. My walking has helped me to lose ten pounds. I feel better and don't begin my working day with all the frustrations caused by driving or standing on a packed bus. I can also work out some of the problems to be faced in the office along the way.

The value of walking in contributing to a dynamic old age was highlighted in the following *New York Times* article:

> I have been living among the oldest people in the Western hemisphere—*viejos,* as they are called in their native Spanish language—in the remote Ecuadorian village of Vilcabamba. . . . A bicycle, no less than a car, is unavailable to most of them. They look upon the horse or burro as an expensive luxury, a diversion. So they walk. They walk to and from work. They walk to get from here to there. . . . Necessity is the mother of fitness and well-being to these aged mountain people, who exemplify the old saying that each of us has two "doctors"—the left leg and the right leg. . . .
>
> Just as the viejos lengthen their lives with their workaday routine on foot, so we endanger our health and shorten our lives with our immobile luxuries. Perhaps the most important benefit of exercise is its retarding effect on the process of arteriosclerosis, clogging of the arteries with fat.
>
> The viejos apparently do not suffer from bad arteries or heart

attacks. I saw no examples of fractured legs or arms. They stay flexible and hardy by a simple rule: Keep moving, don't stop, now or ever.[13]

There are those who find jogging an ideal alternative. This form of transportation, however, normally involves an entire change of clothes. Jogging to and from work could still be a great timesaver, though, enabling you to obtain your physical exercise as part of the working day.

I firmly believe that you should walk or jog to and from work whenever possible. Person power is a delightful form of exercise, lessens frustrations and provides a most economical means of transportation. It helps if you have a jogging companion. Most people who live within one or two miles of their work should give serious thought to walking or jogging. In the years ahead the energy crisis may well require the exercising of person power from time to time. Why not be in shape should such a moment come?

[13]Grace Halsell. "Wisdom on the Hoof." *The New York Times,* April 6, 1975, p. 14.

9

LARGE APPLIANCES & OTHER MAJOR EXPENDITURES

The cost of major appliances and other items covered in this chapter is the third largest expenditure that most people make over a lifetime, after home and cars. Table 9-1 shows the outlay made by one middle-income family for major appliances, including repairs, in a recent seven-year period:

TABLE 9-1   Purchase and Maintenance Cost of Major Appliances for Family X, 1970-77

Item	Cost
1. Refrigerator	$ 395
2. Oven	285
3. Freezer	275
4. Dishwasher	240
5. Clothes washer	195
6. Range	175
7. Clothes dryer	145
8. Repairs	385
Total	$2095

The figures quoted above apply, of course, in one case only. Each family must determine its own appliance needs and the life of these machines will vary depending upon their quality, use and maintenance after purchase. Two things are certain, however: 1) Given the sums involved in purchasing appliances and and other major items, it is essential to have as much information as possible in order to select the product or service best suited to your needs and pocketbook; 2) the purchase of major appliances should be planned over a period of time appropriate to your pocketbook. This planning should include the budgeting of funds for the purchase of needed items.

This chapter will deal with the buying of appliances and other large items employing a managerial approach, with special emphasis on repairs and service contracts. The clothes washer will be the focus of our analysis, although the same process applies to other large expenditures as well.

LARGE APPLIANCES AND THE MANAGEMENT APPROACH

The management process presented in Chapter 1 can be applied successfully to the purchase of all major appliances and other items requiring large expenditures. To arrive at a sound buying decision, you must *plan* wisely, *implement* your plan and *check* to see that your plan has been properly executed.

Whether you build your home (Chapter 11), or have a contractor do the job, it is essential to estimate all major appliance costs in order to stay within your total budget.

A LOOK AT CLOTHES WASHERS: DETERMINING YOUR OBJECTIVE

Planning is all-important in buying expensive items. Thus, your initial consideration in purchasing a clothes washer should be to determine your objective. What type of machine will best meet your needs? To find the answer you will have to reply to the questions *what, when, where, how and why*.

TABLE 9-2 Format to Help Determine Which Appliance Is Best for You—Clothes-Washer Types

	A	B	C	D
Price What does it cost?	$	$	$	$
Size Does it fit available space and appropriate with clothes dryer?	Yes __ No __	Yes __ No __	Yes __ No __	Yes __ No __
Suitability Does it meet our needs? (objective)	Yes __ No __	Yes __ No __	Yes __ No __	Yes __ No __
Simplicity Does it have only the extras that we require?	Yes __ No __	Yes __ No __	Yes __ No __	Yes __ No __
Repairs Does the company or manufacturer have a nationwide service organization?	Yes __ No __	Yes __ No __	Yes __ No __	Yes __ No __
Warranty–Factory How good is it?	Outstanding__ Good __ Fair __ Poor __	Outstanding__ Good __ Fair __ Poor __	Outstanding__ Good __ Fair __ Poor __	Outstanding__ Good __ Fair __ Poor __
Warranty—Dealer How good is it?	Outstanding__ Good __ Fair __ Poor __	Outstanding__ Good __ Fair __ Poor __	Outstanding__ Good __ Fair __ Poor __	Outstanding__ Good __ Fair __ Poor __
Return Policy of Store Is it fair?	Yes __ No __	Yes __ No __	Yes __ No __	Yes __ No __
Durability What is its lifespan under normal usage to include frequency of repairs?	Outstanding__ Good __ Fair __ Poor __	Outstanding__ Good __ Fair __ Poor __	Outstanding__ Good __ Fair __ Poor __	Outstanding__ Good __ Fair __ Poor __
Overall Scores by *Consumer Reports* How does it rate them?	First__ Second __ Third __ Fourth __ or less __	First__ Second __ Third __ Fourth __ or less __	First__ Second __ Third __ Fourth __ or less __	First__ Second __ Thid __ Fourth __ or less __
Reputation of Dealer How good is it?	Outstanding__ Good __ Fair __ Poor __	Outstanding__ Good __ Fair __ Poor __	Outstanding__ Good __ Fair __ Poor __	Outstanding__ Good __ Fair __ Poor __
Resale Value If I need to sell it, is there a market?	Yes __ No __	Yes __ No __	Yes __ No __	Yes __ No __
Comments of Relatives and Friends What has been their experience with similar models?	Outstanding__ Good __ Fair __ Poor __	Outstanding__ Good __ Fair __ Poor __	Outstanding__ Good __ Fair __ Poor __	Outstanding__ Good __ Fair __ Poor __

First, *what* type of washer do you want to buy? Factors to consider include size of family, and availability of funds for initial purchase as well as for upkeep. It can be helpful if you compose a checklist of points you wish to consider in making your purchase. Table 9-2 presents a format that can be modified to meet your requirements.

If your checklist indicates that low cost and minimum repairs are of prime importance, the bottom-of-the-line model (the no-frill, lowest-priced unit) may be the answer. Contrariwise, the top-of-the-line, with all the extras, may be your choice. But if you choose the latter, be prepared to pay the price in higher initial cost, greater upkeep and more energy usage in terms of water and electricity or gas. In either case you should look for a quality machine manufactured by a company with a nationwide service organization to properly install and repair it.

Moving on to your next consideration, *when* is the best time to buy a clothes washer? In principle, you can cut down on costs if you buy at sale time. But be sure to select the model you want, not an old machine that has been modified because of problems. Or, if a major breakthrough produces a vastly improved model in terms of performance, efficiency and economy, you may choose that moment to sell your old washer and buy a new one. But be prepared to pay more for "the latest thing" even though it may not yet be free of bugs. Beware, as well, of impulse buying sparked by attractive ads or a glib salesman. This can lead to costly mistakes. Many people simply defer buying until their old machine wears out.

Where do you want to purchase your clothes washer? If you can obtain a fair price in your neighborhood, there is usually a considerable advantage in buying close to home. If you have a good relationship with the manager or owner in question, he may make a special effort to keep your business. If you travel a long distance to save a few dollars, the costs for gas and use of your valuable time can exceed price savings. Furthermore, if major problems *do* arise, it is much more convenient to deal with respectable local businessmen than with indifferent strangers.

How do you go about purchasing a clothes washer? Should you use cash? Credit? Make a minimum down payment and borrow the remainder? In my view you should *always pay cash for major appliances and the other large expenditures* we will discuss in this chapter. Why pay from 18 to 42 percent extra to purchase an appliance? That is what the money would cost if you went to a bank, loan company or had the store finance it. Thus, a $300 appliance could cost from $354 to $426 if you borrowed the entire amount for one year. This figure could be even higher if the loan were for three years. Besides, if you pay cash there is a good chance of obtaining a lower price than on a credit purchase (see Chapter 6). Remember, your aim is: "Get out of debt and stay out."

Why do you need to buy a clothes washer? It may be the most economical way to handle your laundry needs. One young family computed costs of using their apartment building's washing machine for a year and found that they were spending $254.80. A bachelor who had previously patronized "washaterias" said that his machine paid for itself in two years. And he commented: "I used to waste precious time and gas lugging my wash around. Besides, it was frustrating waiting for a washer to become available. It seemed as if every time I had something important to do all the machines would be full."

Once you have found the answers to what, when, where, how and why, you can state your objective as follows: We will buy a low-end-of-the-line quality machine, preferably at sale time or during another period of advantageous prices. Our purchase will be from a reputable neighborhood dealer, for cash, in order to cut dollar costs and save time.

Establishing Guidelines

Now that you have determined your objective you are ready to proceed with your planning. Guidelines to keep in mind include the following:

1. Obtain brochures about available models offered by various appliance companies. This information can be obtained from stores and/or manufacturers.
2. Stay within your budget. Be sure you consider both initial outlay and the cost of service contracts and annual upkeep. The cheapest machine could be the most expensive in the long run.
3. Consult with friends and relatives who use the model you are considering. Their experiences can be most helpful.
4. Determine your personal needs. These include load capacity, number of settings, available room space and color coordination.
5. Read reports about clothes washers by such respected organizations as Consumers Union, Consumer Reports, and the Better Business Bureau. Their literature should be available in your local library.
6. Plan, if possible, to buy at a time when dealers are hurting for business. For example, in the 1974–75 economic recession many firms had high inventories and some great bargains were available, including factory rebates. And take advantage of sales.
7. Obtain prices on the model you are considering from a minimum of three reputable stores.
8. Make certain there is a reputable nationwide service organization to handle repairs and provide service within and beyond the warranty period. You may think your present home will be permanent, but moves can occur unexpectedly. It is nice to have a service department in your new neighborhood. General Electric Company's major appliance trucks have the following slogan painted on their side panels: "Customer care . . . Everywhere."
9. Obtain copies of warranties of machines you are interested in buying.

Study them carefully to ascertain what free services they will provide and for how long. This differs according to the manufacturer. Likewise, find out what free services, if any, your dealer provides.

10. Check to see what is guaranteed in the service contract, its inclusive dates and the annual cost. Be sure that the period covered by the contract begins after the warranty expires. Why pay for double coverage? Furthermore, the cost of a service contract should not exceed your estimated normal annual repairs. Ask yourself if such a contract is really desirable. You may find it preferable to set aside your own funds for this purpose, earmarking say, fifty dollars, for repairs. And remember to keep adding to that sum. Repair costs increase as the machine ages.

Coping With Dealers

Once your planning is complete you are ready to talk knowledgeably with appliance dealers. Many people automatically pay the asking price on a major appliance. This delights stores and their salespeople, since dealers may pay from 50–70 percent of list price for their appliances and salespeople get commissions based on the dollar value of each sale. Don't be afraid to suggest a lower price once you have decided to buy a particular washer. It helps if husband and wife shop together because one often picks up features about the washer that the other has missed. Take your checklist along (Table 9-2) when you tackle the dealers. Other points to consider include:

1. Color—Does the unit match your decor?
2. Controls—Are they conveniently placed and durable? Does the machine load easily? Are the filters handy?
3. Type—Is the washer automatic or semiautomatic?
4. Credentials—Does the machine have the Seal of Approval from Underwriters Laboratory or another recognized independent testing organization?
5. Refinements—Does the unit have all the features you desire, such as: a) cold, warm and hot controls for both wash and rinse-water temperatures? b) special basket for fragile garments? c) three-cyle speed to take care of varying washing needs? d) a matching dryer?

My own view is that extra features are usually an unnecessary expense. All quality low-end-of-the-line machines we have purchased have done a good job cleaning our clothes provided we followed the manufacturer's instructions.

Look out for "bait and switch" tactics. One couple reported the following sad story: "We noted an ad on a clothes washer sale and hurried to the store. The salesman showed us the $99 special but said it had been sold. He then led us to the $279 model. 'This has it all,' he remarked. His smooth talking and promise of easy credit terms seemed to mesmerize us and we closed the deal. And to think we are both recent college graduates with majors in psychology! Six months later we lost our machine because we couldn't meet the payments."

Checking Your Machine After Purchase

The final management function involved in buying a washing machine is *checking* to see that the unit works properly in your home. The machine should be delivered and installed promptly after purchase. Be there when it arrives. Check to be sure it is the model, color and size that you ordered and has arrived undamaged. You should also question the serviceman regarding its care and functioning. Note how the installation is done, including proper grounding. Then if a minor problem arises, you may be able to fix it yourself. Our repairman tells us he has often been called to homes where the only problem was a plug pulled out of its socket or a blown fuse.

Read the owner's manual carefully. Then put the clothes washer to work at once. If there is any difficulty contact your dealer. He should quickly repair or replace the machine. There is an advantage to charging your purchase, provided you pay no interest. If there is a major defect it is surprising how promptly stores respond if money is still due them.

OTHER MAJOR APPLIANCES

The management approach to buying a washer also applies when choosing other large appliances. Keep the above techniques in mind as we briefly explore the purchasing of clothes dryers, dishwashers, compactors, disposals, refrigerators, freezers and ovens.

CLOTHES DRYERS

A newlywed couple bought a clothes washer immediately on moving into their home but waited six months until they could pay cash for their dryer. The wife commented: "I hung the clothes outside to dry most of the time. It was worth the inconvenience to avoid making a loan. In return for our paying cash the manager reduced the price by 20 percent."

An important consideration in dryer selection is whether you want a gas or electric model. With rising energy costs you should investigate resources in your community. Normally, gas dryers are more reasonable to operate. The initial purchase price, however, is greater. Keep in mind that for all except small-unit gas dryers, you will need a 220–240-voltage connection.

If you plan to wash items like tennis shoes, it is helpful to buy a machine that has a nonmovable shelf. Heavy-soled shoes bouncing around in a dryer may damage the unit.

What about a combination washer-dryer? People we know who have bought these regret it. They feel that such machines neither wash nor dry as well as they might. In fact, these units are no longer being manufactured and I would recommend against buying a secondhand machine. There are, however, small-load washers and dryers that stack one above the other. A bachelor friend who bought these units commented: "They are space savers but took only a small amount of my laundry. I prefer to do my washing weekly so replaced them with two large-capacity units. Sears was asking $218 for the washer and $148 for the dryer but their pair price was $358, so I saved $8."

DISHWASHERS

A dishwasher can be a real boon—particularly for a large family—but for the single person who seldom eats at home it may be an unnecessary luxury. Both the original investment and the annual upkeep—soap, water, electricity and repairs—should be considered carefully by the prospective buyer.

In selecting a dishwasher check the features of several models in each make. Buy the one that will best serve your needs for the life of the machine. Do you require a heavy-duty unit? Large size? Gentle cycle? Special insulation to reduce noise? Overflow protection? Soft-food disposer?

Make certain that you have a grounded electrical outlet whether you use the dishwasher in a house, apartment or mobile home.

Dishwashers may be classified in three categories:

1. *Built-ins.* These units are normally already installed when you buy a new home. They are frequently found in apartments as well. If you build your own home, or have a contracter do the job, you will have an opportunity to select your own make, color and style. The same holds true if you decide to remodel your kitchen. Should you be considering major improvements (see Chapter 11 and 14), it is essential to select a qualified carpenter, painter, plumber and electrician. Skilled master electricians and plumbers can be most helpful in seeing that your good-quality dishwasher is installed properly.

2. *Convertibles.* A convertible dishwasher is both portable and heavy enough to become a built-in if necessary. It is an advantageous buy if you need a dishwasher immediately but later plan to remodel your kitchen or build your own home. At that later date it can be converted to a built-in.

3. *Portables.* Your living quarters may not accommodate a built-in unit. An alternative is the easy-to-store portable which can be rolled to the kitchen sink and connected to the faucet when needed. Prior to purchase, check each unit to be sure the wheels move properly. One owner complained: "It isn't worth the effort to struggle with our portable and hook it up each evening. We still do our dishes by hand most of the time. And if we let the pots and pans pile up for a couple of days the machine is too small to handle them."

COMPACTORS

A home compactor is a relatively new appliance that compresses accumulated trash into about 25 percent of its original size. There is an advantage to having only one or two bags of debris to carry to the outside garbage container each week. But remember, although the volume is reduced, *the weight remains the same* and could represent too heavy a load for feeble or elderly people. Other factors to consider are the additional space required in the kitchen for such units, the noise they make and the safety element. The machine has considerable crushing power and care must be taken with children around. Although a key is required to operate these units, some youngsters have a way of finding the unfindable.

If you are interested in buying a compactor, check a number of makes and observe them in operation prior to purchase. At that time determine how easy or difficult it is to replace disposal bags. Likewise, find out the cost of such bags. This can vary considerably among compactors.

DISPOSALS

We have found our GE food disposal to be both a timesaver and a bug reducer. In our hot southern climate it is important to dispose of food waste promptly or the cockroaches come calling. Our unit is a *continuous-feed* type with an off-and-on switch located on the way near the kitchen sink. Such models function only when tap water is running. It is important to read the instructions that accompany these units. If you have a home with the unit already installed, I suggest you write to the manufacturer for directions. Our unit does not dispose of certain items like banana peels, corn husks and other fibrous foods, although it does a good job on about everything else with minimum racket. However, it does distort the TV picture, often causing me to miss out on that vital piece of news.

A second type of disposal is the *batch feed*. It can only be operated when a special device is locked into position. This safety factor may be useful for your needs. But it does add another step to the disposal process.

REFRIGERATORS

This essential household item is normally the most expensive major appliance you will buy. It is also the most costly to maintain because of its energy usage. Therefore, it pays to choose your unit with care.

The most popular unit on the market is the combination refrigerator/ freezer, although simple refrigerators are also available. The combination unit varies in size beginning with a small model designed for efficiency apartments, or homes with dens and recreation rooms. The refrigeration component may measure as little as four cubic feet, with a six-cubic-inch freezer. In contrast, the large machines may have twenty cubic feet of refrigeration space and eight cubic feet of freezer space. It is important for you to estimate both the amount of space you currently need and what you will require during the life of the refrigerator (average life span is fourteen years).

You should also decide on the features you want. An ice-water dispenser? Frost-free freezer unit? Automatic ice maker? Side-by-side refrigerator and freezer? One family decided against the cost of a water dispenser because the community was reported to have water with cancer-suspect contents. They chose instead to buy bottled water with its own cooling dispenser.

Prior to purchase, it is essential to determine the space available in your kitchen. Also give careful thought to the manner in which you want your refrigerator door to open. You have basically three choices:

1. Single door. One door opens both the freezer and the refrigerator unit, making this model relatively inexpensive. But energy-wise it can be costly if the family opens the unit frequently.
2. Two-door combination with the freezer unit on top or bottom. The former is the more popular. Our family prefers the freezer door on the bottom since we open that door less frequently and find that the added height this arrangement gives to the refrigerator unit makes it easier to insert and remove items.
3. Side by side. These units are normally more expensive because of their larger size. The freezer in particular is larger. Before buying, ask yourself: Will I use all this storage space? And do I have adequate room in my kitchen to accommodate it?

Service and Warranty

What about service and warranty? Prompt service at a fair price is very important in the selection of a refrigerator. You can lose hundreds of dollars in spoilage if service is delayed. It also pays to have a helpful neighbor with extra space in his freezer in case of catastrophe!

At the time of this writing our Sears refrigerator is eight years old. We have no service contract because we have set aside funds to cover service costs (and already paid over $100 in service bills). Our service contract would have cost $22.95 per year—representing a healthy annual profit for Sears which we hoped to eliminate.

Recently we noted that our refrigerator was not cooling properly. We called the Sears service department on a Thursday morning and a serviceman came that afternoon. He said we needed a new heating unit, but that he would not be able to install it until Monday afternoon. This required taking our frozen items to a neighbor.

The charge for his work was as follows:

Price of Heater	$17.35
Job Charge (labor)	26.00
Basic Charge (home call)	9.95
Tax	3.20
Total	$56.50

I asked the serviceman what warranty Sears offered, because there was no indication on the invoice given me. This is unlike General Electric, for example, which spells out its warranty. Sears also returned only half of the invoice that I had signed. The serviceman then said: "We provide one year on parts and ninety days on labor and service at no charge." I asked him to put that statement on my invoice.

In my view Sears should include this warranty on each receipt given the customer. It should also return a complete copy of the invoice. A check with the Sears service manager indicated that the repairman's statement was not completely correct. Instead of ninety days on labor, it is one year. He said Sears did not have to put the warranty in writing because its terms were better than those of competitors. He also said that Sears service goes beyond its warranty, as everyone knows and as the sign above his door states: "Satisfaction guaranteed or your money back."

Prior to the serviceman's departure I asked if there was anything else wrong with the refrigerator. He looked it over and said: "The gasket in your freezer unit is split. You are losing cold air and the piece will need to be replaced within a few months." I replied: "It makes sense to replace it now. I'd save a nine ninety-five house call and, more important, an hour of my time." The new gasket was put on in about twenty minutes. When I checked it, however, I discovered that cool air was still escaping from the freezer unit. The repairman spent another five minutes making the gasket snug. Moral: Always check repair work *while the serviceman is present*!

Charges as follows:

Price of Gasket	$12.50
Job Charge (Labor)	19.50
Tax	1.92
Total	33.92

After the serviceman's departure I added up the bill and found that he had charged me $34.92. It also pays to check the addition and read other parts of the invoice in the serviceman's presence!

FREEZERS

There are two types of freezers on the market—upright and chest. The prime advantage of the upright is its accessibility. But the chest model provides greater storage space. Prior to purchase you should ask yourself: "Do I really need a separate freezer or is the section in my refrigerator sufficient?" All too often we have visited friends whose freezers contain only a handful of items although these units represent a serious investment both in terms of the original price and the maintenance. One solution is buying secondhand—either from stores that sell reconditioned units or from individuals who advertise their appliances for sale. A couple we know bought a virtually new freezer for forty-five dollars from their next-door neighbors who were unable to place it in their new home. They stock it with meats, fish and poultry in large quantities at wholesale prices, dating stored items so that those with the earliest date will be used first. They also have a refill system for when supplies descend to a certain level, recording their stock in a notebook adjacent to the freezer.

OVENS

The development of the microwave oven was an excellent technological breakthrough. There are three other oven types on the market as well, but let's take a look at this glamour oven first.

1. *Microwave.* This is the most expensive of the available units, although prices have dropped considerably since its introduction. The big advantage is its ability to cook quickly. If speed is important to you, you may wish to consider a microwave model. If your present cooking unit functions well, however, I would suggest keeping it until it wears out, by which time the microwave oven will have been improved. However, for those who are currently furnishing a new home, the microwave may be an appropriate solution. It offers real energy savings because of the shorter cooking time involved. Specialized cookbooks are available to help you use and enjoy this appliance. You might wish to look into possible leakage radiation. There has been some discussion of safety hazards in connection with certain microwave ovens. Check *Consumer Reports* for their latest findings on various models prior to purchase.

2. *Free-Standing.* This type, as the name implies, can stand alone in any kitchen location. It has a finished appearance on the front and sides; thus it can be placed wherever you wish.

3. *Built-in.* This unit has two separate parts—an oven which fits into the wall and a tabletop range. The latest development in ranges is the ceramic top, whose surface provides counter space when the unit is not in use. But you pay for this extra space and attractive appearance—from two to four times the cost of a conventional coil cooking top. Sears' lowest-priced coil unit is a third the price of the ceramic-top model, which sells for $299.

4. *Drop-in and slide-in.* These ovens, as the name implies, require precise cabinet sizes so that they can be placed in the appropriate space.

Other features. Ovens are available in gas or electric as well as in single or double units. It is also possible to obtain self-cleaning or continuous-cleaning models. The self-cleaning unit, we have found, cleans well but it must reach 900 degrees Fahrenheit to do its job. This is an expensive energy user. The continuous-cleaning unit does not do as thorough a job and some hand cleaning of burners, for instance, is required. Sears no longer sells self-cleaning units. The cost of Sears' built-in single gas oven is $359, the electrics vary from $229 to $599.

REPAIRS ON APPLIANCES

There have been many complaints in recent years about the poor quality of repair work in general. This is especially true in regard to appliances (a *Life* magazine article quoted in Chapter 14 highlighted this situation). If you buy from a first-rate appliance firm with a nationwide service, however, you can significantly lessen your woes.

Always be present when repairmen come calling! Not only should you oversee the job, but if a serviceman has overlooked something, as in the case of the loose freezer gasket cited earlier, you can call it to his attention. Careful observation can teach you how to do simple jobs yourself and you can gain valuable advice on the care of your equipment by asking questions. One of our neighbors related this pleasant experience he had when the General Electric (GE) repairman came to service the family's tabletop range and self-cleaning oven:

> The repairman arrived promptly at 8:00 A.M., and went right to work replacing a damaged coil in the electric range. He then showed me how to clean the control buttons and suggested placing aluminum pans beneath each of the four burners to keep the underneath area clean. "Grease is the greatest enemy of porcelain," he explained. "It eats it up." He then removed the oven door and replaced the broiler heating unit. Upon completion of the job, he turned on the self-cleaning unit and explained how the control dials work. Prior to leaving, he checked our GE dishwasher and disposal and suggested that chicken bones and small steak bones be put in the disposal to self-clean the rubber grommet. After neatly piling up all the discarded parts, he wrote out two service invoices with charges as follows:

Job Price (labor)	$10.70		Job Price (labor)	$10.70
Parts—Small burner coil	18.50		Parts—Broiler heating unit	20.65
	$29.20		Home call	9.25
Tax	1.75			$40.60
Total	$30.95		Tax	2.44
				$43.04
			Grand total	$73.99

I signed both copies of the invoice and received the original for my file. You will note that I paid $9.25 for this home call. If he had made two home calls, one to repair each item, I would have been charged an additional $9.25. On leaving, the repairman pointed out that the invoice listed labor and parts guarantees as follows:

> The labor service performed on this invoice for which you were charged is guaranteed for thirty days. If the same fault should occur within that time, no charge will be made to do the same repair.

> The parts for which you were charged on this invoice will be exchanged by General Electric or Hotpoint should the part(s) become inoperative through normal use within one year of date of service. Subject to service labor charges after 30 days from the date of service for which you were charged.

I escorted him to the door at 8:35 A.M. The equipment works fine and the service was courteous, prompt and efficient.

OTHER MAJOR EXPENDITURES

Now let us look at financial aspects of other large expenditures, including travel, furniture, stereo systems, pets, weddings, divorces and funerals.

TRAVEL

Vacations can be costly or cheap depending on such factors as mode of travel, lodging, distance and degree of luxury desired. Again it is important to make a budget beforehand and stick with it. Your annual budget should include a vacation allotment. And try to make your time off a relaxing experience. As one manager advised his assistant: "The idea is to come home rested—not to rest up when you come back to work."

Living and Vacationing Abroad

The spread of American government and business activities throughout the world has created opportunities for many Americans to live overseas, thereby reducing the expense of vacations abroad. The United Nations and regional organizations like NATO and SEATO also offer work in foreign lands. And the current rapid progress in transportation permits the traveler today to reach any part of the globe within a few hours.

After living in Europe and the Far East for seven years, I realize how rewarding foreign travel can be. I tell my venturesome friends that they should be able to put their necessary possessions in a single suitcase and be ready to travel overseas on one day's notice. I also suggest that newly married couples rent both an apartment and furniture, limiting their worldly possessions primarily to cash, bonds and stock, so that they can enjoy instant mobility.

Should you decide on a position abroad, it is important to be familiar with the financial aspects involved. Be sure that you have full information on the local rate of exchange, living costs, modes of travel, customs and taxes, and duties imposed on foreign items brought into the United States. Prior to my arrival in Paris, I relied on a friend to take care of hotel accommodations. When I found that the first day's lodging had amounted to eighty-five dollars, my French seemed to improve miraculously, and after a prudent search I moved into better lodgings for nine dollars a day. In another instance, I exchanged francs aboard ship and found that the steamship line was shorting me 10 percent. Foreign exchange rates are quoted in *The Wall Street Journal.* These quotations serve as a general guide, but it is wise to shop for the best deal—provided it is legal.

FURNITURE

Let us begin by assuming that you are newly married, have just obtained your first full-time jobs and want to furnish your apartment. In doing so, it is important to employ the following guidelines:

1. Buy good-quality items. They last longer, give greater satisfaction during usage and in many cases they end up costing less than cheaper merchandise because of greater durability and higher resale value.
2. Itemize your overall furniture needs.
3. Make a budget of estimated costs based upon the list compiled in entry #2 above.
4. Establish a purchase priority list. What are the most essential items? Ask yourselves: "Do we really need it?" One couple told me: "We bought only a dining and bedroom set when we were first married. That plus our wedding gifts was all we needed. How wise that decision turned out to be! We were offered a great job opportunity in another city and snapped it up. Keeping furniture to the minimum slashed our transportation costs and made the move a cinch."
5. Look for good furniture buys in places like Goodwill, Salvation Army, homes of friends in the process of moving and garage sales. If you collect antiques, visit old farmhouses or secondhand stores.
6. Keep in mind that retail stores may mark items up 50 percent or more. In addition, you will be faced with high carrying charges if you buy on time. Find out if discount houses are available in your community. Also watch for special sales. Be a good bargainer when it comes to buying furniture from "wholesale houses." Don't settle for the first price they offer. As one salesman put it: "What you want is our *lowest* low price. We have a 20 percent range and if you don't ask, you don't get it."

7. Always give first consideration to the quality of the company. Does it stand behind its merchandise?
8. Talk with friends. Obtain their views on good buys. You may wish to develop your own checklist patterned after the format suggested for appliances (Table 9-2). If feasible, you should visit at least three stores prior to making a decision. But don't spend a lot of time looking for and bargaining over small items. Concentrate your efforts on the expensive merchandise. A colleague related this tale: "My wife and I spent eighteen hours shopping in search of a table under ten dollars that would perfectly match the decor of my study. We ended up buying the first table we had looked at a week earlier. What a frustrating waste of time!"

STEREO SYSTEMS

Anyone with teenagers knows more about stereos than he might like. I did, however, feel that I was being repaid in part for enduring years of assault to my central nervous system when my younger son, Tom, volunteered to provide the expertise on stereos for this chapter. I also suggest you consult the latest issues of *Consumer Reports, Hi-Fi Stereo Buyer's Guide,* published six times yearly by Davis Publications, Inc., 229 Park Ave., New York, N.Y. 10003, and *Stereo,* published four times yearly by ABC Leisure Publications, Great Barrington, Massachusetts 01230.

Choosing Your Stereo

Three factors should be taken into consideration prior to buying a stereo system:

1. Total System Budget (TSB): This represents the sum you have available to spend initially and for upkeep on your stereo needs. It can vary from $100 to $5,000 and more, for the initial investment. Upkeep for records and additional equipment can range from a few dollars to thousands.
2. Who the system is for: It seems unwise to spend large amounts on a stereo for a very young member of the family who may soon change his interests or might damage the equipment.
3. Where the system will be used and how often: Most apartments prohibit undue noise, so a powerful system normally would be unwise for an apartment dweller. If the system will be in constant use, buy durable quality equipment. If it is mostly for show, don't waste money on high-priced components.

Available Systems

There are three main types of stereo systems. One is the compact system, which consists of a receiver (radio), turntable (record player), speakers and sometimes a tape player-recorder (cassette and/or 8-track). The compact system can be bought in its entirety as a package deal.

The second type of system is referred to as the component system. Here receivers and/or amplifiers, turntables, tape decks, speakers and headphones are bought separately. This alternative is far more costly than the purchase of a compact system but the quality of equipment is much better.

The third variety is the console system, a self-contained unit that includes speakers, receiver, turntable and sometimes tape deck.

Let us examine these three systems more closely.

A. Compact System
When buying a compact system, one should check for the following features:

1. Magnetic cartridges in the tone arm of the turntable. These are much superior to ceramic cartridges and put less wear and tear on records.
2. AFC switch. This handy switch helps pull in weak stations and prevents them from fading in and out.
3. Dust cover. A totally enclosed dust cover is essential. It is preferable to buy a system in which you can play records with the dust cover on. This keeps particles from landing on the record's surface.
4. Cueing. A lever along the side of the tone arm that enables you to raise and lower the arm from the record without taking a chance on scratching the record by manual placement of the arm.
5. Headphone jack. This is found on most systems and enables one to plug in headphones for private listening.
6. Fast-forward feature. If the system comes with a tape player, it is advisable to have it equipped with a fast-forward button/switch. This allows you to advance the tape to select music without having to wait for the music to come on automatically. This can be a timesaver.
7. Woofer and tweeter. The speaker should have a woofer (for bass) and a tweeter (for treble). The woofer decodes the low bass music sounds from such instruments as the drums and tubas. The tweeter decodes the high-frequency instruments such as cymbals, guitars and flutes. The speakers themselves should be fairly heavy. Unfortunately, many models sold with compact systems are poorly constructed and blow out within a short while. Check speakers carefully because some unscrupulous dealers have been known to fill speakers with sand to make them heavier.

Here again, don't buy the first merchandise that you see. Shop around for the best deal you can find. Zenith, Sony, Panasonic, General Electric, Superscope, Realistic and Lloyd's make some of the best compact systems available. You can try to bargain, but dealers seldom reduce the price of compact systems except at special sales.

B. Component System

When buying a component system *never* buy anything but *name brands*. Components are expensive and thus should be of high caliber. Unknown makes may be inferior in quality and provide no warranty. Let's look at the different components one by one.

Receivers / Receivers and/or amplifiers are the most expensive part of the system, and the most basic. It is into the receiver that everything else is plugged and the receiver powers the turntable and tape deck. An acceptable receiver starts at $150 to $200. About 40 percent of your total system budget (TSB) should be spent on this unit. Example:

```
$300 receiver
 200 speakers (a pair)
 150 turntable
 150 tape deck
─────
$800
```

Many people are fooled by slick-talking salesmen, who boast of a receiver's tremendous power. A receiver should be judged on its appearance, sound, practicality and its *efficient* use of power. Marantz, Sony, Sansui, Pioneer, AKAI are some of the best makes.

Turntables / Anyone who spends more than $250 on a turntable may well be wasting his or her money on a fancy exterior. A turntable should have cueing, a heavy platter (this is where the records are placed) and a quality tone arm. Among the better turntables are Dual, BIC, JVC, Garrard and Pioneer. There are two types of turntables—manual and automatic. The difference between the two is that a manual turntable requires you to change each record after it is played. An automatic turntable permits records to be stacked so they don't have to be constantly replaced. I prefer a manual turntable because stacking a record shortens its life.

Tape Decks / There are three types of tape decks:

1. 8-track. Since these are relatively new and unperfected, there are few good 8-track recorders available. If you want to buy one, don't spend less than $150.
2. Reel-to-reel. These are the best tape decks available if you can afford them. Any reel-to-reel under $300 may not be of good quality.
3. Cassettes. This is my son's preferred type. It is more affordable than reel-to-reel and extremely dependable. Don't buy one without a Dolby Noise Reduction switch (this reduces "hiss" and "boom" while re-

cording) and don't spend less than $150 on a cassette deck. AKAI, Sony and TEAC are among the best makes.

Speakers / Buy speakers according to the power of your receiver/ amplifier. Specifications for speakers are usually provided with the receiver and/or amplifiers. Don't buy anything but brand-name speakers. JBL, Pioneer, Jensen, EPI or Bose are the best brands to buy. Speakers are the most important part of your system because they are the only part that you hear. So take your time in order to select the right ones.

Headphones / This item is invaluable for private listening and the well-being of others (especially parents). Headphones should have individual volume controls and be comfortable to wear for long periods of time.

When shopping for a component system—take your time. It is wise to buy the receiver first, then speakers, turntable and finally tape decks.

Only buy component systems from stereo "warehouses" and wholesalers. Avoid department stores, where this type of merchandise is normally more expensive and the stock less complete. You can dicker over the price at stereo "warehouses" and wholesalers. *Never pay list price for component systems.* Tape decks, receivers, turntables and speakers are frequently priced at least $50 to $75 higher than what dealers expect to receive.

C. Console System

When buying a console system, check for these features in addition to the points indicated above for similar equipment in a compact system: 1) a place for record and tape storage; 2) a solid cabinet with sturdy legs.

A console system is usually bought for a living room or den. It is better to buy a component system if you can afford it because stereo consoles are generally of lower quality.

Among the better console systems are RCA, Zenith and Magnavox. A good console system will normally cost at least $300. They are available in department stores, discount houses and specialty shops, and can periodically be bought on sale. Here again, always bargain before you close the deal.

Quadraphonic Sound

Quadraphonic sound in a stereo system may interest you because of the potentially better-quality reproduction achieved through the use of four-channel receivers. For information on a quadraphonic system I recommend that you read *Consumer Reports'* excellent article titled "CU's First Look at Four-Channel Receivers" (June, 1975). It points out that to build a quad system from scratch could cost $1,200 or more.

Quad systems are becoming popular as they do sound better than stereo. A drawback is that you need a large room and four identical speakers for quadraphonic systems to be most effective. Quadraphonic records and tapes normally cost a dollar or two more than stereo albums and tapes. And this could result in your spending a lot more money.

PETS

A wide variety of animals give humans pleasure. The most popular of these is the dog and thus we will focus on canines here. As will be pointed out in Chapter 13, dogs are not only companions but can also be excellent protectors of the home. An example of the initial cost and upkeep of a Shetland sheep dog is presented in that chapter.

Cost of Dog Owning

Dogs may be classified according to their relative size. Small dogs are those whose weight does not exceed twenty-five pounds. A survey in our area indicated that the initial cost of a dog is not a function of its size. Contrariwise, size *does* have an effect on the cost of raising and maintaining a dog. For example, a toy poodle averages between five and ten dollars per grooming, while an Irish setter can run as high as twenty-five dollars. Annual charges for breeds requiring regular care (Table 9-3) approximate the following, according to a local grooming parlor:

TABLE 9-3   Sample Yearly Grooming Costs

Size	Annual Grooming Charge
Small	$108
Medium	118
Large	200

Feeding an animal is normally the most expensive annual cost. Table 9-4 relates to dry food costs only:

TABLE 9-4   Sample Yearly Feeding Costs

Size	Annual Cost—Dry Food Only
Small	$50– 100
Medium	125– 240
Large	250–1000

If you prefer to give your pet a "luxury" diet, such as canned or packaged foods, the above costs can be as much as 100 percent higher.

A second expense factor is annual medical care (Table 9-5). Shots in the first year may cost sixty dollars from a private veterinarian as follows:

TABLE 9-5   Cost of Immunization for First 12 Months

6 weeks	$15
8 weeks	15
10 weeks	6
12 weeks	15
6 months	9
	$60

After the first year, booster shots and vaccines approximate twenty dollars annually. These vet costs can be cut if you take your pet to the local SPCA, where first-year shots should total about twenty-one dollars, with an average fifteen dollars annually thereafter.

Another possible medical cost is for neutering and spaying. The average cost in our community is thirty-two dollars for neutering and thirty dollars for spaying.

In addition to the above expenses, a dog may become ill or be injured. Care, medicine and boarding can be costly indeed. For example, a friend's collie ran through a plate-glass door and suffered severe gashes. The total bill amounted to $150.00 for medical care and a stay of four days at the vet hospital.

A word of advice to save a potential veterinary bill. Frequent brushing is very important in most breeds. It prevents the buildup of bacteria. Infested 'dead skin is the forerunner of "mange," an expensive and troublesome skin disease in dogs.

Another potential expense to dog owners is damage to household furnishings and fixtures. It helps to have the right size dog for your home. A small dog is ideal for an apartment or duplex with no grounds. A large dog in such an environment can cause considerable damage. Besides, it isn't fair to large dogs to keep them cooped up.

Table 9-6 provides a "recap" of the first-year cost of a medium-sized dog as reported by one owner:

TABLE 9-6   Outlay for My Cocker Spaniel
During First 12 Months

purchase price	$150
cost of medical care	56
cost of food	130
Total	$336

If we assume an average life span of twelve years, the total cost of ownership could range from $2,000 to $10,000, or more. Thus, owning a dog can be a major long-term expenditure, with the initial purchase being only a minor part of the cost.

You can, of course, do things more cheaply. A high-school-student neighbor arrived at the following solution. She befriended a senior citizen in our locality who gave her the pick of the litter of Irish setters. She groomed the animal herself and his food came mainly from table scraps. Her good care kept veterinary costs to a minimum. Within two years she was making the dog available for breeding purposes. The money received paid for his keep. You may not have the good fortune to receive such a lucrative gift but often delightful nonpedigreed animals are available at virtually no cost. If interested, read the local newspaper ads and contact your SPCA.

WEDDINGS

The cost of marriage can range from the no-expense common-law variety to exclusive society events costing thousands of dollars. In deciding what kind of wedding they prefer, couples will find it helpful to follow the management approach presented in this chapter.

It is the parents of the bride who normally bear the financial burden of a wedding. Therefore, it is important for the bride-to-be and her family to work closely together in making the arrangements.

Essential to any successful wedding is the development of a budget itemizing all costs involved. Weddings fall into two major categories: justice-of-the-peace ceremonies and formal church or synagogue weddings. First let us look at costs reported by one young couple for a justice-of-the-peace wedding in our area. Keep in mind, however, that it would be easy to spend ten times this amount. Therefore, all costs should be determined in advance.

Justice-of-the-Peace Ceremony

1. Marriage license $ 3
2. Physical examination   20
   This fee may vary depending upon the physician and the area.
3. Justice of the peace   10
4. Ring   95
   Ring prices differ greatly, depending on individual choice. This couple bought a moderately priced wedding set for a double-ring ceremony, $30 for his and $65 for hers. It is the size and quality of the diamond that determine the price; one jewelry store wanted to charge them *$175* for the same quality and size diamond. *Be sure to shop at least three stores prior to making a decision.*

5. Miscellaneous

This can vary from a sizable figure to zero for this working couple who lived with their parents and spent a honeymoon in the same community with friends. Your budget should list any expenditures for clothing, honeymoon, parties, gifts to people who stand up with you, engagement ring, housing and furnishing expenses. A justice-of-the-peace ceremony requires little preparation. Money saved by this couple was put toward things they would need later for their apartment.

TOTAL COST $128

Formal Church or Synagogue Wedding

Planning for a formal wedding can begin a year in advance if it is to be a major affair. Normally, at least four months are required.

Here are the costs reported by a young bride in my class. She considers these expenses to be fairly standard for a formal wedding ceremony.

1. Bridal gown	$ 200
Features affecting the price include material, style and handwork.	
2. Veil	50
3. Bridesmaids' dresses	200
Styles mostly simple. Materials used for this summer ceremony were soft and lightweight fabrics ($100 each).	
4. Hats with ribbons ($15 each)	30
Traditional bridal hats, pillbox-style with short veil, would have cost $160.00.	
5. Shoes	20
6. Gloves, long	10
7. Men's tuxedos (rental of long tails and other equipment) ($30 each)	90
8. Rings	295
Mounted sets—both his and her rings with the engagement ring	
9. Physical examination	25
10. Marriage license	3
11. Gifts for bridesmaids and best man	30
12. Transportation—limousine	50
13. Invitations	30
14. Thank-you notes	10
15. Stamps	13
16. Toasting glasses	5
17. Garter	3
18. Guest book	4
19. Napkins	8

20.	Ring pillow	5
21.	Wedding album	7
22.	Cake knife	4
23.	Souvenir matches	12
24.	Wedding candles	16
25.	Bridal bouquet	30
26.	Flower-girl basket	10
27.	Bridesmaids' bouquets ($15 each)	30
28.	Flower for groom	3
29.	Corsages for mothers	15
30.	Flowers for the church	100
31.	Flowers for the reception hall	50
32.	Reception hall	175
33.	Music–band: four hours	300
34.	Food and drink for 100 people	2,000
35.	Wedding cake	175
36.	Clergy fee	25
37.	Organist	15
38.	Photographer	150

The photographer took a set number of pictures for this price. Special shots or extra photos would have cost more.

39.	Parties before wedding	216
40.	Honeymoon	1,120
41.	Clothing and luggage for honeymoon	367

TOTAL COST $6,001

A young friend commented on her wedding as follows: "We had intended to be practical about our wedding. But every girl dreams about getting engaged and married. Jewelry salesmen, bridal consultants, photographers and so on know that it's an emotional thing and they play on it. I loved the whole thing but it cost far more than my parents could afford. We should have begun by deciding what was best for us *within our budget.*"

DIVORCE—A GRAND RIP-OFF?

Divorce is often a costly financial burden, only a small part of which may be attributable to its legal aspects. Like other major expenditures, it helps if you approach it from the management viewpoint, determining the major problems and deciding how best to solve them. This would include reaching an amicable settlement that could be a real money saver. Your objective should be to keep lawyer fees and other costs to a minimum. It helps if a couple can do adequate *planning* to include determining in advance how they will divide up their property. Points that might be resolved include: Is a lawyer necessary? Can we use the same lawyer? Can we agree to a fair settlement of the property? If there are children involved, can we agree on their support costs? Can we allow sufficient time to sell expensive items like a home and certain furnishings in order to receive fair prices? I mentioned this approach to a divorcée and she responded: "Your theory is great and I wish we could have done it that way. But we despised each other and didn't so much as communicate for six months." Here is what the split cost her. The husband, of course, must have had heavy added expenses, too, but the wife had the children to look after as well.

Legal Costs:

1.	Lawyer's fee for legal separation	$300
2.	Lawyer's fee for divorce	300
3.	Fee charged by attorney for correspondence (one letter and a short meeting in his office, plus three phone calls)	100
4.	Retainer fee for lawyer in Washington. Later she decided to file in her home state.	250
	Total legal costs	$950

Other Costs:

5.	Sold a large old car and bought a new compact to make the trip home safely	$3,000
6.	Trip home including food, gas, motel expenses and other incidentals	350
7.	Household furnishings moved by major carrier. If the wife were to do it again, she says, she would rent a van and drive it herself. This could have been done for about $400.	2,125
8.	Deposit on newly rented apartment	100
9.	Deposit on utilities	25
10.	Deposit on telephone	75
11.	School fee for three children for 1 year	540
12.	School uniforms	120
13.	Family counseling. One child had a particularly difficult time adjusting to the divorce and all the inherent changes.	1,150
14.	Estimated cost on belongings left behind or given away after dividing the property. This was necessary because of limited space and the high cost of transportation. In estimating this figure some items were left that one cannot put a price tag on.	600
15.	Estimated loss because of quick sale of home. The couple accepted the first offer because they really needed the money and were anxious to split.	3,000
16.	Loss of wife's small business—teaching music lessons at home	1,040
17.	Wife forced to find full-time employment. This required putting the youngest of her four children into a nursery school at $80 per month. Each summer it meant	1,560

camp for the other three at a cost of $600. Without a college degree, and being taxed as a single person, she realized little financial gain from her $2.75-per-hour job. This made leaving the children in order to work even more frustrating.

Total nonlegal costs	$13,685
GRAND TOTAL	$14,635

A male viewpoint on divorce came from a twenty-five-year-old acquaintance: "I was lucky. We had no children and our marriage lasted only two years. Neither of us had saved any real money or acquired valuable possessions. The financial expenses of the divorce amounted to only $475. But I still love her and the emotional costs have been enormous. I must have aged five years in the past two months. I've gained fifty pounds and my doctor bills have increased from zero to over $3,000. My advice is to take your time before getting married. Live together first, if necessary, in order to be sure."

Another important financial reason for taking your time in selecting a mate was presented by a middle-aged divorcée: "I have been divorced for four years and still feel the financial impact as well as a certain social stigma. My married girl friends no longer invite me over. It may be that in their mind I present a threat to their marriage, or perhaps it's because my lower income from alimony and child support payments prevents me from entertaining them as lavishly as they would like. Thus, my circle of friends is primarily made up of people who are separated or divorced. I have never met a divorced man or woman who felt that they had been given a fair deal financially, and in truth, both parties suffer financially. When a man's income is cut one-third to one-half and a woman with children receives one-third to one-half the amount she is accustomed to, major changes in life-styles inevitably follow."

FUNERALS

A friend recently told me this story:

The worst emotional experience of my life was when the police notified me that my parents had been killed in an automobile accident. I was overcome with grief and had no idea of what arrangements had to be made. This was my first encounter with death of a loved one and it proved to be a nightmare. I was in no condition to evaluate suggestions made by the funeral director, florist, clergyman and friends. As a result, my parents' funeral costs were exorbitant and three years later I am still paying off bills. How helpful it would have been to have known in advance what death involved—particularly the expenses. But like many others, I avoided any discussion of the subject until it was too late. Yet it is the one thing we can be 100 percent certain will occur. I might have studied appropriate literature, visited funeral parlors and compared cemeteries to become familiar with all costs. To compound matters, my parents left no will or instructions. Perhaps I had a guilt complex about not seeing them often enough and wanted to make it up with the best of everything, particularly since they were so well liked in the community.

What are the expenses involved in a funeral? The following price scale is based on a survey made in one large community.

Fees paid to funeral home. (Although the following fees are usually payable to the funeral home, some are passed on to other parties—often at no profit to the funeral home.

1. Casket fees

Price of casket	$110 –	$6,500
Additional casket fees	500 –	800

These additional fees include the following professional services: use of funeral home; transferring remains to funeral home; maid and porter service; receiving, recording and arranging flowers; delivery of flowers to cemetery; sympathy cards. These professional services are not itemized by funeral homes because they are considered part of the total service.

2. Transportation fee

Funeral coach	60 –	80
Limousine (per car)	26 –	30

3. Preparation fee

55 – 70

(This may not be itemized but only a lump preparation fee, submitted by the funeral director.)

Embalming	55 –	70
Bathing	10 –	11
Dressing	3 –	4
Shaving	4 –	5
Cosmetic work	25 –	40
Hairdressing	18 –	20

4. Clothing fee

(This can be saved if clothing is provided by the family of the deceased.)

Suit or dress and underclothing	30 –	85

5. Newspaper fee

First day	14 –	14
Second day	13 –	13

(Additional charge over twenty lines)

6. Miscellaneous fees

Rental of veil	$ 5 –	$ 6
Recording certificate	7 –	7
Vigil lights	3 –	4
Palms	11 –	11

7. Transportation-out-of-town fees

Receptacle box	60 –	60
CMAS (Canvas bag provided by airlines)	35 –	35

Fees paid to funeral home for outside expenses

1. Sexton fees	$ 50 –	$150
(Opening and closing of tomb)		
2. Certificate fees		
Photo certificates (per copy)	2 –	2

Funeral expenses in some communities are subject to only 50 percent of the regular sales tax because half of the funeral is considered a service

Grave-site expenses

Bronze markers	$ 75 –	$300
Stone monuments	60 –	250
Tomb	3,000 –	30,000

For those who wish to consider cremation the fees are as follows:

Cremation	$125 –	$300
Urns (for one person)	50 –	250
Urns (for more than one person)	100 –	500
Niches to hold them in columbarium or vault	35 –	750

Transportation may also have to be considered, as there are no crematoriums in some states.

On the plus side, if a veteran dies there are Veteran's Administration allowances as follows:

Burial allowance	$250
Flag to drape casket	
Plot allowance (for those not buried in a national cemetery)	150
Total allowance for veterans	$400

As you can see, funerals vary tremendously in price, and funeral homes in the same community may vary considerably for comparable services. Check prices with care. Most important, however: Determine the reputation of the home and the quality of its services.

Many funeral homes now have plans for those who wish to pay for their funerals in advance either in a lump sum or in monthly installments. But isn't it wiser to set aside your own money for this purpose and have it draw interest in a bank, savings and loan association or credit union? Besides, the home might go out of business before you need its services, or you might find a less costly arrangement elsewhere. You can also buy insurance to cover funeral costs from salesmen who collect fifty cents to a dollar each week. This is very popular in some areas but is obviously much too costly! You would be wiser to take out a regular life-insurance policy.

The National Funeral Directors Association indicates that Americans pay approximately $1,000 for a conventional adult funeral. But in cities with elaborate tombs and many traditions, the cost usually runs much higher. Be sure you get what you pay for. A business friend of mine had this story to tell:

> I was responsible for making the funeral arrangements for my brother. We paid for a stainless-steel casket even though we really couldn't afford it. At the funeral parlor I noted the casket's very fancy design. It seemed most unusual for metal. On touching the casket, I discovered that it was not steel but plastic. After pointing this out to the director, he said, "Oh we made a mistake. I'll correct that after we close at ten this evening." That could have been a mighty big mistake—about $900. Rest assured, I checked the next day to see that my brother was buried in the casket we paid for.

OTHER BIG EXPENSES

Space prevents discussing further major expenditures here (other such expenses might include sewing machines, television sets and camera equipment). However, whatever the item, the approach should be the same as that utilized earlier in this chapter. *Plan* wisely to include the amount of money available within your overall budget; *implement* your plan; and *check* to see that your plan has been properly completed. If you follow this concept for all your major-appliance and other large-equipment expenditures, you should spend less, be able to afford more and receive greater enjoyment from your possessions because they will cause you fewer problems.

Similarly, the same approach should be taken for those more solemn eventualities that we all have to be prepared for.

Part Three

HOUSING

Housing may be either a major expenditure or a major investment. For people who rent, it comprises about 25 percent of the budget. However, if you build or buy a quality home, it can be one of the most profitable places to put your money. Here again, the key to success is utilizing sound management principles. Because housing is so important to so many people, seven chapters have been devoted to this subject. All the topics discussed in Part Three explore ways to obtain better housing at lower cost.

Chapter 10 examines the various types of available housing and the pros and cons of renting or buying. The following chapter documents one family's experience in subcontracting their home. Advantages in subcontracting include: saving up to 25 percent in cost; completing the job in up to one-third the time; assuring yourself a better-quality home. Succeeding chapters examine financial aspects of landscaping, including gardening; protecting your property; maintenance, repairs and improvements; swimming pools; and moving.

10

SHOULD I RENT OR BUY?

As members of today's mobile society, we are constantly confronted with problems caused by relocation. Chief among these is choosing new dwelling space, one of the most important decisions we must make. Since it cannot be made in a vacuum, this decision is by nature extremely complex.

This chapter will investigate the two major approaches to housing—rental and purchase—and examine the kinds of dwellings available in both categories. We will also discuss ways of financing a new home. In Chapter 11, we will examine a third option—building one's own home utilizing a managerial approach. Since, as we shall see, the same basic concepts apply to both buying and subcontracting homes, I suggest a careful reading of both chapters by all prospective homeowners.

RENTING VS BUYING

CAREER FACTORS

The basic issue to consider in regard to renting vs. purchasing a home is whether you intend to sink your roots deep into a particular community or travel extensively, taking on a job that requires frequent changes. Some people will sacrifice higher pay and job promotions in order to stay put. Family ties, familiar climate, pace of life and pleasant living may be factors in such decisions. Generally speaking, buying a home seems the best situation for people who enjoy stability. In contrast, it is often better to maximize mobility by renting if you are in the Foreign Service, work for the Peace Corps, have joined the military or are employed by an international corporation. Renting not only gives you a better idea of whether such careers are to your liking but also provides an opportunity to build a money base for a substantial down payment on a house at some future date. (There are, however, some situations in a career requiring frequent relocation in which buying is the better deal. Some companies, for example, pick up the tab for all moving expenses and will permit you to buy a home on a no-loss basis. Upon your transfer, the corporation will reimburse you for your original purchase price, although you have the option of trying to sell the house yourself at a profit.)

AVAILABILITY OF HOUSING

It is easy to list the advantages of both rentals and purchases but actual choices are often severely limited by the area in which you live. Both in the United States and overseas, there are communities where the housing situation is critical. Frequently there is a considerable waiting period for appropriate rentals, necessitating an additional move, with its attendant expenses and other tribulations. Although recent apartment construction has alleviated the shortage to some extent, rental opportunities in certain areas may be limited and overpriced in relation to value received. In such instances you may be tempted to buy. Of course, you may find the reverse situation as well—low rentals and homes at bargain prices in locations such as Cape Kennedy shortly after the NASA cutback.

However, the housing boom that began in California in 1976 spread eastward and resulted in waiting lists for homes under construction in a number of U.S. communities. This scarcity, coupled with inflation, caused new-home prices to rise over 10 percent in one year. (New homes doubled in price between 1970 and 1977.)

Before making a decision, consider the following questions:

1. Have you done a thorough job of investigating rentals and houses for sale?
2. How long do you plan to remain in the area?
3. How much money have you got to work with?
4. What is the money market—that is, the current interest rates?
5. What does your family want to do? (This is perhaps the most important factor of all as long as you stay within your means.)

BUYING FOR RENTAL PURPOSES

I am frequently questioned as to the wisdom of purchasing a home with the idea of renting it out upon transfer. This approach can be costly. It is advisable to be close to the property you own. Absentee ownership is difficult. Maintenance problems, sudden transfer of tenants and delinquent accounts are troublesome problems from a distance of hundreds or thousands of miles.

BUYING FOR RESALE

Should you decide to buy for resale (occupancy of under three years), you should as a general rule make the lowest down payment possible. This will facilitate transfer of ownership. It is difficult to find someone with the large lump sum necessary to buy you out if you have made a considerable investment. Furthermore, your monthly payments should be spread out over a long period of time, bringing them within the reach of more potential purchasers. Take advantage of GI and FHA loans where appropriate. In contrast, if you have found your ideal locality, make the maximum down payment on a home and pay off the balance as rapidly as possible.

When Is the Best Time to Sell?

Experience indicates that when you are subject to transfer, it is invariably the wrong time to sell. It is important to remember that property, in time, will bring a seller whatever price a buyer is willing to pay. It usually takes a fair amount of time and effort to obtain a good deal in either buying or selling. For those subject to frequent transfer, this "shopping opportunity" is not always feasible and they may be forced to "dump" their homes on the market at a considerable

191

loss in order to get back a part of their equity that is needed for other expenditures.

TIPS ON BUYING

Prominent banks and real-estate firms in your community are good places to secure appropriate home-buying (and selling) information. However, you may want to avoid using real-estate brokers initially. This could save you a 6 percent commission on each end of the transaction. For example, a home listing at $20,000 may cost an extra $1,200 if bought or sold through a realty firm. If you can't make a direct purchase or sale, you can always turn to the agent.

Houses, like securities, should be purchased only by those with adequate background and an understanding of the problems involved. It pays to investigate carefully before purchase. After all, a home is the largest single investment a person normally makes in his lifetime. And remember, the energy shortage will be with us for a long time. Therefore, it is of vital importance to select a home that will minimize energy costs.

ADVANTAGES OF RENTING

There are four main advantages to renting your home:

1. *Mobility.* The key advantage to rental on a monthly basis is the freedom of motion it provides. You can pack up and leave at any time with no financial worries about selling the property. For this reason renting usually is the best solution for young people. If, on the other hand, you have found a fine apartment or house and are reasonably sure that you will not be moving for, say, three years, then it may be to your advantage to have a lease for that period. It prevents the landlord from either raising the rent or evicting you before you are ready to go. But don't get tied up in a long-term lease with no escape clause unless you plan to stay put.

2. *Freeing of funds for other investments.* Sums needed for home down payments and closing costs, as well as major maintenance expenses, can be used instead for business, real estate, hobbies, the stock market or other purposes.

3. *Less work.* House and apartment tenants feel less obligation toward maintaining their dwellings since they lack true "pride of ownership."

4. *Timesaving.* It usually takes a lot more effort to buy than to rent. The problems of securing the property, going through the closing and worrying about the soundness of the investment are time-consuming and draining. And once the purchase is made, some people become virtual slaves to their homes.

ADVANTAGES OF BUYING

From a buyer's viewpoint, the advantages of home ownership can be itemized as follows:

1. *Freedom.* It can be pleasant indeed to be "king of the castle" and do as you please. As a friend who recently bought his own home put it: "How sweet it is to be rid of landlords with their list of rules and regulations!"

2. *Pride of ownership.* This intangible element can add tremendously to a family's peace of mind.

3. *Profitable investment.* A house is an investment that may increase in value faster than the cost of living. You are building an increasing equity with each monthly payment.

4. *Sense of belonging.* Home ownership provides the opportunity to sink your *roots* deep into the community. Neighbors who buy with the same intentions tend to have common interests.

RENTING VS. BUYING: WHICH COSTS MORE?

Cost comparisons may be made by utilizing the format presented in Table 10-1. This hypothetical case assumes a family of three and is based upon comparable living areas in a local community.

The cost comparison indicates greater overall dollar expenditure for the homeowner. Keep in mind, however, that his property taxes and a good slice of his monthly interest payments are tax-deductible. Over a year's time, this makes *buying only slightly more expensive than renting.* In some areas, even without the tax advantages, it is actually cheaper to buy.

The figures cited in Table 10-1 will vary from locality to locality. Furthermore, they are not completely valid, because of differences in types of dwellings, locations within the community, floor plans, age of buildings and other factors. Therefore, this table should be considered a general guide only.

TABLE 10-1 Cost Comparison: Rental vs. Purchase

	Rental (2-bedroom apartment)	Purchase ($22,000 2-bedroom house)
Monthly payment	$300	$235*
Taxes (property)		45
Insurance (house)		35
Upkeep		50
Utilities (gas, electricity, water)	100	100
Phone	15	15
	$415	$480

*Includes principal and interest, but little goes to principal in early years.

TYPES OF HOUSING AVAILABLE FOR PURCHASE AND HOW TO FINANCE THEM

Should you decide to buy, several kinds of accommodations are available. Let us begin by looking at the most common of these alternatives.

CONVENTIONAL HOME

The conventional home continues to be the most popular form of accommodation. In 1976, 1.7 million such homes were built, a number that failed to meet the needs of many lower income families. High costs for land, mortgage money and materials were primary factors in preventing people from buying homes. The future demand for conventional homes will be tremendous. The nation's goal for housing was stated in the Housing and Urban Development Act of 1968: "A decent house and a suitable environment for every American family." The Ninetieth Congress felt that this objective could be reached in 1978, with the construction or rehabilitation of nearly 28 million housing units. The plan calls for construction of 20 million private houses, rehabilitation of 1.7 million and government-assisted construction of 6 million new dwellings. Due to the energy shortage, rising home prices and high interest rates that first became apparent in 1973, actual figures will fall far short of the congressional goal.

A conventional home is the goal of the majority of families in this country. The choices available depend on the prospective buyer's financial resources. Many lending agencies say that you should spend no more for a house than two and a half times your yearly salary before taxes. Thus, if you make $9,600, you can afford a $24,000 home. The U.S. Department of Housing and Urban Development states that "a homeowner should not pay more than 25 percent of income for monthly housing expense (payment on the mortgage loan plus average cost of heat, utilities, repair and maintenance).[1]

Virtually all homes are purchased with the assistance of some form of loan arrangement. Let us look at the principal sources available.

GI LOAN[2]

Since the end of World War II, more than 9.3 million people have purchased homes with the assistance of GI loans under the guaranteed-home-loan

---

[1]U.S. Department of Housing and Urban Development. *Wise Home Buying.* Washington, D.C.: U.S. Government Printing Office, March 1972, p. 4.

[2]The phrase "GI loan" means "a loan made by a private lending institution to a veteran for any eligible purpose, pursuant to Title 38, United States Code." From "Loans for Veterans," VA Pamphlet 26-4, revised March 1975, p. 2.

program of the Veterans Administration (VA). Between 1945 and April 1976, over $122 billion had been made available in loans under the VA program. For those of you in school who are veterans, or who may be eligible for a GI loan, this topic is worth your study.

The present maximum rate of interest on a GI loan is 8¾ percent. The VA will guarantee no more than 60 percent of a loan in an amount not to exceed $17,500. Eligible persons must first apply to a lending agency. The major firms doing this type of business are mortgage brokers and some savings and loan associations. If the lender agrees to the loan, the VA orders an appraisal, normally by an independent appraiser who sets a value on the property. Although a GI loan can far exceed the appraised value, any differential must be paid for by the purchaser.

In determining how much you should pay for a house, it is essential that you inspect it thoroughly. It is wise to utilize a checklist such as the one in Figure 10-1. And it helps to estimate your financial payments by itemizing the costs listed in Figure 10-2.

Figure 10-1 Checklist for buying or building a home.

CHARACTERISTICS OF PROPERTY (proposed or existing construction)

Neighborhood

Consider each of the following to determine whether the location of the property will satisfy your personal needs and preferences:

Remarks

Convenience of public transportation ☐
Stores conveniently located ☐
Elementary school conveniently located ☐
Absence of excessive traffic noise ☐
Absence of smoke and unpleasant odors ☐
Play area available for children ☐
Fire and police protection provided ☐
Residential usage safeguarded by adequate zoning ☐

Lot

Consider each of the following to determine whether the lot is sufficiently large and properly improved:

Size of front yard satisfactory ☐
Size of rear and side yards satisfactory ☐
Walks provide access to front and service entrances ☐
Drive provides easy access to garage ☐
Lot appears to drain satisfactorily ☐
Lawn and planting satisfactory ☐
Septic tank (if any) in good operating condition ☐
Well (if any) affording an adequate supply of safe and palatable water ☐

Exterior Detail

Observe the exterior detail of neighboring houses and determine whether the house being considered is as good or better in respect to each of the following features:

Porches ☐
Terraces ☐
Garage ☐
Gutters ☐
Storm sash ☐
Weather stripping ☐
Screens ☐

Interior Detail

Consider each of the following to determine whether the house will afford living accommodations which are sufficient to the needs and comfort of your family:

Rooms will accommodate desired furniture ☐

Dining space sufficiently large ☐
At least one closet in each bedroom ☐
At least one coat closet and one linen closet ☐
Convenient access to bathroom ☐
Sufficient and convenient storage space (screens, trunks, boxes, off-season clothes, luggage, baby carriage, bicycle, wheel toys, etc.) ☐
Kitchen well arranged and equipped ☐
Laundry space ample and well located ☐
Windows provide sufficient light and air ☐
Sufficient number of electrical outlets ☐

CONDITION OF EXISTING CONSTRUCTION

Exterior Construction

The following appear to be in acceptable condition:

Wood porch floors and steps ☐
Windows, doors, and screens ☐
Gutters and wood cornice ☐
Wood siding ☐
Mortar joints ☐
Roofing ☐
Chimneys ☐
Paint on exterior woodwork ☐

Interior Construction

Plastic is free of excessive cracks ☐
Plaster is free of stains caused by leaking roof or sidewalls ☐
Door locks in operating condition ☐
Windows move freely ☐
Fireplace works properly ☐
Basement is dry and will resist moisture penetration ☐
Mechanical equipment and electrical wiring and switches adequate and in operating condition ☐
Type of heating equipment suitable ☐
Adequate insulation in walls, floor, ceiling or roof ☐

The following appear to be in acceptable condition:

Wood floor finish ☐
Linoleum floors ☐
Tile floors—vinyl asbestos, asphalt ☐
Sink top ☐
Kitchen range ☐
Bathroom fixtures ☐
Painting and papering ☐
Exposed joists and beams ☐

Source: *To the Home-Buying Veteran,* VA pamphlet 26-6 (current edition), Veterans Administration, Washington, D.C. 20420.

195

Figure 10-2 Format for estimating costs of purchasing a home.

```
Downpayment  .........................    ____  ┃ Add these
Closing charges:                                ┃ to get your
    Title search and clearance .............    ____  ┃ TOTAL
    Various legal fees  ...................    ____  ┃ INITIAL
    Other changes  ....................    ____  ┃ CASH
            TOTAL INITIAL COST........    ____  ┃ OUTLAY
Size of monthly payment on mortgage .......    ____
Monthly payments on taxes and assessments....    ____
Monthly payments on insurance ............    ____
            TOTAL MONTHLY PAYMENT .    ____  ┃ Add these
Probable fuel cost (average per month) .......    ____  ┃ to get your
Probable monthly utility cost (lights, water, gas,    ┃ TOTAL
    etc.)..............................    ____  ┃ MONTHLY
Estimated monthly maintenance and repair           ┃ COST
    expenses ...........................    ____  ┃
            TOTAL MONTHLY COST......    ____
```

Source: *To the Home-Buying Veteran,* VA pamphlet 26-6 (current edition), Veterans Administration, Washington, D.C. 20420.

Let us assume that your inspection indicates the house is a good buy, your financial estimate convinces you that you should have no trouble meeting payments and you qualify as a veteran. It would then be advisable to utilize the GI loan, which provides the following advantages:

1. The interest rate is normally lower than the going rate elsewhere. For example, the VA charges 8¾ percent, whereas in most areas conventional loans are running between 9 and 9½ percent.
2. With a VA-guaranteed loan you have the right to repay your loan at any time without penalty.
3. An independent appraisal of the property in question is made by the VA for fifty-five dollars. This appraisal is made known to you.
4. No down payment is required.
5. The loan may be made for up to thirty years.

The disadvantages you may encounter are these:

1. There will undoubtedly be red tape involved in dealing with the government.
2. Add-on points[3] are often charged that may absorb much of the savings gained from the lower interest rate. Although the VA will not permit point payments legally, there are ways to do this "under the table." For example, if a home builder charges $20,000, he may hold this price for the GI purchaser but lower it to $19,200 for a conventional 9 percent loan. This means that he has added in a four-point charge, or $800, to compensate for the lower rate of interest.

[3]A one-time charge, based upon the amount of the mortgage, that may be made by lending agencies. One point is equal to a 1-percent additional cost for one year.

FHA

The Federal Housing Administration (FHA) also provides an opportunity to obtain a loan at less than the going rate. The FHA, like the VA, guarantees a loan for the lending agency. The procedure is similar, in that you must begin by going to a lending agency to get its approval for a loan. The next step is for the FHA to make the property appraisal. Anyone who has good credit, steady income and the necessary cash down payment is eligible for an FHA loan. At the present time, the maximum mortgage that the FHA will guarantee for a single-family dwelling is $60,000.

The FHA calculates the maximum insurable loan by taking:
97% of the first $25,000 (the lower of the sales price or appraisal value)
95% of the excess.

CONVENTIONAL LOANS

The key advantage to the conventional loan is that it eliminates governmental red tape. However, it is often more costly; furthermore, in periods of high interest rates the lending agencies are more selective and these loans may be difficult to get.

In the 1975 capital market, it was generally not possible to secure the best deal on a conventional loan. Two examples illustrate the picture. First, the branch manager of a large savings and loan firm told me that he was making no GI or FHA loans—there were better opportunities in the regular home loan. He was making conventional loans up to 80 percent of appraised value. On a $40,000 home, this meant a $32,000 maximum loan, with an interest charge of 9 percent and monthly payments to be completed in twenty years. A buyer therefore had to have $8,000 of his own money available or secure a second mortgage from some other source—at a higher rate of interest.

In the second case, a prominent lending institution on the West Coast was requiring a 25 percent down payment on a new $50,000 house. Although the bank would loan $37,500 at a 9¼ percent rate, they stipulated that if the prime interest rate was raised before the contract was closed, the borrower had to pay the higher price. In addition, they would not grant the loan for a period in excess of twenty years. Consequently, monthly payments, including interest, taxes, insurance and so on, approximated $550. Other costs of closing the deal amounted to an added $2,000 (tax reserve, title company fee, recording fee and such). In this situation, the buyer had to muster at least $14,500 to obtain the $50,000 house, aside from the cash he may have needed for furniture and other necessities.

REAL ESTATE SETTLEMENT PROCEDURES ACT

Speaking of closing or settlement charges (Figure 10-2), a recent law requires complete disclosure of all these costs.

The Real Estate Settlement Procedures Act of 1974 (Public Law 93-533), as amended in 1975, requires use of a standard form for advance disclosure of settlement costs and to record actual charges incurred at settlement in all mortgage transactions involving federally related loans. This law became effective in June 1975. In my view, it is very helpful to the home buyer because it enables him to know exactly what costs he may pay prior to the actual closing time. All disclosure settlement costs must be itemized for both the borrower and the seller.

HUD's first printing of the *Settlement Costs* booklet contained a statement that made Realtors very unhappy. The comment appeared in the section titled: "Understand the Role of the Real Estate Broker" and read: "The broker's principle interest at settlement is to get the transaction closed and his fee or commission disbursed."[4]

The action taken by the Realtors was reported recently in our local newspaper under the caption: "Book Offensive, HUD Changes It." The article stated:

> National Association of Realtors president Art Leitch huddled with HUD general counsel Robert Elliot, NAR's publication reports, and so now future copies of the little book will read:
> "It is up to you to review the documents carefully. Although the broker may offer helpful advice, keep in mind that you are the one who is spending the money to buy a home and are entitled to a full understanding of the costs. The broker has a substantial interest at settlement to complete the transaction. Also bear in mind that the obligation of the seller's broker is to represent the seller and in this connection, the seller may be interested primarily in closing the transaction as soon as possible."[5]

The power of NAR is apparent from the prompt action taken by HUD to modify its booklet. This points up the importance of consumers having a strong national organization to look after *their* interests.

[4]*Settlement Costs.* A HUD Guide. Washington, D.C.: U.S. Government Printing Office, 1975, p. 19.
[5]New Orleans *Times Picayune,* November 19, 1975, p. 15.

198

ENERGY CONSERVATION

Every potential home buyer or home builder should give serious consideration to the future energy situation in the United States. It is apparent that this problem will increase in the years ahead. President Carter said that the energy shortage "is the greatest challenge that our country will face during our lifetime." How does this affect the potential homeowner of tomorrow? He should check with care the size and energy efficiency of a home prior to purchase. Does it have adequate insulation (approximately eight inches of fiberglass in the ceilings and six inches in the exterior walls)? Are the windows and other glass areas insulated or double-glazed? Are the exterior doors adequately insulated? Are heating and cooling units the most efficient and economical? Do I need all this floor space? What are current and projected utility rates? What about location in relation to work? Questions on energy conservation should be answered to your satisfaction prior to purchase.

Present homeowners should study with care the possibility of providing better insulation and making other energy-saving improvements. This study should consider the dollar value of legislation proposed by Congress in 1977: "The home-insulation credit is 20 percent of outlays up to $2,000, with a maximum of $400 which is deductible from taxes due. The installation of solar-energy systems or windmills is 30 percent of the first $1,500 expended, plus 20 percent of any additional outlays up to $10,000." Although the amounts may be modified, an Energy bill should become law this year.

COOPERATIVE APARTMENTS

A cooperative apartment, as the name implies, is one whose purchase involves the sharing of ownership of a building and land. The building is constructed for a group of people who incorporate for this purpose. Their ownership is reflected in their shareholdings, which enable them to reside in their apartments. Each owner also has the privilege of using the land and sharing the common building facilities. The responsibility for maintenance of the building, including payment of taxes, rests with the corporation. It obtains funds for upkeep from the apartment dwellers. Each apartment owner has a single vote in management affairs. An individual owner in a cooperative cannot sell his apartment to another person without the consent of the other members of the cooperative, a restriction that sometimes presents serious problems with respect to contemplated sales. The method of financing a cooperative is similar to that used to obtain a conventional housing loan.

CONDOMINIUMS

Condominiums are apartment buildings, often of the luxury type, in which title to each apartment rests with the purchaser. Ownership also includes a pro-rata share of all land and improvements. Often the builder can borrow virtually all the money required and sell each of the apartments before the construction is completed.

During a recent visit to Miami, Florida, I looked at a number of condominiums. Although some of the least expensive units could be purchased for as little as $20,000, the majority ranged far in excess of this figure—not surprisingly, in view of their location. One luxury unit published a proposed price schedule for its apartments that ranged from $90,500 to $142,500, not including the annual maintenance costs, which ran upwards of $210 per month.

Although a condominium, in contrast to a cooperative, allows you to sell to whomever you please, you could be faced with the problem of finding a buyer. In the meantime, you have made a heavy fixed investment with money that could be earning interest, and in periods of high yields the interest can be a considerable sum. Your monthly assessment may approximate the cost of apartment rent, and as the building ages, these maintenance expenses increase.

Financing arrangements on condominiums vary. Some of the luxury units I investigated were asking 50 percent of the total selling price as a down payment, with the remainder to be paid within twenty years. In contrast, others were advertising small down payments with long-term settlement dates. One such ad read, "Purchase price of $25,990; with 10% down payment of $2,600 and monthly payments at $213 per month for the first seven years and then $160 per month for the next 23 years. Each payment includes principal and interest—annual percentage rate of 8½% per annum."

MOBILE HOMES

There has been a healthy rise in the use of mobile homes in the past ten years. Mobile units accounted for only 8 percent of all new single-family dwellings in 1960, but sixteen years later, they had increased to over 35 percent. Over 800,000 mobile homes were sold in 1976; families living in this type of unit numbered 9 million. The majority of purchasers, accounting for over 50 percent, were young married couples.

A primary advantage of mobile-home living, in contrast to conventional residences, is the lower initial cost. The average two-bedroom unit can be purchased for $8,000 to $10,000, although prices range from $6,000 to $50,000, and even higher for custom jobs. A problem in purchasing a mobile home is choosing from among the myriad of manufacturers in the business—more than two hundred of them. It is important not only to obtain a good-quality home but to make the purchase from a reputable dealer (there are 8000 dealers in business today) who will stand by his product. If you buy a used mobile home, check the going rates as published in the *Official Mobile Home Market Report.*

Although the average mobile home sells for $8,000 to $10,000, financing charges should be considered in determining what your true cost would be in making such an investment. It is possible to obtain conventional loans on mobile homes for periods of from seven to ten years. One plan (Table 10-2) uses the following basis for determining the length of the loan. Calculations are based upon the factory invoice price, not including transportation cost to dealer.

TABLE 10-2   Loan Schedule for Mobile-Home Purchase

Price	Length of Loan
Up to $3,500	84 months
$3,501 to $4,500	96 months
$4,501 to $5,500	108 months
Over $5,500	120 months

Lending agencies indicate that, in theory, loans could be made with a minimum 10-percent down payment, the remainder of the price to be covered by a single first-mortgage loan. However, the maximum advance is based upon the factory-invoice price (see Table 10-3).

TABLE 10-3   Mobile-Home Costs

Selling price ($6,000 + $360 sales tax)		$6,360
Coach factory invoice price	$4,550	
Sales tax (6%)	360	
Extra cushion added	300	
Maximum loan		5,210
Down payment required		$1,150

Now let us see what it will cost, in terms of one lender, to borrow $5,210 in the current era of high interest rates.

It is necessary that you carry insurance during the life of the loan. On the assumption that you obtain a seven-year loan, the insurance cost is $717, which increases the loan to $5,927. This results in a monthly payment of $108.92, for a grand total of $9,149.28. According to the bank, this represents a 12.93 percent simple-interest rate. In order to arrive at your total expenditure, add the $1,150 down payment, and you will find that your mobile home is costing you approximately $10,300.

Many lenders will also try to sell you credit life insurance. This insurance means that if anything happens to the owner, his designated heir would have the coach free and clear. A bank executive told me, "We encourage dealers to push credit life because we receive a nice cut of this insurance sweetener ourselves."

I asked how much the mobile home would cost on a monthly basis if credit insurance were taken and was told that it would come to a total of $118.40 per month, or $9,945.60 over a seven-year period. When you add the $1,150 down payment, the total exceeds $11,000! This appears a bit high for a mobile home that cost the dealer $4,550 plus shipping charges.

Certain lending agencies exercise leverage on dealers. An official put it this way: "We provide certain dealers with a line of credit. Naturally, we expect them to use our bank with respect to any customer sales. They don't have a legal obligation, but there is a real moral responsibility. In this period of tight credit, they know we can cut off their credit quickly. We are pleased when dealers push such extra equipment as air conditioners and king-size beds."

When I pointed out that mobile-home builders claim that all you need to do is move in, he said, "That's true, but if extra equipment can be sold, it swells that loan."

The GI loan can also be utilized for mobile-home purchases under certain conditions. In order for such a home to be eligible, however, a lot must be purchased and the unit immobilized thereon as part of the property—that is, the wheels must be removed and the coach must be affixed to a solid foundation with permanent hookup to all utilities. The loan period for a mobile home may not exceed twelve years. Mobile homes are also eligible for FHA loan guarantees.

Prospective home buyers should give serious consideration to the purchase of a good used mobile home. A bank official told me, "It is possible to find tremendous deals near military bases. No officer wants a repossession to blot his credit record. On occasion, a man ordered overseas may be desperate to find a purchaser, and will amost *give* his mobile home away. Loans on used homes, of course, are far more difficult to obtain, particularly if the home is more than two years old. However, if the prospective buyer has good credit, we would consider letting him assume the payments."

QUALITY AND SERVICE

As mentioned earlier, there are over two hundred mobile-home manufacturers and 8,000 dealers in the United States. Since each category has its share of "quick-buck artists," it is wise to shop around for good-quality coaches and honest, reliable and well-established dealers.

Before making your final choice, go to a mobile-home park and talk to some of the owners. They can be helpful in pointing out good and bad features of their equipment. Your bank loan specialist in this area can also offer sound advice. Take a hard look at the workmanship of mobile homes produced by the leading manufacturers. Examine the quality of the furniture, the strength of the walls and flooring. Is the bathtub built to adult specifications? What about the other plumbing facilities and fixtures? Check the thickness of the doors and the way the windows are hung. Don't hesitate to test the electrical outlets and other fixtures for workability.

Of course, the mobile home is not mobile at all. You can't move the average unit with your car; a sizable truck is required for that purpose. Before you buy, be sure that you have found a suitable park or lot to which to move your new home, and a dealer who will pay for all setup costs. If you are in a hurricane area, make certain that the mobile home is properly grounded so that high winds don't turn it over. Again, be sure that the dealer is reliable; it is one thing to have a ninety-day factory warranty, but another to get the dealer to provide the necessary service within that period.

MOBILE PARKS

There are vast differences in the quality and service offered by various parks utilized by mobile homes. The parks range from luxurious home sites offering conveniences found in apartment living, to ugly eyesores that furnish a miserable existence—noisy, dirty and badly lacking in service. According to one dealer, there is a correlation between mobile-home sales in an area and the quality of its mobile parks. He commented: "The more homes sold, the better the quality and service of the mobile parks."

RECREATIONAL HOMES

Outdoor living beckons to an increasing number of Americans each year. The facilities involved are usually occupied only for recreational purposes, although some people make such dwellings year-round homes. I know a young college instructor who lives full-time on a small houseboat. Recreational homes range from tent campers costing $300 to elegant motor dwellings with price tags that exceed $100,000.

MOTOR HOMES

A relatively recent innovation is the motor home, which is truly mobile and is used primarily during vacations. It normally represents an expensive investment. The cost may range from $11,000 to $100,000 or more.

A motor home permits the owner to stop in any locality without needing to use the motor-park facilities. It is a completely self-contained unit. The method of financing is similar to that used for the purchase of mobile homes. The only difference is that insurance rates are higher for this vehicle on wheels. This is not an item normally purchased by families with limited means, because of its high cost and restricted use.

The energy crisis had an adverse impact on motor homes. A full-sized motor home averages approximately seven miles per gallon. One motor-home executive commented, "Our feeling is that people aren't going to be interested in buying a vehicle that uses more gasoline than a car."[6] However, sales increased markedly in 1976, with the easing of the recession and greater availability of gasoline.

OTHER CHOICES

There are many other types of recreational "homes." One family we know who live in a balmy southern clime make their year-round home in a tent. A young teacher friend spends each summer vacationing in her camper. Other potential home choices include standard trailers, houseboats, truck campers, van conversions and tent campers.

RENTAL OPTIONS

Most of the above housing options—from apartments and houses to boats and mobile homes—are available on a rental basis. As in a purchase, you will want to decide which alternative best meets your needs.

In the current housing market, there are opportunities to rent with the option to buy. Thus, if you like a home or condominium that you are renting, you can buy it at a later date. This alternative allows a thorough check of the house while renting it; an opportunity to raise down-payment money; and time to decide if you really like the community.

If you are interested in a motor-home vacation, you may wish to rent a vehicle. Our neighbor has a family of eight and finds it a delightful way to vacation each year. His rental cost, in 1977, for a four-week trip from New Orleans to California was as follows:

$$\$250 \text{ per week} \times 4 = \$1,000$$
$$12 \text{ cents per mile} \times 4,000 = \underline{\quad 480}$$
$$\$1,480^*$$

*A refundable deposit of $400 was required for the four-week period.

[6]"Motor Home Makers Have Plenty of Trouble as Gasoline Runs Low." *The Wall Street Journal,* December 5, 1973, p. 1.

FOR SINGLES ONLY

A fairly recent housing concept that has been well received in a number of localities is the rental apartment complex for single people. This provides a social atmosphere with swimming pool, clubhouse, dance area, bar and entertainment. A visit to one building supported the fact that it provides a "swinging" atmosphere. A local apartment advertises, "For Young Singles— Where the Action Is."

11

SUBCONTRACTING YOUR HOME

"I understand you built your dream home in two months and saved a bundle of money. Will you tell us how you did it?" This is the way the president of a university alumni club recently invited me to speak at one of his club meetings on a subject dear to my heart. As usual I acquiesced, ever-eager to share the king-sized challenges and tremendous psychological and economic rewards that come with subcontracting your home. This chapter, an outgrowth of such lecture presentations, incorporates questions that my audiences have raised.[1]

One of the queries I frequently receive is "Do you consider this a wise time to build?" My answer is yes. *If you intend to live in a community for at least three years, you should do well by making such an investment.* The longer you wait, the more housing materials and labor will cost and the more complex the energy situation will become.

Another common question is "What made you decide to build?" We had never owned a house until eleven years ago, due to constant moving. Our first purchase, a "spec" (speculation) home, built solely to make a buck for the contractor, proved to be a near-disaster. Living in it convinced us that we could do a better job ourselves. Our move to New Orleans provided the opportunity to try our hand at subcontracting, and we jumped at the chance.

Before giving you the details of our experience, however, I would like to interject a cautionary note. Please keep in mind as you read this chapter that subcontracting entails what can be disastrous risks. I therefore urge you not to try to duplicate my experience unless you have a managerial and financial background. Face your limitations squarely before embarking on a venture of this kind. In our case the risks were less than those posed by available alternatives and the rewards more satisfying.

Even if you decide not to do your own subcontracting, this chapter should enable you to work more efficiently with your architect and contractor. It also contains information of value to potential home buyers. The better one's understanding of home construction, the higher one's chances of getting a fair deal!

THE PLANNING PHASE

My wife and I counted on management concepts working for us in subcontracting our home—and work they did! The first management function, adequate planning, is in fact the key to successful home building. Proper

---

[1]We kept comprehensive notes dating from the initial planning of our home, as well as a daily diary during the construction phase including both planned daily activities and actual accomplishments. This information became a book which I recommend to you: *Do-It-Yourself Contracting to Build Your Own Home: A Managerial Approach* (Radnor, Pennsylvania: Chilton Book Company, 1974).

planning includes reading available literature,[2] speaking with building experts and observing quality residential construction firsthand. Serious consideration must also be given to location, design, expenditures, time available for the project and selection of subcontractors and materials. If the planning stage goes well, all the other steps should fall into place. We spent several months doing our preparatory work. Notice the word "we"; such a project can fall flat on its face unless husband and wife work as a team. If a couple has widely divergent tastes and quick tempers, building a dream house can quickly become a nightmare.

CHOOSING A LOCATION

Location is of prime importance. Look for the lot that best meets your needs, then line up a few alternative choices. We were looking for the following: acceptable walking distance to work; professional residential area; proximity of good public schools for our children; high ground to provide relative safety in the event of hurricanes; area where property values were rising. Although we looked at homes within a twenty-five-mile radius of the university, we kept coming back to a fine location that was only a seven-minute walk to my office. In spite of the relatively high price of its lots, this was the area that best met our requirements.

Another element of importance to us was privacy. Two attractive brick homes nearby plus the six-foot-high fence we would build behind the house would block the neighbors' view of our backyard. To the sides, fencing would prevent the curious from peering at our patio—and you need privacy if you like sunbathing and midnight skinny-dipping.

Our selection of a centrally located site was influenced by reduced travel costs—it meant we could get along with one car. The area also had a strong neighborhood association that checked to be sure homes met minimum specifications. Pride in the neighborhood was encouraged; there was a garden club and a women's group that sponsored talks by members of the police and fire departments and by prominent local officials.

ARRANGING FOR PURCHASE

Once our decision was made, the next step was to arrange for purchase of the desired lot. The owner was willing to negotiate, and working through an able

[2]The federal government has good documents available. Pointers can be obtained from two HUD publications, *Minimum Property Standards (One and Two Family Dwellings)*, HUD No. 4900.1, 1973 edition with amendments; and *Manual of Acceptable Practices*, No. 4930.1, 1973 edition. Helpful information can also be acquired from the Department of Agriculture publication, *Wood-Frame House Construction*, Agriculture Handbook No. 73, USGPO, Washington, D.C., Revised April 1975.

real estate agent we arrived at a fair price—fair in comparison with similar lots recently sold.[3] Next we hired a lawyer, first securing his itemized charges, and initiated the necessary title search. The purpose of this search is to determine if the lot is clear of prior claims; title insurance, another necessity, protects you in the event that it is found that you don't really own "your" property. Once the "Agreement to Purchase" was signed, we moved to the next planning phase.

DECIDING ON PLANS AND MATERIALS

A young architect's assistant—not a licensed architect, but extremely competent—who had just gone into business, was delighted to prepare our plans for a reasonable fee. We had already developed our own drawings of the house, as well as detailed specifications. Our draftsman made up ten sets of drawings (five plans per set: foundation; square footage; elevation; plot; typical interior wall sections) and ten copies of a Description of Materials (see below). It is important to be specific about materials for every item in your home—foundation, exterior walls, floor framing, roofing, windows, interior doors and trim, cabinets, heating, plumbing and so on. Regarding roofing, for example, we specified "Asbestos shingles—Johns-Manville, American Colonial" rather than simply asking for "asbestos shingles," since there is a great deal of quality and price difference in the variety of roofing available to builders. We quickly learned, incidentally, that it pays to buy the finest materials. In the long run, the cost differential is recovered in durability, reduced heating and cooling bills and increased esthetic satisfaction.

The preparation of a detailed list describing all materials and equipment required for your home (Description of Materials) may sound like a huge task, but this is not the case. Your designer will probably have sets left over from previous work, and good builders also have copies. The owner of a home you admire will sometimes lend you his specifications. Once you have several Descriptions of Materials in hand, you need only make appropriate modifications to suit your needs.

OBTAINING BIDS

After the plans and Description of Materials are completed, it is wise to present full sets of each to three respected builders in the community. They will give you their prices to construct this exact house. You can then compare these bids with what you can build the house for yourself. Keep in mind that if you want any additions after signing with a builder, they will cost you extra. I checked with fourteen people who had contracted to have their homes built and found

---

[3]We could establish this readily since the sales prices of all lots appear weekly in our local paper.

that their original estimates had been increased by 6 to 20 percent because of additional builders' charges. One of my neighbors had a patio overhang extended four feet—to the tune of an extra $800. Bear in mind also that there will be other heavy costs before you are settled, such as landscaping, fence and drapes. Therefore, when we estimated our budget, every cost we could think of was itemized in the estimate—including our moving expense. Your itemized budget becomes a significant planning tool. I used the format shown below in Table 11-1. Itemize every cost in your budget; you can obtain a form for this purpose from a lending agency.

Once you have listed all the items necessary to build your home, it is time to obtain prices from subcontractors and supply houses.[4] Leads on the most reliable firms can be obtained from 1) successful builders, 2) observation of quality homes in progress and talks with the subcontractors concerned

TABLE 11-1 The Stillman Budget

Item	First Estimate	Revised Estimate	Actual	Contracted with: (Name, address, phone, principal to contact)
Preliminary costs: (Includes such items as lot, taxes, insurance, lawyer's fee, building permit, and survey)				
Foundation:				
Piling (#9) . . .	950.00	912.00	912.00	Smith Pile Drivers, Inc. 121 Richton Avenue 711-3000 Mr. John Smith
Materials:				
Lumber . . .	5,579.79	5,641.50	5,766.14	Doe Lumber Company 5164 Collins Avenue 401-6111 Mr. J. J. Doe
Total*	xxx	xxx	xxx	

*In arriving at your total, you may wish to pay yourself a fair return and include this figure in the overall price. I based my economic opportunity cost on the fact that if I hadn't spent twelve hours per day on this job for two months, I would have done other productive work. However, if I had contracted with a builder, there would also have been time expended. Four people I queried indicated they averaged three hours per day on the job over an eight-month period. Buying a new or used home also involves putting in time—loan negotiations, etc.

[4]We contacted approximately 150 sources of supply and subcontractors in order to select 49.

and 3) friends who did their own subcontracting. We used all three sources and found them invaluable.

Our plan called for obtaining three bids whenever feasible. We did not always take the lowest bid or accept the first price. In order to secure bids on lumber, electrical requirements, plumbing and so on, it is necessary to provide these firms with your plans and Description of Materials. This is the primary reason for having ten sets made.[5] Insist that all copies be returned. Inevitably a few of them will disappear along the way.

Once we had ascertained the best deals, it was only a matter of tabulating the prices to determine what our overall building costs would be. We compared this total with what the three builders would have charged and found a 25-percent differential with even the lowest bid.

SETTING UP FINANCING ARRANGEMENTS

We were now in a position to visit lending agencies, facts in hand. After all, money is the catalyst that makes any business transaction come together.

My wife and I decided that with interest rates high, it paid to make a maximum down payment. Why let the bank charge us 9 percent when our money only earned 5 percent? The question of points was also given a hard look. The number of points charged ranged from as low as two to as high as six. On $20,000, this one-time charge would amount to $1,200 at the highest rate. Another "hidden" cost was supervision by the lending agency, which varied from zero to one percent. I observed the amount of supervision given my neighbor's home—about thirty minutes of casual observation during the entire construction period. I can think of better ways to spend $200.

As regards insurance and taxes, the lending agencies love to take care of these items for you. A doctor friend told me that his bank representative had advised him to let them handle these things for him, since they could get a better tax assessment. The doctor commented, "My family has lived in New Orleans for four generations; we know all the tax angles and can get the best deal. What this institution wanted was for me to pay my taxes up to a year in advance. They would invest my money until payment was due—a great deal for the bank, but I was getting taken. On insurance, I found their rates higher than the company we use for my medical affairs! You can imagine what I told the fellow!"

My own view is that you should cut your borrowing costs to the minimum. It makes good sense to pay your own taxes and insurance. Shop around for insurance, and obtain the policy best suited to your needs. During construction, it is also desirable to obtain a policy protecting you from such

---

[5] The city and our local Levee Board also required copies for their files.

risks as injury to workmen and others,[6] theft, destruction of materials and damage to neighbors' property. Such coverage can be obtained locally. Home insurance is discussed in further detail in Chapters 13 and 18.

CLOSING

By about this time, you should be thinking of closing the property deal and taking ownership of the land. This can be accomplished quickly with the assistance of your lawyer. Be sure that all costs are spelled out for buyer and seller. These may include the following: mortgage certificate; paving certificate; conveyance certificate; tax certificate; registration of act in conveyance office; registration certificate; cancellation of mortgage registration in archives; passing of act of sale; preparation, order and obtainment of certificates; conduction of title examination; execution of release of mortgage city taxes (to buyer) and state taxes (to seller). Check your figures carefully. For example, I found that the lawyer wanted to compute taxes (city and state) from the first of the month. However, we closed on the tenth. A computation to that date resulted in dollar savings. Such costs add up rapidly.

IMPORTANCE OF TIMING

The final planning tool I utilized was a modified PERT (Performance Evaluation and Review Technique) concept (see Figure 11-1). PERT provides a technique for "planning the step-by-step development and completion of a project."[7] It is a valuable tool to "help identify potential bottlenecks and determine ways of choosing between the resultant delays or alternative approaches that will reduce delays."[8]

The time factor was crucial in establishing my critical path.[9] I had only two months to build the house, because of school commitments in September. Therefore, I developed a schedule that seemed feasible—a two-month schematic diagram (Figure 11-1) that was an optimistic approach—and also an alternative three-month schedule allowing for unplanned incidents.[10] Dates for

---

[6]Subcontractors often have this insurance. If this is the case, it is important to obtain written evidence before they begin work. The "Certificate of Insurance" should be from a reliable company. It itemizes type of insurance (employer's liability, workmen's compensation, comprehensive general), policy number, expiration date and limits of liability.

[7]W. Haynes, J. Massie and M. Wallace, *Management: Analysis, Concepts, and Cases,* 3rd ed. (Englewood Cliffs, N.J.: Prentice-Hall, Inc., 1975), p. 225; also note, pp. 452–57.

[8]Ibid., p. 263.

[9]A management concept that charts the sequence of events that leads most quickly to the completion of a task.

[10]My friends told me that an estimate of three months was still too optimistic because comparable houses in the area took from six months to a year and a half from the initial on-site work until actual move-in.

Figure 11-1 PERT chart used for building phase.

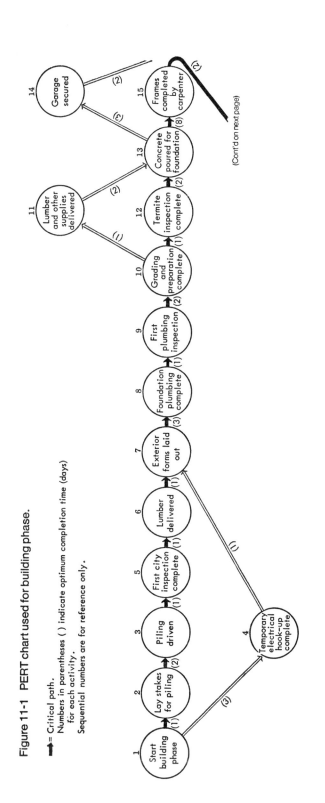

= Critical path.
Numbers in parentheses ( ) indicate optimum completion time (days)
for each activity.
Sequential numbers are for reference only.

(Cont'd on next page)

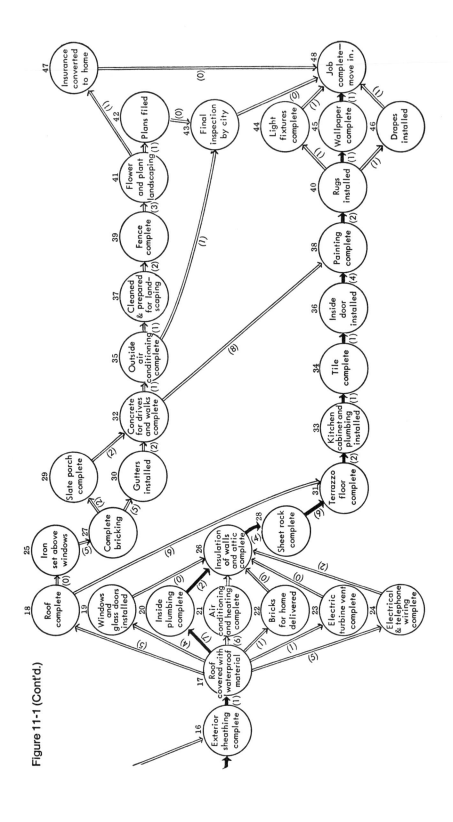

Figure 11-1 (Cont'd.)

subcontracting such work as plumbing, electrical work, flooring, foundation, carpentry, roofing, bricking, fence and pool were firmed up and plotted on my chart. The detailed schedule, much like a budget, provides both a plan and a control technique.

A timetable listing events in chronological order can also be of valuable assistance. It requires that you list all major steps in building your home. A model timetable is shown below:

STILLMAN'S MANAGERIAL APPROACH TO HOME BUILDING

1. Begin building phase. Discuss techniques to meet needs—PERT, management model, organizational and control steps.
2. Lay stakes for piling.
3. Piling driven.
4. Temporary electrical hookup complete.
5. First city inspection complete.
6. Lumber delivered.
7. Exterior forms laid out.
8. Foundation plumbing complete.
9. First plumbing inspection.
10. Grading and preparation complete.
11. Lumber and other supplies delivered.
12. Termite inspection complete.
13. Concrete poured for foundation.
14. Garage secured.
15. Frames completed by carpenter.
16. Exterior sheathing complete.
17. Roof covered with waterproof material.
18. Roof complete.
19. Windows and glass doors installed.
20. Inside plumbing complete.
21. Air conditioning and heating complete.
22. Bricks for home delivered.
23. Electric-turbine vent complete.
24. Electrical and phone wiring complete.
25. Iron set above windows.
26. Insulation for walls and attic complete.
27. Bricking complete.
28. Sheetrock complete.
29. Slate porch complete.
30. Gutters installed.
31. Terrazzo floor complete.
32. Concrete for drive and walks complete.
33. Kitchen cabinets and plumbing fixtures installed.

34. Tile complete.
35. Outside air conditioning complete.
36. Inside doors installed.
37. Grounds cleaned and prepared for landscaping.
38. Painting complete.
39. Fence complete.
40. Rugs installed.
41. Flower and plant landscaping complete.
42. Plans filed.
43. Final inspection by city.
44. Light fixtures complete.
45. Wallpaper complete.
46. Drapes installed.
47. Insurance converted from construction to home.
48. Job complete. Move in.

IMPLEMENTING YOUR PLAN: THE BUILDING PHASE

The planning stage is now complete and it is time to move on to the second phase of the management function: doing what you have planned. The first step in phase two is to make a survey, thus ascertaining that the land you are constructing on is yours. Also take the time to recheck local requirements to be sure that you are building in accordance with city and subdivision restrictions. Even though your plans and specifications have been approved by government authorities, it pays to be familiar with local restrictions during construction.

SELECTING WORKMEN

It is now time to contact that first-rate carpenter you have already selected. He can help you immeasurably. You pay more if he gives you a "turnkey job"—meaning that he is available from the time he lays out the forms for the foundation until the house is completed and the key is turned over to you—but it's worth it.

There is no substitute for really experienced "subs" (subcontractors). I found mine to be great people, full of common sense, loyalty and pride of workmanship. Dealing with them has convinced me that our current teachings in personnel and management—emphasizing human understanding, motivation, self-actualization, coordination, communication and incentives—make sense. At times, I had six or seven different subs working together—carpenter, heating and air-conditioning expert, plumber, painter, roofer, sheet-metal man and pool people—in a truly compatible fashion!

You may prefer to avoid possible conflict by taking it slowly and having only one subcontractor on the job at a time; but time is money. Besides, a more leisurely approach results in greater material loss (theft and pilferage) and prices keep rising each day! Delay seems to build on delay. Therefore, as boss, your big job is to be on the job. As mentioned earlier, I worked approximately twelve hours a day on my house, including time on the site, taking care of financial records, doing the buying and coordinating the day-to-day activity.[11] I even participated in the building process wherever feasible—assisting in installation of heating and air conditioning, hauling and sorting bricks and providing delivery service to meet emergency needs.

IMPORTANCE OF BEING ON THE JOB

Any building project requires prompt decisions daily, and if you are not present, the sub may walk off the job. After all, he is paying his people by the hour. If you don't have the necessary materials or if you're not there to tell him what's expected, why shouldn't he leave? And it could be a long time before he returns—another job may take priority.

Your presence on the job also prevents mistakes. Suppose, for example, that you are paying the carpenter to put up paneling. If he does so before the insulation has been completed, you may never find out why it costs you so much to heat or cool the house.

PRODUCTIVE USE OF WEEKENDS

We were normally free of workmen on weekends. This permitted my wife and me to shop for desired materials, clean up work areas and bring records up to date. Whenever possible, we conducted business involving the house on weekends at our housing site. It saved time to have representatives visit us with samples and catalogues of rugs, drapes, lighting fixtures and so on. We also found that the subs in New Orleans love being able to use the weekends for

---

[11]Most people can't spare this block of time, but instead use vacations, weekends and evenings. Some couples share the supervision. Others hire someone to oversee the project when they cannot be available.

fishing and other entertainments. It cut costs and increased productivity to provide this time off. Most important, subs usually charge time and a half (sometimes double time) for Saturday and Sunday work.

CONTROLLING WHAT YOU HAVE PLANNED

While walking to my office recently, I observed three homes under construction. In each case, the work had come to a standstill. In the first instance, the mortar was not available for the bricklayer, so he had left for another job. At the second house, the electrical inspection had not been made because the contractor had failed to contact the proper city department. At the third site, there was conflict between the carpenter and builder over the terms of payment.

These delays could have been prevented if the builders had taken adequate control measures in accordance with the final phase of the three management functions. Before we examine the specific checks that can be made, let's see how these three functions interact in the process of subcontracting your home.

Assume that you *plan* to clean up the building site at 7:30 A.M. While tidying up (*doing*) you uncover damaged lumber (*checking*). You should then devise a plan for its return and replacement. Concurrently, other subcontractors working for you will be performing their various *planning, organizing* and *controlling* functions. It is evident that you as manager cannot perform each of these functions in isolation. Therefore, you might consider them as part of your management bag of tools, elements which must be utilized harmoniously to get the job done efficiently.

SPECIFIC CONTROLS AND INSPECTIONS

In order to determine the effectiveness of your planning and organizing functions, you must apply certain control techniques. The resulting data permits insights into performance standards and enables the home builder to take remedial measures where appropriate. Here are some of the specific controls you as a home builder might use:

1. On-the-spot-inspections. The more time you spend on the job, the greater your control. Being on the spot gives you the opportunity to check both the quality of work and the materials being utilized. Suppose you are fussy about the exact shade of paint used in each room. Your presence will permit you to alert your painter at once if the color isn't quite right. It is better to establish this after a stroke or two of the brush than when the entire interior of the house has been painted.

You can also check *upon delivery* such supplies as fencing material. If your inspection reveals a number of poor-quality boards with large knotholes, you can demand replacements. In contrast, if the fence is installed before the shoddy material is discovered, it is more difficult to convince the subcontractor to replace it.

Being on the job enables you to prevent unnecessary delays. If a subcontractor is absent, you can call his home or office to find out why and arrange for other work to be done. Likewise, if supplies are not delivered on schedule, you can take action to obtain them—either by placing a phone call requesting prompt delivery or by picking them up yourself. You will also have a chance to talk with your subcontractors about juggling schedules to preclude delays.

The significance that home buyers now place on inspections was discussed in a report titled "Homeowners Outraged by New House Defects and Delays in Repairs":

> Prospective buyers also are becoming more cautious about choosing a home in the first place. Many, for example, are having new houses inspected by Mr. Heyn's inspection service before closing contracts. Mr. Heyn, who founded the service in 1969, says he had expected most of his customers to be people buying 20- to 30-year-old houses. "The biggest surprise is that over 50 percent of our business is new-house inspection," he says.
>
> Most of the complaints around the country involve houses constructed by production builders, those who build from a number of basic designs. But even buyers who use custom builders are becoming more skeptical. Roland Eppley, president of Eastern States Bankcard Corp., had Mr. Heyn's men inspect his custom house in Manhasset, N.Y., during four different stages of construction.
>
> Mr. Eppley, who paid more than $100,000 for the house, says the added $260 he paid Mr. Heyn's firm "gave me peace of mind."[12]

Think how effective your control can be with continual on-the-job inspections, as compared with the above four visits.

2. Other inspections. Visits from loan-agency officials as well as electrical, plumbing and other city inspectors can provide splendid means of checking the quality of workmanship and material. I sensed that investigators took a greater interest in making thorough inspections when I was present. Even when they approve the work, it can be helpful to ask their advice on what could have been done to make it better.

[12]*The Wall Street Journal,* April 3, 1973, p. 1.

If irregularities should be found, take prompt action to correct them. Such corrections should be made in a friendly working relationship with your subcontractors.

Another kind of inspection I found helpful was visits from those friends whose views on workmanship and materials I valued.

An important inspection is made when the house becomes available for occupancy. You should plan to move in within seventy-two hours after completion. If necessary, peripheral work can be finished when you are in residence. The advantage of being in the home is that you have a twenty-four-hour check on all aspects of the job. Be sure to check everything with care. Even if it's wintertime, be sure to try out the cooling system.

3. Meetings. Each morning, I met with my subcontractors upon their arrival. We discussed the day's work and any problems that needed to be resolved. Prior to their departure, we confirmed the time they would be at work the next day. As a result of these sessions, the subcontractors would notify their workers of any change. It also meant that we were all alert to matters of common interest and any problems that might arise.

Such meetings also offered the opportunity to exchange ideas. Skilled craftsmen, with their many years of experience, have much to teach about various aspects of home building. They take pride in their work and are critical of the workmanship of others. Having them point out deficiencies gives you the facts with which to back up requests for corrective action.

In order to prepare properly for these daily sessions, it is essential for you to do your homework the night before. Review your PERT chart, plans, Description of Materials, timetable and budget. Subcontractors' time is valuable, and they normally work right along with their people. These sessions should be brief, and ideally should be held while the work is in progress.

Frequent topics of discussion during such sessions include interpretation of the architect's drawings, deadlines, materials needed, inspection requirements and payments. Try to provide an atmosphere that will encourage the subs to express their views.

Comments of workers are also useful. Some of my workmen would arrive on the job before their boss, giving me the opportunity to learn from them.

Another good time to rap with the subs and their workers is during lunch breaks, when everyone is generally in a relaxed and congenial mood. Encourage everyone to present his views on what can be done to make yours a better house. Lunch gatherings also serve as a good time to brainstorm a new idea or propose a modification. By brainstorming, I mean obtaining the maximum number of ideas regardless of their quality. Your next step is to weed out the most feasible proposals. Topics we discussed included changing the pitch of the roof, increasing the size of the breakfast nook and whether or not to use a new plastic material. These sessions can help you arrive at sound decisions.

4. Payment by check. It is wise to make the vast majority of payments by check and to obtain receipts. You will need cash, of course, to buy an occasional drink or a handful of screws; but keep a record of these small expenditures— they add up!

It is wise to endorse the back of the check, indicating the purpose of the payment: "Final payment for painting home at 1526 Edison Avenue, per contract #201."

Prior to return of your monthly statement, you may need to show your loan agency that payment has been made. Your receipt will serve this purpose. It can be valid even if written on a scrap of paper, as long as it is signed by a responsible person in the organization. Take advantage of any discount offered for early payment; otherwise, wait until the due date.

Don't hesitate to stop payment on a check if you find that material is defective or work has not been done as promised. It may be the best way to see that appropriate corrective action is taken. Money is the best incentive for getting a job done. Once payments are completed, you have lost your bargaining power. I recommend that 10 percent be withheld on major jobs until you make a final inspection.

5. Budget control. Your budget can serve as a planning and control document. The figures indicate the several estimates of what the various items cost. Their total provides you with an indication of the money required to build your home. This information enables you to talk intelligently with your lending agency.

Your estimate, however, does not always coincide with actual costs. In most cases, cost exceeds the amount planned for in the budget. If you have established price agreements with your subcontractors, cash adjustments should be minor unless plans have been changed in the meantime. Supplies are a different story. In 1973, for example, prices on key lumber and plywood products increased by 20 to 30 percent in seven weeks. However, if you use your budget effectively as a control device, this variation between estimate and actual cost can be minimized by promptly posting the actual price paid for each item. You should then check carefully to see if you have exceeded your estimate and by what amount. The real value of budget control will be realized only if you take positive action to correct the problem.

Let's assume, for example, that after the foundation work has been completed, you find that your budget estimate has been exceeded by 5 percent. The problem is obvious—you spent too much. What can you do about it? After obtaining the facts and determining the problem, you should proceed, in management terminology, to "look at alternatives." One solution would be to ask your loan agency for more money, on the basis that the cost of the entire project will increase by 5 percent. A second alternative might be to substitute lower-quality materials on the remaining construction in order to make up the difference. A third possibility could be to eliminate something from the house. After weighing the various alternatives, you will be ready to make a sound decision. The management approach involved here utilizes the following sequence: Obtain the background facts; determine the problem; look at the alternatives; decide which alternative to implement.

6. Filing System. As discussed in Chapter 2, a good filing system is a timesaver and can be an effective control technique. If organized properly, it permits you to find essential information quickly should you have to make a sudden decision. I kept my home-building records in manila folders in a file cabinet. Each subcontractor and supplier had an individual file; and such items as checks, budgets, PERT charts and photographs were filed separately in alphabetical order for easy reference. Keep your filing system simple.

7. PERT. As mentioned earlier, PERT is a splendid planning and control document and should be followed with care during the building phase. Just as your budget serves as a money control, PERT permits you to keep your construction work on schedule. It not only enables you to determine how long it will take to finish the job but points out the numerous tasks that can be done *concurrently* in order to minimize completion time. For instance, if a strike should occur in the cement industry and your schedule shows it is time to lay the driveway, your PERT chart can assist you in selecting a feasible alternative.

However, regardless of how well it is conceived, a planning document like PERT cannot foresee all eventualities. And PERT is only as valuable as you make it.

8. Photographs. My Minox camera was a useful control device. It was small enough to carry in my pocket, and it enabled me quickly to make a permanent record of any potential problem. For instance, if I questioned the soundness of a shipment of lumber at the time of delivery, I took a picture of it with the company truck in the background, or included the man who made the delivery in the photo.

If you intend to do any future building, photos can be valuable in reviewing the step-by-step process and helping you to make improvements the next time around. I would like to have taken movies of the entire home-construction process. After all, sports teams make good use of film to analyze their strengths and weaknesses and those of their opponents. Management's way of winning is to make a healthy profit, and to do this, it helps to have a championship team.

9. Communication. Again I want to stress the importance of talking

with your workers, suppliers, subcontractors and other builders. The information you receive can be invaluable.

When you give instructions, be sure that what you say is clearly understood. One way to guarantee effective communication is to have the person repeat to you what you told him. Keep in mind that workers and suppliers often have their own special vocabulary. If you have any concern that your orders may be misunderstood, *put them in writing.*

10. Legal action. Another control measure is positive followup action, but take only the amount of action necessary to get the job done. If a subcontractor or supplier has failed to meet his commitment, you may wish to proceed as follows:

a. Call the person in question, courteously explain that the work was not satisfactory and set a time for it to be corrected. By referring to your written contract you can refresh his memory as to the terms of your agreement.

b. Make a second phone call, firmly explaining that you expect the work to be done, and set a second deadline.

c. Write a letter stating that you will take necessary legal action if the work is not done within a specified time. Send copies of letters to appropriate parties including the Better Business Bureau, a local consumer-affairs office, Ralph Nader and the Special Assistant to the President for Consumer Affairs.

d. Proceed with the necessary legal action. You may find that filing suit in the small claims court is sufficient to obtain the amount of damages due you. If not, secure the services of a lawyer. Your chances of being successful in a legal battle are improving since the "buyer beware" doctrine[13] is no longer as valid as it once was. This change is pointed out in the article on homeowners' complaints quoted earlier in the chapter:

> Mr. ____ says he'll sue ____ if necessary. In the past, most courts have routinely sided with builders, citing the "buyer beware" doctrine. But the Research Institute of America, a business advisory service in New York, says that courts in 19 states have changed, often ruling in the homeowner's favor in suits over such things as faulty wiring, poor grading, or badly installed ductwork.[14]

---

[13]The "Buyer Beware" (*caveat emptor*) doctrine is a principle in business that, without a warranty, the buyer of merchandise takes the risk of quality upon himself.

[14]*The Wall Street Journal,* April 3, 1973, p. 1.

Don't waste your time and energy quibbling over minor points to satisfy your ego. But once you decide that something is important, proceed with vigor to gain a fair settlement. In theory, careful step-by-step planning and checking on both workers and suppliers will preclude having to take drastic steps. But it's wise to be prepared for trouble. Someone in whom you have great trust and confidence *could* let you down.

12
LANDSCAPING, INCLUDING GARDENING

Webster defines landscaping as changing "the natural features of a plot of ground so as to make it more attractive, as by adding lawns, trees, bushes." Here again, the key to success is good planning. From the moment of purchase, you should consider what you desire in terms of patio, driveway, lawns, garden space and so on for your property and set aside funds for these purposes. This will permit you to implement your plans as quickly and inexpensively as possible once you have moved into your new home.[1]

TAILORING YOUR LANDSCAPING TO YOUR LIFESTYLE

Landscaping gives you an opportunity to be creative; it should reflect your personality and appeal to your aesthetic sense. At the same time, you must approach it realistically, taking into consideration the possibility of resale, the time available for maintenance, costs involved and future needs based upon the changing composition of your family. If you have a large, busy household or numerous other interests, you probably will not have much time to devote to keeping up your grounds. Simplicity may be your primary aim. To the dismay of environmentalists, you will want to rely on extensive use of concrete and a minimum of lawn, shrubs, flowers and trees.

WHAT WILL IT COST?

To keep landscaping costs to a minimum it is important to budget an adequate amount of money for this purpose during the planning stage. Too many families try to cut corners here, either failing to face their landscaping needs squarely or preferring to deal with them at a later date. This results in extra costs and an unsightly property. Good planning allows you to make your residence attractive from the start and carry out subsequent improvements at minimum expense.

HOW DO YOU GO ABOUT LANDSCAPING YOUR HOME?

There are several approaches you may wish to consider in landscaping your home. Here are some of the possibilites.

[1]The material in this chapter has been extracted from *Do-It-Yourself Contracting to Build Your Own Home: A Managerial Approach,* Richard J. Stillman, © 1974, reprinted by permission of Chilton Book Company.

OBTAIN ADVICE FROM THE COUNTY AGENT AND LAND GRANT UNIVERSITY

County agents can be found in every state. They work with a land-grant university and are paid in part from funds provided for by the Department of Agriculture. If there is no county agent nearby, you can write your land-grant university. In Louisiana, for example, you would write to: Director, Cooperative Extension Service, Louisiana State University and Agricultural and Mechanical College, Baton Rouge, Louisiana. Some of the free publications available are titled: *Enjoy Your Home Grounds, Diseases and Insects of Lawn Grasses, Plan Landscapes for the Family* and *Roses.*

The university will also test the soil in your yard to determine what may be needed to improve it.

SECURE A GARDENER

Talk with neighbors who have well-kept yards and find out who is taking care of them. Select the best-qualified individual to plant your grass, shrubs and flowers.

HIRE A PROFESSIONAL LANDSCAPER

Contact a professional landscaper and have him prepare a design for your property along with an estimate of what the entire job will cost. You should try to obtain three bids.

DO IT YOURSELF

In order to keep your costs at a minimum, it may be necessary to "do-it-yourself." Landscaping your own property, particularly if you have a small lot, is not a difficult task. You can get splendid ideas from reading available literature (see Bibliography) and observing attractively landscaped homes.

One of our neighbors went to a professional landscaper initially but could not afford his price. He also obtained an estimate from a local gardener. He then figured what it would cost if he did the job himself, including buying materials and equipment. He found that it was considerably cheaper to use his own labor. Today he has one of the most attractive yards in the neighborhood.

CREATING A LAWN

If possible, your lawn should be established shortly after you move in. Not only will it add to the attractiveness of your property, but in the event of heavy rain, it can keep your soil from being washed away. Begin by determining what type of grass does best in your area. In New Orleans we looked at three varieties: St. Augustine, Zoysia Matrella and Bermuda. We selected St. Augustine after discussing it with the county agent and observing the successes and failures of our neighbors. It provides a thick carpet and, in our locality, gives an attractive appearance all year round.

We decided to build our lawn four to five inches above our walk and bought three loads of topsoil for this purpose. Instead of doing the job ourselves, we hired a gardener who had done quality work in the neighborhood. He purchased the grass, shrubs and fertilizer. Next time, we plan to do our own planting. The gardener made a profit on the materials and received a healthy hourly return for his work.

The quickest way to have a finished look is to buy sufficient sod to cover your entire lawn area. But this is expensive. Our gardener bought enough sod to cover about one-third of the area and, by distributing it well, the entire lawn was covered within three months. The least costly solution would have been to plant cuttings. But using this method would have increased the time needed to complete the lawn by several months.

SPECIFIC STEPS TO LAWN GROWING

If you decide to grow a new lawn yourself, here are some specific steps suggested by Winona Guedry in *Enjoy Your Home Grounds:*[2]

1. The first work to do is to level the outdoor area so as to have surface drainage away from the house. If you remove some of the topsoil, save and use it. Be careful when leveling under trees.
2. Plow, grade and harrow. You may have to haul soil to fill in low spots.
3. Add organic matter, such as barnyard manure, peat, compost, well-decomposed sawdust, gin trash or well-rotted rice hulls. For an average 75 x 150 feet, use 1 ton of barnyard manure or equivalent and 150 pounds of 3-12-12 or 0-14-7 fertilizer. If you do not add organic matter, use 150 pounds of 3-12-12 or 6-8-8. Work it well into the soil.
4. Rake until the seedbed is very fine; then roll.
5. You are now ready to seed, sprig or sod your lawn.

MAINTAINING YOUR LAWN

Once you have an attractive lawn, how do you go about maintaining it? You can

[2]Cooperative Extension Service. Baton Rouge, Louisiana: LSU. Courtesy of Louisiana Cooperative, p. 2.

do the work yourself with the help of a lawn mower and edger. The grass may require cutting once a week in the growing season. A relatively small lawn is easy to maintain and doing so is a splendid form of exercise. Amos Alonzo Stagg, the great University of Chicago football coach, was still cutting his grass at age ninety-nine.

Should you decide to have a gardener take care of your yard, the charge in our area for a weekly visit is forty to fifty dollars a month. The quality of the work you get for your money ranges from excellent to adequate.

My own view is that there is no substitute for personal attention. It can be argued that your time is valuable and could be better utilized elsewhere. This is true in many cases on a purely monetary basis, but doing your own land-scaping can provide a delightful change of pace and needed relaxation. Cutting the lawn, tending the shrubs and flowers and maintaining the pool is healthy exercise for the entire family.

A third approach to lawn maintenance, which can be combined with one of the above, is to utilize a lawn-care company. Such firms treat your lawn a specified number of times a year. The annual cost for this service is normally based on the square footage involved. If, for example, a lawn covers 5,000 square feet, the charge may vary from $170 to $220. The company will usually make four to five visits during the growing season.

If you decide to use a lawn-care company, investigate it first. Points you will want to determine include whether the company is reliable; whether it is known for good work; and whether you have the right to terminate the agreement without penalty.

A TRUCK GARDEN OF YOUR OWN

Given the high cost of living, growing your own fruit and vegetables can be a great way to save money. It also should have appeal for the health-minded and the environmentalist. Indeed, growing food for your table can be immensely rewarding, but it is important to realize from the start that it can be demanding, discouraging and in some areas expensive as well. A neighbor in New Orleans tried a small vegetable garden, specializing in tomatoes. He found, however, that before he could apply protective measures insects had eaten the green fruit. After six months, he gave up the project as an impossible task.

In contrast, a friend who lives nearby has successfully kept a garden for years and spends much of his spare time pursuing this hobby. If you are interested, I suggest that you contact your local county agent for advice on soil maintenance and information on which crops do well in your locality.

A GARDEN FOR THE CHILDREN

What about a garden for youngsters? It is immensely satisfying to direct a child's energy toward projects that can be useful in adult life and an appreciation of the soil certainly falls within this category. There is an interesting article in the March 1973 issue of South Central *Bell Notes* pointing out how to start a small flower garden. The instructions apply to raising fruit and vegetables as well:

> Looking for something different or unusual to do with your child for coming holidays and vacations? One of the most stimulating things you can do is help your child plan and plant his first garden. Observing how living things grow will be rewarding and exciting.
>
> A child's first garden should be a small one, about 3' x 6', with flowers that are easy to grow. First choices should be annuals. They must be planted each year, but the rewards of your youngster's first efforts are almost immediate.
>
> In choosing the flowers to plant, the marigold is a popular choice, with many varieties available. Other favorites are zinnias and petunias. If your child likes flowers for their smell as well as their color, sweet alyssum would be a good choice.
>
> All these plants do well even in poor soil and thrive on lots of sunlight. Most will bloom from seed in six to eight weeks and will last until first frost.
>
> Even a small garden will require weekly care. After preparing the soil, planting, and marking the rows, watering and weeding will keep a youngster busy, but happy and proud as he is rewarded with flowers from his private domain.

ROSES AND OTHER FLOWERS

Our family loves roses. We have been saddened, however, to discover that the two plants in our backyard do not seem to thrive on love alone. Two horticulturists point out below the appeal of this fragrant flower and the work involved in its successful cultivation:

> Roses are one of the most interesting and popular of all garden plant materials. For centuries, the universal appeal of the rose has been due to its versatile landscape uses as well as its cut flower quality. Few plants can supply color for such an extended period. . . . Do not consider growing roses unless you are willing to devote special attention to the control of insects and diseases. No factor in growing roses is more important than a

systematic program for insect and disease prevention and control. . . .
Both insects and disease pests can cause real concern. Yet, for individuals
who are truly fond of roses, the pleasure of having roses will justify the
expense and time required to keep insects and disease problems to a
minimum.[3]

My good friend Wes Strauch has been very successful in raising roses and
lectures on the topic. He believes that the best way to start a rose garden is to
limit yourself to two or three bushes. A bush can be bought for as little as $1.25,
but a high-quality plant costs $6 to $7. Wes emphasizes that to have a first-class
rose garden "you must devote a lot of time and study—you must be all wrapped
up in it."

There are many other flowers available for those individuals who may
wish to accept a lesser challenge than the rose. A good deal of research in recent
years has made it easier to raise beautiful flowers. Frederick C. Klein writes:

> Professional flower breeders are applying techniques previously used in
> the development of food crops to produce plants that are more vigorous,
> uniform, and disease-resistant and are freer-flowering and easier to grow
> than anything that has been available before. Roughly two-thirds of the
> flower varieties that home gardeners will plant this spring didn't even
> exist 20 years ago. . . .
>
> In years past, many American gardens consisted primarily of such
> perennial bloomers as roses, lilies, phlox, and delphiniums, whose
> success depends largely on the gardener's skill in periodically pruning
> and dividing his plants and shielding them against bad weather. This
> sort of gardening continues, of course; flower fanciers tend to gravitate
> to these more challenging types once they have mastered simpler ones.
>
> Increasingly, though, gardeners are planting annual flowers from
> seed or purchased plants, and they are getting results that once went
> only to the highly skilled. "It used to take a green thumb to have a good
> garden; now all it takes is a dirty hand," says William Carlson, associate
> professor of horticulture at Michigan State University and executive
> secretary of the National Association of Bedding Plant Growers.[4]

The above article also points out that although "no one knows exactly how
many Americans tend a patch of flowers during the summer . . . estimates
range as high as 20 million." An incentive to some is the W. Atlee Burpee
Company offer of $10,000 to the person who finds a pure white marigold in his
garden and sends in seed that can produce a similar one.

---

[3]Newil G. Odenwald and Claude Blackwell. *Roses.* Baton Rouge, Louisiana: Cooperative
Extension Service, LSU, pp.1 4–15 (courtesy of Louisiana Cooperative).
[4]Excerpt from *The Wall Street Journal*'s article of April 30, 1973 © 1972 Dow Jones &
Company, Inc. All rights reserved.

LANDSCAPING EXPENDITURES

What should you budget for landscaping? This will vary for each family. Table 12-1 lists our initial expenses.

Once the landscaping is completed, you will be faced with yearly maintenance. Expenditures will depend upon how much of the work you do yourself, the size of your yard, where you live and climatic conditions (Table 12-2).

You may wish to keep detailed records of your landscaping costs and a progress report of work being done by the family. Good luck!

TABLE 12-1   Stillman's Initial Landscaping Costs

Grass	$ 75
Fertilizer	62
Soil	45
Gardener	175
Plants	142
Seeds	25
Edger (electric)	57
Lawnmower (electric)	125
Basic gardening tools (rake, shovel, broom, hoe, trowel, cultivator)	28
Hoses, nozzles, sprinkler	59
Total initial costs	$793

TABLE 12-2   Stillman's Annual Upkeep on Property

Plants	$ 74
Seed	25
Fertilizer	39
Tools	36
Water	24
Repairs	36
Total annual cost	$234

13
PROTECTING YOUR PROPERTY

(continued on p. 234)

Crime is now the number one concern in our cities and the home is the prime target. Unfortunately, most people do not provide adequate protection until a burglary has occurred. Approximately $300 million in personal property was stolen last year; only $15 million was recovered. Families are concerned not only about the rising number of burglaries but about their personal safety.[1]

My weekly half-hour radio program has touched upon many timely topics but none has brought greater response from my listeners—both in letters and phone calls—than the program devoted to protective measures for the home. Most listeners expressed concern and a desire to eradicate the evils that lead to crime. One woman wrote: "I liked very much what you said about working on long-range plans to improve our society so that securing ourselves from one another becomes less necessary, for this certainly is the basis of the entire issue."

Indeed the ultimate goal should be to improve the quality of American life. In the meantime, however, we must face facts. This chapter discusses what you can do to protect your home now. As you read through it, you should find it helpful to refer to Figure 13-1 which lists available protective measures and their costs. As you will see, the price of a safe home varies from zero to very high.

A MANAGERIAL APPROACH TO HOME SECURITY

A good manager will look at a variety of security systems in order to determine which will best meet his needs in relation to the money he can afford to spend. This is another area in which foresight pays off. By considering the financing of safety requirements in the initial planning of your home, the interest will be at the current first mortgage rate. Should you decide to make the same purchases later, the costs could range from 9½ percent to 42 percent.

No security plan, however, will be effective unless it is based on a systematic consideration of *all* your home-protection needs. Locks, for example, are worthless if you don't have a sound method of checking to be sure they are secured. Likewise, if you have a fixed amount of money available, you must establish priorities and decide what will best meet your requirements. Security, in turn, should be viewed in the context of your overall housing requirements. This means that you should decide ahead how much to allocate for security in relation to plumbing, electrical equipment and all other expenses. If you wait to consider protective measures until the house is nearly complete, you may have no money for such "extras" as quality locks.

[1]The material in this chapter has been extracted from *Do-It-Yourself Contracting to Build Your Own Home: A Managerial Approach,* Richard J. Stillman, © 1974, reprinted by permission of Chilton Book Company.

Figure 13-1 Protective measures and their cost.

Items	None	Minor ($1-$10)	Average ($11-$100)	Expensive ($101 up)
Alarm system				x
Alert to tricks	x			
At home appearance		x		
Dog		x	x	x
Escape routes	x			
Fence				x
Garage				x
Guns		x	x	x
Insurance				x
Iron doors and windows				x
Lighting			x	
Locks			x	x
Marking equipment		x		
Neighbors	x			
Pictures		x	x	
Police assistance	x			
Security checks	x			
Security during construction		x	x	x
Sitter service				x
Store valuables			x	
Top secret measures		x	x	x
Unpunctual hours	x			
Windows secured		x	x	
Wireless equipment				x

EFFECTIVE PROTECTIVE MEASURES

Here are some of the security measures currently available for home protection.

DOGS

A good dog can be a valuable means of protection; a penetrating bark can both frighten off would-be intruders and alert members of the family to take other precautionary measures such as calling the police, turning on the alarm system or securing weapons.[2] If you desire information about where to obtain a trained watchdog, contact the canine division of your police department or a private guard agency. These animals cost from $150 to $300, and two of the best breeds are German shepherds and Doberman pinschers.

[2] I would like to stress the fact that guns are very dangerous and may cause more harm than good. I was a Regular Army infantry officer for twenty-three years and have had several close calls as a result of guns being "accidentally fired."

You must be prepared, however, for the fact that a watchdog may turn on a member of the family. We have all heard horror stories to this effect. Also, dogs can be quite expensive (see Chapter 9). Table 13-1 lists the initial cost and maintenance for a small-size thoroughbred in one community:

TABLE 13-1   Cost of Acquisition and Annual Maintenance of Thoroughbred Dog

Initial Cost	
AKC registration	$ 5
License	6
Initial examination	8
Purchase price	150
	$169

Annual Cost	
Food	$106
Toys	10
Tags	6
Visits to veterinarian	80
	$202

It is, of course, possible to eliminate the purchase price by obtaining a dog from a friend or the SPCA, although in our community the SPCA requires payment of eighteen dollars to cover the cost of shots and license.

A dog requires daily care. If you take a trip, it may mean placing him in a kennel or leaving him with a friend or relative. This eliminates your home protection during your absence.

MARKED EQUIPMENT

Obtain an engraving tool that will enable you to mark your social security number or driver's license number on such valuable equipment as radios, televisions and tape recorders.

Our community has an excellent procedure for identifying property. It operates under jurisdiction of the police department and works as follows:

1. Fire stations loan out marking equipment accompanied by an instruction sheet and a form on which to list valuable items.
2. When the police department has been notified that the valuables have been appropriately marked, they mail the homeowner two sets of decals.
3. The homeowner places the decals on his windows to inform all concerned that his equipment is marked.

237

4. The completed list of valuables is placed in the owner's safe-deposit box at the bank.

A number of cities have adopted a similar program. Those persons interested in further information about "Operation Identification" should write to the New Orleans Police Department.

LOCKS

Various locks provide varying degrees of security. Four major categories are used on exterior doors:

Key in the Doorknob

This is the lock used in the majority of homes. It is the easiest to force and the least expensive. Builders favor it for the construction of speculation homes.

Our carpenter swiftly demonstrated how he could enter our home with this type of lock. With a twist of a wrench he had the door open. He also showed me how to gain entry by inserting the blade of a pocketknife between the latch and the door frame despite the fact that the lock in question had a trigger bolt which was supposed to prevent such access.

The carpenter went on to emphasize that, although a lock itself may be strong, it is of little value unless the door has good hinges, is securely encased in a solid frame and is made of a sturdy material. It takes little time and effort on the part of a burglar to break the panel of a weak door or knock off the latches and gain quick entry.

Dead Lock

This lock is installed in the face of the door and is available with or without a key. Its installation requires drilling sizable holes in your door and frame. A dead lock normally has a rectangular-shaped metal projectile which is inserted into the hole of the frame to lock the door. The longer and larger the projectile, the more difficult it is to pry the door apart. Since there is no beveled edge or spring mechanism on the dead lock, insertion of a penknife or other object cannot open it.

Vertical Bolt

This is an auxiliary lock (also a dead lock) which is screwed onto the door and frame. It prevents a burglar from jimmying the door because it contains a pin that fits into a plate. We use vertical auxiliary locks in our home ($16 each) and find them most practical. Unless you are extremely handy, I would suggest having a locksmith do the work. The current installation price in our area is $20 to $25.

Special Locks

You may wish to consider a lock which when picked or forced triggers an alarm. There are also pick-proof cylinder locks that are difficult for the professional burglar to open. Or bar locks can be purchased to install at the base and top of your doors. To lock them, metal projections are inserted in the ceiling and floor.

In order to choose wisely from the large selection of quality locks available today, I suggest that you visit several locksmiths and examine their merchandise. Also consult with security officers at several major companies in order to determine what types of locks are best suited to your needs.

GUNS

A rifle or pistol can be an effective means of protection *if* you know how to shoot it accurately and can keep it close at hand. Some homeowners keep a loaded weapon under their pillow or in a nearby table drawer, but this is very risky. A mistake could be fatal. There is an added danger in households with children. In order to prevent their playing with weapons, *you must put firearms in a safe, locked place and separate ammunition from the guns.* These extra safety measures, however, could mean that a weapon would be unavailable if needed in a hurry.

Should you decide to buy a gun, register it with the police. Check with them to see if it is possible to receive instructions on how to use it properly. Pistols, in particular, require considerable training to assure good marksmanship. You must practice continually to keep up your expertise. Perhaps there is a local gun club that you might wish to join. Be sure to clean your weapon periodically so that it functions when needed.

Again, I wish to emphasize that weapons are very dangerous and may cause more harm than good.

NEIGHBORHOOD SPIRIT

It pays to be friendly with your neighbors. Try to get together and work out a method of mutual cooperation. If you plan to be away, let the people next door look after your property, reporting anything suspicious to the police. Do the same for them when necessary. Neighborhood security is greatly improved by teamwork. You may therefore decide to organize a group of local homeowners into a patrol. Should it be necessary you may even want to hire a private organization to cope with security matters. The greater the number of neighborhood families involved in an effort, the more successful it will be.

POLICE ASSISTANCE

Help the law work for you. Do your part by contacting your local police department and asking their views on security measures. They may send an officer to your home to offer advice. You may also wish to have a policeman speak on home protection at a neighborhood meeting. He can provide excellent precautions that apply to your specific locality. It will also give you an opportunity to ask questions. At a recent meeting in our area, a speaker gave worthwhile advice on safeguarding homes against criminals, and tips for vacationers (see Figure 13-2).

Figure 13-2 Advice for safeguarding your home.

KEEP outside lights on all night to illuminate all sides of your home.
MAKE sure that the area between the home and detached garage is lighted.
STORE expensive jewelry in a safe deposit box.
IF you leave the house, close the garage door. An open garage door is an open invitation to the daytime burglar.
LEAVE lights on in the house when you are away for the evening.
BEFORE you leave for a vacation, inform the police and a neighbor. Leave window shades and blinds at a normal level and make sure that milk bottles and newspapers do not accumulate at your door. Ask post office to hold mail.
DON'T give keys to strange service men. Separate auto keys and house keys. Check references of maids and cleaning people. Keys are easily duplicated.
LOCK windows and doors—including the side doors—when you retire. Use a supplementary chain lock.
LOCK attic windows. Lock garage too.
PUT a strong short chain on your door.
DON'T leave your door unlocked, even when you're in the house.
KEEP the door chained when a stranger knocks until you are satisfied his purpose is legitimate.
DOUBLE-LOCK your door when you leave.

ALWAYS test your doors to make sure you have locked them before leaving.
SEE that shrubbery that might provide an easy hiding place is kept trimmed.
CHECK thoroughly the references of maids or service people who are given access to your home.
MAKE sure all screens are secured from the inside.
A DOG provides warning and protection.

Tips for Vacationers

STOP all deliveries such as newspapers, milk, and laundry. Ask a neighbor to remove mail from mailbox daily and remove circulars and brochures left at the house.

LOCK all windows and doors securely.

USE a light meter which turns on a lamp and outside lights at dusk.

IF absent for an extended period, arrange to have your lawn mowed, preferably by a relative or trusted neighbor.

NOTIFY police that you will be on vacation, giving address, date and time of departure, and date and time of return.

MARK personal belongings with your driver's license number.

Showing an interest in your police force will make them more alert to your problems. Cooperation is a two-way street. You may find it helpful to ask them to patrol your area more frequently. In addition to the city protection, your locality may have its own police force. If so, contact this group.

Call the police whenever you see a suspicious person, strange vehicle or unusual action in your neighborhood. The following loss might not have occurred if the police had been given an opportunity to present their views on security measures. As the story was related to me, a neighbor observed a man loading a television set onto a truck outside the house of a young working couple. She assumed that he was a TV repairman and, walking across the street, asked if he could take her TV set back to the shop with him as well and make the necessary repairs. He was most obliging, saying: "I won't charge you for pickup service and will bring the set back next Tuesday." The following Wednesday, when the television set had still not been returned, she knocked at her neighbors' door when they got home from work and asked: "Have you gotten your television set back from the repair shop?"

"What do you mean?" they replied. "We don't have a TV any more. Our house was robbed last week and they took the set with them."

BURGLAR AND FIRE-ALARM SYSTEMS

A burglar-alarm system can provide both psychological and physical protection. A potential burglar may be psychologically deterred if he sees an on-off lock device with a red lamp and alarm bell housed in a tamper-proof box outside your front door. You can also place warnings in the form of decals in your window.

The physical deterrent is supplied by the system itself, which triggers an alarm should entry be made through a door or window. The theory is that the noise will frighten the burglar away. Emergency switches can also be installed in various parts of the house, allowing you to sound the alarm from any room if you hear something suspicious.

In some communities the house alarm system can be connected directly to police headquarters. In other localities, the home can be tied into the alarm company's office, which in turn contacts the police. There is a monthly charge for this central hookup.

Alarm systems are expensive, varying in price from $700 to $2,500 and up. Therefore, it is important to check to be sure that you are dealing with a reputable firm that will back up its equipment.

The alarm-system decision should be made in the planning phase of homebuilding. Not only is it more reasonable to have the installation done during construction, but this permits you to benefit from your system's protection from the moment you move in. Prepare your specifications and be precise in your requirements. If possible, obtain three bids based on free estimates. These should be submitted after a study is made of your house plans and alarm-system specifications.

You should also consider installing an effective fire-alarm system. One type has a fire-alarm circuit which, when broken by fire, sounds a warning horn. It is also possible to install a unit that detects smoke or heat and activates an alarm. By having the combination of heat, smoke and fire detection, your chances of being warned in time increase. But such systems are expensive. If you have a multiple-story home, an adequate fire-alarm system would appear to be a more important requirement.

There are heat-and-fire detection devices available that can be installed for individual rooms in a home. They can be bought for about fifty dollars and are easy to install. However, a locksmith said: "Such devices are not so dependable because they are battery-operated. If the battery fails, you have no protection. I recommend that you pay to have an entire burglar-and-fire alarm system installed. This wouldn't be much more expensive than the heat-and-fire-detection system. Such a system ties in with your electrical outlet and the auxiliary-battery unit is used only if you have a power failure.

ENCLOSED GARAGE

It is wise to keep your bicycle, car and other equipment under lock and key. Our younger son, Thomas, recently left his bike at the front-door step on a Sunday afternoon. It was gone—permanently—when he returned a few minutes later.

Install necessary locks on all garage doors and make daily checks to be sure that they are secured. An automatic electric garage door is a convenience, saving you from having to lock and unlock the door each time you enter or leave with your car.

IRON DOORS AND WINDOWS

Increasing numbers of homeowners are installing iron grills at their entryways and windows. Used sparingly, grillwork has a certain charm; however, if placed at all windows and entrances, it tends to make a house look like a prison.

Grill work is expensive and requires good locks to be effective, but it does provide added security since it constitutes another barrier to penetrate before reaching the interior of the house. Still, if you put an iron door at your front entry only, your home remains vulnerable at other entrances and windows. A burglar will normally seek to enter a home at its weakest location. This is why it is so important to consider *all aspects of security* in devising an effective protection plan.

OTHER SECURITY SUGGESTIONS

STAGGERED HOURS

Avoid establishing a precise pattern for leaving or returning home. This will make it more difficult for people watching your residence to make break-in plans.

AT-HOME APPEARANCE

You may wish to turn on your record player, television or radio before leaving the house. This gives the impression that someone is at home. Your home should appear occupied at all times, since robbers prefer to enter empty houses, where there is less possibility of being identified or engaged in a fight in which they might be apprehended, injured or killed.

PROTECTED VALUABLES

Don't keep your valuables at home. Items of substantial monetary worth should be kept in a safe-deposit box at the bank.

PICTURES

It is helpful to photograph your possessions. Keep one set of pictures in your safe-deposit box. Be sure to update your photographs as you acquire additional items. Your memory can play tricks but your camera will provide solid proof.

ESCAPE ROUTES

Devise a plan that will enable you to leave your home rapidly in the event of a burglary or fire. Your fire department can suggest avenues of escape and alert you as to what to do in case of fire. Upon request, they will come to your home to recommend fire-prevention measures, including proposals for such safety items as fire extinguishers.

SECURE WINDOWS

Nailing or screwing shut windows makes them difficult entry points. However, in the event of fire, sealed windows make escape more complicated from certain locations—particularly if you have a multiple-story residence. Keep a screwdriver, hammer or chair nearby in case you need to open windows fast.

OUTDOOR LIGHTING

A good outdoor lighting system can be helpful. You can obtain lights that come on at dusk and go off at dawn. There is one negative aspect to this sytem, however; illuminating your home can draw it to the attention of a person who might otherwise have ignored it.

FENCING

A fence can be a good way to keep burglars out. Its value is enhanced if the gates are kept securely locked. A fence, however, could also be a hiding place. Once intruders are in a backyard, they can often work unobserved. Thick shrubbery is another potential hiding place.

WIRELESS EQUIPMENT

There are radar devices on the market that alert you to the presence of potential burglars. This equipment can be strategically placed near doors and windows. When a person passes within a certain distance of these mechanisms, an alarm is triggered. An advantage of such devices over wired alarm systems is that the alarm goes off *before* the house is broken into. On the minus side, however, a friend, animal or a high wind can trigger the alarm.

In addition to the motion-detection system, there is also a wireless monitor system available. Small radio transmitters are placed on windows and doors. A master control is also installed; if an entry is made, this device sounds an alarm and automatically alerts the alarm company's office, which in turn calls the police. Installation costs may vary from $300 to $800. A monthly service charge begins at $15.

ALERTNESS TO TRICKS

The following anecdote points out the need to watch for trickery that may result in your home being robbed. While shopping, a woman had her purse snatched. The next day she received a telephone call at home. A man's voice said, "I found your billfold this morning while walking to the office. It has no money in it, but contains your credit cards and driver's license."

The woman was overjoyed and promised a reward for the return of these items. The caller said, "I don't have a car, but if you could meet me downtown at the Namllits Drugstore I could take a few minutes off from work to be there at three o'clock this afternoon. I'll be wearing a brown jacket and striped trousers."

That afternoon the woman went to Namllits at the appointed hour. She waited forty-five minutes but the man never appeared. Upon returning home, she found that her home had been robbed. On reporting it to the police, she was informed that this trick had been pulled the previous week in another section of town.

Other ruses that burglars have used to gain entry include posing as a policeman, FBI agent, repairman or mailman. A fake accident and request for help may lure you from your home. It pays to be alert.

Burglars read about forthcoming funerals, wedding ceremonies and graduations, and note when they will occur. People who announce their vacation plans in the newspaper or elsewhere also play into robbers' hands.

SECURITY CHECKS

Establish a good security-check system. It doesn't pay to install quality devices and not use them. You can buy the best locks, but if you don't keep them secured, they serve no purpose. One home I know of has a sign at each exterior door reminding members of the family to lock it. Another household makes one person responsible for seeing that all doors and windows are locked before bedtime. If you have an alarm system, establish a workable procedure to ensure that it is turned on and off as required.

TOP-SECRET MEASURES

Hearings before Senate committees in 1976 revealed sophisticated devices used by CIA and FBI training personnel. The potential security measures you can develop are limited only by your imagination and availability of money. Things you might want to consider could include installing hidden cameras, recording machines, peepholes, eavesdropping devices to pick up conversations on your property, monitoring your phone, fingerprinting entryways, trip wires and other booby traps. The more unknowns you have, the more protection you'll have against a successful burglary.

IS YOUR HOME YOUR FORTRESS?

Given the funds, you can turn your house into a fort with an alarm system, iron doors and window guards, electronic devices, special locks, watchdogs, elaborate lighting systems and an arsenal of weapons. But is this the way you want to live? Keep in mind that if someone really wants to enter a home, he will. No fortress in history has proved to be invulnerable.

In the long run, we best improve our home security by being concerned about crime in our local communities, states and the nation as a whole. The fortress concept of home security only means that the burglar will turn to a less well-protected residence. The home-security race, like the arms race, is not the most desirable solution.

Figure 13-3 Types of homeowner coverage.

COMPARISON OF HOMEOWNER FORMS	SPECIAL FORM 3		BROAD FORM 2		STANDARD FORM 1	
PERILS (X indicates perils covered)	Dwelling	Personal Property	Dwelling	Personal Property	Dwelling	Personal Property
Fire and Lightning	X	X	X	X	X	X
Windstorm, Tornado, Hail	X	X	X	X	X	X
Explosion	X	X	X	X	X	X
Riot, Civil Commotion	X	X	X	X	X	X
Damage by Aircraft and by non-owned Vehicles	X	X	X	X	X	X
Smoke	X	X	X	X	X	X
Removal	X	X	X	X	X	X
Vandalism and Malicious Mischief	X	X	X	X	X	X
Theft	X	X	X	X	X	X
Breakage of Glass	X		X		X	
Damage by Owned Vehicles	X	X				
Damage From Falling Objects	X	X	X	X		
Weight of Ice, Snow, or Sleet	X	X	X	X		
Collapse of Building or any part thereof	X	X	X	X		
Accidental Discharge, leakage or overflow of Water or Steam	X	X	X	X		
Sudden and Accidental Tearing Asunder, Cracking, Burning, or Bulging of Steam or Hot Water Heating Systems	X	X	X	X		
Freezing of Plumbing, Heating and Air Conditioning Systems and Domestic Appliances	X	X	X	X		
Sudden and Accidental Injury from Artificially Generated Electrical Current to Fixtures and Wiring When Fire Ensues	X	X	X	X		
"All Physical Loss" Covers all damage to Residence, unless policy terms specifically exclude coverage. (This is broadest residence insurance available.) Includes loss by Rain, Snow, Chemicals, Hole Broken in Wall while Moving Furniture, etc. Among standard exclusions are losses from hazards such as Flood,* Termites, Wear and Tear, Deterioration, Smog, War Risk, Nuclear Reaction, and Earthquake.**	X					

* Flood insurance is not available as a part of, or an endorsement to, any homeowner's policy. In many areas, flood insurance is available through a separate government sponsored policy that is issued by a company specifically assigned the responsibility for each area. Upon request, we will furnish information regarding flood insurance.

**Earthquake coverage is available upon request for an extra premium charge.

Source: Armed Forces Co-operative Insuring Association, Fort Leavenworth, Kansas.

INSURANCE[3]

HOMEOWNER INSURANCE

Another important form of security is the acquisition of appropriate insurance with a reputable, first-rate company. A homeowner's policy may give you all the coverage you need. Such policies insure your home against fire, lightning, wind, hail and many other perils. It is important to determine what these other perils include. Figure 13-3 lists the variations among one company's Forms 1, 2 and 3. The advantage to Form 3 coverage is apparent in that it covers "all physical loss." This is the broadest type of coverage and the kind I recommend.

Whatever type of policy you choose, read it carefully to ascertain exactly what it provides, and reappraise your belongings annually to be sure that you are adequately protected in light of the rising cost of replacing possessions.

An important aspect of the homeowner's policy is the comprehensive personal liability insurance (CPL) it offers. (If you rent, the CPL can be obtained separately.) This coverage provides protection should you or any member of your household be held legally liable for actions resulting in accidental injuries to others or accidental damage to the property of others. Coverage applies to personal and sports activities, and it is effective both on and away from the premises and inside and outside the residence.

The following are selected situations in which the CPL insurance would be effective:

1. A deliveryman or guest is injured in your residence.
2. You accidentally injure someone while engaged in golf, hunting or horseback riding.
3. One of your children injures a playmate with one of his toys.
4. Your pet bites someone.
5. A fire spreads from your property to the property of others.

FLOOD INSURANCE

The major flood devastation of Hurricane Camille in 1969 was in the area along the Gulf Coast, from just east of New Orleans to Mobile, Alabama. It was estimated to have caused $1.5 billion in damages, and 284 lives were reported lost. Among the tragedies resulting from Camille were cases of families who were paid almost nothing on property they had felt was appropriately insured since they had been paying hefty premiums each year for this purpose. One woman interviewed on TV reported that she had received $272 on a property loss of $5,000. The agent had informed her that almost all the loss was caused

---

[3]For further discussion of insurance topics see Chapters 17 and 18.

by flood, not wind, and therefore she was not protected. He hadn't mentioned this lack of coverage when he sold her the policy.

Such tragic financial losses were a common aftermath of Camille. As a result, the federal government has been taking steps to alleviate problems like this in the future. In mid-1970, the U.S. Department of Housing and Urban Development announced that 213 flood-prone American communities in 31 states were eligible for flood insurance. People in these areas may purchase insurance at federally subsidized premium rates. The maximum amounts range from $17,500 for single-family homes up to $30,000 for two- to four-family dwellings. Rates vary from forty to fifty cents per $100 of insurance, depending on the value of the structure. Contents also may be insured up to $5,000, with rates of fifty to sixty cents per $100 of insurance. This insurance protection is available through local agencies. I was informed by an area agent that on a $17,500 single home, the premium would be $70 per year. To obtain $5,000 in personal-property coverage, it would cost $25.

The National Flood Insurance Act of 1968 states that "anyone who does not choose to buy flood insurance in a community which is eligible will not be able to get federal financial disaster aid for flood losses that occur after one year from the date his community became eligible to the extent that the loss would have been covered by flood insurance."[4] It is wise to take advantage of this type of insurance. If you live in a flood-prone region be sure that you have proper coverage.

SECURITY DURING CONSTRUCTION

During the construction of your home, take our appropriate insurance. If an individual is working directly for you, see that he is covered in the event of injury. Also make certain that your subcontractors are properly insured (see Chapter 11).

The following measures can be taken to keep physical losses at a minimum while building your home:

1. Enclose your garage promptly so that it can serve as a locked storage area for tools and other materials.
2. Build your home rapidly. The less idle time, the better.
3. Order out only the amount of supplies needed to accomplish the immediate jobs.
4. Ask your neighbors to keep an eye on the construction site.
5. Pay for protection. In one area I know much of the vandalism was done by youngsters living in the neighborhood. They turned over

[4]New Orleans *Times Picayune,* August 16, 1970, sec. 3, p. 3.

paint cans, wrote obscene words on doors and walls, broke windows, bent pipes and took materials. To combat this, a builder asked one of the young toughs to "protect" his property.

A house under construction is a fascinating place for children and draws them like a magnet. You can expect some damage unless there is twenty-four-hour supervision. One builder in our area hires a night watchman who comes on duty as the subcontractors are leaving each evening. He found his losses from vandalism were so great that it was cheaper to have a person protect his construction sites on a continuing basis.

6. Make surprise visits to the site during the weekend and evening hours.
7. Enclose your house as soon as possible. Prior to installation of your permanent doors, your carpenter can nail up plywood sheets each evening.
8. Watch tools. It is important to alert workmen to the need to protect their tools while they are on the job. In some locations, it is unsafe for carpenters to leave their hammers or saws unguarded for a moment. In my own case, when I was helping to install the air-conditioning unit, my job was to rivet the ducts together. When it got to 120 degrees in the attic, I decided to take a break. When I returned, the riveting gun was missing. I never recovered it, but fortunately my insurance company paid for it.

14

MAINTENANCE, REPAIRS, IMPROVEMENTS

Effective home management entails knowing how to foresee and counteract the ravages of aging and wear and tear on your home and equipment. Upkeep problems increase with time, and this chapter is devoted to helping you cope with them. A special section deals with how to carry out home improvements appropriate to your pocketbook and family needs.[1]

MAINTENANCE

Maintaining your house means keeping it at a certain level of efficiency and good repair. If you have bought a new house or done a quality job in building a home of your own, your maintenance should be minimal. In Chapter 11 we pointed out the importance of planning a home that can be easily cared for.

IMPORTANCE OF PREVENTIVE CARE

Preventive maintenance—taking proper care of your equipment *prior* to its breaking down—can forestall many major repairs. The advantages of good upkeep are twofold: the equipment will last longer and your repair bills will be reduced. Be sure, however, to start out with quality equipment which has been properly installed. The best maintenance will be wasted if the construction is poor and the equipment inferior. Should you find yourself stuck with shoddy merchandise, replace such items as quickly as possible.

Maintenance expenses can be increased considerably by poor planning. For example, at a recently completed home near ours, the owner wanted a patio that would be well protected. The architect devised a rectangular area surrounded on three sides by the house and on one side by the garage, completely enclosing the space except for the open ceiling. The owner was delighted by the look of the completed job. But his happiness was short-lived. After the first heavy rain, the patio flooded. No drainage had been provided and the only way to remove the water was to bail it out. The lowest estimate to remedy the situation was $950. Our neighbor decided to live with the problem for six months and, during the rainy season, had a serious maintenance problem.

TOOLS AND STORAGE

In order to maintain your equipment properly you need good tools and a satisfactory place to store them. In planning your home, provide adequate space for this purpose. I recommend setting aside an area in an enclosed

[1]The material in this chapter has been extracted from *Do-It-Yourself Contracting to Build Your Own Home: A Managerial Approach,* Richard J. Stillman, © 1974, reprinted by permission of Chilton Book Company.

garage, basement or utility room. You may wish to purchase a small shed[2] that could be located in your backyard. We keep our tools in the dressing room of our garage, adjacent to the swimming pool (see Chapter 15). A pegboard makes them readily available; I built shelving immediately below the board to store nails, tape, oil and other supplies. You should have a nice store of nails and lumber to start with since all leftover building supplies belong to you.

Arrange your tools neatly and keep them in first-class condition by cleaning and oiling them frequently. Insist that anyone who uses them return them to their proper place.

Tools are expensive and should be protected. If they are stored in a garage, keep the door locked. Buy only those tools that fill your specific maintenance and repair needs. The cost of a set of quality tools (including a toolbox) geared for routine tasks, varies between $150 and $250. The items that I use most frequently are assorted saws, hammers, screwdrivers, pliers, wrenches and drills.

RECORD KEEPING

The file system suggested in Chapter 2 should include folders for maintenance, repairs and home improvements. Keep warranties and instructions on how to care for your equipment. You may also wish to devise a checklist that will serve as a reminder to see that these items are properly maintained. Items that need regular surveillance include heating and cooling units, floors, fences, refrigerators, ovens and dishwashers; termite inspection and painting are also matters to consider periodically.

PROMPT CORRECTIVE ACTION

Maintenance chores should be tended to promptly, utilizing quality materials. If loose screws or gate hinges are left untended, for example, a door could break off and repairs would be expensive. By doing simple jobs like oiling appropriate equipment and tightening the screws on your appliances and doors, you can avoid major problems. Wood fences should likewise be examined periodically for loose knots, since once a knot is lost, it is necessary to fill the hole with a substitute material. This will be more expensive than a preventive squirt of glue and do a less attractive job.

MAINTAINING YOUR COOLING UNIT

Central air conditioning is an expensive investment in warm areas—both in

[2]A 12- x 18-foot lawn building costs $450 to $560 and can store considerable equipment. Extra items designed for this building include shelving, tool rack, pegboard and workbench.

original cost and upkeep. In order to have your system perform economically, it is important to keep it operating efficiently. In this era of rising fuel costs *I cannot overemphasize the importance of adequate insulation.* What steps should you take to maintain a quality unit? Our local utility advises its customers as follows:

Clean or replace filter at least every month during the summer. Dirty filters put an added strain on your air conditioning, and on your cooling bills, too, so keep them clean.

Set thermostat at highest setting that keeps you comfortable—and leave it there. The lower the setting, the longer your unit will run and the more it will cost to operate.

Keep windows and doors closed—unnecessary opening of windows and doors lets in outside air that must be cooled and dehumidified.

Keep hot sunlight out—use draperies, awnings, shutters, or shades to keep the sun out.

Have system checked annually—a check of the mechanical operation of your system by a qualified serviceman is important for efficient, economic operation.[3]

PAINTING

You can save substantial sums by painting your own home. Doing the job yourself, however, requires considerable hard work and time. If you decide that the interior needs painting, work in one room at a time over an extended period so that the project does not become a major undertaking. It is helpful to divide the work up among family members.

Last year, I found it necessary to paint the outside of our house. We began by getting estimates from three firms that specialized in home painting and had a good reputation in the community. Their prices varied from $550 to $725. I then went to several job sites where painting was in progress and, after watching the workmen, talked to several painters about working for me in their spare time. Two came to my home and gave me estimates. In one case, I was told that the job would cost $4.50 an hour if I supplied all the equipment, including brushes and paint. The second applicant preferred to supply his own paint and equipment. His price was $7 an hour.

I next went to a first-class paint company and priced brushes and paint. Finally, after receiving all the good advice I felt I needed about how to prepare the outside of a house for painting, I decided to do the job myself. Needless to say, the following price comparison influenced my do-it-yourself decision:

---

[3]"How the Weather Usually Means Higher Public Service Bills," *Homemaking.* New Orleans Public Service, June 1973, p. 3.

Painting contractors	$550–725
Painters	$305–380
Our family	$76*

*Cost for brushes, sandpaper, paints, mildew remover, rollers, masking tape and so on.

Fortunately, my older son Richard offered to paint if I would do the necessary preparation. This helped tremendously but the project still turned out to be more than I had bargained for in terms of time and effort. I began the preparation process by removing the flaked paint. The paint on the house luckily required very little sanding; but this was not true for our gates, which had been covered with both latex and an oil-based paint—a mixture so tenacious that it had to be burned off. In addition, I was faced with caulking, puttying, securing loose nails and removing mildew.

The final preparatory step prior to painting was to protect our brick, windows, doorknobs, shrubs and driveway from paint splotches. Careful use of old sheets, newspapers and masking tape did the trick. It is much easier to take these protective measures than to remove unwanted paint. Another chore was cleaning the brushes and removing paint from the ladder each evening after my son finished working.

What about equipment? Our experience proved that it is very important to buy quality paint, brushes, rollers and materials. We bought the best grade latex based paint at nine dollars per gallon. The price differential is minor and this extra cost is recouped in a longer-lasting, better-looking paint job. We used a roller wherever practical. It covered well and enabled my co-worker to complete the job more quickly. Brushes were used on trim and spots missed with the roller.

Paint stores can match any color and they will shake the containers so that the paint is ready to be applied. Make the best estimate you can as to the amount of paint you will use. It is best to underbuy; you can always go back for more.

Painting, especially a job of this magnitude, requires good management. The preparatory work, including purchasing the necessary equipment and preparing the surfaces in question, must be done properly. You should strive for and assure that you get a first-class job.

REPAIRS

If you want to get an item repaired promptly and properly, it is wise to learn to do it yourself. Today's abundant life-style has brought a multitude of marvelous gadgets and equipment to many households. But how often have you heard:

"The stupid thing won't work!"
"Broken? I just bought it yesterday!"
"That serviceman promised to be here last week. What happened?"

In the future, American families will probably have even more material possessions; thus, repair problems can be expected to increase. In a chilling article on "The Horrors of Home Repair," *Life* magazine took a hard look at the difficulties of getting things fixed. The author stated:

> Our craftsmen have become what amounts to a New Class: an elite body—inaccessible, accountable only to themselves and enjoying, for all their public indifference, an unprecedented growth in demand for their services. In doing so, they often seem to have done away with the once-proud ethics of their crafts: as manufacturers learned to apply obsolescence to their [products] craftsmen now appear to practice it, and generously, in their services. The object is to get in, get the money, and get out swiftly, leaving the pieces to fall behind them. The worse the job any one of them does, the sooner another one of them is called upon to redo it and the more work there is for everybody.[4]

THE DO-IT-YOURSELF PHILOSOPHY

A partial solution to the problem of repairs is the utilization of a very "available resource"—yourself. Too many members of our society remain oblivious to the fact that their own hands can be useful in making repairs. It would be prudent for more of us to learn the basics of repairing electrical items, maintaining our cars, handling a power mower without getting hurt, painting our homes or taking care of outboard motors. But remember when undertaking repairs to read all written instructions carefully and, if you need professional help, to consult a reputable firm.

The benefits to be derived from a do-it-yourself philosophy are not only the money saved and the physical exercise involved, but also the mental satisfaction that comes from accomplishment—and in many cases, a finished job that is superprofessional, thanks to personal interest and pride.

[4]William A. McWhirter. "The Horrors of Home Repair." *Life,* June 5, 1970, p. 58. (Copyright: *Life* magazine, © 1970–1972 Time Inc., William A. McWhirter)

REPLACEMENTS

From time to time, you will have to replace even the best-maintained, highest-quality equipment. Everything eventually wears out. Regular inspection should enable you to approximate when replacements will be needed and permit you to sell, trade or replace items while they are in working condition.

In considering replacements, keep in mind that new and better products are constantly being made available to the public. Our nation is currently spending $35 billion annually on research and development in contrast to less than $1 billion forty years ago. We can expect this trend to continue. Keep abreast of the latest advances—not only for their convenience now, but also as future selling points in the event that you decide to sell your home.

Prior to replacing a piece of equipment, check carefully into the newest items available. For example, our pool will soon be needing a new filter. The present one uses diatomaceous earth and requires pulling up a plunger to backwash. This is a difficult and time-consuming chore. There is now a filter on the market which eliminates these problems. One manufacturer, Harmsco, states, "... we call it the Freedom Machine because that's what it gives you. Freedom from four-way valve maintenance. Freedom from sand blowback. Freedom from diatomaceous earth. Freedom from separation tanks. And freedom from excessive water consumption." I really look forward to buying a filter with these features.

HOME IMPROVEMENTS

Effective home planning takes future improvement projects into consideration. Let's assume that you want to make a major improvement in your home. Suppose, for instance, that you initially completed only the first floor of your home but now want to finish the upstairs. Or perhaps you want to add an enclosed garage, den or extra bedroom to your house. These improvements can be best accomplished if they have been foreseen in the planning stage.

Once you have decided to make a major improvement, you should follow the management approach emphasized throughout this book. The specific management information pertinent to building a swimming pool (Chapter 15) should also be reviewed. Take time to plan exactly what you want. In my capacity as a management consultant, I was recently asked by a business executive, "Isn't it wasteful to spend so much time planning?" My response: "Think back to all the hours it took you to settle your last labor dispute. All the meetings, bitterness and court action could have been avoided with adequate planning."

THE PLANNING PHASE

Again, the best time to prepare for home improvement projects is during the planning stage. The following story told to me recently by a successful contractor brought home to me once more the importance of making changes no later than during the blueprint stage.

> You can take an eraser to correct a rough drawing. Even if your design is finalized, you can modify it and a new set will cost only $75 to $100. But it really becomes expensive when the building is underway. Recently we contracted to add a new wing to an old house. The foundation had been poured. The framing, bricking, plumbing, and electrical wiring were also completed. At this point, the housewife decided to move her kitchen sink one foot to the right. She thought we were cheating her when our estimate indicated it would cost $1,400. I told her this change meant I had to contact the subcontractors involved for their changes. Numerous modifications would have to be made, otherwise the plumbing fixture would go right through the window. The electrician would have to modify his wiring. I needed to call back the carpenter to change the cupboards, etc. The client recognized the hard way that she should have taken more time initially to plan her kitchen.

Adequate planning also means checking with care prior to selecting a firm to make a major improvement in your home. Try to obtain three estimates and secure a written contract.

PROTECTING YOURSELF AGAINST CONTRACT ABUSE AND SWINDLERS

A word of caution about contracts. Unfortunately, people usually receive them at the most inopportune time—just before they are asked to sign on the dotted line. Contract agreements should, in fact, be studied with care well in advance of closing the deal. If necessary, let your lawyer look your contract over.

Here is what happened to a friend of mine when he failed to read the fine print:

> We decided to add a guest house in our backyard. I found the name of a contractor in the phone book and proceeded to call the owner of what I will call "Goodluck Industries." That evening he came to our house and quoted a price of $6,600. I signed the contract with the understanding that work would begin within thirty days. A week prior to his starting, I

became concerned and proceeded to check him out with the BBB. To my dismay, I found that the owner of "Goodluck Industries" was a fraud. He never finished a job. But the contract specified that in the event of cancellation, I must pay a penalty of $660 even though no work was ever done. I went to my lawyer and, after much effort, including threatening legal action, I bluffed my way out of it. But the time expended cost me $3,350 in lost business.

Mrs. Nell Weekly, head of the New Orleans Office of Consumer Affairs, offers six excellent suggestions and a reading list to help you prevent being taken in a home-improvement swindle:

1. Get bids from several reliable contractors. Best sources of information on reliability are the Better Business Bureau (checking under both firm's name and contractor's name) and references from customers. Call the Remodelers Council and inquire about the arbitration provisions in their contracts. If this is important to you, make sure your contractor agrees to it.
2. Get it in writing, including details on work to be performed, guarantees, and specifications of materials to be used. Total cost and schedule of payments should also be in the contract. The most advantageous contract for the consumer reserves a substantial final payment to ensure that all work will be completed. Never make an advance payment for a special price or permit use of your home for advertising.
3. Do not sign contracts with door-to-door salesmen. Do not allow people to "inspect" your roof or heating system or your home for termite damage unless you have called them. Unnecessary work has been done and some homes actually damaged by roving "specialists."
4. Be wary of package deals which include financing. Shop as carefully for your money as you do for your contractor. Think twice before agreeing to mortgages; investigate FHA loans.
5. Make sure your contractor has a building permit.
6. Never sign a completion certificate until all work has been completed to your satisfaction.
7. For additional information, read: Chapter II, "How to Avoid Swindles on Home Improvements," in *Consumer Swindles and How to Avoid Them*; "Home Improvements for Love of Money" in the January issue of *Money* magazine; and Better Business Bureau publications, including *Tips on Home Improvements* and Safeguard Bulletins 5 and 12.[5]

[5]"How to Avoid Being 'Had.'" *Dixie Roto Magazine,* New Orleans *Times Picayune,* May 6, 1973, pp. 37, 48.

BUDGET ASPECTS

What should you budget for home improvements? Ideally, you should save up enough money to cover all possible costs. Why pay a high rate of interest? For those who cannot pay cash, however, let's take a look at the terms offered by one major firm.

Home-improvement credit plans and the Sears solution / Sears offers three credit plans that can be used to make home improvements.

1. *Revolving Charge Account.* The finance charge is determined by applying a periodic rate of 1.5 percent per month (annual percentage rate of 18 percent) to the average daily balance. A loan of over $500 must be paid within ten months. If paid within thirty days of billing date, there is no interest cost.

2. *Easy Payment Plan.* The annual percentage rate of the finance charges is 20 percent. You have up to thirty-six months to pay, depending upon what you purchase.

3. *Modernizing Credit Plan.* The annual percentage rate of the finance charge is 14.75 percent. You have up to five years to pay. On $2,000, for example, your interest for five years amounts to $792.

Sears credit personnel have informed me that, generally speaking, the company does not require any security on small loans—sums of up to $2,000. The loan decision is based in large measure on a person's character and standing in the community. In contrast, a savings and loan association in our area currently charges 8½ percent but requires a mortgage. As pointed out in Chapter 15, one local loan company is offering home-improvement loans for 14.1 percent, but it expects the borrower to take out a life-insurance policy. Our local banks charge approximately the same as Sears.

Sears makes improvements in such areas as fencing, central cooling, heating, roofing, windows, doors, gutters, siding, ceiling tiling, awnings, carports, carpeting, built-in dishwashers, blown-in insulation, bathrooms, water heaters and kitchens. Their guarantees read as follows:

> All installation labor provided through Sears shall be performed in a neat, workmanlike manner in accordance with generally accepted trade practices. Further, all installation shall adhere to all local laws, codes, regulations, and ordinances. Customer shall also be protected by insurance relating to Property Damage, Workman's Compensation, and Public Liability. . . .
>
> In addition to any guarantee which may be extended to you covering the product you have purchased, Sears, Roebuck and Co. guarantees the workmanship involved in the installation of the product

as follows: Should any defect appear in such workmanship within one (1) year from date of installation, Sears will upon notice from you, cause such defects to be corrected at no additional cost.

A firm like Sears both provides the loan and makes the home improvements. But if you shop around, you may be able to obtain a lower-priced loan and have the job done at less cost. Be sure, however, that you are dealing with reliable companies.

15

SWIMMING POOLS

There are over one million swimming pools currently on the property of homeowners throughout the United States. In some wealthy residential areas, virtually every backyard contains a permanent pool. It should be remembered, however, that a pool is a major investment whose initial cost approximates that of a luxury automobile. Hence, prospective pool owners should think carefully before reaching a decision. This chapter reviews some of the pros and cons of pool owning with tips on how to proceed for those who decide to "take the plunge."[1]

ADVANTAGES OF POOL OWNING

EXERCISE

Swimming is a delightful and invigorating form of exercise for the entire family. A pool also serves as a training ground for the development of expertise in such areas as lifesaving, scuba diving and water polo.

ENTERTAINMENT

Poolside get-togethers are an enjoyable way to entertain relatives and friends. You can barbecue nearby and spend an afternoon or evening of pleasant exercise and good conversation in a picnic environment.

INCREASED PROPERTY VALUE

A pool can increase the value of your home by a sum over and above the installation cost.

STATUS SYMBOL

Pool ownership is one way to keep up with the Joneses if you feel the need.

AESTHETICS

An attractive pool in a tastefully landscaped yard can provide a pleasant view from your patio or elsewhere in your home. There is also the satisfaction of creating your own design.

GENERAL SAVINGS

If you and your family now belong to a swim club or other facility, pool

---

[1]The material in this chapter has been extracted from *Do-It-Yourself Contracting to Build Your Own Home: A Managerial Approach,* Richard J. Stillman, © 1974, reprinted by permission of Chilton Book Company.

ownership can result in dollar savings. One of our neighbors, who dropped his swim-club membership when he built his pool, reports that it has saved him considerable travel time and gasoline.

PRIDE OF OWNERSHIP

A pool owner gets real satisfaction from knowing that he can do as he pleases about his pool's maintenance and decor.

DISADVANTAGES OF POOL OWNING

COST

The pool owner's initial outlay is a hefty $5,000 to $15,000 (I am speaking here of quality in-the-ground pools, not inexpensive, above-the-ground models).

In addition to the cost of the pool itself, you must consider the outlay for decking, backyard lighting, landscaping and fencing.

After the pool is built, you will be faced with maintenance expenses which may vary from $400 to $1,500 a year, depending upon how much work you do yourself, the size of the pool, the kind of repairs, where you live and climatic conditions. Our own annual costs are summarized below:

Acid and algaecide	$ 18
Chlorine	120
Diatomaceous earth	12
Electricity	160
Pool equipment	80
Repairs	140
Total Annual Cost	$530

A weekly cleaning service costs about $500 a year and a pool heater adds approximately $120 to the gas bill. Thus, our yearly expenses could have been increased to $1,150.

UPKEEP

Pool ownership is a constant responsibility. If you want to hire someone to maintain your pool, you must find a reliable firm and assure that the work is done properly. Even the owner with a maintenance contract is faced with day-to-day upkeep, insurance questions and the necessity to take safety precautions.

ACCIDENTS

A pool can be the cause of numerous, and sometimes fatal, injuries. It represents a constant hazard for toddlers. Be sure to equip yourself with first-aid equipment, a knowledge of artificial respiration, and appropriate insurance coverage.

USABILITY

Will the pleasure and use you get from your pool be worth the worry? A pool's novelty wears off quickly and don't forget that the composition of your family will change over the years. Then, too, many people prefer the congeniality of a club or public swimming facility.

FINANCIAL LOSS

Your pool could be a drawback when you decide to sell your home. Many people don't like pools or feel they don't need one. A factor in making your decision should be whether or not pools are common in your neighborhood.

A MANAGERIAL APPROACH TO POOL BUILDING

If you decide to build your own pool, it is important to follow the management concepts emphasized throughout this book. Your objective might be "to have a quality swimming pool built within thirty days at a minimum cost." You must *plan* your pool wisely, *arrange* to have it built in accordance with your plan and make adequate *checks* to ensure construction as specified in the contract. Achieving your objective requires the efficient use of three resources: men, money and materials. Delineating your objective, determining the resources available and understanding your managerial functions should put you in a good position to make solid decisions.

SELECTING YOUR LOT

The ideal time to decide if you want a pool is *prior* to purchasing your land or home. If you decide to become a pool owner, select property that affords privacy. We considered it important to find a lot set in such a way that our neighbors could not look directly into our backyard and where the buildings facing our patio were attractive. The brick garages of our neighbors provide both privacy and a pleasant view.

And don't forget shape and size. Will your lot's dimensions be adequate for the type of pool you desire?

FINANCING YOUR POOL

If you build your swimming pool simultaneously with your home, it becomes part of the total financial package. Thus, if the current mortgage rate is 7½ percent, that is what it will cost to finance your pool. If, however, you wait until after the house is completed, you must obtain a home-improvement loan. The difference is approximately 2 percent, based upon charges of a local savings and loan association. In contrast to the savings and loan 9½ percent charge, a finance company advertised real-estate loans at 14.1 percent. The ad read: "Homeowners, now you can get $3,000 to $13,000 when secured by a first or second mortgage."[2] Their rates were spelled out as follows:[3]

Amount Financed	Monthly Payment	Months to Pay	Total of Payments	Annual Percentage Rate
$3,000	$ 70.00	60	$4,200.00	14.1%
$5,000	$116.66	60	$6,999.60	14.1%
$7,000	$163.33	60	$9,799.80	14.1%

If you select a finance company, your loan must normally be secured by a mortgage to obtain their lower rate. Otherwise, it could cost up to 42 percent. Length of payment is listed as five years in contrast to the much longer loan period if you build the pool at the time the house is constructed. Note also how interest charges mount up; if you borrow $7,000 for 60 months, it costs you $2,799.80.[4] Should you decide to build later, I recommend that you save your money and pay cash for the pool.

ADDITIONAL CONSIDERATIONS

Once you have determined your financial needs and found a desirable lot, there are other factors to consider.

Basic Planning

As stated earlier, it is best to plan your pool concurrently with the rest of your home and include it in the initial house sketch. To help you develop a suitable drawing, look at a number of other home pools. Current articles and books on the subject will bring you up to date on the latest technical and aesthetic developments. Be sure to consider your pool as part of the total home picture, relating it to your landscaping, patio, fencing, garage and the house itself.

[2]"Associates Financial Services of America, Inc." New Orleans *Times Picayune,* May 22, 1973, p. 5.
[3]Ibid.
[4]You may be asked to take out a life-insurance policy for $534 (if not, you would be required to assign a $7,000 portion of your present policy for the life of the loan). An accident and health policy is encouraged, amounting to $602. Thus, your cost could be increased to $3,936.

Selection of a Builder

Considerable time and study should be given to selecting a company to build your pool.[5] Contact experienced people and obtain their views on the quality of construction, costs, time required, and the reliability of various firms. It pays to call your bank, Better Business Bureau and the local consumer-affairs agency. You should also find out whether a builder belongs to the National Swimming Pool Institute.[6]

Make a point of visiting pool builders at their offices. You can get a good idea of an overall operation by observing its headquarters. Also visit homes where pools are under construction and talk with the workers. Note the quality of their workmanship. Building a quality pool requires good supervision and skilled craftsmen.

You also should ask pool builders if they will furnish you with a certificate of insurance from a recognized company. The certificate will indicate the type of insurance, its expiration date and the limits of liability. Insurance coverage may include workmen's compensation, employer's liability, bodily injury (except car), property damage and automobile liability. The certificate will include a statement to the effect that "in the event of cancellation of said policies, the company will make reasonable effort to send notice of such cancellation to the holder at the address shown herein, but the company assumes no responsibility for any mistakes or for failures to give such notice." Another means of protection is to have the company obtain a bond. Then, if the work is not in accord with the contract, you would have an insurance agreement covering a stated financial loss.

Here again, when possible, make your selection from three competent firms. Determine which one will give you the best deal, including quality, price and service. It will be necessary for you to furnish all bidders with specifications and a preliminary sketch to ensure that they are bidding on the type of pool you want.

Specifications

The better your sketch and the more detailed your specifications, the more accurate the bids should be. In the case of my own pool, I grouped my specifications into four major categories: size, design, construction and equipment:

---

[5]You may wish to consider subcontracting your pool in a manner comparable to that described in Chapter 11 for homes. If so, the procedures outlined in that chapter (PERT, a timetable and so on) should prove helpful.

[6]This organization can be helpful in providing you information and literature on pools. Their address is: 2000 K Street, N.W., Washington, D.C. 20006.

Size / 14 to 21 feet wide and 32 feet long; 4 feet at the shallow end to 8 feet at the deepest point.

Design / Free-form

Construction / Pneumatically placed monolithic Gunite 5 to 10 inches thick; reinforced with ½- and ⅜-inch steel bars, to be placed 12 inches both ways (vertically and horizontally) in the shallow end and 6 inches both ways in the deep end.

1. Steps: Gunite custom-built steps (three) in shallow-end corner.
2. Tile: 6 by 6-inch blue trim around entire pool.
3. Coping: 8-inch brick around entire pool.
4. Deck: None. (We had the subcontractor who prepared our patio and foundation do the decking with the same wash-gravel material. His cost was much lower than the pool company's.)
5. Interior finish: Genuine pure-white marble deluxe interior pool finish.
6. Other: Concrete filter slab to support tank and equipment.

Equipment /

1. Filter System: Swimquip model # MKW hi-rate diatomaceous with 25 square feet of filter area, stainless-steel filter tank, 1-horsepower, 220-volt motor, hair and leaf strainer, face piping, fittings, suction valves, automatic air relief and pressure gauge.
2. Heater: None. (We decided not to install a heater since New Orleans weather permits swimming five or six months a year in unheated water. In colder weather, we don't care to swim outdoors. Provisions were made, however, for a heater to be installed later. Space was left for it next to the filter system and a gas stub-out was installed nearby. A pool heater may vary in price from $500 to $1,200 depending upon size, quality and installation charges.)
3. Chlorinator: Custom-built tiled chloramatic feeder.
4. Diving board: Deluxe 8-foot genuine Douglas fir, turquoise coat with white sand, tread-top surface and stainless-steel supports.
5. Ladder: None. (We felt that a ladder clutters up a small pool and is a needless expense, especially if you have steps.)
6. Vacuum cleaner: 10-inch vacuum cleaner with 30-foot floating hose and 16-foot handle. (There is a vacuum cleaner on the market that will automatically clean the floor and sides of a pool, but it is expensive—$330 to $500.)
7. Wall brush: Deluxe 17-inch nylon brush with aluminum bracket and 16-foot handle.
8. Leaf skimmer: Deluxe hand skimmer with a plastic screen and 12-foot handle.
9. Test set: Dial-a-Test set with case.

10. Thermometer: None. (If you buy a heater, the thermometer could be a useful item. The hand test suits my needs—if it's too cold, I don't go swimming.)

11. Safety rope: None. (We installed the Cycolac cup anchors. If necessary, the safety ropes could be purchased later to separate the shallow end from the deep end.)

12. Underwater light: Chrome-plated 500-watt daylight-blue type complete with lens, bulb, deck box and switch at filter area.

13. Time clock: Automatic time clock for filtration equipment. (This enables you to regulate the time you wish the pool filter system to operate. It may vary from zero to twenty-four hours a day.)

14. Fill spout: None. (You may wish to buy a chrome-plated brass one-inch fill spout; it is utilized to add water to the pool and would have been placed under our diving board. I once bumped my head on a spout at a neighbor's pool because it was hanging over the edge. The injury potential and added cost convinced me that it would be better to install a water outlet near the pool and use a hose. This has proved satisfactory. I also use the hose to wash down the deck and water the shrubbery.)

15. Main drain fitting: 8-inch drain frame and grate.

16. Vacuum wall fitting: Vacuum fitting located in skimmer.

17. Return water fitting: Twin-jet returns with whirlpool action.

18. Skimmer: Deluxe superflow self-adjusting type.

19. Other: 135 feet of 4-inch Orangeburg pipe to be installed to storm sewer drain with three grills. Four gallons of muriatic acid, 40 pounds filter aid, 1 gallon tile cleaner, and 100 pounds of chlorine. The pool supplies furnished initially lasted us for three months.

When to Build

If you subcontract your home, begin building your pool after the pilings have been driven. At this point, your entire lot will still be easily accessible. If you wait until your home is completed, it could be difficult for the pool builder to work with his equipment. I have seen cases in which dirt had to be shoveled by hand and removed in wheelbarrows. This can increase the cost of your job considerably.

Construction of a pool is messy work and you will be faced with a real clean-up task if your home is already occupied and landscaped when the building begins. Should this be the case, however, begin construction as soon after occupancy as possible so that you can enjoy your pool for the maximum time. If you build your pool and home simultaneously, it is important to have some form of temporary protection, such as fencing, to keep out stray animals and youngsters. You should also have the necessary insurance to protect you from various types of injuries (see Chapter 18 regarding homeownership and CPL insurance coverage).

THE BUILDING PHASE

It is important to be on the spot while your pool is being built in order to assure that the sketch and specifications are actually being implemented. The following aspects of the construction process deserve special attention:

Design

Stakes will be placed to indicate the layout of the pool. Be sure that the area marked out conforms to your drawing by verifying its dimensions and location. Review any city and subdivision requirements pertaining to swimming pools.

Excavation

See that the excavation equipment does not damage sidewalks, neighboring property or your building material. After the hole has been dug, measure the depth to determine that it complies with the specifications. Trucks will haul away the dirt; if you plan to build up your front yard, make certain that sufficient soil is left for this purpose.

Preparation

Once the digging is completed, the workers will smooth out the bottom and edges of the excavation to make it conform precisely to the pool sketch. In my case, this required the services of three men for eight hours.

The main drain was then formed up and a load of shells placed at the bottom of the pool. Next, steel bars were put in the pool and secured by ties.

After pipe has been laid from the main drain to an outlet at the top of the pool, concrete is sprayed against the sides. This is referred to as a Gunite process.[7] It takes a powerful man to handle this pneumatic spray gun and it is interesting to watch this process. We checked to see that approximately five inches of concrete had been laid on the floor and ten inches on the sides. Other tasks including coping, tiling, and installing drainage, electrical equipment and a filtering system.

The plastering of the pool is another interesting process which results in a white marble interior finish. Once the coating is dry, the pool should be filled with water. After the diving board is installed, decking can be completed for the pool area, driveway and patio.

As soon as the work on your pool has been completed, inspect and test the equipment. Be sure that there are no leaks. Withhold final payment until the city inspectors have given their approval.

---

[7]You may desire to use another type of coating such as metal, fiberglass or vinyl. Check to find out which is best suited to your area and pocketbook.

POOL-SCAPING

We positioned our pool so that it could be seen from the den and lie adjacent to the patio. Since we wanted a diving board, we decided on an eight-foot depth for the deep end to minimize possibilities of injury. Our shallow end is four feet deep in order to allow good swimming in all areas. The wide steps at the shallow end are both convenient and graceful.

The pool's red brick coping blends with the color of our home and, in this area, brick is reasonably priced. The wash-gravel decking conforms with our driveway and patio.

Two doors lead to the garage. One provides access to a storeroom for pool equipment—chemicals, diatomaceous earth, acid and hose for the vacuum cleaner. The other door leads into a dressing room where towels, swim suits and general tools (see Chapter 14) are kept.

POOL MAINTENANCE

A swimming pool requires considerable care, but good care is rewarded by a handsomer pool and a lower repair bill. I recommend that you or a member of your family clean your pool. It is good exercise and alerts you to any existing problems.

During the swimming season, you will need to add frequent doses of chlorine and acid to maintain clear sparkling water. Check your acid and chlorine content daily, utilizing your test kit.

Chlorine and acid can be dangerous; handle them with care. The following warning appears on the chlorine container:

> This material contains chlorine. When measuring any chlorine product, use only a scoop or container that is non-flammable and to be used exclusively for the bleach. Scoop or measure should be made of plastic, enamel or metal. Scoop must be completely dry, clean and free of any foreign matter, liquid or solid. Chlorine is a strong oxidizing agent. Contact with heat, acids, greasy rags, paper or any organic or oxidizing materials (such as vinegar, paint products, beverages, tobacco, cleaners, soap products, pine oil, kerosene, paper, rags, gasoline, mineral spirits) may cause fire. In cast of fire, douse liberally with water.
>
> Never mix chlorine bleaches with anything except water. Avoid contact with the eyes.[8]

Vacuum your pool weekly, clean the tile, skim the pool surface, backwash the filter, wash the deck and empty the skimmer basket. It is desirable to have your pool inspected yearly by a specialist.

A personal daily inspection is also important. Pranksters occasionally

[8]Olin, HTH Dry Chlorine, Olin Corporation, Stamford, Conn.

toss items over the fence which not only are unsightly but can clog the filter system. Copper pennies, nails and bobby pins cause rust marks if not removed promptly. Should rust spots occur, remove them with an abrasive compound.

Get qualified advice on how to maintain pool equipment and service the pool. Learn, for example, what to do when the filter system loses its prime—that is, when there is no more water in the pipes. Why call a repair man and pay ten dollars or more per visit when you can handle this yourself? Study your instruction manual carefully and go over the procedures several times with the pool representative. Be sure that you understand exactly how everything works. Mistakes can be costly. For example, if you close off all the valves and turn on the motor, leaks will develop quickly.

POOL SAFETY

Never forget that a pool can be dangerous. Here are some rules that you should establish:

1. Never swim alone.
2. Have a lifeline handy that can be thrown to a person in trouble. We use a garden hose.
3. Don't allow running or horseplay around the pool.
4. Wait at least an hour after eating before swimming.
5. If you have guests, check to see if they can swim. If not, use a safety rope to block off the deep end.

16

MOVING

As veterans of nineteen moves, my wife and I feel that we qualify as experts in this domain. We learned from each move and the principal lesson we mastered was the importance of good management.

This chapter will therefore be devoted to showing you how to utilize a management approach in making your move. Again, in accordance with good management procedure, you will want to determine your objective, *plan* carefully, *implement* your plan and *check* to see that the move is properly completed. Keep in mind that performing these duties requires close supervision and the better the supervision, the more successful the move.[1]

THE PLANNING PHASE

In planning your move, the following points deserve special consideration:

REDUCTION OF HOUSEHOLD POSSESSIONS

If, like our family, you have made frequent moves, you know that each change of location makes the task of packing, transporting and unpacking your possessions more difficult. Accumulated belongings can present a mountainous problem with the passing of time. My wife's solution is a simple: "If in doubt, pitch it out." By pitch it out, of course, she doesn't mean throwing things away. Items of worth can be disposed of by advertisement, garage sale or through a thrift shop. The Salvation Army and Goodwill Industries are delighted to receive a call and will pick up any merchandise you wish to donate to them.

The advantages of keeping your household possessions at a constant minimum are twofold: 1) a marked reduction in shipping costs at moving time; 2) a considerable saving of time and effort in preparing for your move and settling into your new location.

In planning your move you should consider selling your furnishings at your present site, taking only valuable items with you. If you offer to sell your home with the drapes, rugs, basic furniture and major appliances included, this can present a more attractive deal to some people. It may be possible to dispose of an apartment or to rent a furnished house in the same way. I know of several instances in which owners have sold their condominiums furnished and made a healthy profit. Many people like the idea of taking over a tastefully furnished residence and moving in with no concern about decorating.

If you decide to reduce your household possessions, it will also enable

---

[1]The material in this chapter has been extracted from *Do-It-Yourself Contracting to Build Your Own Home: A Managerial Approach,* Richard J. Stillman, © 1974, reprinted by permission of Chilton Book Company.

you to start out fresh in your new home. Perhaps the old furnishings are not appropriate to the new surroundings. When determining what to keep, weigh such factors as the cost of buying new furniture.

SELECTING THE BEST MEANS OF MOVING

Use a moving company with a well-established reputation. Check with neighbors and friends who have recently moved to get their recommendations. If possible, obtain estimates of costs from three competent firms in order to have a basis for comparison. If you plan to store some of your household goods, visit the company warehouse. Consider the alternative of hiring a van and doing the packing and moving yourself. This can be a major undertaking, but for intracity moves or short hauls, it can be accomplished at a savings in money, time and breakage (more about the "do-it-yourself approach" at the end of this chapter).

ALLOCATION OF ADEQUATE FUNDS

In determining your budget requirements, be sure to allow yourself adequate move-in funds. By move-in funds I mean money to cover both moving costs (storage and moving) and the cost of new furnishings and appliances required at the time you first enter your new home. If you have to make stops along the way, include an allowance for family travel expenses.

You may work for a company that will pay for your entire move and will also guarantee that you do not take a loss in selling your old home. Even in such circumstances, however, your move can be more agreeable if you follow sound management concepts.

ESTIMATING MOVING EXPENSES

You should be able to estimate your moving costs with reasonable accuracy. Each carrier you contact will send an estimator to your home to determine the total charge involved. Be sure to show him everything you plan to send by van so that his bid will be accurate. Likewise, let him know what extra furnishings you may purchase prior to moving. Well in advance of your move you should obtain a copy of the carrier's "estimated cost of services" form. The various services that determine the cost of a move are: transportation; valuation charge; pickup and delivery for storage in transit; storage in transit; warehouse handling; special servicing of appliances; hoisting, lowering or carrying pianos and heavy articles; packing and unpacking services; purchase of barrels, boxes, cartons, mattress covers, crates and containers.

You may wish to come up with your own estimated total weight. Such an undertaking serves as a check on the estimator and may further encourage you to eliminate some of your possessions by sale, donation and the trash pile.

STORAGE CONSIDERATIONS

If it is necessary to put your furniture in storage, check the warehouse you plan to use with care. Find out exactly where your furniture will be placed and, if possible, visit your possessions in storage.

You can make storage arrangements directly with a local warehouse or secure an agreement with a major carrier. If you have an agreement with an interstate van line, the terms and conditions of your contract apply to the storage as well as the move. In contrast, if you use a local warehouse, the terms are whatever you arrange with that firm.

Normally, the carrier will set a time limit for "temporary storage" of no more than 180 days. After that date your belongings go into "permanent storage" and the warehouse rules apply. This is another reason for finding a permanent place to live prior to moving to your new location. The longer your possessions remain in storage, the greater the risk of damage or loss.

If you subcontract your home, it gives you good control over the completion date and ample time to prepare for a successful move. Your PERT chart (see Chapter 11) and timetable will enable you to determine when the house will be ready and you can make definite arrangements with the moving company of your choice. This move should be taken into consideration during the planning phase of your home.

RECORDING OF POSSESSIONS

Keep an up-to-date record of your possessions. This should include the original cost, year purchased and estimated present value. If losses are sustained, you will then have appropriate evidence to support your claim. This list can also be helpful in the event of household burglaries, as discussed in Chapter 13. Most large moving companies supply forms for this purpose.

USE OF CHECKLISTS

Make a checklist of every step of your move as indicated in Figure 16-1 at both your present and new address. Well in advance of your move, study this checklist with care. It contains some excellent suggestions and you may wish to act on them before and during your move. Without an effective reminder, it is all too easy to forget something important in the busy days before your departure.

TRANSPORTATION OF VALUABLES

Be sure that all valuables and heirlooms are properly insured and, when possible, move them yourself. Under no circumstances should you ship them in a regular move. Some people also carry bedding rolls, kitchen utensils and

Figure 16-1 Checklist of arrangements to be made when moving.

☐ Change address, get records, trip arrangements.

☐ Collect and sort mail for listing address changes.

☐ Notify post office of move and fill out change of address cards.

☐ Send address change to friends and businesses.

☐ Get all medical and dental records.

☐ Check and clear tax assessments.

☐ Have your W-2's and other tax forms forwarded.

☐ Notify local draft board if any member of family is subject to draft.

☐ Transfer insurance records, check auto licensing requirements.

☐ Notify school and make arrangements for sending transcripts of school records to new school.

☐ Have letters of introduction written.

☐ Arrange for transfer of jewelry and important documents.

☐ Close charge accounts.

☐ Arrange shipment of pets and any immunization records.

☐ Make travel plans.

☐ Get hotel reservations, and make note to reconfirm.

☐ Collect all clothing or items to be cleaned or repaired.

☐ Return things borrowed—collect things loaned.

☐ Have bank transfer accounts and release safe deposit box.

☐ Arrange to disconnect utility services.

☐ Arrange to connect utility service at new home.

☐ Have farewell parties and visits.

☐ Make arrangements to have heavy appliances serviced for move.

☐ Give away articles you don't plan to take along, give to charitable organizations, get signed receipt for tax purposes.

☐ Dispose of all flammables.

☐ Have car inspected and serviced.

☐ Pack suitcases ahead of time.

☐ Select traveling games.

☐ Set things aside to pack in car

☐ If you haven't made arrangements with your mover to do so, take down curtains, rods, shelves, TV antenna if agreement with new owner authorizes this.

☐ Start packing suitcases you can live out of, if necessary for the first day in your new home.

☐ Line up a baby sitter for moving day so you can look after moving.

☐ In a special carton place items you will need in the first few hours in your new home: soap, towels, coffee, cooking pot, etc. Mark this carton with sticker "Load Last—Unload First!"

☐ Make up special cartons with "Do not move" for articles to be taken in car.

☐ Empty and defrost your refrigerator and freezer and let them air at least 24 hours. Also clean and air your range.

☐ Line up a simple breakfast for next morning that won't require refrigeration or much cooking. Use paper plates.

☐ Finish packing personal belongings, but leave out the alarm clock!

☐ Get a good night's rest.

☐ Be on hand the day of your move, or have someone there authorized to answer questions.

☐ Accompany the van operator while he inventories your possessions to be moved.

☐ Make last minute check on your appliances to see that they have been serviced.

☐ Sign (and save your copy) of bills of lading and make sure delivery address and place to locate you enroute are correct.

☐ Advise driver exactly how to get to new residence.

☐ Also delivery date or dates.

☐ Ask that you be advised of final cost. (This will be determined after van is weighed.) Then, if you have not arranged for time payment of move, or your company is not paying for it, make sure you'll have the needed cash, money order or certified check to pay before van is unloaded at destination because carriers require payment before unloading.

☐ Strip your beds, but leave fitted bottom sheets on your mattresses.

☐ Before leaving house, check each room and closet, make sure windows are down and lights out.

☐ Upon arrival at new location, call the Mayflower agent immediately to leave address and phone number where you can be reached and when, so you can make final arrangements for delivery.

☐ Be on hand at unloading and have a plan for placement of your furniture.

☐ Check all electrical fuses. Sometimes pennies have been used as substitutes!

☐ Check the condition of your belongings. If any items are missed or damaged, note this on your inventory sheet and shipping papers; then report such information to your Mayflower agent who will take care of it for you.

☐ If your utilities haven't been connected, call them for this service, and have them check your appliances for proper operation.

Source: Moving Kit, copyright 1970, Aero Mayflower Transit Company, Inc.

other necessary items in their car so that if the shipment arrives late, they will have adequate means of surviving in a minimal way until their possessions arrive.

ADEQUATE LOSS PROTECTION

How much protection should you have on your shipment?[2] If you decide against additional protection for your household possessions, in the event of damage you will only be paid at a rate of sixty cents per pound per article. Suppose, for example, that you have a lightweight bicycle that weighs ten pounds, cost you $250, and was purchased just prior to shipment. Should it be hopelessly damaged during shipment, you would receive $6 and suffer a loss of $244. You can, however, pay an extra amount of money for greater protection. You have two alternatives: You can either determine the value of your entire shipment and be covered for this amount in the event of a complete loss, or not set a valuation. In the latter case, the mover's maximum liability is automatically set at $1.25 times the weight of your shipment in pounds. Thus, if the net weight of the load totals 5,000 pounds, you would receive $6,250 in the event of a total loss.

The bill of lading reads as follows with respect to the valuation:

Unless the shipper expressly releases the shipment to a value of 60 cents per pound per article, the carrier's maximum liability for loss and damage shall be either the lump value declared by the shipper or an amount equal to $1.25 for each pound of weight in the shipment, whichever is greater. The shipment will move subject to the rules and conditions of the carrier's tariff. Shipper hereby releases the entire shipment to a value not exceeding

_____

(to be completed by the person signing below)

NOTICE: The shipper signing this Request For Service must insert in the space above, in his own handwriting, either his declaration of the actual value of the shipment, or the words "60 cents per pound per article." Otherwise, the shipment will be deemed released to a maximum value equal to $1.25 times the weight of the shipment in pounds.

Should your merchandise be lost en route, you receive a cash payment based on the type of protection you selected. If your belongings are merely damaged, however, the carrier has the choice of either restoring the damaged articles to

---

[2]In this instance, we are referring only to motor shipments of household goods by common carriers operating in interstate and foreign commerce. If you are making an intrastate move by a local carrier, you should determine his protection.

278

the condition in which they were taken from your home or paying you the actual value less depreciation.

Keep in mind that the coverage you receive is not called insurance. In fact, the Interstate Commerce Commission actually prevents movers from selling insurance. The ICC views your protection as a matter that affects "the liability of the mover for loss or damage to your goods."

USE OF THE ICC PAMPHLET

The ICC has prepared a pamphlet titled *Summary of Information for Shippers of Household Goods* which should be studied by every prospective shipper. The ICC has made it mandatory for all carriers to provide their customers with copies of this publication. However, an ICC study indicates that about 18 percent of those shipping household goods had not received a copy of the pamphlet.

I urge you to read the ICC booklet from cover to cover well in advance of your move. Its following list of do's and don'ts deserve special attention.

DO
Read this information booklet entirely.

Select your household goods mover with care.

Be sure that agreements between you and the carrier are in writing and on the order for service and the bill of lading.

Examine and make sure that physical inventory record of your household goods is accurate as to number of items, condition of furniture, and so on.

Make sure you understand the limited liability of the household goods carrier.

Schedule your departure and arrival with enough flexibility to allow for possible failure on the part of the carrier to meet exactly his scheduled time.

Accompany, if you can, your carrier to the weighing station for weighing of your shipment.

Advise the carrier of a telephone number and/or address where you can be reached en route or at destination.

Request a reweigh of your household goods if you have any reason to believe the weighing-in not accurate.

Be certain that everything on the inventory is accounted for before the van operator leaves either origin or destination.

File a claim for any loss or damage noted on the delivery papers as soon as possible.

DON'T
Fail to read this information booklet entirely.

Believe an estimate is a final cost of your move.

Expect the carrier to provide boxes, cartons, barrels, or other packing material free of charge.

Expect maid service and appliance service free of charge.

Fail to make arrangements to have in cash or certified check the maximum amount shown on the order for service unless credit has been arranged for in advance.

Plan to leave your old residence until the moving company leaves, unless you have a friend or neighbor acting in your behalf.

Expect your household goods to be unloaded until you have paid at least the maximum amount shown on the order for service in cash or certified check unless credit has been arranged for in advance.

Sign any receipt for your household goods until you are certain that they are all delivered and that there has been no apparent damage that has not been noted on the shipping papers.[3]

The ICC has over eighty offices in major cities throughout the United States. Each office employs a minimum of two people who are available to answer your questions and provide other assistance within their areas of responsibility.

IMPLEMENTING YOUR MOVE PLAN

IMPORTANCE OF SUPERVISION

You or a member of your family should be on the spot during both the packing phase and the move itself. Your personal supervision will normally result in workmen taking greater care. It won't take long to judge if you have a good crew. If they are sloppy and hurry the job, inform the head man. If this brings no improvement, contact the local office immediately and request a responsible supervisor.

PREPARING FOR THE PACKERS

Plan for the packers' arrival. Have your household possessions neatly arranged and provide adequate space for the workers. Items to be packed should be clean and readily available.

Observe the packers' work carefully. You can learn much from professionals about how best to protect your china and crystal for a safe move. This knowledge will be useful should you ever decide to do-it-yourself.

You may wish to code your containers. A marking system will help you to place possessions quickly in the correct rooms of your new home. Should any breakage occur while your items are being packed, make a notation on the bill of lading. Likewise, if the packers indicate that your furniture is gouged,

[3]ICC. *Summary of Information For Shippers of Household Goods*, Washington, D.C.: U.S. Government Printing Office, p. 4.

scratched or otherwise damaged and you disagree, state your disagreement in writing. This written statement will be essential on submission of your claim.

OVERSEEING THE LOADING

Once the movers start taking furnishings from your residence, you should have a system of checking each item that is placed in the van. This check also gives you an opportunity to see if other peoples' furnishings are already aboard. Unless you are able to fill a van with your own belongings, it will normally take on other household possessions en route in order to assure a full load. This may delay the arrival of your shipment.

WEIGHING YOUR POSSESSIONS

Before the moving van sets off for your new home you should receive a bill of lading. This is your receipt for your household possessions and will indicate the weight of the van prior to receiving your merchandise (tare weight). You may wish to follow the van to the weighing station to determine the weight of your load. The weight of the van with your belongings aboard is called the gross weight. Your moving charge is calculated on the net weight (gross weight minus tare weight). Once the net weight has been established, you can call the carrier's local office and obtain the transportation cost of your shipment.

If you have any concern about the accuracy of the weight of your household possessions you can request that they be reweighed before they are unloaded. But unless this second weighing shows a certain established variation in the weight, you will be required to pay a reasonable charge for it.

CHECKING ON YOUR MOVE

THE UNLOADING PHASE

Try to be at your new home prior to the arrival of the van. This is the time to check carefully each of your possessions. If you keep the carrier waiting, you may find that your shipment has been placed in storage. This can be expensive. Find out how long a van will wait prior to leaving your residence.

It helps to have a sketch available on moving day showing the approximate placement of your furniture in the various rooms of your new home. Frequent switching of furnishings is hard on movers. One family I know takes photographs of their possessions as they are placed in their old home. They find that referring to their photos on moving into their new abode enables them to resettle more quickly. As noted in Chapter 13, pictures are also an excellent way of recording what you own.

Check each item as it comes off the van for possible damage. Make appropriate notations on the inventory, delivery receipt or bill of lading.

If your agreement calls for unpacking, be sure that all items are removed from the cartons and placed in the closets, cabinets and drawers that you designate. Again, make notation of any damage found.

PAYMENT

Th movers will be anxious to complete unloading, have you sign for the merchandise and receive payment. But payment for your shipment should not be made until you are satisfied that all work has been completed in accordance with the contract. Make certain that you have listed all damaged and missing items and that this list appears above your signature. *Don't let yourself be rushed.*

Unless you have been given credit by the mover prior to delivery, payment must be made in cash, certified check, money order, traveler's check or cashier's check.

SUBMITTING A CLAIM

If, after checking for damaged and missing items, you wish to complain, submit your claim promptly and follow up to see that you get a fair deal. The ICC states in the pamphlet mentioned earlier:

> If you need to file a claim, the earlier this is done, the quicker the mover can make settlement. We cannot stress enough that your best proof of claim is notation on the bill of lading, inventory, or delivery receipt at the time of delivery. If you should later discover that an article was lost or damaged and you have proof that such loss or damage was caused by the mover, you can still file a claim for such loss within 9 months after the move. Your claim is much more difficult to process if it is delayed or presented some time after your goods have been delivered.[4]

SHORT-DISTANCE MOVES

We have discussed the long-distance move, but what about short hauls? If you remain in the community in which you presently live, you have additional options in deciding how to proceed. Your choices include: employing a large carrier; using a local firm that specializes in short-haul moving; renting a truck and driver; renting the truck and driving it yourself; moving the possessions yourself, using family transportation; or a combination of these.

[4]Ibid., p. 6.

If you have the time and energy, there is no question that you can save considerable money and do a splendid job by taking on much of the responsibility yourself. Over the years, we have found that our most successful moves have been those that we did on our own. But be prepared for hard work! When we moved across the street while living in Arlington, Virginia, for example, it took three of us two full days to move 8,000 pounds. We also had help from several neighbors. If you are moving into a house you have built yourself, get installed as quickly as possible after its completion. This will prevent pilferage and theft of items you may have placed in your new home once it seemed well secured.

If you "do-it-yourself," your automobile can be useful for transporting small items. You can rent a truck for the rest and perhaps hire a college student to assist you with your move.

Part Four

INSURANCE & SOCIAL SECURITY

This fourth section points out the importance of insurance in relation to your total personal-finance program.

Insurance can provide dollar protection for you and your family. The amount required will vary with each individual. Obviously, an elderly person with no car will have far different auto insurance needs than a three-car family with four teenagers. Due to the many factors that enter into making a wise insurance decision, I recommend that you review the chapters on Budgeting, Clothing and Personal Care (Including Health Maintenance), Transportation (Highlighting Cars), Large Appliances and Other Major Expenditures, Part III on Housing, and Part VII on Taxes, Retirement and Estate Planning before settling on an insurance program.

17

LIFE INSURANCE & SOCIAL SECURITY

(continued on p. 288)

Life insurance and social security are two important sources of protection for you and your family. It is therefore important to familiarize yourself with the benefits they provide. A careful reading of this chapter, which examines these two vital areas in depth, and the following chapter, which considers other available insurance options, will help you determine your overall insurance needs and assist you in setting up a comprehensive insurance program tailored to meet them.

LIFE INSURANCE

PURPOSE OF LIFE INSURANCE

Why do you need life insurance? Its primary function is to provide money for someone or something in the event of the policyholder's death. Therefore, sufficient insurance protection should be an essential element in the financial portfolio of anyone with personal responsibilities. This protection can take the form of investments, a commercial policy or a group policy offered at nominal rates at your place of business. For those in the armed services, the government provides excellent family benefits at little cost. Such sources of financial protection should be given due consideration in the determination of your overall life-insurance requirements.

Suppose, however, that you have no family, no obligations and no wish to leave anything to charity. You may well say, "Who needs it? I'll enjoy my money myself!" (At the other end of the spectrum, you can skimp to maximize savings for insurance purposes, betting on dying young and leaving a sizable fortune for others to enjoy.)

CHOOSING AN INSURANCE COMPANY

An insurance policy is only as good as the company behind it. Therefore, it pays to take a hard look at available facts prior to signing a contract. It is wise to select a well-established company with a fine reputation, a healthy growth rate and competitive prices.

There is much good material on insurance companies in *Life Financial Reports* and *Life Rates and Data,* published by the National Underwriter Company, 420 East 4th Street, Cincinnati, Ohio 45202. In addition to this information on specific companies, you may wish more general background on insurance itself. If so, I recommend your reading the *Life Insurance Fact Book,* current edition, published by the American Council of Life Insurance, 1850 K Street, Washington, D.C. 20006. All of the above publications should be available at your library.

HOW MUCH INSURANCE DO YOU NEED?

The odds are very much against your dying as a healthy young person (those required to travel frequently by car or plane, or holding high-risk jobs, should of course give special attention to their insurance needs), but your chances of hitting the insurance jackpot increase with age. Death gets us all in the end, but by that time you should have a tidy sum of savings and other investments. How much insurance you want to leave is your decision. It is helpful to keep in mind the other assets that you will be leaving to your heirs.

I believe that life insurance should be purchased solely as protection in the event that you die before you have accumulated a nest egg to meet the needs of your heirs or to provide a legacy for whatever purpose you desire. If you accept this approach, *you should buy the cheapest form of life insurance available*—term or group (we will discuss the various types of insurance below). By following my overall investment policy, you can accumulate alternate forms of insurance in the form of cash reserves, bonds, stocks, real estate and other assets while paying your insurance premiums. A check of insurance company holdings proves that *they* place *their* funds in the above investments, so why pay a middleman a high fee to do this for you once you have assured yourself the necessary insurance protection?

TYPES OF INSURANCE PLANS

The insurance business is booming in America today. There was $2,139 billion worth of life insurance in force at the end of 1975. The average amount of life insurance protection per family in the United States in 1975 was $28,100.

Life insurance companies in the United States in mid-1975 numbered 1,797, of which 1,652 were stock companies owned by shareholders and usually not paying dividends on their policies. Mutual life insurance companies numbered 145, but accounted for slightly over half the life insurance in force. Mutuals do not have stockholders and normally issue policies that pay dividends. This fact does not lower the net cost of mutual insurance because the premiums charged reflect this dividend differential.[1]

There are four major categories of life insurance available today: ordinary, group, industrial and credit. This chapter will deal primarily with the first two categories—ordinary and group. In the case of ordinary life insurance, each individual must decide which type of policy is best suited for him. This is a far more complicated matter than group coverage, which is usually provided by the employer and gives the employee no choice but to accept the plan or not participate.

---

[1]American Council of Life Insurance, *Life Insurance Fact Book,* 1976.

Industrial insurance policies should not be confused with the excellent group insurance available to workers in many industrial organizations. The title "industrial" is misleading. Industrial policies are in fact ordinary life insurance; but they are categorized separately because they are written in small amounts and collected weekly or monthly by agents going from house to house. This is the most expensive type of insurance available.

> The average size of industrial policies in force was $570 in 1975. Total industrial life insurance coverage in the United States was $39.4 billion at the end of 1975. This coverage was issued under 70 million industrial life insurance policies.[2]

The above figures point up the fact that securing small amounts of money from a large number of people can be big business—and most profitable for the insurance salesmen and their companies.

You will encounter credit life insurance if you borrow money. Its purpose is to protect the lender in case you should die prior to repayment of the entire debt. It is utilized by such lending agencies as furniture stores, banks and small-loan companies. From the borrower's standpoint, this is just another expense in the high cost of using someone else's money. The lender normally makes a large profit on this credit insurance.

> The amount of credit life insurance in force in the United States increased $10.2 billion during the year 1975, to a total of $112 billion at the year end.[3]

ORDINARY INSURANCE

Let us now examine the ordinary-insurance category. It has the largest amount of insurance in force ($1.083 trillion) and the greatest number of policyholders (134 million). Ordinary offers a variety of policies to meet any individual need. We will discuss the four principal types and several special types.

Ordinary Life

The ordinary life (or straight life) insurance policy offers protection by the payment of a fixed premium throughout the lifetime of the insured. Ordinary life calls for the lowest premium payment of any of the permanent plans, thus affording the largest amount of permanent protection per dollar of premium paid. After the first policy year, the accumulated cash value may be utilized for

[2]Ibid., p. 31.
[3]Ibid., p. 31.

one of several purposes: paid-up insurance, extended-term insurance (see below), cash loans or cash surrender.

This is the most common type of insurance held by American families. Premiums continue for life, and the face value of the policy is payable at death. A check of one successful company indicated that as of December 31, 1976, it had 93,795 ordinary life policies out of a total of 110,608.[4]

The advantages of this type of policy are the relatively low cost and the accumulation of cash values. The latter permits cashing in the policy and receiving a limited amount of money in relation to the amount paid, or borrowing against it. To borrow your own money, insurance companies charge you 5 to 6 percent. A disadvantage of ordinary life is that the insured may not always be able to meet the premiums. It is important to remember that these are lifetime payments. The possibility of failure to meet future payments is increased when a large proportion of earnings is placed in such insurance. Another consideration is the inherent weakness of life insurance itself—the lack of protection against inflation.

Ordinary life may be purchased on a guaranteed-cost (given price) or a participation basis. A participation policy, while higher in initial cost, after the second year pays the insured dividends that may be applied toward the premium payments. Detailed computations may be necessary to determine whether the dividend or nondividend policy is the better deal.

The disadvantage of life payments cited above is not as great as would appear at first glance. If at some future date the insured is no longer able to maintain payments, he has the privilege of converting to a paid-up policy of lower value and making no further payments. The option is often taken by retirees whose insurance needs decline along with their income.

Fixed-Payment Life

The fixed-payment (or limited-payment) life policy provides insurance protection throughout the lifetime of the insured by the payment of a fixed premium for a period of twenty (twenty-payment life) or thirty (thirty-payment life) years. At the end of this period, payments cease but the insurance continues in force, and guaranteed values continue to accumulate. Also, such dividends as may be declared on a participating policy will by payable throughout the lifetime of the insured. Premiums for the twenty-payment life policy, however, are higher than those for ordinary, or thirty-payment life, because the policy becomes fully paid up in twenty years.

Under the limited-payment plan, the period of premium payments is tailored to the individual's requirement. Fixed-payment policies are of two

---

[4]Army Mutual Aid Association. *98th Annual Report* (for the year ending 31 December), 1976, p. 21.

varieties, designed to mature either at a specific future date or at a given age. These policies have the advantages of being paid up at a definite time and of building cash values more rapidly than similar amounts of straight life. The major disadvantage is cost. The amount of protection that can be bought per dollar of premium is lower than with group, term or straight life. This is an important consideration since most life insurance is bought by the young family man of modest income.

There are variations of the standard policy. For example, at least one insurance company has what they call a Modified Life 5-10 Policy. After purchasing, say, a $10,000 policy, for the first five years the insured pays 50 percent of the annual premium, and the full premium thereafter. At the end of twenty-seven years, the policy is fully paid up. However, if the insured continues premium payments for the next eight years, the policy becomes an endowment that would pay, at age sixty-five, $14,265. The total cash outlay for such a policy is $8,100. This modified policy overcomes one of the major objections to fixed-payment life: It provides good protection to the insured at a time when his income is low and his need for insurance can be high. A major drawback to this type of policy is the fact that five years from now his premiums will double, perhaps at a moment when he can ill afford it.

Endowment

A majority of endowment policies are of the twenty-year variety. As noted above, they call for a fixed-premium payment over a twenty-year period. At the end of this time, unless the policy matures sooner by death, the full amount is payable to the insured, either in one sum or in monthly installments normally ranging in number from 36 to 240, as he may elect. The premium for this type of contract is higher than the premium for ordinary, twenty- or thirty-payment life plans, because the contract not only provides for full payment to the insured if he is alive at the end of the endowment period, but guarantees full payment to his beneficiary if he should die at any time during the twenty-year period.

Another variety of this policy is the endowment at age sixty. This policy, otherwise identical with the twenty-year endowment, provides for fixed-premium payments only until the insured is sixty years old. There are other varieties of endowment policies that can be tailored to fit your needs.

Endowment insurance is designed as a life-benefit policy. In 1975, for example, life insurance companies paid out $946 million in matured endowments, as compared to $9.2 billion in death benefits. A person buying an endowment is paying for both protection and a savings account. Therefore, his premiums are higher than those required by other types of insurance for the same amount of protection. Insurance companies take both the savings and the protection portions of your endowment premiums (less a big chunk for expenses) and invest them.

How well have the insurance companies done with their investments? The rate of interest they have paid in the past ten years ranges from 2½ to 4 percent for some of the mutual companies. Check your local bank and you will quickly see that you can beat that return. Endowment policies are also prime targets for loss due to inflation. Since they are long-term contracts, as they mature they may only partially fulfill the need for which they were obtained in the first place. Like long-term bonds (see Chapter 20), they often fail to keep up with loss in the purchasing power of the dollar.

An endowment policy can, however, be a means of encouraging saving. Insurance companies insist upon payment of your premiums on penalty of cancellation. The company has no compunction about voiding a lapsing policy.

In a Roper survey, it was found that a large percentage of the public thinks of life-insurance premiums as a debt similar to mortgage payments. Even during the depression, most policyholders paid their insurance premiums. However, for those who do default, the primary purpose of insurance—protection—is defeated. Default often occurs when protection is most needed.

Term

Term insurance provides for a level premium rate for a set period, often sixty months (five years), after which the policy terminates and becomes void unless renewed or changed to some other form of coverage. Payment of the premium for the sixtieth month automatically renews the term insurance for an additional five-year period, at a correspondingly higher premium rate.

Term insurance has been classified as "pure protection" insurance. When you buy a term policy, it is sunk cost; that is, there is no cash value being accrued. If you live to the end of the insurance period, you have only a pile of receipts to show for your premiums. Dollar for dollar, it's the best deal—it is similar to car or fire insurance, in that you pay for insurance protection only.

The simplest and oldest form of term insurance is declining-term insurance. This is very reasonable. A few years ago, there was an insurance company in the Midwest that would sell a $10,000 policy for $44 a year if the insured was under thirty-five years of age, with no medical examination required. The fly in the ointment was that each year the value of the policy declined sharply.

A second type of term insurance provides for payment of the face value of the policy in case of death during the term for which the policy is issued. This type is popular with young families, because of low cost, renewability and the conversion privilege (see below). A term policy is renewable, usually for the face value of the original, without the need of a physical up to age sixty-five. The major mutual or stock companies normally do not offer term insurance to people over sixty-five, and never to those aged seventy or more.

A term policy may be convertible into ordinary life, fixed-payment or endowment. The type of conversion varies with insurance companies. One company offers a five-year renewable and convertible term and a ten-year convertible term. In both policies, the conversion clauses are similar:

> The policy may be converted on an elective basis without evidence of insurability at any time not later than the policy anniversary on which the Insured's age nearest birthday is 62 years. Conversion may be to any level premium whole life policy or endowment under the new policy, provided that the term policy is in force on the date of exchange with all premiums duly paid.[5]

The major attraction of term insurance is its low cost. A $10,000 renewable term policy can be purchased for approximately $55 at age twenty-five. This includes not only accidental death benefits equal to the face value of the policy, but a waiver of premium due to disability as well. However, at each renewal the cost of the insurance goes up without a corresponding increase in protection. At age thirty, premiums approximate $59; at forty-five, $116; and by age sixty, the cost reaches $350. The waiver of disability is no longer available at age sixty.

The key to successful use of term insurance is to employ it early and then build your own insurance nest egg through other investments. If you go the long route in either term or convertible term, it can be costly. Let us consider the following example. At age twenty-five, Mr. X purchases a $10,000 ten-year convertible-term policy and converts at the end of the period. He would pay $58 a year for the first ten years and $245 thereafter. Mr. Y, at age twenty-five, purchases a participating ordinary life policy for $10,000 at a premium of $183. At age forty. Mr. X has had a total insurance cost (premiums minus cash value) of approximately $1,200, while Mr. Y's cost was $885. The cost gap widens over the years.

SPECIAL POLICIES

In addition to the four major types of ordinary policies discussed above, there is a fifth group that combines the features of ordinary life, endowment and term policies. Such combinations are expensive but in theory give greater protection and savings than the ordinary policies.

Family Security Policy

One company sells a special policy that it calls a Family Security Policy. This plan provides monthly income protection for twenty years, along with permanent insurance payable at death. Its cost is considerably lower in the early years

---

[5]Excerpt from the INA Five-Year Renewable and Convertible Term Policy.

than that of a straight life policy with a family-protector rider of comparable coverage. Of course, cash values accrue very slowly under such a plan. Each unit consists of $1,000 of face amount.

Family Policy

A second combination of ordinary life and term insurance is what another company calls a Family Policy, covering all family members. It provides for $5,000 in straight life on the head of the household, a $1,500 term policy on the wife that is in force until the insured's sixty-fifth birthday and a $1,000 term policy on each child up to age twenty-five. Both the term contracts are convertible into other types of policies, with restrictions, and the cost of the accidental-death benefit and disability waiver are included in the premium. The advantage of this type of policy is that each new member of the family is automatically insured at the age of fifteen days, thus saving this additional expense.

Jumping Junior Policy

A third special plan called the "jumping junior" policy has a face value of $1,000 until age twenty-one, when the face value jumps to $5,000. Premiums are payable to age sixty-five. In addition, another $5,000 worth of permanent-type insurance can be purchased at age twenty-one without medical examination or proof of insurability. There are a multitude of additional policies to choose from and an insurance company will tailor a program to meet your desires.

DETERMINING THE MOST ADVANTAGEOUS ORDINARY POLICY

Which of the four principal ordinary policies is best for you—straight life, fixed payment, endowment or term? Obviously, each person must decide what his own needs are in relation to a total investment program. Whether or not you intend to assume family responsibilities certainly makes a difference in your insurance needs. I personally favor term insurance for any young person.

Some years ago, Kiplinger's magazine *Changing Times* took an interesting approach. The publication investigated the amount of insurance protection that $150 a year would buy. After giving consideration to straight life, limited payment, endowment and term policies, *Changing Times* favored straight life. In comparing death benefits at age twenty-five the magazine found that straight life gave $12,000 in protection, limited payments (to sixty-five years of age) and provided $10,700, while a twenty-year endowment gave only $3,800.

It is apparent, however, that in comparing straight life and term, the latter gave far more protection for the insurance dollar. Yet, if one looks at the total insurance cost (TIC), straight life may still be the better buy. A $10,000 term policy would cost a twenty-five-year-old about $500 in premiums over a ten-year period. The same amount of ordinary life would require payments of $1,430, but the policy would have a cash value of $1,135. Accordingly, the straight life TIC would be only $295, making it $205 cheaper than the term policy over a ten-year period. In addition to TIC savings, annual premiums will narrow so that by age forty-five, renewal of insurance will approximate straight life. From the Kiplinger presentation, it may be argued that for a given amount of insurance, ordinary life is preferable to term provided that one can afford the higher premiums. I do not agree, because if my total financial program is followed, a person would be reducing insurance payments over the years (other than group), and buying growth investments.

GROUP LIFE INSURANCE

Group insurance, as the name implies, is issued to a group of people under one master policy. A number of organizations, both private and public, have such policies for their employees. These group policies normally do not require medical examinations.

The major advantages of group insurance are the low premium and the excellent protection when you need it the most—during the early years of employment. I strongly urge that if you have the opportunity to participate in such a program, you take full advantage of it. By paying minimum rates for insurance with maximum protection, you can put your other savings in investment areas with a greater dollar return. With each dollar saved in bonds, banks or other investments, you are in fact providing both savings and insurance. Let us assume that at the end of five years you have a group policy for $15,000 and another $10,000 placed in the bank and U.S. savings bonds. In such a situation, you have, in fact, $25,000 in insurance. In all investments, your aim is to maximize each dollar to your advantage. Group insurance is one way to do this.

Let us consider a specific group policy—the one available to employees of Louisiana State University—as an example of the low premium and good benefits offered by group plans. To begin with, the university pays half of the insurance premium. Life coverage of $20,000, for example, costs the employee only $11 per month. Such a benefit is offered by many other organizations as well. Some, in fact, pick up the entire tab. It pays to check all these benefits before arriving at your who-to-work-for decision.

Be sure to investigate the options available in any group plan with respect to your dependents.

VARIABLE INSURANCE

An interesting new development in life insurance is the variable policy. It is available in limited-payment form only. Those who buy such policies will find their premiums and benefits to their heirs varying over the years. The objective of a variable policy is to keep up with inflation.

Insurance companies offering variable policies plan to invest the premium in quality common stock, in order to keep abreast of rising consumer costs.[6] Unfortunately, however, many common stocks over the past several years have failed to show growth, and a number have declined during this era of rapid inflation.

The variable policyholder is protected in the event that his company's portfolio of stocks declines below the estimated value of the policy. The insurance firm is required to pay the beneficiary an amount at least equal to the face value. Contrariwise, if the stock investments should enhance in value, payment to the heirs would exceed the face amount. For example, if you buy a $5,000 variable life policy, you can be assured that your heirs will receive a minimum of $5,000 upon your death. However, if the common-stock investments of your particular company are successful, your beneficiaries could receive $6,000, $7,000 or more. For this privilege, of course, you can expect to pay higher premiums. The higher the common stock in the company portfolio rises, the greater your premiums. It has been estimated that variable-policy premiums will generally be about 10 percent higher than the regular fixed-payment variety.

In addition to the higher cost, another problem with the variable policy is the inability to determine precisely its loan or cash-surrender value. In choosing this type of insurance, the possibility that one day you will want to borrow money on your life-insurance policy should be taken into consideration. The stocks involved may go down at the time you need the loan from your insurance company. Of course, the possibility exists that the stocks will rise sharply; either way there is always an element of uncertainty surrounding variable policies. In contrast, you always know the exact amount available in a regular policy in each of the years ahead.

From a buyer's viewpoint, it is good to know that all variable insurance comes under the jurisdiction of the Securities and Exchange Commission (SEC). This regulatory federal agency requires companies issuing variable policies to be registered with the SEC and to establish prudent controls. Prior to buying a variable policy, be sure first to study any available literature, including the prospectus and current annual report.

In sum, a variable policy could provide your beneficiary with more

---

[6]Some mutual funds are now also selling variable life policies.

money than a fixed life policy. However, in return for the possibility of a larger final payment, you would pay greater yearly premiums. In my view, it is wiser to buy a fixed amount of insurance for a set price. The difference could then be placed directly in common stock. Otherwise, you are paying a middleman-cost by having the insurance company invest in growth securities.

In addition to the sizable administrative cost charged by insurance companies, their investment program might not coincide with your specific stock-market objective. Furthermore, the common-stock gain in your insurance policy may be subject to estate taxes. You should check this point carefully in doing your estate planning.

Keep in mind that variable policies will show remarkable differences in growth. Their success or failure will depend largely on the managerial skill and objectives of each insurance company. Look, for example, at the wide differences in the growth rates of mutual funds—even those with comparable objectives. In view of the fact that variable policies are so new, there is no track record to show which insurance firms have been most successful—another reason against selecting such a policy at this time. If you are interested in this type of investment, I suggest that you wait and see who comes out well in the next several years. In the meantime, you can be protected by investing in a term or group policy and putting the remainder in such growth areas as quality common stock, sound real estate or profitable hobbies.

SOCIAL SECURITY

WHO IS COVERED?

Social Security, like life insurance, is a form of protection. It protects you and your family against the risks of being stripped of income because of death, prolonged disability or retirement. In addition, about twenty-two million people aged sixty-five and over (nearly all of the nation's elderly population) can count on help in paying their doctor and hospital bills.

The Social Security Act was passed by Congress in 1935, in the midst of the depression. Its primary purpose was to provide a retirement income to people who had had money deducted from their paychecks for this purpose during their working years. This act has had many amendments over the years, and now the Social Security insurance system provides protection for millions—about nine out of ten of all working Americans. Although retirees receive the largest share of Social Security payments (over 50 percent), there are substantial amounts paid for survivor benefits, disability, and hospital benefits under Medicare.

The following cases indicate the broad coverage of Social Security today:

Mrs. _____ was left with five small children when her husband, a milkman, died of a heart attack at age twenty-nine. She will get monthly checks for herself and her children until they are eighteen, plus checks for each child aged eighteen to twenty-two who stays in school. And when Mrs. _____ is sixty, she will be eligible for widow's checks for herself. Altogether, the family may collect well over $100,000.

Or take Mrs. _____, whose husband, a garage mechanic, died at age twenty-seven in an automobile accident. They had three small children and were expecting a fourth. Mrs. _____ and her children may eventually get more than $115,000.

Each month a check goes to Mr. _____ of Hattiesburg, Mississippi, who was born on July 4, 102 years ago.

Another goes to a baby girl, born seven months after her twenty-one-year-old father was killed in an automobile accident. A third goes to a young widow, whose husband was killed in Vietnam, leaving her with a two-year-old boy. A fourth goes to Mr. and Mrs. _____ and eight of their children, because Mr. _____ has been in a hospital bed ever since he was hit by a stray bullet during a fishing trip. A fifth goes to nineteen-year-old triplets, whose father retired in 1958 and who are now enrolled in college. A sixth goes to a retired lawyer. A seventh goes to a ninety-seven-year-old gentleman, and it has been his sole source of income for the past thirty years.[7]

RECENT LEGISLATION

The year 1972 marked the passage of major amendments in the Social Security law. This new legislation brought greater protection and higher payments to millions of Americans beginning in 1973. The 1972 amendments provided for a 20 percent increase in Socal Security payments and automatic increases in cash benefits in succeeding years, to keep pace with increases in the cost of living. Listed below are other specific areas in which the recent amendments have been beneficial.

Disability

Thanks to the 1972 legislation, a person who became disabled before age twenty-two can receive childhood disability benefits if one of his parents is entitled to retirement or disability benefits or dies after working long enough

[7]*Social Security, What It Means to You,* p. 2. U.S. Department of Health, Education and Welfare.

under Social Security (see "work credits"). The new law also provides that monthly payments can be resumed if an adult who received childhood disability checks and then recovered becomes disabled again within seven years after his previous disability ended.

Although the new disability provision is an improvement over the former legislation, there is considerable criticism about the current coverage, because a person must have been disabled before age twenty-two in order to be eligible. Since tragic automobile accidents, for instance, occur daily on our highways, totally or partially disabling motorists and/or pedestrians, many people believe that any eligible party, regardless of age, who becomes disabled should be protected by Social Security.

Student Benefits

Starting in 1973, a full-time student's checks no longer stop when he reaches age twenty-two, but continue through the end of the quarter or semester in which his birthday occurs if he has not completed undergraduate requirements. If he attends a school that is not run on a semester or quarterly basis, checks continue until he completes his current course or for two months after the month he reaches age twenty-two, whichever comes first.

Benefits for Grandchildren

Children may now be eligible for Social Security benefits based on a grandparent's earnings if the natural parents are disabled or dead, and if the grandchildren are living with and/or supported by their grandparents.

Duration of Marriage in Accident Cases

A widow (or dependent widower) and stepchildren of a worker who died accidentally or in the line of duty while on active duty in the Armed Forces can now get survivor benefits regardless of the length of time the marriage lasted. Previously, the marriage must have lasted at least three months for any survivors to get benefits.

Benefit Increases for Widows

The benefit for a widow (or dependent widower) who starts getting benefits at age sixty-two or later can now range from 82½ percent to 100 percent of the husband or wife's full benefit, instead of being limited to 82½ percent as in the past. The survivor's benefit rate depends on the age at which he or she begins receiving benefits, as well as the benefits the deceased husband or wife would be getting if he or she were still alive.

Special Minimum Benefit

The 1972 legislation provides a special minimum benefit at retirement for people who worked under Social Security for more than twenty years. This law helps those who had a low income in their working years. The amount of the special minimum depends on the number of years of coverage.

Figuring Men's Benefits

Benefits for men who reach age sixty-two in 1975 or later are now figured the same way as they are for women. Under the new law, a man and woman who are the same age have equal benefits if they had equal earnings. The work credits required to qualify for benefits are now also similar for men and women.

Delayed-Retirement Credit

A worker who does not receive benefits before age sixty-five and who delays his retirement beyond age sixty-five will get a special credit that can mean a larger benefit. The credit adds to a worker's benefit 1 percent for each year (1/12 of 1 percent for each month) from age sixty-five to age seventy-two for which he did not get benefits. The credit applies only when a worker has earnings after December 1970. The increases became effective January 1973. Benefits of dependents or survivors are not increased.

The delayed-retirement benefit beyond age sixty-five has been criticized as not going far enough. At present, a person can work after sixty-five up to a certain dollar amount, and receive Social Security cash benefits. At age seventy-two, he can receive all his dollar benefits regardless of his income from work. It has been argued that every person who continues work beyond sixty-five should be entitled to receive all his cash retirement benefits at sixty-five if he so desires, regardless of his income from work. After all, it was his money that was put aside by the Social Security Administration for this purpose (a form of insurance protection). Why shouldn't payments be made to him at the time he desires to receive them? He may decide to accept the bonus of the delayed-retirement credit and wait until age seventy-two. But it should be his choice.

Other Improvements

The 1972 legislation also took constructive measures in regard to disability claims after death; new benefits for people disabled by blindness; benefits for divorced women; and wage credits for Japanese-Americans.

If you have any questions in these or any other areas pertaining to Social

Security, it is important to call your nearest Social Security office. Look in your phone book under "Social Security Administration." If you have no such office nearby, write to the Social Security Administration, U.S. Department of Health, Education and Welfare, Baltimore, Maryland 21201.

CASH BENEFITS

The higher your earnings (up to the current ceiling of $17,700), the higher your monthly Social Security benefits. A person who was under age sixty-five and disabled in 1976, for instance, might have received $223.20 per month if his average yearly earnings after 1950 amounted to $3,000. In contrast, if he had averaged $5,000, his payments would have been $304.50. A retired worker (aged sixty-five or older) would also be paid the $223.20 based upon $3,000 earnings, or $304.50 based upon $5,000 earnings.

HOW TO ESTIMATE YOUR SOCIAL SECURITY RETIREMENT CHECK

Your Social Security card bearing your Social Security number is the equivalent of a valuable insurance policy. During your term of employment, your employer deducts a specified amount from your salary which eventually makes you eligible for certain benefits. One of these benefits is the receipt of monthly payments upon retirement. The amount of the payments is dependent upon the earnings that you make while you are working.[8]

How can you make a rough estimate of what your retirement check will be? If your retirement is some years away, it's likely that your benefits will be higher than you estimate. This is because it is now guaranteed by law that Social Security benefits will be inflation-proof. Benefits will be increased automatically in future years to keep pace with changes in the cost of living. The first automatic increase took place on January 1, 1975.

Your benefit check could also vary from your estimate because your earnings in future years may not be exactly what you expect. When you apply for benefits at your Social Security office, they will figure the exact amount of your monthly check.

A retired worker can get full monthly checks at age sixty-five. So can his wife, age sixty-five or older, and his dependent children. Reduced payments can start as early as age sixty-two for a worker or his wife.

---

[8]Source of information in this section is U.S. Department of Health, Education and Welfare, Social Security Administration, DHEW Publication No. (SSA) 76-10047, November 1975: *Estimating Your Social Security Retirement Check.*

Work Credits

Before you get a Social Security retirement check, you need to have credit for a certain amount of work under Social Security. Table 17-1 shows how much credit you need:

TABLE 17-1   Credit for Work Under Social Security

If you reach 62 in	You need credit for this much work*
1978	6¾ years
1979	7
1980	7¼
1981	7½
1983	8
1987	9
1991 or later	10

*No one ever needs more than ten years of work.

If you stop working under Social Security before you have the amount of credit noted in the table above, you are not eligible for retirement benefits. But the credit you've earned will stay on your record, and you can add to it if you return to work in a job covered by Social Security. You can request a statement of your Social Security earnings at any time; request forms are available at all Social Security offices.

Estimating Your Benefits

By following the directions below, you can calculate the approximate sum you will receive from Social Security upon retirement.

Step 1. Your retirement check is based on your average earnings over a period of years. Based on the year you were born, pick the number of years you need to consider from Table 17-2. Write the number of years here ____.

Step 2. Fill in the worksheet (Table 17-3). Column A shows maximum earnings covered by Social Security. In Column B, list your earnings beginning with 1951. Write "O" for a year of no earnings. If you earned more than the maximum in any year, list only the maximum. Estimate your earnings for future years, including any years you plan to work past age sixty-five. Stop at the year before you retire.

TABLE 17-2 Data to Compute Retirement Income

Year you were born	Men	Women
1909	18 years	15 years
1910	19	16
1911	19	17
1912	19	18
1913	19	19
1914	20	20
1915	21	21
1916	22	22
1917	23	23
1918	24	24

TABLE 17-3 Worksheet

Year	A	B
1951	$3,600	$
1952	3,600	
1953	3,600	
1954	3,600	
1955	4,200	
1956	4,200	
1957	4,200	
1958	4,200	
1959	4,800	
1960	4,800	
1961	4,800	
1962	4,800	
1963	4,800	
1964	4,800	
1965	4,800	
1966	6,600	
1967	6,600	
1968	7,800	
1969	7,800	
1970	7,800	
1971	7,800	
1972	9,000	
1973	10,800	
1974	12,600	
1975	14,100	
1976	15,300	
1977	16,500	
1978	17,700	
1979	22,900	
1980	25,900*	TOTAL
TOTAL		$

*The maximum amount of annual earnings that count for Social Security will rise automatically in future years as earnings levels increase. Because of this, the base in 1981 and later may be higher than $25,900.

TABLE 17-4 Monthly Retirement Benefits

	For Workers				For Dependents[1]				
Average yearly earnings	Retire-ment at 65	at 64	at 63	at 62	Wife at 65 or child	Wife at 64	Wife at 63	Wife at 62	Family[2] benefits
$923 or less	$101.40	$94.70	$87.90	$81.20	$50.70	$46.50	$42.30	$38.10	$152.20
1,150	123.60	115.40	107.20	98.90	61.80	56.70	51.50	46.40	185.40
1,500	150.10	140.10	130.10	120.10	75.10	68.90	62.60	56.40	225.20
2,000	169.80	158.50	147.20	135.90	84.90	77.90	70.80	63.70	254.70
2,500	189.80	177.20	164.50	151.90	94.90	87.00	79.10	71.20	284.70
3,000	209.70	195.80	181.80	167.80	104.90	96.20	87.50	78.70	320.60
3,500	227.30	212.20	197.00	181.90	113.70	104.30	94.80	85.30	368.70
4,000	246.80	230.40	213.90	197.50	123.40	113.20	102.90	92.60	421.80
4,500	266.70	249.00	231.20	213.40	133.40	122.30	111.20	100.10	474.80
4,750	277.70	259.20	240.70	222.20	138.90	127.40	115.80	104.20	504.10
5,000	286.10	267.10	248.00	228.90	143.10	131.20	119.30	107.40	528.10
5,250	296.70	277.00	257.20	237.40	148.40	136.10	123.70	111.30	554.60
5,500	304.70	284.40	264.10	243.80	152.40	139.70	127.00	114.30	566.60
5,750	314.90	294.00	273.00	252.00	157.50	144.40	131.30	118.20	581.30
6,000	323.40	301.90	280.30	258.80	161.70	148.30	134.80	121.30	593.30
6,250	331.50	309.40	287.30	265.20	165.80	152.00	138.20	124.40	605.40
6,500	341.70	319.00	296.20	273.40	170.90	156.70	142.50	128.20	619.90
6,750	351.50	328.10	304.70	281.20	175.80	161.20	146.50	131.90	632.60
7,000	362.40	338.30	314.10	290.00	181.20	161.10	151.00	135.90	645.80
7,250	373.30	348.50	323.60	298.70	186.70	171.30	155.70	140.10	659.20
7,500	384.20	358.60	333.00	307.40	192.10	176.10	160.10	144.10	673.10
7,750	395.20	369.60	343.20	316.80	197.60	181.20	164.70	148.20	691.60
8,000	402.00	375.20	348.40	321.60	201.00	184.30	167.50	150.80	703.60

[1]If a woman is eligible for both a worker's benefit and a wife's benefit, the check actually payable is limited to the larger of the two.
[2]Worker 65 or older, wife under 65 and one or more children.

Step 3. Cross off your list the years of your lowest earnings, until the number of years left is the same as your answer to Step 1. (You may have to leave some years of "O" earnings on your list.)

Step 4. Add up the earnings for the years remaining on your list. Write this figure in the space marked TOTAL at the bottom of Table 17-4 and here: $____.

Step 5. Divide this total by the number posted for Step 1. The result is your average yearly earnings covered by Social Security. Write the figure here: $____.

Step 6. Consult the Monthly Retirement Benefits (Table 17-5). Under the heading "For Workers," find the average yearly-earnings figure closest to your own. Look over to the column listing your age at retirement to see approximately how much you can expect to get. Write the figure here: $____.

Step 7. If you have an eligible wife or child, or both, look under the heading "For Dependents" to determine approximately how much they will receive based on the same average yearly earnings you used to figure your own check. Write the amount of any dependents' benefits here: $____.

Step 8. Finally, add the figures posted for Steps 6 and 7 to see what your approximate total family retirement benefits will be under Social Security. Write the figure here: $____.

Maximum Benefits

Some people think that if they have consistently earned the maximum amount covered by Social Security, they will get the highest benefits shown on Table 17-3. This isn't so. The most a worker reaching age sixty-five in 1976 could have received was $387.30. This is because the maximum amount of earnings covered by Social Security was lower in past years than it is now. Those years of lower limits must be counted in with the higher limits of more recent years to figure your average earnings and thus the amount of your monthly retirement check.

SOCIAL SECURITY'S RISING COSTS

The additional benefits made available to Social Security recipients over the years have taken their toll in increased expenses. To cover these costs, workers' payments have been increased. This has been accomplished by increasing both the tax rate and the tax base.

In December 1977, Congress passed a Social Security funding bill that will more than triple payroll taxes for many workers by 1987. The following two tables provides a comparison between the old and current law.

TABLE 17-5 Salary Subject to Social Security Deductions

	Current Law	Old Law
Calendar Year	Salary Base	Salary Base
1977	$16,500	$16,500
1978	17,700	17,700
1979	22,900	18,900*
1980	25,900	20,400*
1981	29,700*	21,900*
1982	31,800*	23,400*
1983	33,900*	24,900*
1984	36,000*	26,400*
1985	38,100*	27,900*
1986	40,200*	29,400*
1987	42,600*	31,200*

*Estimated

TABLE 17-6 Social Security Contribution Rate (Employer-Employee, Each)

	Current Law	Old Law
Calendar Year	Tax Rate	Tax Rate
1977	5.85%	5.85%
1978	6.05	6.05
1979	6.13	6.05
1980	6.13	6.05
1981	6.65	6.30
1982	6.70	6.30
1983	6.70	6.30
1984	6.70	6.30
1985	7.05	6.30
1986	7.15	6.45
1987	7.15	6.45

Note that in the year 1977, the employee contributed 5.85 percent under the recent law. By 1987, this percentage increases from 5.85 to 7.15 percent. Let us assume that in 1977, a person earned $16,500. His Social Security payment for that year would have been $965.25. By 1987, a person who earns $42,600 would pay $3,045.90 (see Table 17-7). The employer must also pay into the Social Security system, in the same amount as that deducted from each employee.

The person who is self-employed must contribute a higher percentage of his earnings, as indicated in Table 17-7.

TABLE 17-7 Social Security Payroll Taxes for Workers

Current Law

Calendar Year	Wage Base	Tax
1977	$16,500	$ 965.25
1978	17,700	1,070.85
1979	22,900	1,403.77
1980	25,900	1,587.67
1981	29,700	1,975.05
1982	31,800	2,130.60
1983	33,900	2,271.30
1984	36,000	2,412.00
1985	38,100	2,686.05
1986	40,200	2,874.30
1987	42,600	3,045.90

SOCIAL SECURITY'S FUTURE

The fact that more people are living longer, with greater numbers receiving Social Security benefits, has resulted in the failure of the system to be self-supporting. When Social Security was first established, there were about twelve workers supporting one retiree. Today that base has been reduced over 60 percent. To partially compensate for this loss both the wage base ($16,500 in 1977) and the contribution rate (5.85 percent in 1977) have been increased markedly since 1935. The recent law will provide additional funds for Social Security needs, but is still not sufficient in the long run. Unless additional funds are obtained through such measures as imposing Social Security taxes on all earnings, and increasing the contribution rate, the system could go broke. I feel sure, however, that the U.S. Government would divert other revenue to assure that certain payments are made to all recipients who earned them. In my view, we can expect Social Security pensions to continue, to include cost-of-living increases, financed in part by higher payments from the working-age group. The federal government will make up any deficit by dipping into other funds.

18

CAR, PROPERTY, LIABILITY, ACCIDENT & HEALTH INSURANCE
(Including Medicare)

(continued on p. 312)

Most members of the work force can normally expect to have acquired a car, household property and family responsibilities within a reasonable period. With these acquisitions comes the need for adequate protection. The importance of appropriate life insurance was discussed in Chapter 17. This chapter will investigate the other components of a sound insurance program. The number of dollars to be invested in insurance coverage will, of course, vary with the individual.

Special attention will be devoted to the area of car insurance and the high, sometimes prohibitive, cost of automobile coverage for the young. We will also investigate the areas of property, accident and health insurance, including Medicare, stressing the importance of liability coverage in most insurance areas.

CAR INSURANCE: DETERMINING YOUR OBJECTIVE

Auto insurance permits a pooling of resources in order to transfer the burden of loss from an individual to a group that pays for this privilege. From a personal-finance standpoint, your objective should be to *make the minimum contribution for a policy with the maximum coverage.* This requires shopping around for the best rates and never accepting insurance proposals by an auto dealer without making valid comparisons. As we shall see, young people are paying high rates today and should examine with special care the types of companies available, coverage provided and net premiums.

TYPES OF INSURANCE COMPANIES

Stock vs. Mutual

There are two principal types of auto insurance companies: stock and mutual. A stock company, as the name implies, is owned by shareholders. Consequently, a portion of the profits generated by premiums goes to owners of stock, in the form of cash dividends. A mutual company belongs to the policyholders and distributes its net earnings through premium rebates, which can amount to as much as 50 percent. In addition to the regular mutual company, there are also a few that are "assessable,"—that is, when operating losses occur, members may be assessed additional amounts. Thus, although such mutuals may, at times, provide maximum savings to their policyholders, their rates can exceed those of standard mutuals thanks to assessments. It is difficult to estimate annual payments to an assessable mutual, because their rates have been known to increase more than 100 percent in a given year.

Selective Membership

Another type of auto insurance company deals with select membership. For example, the United Services Automobile Association restricts eligibility to certain military personnel. The Insurance Exchange of the Automobile Club of Southern California provides insurance only to members of its motor club.

TYPES OF AVAILABLE COVERAGE

There are six major categories of automobile-insurance coverage: bodily-injury liability; property-damage liability; medical payments; comprehensive (excluding collision); collision; and uninsured motorists. As we examine each category, remember that company terms vary. It is extremely important to read with care the fine print in a policy before buying it.

1. *Bodily-injury liability* insurance pays for injury, sickness or disease—including death resulting therefrom—imposed on others, for which the insured may be legally liable. This includes damages for health care and loss of services that may result from an accident involving the insured's automobile. It also protects the insured from claims or suits that are the result of an accident. It is particularly important to have adequate protection in this area in view of the high awards being rendered by the courts today. The difference in insurance cost between $10,000/$30,000 and $100,000/$300,000 bodily-injury coverage is relatively small for the significant additional security.

2. *Property-damage liability* protects the insured from financial loss due to injury to, or destruction of, the property of others. This protection would include damage to other cars, homes and buildings. It does not provide protection for destruction of your own vehicle.

3. *Medical coverage* pays all reasonable expenses incurred from within one year from the date of accident for necessary medical, surgical, X-ray and dental services. This coverage applies to the insured and his immediate family, whether they are riding in a car or walking. Passengers are usually covered if riding in the insured's car, but this is subject to the terms of the policy.

4. *Comprehensive coverage* protects the policyholder against loss caused by circumstances other than collision. It includes breakage of glass and loss caused by missiles, falling objects, fire, theft, windstorm, hail, water, flood, larceny and so on.

5. *Collision insurance* pays for loss to your own automobile or a nonowned vehicle and does not include other cars involved in an accident. This is the most expensive type of automobile insurance for complete coverage, and the majority of contracts are written with a deductible clause. This means that the insurance company agrees to pay only for the amount of each loss in excess of the established deduction. Most deductible clauses provide that the insurer pays the actual cash value less $50, $100 or $150. I personally believe that $100 deductible is sufficient for your vehicle in the event of collision.

6. *Uninsured-motorist coverage* protects the insured driver from the uninsured driver in the event of damages from bodily injury. Coverage extends to the policyholder and his immediate family, whether riding in a car or walking. This protection is desirable in view of the fact that the uninsured motorist may have little or no money or property.

Other special types of coverage may also be available, such as emergency road service.

INSURANCE RATES

Insurance rates vary depending upon several factors. Most states are divided into numerous territories for the purpose of determining rates. For example, a person living in Boston, Massachusetts, may pay twice as much for his automobile insurance as one living in a rural area of the same state. Other considerations include the type of vehicle; its use; and the age, sex, occupation and previous record of the driver.

Despite the continuing rise in insurance costs, there are ways to save money. Drivers who are free of accidents and traffic violations for a set period may have their insurance reduced as much as 25 percent. A person who owns two cars should have them both insured in the same policy, as this often permits a 20-percent discount. Some students have Dad include their car in his policy. That's great if you can swing it. All insurance companies offer some scheme by which you can economize and still have the necessary protection. Deductible insurance is one example.

It is important to list your car properly. A vehicle used for pleasure only is insured much more cheaply than one required for business. Your car agent may overlook this point. Keep in mind that the more expensive the policy, the more money the agent receives in commission.

Driver's training is another way to have rates discounted. Most companies reduce premiums by 10 percent if the insured has had recent driver's training. Also, some companies are giving discounts for students who have done well in their studies.

CHOOSING AN INSURANCE COMPANY

When you buy auto insurance, determine exactly what coverage you will need. Naturally, the overall cost of the policy is important, but selection of a fine company is paramount. In choosing a firm, check into its past history; reliability and financial stability have no substitutes. Some people have found out too late that their company does not possess the funds to pay its claims. In the past ten years, many companies accepting "high-risk" clients have become insolvent, leaving over $500 million in unpaid claims.[1]

---

[1] These "high-risk" insurers have been called "excess-premium writers" or "surplus lines."

A splendid way to make price comparisons was presented in a *Consumer Reports* article published some years ago. Its emphasis was that "pricing car insurance is a do-it-yourself project and a rewarding one."[2] The study on which the article was based indicated that by checking on prices charged by different companies, you could conceivably cut your insurance bill by more than 30 percent.

The importance of choosing your car-insurance company with care is illustrated by the following personal-case presentation made by one of my students in class.

The John Smith Case

Recently, three members of the "John Smith" family were involved in a serious accident in northern Illinois. The accident occurred at the intersection of two state routes. Despite a number of unanswered questions concerning the accident, the driver, Mr. Smith, was charged by the State Highway Patrol for failing to yield the right-of-way. Consequently, Mr. Smith was held responsible for all bodily injury and property damage at the scene of the accident. Of the three cars involved in the accident, two of them were "totaled." Three people were injured, fortunately none very seriously.

The worst news was yet to come. Less than twenty-four hours after the accident, Mr. Smith was informed by his insurance company that he was not covered. This was a real shock, since he had been paying premiums for six years. The insurance company claimed, however, that there had been a policy lapse. Mr. Smith argued that he had a record of sending a check for the amount due. Somehow this check had been lost, having never been received by the insurance company and therefore not cancelled.

The company stated that it had informed Mr. Smith of his policy lapse, although he had never received this notification. Neither of the two loan companies that financed the car was sent a lapse notice. Nevertheless, the insurance company claimed that it had a record that proved it had sent such information.

To further complicate the situation, Mr. Smith was advised that the other car he owned was fully insured; that both cars were insured on separate policies; and the policy that had lapsed was the car involved in the accident.

The student relating the John Smith story summed it up as follows:

This accident proved to be a very costly lesson. The insurance company did not possess the integrity Mr. Smith had expected. Equally important

---

[2]"Auto Insurance: The Price Factor." *Consumer Reports,* July 1970, p. 426.

is the negligence of the agent involved. There was no reason for the two cars to have been insured on separate policies, as this is more expensive. A responsible agent would have made sure that both cars were insured on one policy to save money. Furthermore, after the company informed the agent of the lapse, he should have checked as to why Smith was paying on one policy and not the other.

As a result of this unfortunate situation, Smith now has insurance with a more reliable company, but the total cost of damages and possible lawsuits must still be paid. It is absolutely necessary for the motorist to investigate a company and its history with care before he decides on an insurance policy, especially as regards their payment of claims. Smith isn't the first person to have been taken by an insurance outfit and I doubt that he will be the last.

ACCIDENT PROCEDURE

Assume that, like John Smith, you have an accident. What should you do? Above all, keep your cool. You should also consider taking the following steps, recommended by one firm. Most companies furnish similar guidelines but many of us fail to read them. It is recommended that such instructions be kept handy in the glove compartment of your car.

1. Call an ambulance for anyone seriously injured.
2. Get names and addresses of all persons in the other car, descriptions of cars and license numbers.
3. Be sure to obtain names and addresses of all witnesses.
4. Measure any skid marks made by either vehicle.
5. DO NOT ADMIT RESPONSIBILITY. Make no statement regarding the accident except to authorized claims representatives and the police.
6. Comply with state laws by filing the required Motor Vehicle Accident Report and send a copy to the Home Office.
7. DO NOT DISCLOSE YOUR POLICY LIMITS TO ANYONE.
8. Report the accident immediately. Failure to do so may jeopardize your insurance protection and may result in loss of your driving privileges.[3]

NO-FAULT INSURANCE

"I will not be blackmailed by an industry," stated Governor Francis Sargent of Massachusetts on August 13, 1970. The occasion was the signing of the No-Fault Insurance bill that, in effect, reduced auto premiums by 15 percent in his

---

[3]United Services Automobile Association. *Directory of Automobile Claims Representatives,* 1976-1977 edition, San Antonio, Texas.

state. According to the governor, the $400 billion insurance industry had exerted enormous pressure to prevent passage of the bill. As one young Bostonian put it earlier that year when queried on TV about the trend in insurance costs: "The way things are going, my premium would be about $1,000 a year on a new car, and I just can't afford those rates along with the monthly car payments."

The new law requires third-party auto insurance for all drivers and makes it mandatory for insurance companies to pay the initial $2,000 in accident claims at once, regardless of which driver is at fault.[4] Insurance companies responded promptly to the No-Fault bill, with three of the major firms ceasing to write policies in the state of Massachusetts. The governor indicated that he would have the state provide the coverage if the private companies failed to offer such protection.

General concern over various aspects of car insurance stimulated Congress to order a study by the Secretary of Transportation of the current system of liability protection. The findings stated that less than 50 percent of individuals seriously injured in auto accidents received any payment under the fault system of insurance. An article in a 1970 issue of *Consumer Reports* anticipated the concern of many drivers today:

> Automobile insurance companies make their living by selling financial security against accident losses. Yet this industry has managed to instill a sense of financial insecurity in the motoring public.
>
> Millions of policyholders are hard-pressed to pay ever-rising premiums. Car insurance rates have just about doubled in the past 20 years and continue to increase at an accelerating pace. Some people—especially young men—are being priced out of the market. Countless others risk having their car insurance priced out of reach with every claim filed against their policy.
>
> Millions of policyholders stand in peril of having their protection discontinued because their insurance company no longer wants to cover them. Car insurers have canceled or refused to renew the policies of 14 percent of all policyholders at some time in their lives. . . . 55 percent of policyholders have heard of other people whose policies were canceled or not renewed. Thus does anxiety in the motoring public spread like ripples around those directly involved.[5]

In the eight years since Governor Sargent established no-fault insurance in Massachusetts, thirty-one states have adopted some form of this new concept.

---

[4] No-fault is a system of car insurance in which the insured firm pays the policyholder for his own personal or bodily injury. It does not require proving the other person is responsible to collect.

[5] "Auto Insurance: The Quality Factor." *Consumer Reports*, June 1970, p. 332.

Furthermore, Congress has considered authorizing a no-fault auto insurance bill. The Hart-Magnuson Bill, S-354, passed only the Senate in May 1974. It was designed to allow four years for each state to pass a no-fault law, with a provision that S-354 would apply for any state not having its own no-fault law by then. Several other federal no-fault bills have been proposed, but these have failed. They meet strong opposition from trial lawyers, who make over a billion dollars annually from handling personal-liability cases.

It is important to remember that even with a no-fault program you need other car insurance—liability coverage for bodily injury, property damage and uninsured motorists. Reason: Most states with no-fault restrict the right to sue but they do not eliminate it. There is also considerable variation in the amount and type of coverage among the states. For example, Pennsylvania, Michigan and New Jersey have unlimited compulsory no-fault in contrast to Massachusetts, Virginia and South Dakota with a $2,000 limit.

CAR INSURANCE AND THE YOUNG DRIVER

The higher cost of car insurance for young people is worth special emphasis. It is recognized that young people have a greater probability of car accidents according to actuarial tables and should pay a higher rate. Nevertheless, in a number of cases, these rates have become prohibitive. The effect of such discrimination against young drivers has been brought home to me time and again in my classroom.

My students feel strongly that this attitude is unjust, because it forces them to turn to high-risk companies that charge exhorbitant rates. Those who cannot obtain such premium money must either give up driving or take the chance of operating a vehicle without coverage, thereby placing additional mental strain on the people involved and adding to the possibility of further accidents.

Indeed, during classroom discussions about car insurance my students, almost without exception, have had sad tales to tell. They are unanimous in the belief that protection is most needed during the learning years of driving—yet premiums are highest at this time, and "good" companies are apt to drop a young policyholder if he has one or two accidents. (An agency manager told me, "We do make exceptions, but what we shoot for are the best drivers who have a consistently clean slate. If a young driver is in trouble but his father carries plenty of other insurance with us, however, we might go along with him one more time. Let's face it, it's all dollars and cents with us.")

Driving, my students feel, improves with experience. Thus, more accidents should be expected from the younger-age group. To penalize youthful drivers so drastically, by revoking their insurance or making the rates exhorbitant, seems unreasonable. Furthermore, the number of accidents a young person has should not be the governing criterion for revoking insurance. Other considerations should be weighed, such as the person at fault and the number of years of experience. It was also pointed out that the person who pays premiums for, say, twenty years without making a single claim against the company gets a bum deal. He doesn't get the next ten years free, but goes right on paying the rising annual rates. Thus, whether drivers are accident-prone or accident-free, the insurance companies get the best of the deal.

The courageous action of the Massachusetts governor in signing the No-Fault Insurance bill, was applauded by the class, for they recognized that insurance firms have monumental financial resources for lobbying purposes at both the state and national levels. It seems only right that if private insurance firms cannot meet the legitimate needs of a group in our society, we should seek alternate solutions that make it a state and federal responsibility.

The class suggested that youthful auto insurers band together in order to make their positions understood and to obtain necessary auto insurance at fair rates.

PROPERTY INSURANCE

There are many kinds of property insurance available to meet your needs. We will examine the most common here. Keep in mind that terms will vary from company to company and that you can secure protection for almost any risk—provided you are willing to pay the price. (Take the case of earthquake insurance, for example. Few in the group whose homes were ravaged in the San Francisco area in 1957—the worst such quake since the 1906 disaster—were insured because of the high cost of coverage and the long period since the last time any substantial earthquake damage had been done. The charge for three years' coverage approximated $100 for a $20,000 home. However, this rate is predicated on a 5-percent deductible basis; the homeowner in this case would pay for the first $1,000 in earthquake damage. Hence, as one long-time resident of San Francisco put it: "This type of insurance is too expensive in relation to value received. I put these funds to work building security in stocks, bonds, land and pertinent insurance. My other investments are really a form of insurance.")

Most firms are delighted to build an insurance program especially tailored for you. It helps to know first what your requirements are, and no one can judge that better than you. Again, remember to seek out well-established companies that will provide you with the desired coverage and service at reasonable rates.

HOMEOWNERS' COVERAGE

Homeowners' policies and the comprehensive liability insurance (CPL) they include were discussed in detail in Chapter 13. It is worth noting here, however, that the special medical-payment and property-damage clauses that form an integral part of the CPL insurance do not necessarily require legal liability to be effective. The insured's obligation may be moral rather than legal. Payment under these clauses may be authorized by the insurance company without resorting to a court trial.

FLOOD INSURANCE

I would like to stress once more the importance of coverage against flood damage if you live in a flood-prone region. Refer to Chapter 13 for a rundown of existing legislation in this area as well as an explanation of types of available coverage.

BOATOWNER'S POLICY

This package provides "all-risks" of physical-loss protection for inboard or outboard motorboats and sailboats, including motors, attached and unattached equipment, accessories and boat trailers. The policy furnishes watercraft liability for bodily injury, property damage and medical payments. The watercraft liability is written only in conjunction with the "all-risks" of physical-loss coverage.

PERSONAL PROPERTY

There are two types of coverage you may obtain with respect to your personal possessions. First, the basic personal-property coverage protects against losses from fire, lightning, smoke, flood, earthquake, wind, explosion, certain transportation hazards and other related threats to personal property. The second personal-property policy protects against losses from such events as theft, burglary, larceny, holdup, riot, civil commotion, loss (including cash to $100) and breakage of gemstones. This protection, in combination with the basic, provides an "all-risk" floater protection.

For the past several years, the ratio of loss indemnities to premiums has been steadily rising because of increased claims, particularly in urban areas. This rise is aggravated by the increased rate of inflation in replacement costs, particularly in the case of valuables, so heavily insured under this coverage. As a result, premiums are increasing each year. A number of wealthy people no longer wear their jewels; they keep them in a safe-deposit box as a form of investment and wear imitations.

FARMOWNER'S POLICY

This policy insures eligible farm buildings and farm personal property, as well as your farm residence. It includes theft coverage, farmer's comprehensive personal liability and additional living-expense insurance in one complete package policy. If a farm fire policy is more suitable, it is possible to obtain such protection, and you may order liability coverage under a separate farmer's comprehensive personal-liability policy.

LIABILITY

Liability insurance protects the policyholder against claims arising from property damage and bodily injury. There are two categories of liability insurance: comprehensive and car. Homeownership and comprehensive liability insurance (CPL) were discussed in Chapter 13. Auto insurance liability coverage was discussed earlier in this chapter.

It is extremely important to have adequate liability coverage. As your assets grow you will need increasing protection. Keep in mind that you become a more desirable person to sue as you acquire more worldly treasure. In addition to general liability insurance you may wish a personal-catastrophe policy. This umbrella liability insurance extends your coverage to more situations. In order to buy an umbrella policy you must already have established minimum general liability insurance on your car and home. You can then obtain $1,000,000 or more of umbrella protection.

ACCIDENT AND HEALTH INSURANCE

There are a variety of accident and health policies available. Some furnish extensive coverage, and others provide auxiliary protection.

GROUP PLANS

A number of companies and government organizations offer group policies for health and/or accident. Whenever possible, it pays to take advantage of this protection. The rates are reasonable, and in some cases the organization pays for part of the cost.

The type of health coverage offered by one organization appears in Figure 18-1. Plan A lists the benefits under the major medical program. Note that the monthly rate for one person is $1.80 under the basic plan and $4.18 for major coverage. As a single person, going into your first job, you can't afford not to take advantage of such an opportunity. The family plan is also a bargain.

Figure 18-1 Two medical plans available under a group policy.

PLAN "A"

SCHEDULE OF BENEFITS
BASIC MEDICAL EXPENSE BENEFITS

Payments will be made for the expenses charged to you, UP TO the maximum amounts listed below. Unless otherwise specified the same amount applies to the Employee and each Dependent. Pregnancy expenses are paid under Pregnancy Benefits only.

HOSPITAL BENEFITS—Subject to the Deductible Amount of $25.00 (See Deductible Below)

Basic Room and Board Daily Rate—Employee	$	13.00
Dependent		12.00
Basic Maximum during any disability Employee		403.00
Dependent		372.00
Other Hospital Expenses—Maximum during any disability: 100% of such expense incurred up to.................... and then 75% of the next $2,000.00 of such expense incurred.	$	300.00

DEDUCTIBLE AMOUNT:
$25.00 during each period of hospital confinement as a registered bed patient, provided that if an insured person who has been released from a hospital and again becomes confined in a hospital for the same cause or causes or for complications therefrom within one month after the commencement of the first period of hospital confinement, the subsequent confinement shall be considered part of the earlier period of confinement.

AMBULANCE BENEFIT—Maximum amount per trip.	$	10.00

SURGICAL BENEFIT

Maximum for any procedure in accordance with Schedule of Operations form	GSS-3	
Maximum amount during any disability (see pages 22 and 23)	$	300.00

PLAN "A"

SCHEDULE OF BENEFITS—CONTINUED

IN-HOSPITAL DOCTOR CALL BENEFIT

Daily Medical Benefit	$	3.00
Maximum period during any disability.		50 days

SCHEDULED DIAGNOSTIC LABORATORY AND X-RAY BENEFIT

Maximum for any test or X-Ray examination as per Schedule (see pages 15 and 20).	GLX-1	
Maximum amount for any one accident	$	25.00
Maximum amount for all sickness during any period of twelve consecutive months.	$	25.00

PREGNANCY BENEFITS
Hospital and Non-Hospital Pregnancy Expense Benefit

Maximum Amount with hospital confinement	$	100.00
Maximum Amount without hospital confinement	$	50.00

OBSTETRICAL PROCEDURES—Maximum amount as listed below:

Miscarriage	$	25.00
Delivery of child or children		
(a) By Caesarean section.	$	100.00
(b) By any procedure other than Caesarean	$	50.00

NOTE: For female employees, the above PREGNANCY BENEFITS and OBSTETRICAL PROCEDURES are payable only if she had one or more dependents enrolled for Dependents insurance on the date her pregnancy commenced.

YOUR MONTHLY CONTRIBUTION FOR THE "PLAN A" BENEFITS.—Basic Plan

Individual Employee Only	Family Plan
$1.80	$6.80

PLAN "B"

SCHEDULE OF BENEFITS
MAJOR MEDICAL PLAN

Major Medical Expense Benefits but not the Pregnancy Expense Benefits included under Plan B are subject to the Deductible Amounts specified below. Plan B provides the same coverage for both an employee and his insured dependents.

"Dependents" are your spouse and your unmarried children, including step-children, and any children living with you and dependent upon you provided the first adoption papers have been approved by a court, who are at least 10 days but (a) less than 19 years of age, or (b) less than 23 years of age if attending an educational institution and depending upon you for financial support. Dependents who are in full-time military, naval or air service, and spouse who is eligible for insurance as an employee and has elected to be insured as an employee, are not eligible for dependent insurance.

PREGNANCY EXPENSE BENEFITS—Maximum Amount.	$	150.00

NOTE: For female employees, the above PREGNANCY BENEFITS are payable only if she had one or more dependents enrolled for dependent insurance on the date her pregnancy commenced, or if her husband was insured as an employee on the date her pregnancy commenced.

MAJOR MEDICAL EXPENSE BENEFITS
DEDUCTIBLE AMOUNT, during each calendar year with respect to each insured person.

	$	50.00

of Covered Expense incurred while the insured person is hospital confined as a registered bed patient, with a separate Deductible Amount of $100.00 applying to all other Covered Expense.

PERCENTAGE PAYABLE. For covered expenses incurred in excess of the Deductible:

a. Hospital room and board charges (but not to exceed $20.00 per day) and other charges made by the hospital on the days for which a charge is made for room and board, excluding expense incurred for professional, medical and surgical services, other than charges for the administration of anesthetics.

(1) 100% of the first $500.00 of such expenses
(2) 80% of such expenses in excess of $500.00

b. All other expenses not referred to in "a" above: 80% of such Covered Expenses.

Maximum Aggregate Amount, with respect to each insured person		$10,000.00

DEDUCTIBLE CARRY-OVER PERIOD: Last 90 days of each calendar year.

YOUR MONTHLY CONTRIBUTION FOR THE "PLAN B" BENEFITS.—Major Medical Care.

Individual Employee Only	Employee and One Dependent	Employee and Two or More Dependents
$1.18	$10.22	$11.00

Source: *Group Hospitalization Benefits for Faculty and Staff of LSU*, pp. 2–4.

323

If you enter the armed forces, you will find that they have a splendid health program. Your dependents can use the regular military facilities, when available, or obtain the services of a civilian physician. Under the "Uniformed Services Health Benefits Program," the patient is required to pay the first $50 of any medical expenses ($100 for a family), and after that pays only 20 percent of his annual medical costs. The government picks up the remainder.

Another example of an organization policy is the all-risk group accident insurance program. This coverage affords protection supplemental to the benefits provided under a group life-insurance plan, group disability plan, workmen's compensation or the employee's private insurance program. This particular insurance protection provides 24-hour, 365-day coverage against accidents at work, at home, at play and while traveling anywhere in the world. The cost is 52 cents per month per $10,000 of coverage.

There are a number of auxiliary health-coverage plans. For example, you can obtain protection for the differential between the 80 percent military coverage (under the Uniformed Services Program) and your total medical expenses. Similar additional insurance can be secured for those under Medicare. My own view is that, as a rule, the high cost is not worth the limited added coverage. However, if you have no group-type health or accident protection, I strongly advise you to obtain a good commercial policy that is available from Blue Cross/Blue Shield, private medical groups and insurance companies. The number of dental insurance policies has increased rapidly in recent years; over 15 million individuals are presently covered. You may wish to include such protection as part of your total health-care package.

MEDICARE

DETERMINING ELIGIBILITY

Medicare is a program of health insurance under Social Security set up to help millions of Americans age sixty-five and older, and many severely disabled people under sixty-five, to pay the high cost of health care.[6] In order to determine your health insurance needs at age sixty-five or older, it is essential that you be familiar with the major provisions of Medicare. Although virtually all people aged sixty-five or older are eligible for Medicare benefits, it also covers disabled people who have been getting Social Security for two years or more and people insured under Social Security who need dialysis treatment or a kidney transplant because of chronic kidney disease. Wives, husbands or

---

[6]Sources: *Your Medicare Handbook* and *A Brief Explanation of Medicare* by U.S. Department of Health, Education and Welfare, current editions.

children of insured people may also be eligible if they need kidney dialysis or a transplant.

To find out whether or not you are entitled to Medicare, and to make sure that you get full Medicare protection starting with the month you reach age sixty-five, check with your Social Security office two or three months before your sixty-fifth birthday. If you are not receiving monthly Social Security checks, you should be contacted by mail a few months before you are sixty-five. If you are a disabled person who has been receiving Social Security disability benefits for two years or more, you will get hospital insurance automatically. You will receive information about Medicare in the mail and need do nothing now.

THE TWO ASPECTS OF MEDICARE

There are two phases to Medicare—hospital and medical insurance. The hospital-insurance phase helps pay for the care you receive as a patient in a hospital and for certain follow-up care after you leave the hospital. The medical insurance phase helps pay for your doctor's services, outpatient hospital services and many other medical items and services not covered under hospital insurance.

Hospital Insurance Protection

Everyone aged sixty-five or older who is entitled to monthly Social Security or railroad-retirement benefits gets hospital insurance automatically without paying monthly premiums. You don't actually have to retire to get hospital insurance protection; even if you keep working after you are sixty-five, you will receive this protection if you have worked long enough under Social Security or railroad retirement. Table 18-1 shows how many quarters of coverage are needed for hospital insurance:

TABLE 18-1   Relationship of Work Quarters Necessary to Hospital Insurance and Age

Year you reach 65	Quarters of coverage needed*
1978	24
1979	25
1980	26
.	.
.	,
.	.
1993	39
1994 or later	40

*No one ever needs more than 40 quarters of coverage. The coverage needed increases yearly by one until the maximum of 40. In general, you get credit for quarters of coverage based on wages in increments of $250. A person receives a maximum of four quarters credit annually if he receives $1000, or more, any time during the year. If you are paid wages of $250 (but less than $500) during the year, you would receive one quarter of coverage.

People 65 or older who are not automatically entitled to hospital insurance can buy this protection for a monthly premium of thirty-three dollars. Coverage can begin no earlier than the month you are sixty-five. To buy hospital insurance, you will also have to apply for it and pay the monthly premium for medical insurance.

Hospital Insurance Benefits

Your hospital insurance helps pay the cost of medically necessary covered services for the following care:

1. Up to 90 days of inpatient care in any participating hospital in each benefit period.[7] For the first 60 days, it pays for all covered services after the first seventy-two dollars. For the 61st day through the 90th day, it pays for all covered services except for eighteen dollars a day. Care in a psychiatric hospital has a lifetime benefit limit of 190 days.
2. A "lifetime reserve" of sixty additional inpatient hospital days. You can use these extra days if you ever need more than ninety days of hospital care in any benefit period. Each lifetime reserve day you use permanently reduces the total number of reserve days you have left. For each of these additional days you use, hospital insurance pays for all covered services except for thirty-six dollars a day.
3. Up to 100 days of care in each benefit period in a participating skilled nursing facility—a specially qualified facility which is staffed and equipped to furnish skilled nursing care or rehabilitation care and many related health services. Hospital insurance pays for all covered services for the first twenty days and all but nine dollars a day for up to 80 more days, but only if:
   a. your medical needs require daily skilled nursing or rehabilitation care;
   b. a doctor determines that you need extended care and orders your care;
   c. you have been in a participating (or otherwise qualified) hospital for at least three days in a row before your admission;
   d. you are admitted generally within fourteen days after you leave the hospital; and
   e. you are admitted for further treatment of a condition for which you were treated in the hospital.
4. Up to 100 home health "visits" from a participating home-health agency for each benefit period, but only if:
   a. the continuing care you need includes part-time skilled nursing care or physical or speech therapy;

[7]A "benefit period" begins the first time you enter a hospital after your hospital insurance starts. It ends after you have not been an inpatient for sixty days in a row in any hospital or in any facility that mainly provides skilled nursing care.

b. you are confined to your home;
c. you were in a participating (or otherwise qualified) hospital for at least three days in a row;
d. a doctor determines that you need home health care and sets up a home health plan for you within fourteen days after your discharge from the hospital or a participating skilled nursing facility; and
e. the home health care is for further treatment of a condition for which you received services as a bed patient in the hospital or skilled nursing facility.

Services Covered by Hospital Insurance

Covered services in a hospital or skilled nursing facility include the cost of room and meals (including special diets) in semiprivate accommodations (two to four beds), regular nursing services and services in an intensive-care unit of a hospital. They also include the cost of drugs, supplies, appliances, equipment and any other services ordinarily furnished to inpatients of a hospital or skilled nursing facility in which the insured receives treatment.

Services Not Covered by Hospital Insurance

Hospital insurance is basic protection against the high cost of illness after you are sixty-five or while you are severely disabled, but it will not pay all of your health-care bills. No payment will be made for:

1. Doctor bills. (They are, however, covered if you have medical insurance.)
2. Private-duty nurses.
3. Cost of the first three pints of blood needed during a benefit period while you are an inpatient in a hospital or skilled nursing facility.
4. Convenience items requested by you, such as a telephone or television set in your room.
5. Care a patient may get in a hospital or skilled nursing facility when the main reason for the patient's admission or stay is his or her need for help with such things as bathing, eating, dressing, walking or taking medicine at the right time.

Coverage of Hospital Services Outside the United States

Payment will usually be made under Medicare for services only in the fifty states, the District of Columbia, Puerto Rico, the Virgin Islands, Guam and American Samoa. However, under the following conditions, payment[8] will also be made for certain services outside the United States:

[8]Whenever feasible, you should check prior to entry, on the amount of payment that will be made by hospital insurance for services outside the U.S.

1. If a foreign hospital is closer to your home than the nearest U.S. hospital which can provide the care you need, hospital insurance will help pay for the covered services you receive in the foreign hospital.

2. If you are in the United States when an emergency occurs and a foreign hospital is closer than the nearest U.S. hospital which could provide the emergency care you need, hospital insurance can help pay for the emergency care.

3. If you become ill or are injured while traveling through Canada between Alaska and another state, hospital insurance can help pay for inpatient care in a Canadian hospital.

Financing of Hospital Insurance

The hospital-insurance aspect of Medicare is financed by special contributions from employees, their employers and self-employed people. Each group pays the same rate. The contribution rate is 0.9 percent of the first $14,100 of yearly earnings for 1975.

Financing of Medical Insurance

Medical insurance is financed through monthly premiums paid by the insured party and by payments from the federal government which by law must cover at least one-half the cost of the total program. Premium amounts are reviewed each year to ensure that the program remains on a pay-as-you-go basis.

A 1973 change in the law, however, limits future increases in your medical-insurance premium. Even if program costs go up because of higher charges for medical services, your premium cannot be increased by more than the percentage of any general Social Security benefit increase since the last premium amount was established. If your premium plus the equal amount paid by the government is not sufficient to keep the program financially sound, the additional amount will be paid from general revenues.

The present basic premium is $6.70 a month plus 10 percent for each twelve-month period a person could have been enrolled for medical insurance but was not.

Medical Insurance Benefits

Medical insurance will help pay for the following services:

1. Physicians' services anywhere in the United States—in the doctor's office, the hospital, your home or elsewhere—including medical supplies usually furnished by a doctor in his office, services of his office nurse and drugs he administers as part of his treatment which you cannot administer yourself. There is a limit on payment for

covered psychiatric services furnished outside a hospital. Physicians' services outside the United States are covered only if they are furnished in connection with covered care in a foreign hospital.

2. Outpatient hospital services in an emergency room or an outpatient clinic of a hospital both for diagnosis and treatment.

3. Up to 100 home health "visits" each calender year, but only if:
   a. you need part-time skilled nursing care or physical or speech therapy services;
   b. you are confined to your home;
   c. a doctor determines that you need home health care;
   d. a doctor sets up and periodically reviews the plan for home health care;
   e. the home health agency is participating in Medicare.
   These visits are in addition to the posthospital visits you receive if you have hospital insurance.

4. Outpatient physical therapy and speech pathology services—whether or not you are homebound—furnished under supervision of participating hospitals, skilled nursing facilities or home health agencies; or approved clinics, rehabilitation agencies or public health agencies under a plan established and periodically reviewed by a doctor.

5. A number of other medical and health services prescribed by your doctor such as diagnostic services; X-ray or other radiation treatments; surgical dressings, splints, casts, braces; artificial limbs and eyes; certain colostomy-care supplies; and rental or purchase of durable medical equipment such as a wheelchair or oxygen equipment for use in your home.

6. Certain ambulance services.

7. Certain services by chiropractors.

8. Home and office services by independent physical therapists with certain payment limitations.

Services Covered by Medical Insurance

Each year, as soon as your covered medical expenses go over sixty dollars (the annual deductible), medical insurance will pay 80 percent of the "reasonable charges"[9] you incur for all covered services during the rest of the year regardless of the number of bills you have.

There are four exceptions to this general rule:

1. Laboratory and radiology services by doctors while you are a bed patient in a hospital are paid—without your meeting the sixty-dollar deductible—at 100 percent of the "reasonable charge."

[9]"Reasonable charges" are determined by the Medicare carrier—the organization selected by the Social Security Administration to handle medical-insurance claims in the area where you receive services.

2. Home health services are covered at 100 percent after the sixty-dollar annual deductible.
3. Payment for services of independent physical therapists is limited to a maximum of eighty dollars a year.

Services Not Covered by Medical Insurance

Medical insurance does not cover certain services or supplies. Among these are:

1. Routine physical checkups.
2. Prescription drugs and patent medicines.
3. Glasses and eye examinations to fit glasses.
4. Hearing aids.
5. Immunizations.
6. Dentures and routine dental care.
7. Orthopedic shoes.
8. Personal-comfort items.
9. The first three pints of blood you receive in each calendar year.

Sources of Information on Medicare

Call any Social Security office for more detailed information about Medicare or any other form of Social Security program. I recommend that you ask for a copy of *Your Medicare Handbook*. It provides information on the various aspects of Medicare, including how to submit medical-insurance claims.

Part Five

FIXED-INCOME INVESTMENTS

This fifth section looks at how to invest money wisely in various types of bonds and other sources that provide a fixed rate of return. For the past few years it has been possible to receive historically high interest by purchasing bonds from some of our safest institutions. A wise money manager should weigh opportunities in fixed-income instruments against such other purchases as stocks, real estate, hobbies, commodities and investment companies. Good timing is essential in creating an effective portfolio. This means buying the appropriate security at the time when you can get a good deal. To accomplish this requires an understanding of *all* investment opportunities available. Therefore, I suggest reading Part Six and reviewing Chapters 1 and 2 before settling on an investment program.

19

BANKS, SAVINGS & LOAN ASSOCIATIONS, CREDIT UNIONS & THE MONEY MARKET

(continued on p. 334)

IMPORTANCE OF CASH RESERVES

"1 can't believe I could have been so stupid. Here I was laid off as a result of the energy crisis! I had thought my job was secure—my company had spoken glowingly of our future together—so I had nothing put aside for an emergency."

This grim tale was echoed many times during 1974–1976, when unemployment reached the 9-percent level. Both white- and blue-collar workers were hard hit, sometimes with disastrous results. Many families, forced into heavy debt at high interest costs, learned too late about the importance of cash reserves.

WHAT ARE CASH RESERVES?

A cash reserve is money saved that is immediately obtainable in the event you need it. This chapter will examine the sources through which you can effectively build up such funds.

I use the word "effectively" because cash in a mattress does not provide an effective buildup, nor does money stowed away in a safe-deposit box at a bank. The box provides maximum safety, since you can get those same dollars quickly; but this money draws no interest (income) and a fee is being paid for the use of the box. Furthermore, if we accept the long-term trend as being inflationary, then the dollars in the safe-deposit box are *not* completely safe, since their future buying power will diminish rather than grow.

If safety of principal is the first objective, there are better choices than hoarding dollars. These alternatives include putting your funds into banks, savings and loan associations, credit unions and the money market. During the course of this chapter we will examine each of these alternatives in turn. In every instance, you will be putting your money to work. Benjamin Franklin expressed it this way: "Money makes money, and the money money makes, makes more money." To support his concept, he bequeathed $5,000 in 1791 to the citizens of Boston, with the understanding that it be allowed to accumulate interest for one hundred years. A century later, the $5,000 had increased to $311,000.

How Large Should Your Cash Reserve Be?

The amount to be placed in the cash reserve depends on individual requirements and will therefore fluctuate. Normally, I suggest that the reserve comprise four months' salary. This sum can be lowered for those with no family requirements or heavy expenditures, while a larger amount may be needed by persons with large families, home-purchase plans and other responsibilities. As noted above, the purpose of a cash reserve is to provide funds when you need them. Check on any restrictions that may be imposed in the event that you want the money immediately.

SELECTING THE APPROPRIATE FINANCIAL INSTITUTION

Never sacrifice safety of principal for a small differential in interest. Be sure to place your money in banks, savings and loan associations and credit unions that have good track records. There is no substitute for long-term success in the areas of growth, profit and sound management. But most important, how is the organization in question currently doing and how can it be expected to do in the future, based on present observations? Answering these questions requires your frequent reappraisal of the institutions in which you have placed cash reserves. (The case of the Penn Central Transportation Corporation, whose demise is discussed in Chapter 22, exemplifies the need to follow investments closely.)

"RULE OF 72"

A simple method of measuring how rapidly your money grows at a given rate of interest is called the "Rule of 72." By dividing the rate of return into 72, you will obtain the number of years required to double your money at that rate. Savings at 4 percent double in eighteen years ($72 \div 4 = 18$). Similarly, savings at 6 percent will be worth twice as much in twelve years. These figures pertain to interest compounded annually; if your bank compounds interest on savings accounts semiannually or quarterly, doubling your money will take a shorter period of time. This points up the value of making your money work hard for you.

　　　Let us now turn to the various savings media that may provide you with an effective buildup of cash reserves, remembering that diversification of funds into a variety of good investments is the key to sound financial management. After you meet insurance requirements, cash reserves should be the first line of dollar defense in the development of a diversified portfolio, and those reserves should be established in the following sequence: 1) checking account; 2) savings account in a bank, savings and loan association or credit union.

BANKS

PURPOSE

Banks furnish a variety of services. You must be familiar with these services in order to use them to your advantage. Like other businesses, banks vary from strong financial institutions to those on the brink of bankruptcy. It is essential to select a well-established commercial bank that is a member of the Federal Deposit Insurance Corporation (FDIC) discussed below. Services might include safe-deposit boxes, checking and savings accounts, certified checks, bank drafts, money orders, a variety of loans, trust and estate management, financial advice, coins and currency for public use, foreign-exchange information, U.S. savings bonds, credit cards and travel aid. If you are moving to another community, your bank can provide a helpful letter of introduction.

ROLE OF THE FEDERAL DEPOSIT INSURANCE CORPORATION (FDIC)

Every account in member banks of the FDIC up to $40,000 is insured. "The Federal Deposit Insurance Corporation insures only deposits in national and most state banks, including commercial and mutual savings banks. Insured banks are required to display the official FDIC sign at each teller's window or station."[1]

The FDIC protects bank depositors as follows:

Each bank approved for deposit insurance must meet high standards. Adherence to these standards is determined regularly through bank examinations by federal or state agencies. If, despite these precautions, an insured bank gets into financial difficulties and must be closed for purposes of liquidation, the Federal Deposit Insurance Corporation is on hand promptly with cash to protect the depositors. The Corporation usually begins payment to the depositors within ten days after the date of final closing.[2]

It is interesting to note that the FDIC insures against only the closing of a bank. The leaflet quoted above poses the question, "Does the insurance protection afforded by the Corporation extend to losses sustained by depositors in any fashion other than through the closing of an insured bank?" The answer: "No."[3]

BANKS AND THE FEDERAL RESERVE SYSTEM (FRS)

To further ensure the safety of your deposits, I recommend that you choose a bank that belongs to the Federal Reserve System (FRS).

The FRS was organized in 1913 under the Federal Reserve Act, whose stated purpose included ". . . [establishing] a more effective supervision of banking in the United States. . . ." Much has been accomplished since that date

[1]*Your Insured Deposit,* leaflet provided by the Federal Deposit Insurance Corporation, 550 17th Street, N.W., Washington, D.C. 20429, p. 2.
[2]Ibid., p. 2.
[3]Ibid., p. 3.

to improve the banking environment. In 1975 there were nearly 6,000 member banks. Top policy emanates from the Board of Governors of the Federal Reserve System in Washington, D.C. There are twelve Federal Reserve Banks under Washington's supervision.

Bank membership, obligations and reserves are highlighted in the following Federal Reserve publication:

> All national banks in the United States are required to be members of the System, while state banks are admitted to membership upon application if they meet certain requirements. On December 31, 1973, there were 13,700 commercial banks in the country, of which 5,800 were member banks. Although the member banks accounted for only 42 percent of the total number of commercial banks, they held approximately 80 percent of total commercial bank deposits.
>
> Member banks assume certain obligations. They become subject to numerous safeguarding provisions of the Federal Reserve Act, among which are those pertaining to affiliations with securities and investment companies, interlocking directorates, removal of directors and officers because of unsafe or unsound practices, payment of interest on deposits, and branch bank relations. State bank members are subject to examination and supervision by the Federal Reserve System.
>
> Member banks also must keep reserves, in cash or on deposit with their Reserve Bank, equal to certain proportions of their various types of deposits. They are also required to subscribe to the capital of the Federal Reserve Bank of their district in an amount equal to 6 percent of their capital and surplus.[4]

CHECKING ACCOUNTS

A checking account can be a valuable financial tool. Put to work properly, it can save you time and money. Ineffectively employed, it can be expensive and cause embarrassment because of checks returned marked "Insufficient" Funds." A regular checking account draws no interest. Therefore, it is desirable to keep your balance at a minimum consistent with monthly expenses. Whenever feasible, I suggest that your take-home pay be sent to the bank for deposit to your checking account.

Beware of service charges. After one of my lectures to a municipal government society, the wife of a member told me that she was paying 15 cents a check on an average balance of $50 per month. Each month she cashed approximately ten checks averaging $5 each. Her charge for this service was $1.50 a month. Thus, she was paying 36 percent a year for the privilege of having this small account. By maintaining a minimum monthly balance, she

---

[4]*The Federal Reserve System,* pamphlet prepared by the Federal Reserve Bank of Atlanta, Sixth Federal Reserve District.

could have eliminated this service charge. Some banks, for example, cash up to ten checks free of charge, as long as a minimum balance of $100 is maintained at any time during the month. On the assumption that the $100 could be invested at 5 percent, the lady in question would save 31 percent annually by keeping a minimum balance in a checking account in such a bank.

Shop around to find a well-established bank that will give you the best service for the lowest price. For example, in contrast to the bank that allows up to ten checks per month free with a minimum balance of $100, another institution may required $700 minimum balance for a comparable number of checks.

Free Checking Accounts

The current era of money shortage finds banks aggessively using new means to attract deposits, including the offer of free checking accounts. According to a *Wall Street Journal* report:

> Summit & Elizabeth Trust Co., a $175 million bank based in Summit, New Jersey, for instance, offers a free checking account to anyone who requests and qualifies for a $400 to $5,500 overdraft, or standby, line of credit. And the standby line goes to anyone judged credit-worthy. Sterling National Bank & Trust Co., New York, tries a different tack. It will give a free account to anyone depositing $1,000 or more into one of four types of savings accounts it offers.[5]

The article concludes with another example to support the thesis that the rich get richer:

> Lawyers and accountants often don't have to go to such lengths. Banks frequently extend free checking-account services to them regardless of the size of their balances, in the hope of profiting from the client business these professionals may bring in. Bankers concede reluctantly that some major corporate executives also wheedle a free checking account for themselves on the same basis.[6]

In our city, several banks cash an unlimited number of checks at no charge to those persons maintaining a $300 minimum balance. My bank has a $1,000 minimum, and I asked the branch manager why he wasn't competitive. He replied, "You didn't question the higher figure. We don't announce it, but to be competitive I can give you the same three-hundred-dollar minimum."

---

[5]"Free Checking by Banks Holds Some Pitfalls for Consumers." *The Wall Street Journal,* July 17, 1970, p. 15.
[6]Ibid.

Interest-Bearing Checking Accounts

A recent development in the checking-account arena is an arrangement whereby you can receive interest on your balance and draw "cheques" against the entire amount. When I questioned the president of my bank about this arrangement, he replied, "Your money should be safe since the bank you cite is a member of the FDIC. However, as members of the Federal Reserve System we are not permitted to pay interest on checking accounts."

Effective January 1, 1974, Congress authorized two states, Massachusetts and New Hampshire, to offer interest-bearing checking accounts. These accounts are known as "negotiable orders or withdrawal" (NOW) accounts, and are available at commercial banks, savings and loan associations and mutual savings banks in those states. The federal banking agencies set a 5-percent interest-rate ceiling on these accounts. You may wish to write congressmen and senators from your state recommending that they vote to authorize all financial institutions throughout the United States to pay interest on checking accounts.

Checks can be legally written in a variety of formats, as long as they inform the bank whom to pay and the amount to be paid, and include the genuine signature of the depositor.

SAVINGS ACCOUNTS

The second area in which banks provide a means to build an effective cash reserve is through a variety of savings plans. In 1976, commercial banks' passbook rates varied from 5 to 5½ percent, depending on the type of account and the locality. On large amounts, banks in 1974 issued generous certificates of deposit (CDs).[7] CDs of three-to-six month duration were quoted at 12 percent for amounts of $100,000 or more. However, money rates fell markedly by 1977 and at this writing top rates paid by major banks on CDs of six months' duration are only bringing buyers 5.6 percent. In contrast, smaller certificates of six-year duration were available with a $1,000 minimum, and commercial banks were permitted to pay up to 7½ percent on them if they were held for six years.[8] One local bank, however, was paying only 6½ percent on the small CDs of 2½- to 4-year maturity. On thirty- to eighty-nine-day certificates, the interest rate quoted was 5 percent.

It was apparent that the high short-term rates in 1974 gave the large investor an opportunity to make a lot of money. For a short time, in 1973, it had looked as if the monetary authorities were going to give people with limited

---

[7]A document containing a promise by a financial institution to pay the depositor the amount of money placed in the institution with interest at a fixed rate on specified dates.

[8]Savings banks were authorized to pay ¼ of 1 percent higher (7¾ percent) than commercial banks.

funds a fair break in the money market. At that time, the Federal Reserve Board, Federal Deposit Insurance Corporation and Federal Home Loan Bank Board permitted savings banks, savings and loan associations and commercial banks to remove all ceilings on CDs with a face value of at least $1,000, falling due in not less than four years. This act gave people of limited means an opportunity to buy CDs at yields from 8 to 10 percent. They invested hundreds of millions, primarily by withdrawing funds from conventional savings banks and savings and loan accounts. But this fair deal was short-lived. A *Barron's* editorial commented as follows:

> Faced with a loss of deposits (albeit on a smaller scale relative to total resources than in previous periods—1969–70 and 1966—of disintermediation), savings and loan associations and savings banks swung into action. In recent weeks, according to the *American Banker,* "Members of the savings and loan industry have been bombarding Congress with letters, telephone calls and telegrams urging adoption limits on 'wild card' savings certificates. The latter sped through the Senate Monday night [October 1] and the House on Tuesday [October 2]." Last week the FHLBB, FDIC and Fed moved to comply. For commercial banks they set a ceiling rate of 7¼%; for savings banks and savings and loan associations, one of 7½%. They also listed a previously imposed restriction limiting the issuance of such certificates to 5%–10% of an institution's assets.
>
> Score a point for the federal banking agencies, which had the wisdom in early July to scrap the ceilings, and then, under duress so to speak, put them high enough to keep the damage to a minimum. But three jeers for Congress, the lower chamber of which, out of a total membership of 435, boasts exactly 107 (including nine on the House Banking and Currency Committee) with what the *Congressional Quarterly* describes as "an interest—usually stock ownership—in banks, savings and loans or bank holding companies." Whether or not because of such close ties, the lawmakers handled the issue with what can only be called indecent speed. No committee hearings were held and no witnesses were called. In the upper chamber, where a colleague's birthday can elicit congratulations covering a score or more pages in the *Congressional Record,* Senate Joint Resolution 160 elicited comment—all, with fine bipartisanship, favorable—from precisely three solons. House debate consumed no more than an hour or so. Without further ado, or a final tally of the votes, both chambers overwhelmingly gave their assent.
>
> To judge by the *Record,* only one member of Congress, Rep. John H. Rousselot (R., Calif.), had the good sense to demur. Here is what he told his colleagues: "My major concern about this legislation is that we do not know the total impact. There were no hearings in the Senate. We had no hearings in the Committee on Banking and Currency in the House. We ran it through in 20 minutes today. I tried to get some time to ask some questions, but I was denied the opportunity, which I believe was unfair. This was not unanimously passed by the committee. The vote was taken by voice.

"The problem is that once again we are legislating in the dark. . . . Several of my colleagues have said, 'John, do not get excited. We will just pass this and show them we are trying to do something.' That kind of action is deceitful. I believe that is absolutely why the Congress gets a reputation of not knowing what it is doing. I believe it is wrong to legislate that way.

"Some day we may learn the lesson of allowing the free marketplace to make the final decisions, rather than inserting the Federal Government into the breach." Second the motion.[9]

This action of Congress, in ordering the setting of interest-rate limits, again points up the need for a powerful lobbying force in Washington that looks to the interest of the consumer (see Chapter 3). We will examine the need for consumer protection in the area of savings institutions at the end of the chapter.

Types of Savings Accounts

After acquisition of a minimum-balance checking account, investment in interest-bearing savings accounts is wise. Banks are delighted to open such accounts for you. Normally, you must start with a $5 minimum deposit. Interest is usually paid quarterly or semiannually. You make withdrawals as needed, but those made before due dates usually lose all interest. For example, if interest is paid on January 1 and July of each year, and the depositor invested $500 in a savings account on January 25 and withdrew it on June 20 of the same year, he would receive back only the $500 deposited. Some savings institutions, however, do pay interest from date of deposit to date of withdrawal.

The regular passbook interest rate in our community at this writing is 5 percent. There is a Gold Star Pass Book account that pays 5½ percent, but it carries definite restrictions to go along with the extra percent, including, among others, a minimum initial deposit of at least $100. Investigate the special possibilities in your neighborhood and read a copy of the rules before making your decision as to a regular or a special account.

Most banks have Christmas savings plans. But check such schemes carefully; they may be fine for the bank but costly for you. Banks spend a lot of money advertising the advantage of saving weekly so that you will have a nice nest egg for Christmas shopping; one bank even offers a tiny cookbook to such savers. But these plans often pay no interest. However, in this era of tight money, some banks are now offering to pay the going rate of bank interest on Christmas savings plans.

Although there is usually no charge for keeping money in a savings account, there are exceptions. One of these involved a Midwest bank, located

---

[9]"No More Wild Cards: Congress Has Dealt Savers out of the Money Game." *Barron's,* October 22, 1973, p. 7.

within walking distance of a university, which has a large percentage of student accounts. Students were wisely using their savings accounts like checking accounts by making only small withdrawals to meet their expenses. This caused the local bank to put a twenty-five-cent charge on all savings-account withdrawals numbering over six in any one interest period. In some cases such action could result in a high interest charge in relation to the amount deposited, provoking serious protest.

SAVINGS AND LOAN ASSOCIATIONS

PURPOSE

Savings and Loan (S and L) associations are privately owned financial organizations administered by a board of directors. They provide loans for repairs, construction, purchasing or financing of homes and other real estate. In

Figure 19-1 Balance sheet, Greater New Orleans Homestead Association.

ASSETS

First Mortgage Loans	$ 78,803,715.13
Home Improvement Loans and Other Loans	2,286,486.83
Loans on Savings Accounts	1,043,445.91
Cash on Hand and in Banks	325,330.31
U.S. Government and Agency Obligations	2,757,870.00
Stock in Federal Home Loan Bank	672,100.00
Prepaid Federal Insurance Premiums	140,327.49
GNMA & FHLMC Investments	2,490,351.13
Other Investments	4,740,000.00
Bldg., Leasehold, Furn. and Fix	423,499.99
G.N.O. Consumer Loans	659,554.29
Other Assets	469,342.98
	94,812,024.06

LIABILITIES

Savings Accounts	86,873,919.32
Advances from Federal Home Loan Bank	238,650.00
Loans in Process	875,314.30
Advance Payments for Taxes and Insurance	478,523.82
Other Liabilities	354,402.32
Unearned Discounts	1,262,887.53
Reserves and Surplus	4,728,326.77
	94,812,024.06

Source: Greater New Orleans Homestead Association, Statement of Condition, December 31, 1975.

Louisiana, the state-chartered companies are called "homestead associations." Other names used include building associations, building and loan associations, savings associations and cooperative banks.

S and L associations generate their money from depositors who establish share accounts. Deposited funds are used mainly to make loans secured by home mortgages. These associations also invest a small amount of their funds in other areas. Figure 19-1 presents the recent balance sheet of a local association. The bulk of its assets are in first-mortgage real-estate loans; however, it also has money invested in U.S. government obligations, loans secured by share accounts, Federal Home Loan Banks (FHLB) stock, Government National Mortgage Association (GNMA) investments (see Chapter 20) and seven other listed assets. I asked one manager if his association earned interest on money deposited with local banks (Cash on Hand and in Banks). "No," he replied, "but prior to issuing our semiannual statements, we like to beef this figure up. It makes good window dressing for our customers. You can rest assured we reduce it the next day to have it earning interest in some investment."

SAVINGS AND LOAN CHARTERS

Savings and loan associations are chartered under federal and state laws. The Federal Home Loan Bank Board is the chartering agent for the U.S. government. Before granting a charter the board, by law, passes upon 1) the charter and responsibility of the applicant group, 2) the need for such an institution in the community to be served, 3) the probability of its usefulness and success, and 4) the effect of a new association on existing institutions of a similar nature.[10]

State associations are chartered by state banking commissioners, who are usually guided by the same standards as those applied by the Federal Home Loan Bank Board.

SAVINGS AND LOAN INSURANCE

Savings and loan associations are insured by the Federal Savings and Loan Insurance Corporation (FSLIC). The FSLIC provides insurance on each savings account up to $40,000 in all federally chartered savings associations and in state-chartered associations that apply and qualify for membership. A majority of S and Ls are FSLIC members.

The FSLIC has a splendid record in paying insurance claims when an institution is declared in default. However, it attempts to arrange for the absorption of a failing institution by a strong one nearby, so that accounts can be transferred intact.

---

[10]Federal Home Loan Bank Board. *Rules and Regulations for the Federal Savings and Loan System,* current edition.

Those placing funds with S and L associations are legally shareholders and are purchasing savings shares. Should withdrawal requests exceed available funds, an S and L may require a thirty-day notice. If, after thirty days, the S and L is still unable to meet demands, it may institute a rotation plan of repayment. Under this system, withdrawal requests are numbered and filed in the order received. If a shareholder in a federal association has invested $1,000 or less, he is paid off when his request is reached; if his request is more than $1,000, he is paid $1,000 when his number is reached. His request is repeated until all requests are fully met or until the association is declared in default. In cases of default and closure, the insurer usually begins payment of shareholders within ten days. Rotation rules for state-licensed associations vary.

If an S and L is a member of the Federal Home Loan Bank System, it can borrow up to 50 percent of its total savings balance from a Home Loan Bank to meet an emergency. Most S and L associations are "mutual" organizations, so called because the shareholders have voting rights and theoretically own the capital of the institution. A number of associations are capital-stock, or "guarantee," associations, which means that in addition to the savings shares there is another class of stock, the holders of which own the association's equity.

SAVINGS AND LOAN DIVIDENDS

There is no restriction under federal law, or under the statutes of most states, that limits dividend rates for associations. Over the years, S and Ls have paid slightly higher returns on savings than banks have. At the present time, most associations offer a variety of plans, with rates ranging from 5¼ to 7¾ percent. Figure 19-2 lists seven different plans of one association. The passbook plan

Figure 19-2 Savings plans of the Greater New Orleans Homestead Association, 1977.

Type of Account	Plan	Description of Savings Plans	Rate Per Annum	Earnings Information
REGULAR PASSBOOK	"A"	$10.00 minimum. Add or withdraw any amount at any time without penalty, after money has been invested ten (10) days. This is the favorite account of most savers. Earn on a "day in to day out" basis.	5.25% *5.39%	
TELEPHONE TRANSFER ACCOUNT	"B"	$1,500 minimum. This is a regular passbook account with the added convenience of being able to transfer funds to or from your checking account in a minimum amount of $500. Transactions made in person may be made in any amount.	5.25% *5.39%	Earnings are compounded on a DAILY basis and are paid the end of each March, June, September and December.

Type of Account	Plan	Description of Savings Plans	Rate Per Annum	Earnings Information
FULL-PAID CERTIFICATE	"C"	Save in $100 units. A negotiable certificate which should be safeguarded against accidental loss. Investments must remain in account until end of earnings distribution period to earn at stated rate.	5.25%	You may elect to have earnings mailed to you or allow them to remain in your account and enjoy additional earnings.
90-DAY NOTICE ACCOUNT	"D"	$100 minimum. Withdrawals may be made only during the ten days following the end of each quarterly period or by providing a written 90-day advance notice.	5.75% *5.91%	
BONUS ACCOUNT	"E"	$1,000 (minimum) earn at 5.25% per annum. After 90 days, receive bonus at rate of ½% per annum. Withdraw between quarterly interest period and earn 5.25% rate to date of withdrawal. Additional deposits to this account not permitted. No interest earned if funds withdrawn during first 90 day period.	5.25% Bonus ½%	Monthly interest checks available upon request on accounts with a balance of $2,500 or more.
SINGLE PAYMENT CERTIFICATE	"F"	$1,000 (Minimum). Issued to mature in 1 year, but less than 30 months. Automatically renewable if not notified.	6.50% *6.72%	PLEASE NOTE: A substantial interest penalty is incurred when certificates are cancelled prior to maturity date. Please inquire as to exact regulations.
	"G"	$1,000 (Minimum). Issued to mature in 2½ years, but less than 4 years. Automatically renewable if not notified.	6.75% *6.98%	
	"H"	$1,000 (Minimum). Issued to mature in 4 years, but less than 6 years. Automatically renewable if not notified.	7.50% *7.79%	
	"I"	$1,000 (Minimum). Issued to mature in 6 years. Automatically renewable if not notified.	7.75% *8.06%	
KEOGH PLAN	"J"	Retirement Plan for self-employed persons. Full information available upon request.		
IRA PLAN	"K"	Retirement Plan for employed persons whose company offers no retirement benefit. Full information available upon request.		

EARNINGS COMFOUNDED DAILY AND PAID QUARTERLY *When earnings are left in account one year.

normally accounts for more than 50 percent of the business; an S and L official explained the passbook's popularity to me as follows: "A customer came to me yesterday with five thousand dollars and wanted a higher return than the passbook rate. But after I had explained all the ramifications and penalties involved in an alternate plan, she said, 'Oh, that's too complicated. I'll stay with the passbook.' " The S and L manager was, of course, delighted that she took the lower rate. Associations locally are charging 9 to 10 percent on mortgages, so the 2- to 5-percent spread permits a healthy profit, since, as noted above, S and L deposits are almost entirely loaned out in high-yielding mortgages.

CREDIT UNIONS

PURPOSE

A credit union may be viewed as a cooperative organization. It is comprised of a group of people who pool their money to make loans to one another. Members receive interest on their savings based upon revenues derived primarily from loans. These loans are normally of short duration. They are consumer-oriented for such purposes as cars, furniture, medical debts, appliances and emergencies. "The principal goals of a credit union are to provide members with a good return on savings and a source from which they can borrow at reasonable rates of interest."[11]

Credit unions operate under a federal charter and supervision. Membership in each union is limited to a particular segment of the population, such as military personnel at an air base, employees of a university, a manufacturing group or government agency, or an association or trade union. At annual meetings, the members select from within their group a governing board consisting of the directors, the credit committee and the supervisory committee.

HISTORY OF CREDIT UNIONS

Credit unions were first established in the United States before World War I. The Credit Union National Extension Bureau was created in 1921 to provide the legislative, organizational and operational services that fostered their growth. In 1934, the Credit Union National Association[12] superseded the bureau. That same year, Congress passed the Federal Credit Union Act (amended in 1959), which spelled out standards and requirements, including annual verification of the records.

By 1977, there were over 23,000 credit unions in the United States, with 23 million members and $46 billion in assets. They ranged in size from fewer than 100 members to nearly 400,000.[13] The typical credit union that year had 1,000 members and $2 million in assets. There were more than $32 billion in loans outstanding in the United States in 1977.

[11]*Pentagon Federal Credit Union News,* April 1970, p. 1.
[12]Presently titled National Credit Union Administration.
[13]The Navy Federal Credit Union Annual Report listed 394,394 members on December 31, 1976.

GROWTH OF CREDIT UNIONS

About 10,000 credit unions are chartered under state laws, with the others under federal jurisdiction. Credit unions have been the fastest-growing of all financial institutions in recent years. As noted above, they were organized originally to extend short-term credit at reasonable rates of interest to their members. Over the years, however, their operations have expanded to include credit for real estate, consumer durable goods and Thrifty Credit Loan Service as a means of paying monthly bills. A number have acquired the characteristics of a commercial operation instead of a voluntary mutual-aid group.

The National Credit Union Administration in 1974 authorized credit unions to offer their members share-draft accounts. These share drafts were in fact interest-bearing checking accounts. They were so well received by the public that banks became alarmed and threatened legal action. As a result, no new approvals have been granted but nearly 600 credit unions continue to provide this service.

In 1977, a law was passed permitting federally chartered credit unions to make thirty-year mortgage loans as well as twelve-year improvement loans. Prior to 1977, some state-chartered credit unions had made longer-term mortgage loans. Some large credit unions employ full-time professionals and pattern their practices after commercial lenders while maintaining low rates on loans and fair return on savings. However, the typical credit union is still small and has little expertise or professional staff.

VOTING SHARES

Credit union savings shares are sold in five-dollar units; lesser amounts deposited are applied to the purchase of a share. A majority of the association's capital is available for loans to shareholders. In one association I checked on[14] 97 percent of the savings were on loan to its members. Each member, irrespective of his holdings in the credit union, is entitled to one vote in the annual election of the board of directors and its committees. Most laws provide that dividends shall not exceed 6 percent. In some associations, free insurance is provided for the amount of the savings, with a limit varying from $1,000 to $5,000. Thus, if a member dies and has savings of $1,000, his beneficiary would receive $2,000.

HOW SAFE ARE CREDIT UNIONS?

The Bureau of Federal Credit Unions, Department of Health, Education and Welfare, supervises credit-union operation under federal charter, and in most states the state banking commission supervises the credit union under state charter.

[14]Pentagon Federal Credit Union, as of June 30, 1970.

Loans to officers, directors and members of committees are limited to the value of their shares in the organization. Further, such persons may not act as endorsers for borrowers. The accounting records of credit unions are subject to regular examination by government authorities. Protection is also offered the members by surety-bond requirements for those who handle money. Most state laws provide for a ceiling on loans to members. Under federal law, interest on credit-union loans may never exceed 1 percent per month on the unpaid balance, which is 12 percent on an annual percentage rate. Associations will normally vary from 9 to 12 percent in their annual charges.

The safety of savings in a credit union is dependent upon its loan policy, its management, the strength of the employer and the state of the economy. Federal and state supervision of credit unions is not as extensive as that directed at S and L institutions or banks, and credit unions often lack the expertise in management enjoyed by other savings institutions. However, members of credit unions can enjoy the security of having their share accounts insured up to $40,000 by an FDIC-type agency.[15]

Withdrawal of savings from a credit union constitutes a repurchase by the union of shares in the organization. Shares are not transferable to others; they are bought back by the union as funds are available. If no funds are available at the moment of sale, the shareholder must wait his turn for repayment. Credit unions maintain certain cash and government bonds for the purpose of meeting ordinary withdrawals. They also draw on new savings and repayment of loans. They do not, however, have secondary sources to fall back upon in the event that these normal sources are insufficient.

THE MONEY MARKET

The money market is composed of short-term securities. The major categories include U.S. Treasury bills, select U.S. government agency issues (see Chapter 20), bankers' acceptances and commercial paper.

"The money market may be thought of as a group of submarkets, one for each kind of security. No one rate of return prevails in the national money market. The rates of return on various money-market instruments do move in a trend and in harmony, however. Because market rises differ and because liquidity differs, yields also vary."[16] Money rates are quoted daily in *The Wall Street Journal*. Figure 19-3 indicates the variation in interest rates. In 1977, they

---

[15]The Credit Union Share Insurance Bill became law on October 19, 1970. The law (Public Law 91-468) provides for the insurance of members' share accounts up to twenty thousand dollars in the event an insured credit union becomes insolvent for any reason. This law was amended in 1974, increasing insurance to forty thousand dollars.

[16]*Financing a Trillion-Dollar Economy*, MLPFS pamphlet, September 1969, p. 23.

approximated the passbook rate. In recent years the money market had exceeded the passbook rate by 1 to 3 percent.

Here is the market in which savings and loan associations, banks and credit unions invest a portion of their money. It is a very active market in which securities are normally easy to buy and sell, either at the initial issuance or in the secondary market.

This is an ideal place to invest cash reserves as you acquire sizable funds available for investment. My own preference is for Treasury bills, noteworthy for their prime safety factor, liquidity and adequate yield, but all the options discussed below offer fair returns and safety. The drawback to money-market investment is that it requires a large sum of money in most cases. You may also want to invest in government bonds (see Chapter 20).

TREASURY BILLS

Treasury bills are issued on a discount basis, under competitive bidding, with maturities not exceeding one year from the date of issue when the face amount is payable. The most common types are three-month, six-month and one-year bills. If you wish to purchase these bills at original issue, you can do so at Federal Reserve Banks and branches. Bids are invited weekly for the three-month and six-month bills, and monthly for one-year bills. Small purchases are accepted at the average of accepted competitive tenders. Treasury bills are bearer securities, currently issued in denominations of $10,000, $50,000, $100,000, $500,000 and $1 million. Within the same series, exchanges are

Figure 19-3 Over-the-counter quotations on Treasury bills, June 24, 1977.

U.S. Treas. Bills			U.S. Treas. Bills		
Mat	Bid	Ask	Mat	Bid	Ask
	Discount			Discount	
6-28	5.32	4.86	10-18	5.09	5.01
6-30	5.15	4.69	10-20	5.09	5.03
7- 7	4.97	4.75	10-27	5.10	5.02
7-14	4.97	4.75	11- 3	5.11	5.05
7-21	4.97	4.75	11-10	5.12	5.04
7-26	4.97	4.81	11-15	5.14	5.08
7-28	4.97	4.83	11-17	5.14	5.08
8- 4	4.96	4.84	11-25	5.16	5.10
8-11	4.96	4.84	12- 1	5.18	5.12
8-18	4.94	4.82	12- 8	5.19	5.13
8-23	5.01	4.95	12-13	5.20	5.12
8-25	4.99	4.91	12-15	5.19	5.13
9- 1	5.01	4.93	12-22	5.19	5.15
9- 8	5.00	4.92	1-10	5.24	5.16
9-15	5.00	4.92	2- 7	5.27	5.21
9-20	5.02	4.92	3- 7	5.32	5.26
9-22	4.98	4.94	4- 4	5.37	5.29
9-29	5.04	4.96	5- 2	5.41	5.32
10- 6	5.05	4.97	5-30	5.39	5.33
10-13	5.07	4.99	6-27	5.39	5.35

Source: *The Wall Street Journal,* June 27, 1977, p. 22.

permitted for other authorized denominations.[17] An example of the yields on Treasury bills is shown in Figure 19-3.

"The rich get richer and the poor get nothing" was never truer than when the Treasury Department raised the minimum bill denomination, in February 1970, from $1,000 to $10,000. The Department acted after small investors, in increasing numbers, found that this money-market medium provided a 2-percent better return than the savings media. The Treasury's publicity release, in presenting its reasons for the change, quoted the Secretary of Housing and Urban Development, George Romney, as follows:

> The outflow of savings from Savings and Loan Associations, Mutual Savings Banks, and other thrift institutions has aggravated the shortage of mortgage funds and contributed to a serious decline in housing production. To avoid a serious, growing housing shortage, it is essential that we discourage the outflow of funds from mortgage lending institutions. This Treasury action should substantially improve our housing outlook.[18]

There was no suggestion made that large investors and corporations should, conversely, transfer a portion of their Treasury-bill investments into these thrift institutions—a process that could solve the problem without depriving the small investor of his opportunity for greater profit.

The Treasury also cited the increased costs in handling "the extraordinarily large volume of small transactions in short-term Treasury bills." Of course, the Treasury issues small-denomination U.S. Savings bonds (Series E) ranging from $25 to $750, and it does not complain about their size—perhaps because the interest rate was only 5 percent instead of nearly 7 percent when the change was made. The Treasury release stated that the small investor is subject to "sizable charges" in buying Treasury bills from "dealers, banks, and brokers." This isn't necessarily true because investors can purchase newly issued bills at no cost from their local Federal Reserve Bank or branch.

BANKERS' ACCEPTANCES

An acceptance is a time draft which a bank has promised to honor at maturity. Bankers' acceptances are used primarily in the import/export business. The bank substitutes its own credit for that of an importer. Here is an example of how an acceptance is created.[19]

---

[17]Primary source for this background information is *United States Securities Available to Investors,* Department of the Treasury Fiscal Service, Bureau of the Public Debt, Washington, D.C., current edition.

[18]Last paragraph in a press release by the Treasury Department, February 26, 1970.

[19]Source for this material is *Bankers' Acceptances for the Institutional Investor,* Merrill Lynch, Pierce, Fenner & Smith, Inc., Government Securities Division, Money Market Securities Department, 48 Wall Street, New York, New York 10005.

John Doe, a New York importer, wants to buy bananas from José Paz, a Honduras exporter. Mr. Doe asks his bank (First National City) to issue a letter of credit in favor of Mr. Paz. The letter of credit includes shipment details, terms and the amount for which Mr. Paz may draw a time draft on the First National. John Doe promises to pay First National at maturity of the draft (upon receipt of the bananas in New York). First National looks to Mr. Doe for payment under the terms of their agreement. However, Mr. Paz, who is the drawer of the draft, remains contingently liable for the life of the transaction (six months or less). José Paz discounts his draft at his Honduras bank, which has been notified of the letter-of-credit agreement by the First National City Bank. The shipping documents and draft are forwarded by the Honduras bank to First National. Upon its receipt in New York, the draft is stamped "accepted" and signed by a bank official. The draft, now an acceptance, has become an irrevocable obligation of First National. Normally, the bank in Honduras will discount the acceptance. First National may then sell the acceptance to a dealer.

Acceptances are an extremely safe form of investment. There is no record of an investor's ever having sustained a principal loss on an acceptance of a U.S. bank. This safety factor is apparent in the yield the acceptance draws in the money market. Acceptances are usually considered second only to U.S. government issues in safety, and on a par with certificates of deposit.

Bankers' acceptances are issued on a discount basis and may be purchased through a dealer such as Merrill Lynch. They come in denominations of from $25,000 to $1 million and are issued to mature in 180 days or less.

COMMERCIAL PAPER

Commercial paper (CP) consists of short-term negotiable promissory notes issued by large corporations for periods up to 270 days.[20] These notes are normally available in amounts ranging from $100,000 to $1 million. A few dealers sell smaller amounts. Corporations such as General Motors Acceptance Corporation place their own paper and may sell amounts as small as $25,000.

There are three commercial paper ratings: prime, desirable and satisfactory. Paper that is rated prime represents the largest percentage outstanding. Commercial paper is a general obligation of the issuing corporation. In the event of bankruptcy its status as to payment priority, with respect to other fixed-income obligations, has not been clarified.

Commercial paper is sold either by direct placement—by a few major finance companies—or through dealers. Dealers underwrite the commercial paper of several hundred industrial corporations and finance companies. Four

[20]Source for this material is *Commercial Paper: an Expanding Market for the Institutional Investor*, Merrill Lynch, Pierce, Fenner & Smith, Inc., Government Securities Division, Money Market Securities Department, Wall Street, New York, New York 10005.

factors affect the CP rate: conditions of the money market, anticipated rates, comparative yields with other money-market instruments and dealer inventories.

Commercial paper is sold on a discount basis, like bills and acceptances. Yields may be quoted in either fractions or decimal increments. The discount can be computed as follows:

$$\text{Discount} = \text{Face amount} \times \text{Rate} \times \frac{\text{Days to maturity}}{360}$$

There is normally a slightly higher yield from commercial paper than from bankers' acceptances and Treasury bills, but it can be less safe. I recommend buying only the top, prime category. The bankruptcy of the Penn Central Transportation Company in 1970 left a number of people and institutions holding their commercial paper.

THE ROLE OF CONSUMER PROTECTION

Before leaving the subject of savings institutions and the money market, I would like to return to a point mentioned earlier in the chapter—the issue of consumer protection. Some savings institutions are not responsive to customer demands. Take, for example, the "shareholders" of savings and loan associations, who in reality have no voice in management. I once asked an S and L association manager why no proxies were ever issued. He replied, "We find it best to leave them at the office. It saves a lot of headaches. If a shareholder actually requests a proxy, we give him one, but few ever do. If the proxies were mailed, it would result in inquiries. Our eleven-man board keeps tight control."

"What about showing your profit-and-loss statement?" I asked.

"We can't do that because it would divulge our secrets. After all, we have thirty-nine local associations. It might also raise questions about the money we spend for advertising. Let's face it, in this tight money market publicity is expensive. Some associations have given away radios and silver dollars. I've heard that a New York bank even offered TV sets."

Savings and loan associations, credit unions and banks should divulge the same information as do corporations listed on the New York Stock Exchange. Furthermore, members of associations and credit unions should have an important voice in management decisions, just as bank despositors should be able to influence management policy. Unfortunately, there is little regard for the views of the people who supply the funds for the above financial institutions. As a means of having the views of the little depositor or shareholder heard, I strongly recommend that he be represented by at least two directors on every board, and that a transcript of the highlights of these board meetings be made available to all interested parties.

The voice of consumer protest should also be heard in the money-market area. There is no valid excuse for the suppression of $1,000 Treasury bills. And why not have small-lot transactions of commercial paper, bankers' acceptances and certificates of deposit? I asked a senior partner of a large brokerage firm, "Would it be feasible to deal in lesser amounts of money-market securities?"

"Yes," he replied, "I'll look into it." In fact, he did nothing.

At a recent congressional hearing, a senator pointed out that only powerful protests made an impact. Security-minded small investors should unite behind an effective spokesman and insist on a better deal in areas like the money market.

20
BONDS

(continued on p. 356)

In building up an effective investment portfolio, it is wise to follow an orderly progression. In Chapter 19, we discussed the importance of cash reserves, examining the functions of checking accounts and various savings institutions in putting your money to work. Let us now turn to the next link in the financial chain—the bond market—first determining the various types of available bonds, and then examining their place in your portfolio.

What is a bond? It may be defined as a certificate of indebtedness on which the issuing agency promises to pay the holder a precise sum, including an established rate of interest at times specified in the agreement.

In the case of corporate obligations, the bondholder has a higher-priority claim against the corporation than does the stockholder. This applies both to the receipt of income and the return of principal in the event of bankruptcy. If a corporation earns only enough in a particular year to pay bondholders, and it has no surplus or other available sources to obtain funds, the stockholders receive nothing. But in prosperous years, bondholders continue to receive only the established rate of interest, while stockholders, as owners, may share in the high earnings through larger dividends.

The fact that bondholders precede stockholders in payment, however, does not guarantee a bond's safety. During the depression of the thirties, a great many companies failed to pay either bond interest or dividends, although many other corporations met all their obligations. From the investor's point of view, it is desirable to select those issues that have proved they can weather periods of economic adversity. Bonds in the above category are generally those issued by the U.S. government and its agencies, first-rate municipalities and well-established corporations that have excellent management and long records of financial solvency. Let us look first at the federal government issues.

U.S. GOVERNMENT SECURITIES

The federal government has two general classes of interest-bearing public issues: 1) nonmarketable, nonnegotiable securities, and 2) marketable, negotiable securities.[1]

NONMARKETABLE SECURITIES

The two types of nonmarketable, nonnegotiable securities issued by the federal government are Series E and Series H U.S. Savings bonds. The bonds are dated as of the first day of the month in which they are purchased, are issued only in registered form and are payable only to the registered owners during their lifetime. They may not be used as collateral for loans. To compensate for their

---

[1] Primary source for the information on U.S. Government securities is *United States Securities Available to Investors,* Department of the Treasury, Fiscal Service, Bureau of the Debt, Washington, D.C., 1975.

non-negotiability, these securities are not subject to market fluctuations. Neither are they callable for redemption before their extended maturity dates; however, at the option of the owners, the bonds are redeemable before maturity, in accordance with their terms at fixed redemption values.

Series E Bonds

These are appreciation-type bonds issued on a discount basis. Purchase prices, maturity prices and denominations are as follows:

TABLE 20-1 Maturation Schedule for Series E Bonds*

Purchase Price	Maturity Price*
$ 18.75	$ 25.20
37.50	50.40
56.25	75.60
75.00	100.80
150.00	201.60
375.00	504.00
750.00	1,008.00
7500.00	10,080.00

*This maturity price applies to those bonds bearing issue dates beginning December 1, 1973. For specific details on redemption values of Series E bonds, refer to a current *Federal Register* pamphlet published by the De- ment of the Treasury.

The bonds mature five years from date of issue, but they may be redeemed at any time after two months from issue date at fixed redemption values. No interest as such is paid; but the periodic increase in redemption value over the issue price, paid only on redemption, represents interest. When the bonds are held to maturity, the yield or investment return is equivalent to interest at the rate of 6 percent per annum, compounded semiannually. If they are redeemed before maturity, the yield is less. Therefore, this type of invest- ment should be made only when you plan to hold it until maturity.

The bonds may be registered in the names of individuals—whether adults or minors—in single-ownership, co-ownership, or beneficiary forms; and in single-ownership form in the names of fiduciaries and private and public organizations; but not in the names of commercial banks in their own right. Series E bonds are subject to an annual limitation of $10,000 (face amount) for each owner.

They may be purchased at banks generally, or by mail at any Federal Reserve Bank or branch, or at the Office of the Treasurer of the United States, Securities Division, Washington, D.C. 20226. Purchase applications must be accom- panied by payment in full.

Series H Bonds

These are ten-year current-income bonds, issued at par in denominations of $500, $1,000, $5,000 and $10,000. They are redeemable at par at the owner's option six months from issue date, except during the calendar month preceding an interest-payment date. Interest is paid semiannually by check, in varying amounts based on a graduated scale fixed to produce a return of about 6 percent per annum, compounded semiannually, if the bonds are held to maturity. If it shall be necessary to cash them during the first few years after purchase, a lower rate of interest is received.

Series H bonds may be registered in the same forms as Series E bonds and may be purchased from the same sources. Like Series E, they are subject to an annual limitation of $10,000 for each owner, but the limitation does not apply to Series H bonds acquired through exchange of Series E bonds. Thus, as owner of, say, $10,000 in Series E bonds may replace them with an equivalent amount of the Series H even though he already had some Series H bonds.

SPECIAL FEATURES OF SERIES E AND H BONDS

I know of no safer bond purchase than investing in Series E and H government bonds. The reasons for this are as follows:

1. Interest on these issues does not have to be reported in a tax return until the securities are cashed or at the time of final maturity, whichever is earlier. Therefore, a person who wishes to retire at the ripe old age of thirty-eight could begin a Series E program at age thirty-three and save an appreciable amount in federal income taxes by cashing them in and paying the tax after retirement. When the bonds mature he can, instead of redeeming them for cash, exchange them for an equivalent amount of Series H bonds, and the tax on the accumulated interest will be deferred until the H bonds are redeemed. (The Series E bondholder can, of course, report the accrued interest earlier. If this is done, all interest to date must be shown in the current tax return, and each return thereafter must list the annual gain for that year.)

2. The H series is well suited to people who want a periodic income, as its holders receive interest payments by check every six months.

3. Series E bonds can be easily purchased through monthly payroll deduction plans.

4. Both Series E and H bonds are easily convertible into cash; have an assured rate of return and guaranteed redemption values; and are replaced by the Treasury if lost, stolen, mutilated or destroyed.

MARKETABLE SECURITIES

Marketable government securities fell into two categories: Treasury bonds and Treasury notes. Issued through the Federal Reserve Banks as fiscal agents of the

United States and by the Office of the Treasurer of the United States, they are available in series form, each series having similar terms and conditions. Generally, bonds are issues of long term and notes of medium term. Treasury bonds and notes bear interest, are transferable and may be sold in the market. Ordinarily, all such securities may be used as collateral for loans.

Both bonds and notes are available in bearer form. (Bearer securities, the ownership of which is not recorded, are payable to bearer, title passing by delivery without endorsement when interest is due.) Bonds and most issues of notes are also available in registered form, meaning that the names and addresses of the owners are recorded. Interest on these is paid by check drawn to the order of the owner and recorded on the Treasury's books. Registered securities may be transferred by assignment executed by the registered owner or his authorized representative. It is advantageous to purchase marketable government issues in registered form, thus reducing the risk of loss or theft.

Treasury Bonds

Bonds of each series have a fixed maturity,[2] usually more than five years from date of issue, when the principal amount becomes payable. When so provided in the offering circulars, bonds may be called for redemption before maturity at the option of the United States, on and after specified dates, on four months' notice.

Bonds bear interest at fixed rates, payable semiannually. Interest ceases when the principal amount becomes payable, whether at maturity or on earlier call date. Denominations of recent series are $500, $1,000, $5,000, $10,000, $100,000 and $1 million. Within the same series, bonds may be exchanged as follows: 1) for other authorized denominations, 2) bearer for registered bonds and 3) registered for bearer bonds.

Treasury Notes

Notes of each series have a fixed maturity of between one and seven years from date of issue, when the principal amount becomes payable. They bear interest at fixed rates, payable semiannually. Denominations are $1,000, $5,000, $10,000, $100,000, $1 million, $100 million and $500 million. Within the same series, exchanges are authorized 1) for other authorized denominations, 2) bearer for registered notes and 3) registered for bearer notes.

[2]The face amount of a bond.

PURCHASE OF MARKETABLE SECURITIES

Purchase From the Treasury

Marketable bonds and notes may be purchased directly from the Treasury only on the occasion of a public offering. Subscriptions, subject to allotment, may be made at Federal Reserve Banks and branches, and at the Office of the Treasurer of the United States, Securities Division, Washington, D.C. 20226, at such times. Banks and brokerage firms will handle subscriptions for customers, but there is a charge for this service, whereas subscriptions are made free of charge at Federal Reserve Banks and branches. Some banks waive the service charge if you have a substantial account with them.

Prospective purchasers of new Treasury issues should obtain tender forms from a Federal Reserve Bank or branch. Tenders for $500,000 or less from any one bidder entered on a noncompetitive basis are accepted in full at the average price of accepted competitive bids. In lieu of submitting an individual tender, you may wish to use a brokerage firm or bank.

If you are interested in subscribing for future issues of any class of marketable securities, you can get the necessary information from a Federal Reserve Bank or branch or from a bond specialist in a brokerage firm. *The Wall Street Journal* and your local bank usually have this information as well.

Purchase in the Market

After their original issue, Treasury bonds and notes may be purchased in the market, at prevailing market prices. Anyone interested in purchasing them should consult a broker, bank or dealer in these securities. Requests for information on marketable issues may be addressed to any Federal Reserve Bank or branch, or to the Commissioner of the Public Debt, Department of the Treasury, Washington, D.C. 20226.

TAX STATUS OF U.S. GOVERNMENT SECURITIES

Income derived from Treasury bonds, notes and savings bonds is subject to income tax. For purposes of federal taxation, any increase in the value of savings bonds—the difference between the price paid and the redemption value received, whether at or before maturity—is considered to be interest.

All federal government securities are subject to estate, inheritance, gift or other excise taxes, whether federal or state, but are exempt from all other taxation by any state, any possession of the United States or any local taxing authority.

ADVANTAGES OF U.S. GOVERNMENT SECURITIES

The Stability Factor

A criticism presently leveled against bonds in general is that they have failed to keep pace with inflation; that dollars invested in fixed-income securities in recent years do not have comparable buying power today. This cannot be denied. However, this shortcoming must be balanced against the violent fluctuations that have occurred in other types of investments, such as real estate and stocks. Compare the losses in property values and corporate stocks with the depreciation of government bonds for the ten-year period ending in 1932. At that time, the person with government securities was in a far more favorable financial position than his friend with stock and property holdings. Likewise, the person who in 1973–1975 invested his money in long-term Treasury issues found himself with a much higher yield than that enjoyed by stockholders. His principal was intact, while stocks declined 45 percent as measured by the Dow Jones Averages in the period between January 1973 and November 1974. Many properties also declined sharply during the deep recession of 1973–75. And a number of landholders and real estate companies failed because they could not meet their mortgage and tax payments.

What about the future? Based upon what has happened in the past, we cannot forecast the years ahead with certainty. We do know that our society has never been able to eliminate cyclical fluctuations. Accordingly, the wise investor acquires various holdings in order to have adequate protection. Highest-quality bonds furnish a strong pillar in building a diversified investment program; thus, I recommend that marketable government bonds be included in an investment portfolio. If held to maturity, they provide good income coupled with unexcelled safety of principal. Furthermore, at today's prices, a few long-term Treasury issues are selling under par and therefore have a limited growth potential. For example, the 7-percent 1993–98 series can currently be bought at about $950 per thousand, or 5 percent below redemption value. In the meantime, if lower interest rates and the cheaper-money era should return, this would raise their market price. Of course, the converse is also possible. If interest rates should rise above present levels, then the price of bonds would decline further. Nevertheless, a purchaser could be assured of receiving $1,000 by 1998 for about $950 investment now, and during the intervening years the holder would be earning nearly 7½ percent on his investment.

The purchase cost of marketable issues depends on two factors: the brokerage commission and the spread between the bid and the asked price.

This spread is quoted in thirty-seconds of a point and on some issues approximates one point. Fifteen years ago, the spread on the longest-term governments was only 8/32, but costs have risen on all investment transactions. If possible, buy new issues of negotiable bonds and notes to avoid the commission, which can amount to over $1,000 on some long-term bond transactions involving amounts of $100,000. For example, one individual recently paid the following costs on buying $100,000 of 6¾-percent Treasury bonds due in 1993:

$1,000—Spread between bid (93) and asked price (94)
    25—Bank service charge
     3—Phone call to correspondent bank
——————
$1,028

The bid and asked price of Treasury bonds and notes are listed daily in *The Wall Street Journal*. These marketable securities pay up to 25 percent higher a return than U.S. Savings bonds during this era of relatively high interest rates. There is also the appreciation potential on these bonds, in the event that interest rates fall in the years ahead.

Several U.S. Treasury bonds selling below par today offer a feature that is important to estate planning. Under certain conditions, they may be redeemed at par plus accrued interest, for the purpose of applying the proceeds to the payment of federal estate taxes. For those interested in further details, I suggest contacting the Treasury Department.

DRAWBACKS OF U.S. GOVERNMENT SECURITIES

In view of the advantages to buying savings bonds, I am frequently asked why this form of investment is not viewed as a "cash reserve." There are several reasons. Although it qualifies from the standpoint of safety of principal, you cannot obtain your principal during the first two months after purchase, and this may be just the time you are hit with an emergency. Nor can these bonds be used for collateral. Another disadvantage is the lower interest rate in the early years; if funds are needed for an emergency during that time, a savings account would normally provide a higher yield. This is the primary drawback of Series E and H bonds—their low return in relation to other savings media, a problem that has existed since their initial issuance at 2.9 percent in 1941. A 6-percent return in 1975 didn't even keep pace with inflation that year.

The danger in bond purchases other than the E and H Series, including negotiable government issues, is the daily fluctuation based on interest rates. It could happen that when cash is needed, the bonds could be disposed of only at less than the original cost. As an illustration, U.S. Treasury bonds (Series

December 15, 2½ 72/67) were initially sold at par in November 1945 to provide a yield of 2½ percent. Each $1,000 bond had sold as high as $1,065.31 (1946) and as low as $849.60 (1970). In 1971, the 72/67 series was selling for $966.00, to yield 4.7 percent at maturity. This series matured December 15, 1972, but could have been called at the option of the U.S. Treasury on or after December 15, 1967.

It is significant that a call for redemption must be made at par, plus accrued interest. As noted earlier, the Treasury is required to give four months' notice before taking such action. Normally, the call for redemption is made at the most opportune time for the government. With prime interest rates much higher than 2½ percent during the period 1967–1972, it was obviously wise for the government not to make payment until maturity on the series of December 15, 2½ 72/67.

GOVERNMENT AGENCIES AND IBRD

In addition to securities of the U.S. Government, you may also purchase debt issues of agencies that have federal-government participation. These obligations generally provide a slightly higher interest return to the holder. An extremely safe buy from the standpoint of interest on due dates, they have been well accepted in the marketplace. In the past ten years, the number of these securities has increased considerably, owing to the expanded role of the issuing agencies and their need for additional money.

The best known of the above agencies are the Banks for Cooperatives, Federal Home Loan Banks, Federal Intermediate Credit Banks (FIC), Federal Land Banks, Federal National Mortgage Association and the World Bank, or International Bank for Reconstruction and Development (IBRD).[3] These organizations play an important role in the nation's economy by providing significant sources of funds for worthy projects. Their debt issues are listed daily in *The Wall Street Journal.* The yields of the various agencies indicate a limited spread for comparable maturity dates. The figures also reflect the ability of the organizations to attract funds at a return only slightly higher than that of U.S. government issues.

Information about new issues appears in the *Journal* on the page devoted to "The Bond Markets"; also appearing in the *Journal* are advertisements concerning new obligations.

---

[3]For further information on government agencies and IBRD, read *Handbook of Securities of the United States Government and Federal Agencies and Related Money Market Instruments,* The First Boston Corporation, current edition.

These agency issues are excellent additions to the portfolios of banks and other organizations that employ bond experts to determine which yields best fit their needs. However, for most individuals, I recommend staying with a simple program that includes Treasury bonds and/or notes. The rate differential is normally so small that it is not worth the effort involved in acquiring federal agency issues

OTHER PUBLIC-INTEREST AGENCIES

There are a number of other agencies clothed with a public interest that issue debt instruments. These include the Commodity Credit Corporation (CCC), Department of Housing and Urban Development (HUD), Federal Housing Administration, Export-Import Bank of Washington, Farmers Home Administration, Inter-American Development Bank, Merchant Marine and Tennessee Valley Authority.

THE GOVERNMENT NATIONAL MORTGAGE ASSOCIATION

The sophisticated investor may be interested in securities of a relatively new public agency: the Government National Mortgage Association (GNMA). A primary objective of the GNMA is to assist in the financing of more housing by making real-estate mortgage investments attractive to all types of investors. It accomplishes this objective by guaranteeing bonds, participation certificates and pass-through securities. This guarantee is backed by the full faith and credit of the U.S. government. The GNMA has complete authority to borrow from the U.S. Treasury to meet its obligations under the guarantee.

Of the three types of securities guaranteed by the GNMA, the pass-through securities have been the best received. They represent a share in a pool of FHA and/or VA mortgages. An issuer, usually a mortgage banker, will put together a minimum of $2 million of FHA-VA mortgages. The issuer will place them in the custody of a bank and, through the GNMA, issue a pass-through security.

Purchasers of these GNMA pass-through securities receive monthly payments of principal and interest. The average life of these investments is twelve years; the maximum maturity would be thirty years. The high rate of interest for such a safe investment has drawn a good number of astute institutional and private investors. Yield has varied between 6½ and 9½ percent during the past five years. In June 1976, a new GNMA issue provided a 8.33 yield. Before you purchase these securities, however, I suggest that you confer with your banker or broker and become more familiar with the subject. Merrill Lynch is the largest distributor of GNMA modified pass-through certificates.

Prospective buyers should read their pamphlet, titled *Merrill Lynch Explains Pass-Through—The Government National Mortgage Association Guaranteed Securities.*

STATE AND MUNICIPAL SECURITIES

State and municipal bonds—known collectively as "municipals"—are obligations issued by state, cities, school districts, housing and port authorities and other political subdivisions to raise money for a variety of projects. They fall into four categories:

1. *General-obligation bonds* are secured by the full faith and credit of the issuing state or municipality, and all the community's tax resources are pledged to the repayment of the obligation.

2. *Limited-tax bonds* are secured by a partial or limited pledge of the issuer's taxing power (the first two cents of a cigarette tax, for example).

3. *Revenue bonds* are secured by revenues from the operation of a specific project, such as a water or electric system, or a toll road.

4. *Public-housing authority bonds* are primarily secured by the rentals of individual housing projects. If these rents are not sufficient to cover indebtedness, the public-housing authority each year makes up any deficit with funds granted by Congress.

RATING MUNICIPALS

Two services, Moody's and Standard & Poor's, analyze and rate state and municipal bond issues. Rating on thousands of municipals can be found in Standard & Poor's *Bond Guide,* arranged alphabetically by states, and indicating whether the bonds are state bonds, general obligations or revenue bonds.

Standard & Poor's has seven municipal-bond ratings, from the top quality (AAA-prime) down to those in default (D). Moody's has a somewhat similar rating system, ranging from Aaa down to C.

Since bonds should be purchased for safety, I recommend only the AA rating or higher.

PRICING MUNICIPALS

Daily prices of municipals are more difficult to come by than those of corporates or governments, although *The Wall Street Journal* does report the coupon, maturity, bid and asked prices of a few active tax-exempt revenue bonds issued by toll roads and other public authorities. Your stockbroker can give you current bid and asked prices on various municipal issues and information on new issues. Also, *The Wall Street Journal* devotes a daily column to tax-exempts that provides data on planned issues, sales, new listings and other pertinent news.

ARE MUNICIPALS RIGHT FOR YOU?

Municipal bonds may be a desirable purchase as you move up the economic ladder. Interest paid on these bonds is exempt from the federal income tax and most states exempt interest on bonds of their own from state taxes. The wisdom of an investment in municipals would depend upon the tax bracket of the person concerned. I normally recommend their purchase for those whose bracket is 36 percent or higher. Let us assume that a person is in the 36-percent group. If he bought a $1,000 municipal yielding 6 percent, it would provide him an after-tax income of $60 a year. In contrast, a comparable corporate bond might offer a 9-percent yield but the federal income tax bite would leave him with only $57.60. Whether municipals would be a beneficial addition to your portfolio can be determined readily by consultation with your broker.

NEED FOR CAUTION

Before investing in specific municipals, it is important to determine the current and projected ability of a municipality or state to pay its interest on bonds and the principal on maturity. Cities like New York are in deep financial difficulties at this writing. As a result, they are paying very high rates in order to induce buyers for their short- and longer-term securities.

A *Wall Street Journal* article stated:

> Everyone has heard about New York City's intractable problems—the sag toward bankruptcy, the physical deterioration, the high crime rates, the flight of people and businesses, the irritations unlimited. But perhaps not so widely recognized is the extent to which the Big Apple isn't just a rare rotten apple in the U.S. municipal barrel. In many cities, block after block of gutted buildings and rubble-strewn lots suggest that quite possibly much of the barrel may be rotting—a frightening possibility in a nation in which nearly a third of the population lives in cities of 50,000 or more.[4]

[4]"Many Municipalities Lag Behind the Nation in Economic Recovery." *The Wall Street Journal,* June 16, 1976, p. 1.

CORPORATE BONDS

Bonds issued by American and foreign corporations come in a variety of forms ranging from first-class to extremely risky. In 1977, for example, some excellent AAA (top-rated) issues were offered to provide a yield of 8 percent.

The capitalization of corporations may be composed primarily of bonds or consist of a small bond issue with the remainder in common stock. To increase their attractiveness, some corporate bonds are convertible into stock. Corporate bonds may be sold over-the-counter or on a major exchange; it may be easy to dispose of them or almost impossible to find a buyer. Therefore, it is most important to have the necessary facts before making a purchase.

RATING CORPORATE BONDS

Because of the complexity of the corporate-bond market, the potential buyer should be familiar with bond ratings. For example, Standard & Poor's *Bond Guide*, cited earlier, grades corporate bonds in nine classifications, ranging from the highest grade to bonds in default. The facts on corporates treated in the *Bond Guide* include interest rate, due dates, ratings, eligibility, legality, form of bond, call price, price range for three current years, yield to maturity (see below), principal business of the corporation, underwriting information, outstanding debt, financial position, ratio of debt to net property, overall earnings and interim earnings.

The Wall Street Journal publishes information on corporates daily on the "Bond Market" page, including current prices of recent offerings. A look at this information points up the fact that some of these corporate bonds have risen in price since issuance, and the holders have a capital gain if they choose to sell. Contrariwise, others have declined and holders would have a loss if they sold. The *Journal* also publishes the daily transactions of bonds listed on the New York Stock Exchange.

COMMISSION FEES

What about costs? For issues traded on the exchanges, the commission charged is generally $2.50 to $7.50 (per bond) based on the number of bonds in a trade.

FLOATING RATE NOTES

Money managers are constantly seeking new ways to obtain funds for their companies. Their objective is to obtain the needed dollar amount at the lowest possible rate and then employ it at the highest possible rate. Commercial banks are splendid examples. They borrow from depositors at 5 percent and loan such money to borrowers at two, three and four times that rate!

It helps when money managers come up with fresh ideas that can be aggressively marketed to the public.[5] Such an idea was presented, in 1974, by Citicorp[6] (formerly First National City Corporation), a major commercial banking firm.

In July 1974, Citicorp offered investors the opportunity to buy $650 million of their fifteen-year floating rate notes due June 1, 1989. The notes were available in initial orders of $5,000 and subsequent ones of $1,000.

What inducements did Citicorp offer potential buyers? A guaranteed 9.7-percent annual rate of interest through May 31, 1975. And from May 31, 1975 to May 31, 1976, interest would be 1 percent above the average three-month U.S. Treasury bill rate. Buyers could then redeem 100 percent of their principal amount beginning June 1, 1976, plus accrued interest. This redemption opportunity was available every six-month period thereafter, until maturity. *And interest payments by Citicorp would continue to adjust in relation to the Treasury bills until the final maturity date of June 1, 1989*—thus, the name "floating-rate notes."

The Citicorp issue was quickly oversubscribed. Seven other companies then proceeded to issue floating notes. The market soon became saturated. And when short-term interest rates declined markedly, in 1975–1976, the small investor found that he could do better elsewhere. In my view there are better bond and note opportunities than floating issues. Treasury bills provide much greater short-term marketability and the interest differential is minor. This is particularly true in view of the fact that Treasury issues are exempt from state and local taxes, while floating notes are subject to these taxes. Prime corporate bonds provide higher yields over the long term and have comparable safety.

CONVERTIBLES

A convertible bond is one that may be exchanged for a certain number of shares of stock. A bond with this "exchange" sweetener may be issued at a lower rate of

---

[5]Corporations receive splendid support from underwriters who actually provide the mechanism for selling such issues to the public. Three firms (The First Boston Corporation, Goldman Sachs & Co. and Merrill Lynch, Pierce, Fenner & Smith, Inc.) received 1 percent or $6,500,000, in underwriter discounts and commissions.

[6]Citicorp, effective October 31, 1968, became the sole shareholder of First National City Bank ("Citibank") except for directors' qualifying shares. Citibank is the second largest commercial bank in the world in terms of total assets and total deposits.

interest than would a normal bond. It may also be the only way the company can market its issue. Convertibles permit investors to participate in the appreciation potential of common stock, but with relatively less risk. In the event that the price of a stock declines, support may be provided by the bond yield. The appreciation potential of a convertible is determined primarily by the price of the common stock for which it may be exchanged. The built-in safety of a convertible in a declining stock market is based on its status as a debt obligation of the corporation with a fixed-interest rate. The relation between the price of a convertible and the value of the number of shares for which it can be exchanged usually determines how closely the price of the convertible will follow the price action of the common stock.

As a general rule, appreciation prospects are long-term if the premium over conversion value is substantial. If the price of the common stock should decline, the convertible is supported by the yield; the price is unlikely to fall below that of nonconvertible senior securities of the same quality.

The risk of call should be taken into consideration before investing in convertible securities. A corporation usually issues convertible bonds with the intention of effecting their conversion into common stock. Therefore, the convertible securities are unlikely to be called before the common stock is selling at a price that provides the investor with equal value in the exchange.

In 1974, the combination of declining stock prices and increasing interest rates deprived convertible bonds of their two primary price supports. Lower stock prices resulted in lower conversion values, and high interest rates depressed estimated investments values, or the theoretical price floor. As a result, many good-quality convertibles of sound companies were selling at or near historic lows.

The effect of the stock market on convertible bond values can be illustrated as follows. Let us assume that convertible bond X initially sold at par ($1,000 per bond) to provide a 6-percent yield. It can be converted into two shares of X common stock until June 30, 1980. If the common-stock shares are selling at $500 or below, there is no advantage to the conversion feature. However, if X common stock moves to $1,000, X bonds should appreciate to $2,000. In contrast, if the stock declines to $50 and interest rates for this type of bond rise to 9 percent, the 6-percent X bond will sell well below par.

CONVERTIBLES AND YOUR PORTFOLIO

I have already noted that stocks should be considered for income and/or growth, and bonds for their features of safety and fair interest return. Convertible bonds are an attempt to combine the features of each, but they do not provide the best of either. Keep this in mind in terms of an effective investment portfolio.

YIELD TO MATURITY

It is helpful to understand the meaning of yield to maturity in terms of the bonds discussed in this chapter.[7]

Bond tables designed to inform you of the exact yield to maturity for various coupons can be consulted at brokerage firms or banks. A complex formula is utilized for the precise determination of yield to maturity. However, an approximation can be made by utilizing the following formula:

$$\text{Yield to Maturity} = \frac{\text{Annual bond interest} + \dfrac{\text{Discount}}{\text{Years to Maturity}} \text{ or } - \dfrac{\text{Premium}}{\text{Years to Maturity}}}{\dfrac{\text{Purchase price} + \text{Redemption price}}{2}}$$

Let us apply this formula to a 4-percent U.S. Treasury bond. First, let us assume that you made a purchase of a 4-percent $1,000 bond on February 15, 1976, for $1,010 and that it has four years remaining until maturity. The $10 premium disappears during this period because you will only receive $1,000 in 1980. here is how the formula works:

$$\begin{array}{ll}
\$\ \ 40 & \text{Annual bond interest} \\
\$\ \ 10 & \text{(Premium)} \div 4 \text{ (Years to maturity)} = \$2.50 \\
\$1010 & \text{(Purchase price)} \\
\$1000 & \text{(Redemption price)}
\end{array}$$

$$\frac{\$40 - \$2.50}{\dfrac{\$1010 + \$1000}{2}} = \frac{\$37.50}{\$1005} = 3.7\% \text{ Yield to Maturity}$$

Thus the yield to maturity approximates 3.7 percent. It is less than the 4-percent coupon because you paid a $10 premium on the $1,000 bond at time of purchase.

Now let us take an example of a high-interest era and assume that the bond is bought for $800 on February 15, 1976:

$$\begin{array}{ll}
\$\ \ 40 & \text{Annual bond interest} \\
\$\ 200 & \text{(Discount)} \div 4 \text{ (Years to maturity)} = \$50 \\
\$\ 800 & \text{(Purchase price)} \\
\$1000 & \text{(Redemption price)}
\end{array}$$

$$\frac{\$40 + \$50}{\dfrac{\$800 + \$1000}{2}} = \frac{\$90}{\$900} = 10\% \text{ Yield to Maturity}$$

[7]In Chapter 21 "current yield" is presented as it applies primarily to the stock market. However, this concept also is pertinent to bonds.

Thus the yield zooms to 10 percent if you bought a 4-percent bond for $800 four years prior to maturity.[8] It pays to look at various bond issues in order to determine yields to maturity. Good buys in discount bonds are possible in terms of both high interest and a reduced capital-gains tax on redemption.

BONDS AND YOUR PORTFOLIO: AN OVERVIEW

You should buy bonds primarily for safety of principal and a fair income. The simplest and easiest way to do this is systematically to buy U.S. savings bonds through a monthly allotment and, once a sizable number are accumulated, to convert them (on maturity) into negotiable U.S. Treasury issues, thus permitting a higher yield and a limited growth potential.

Timing for bond purchases, as for other investments, is of prime importance. It is foolish to buy long-term Treasury bonds when interest rates are low. Conversely, it is wise to buy them when yields are high. The variation in long-term bond yields is apparent from Figure 20-1. Note that long-term governments varied from less than 4 percent in 1964 to 8½ percent in 1975. The chart also reflects that the spread between corporates (AAA) and Treasuries recently approximated ½ percent.

What portion of savings should be placed in government bonds? In Chapter 19 I recommended that the equivalent of four months' salary be used as the norm for a cash reserve. After this, I suggest that an additional sum equal to the cash reserve be placed in U.S. savings bonds. Upon completion of the cash-reserve and savings-bond goals, capital (up to $10,000) should be divided equally among Treasury bonds, stocks, real estate and other investments. Once the savings bonds reach maturity, they should be converted to Treasury bonds.

Let us take the case of a family with an annual income of $21,000. In accordance with my concept of a diversified investment program, they should deploy funds in the following sequence: 1) cash reserve of $7,000 ($300 minimum-balance checking account and $6,700 in a bank and/or savings and loan association); 2) U.S. savings bonds totaling $7,000; 3) government bonds, quality stocks and other investments evenly proportioned, up to $10,000; and 4) additional funds employed primarily in stocks, real estate and other growth opportunities (see Chapter 21-26). The figures presented in this example should be used as a guide only. The amounts placed in the safety-of-principal categories could be lowered for a single person who has no family obligations and no future requirements for heavy expenditures. In contrast, larger

---

[8]If you had bought the bond at the issue price of $1,000 your yield to maturity would be 4 percent. This is apparent because at maturity (February 15, 1980), the U.S. Treasury would pay you the face value listed on the bond ($1000).

Figure 20-1 Bond yields—long-term Governments, municipal, and corporates.

EQUIPMENT TRUST CERTIFICATE RATINGS

Considering the remarkable record of railway equipment trust certificates over a long period of years, this type of security stands preeminent among railway investments as a class. This is backed by the infinitesimal losses suffered by holders of equipment certificates since the inception of this form of financing in 1868, and their inclusion in pension and related portfolios where there is a specific need for this type of security. While marketability of outstanding equipment trust certificates is somewhat restricted, this is not important in an essentially intermediate-

term obligation of quality. In many instances, specific maturities are acquired so that repayments coincide with requirements of pension or other investment fund objectives.

The better-grade issues are highly desirable as limited-term investments where safety of principal is of paramount concern. Where a moderate compromise with quality is permitted for the sake of a somewhat better yield, the medium-grade certificates deserve consideration, including those of some marginal roads in view of generous yields.

Company	Rating
Alabama Great Southern	AA
Atchison, Topeka & Santa Fe	AAA
Atlantic Coast Line	AA
Baltimore & Ohio	A
Burlington Northern	AA
Canadian Pacific	AA
Chesapeake & Ohio	AA
Chicago, Burlington & Quincy	AA
Chicago & East'n Illinois	AA
Chicago & North Western	A

Company	Rating
Chi., Rock Island & Pacific	BBB
Cin., N. Orleans & Tex. Pacific	AA
Clinchfield R.R.	AA
Colorado & Southern Ry.	AA
Denver & Rio Grande Western	AAA
Great Northern Ry.	AA
Gulf, Mobile & Ohio	A
Illinois Central Gulf	A
Louisville & Nashville R.R.	A

Company	Rating
Missouri Pacific R.R.	AA
New York Central R.R.	NR
New York, Chicago & St. Louis	AA
Norfolk & Western Ry.	AA
Northern Pacific Ry.	AA
Pennsylvania R.R.	NR
Pittsburgh & Lake Erie R.R.	AA
St. Louis-San Francisco Ry.	A
St. Louis & Southwestern Ry.	AAA
Seaboard Coast Line R.R.	AA

Company	Rating
Soo Line R.R.	AA
Southern Pacific Co.	AA
Southern Ry.	AA+
Texas & Pacific Ry.	A
Trailer Train Co.	A
Union Pacific	AAA
Wabash R.R.	AA
Western Maryland Ry.	AA
Western Pacific	A+

LONG TERM BOND YIELDS
YIELD IN PERCENT—INVERTED SCALE

MUNICIPALS
LONG TERM GOVERNMENTS
AAA CORPORATES
△ REVISED—PRIOR DATA NOT COMPARABLE

Source: *Standard & Poor's Bond Guide*, New York, Standard & Poor's Corporation, May 1977, p. 9.

amounts may be necessary for some with large families, home-purchase plans and other responsibilities.

BONDS AND PROFITS

Throughout this chapter we have stressed the safety factor of bond ownership. In closing I would like to emphasize that bonds can sometimes bring in handsome profits as well. The following market figures from 1970–1975 illustrate this fact.

Between 1970 and 1975, bond markets reached all-time peaks in payment of interest rates to holders. MAPCO, Inc. (a leading gas pipeline retailer), for example, was forced to pay an 11-percent rate in 1970, in order to attract the necessary investors. On June 16 of that year, New Jersey Bell Telephone, a top-quality company, was required to price its $100 million of debentures at a price yielding its recipient 9.35 percent. Furthermore, the 1970 peak was surpassed four years later. In September 1974, South Central Bell was required to pay a return of 10.05 percent on its $225 million of debentures. These high returns may never again be available, but there will always be opportunities to capitalize on investments.

Municipal bonds reached their peak in 1975, when the Standard & Poor long-term bond yields for municipals indicated a yield above 7 percent. U.S. Treasury issues provided returns of up to 8½ percent in 1970. And in 1974 the Treasury set a record coupon rate of 9 percent on two issues with maturities due in 1977 and 1980.

People who purchased issues like the 9-percent Treasuries and South Central Bell are not only receiving a splendid return on their money but at times could cash in on a nice capital gain. In June 1977, these bonds were selling as follows:

Issue	Offering Price	Price 1977
9% U.S. Treasury Bonds, Aug. 1980	100	107 20/32
South Central Bell, 10.05%	100	112

Part Six

GROWTH-POTENTIAL INVESTMENTS

An essential element in a successful money-management program is the placing of adequate funds in growth-type securities. To ensure a sound and profitable portfolio, however, I recommend that funds not be placed in growth-potential issues until a person is out of debt (with certain exceptions[1]), has a sound insurance program and possesses adequate cash reserves. This is because purchasers of growth investments run a real risk of principal loss.

Should I concentrate my buying in any particular growth field? My answer to this frequently asked question is that circumstances and opportunities vary with the individual. For example, a family that moves frequently should normally avoid real estate. Individuals shouldn't enter the commodity market unless they can devote adequate time to this highly speculative area. Quality stocks and profitable hobbies, like coin collecting, should be reserved for those with adequate cash reserves.

[1]The three exceptions listed in Chapter 5 are: to obtain an education, buy a home, meet an emergency.

THE STOCK MARKET

QUALITY VS. "MAGIC STOCKS"

"How can I make a fast buck in the stock market?"

"Can you give me some good leads?"

"I bought a thousand shares of a new computer-service company that the salesman said should double in price soon—should I buy more?"

"A friend said his stock paid a twenty-percent cash dividend over the years. Can you believe it?"

"What do you think of those go-go stocks I've been hearing about? Where can I find issues like National Student Marketing and Panacolor?"

These were among the questions friends and clients were asking me prior to the sharp stock-market decline that bottomed in May 1970. During that slump, Panacolor fell from $22.00 per share to $1.75, and Student Marketing plummeted from $32.50 to $2.00. Other "magic stocks" which, according to some salesmen, were sure to provide instant wealth, suffered dramatic losses. Stockbrokers earned up to $150,000 per annum in the 1967–1969 era; but precious few investors who put their hard-earned dollars into go-go issues in 1968 had anything to show but severe deficits a few months later. Between 1973 and 1974, the blue chips[1] of the stock market suffered a sharp decline of 45 percent; but a group of highly speculative issues declined more than 90 percent in dollar value. One of these, Equity Funding Corporation, sold mutual funds and insurance. Prior to the disclosure of massive fraud in its insurance operations, the stock sold as high as $37.25 per share. Today, the stock is worthless.

The moral of the story?

There is no sure road to sudden riches in the purchase of shares in unique situations pushed by high-pressure agents. For every Cinderella story, there are thousands of disappointments and heartaches. It is important to question why you are being singled out to buy an unusual opportunity. Is it goodwill or a chance for the solicitor to make a good profit at your expense? Salespeople receive sizable commissions for completing transactions on these "bargains."

Throughout this book we have stressed the desirability of making quality investments in every area and doing business with firms that are well established and have histories of successful management. This applies as much to investments in stocks and bonds as to the purchase of household appliances, clothing, houses and cars. It pays to invest your money in quality growth stocks of companies with proven reputations.[2]

Furthermore, securities should not be bought without adequate back-

---

[1]Stocks of highly respected major corporations with long records of financial success.

[2]Stocks of corporations that grow at a faster rate than the economy as a whole and put a sizable portion of their annual profits back into the business.

ground and understanding of the problems confronting the investor. It is entirely possible to establish a satisfactory investment program by concerning yourself primarily with a fair return on your money and growth consistent with the economic development of our nation. It's when you try to beat the averages that you run into trouble.

For example, many top-rated stocks today are returning little more than 6 percent in yield, if that. Don't expect a 12-percent return on stock of this caliber—such a yield would imply serious risk. Then again, a fine growth stock may produce no yield. But the same is true of very poor issues. In all cases, careful analysis is required. Techniques of stock evaluation will be discussed in Chapter 22. Let us now examine the nature of stock itself.

TYPES OF STOCK

What is a share of stock? Each stock certificate represents a part-ownership in a corporation. The owner-shareholder receives dividends only after all other obligations against the corporation have been paid.

PREFERRED STOCK

Stock falls into two principal categories—preferred and common. Preferred, as the name implies, normally has priority over common stock in the payment of dividends and assets. Preferred shareholders usually receive a stated dividend rate. However, there are participating preferred issues available that, under specified conditions, are eligible for dividends above the stated rate. A corporation may have more than one class of preferred stock, offering, for example, both preferred and prior-preferred. The prior-preferred stock has priority as to the distribution of dividends and assets over either the preferred or the common. Another type of preferred, convertible-preferred, can be converted into common stock.

COMMON STOCK

The most widely used method of capitalization is through issuance of common stock. Shareholders of common stock are the last shareholders in a corporation to receive dividends and are not limited to any fixed rate of return. Thus, in prosperous earning periods, owners of common stock may receive a high yield on their investment, whereas in poor earning periods they may receive nothing. On the other hand, growth companies like Xerox and IBM provide holders of common stock with small yields regardless of earnings, because they plow profit back into their corporations instead of paying out higher dividends. Owners of IBM and Xerox stock sacrifice immediate dividend return for increases in the market value of their issues. This is a common characteristic of all growth companies.

Since the layman seldom has the time or background necessary to develop a complex portfolio, I recommend that you stick to common stock. Preferred issues combine some features of stock and bonds but in my opinion lack the best qualities of either. They are not as safe as U.S. Treasury bonds and do not offer the eventual dividends or growth potential found in common stock. Common stock in growth corporations is the fourth link in the financial chain, following 1) checking account, 2) savings account in a bank or other financial institution and 3) government bonds.

DETERMINING YIELD

All prospective stockholders should know how to compute yield. This is done by taking the annual dividend (or interest) paid and dividing it by the current market price. For example, if a stock pays a $1.20 annual dividend and is presently selling at $24 per share, its yield is 5 percent. The same method of computing current yield applies to interest on savings accounts or bonds. A bank paying $4.50 per year on each $100 invested gives the investor a yield of 4½ percent. A $1,000 corporate bond paying $40 per year and currently purchased in the open market at $500 yields 8 percent. By determining the yield before purchase, you can compare stock values in terms of expectable income.

It is important to realize that buying and selling securities is done in a free market. That is, the person who sells generally does so because he thinks that the price of the stock is going down; whereas the person who buys believes that the stock is increasing in value. Consider as well that there are many people more skilled than you on the lookout for special situations and bargain issues. Don't try to compete with them. If the "expert"—followed by the crowd— believed that a stock's 12-percent yield meant a good buy, he would have bought the stock himself. And, when stocks do catch on, remember that the effect of heavy demand on a security is to raise its price, with a resultant lower yield.

Actually, yield on your stocks should be your last concern. Stock dividends, after you deduct $100 in any one year are taxable on the same basis as your other income. Therefore, even if your tax bracket is as low as 20 percent (and it probably won't be, if you are in a position to buy stocks), a 5-percent yield will actually give you only 4 percent.

For this reason, it is seldom wise for a person who is under retirement age to buy income stocks. Growth stocks are far more likely to bring you to your million-dollar goal.

THE COST OF TRADING SHARES

BUYING AND SELLING SMALL LOTS

One of my students recently reported the following experience in regard to the high cost of buying and selling small amounts of stock. He had purchased one share of a company listed on the New York Stock Exchange. A short time later, the bank threatened to repossess his car unless an overdue payment was made promptly, and he was forced to sell the stock at the purchase price. His costs are shown in Table 21-1:

TABLE 21-1 Cost of Small-Volume Stock Transaction

Purchase price for one share	$56.00	
Commission paid*	+15.00	
Total cost		$71.00
Selling price	$56.00	
Commission paid	−15.00	
	$41.00	
N.Y. State Tax	−.03	
	$0.97	
SEC fee	−.01	
Amount received from sale		40.96
Net loss		$30.04

*The commission that brokerage firms may charge per order on an amount involving less than $100 is as mutually agreed between the firm and the client.

The student lost $30.04, or approximately 54 percent of the price of the stock and received no dividend during the two-month period he owned it. This loss was due entirely to commissions and other fees involved in buying and selling the share; there was no decline in the price of the stock itself.

A look at the rates in Table 21-2 further emphasizes the high cost of small-share purchases. Note the variation in charges based upon different dollar amounts invested in the purchase of a stock selling at fifty-six dollars a share:

TABLE 21-2 Cost of Small-Share Purchases

No. of Shares	Cost Less Commission	Broker's Commission	Percent
10	$ 560	$ 24.00	4.3
25	1,400	38.75	2.8
50	2,800	56.30	2.0
100	5,600	80.73	1.4
1000	56,000	529.09	1.0

As indicated in the table above, if you purchase ten shares at fifty-six dollars per share, your cost amounts to 4.3 percent, as compared with 2.0 percent on a purchase of fifty shares at the same price. The 100-share purchaser pays only

1.0 percent. Investment companies, banks, foundations, wealthy people and others who make larger dollar purchases make further savings. These investors have sufficient financial muscle to permit them to bargain with brokerage firms for the best deals.[3]

The information in Tables 21-1 and 21-2, as well as the story of the one-share transaction, illustrates the importance of following certain guidelines in purchasing stock:

1. Don't buy stock unless you can afford it. As noted earlier, it is best to be debt-free at the time of purchase.
2. Buy stock in sufficient quantities so that the commission is only a small percentage of the total investment. The long-range goal should be to make round-lot transactions.
3. Be sure to determine all costs before making a purchase or sale.

FIXED COMMISSION RATES

Figure 21-1 presents the commission rates charged by brokers for transactions

Figure 21-1   Minimum New York and American Stock Exchange commission rates prior to May 1, 1975.

On 100 Share Orders and Odd Lot Orders

Money Involved In The Order	Minimum Commission
$ 100—but under $ 800	2.0% plus $ 6.40
$ 800—but under $2,500	1.3% plus $12.00
$2,500—and above	0.9% plus $22.00

Odd Lot—$2 Less

Multiple Round Lot Orders

$ 100—but under $ 2,500	1.3% plus $ 12.00
$ 2,500—but under $20,000	0.9% plus $ 22.00
$20,000—but under $30,000	0.6% plus $ 82.00
$30,000—to and including $300,000	0.4% plus $142.00

Plus (for Each Round Lot)

First to tenth round lot	$6 per round lot
Eleventh round lot and above	$4 per round lot

PLUS On any order involving an amount not in excess of $5,000. the commission computed in accordance with the foregoing provisions was increased by 10%. and on any order involving an amount in excess of $5,000. the commission computed in accordance with such provisions was increased by 15% and then 8%.

In actual practice. the commission charge for bond transaction is usually around $5.00 per $1,000 bond. with some discounts for large quantity orders.

[3]The reduced-rate concept for large transactions became effective December 5, 1968. Before that date, the basic rate had been the same regardless of the number of round-lot (100) shares purchased. However, investment companies and other large institutions had begun making transactions off the NYSE in ever-increasing numbers. Smart "go-between" brokers would find a buyer and a seller, and would complete the transaction for a smaller commission than that charged by the exchanges. This was the primary cause of the lowering of commissions for those who could best afford them.

on the New York Stock Exchange prior to May 1, 1975. This information can give you a basis for comparing current negotiated rates with the old fixed commissions.

NEGOTIATED RATES

On May 1, 1975, fixed commissions on exchanges were eliminated. What brought this change about? In recent years there had been criticism about the fixed commission rates established by the various organized exchanges. Since all firms charged the same price, this precluded the customer's shopping around. A breakthrough occurred in 1968, when it was decreed that commissions on large orders ($300,000 and over) could be negotiated. After considerable study, the SEC ordered that fixed rates be eliminated by the May 1975 date regardless of the amounts involved. As a first step, on April 1, 1974, the SEC authorized brokerage firms to establish their own commission rates on transactions of $2,000 or less. As a result, some firms lowered their commissions and others raised them. Merrill Lynch, for example, lowered its rates by 16.7 percent to 29.5 percent. However, by accepting the lower prices under this special plan, the customer forfeited certain benefits. Merrill Lynch required such investors to buy at the current market price and pay for their purchases at the time the order was placed. The dollars given to Merrill Lynch determined the number of shares to be purchased—to include fractional amounts. The firm kept the securities in its possession; however, if the buyer desired certificates for the full shares, they would be mailed at a prevailing charge. If the customer wanted those services formerly offered for the $2,000-or-under purchase, Merrill Lynch provided them at the established commission rates effective prior to May 1, 1975. By mid-1976 the rates of a number of brokerage firms were above pre-May 1975. See Figure 21-3 for a major firm's rates.

The move to negotiated rates has in general resulted in higher costs for the small investor and reduced rates for institutionalized buyers. Although it is possible in some cases for the little guy to obtain a lower commission charge, it requires astute shopping. Investors should obtain all the necessary facts about costs and benefits before selecting a brokerage firm. For example, if you want the broker only to buy your stock and ship the certificate to you, be sure this is understood. Obtain a copy of the current posted rates. It pays to take your time in order not to be taken.

The opportunity for the small investor to secure lower rates should improve in the future. A recent *Barron's* article pointed out the increased competition for retail brokerage business. The article said that Chemical Bank is expected to offer to individuals facilities to buy and sell stocks through its branches at lower fees than those currently charged by most brokerage houses. Such action, it was reported, could result in other big banks wanting to get a piece of the action.

The article went on to point out how institutions have done well since the advent of negotiated rates, but not the small investor. *Barron's* said:

Last, Best Hope

A potential boon to smaller investors—for whom boons in recent years have been few and far between—these new entrants on the retail brokerage scene have evoked scant hurrahs from older hands on Wall Street. For too many firms, large and small alike, the retail customer is the last, best hope for the good life. Since the onset of negotiated rates on May 1, 1975, institutions have pushed brokers against the wall in their demands for deep discounts on executions. Word is that discounts off old minimum rates range as high as 85%. By contrast, retail commissions not only have shown few signs of cracking but also are often above pre-Mayday levels. The reason, in the words of one wire house executive: "Institutions dictate to us. We dictate to individuals." The public, in short, lacks muscle. As a matter of fact, the lure of the retail commission dollar is attracting plenty of active attention from unexpected sources these days. On June 2, 1976, for example, the specialist firm of Kingsley, Boye & Southwood launched an advertising blitz in the estimable pages of *Barron's, The Wall Street Journal* and *The New York Times* that carried the banner headline: "Why are you paying your broker for services you never use?" It pitched commission discounts of up to 50% off old New York Stock Exchange minimums.[4]

OVER-THE-COUNTER TRADING

The cost on over-the-counter stocks is more difficult to compute than that of a purchase made on an exchange.[5] For example, Figure 21-2 indicates that the bid price on Affiliated Bankshares is fifteen dollars per share and the asked price is sixteen dollars. So if you had bought Affiliated on June 29, 1977, it might have cost you sixteen dollars per share. If you had sold it, you might have received sixteen dollars. Thus, on a hundred-share transaction there would be a hundred-dollar differential, or an almost 7-percent loss. This is a higher commission than if you made a similar transaction on a major exchange. However, Figure 21-2 states, "All over-the-counter prices printed on this page

[4]G. G. Mahon. "Eight Cents a Share—Competition for Retail Brokerage Business." *Barron's,* July 12, 1976, p. 5.
[5]The over-the-counter market consists of the thousands of corporations not listed on organized exchanges.

Figure 21-2 Extract of stock transactions on over-the-counter markets.

Over-the-Counter Markets

4:00 p.m. Eastern Time Prices, Wednesday, June 29, 1977

All over the counter prices printed on this page are representative quotations supplied by the National Association of Securities Dealers through NASDAQ, its automated system for reporting quotes. Prices don't include retail markup, markdown or commission. Volume represents shares that changed ownership during the day. Figures include only those transactions effected by NASDAQ market makers but may include some duplication where NASDAQ market makers traded with each other.

Volume, All Issues, 7,447,900

SINCE JANUARY 1

	1977	1976	1975
Total sales	912,566,176	860,099,651	740,291,842

MARKET DIARY

	Wed	Tues	Mon	Fri	Thur
Issues traded	2,540	2,538	2,535	2,534	2,535
Advances	342	292	416	583	436
Declines	336	434	304	188	245
Unchanged	1,862	1,812	1,815	1,763	1,854
xNew highs	52	57	100	90	74
xNew lows	21	32	16	14	20

x-Based on 4 p.m. Eastern time bid quote.

MOST ACTIVE STOCKS

	Volume	4:00 Bid	Chg.
Gov Employee Insur	472,000	6¼	....
Daylin Inc	117,400	1 9/16	+1/16
De Beers Cons Mines ADR	113,300	3 3/16	+1/16
Penn Offshore Gas B	102,100	14¼	....
Energy Reserve Group	98,400	2⅜	+1/16
Triton Oil & Gas	96,200	9¾	+ ⅞
Nicolet Instrument Cp	93,200	8½	+ ½
Geosource Inc	81,100	23	+ 1
Adolph Coors Co B	79,400	17⅝	....
Penn La Tex Offshore	73,000	6	−1/16

Stock & Div.	Sales 100s	Bid	Asked	Net Chg.
--A A--				
AaronBro .20e	43	9¾	10¾	...
Acady Ins Grp	40	1 15-16	2 3-16	−1-16
AccelratnC .80	71	16¾	17½	...
AcetoChm 5.5i	14	17	18	+ ¼
ACMAT Corp	3	1⅝	2⅛	− ⅛
Acme Elec .28	12	10⅛	10⅝	...
ADA Res .08b	92	4½	4⅞	+ ⅛
AddWesley .40	1	7	7½	...
Advance Ross	16	3	3⅜	− ¼
Advan MicroD	156	25¼	25¾	+ ¾
Advent Corp	15	3¾	4¼	...
AEL Indust A	13	5⅛	5½	− ⅛
Aerosonc .06d	25	2⅞	3¼	...
Air Florida Sy	36	2¼	2¾	...
Affil Bnksh .84	6	15	16	...
AgMet Incorp	16	9	9½	− ¼
Agnico Eagle	87	5	5¼	+ ⅛
AlaBancp 1.32	64	25	26	...
AlaTennN 1.40	7	17½	18½	+ ⅛
Alanthus C .25	25	3¾	4¼	...
Alaska Gold	3	3	3¾	− ¼
Alaska Intl .24	1	5¼	6¼	...
AlexandA 1.40	161	44⅝	45⅛	− ¼
Alex Bald 1.20	75	16¼	16¾	− ⅜
AlicoIncp .17d	1	12¾	13¼	+ ⅛
Allegheny Bv	7	4½	4¾	...
AlliedBncs .84	34	29½	30	...
AlliedTch .05b	70	1 13-16	2 1-16	−1-16
Allied Tele .60	5	14¼	14¾	...
Allyn Bacn .45	2	10½	11	...
Altex Oil Corp	2	⅝	11-16	...
AltonBoxBrd 1	4	16½	17	...
AmbassG .05b	18	12	12¾	− ½
Amarex Incor	103	16⅛	16⅝	+ ⅝
Amco Energy	98	3⅝	4	+ ⅛
Amdahl .05b	230	26	27	+ ¼
Am Aprsl .15b	5	4¾	5⅛	...
AmBkr Ins .24	126	4⅛	4½	...
AmBkTrPa 1g	z58	17	18	...
AmBkrLf .20g	29	4½	5	...
Am Biomedicl	7	2¾	3	...
Cinn FclCo .80	z30	18¾	19¼	...
Circle Inc .85b	49	15¼	15¾	+ ⅛
CitzSthnCp .96	12	15¼	16¼	...
CitSoNBGa .52	302	6½	6⅞	...
CitizenFid 1.44	z65	32¼	33¼	...
Citz UtilB 2.14	24	30¾	31½	+ ¼
CitzUtil A 3.3k	10	36⅜	36⅞	...
City NatlCp 1g	1	22	23½	...
ClarkJl Mfg 1	12	27	28½	...
ClevTrust Rlt	3	3½	4	...
Clevetrust 1.80	53	35¼	36¼	+ ¼
Clow Corp .40	14	9¾	10¼	− ⅛
CoastlStCp .28	15	5¾	6⅛	− ⅛
Cobe Labrator	12	20½	21¼	− ¼
CocCBtCon .52	3	12	12¾	...
CocaCB La .90	6	20⅜	20¾	...
CoCBtlMia .48	61	11½	12¼	+ 1
CCBtlMidA .50	18	14¼	15	+ ⅝
Coherent Incp	12	5¾	6½	− ¼
College Un .18	51	10	10½	...
ColonBnc 1.60	x6	17½	19	...
ColGasEn 1.32	2	10⅞	11⅜	...
ColLifeAcc .32	5	10¾	11¼	...
ColoNatBnks 1	13	16¾	17½	...
CombndIns .80	183	15¾	16⅛	...
Comdisco .40	3	10	10¾	...
ComclClHs .50	5	13⅞	14⅜	...
ComlShrg .70g	7	27	28½	...
CwthNtRs 1.68	2	20	21	...
CmwTlPa 2.08	7	31½	32½	...
Comunc In .48	21	18¾	19¼	...
Commun Prop	15	5⅞	6¼	− ⅛
CompSvc Ntw	8	12½	13½	− ¼
Compuscan In	5	7¾	8¼	...
CmptrAuto .16	42	26	26½	− ¼
Cmptr Comm	184	6⅜	6¾	+ ¼
Computer Con	7	6	6¾	...
ComptrE S .16	41	9⅛	9⅝	...
Computer Ntw	22	5⅞	6⅜	...
Cmptrvisn Cp	71	7⅞	8⅜	...
Comtech Labs	56	7¾	8¾	+ ¼
Comten Incp	136	11¾	12¼	...
1st UtdBcp .60	z18	17¼	18	− ¼
First West Fin	5	2¾	3	− ⅛
Flagship Bank	28	5⅞	6⅜	− ⅛
FlaComBk .76	6	11	11¾	...
Fla Cyprs .10b	12	3½	3⅞	...
FlaGRlTr .64b	2	12½	13½	...
FlaMgMtl .24b	1	10¾	11½	+ ¼
Fla NatlBk .36	18	14¼	14⅝	− ⅛
Flurocarbn .20	6	9	10	...
Flynn Energy	18	8	9	+ ¼
Food Town .12	4	18¾	19¾	...
FoothllGr .22g	6	8⅜	8⅞	...
Forest Oil .60a	151	19½	19⅞	− ⅛
FotomatCp .32	28	11⅜	11⅞	− ⅛
FourPhase Sy	85	15⅜	15⅞	+ ¼
Frankln El .40	9	15¼	15¾	− ⅛
FranklinLife 1	72	23⅛	23½	...
FrasrMtg .75b	2	10¼	11	...
FredkHerr .24	4	4½	5	...
Fremnt G .38b	54	13¾	14¼	− ⅛
Frndly Ice .10	18	11	11¾	− ¼
Froz FdEx .36	z50	9⅜	9⅞	...
Fuller H B .56	193	10	10½	...
Fundng Systm	4	4	5	...
Funtime Incp	7	10¼	11¼	...
Furrs Cafe .40	33	7⅜	7¾	− ⅜
--G G--				
Galaxy Oil Co	219	7⅜	7¾	+ ⅛
Galaxy Oil ut	57	9¼	9¾	+ ¼
Galaxy Oil wt	51	2	2½	+ ⅛
Galvestn H .20	33	18⅛	18⅝	+ ⅛
Gelco Corp .46	x230	17¾	18¼	+ ½
Gelman Instr	27	14¼	15	+ ¼
Gen Automatn	91	7	7½	...
GenAutoPt .96	22	27½	28½	...
Gen Bindg .12	10	9¼	10	...
GenCare Corp	169	11¾	12¼	...
GenCmptr Sys	20	1⅜	1¾	...
Genl Datacom	11	6⅜	6⅞	+ ¼
GenlEnrgy .10	27	17¼	17¾	+ ¼
Gen Hlth Serv	90	4⅜	4¾	+ ⅜
GenOhioSL .20	14	6⅛	6⅝	− ⅛

EXPLANATORY NOTES

z-Sales in full.
a-Annual rate plus cash extra or extras. b-Paid so far this year, no regular rate. c-Declared or paid since stock dividend or split, no regular rate. d-Paid last year. e-Declared or paid in 1977 plus stock. f-Declared or paid in 1976 plus stock. g-Annual rate plus stock dividend. h-Paid this year, latest dividend omitted. i-Paid in stock in 1976. k-Percent paid in stock in 1977. r-Ex-rights. x-Ex-diviidend. y-Ex-distribu tion. (z) No representative quote.

Source: *The Wall Street Journal*, June 30, 1977, p. 22.

are representative quotations supplied by the National Association of Security Dealers through NASDAQ, its automated system for reporting quotes. Prices don't include retail markup, markdown or commission."

Therefore, it is very important to find out the actual costs when buying and selling over-the-counter stocks. Some brokers charge a commission in addition to the spread between the bid and asked prices. Others price the over-the-counter stock at a greater spread than is listed in the papers. Shop around to get the best deal.

It is usual to pay considerably more commission on over-the-counter transactions than on the major exchanges. And since you are normally dealing with a less active market, if you wish to sell in a hurry you may have trouble finding a buyer at a fair price.

SOURCES OF MARKET INFORMATION

THE FINANCIAL SECTION

There is an abundance of factual material about stocks to be found in the financial sections of the major newspapers. The most comprehensive data appears in *The Wall Street Journal*. An understanding of this material is helpful in the selection of appropriate stocks.

Let us look, for example, at Figure 21-3, an extract of daily New York Stock Exchange (NYSE) composite transactions.[6] The volume is the number of shares and warrants that were traded on June 29, 1977: 22,197,280 shares and 223,700 warrants. The fifteen most active stocks (those with the most shares traded) are listed with their volumes and price ranges. There are approximately 2,000 stocks listed on the NYSE, yet you will note that on the day in question, 2,895,900 shares were traded in these fifteen stocks alone—or about 13 percent of the total volume. If you want a ready market for the sale of your securities, it is advantageous to have an issue with a large number of common shares that are actively traded on a major exchange.

In addition to the report on the fifteen most active stocks, the extract cited above provides helpful information on individual issues. Consider the case of American Airlines. Its high and low for the year were 14½ and 8⅝.

---

[6]Quotations on the NYSE now include trades on the New York, Midwest, Pacific, Philadelphia, Boston and Cincinnati stock exchanges and reported by NASDAQ and Instinet.

Figure 21-3 Extract of composite transactions on the NYSE.

NYSE-Composite Transactions

Wednesday, June 29, 1977

Quotations include trades on the New York, Midwest, Pacific, Philadelphia, Boston and Cincinnati stock exchanges and reported by the National Association of Securities Dealers and Instinet.

26 **THE WALL STREET JOURNAL,**
Thursday, June 30, 1977

Wednesday's Volume
22,197,280 Shares; 223,800 Warrants

TRADING BY MARKETS

	Shares	Warrants
New York Exchange	19,000,000	223,700
American Exchange	5,400	....
Midwest Exchange	1,021,000	....
Pacific Exchange	788,300	....
Nat'l Assoc. of Securities Dealers	863,080	100
Philadelphia Exchange	213,700	....
Boston Exchange	85,900	....
Cincinnati Exchange	181,800	....
Instinet System	38,000	....

NYSE—Composite

Volume since Jan. 1:	1977	1976	1975
Total shares	3,081,263,412	3,390,916,427	....
Total warrants ..	14,196,400	12,038,600	....

New York Stock Exchange

Volume since Jan. 1:	1977	1976	1975
Total shares	2,628,501,042	2,904,073,827	2,661,859,390
Total warrants ..	14,157,700	14,857,100	61,748,600

MOST ACTIVE STOCKS

	Open	High	Low	Close	Chg.	Volume
Brit Pet	16⅛	16¼	16⅛	16¼	+ ¼	323,000
Norton Sim	17⅞	17⅞	17⅝	17¾	− ¼	302,100
US Steel	38	38¾	38	38¾	.....	274,400
Inexco Oil	27⅝	28½	27¼	28½	+1⅛	217,000
AtlRichfl	60½	60⅝	60	60⅝	− ⅛	212,100
K mart	28	28¼	27¾	28	− ¼	199,100
PhillpsPet	31⅛	31⅜	31	31⅜	− ¼	187,600
Dan River	12⅛	13⅞	12⅛	13½	+1⅜	170,800
Dow Ch	34⅛	34⅛	33⅝	34	.....	168,000
Un Carbide	49⅛	49¼	48¼	48⅞	− ⅜	152,600
Exxon	52¾	53	52⅝	52¾	− ⅛	149,600
Alcoa	53	53⅛	52½	53	− ⅜	147,500
IBM	263½	265¾	261½	265¼	+1⅛	136,100
Cont Oil	33½	33⅞	33½	33¾	+ ⅛	129,700
Rockwel Int	36⅞	37	36½	36¾	− ½	126,300

1977 High	1977 Low	Stocks	Div.	P-E Ratio	Sales 100s	High	Low	Close	Net Chg.
		— A-A-A —							
39⅜	32⅜	ACF	2	9	108	36⅜	36⅛	36⅛	− ¼
23¼	18⅜	AMF	1.24	10	140	19⅝	19¼	19½	+ ⅛
15⅜	12⅞	APL Cp	1	6	32	14⅛	14⅛	14⅛	......
50¾	36¾	ARASv	1.32	11	32	41¾	41½	41¾	......
23⅝	17¼	ASALtd	.80	..	234	18¾	18¼	18⅜	+ ⅛
12⅜	9⅜	ATOInc	.40	7	103	11⅞	11⅝	11¾	+ ⅛
49⅛	38⅞	AbbtLab	1.20	13	287	44⅝	44	44⅛	− ⅜
13¼	9½	AcmeC	.50	16	32	12	11⅞	11⅞	− ⅛
3½	2⅝	AdmDg	.04	5	9	3	2⅞	3	+ ¼
13¼	11⅝	AdmEx	1.15e	..	10	12¼	12	12¼	+ ¼
5	3⅞	AdmMl	.10e	7	28	4	4	4	......
14⅜	9⅞	Addrsg	.10e	23	421	14⅜	13⅞	14⅜	+ ⅜
37½	28⅜	AetnaLf	1.60	8	541	37⅜	37	37⅜	+ ⅛

1977 High	1977 Low	Stocks	Div.	P-E Ratio	Sales 100s	High	Low	Close	Net Chg.
16	10½	Aguirre		..	33	15¾	15½	15¾	+ ¼
20	15⅛	Ahmans	.40	5	15	17⅞	17⅝	17⅝	− ¼
3⅞	2¾	Aileen		63	32	3¼	3⅛	3⅛	− ⅛
35⅞	22½	AirPrd	.20b	11	268	24⅜	24	24¼	+ ¼
15½	11½	AirbFrt	.60	10	98	12¼	11⅝	11¾	− ⅝
34⅛	28¼	Airco	1.15	7	407	32¾	32⅛	32⅛	− ¾
19⅛	15¾	Akzona	1.20	70	20	16⅛	16	16⅛	......
16⅞	14⅜	AlaGas	1.28	7	3	15¾	15½	15¾	+ ⅛
116½	112	AlaP pf	11	..	z10	114¾	114¾	114¾	+ ½
105	93	AlaP pf	9.44	..	z1000	104	104	104	− ⅞
21½	15	Alaskln	.66	8	132	19	18¼	18½	......
20⅛	17¼	Albany	.80	6	7	17⅞	17¾	17¾	+ ⅛
8⅛	6	Alberto	.36	18	25	6⅞	6⅝	6⅝	− ⅛
23¼	19⅜	Albertsn	.80	9	94	23¼	23	23	− ⅛
29½	23⅛	AlcanAl	.80	14	621	27⅜	27	27	− ⅜
23¾	18⅛	AlcoStd	.96	6	6	22⅞	22⅞	22⅞	− ⅛
23⅛	16⅛	AlconLb	.32	14	74	19¼	18⅞	19⅛	− ⅜
8⅛	5⅝	Alexdr	.40e	7	28	6⅞	6⅝	6⅝	− ⅛
15⅛	11⅞	AllgCp	.60a	7	35	14⅝	14⅜	14⅝	+ ¼
25⅛	20½	AllgLd	1.28	8	11	20½	d20¼	20¼	− ¼
43⅛	39¼	AllgLd pf	3	..	5	40¼	40	40¼	+ ¼
22⅝	19⅞	AllgPw	1.68	8	133	21½	21¼	21⅜	− ⅛
14½	12¾	AllenGp	.70	7	28	14¼	14	14¼	......
22½	20	Allergan	.40	10	54	22⅜	21¾	21⅞	− ¼
51⅜	38¾	AlldCh	1.80	13	195	50⅛	49⅝	50	− ¼
14⅝	12¼	AlldMnt	.64	7	1	13	13	13	......
12½	10	AlldPd	.45e	22	28	10⅞	10½	10¾	+ ⅜
23½	19⅝	AlldStr	1	7	816	23⅛	22¾	22¾	− ¼
56½	53½	AlldStr pf	4	..	z20	55½	55½	55½	+ 1½
4	2¾	AlldSup		..	47	4	3¾	4	+ ⅛
33¾	23½	AllisCh	1.10	7	133	30⅝	30⅛	30⅝	+ ⅛
10⅛	8⅝	AllrtAut	.60	9	4	9¾	9¾	9¾	− ⅛
19	14½	AlphPrt	.72	4	3	15⅝	15½	15½	+ ⅛
59½	50½	Alcoa	1.80	11	1475	53⅛	52½	53	− ⅜
36¾	25	AmlSug	2	6	8	26¼	26	26¼	+ ¼
59¾	42	Amax	1.75	10	171	42	d41½	41¾	− ¼
141	101¾	Amax pf	5.25	..	1	102½	102½	102½	......
59¾	45⅝	Amax pf	3	..	22	45¾	d45½	45¾	+ ⅛
29⅞	21⅝	AMBAC	1	9	60	28¼	27¾	27¾	− ¾
13⅛	10⅜	Amcord	.60	8	22	11½	11⅜	11⅜	......
20⅝	17½	Amrce	1.20	7	9	u20¾	20⅝	20¾	+ ½
37½	33¾	Amrc pf	2.60	..	7	u37⅝	37⅜	37⅝	+ ½
36⅞	29½	AHess	.80b	8	341	36½	35⅞	36½	+ ¼
81¼	66½	AHes pf	3.50	..	103	90	79	80	+ ½
24	18⅛	AAirFilt	.56	10	25	21	20⅝	20⅞	+ ¼
14¾	10	AmAir		5	185	10¾	10½	10¾	+ ⅛
5	2¾	AmAir wt		..	39	3⅞	3¾	3¾	......
22¼	[illegible]	AAir pf	2.18	..	40	21⅝	21⅜	21½	+ ⅛
16¼	13⅛	AmBaker	1	6	20	15½	15⅜	15½	− ¼
48⅛	43	ABrnds	2.92	10	113	46⅝	46⅛	46½	+ ⅛
26	23½	ABrd pf	1.70	..	2	24⅝	24⅝	24⅝	......
46¾	37	ABdcst	1	10	98	43⅝	43	43⅝	+ ¼
12¼	10⅛	ABldM	.50	7	25	12⅛	12⅛	12⅛	......
41⅜	38¼	AmCan	2.40	8	68	40	39⅜	40	+ ¼
24	22¼	ACan pf	1.75	..	27	u24⅛	23⅜	23⅝	......
6¼	4½	BellInd	.08a	5	71	4⅞	4¾	4¾	− ¼
50⅜	45¼	BellCd	4.08	8	24	49¾	49⅝	49¾	+ ⅛
22⅞	19¼	Bemis	1.20	7	84	20⅛	20	20	− ⅛
47	38	Bendix	2	8	55	40½	40	40	− ¾
95	80	Bendix pf	3	..	1	82	82	82	− 1¼
27	21⅜	BenfCp	1.60	6	166	24	23⅝	23¾	− ⅛
60⅜	47½	Benef pf	4.30	..	6	51½	51⅜	51½	− ½
117	96¼	Benef pf	5.50	..	z40	106	106	106	− ¼
30	27½	Benef pf	2.50	..	z50	29½	29½	29½	......
2¼	1⅜	BnfStM		..	7	1⅞	1⅞	1⅞	......
3⅝	1½	BengtB	.08	14	97	2⅝	2½	2⅝	+ ⅛
6¼	4	BerkeyP		14	117	4⅜	4¼	4⅜	......
24	17⅝	BestPd		8	45	21½	21⅛	21⅜	− ⅜

Source: *The Wall Street Journal*, June 30, 1977, p. 26.

Figure 21-4 Stock transactions on six exchanges.

Other Markets

(Selected Stocks; Dually Listed Issues Excluded)

Thursday, June 30, 1977

Toronto Exchange
Quotations in Canadian funds.
Quotations in cents unless marked $.

Sales	Stock	High	Low	Close	Chg.
3152	Abitibi	$9⅞	9½	9⅞	+ ⅛
300	Acklands	$11½	11½	11½	
5668	Agnico E	$5⅝	5½	5⅝	
100	Agra Ind A	$5¾	5¾	5¾	+ ¼
22586	Alta Gas A	$15¼	15⅛	15¼	
8600	Alta Nat	$39½	38	39¼	+1¼
1050	Alliance B	365	360	360	− 5
7600	Alminex	$9	8⅞	8⅞	
26090	Am Bonza	$16¼	15⅝	16¼	+ ⅛
600	Argus C pr	$11⅛	11⅛	11⅛	
750	Atco A	$17⅛	17	17	
23717	Bell Canad	$53⅛	50⅞	53⅛	+ ½
8480	BP Can	$13½	13⅛	13¼	− ¼
1600	Banister C	$13⅝	13½	13½	− ⅛
8164	Bank N S	$20¾	20½	20¾	+ ⅛
3713	Block Bros	$5¾	5¾	5¾	
22650	Bovis Cor	75	70	75	+10
7540	Bralor Res	440	430	440	+ 5
600	Bramalea	$6½	6¼	6¼	
13670	Brameda	149	140	145	
200	Brenda M	$9	9	9	− ⅜
18765	Bridger	$9⅛	9	9⅛	+ ⅛
1700	BCFP	$23	22¾	22¾	− ⅜
1400	BC Phone	$14¾	14¾	14¾	+ ⅜
3600	Brunswk	460	455	460	− 5
500	Budd Auto	$7¼	7¼	7¼	
700	Burns Fds	$9¾	9⅝	9¾	
1200	Cad Frv	$9¼	9	9¼	+ ¼
9278	Cal Pow A	$35¼	35⅛	35⅛	− ¼
4425	Camflo	$11⅞	11¼	11⅞	+ ⅝
1950	Campau A	425	415	425	+10
1800	C Nor West	$7⅛	7	7⅛	+ ⅜
3875	C Pakrs C	$18⅛	18	18	− ⅜
3650	Can Perm	$18⅛	18	18w1	
7665	Can Trust A	$25	24⅞	25	+ ½
2360	C Tung	$10¼	10	10⅛	
303	C Cablesy	$12	12	12	+ ⅜
800	Cdn Cel	$7⅞	7⅝	7⅝	− ¼
100	CGE	$23½	23½	23½	+ ½
11357	CI Bk Com	$24½	23⅞	24	− ½
1754	Cdn Tire A	$34½	34⅜	34⅜	− ⅛
2438	C Uilties	$14⅜	14¼	14⅜	+ ⅛
3300	Cassiar	$9½	8⅞	9½	+ ½
5500	Celanese	345	335	345	+10
19500	Chieftan D	$14⅛	13¼	14	+ 1
10055	C Holiday I	410	400	410	+15
3800	Con Bldg	285	275	285	+10
10100	Con Distrb	360	350	355	+10
6580	Cons Gas	$16½	16¼	16¼	
2324	Con Fardy	295	290	295	+ 3
4900	Conwest	$5¼	495	5⅛	+ ⅛
925	Craigmt	$5⅞	5¾	5⅞	+ ⅛
500	Crush Intl	$8¼	8¼	8¼	
4150	Cyprus	$9½	9⅜	9½	
3487	Denison	$47½	47¼	47¼	
5200	Dicknsn	410	405	405	+ 5
785	Dofasco A	$25⅜	25⅜	25⅜	+ ⅛
400	Dom Store	$16	15⅞	15⅞	+ ⅛
2750	Du Pont	$14¾	14¼	14¾	+ ¾
10100	Dylex L A	$7	6⅞	7	+ ⅛
1497	East Mal	215	208	215	+ 6
1555	Emco	$5¼	5⅛	5¼	
4115	Falcon C	$5¾	5⅜	5¾	+ ⅜
7500	Fibrg Nik A	$33⅞	33½	33⅞	+ ⅜
2590	Fed Ind A	$6	5⅞	6	
20	Francana	$7¾	7¾	7¾	− ⅛
50	Fraser A	$24	24	24	
4725	G M Res	350	340	350	+20
2100	Gibraltar	$5⅞	5¾	5⅞	+ ⅛
3080	Graft G	$18¾	18¾	18¾	+ ¼
4100	Granduc	91	90	90	− 3
120	Gt Oil Sds	$8¼	8¼	8¼	+ ⅛
100	GL Paper	$27½	27½	27½	
900	Gt W Life	$53	52¾	53	+ ½
197	Greyhnd	$16¾	16¾	16¾	+ ¼

Sales	Stock	High	Low	Close	Chg.
100	Talcorp A	$9¼	9¼	9¼	− ¼
100	Teck Cor B	490	490	490	+ 5
1437	Tex Can	$29¾	29¾	29¾	+ ¼
500	Thom N A	$12½	12¼	12½	+ ¼
11217	Tor Dm Bk	$18½	18¼	18½	+ ¼
3400	Torstar B	$14	13⅞	14	
6374	Traders A	$17	16¾	17	+ ⅛
14950	Trns Mt A	$11½	11¼	11½	+ ¼
11528	TrCan PL	$15⅜	15⅛	15⅜	+ ⅛
1314	UGas A	$10¼	10⅛	10¼	
784	Union Oil	$9¾	9⅝	9¾	+ ¼
1600	U Keno	$8¼	8⅛	8⅛	+ ⅜
6000	U Siscoe	$8	7¾	7¾	− ⅛
101200	Upp Can	180	165	175	+14
460	Vestgron	$13½	13	13½	+ ⅜
8900	Voyager P	$8⅞	8¾	8¾	− ⅛
1000	Weldwod	$11¾	11¾	11¾	− ¼
100	Wstburne	$10⅛	10⅛	10⅛	+ ⅛
11350	West Mine	410	385	410	+30
200	Weston	$12⅞	12⅞	12⅞	+ ⅛
380	Woodwd A	$15⅝	15½	15⅝	
620	Yk Bear	410	400	410	+ 5
800	Yukon C	176	175	175	− 1

Total sales 2,859,759 shares

Montreal Exchange
Quotations in Canadian Funds
Quotations in cents unless marked $.

Sales	Stock	High	Low	Clos	Chg.
4073	Bnk Mont	$16⅛	16	16⅛	+ ¼
375	Can Cem	$8¾	8¾	8¾	+ ⅛
100	CanSo Ry	$40	40	40	
1100	Cdn Indust	$19½	19½	19½	
5850	CdnInt Pw	$21¼	21	21¼	+ ⅛
30275	Canron	$24¼	24	24	+ ½
210	Con Bath	$23⅝	23⅝	23⅝	− ⅛
9700	Fncl Col	175	170	175	+5
632	Gaz Metro	$6¼	6¼	6¼	+ ⅛
1474	Imasco	$26½	26¼	26½	+ ¼
250	Power Cp	$8½	8½	8½	− ⅛
385	Price Co	$9⅜	9¼	9⅜	
1220	Royal Bnk	$26⅝	26⅝	26⅝	
5700	RoyTrst A	$16	16	16	
1100	Steinbrg A	$16½	16½	16½	+ ⅜
1430	Zellers	500	495	500	

Total sales 599,077 shares.

Midwest Stocks

Sales	Stock	High	Low	Close	Chg.
800	CarsonPirS	20¼	20⅛	20¼	+ ¼
20	IndMh pf	44	44	44	+1⅛
300	InlandS pf	39½	39½	39½	−2
100	MetroInd	2⅜	2⅜	2⅜	− ⅛
100	Modine	40	40	40	+ ⅛
2200	OsGold Seed	4⅞	4⅞	4⅞	− ⅛
200	StdAmFn	17⅝	17⅝	17⅝	.....
600	StarrBcst Grp	5⅜	5⅜	5⅜	.....

Total stock sales 830,000

Pacific

Sales	Stock	High	Low	Close	Chg.
4500	Almaden	12⅛	12⅛	12⅛	+ ⅛
200	Aloha Airl	4⅛	4⅛	4⅛	− ⅛
8500	AlzaCp	7	6¾	7	+ ⅛
1300	AmFinpfD	9⅜	9 5-16	9⅜	+ ⅛
1003	AmFinpfE	9 3-16	9⅛	9⅛	+1-16
600	AMdBld	7¼	7⅛	7¼	− ⅛
400	AmPacestr	2	2	2	+ ⅛
1000	Amfac pf	13	13	13	+ ⅛
1200	CanSou Pet	2⅝	2½	2⅝	+ ⅛
7700	Cenco	3	2⅞	2⅞	− ⅛
700	ChiefCon Mn	4⅛	4	4	.....
500	ChrisCrwt A	11-32	11-32	11-32	+1-16
1700	Crestmt	17⅛	16⅝	17⅛	+ ½
2400	DantRus	11¾	11½	11¾	+ ½
700	Frawly Ent	5⅛	4⅞	5⅛	.....
1200	Gen Hostwt	3-16	3-16	3-16	.....
2200	Granger Asn	8⅛	7½	7⅝	− ⅜
2500	Hershey Oil	4	4	4	.....
1200	IHOP Cp	2¼	2¼	2¼	.....
800	LaPac Res	15-32	13-32	13-32	.....
1000	McCart	3	3	3	.....
25200	Memorex Cp	25⅛	24¼	25	+ ⅞
300	Merchnt Pet	2¾	2⅝	2⅝	.....
1800	Norris Oil	5⅞	5½	5⅞	+ ⅜
3000	Nytronics	1¾	1⅝	1⅝	.....
1000	PGTrans	13⅝	13½	13⅝	+ ⅛
800	PacRes	8½	8½	8½	− ⅛
100	Schick	1	1	1	.....
100	SilvrDlr	3⅞	3⅞	3⅞	.....
600	SCGspfA	17¼	17	17	.....
1000	Stanwood Cp	2½	2½	2½	+ ¼
3600	UnitCan OG	7	6⅞	7	+ ¼
4100	Zoecon Corp	17⅛	17	17	− ¼

BONDS

Sales	Bond	Issue	High	Low	Close	Chg.
23000	AFinl	9½s80	99¼	99	99¼	+ ¾
112000	AFinl	9½s88	86½	85	85	− ⅛
61000	AFinl	9½s89	86⅝	86½	86⅝	+ ⅛
2000	AFinl	11¾83	105½	104⅝	104⅝	+ ⅛
5000	Brown	9s95f	85	85	85	+1
17000	McCa	7½s91	61	61	61	+ ⅞
5000	StPac	10s89	100	100	100	−1
1000	Stwd	cv6½89	59½	59½	59½	.....

Total sales .... 1,144,000 shares.

Philadelphia Exchange

Sales	stock	High	Low	Close	Chg.
2700	Basic Food	1¼	1¼	1¼	+ ⅛
500	Grolier Inc	⅞	⅞	⅞	
4400	IntBkn pf	7⅞	7½	7½	− ¼
4300	Penn Cntral	1⅝	1½	1½	− ¼
300	Pitt Brew	2	2	2	
3500	ReincGrp wt	14	13⅞	14	

Total Sales 243,000 shares.

Boston Exchange

Sales	Stock	High	Low	Close	Chg.
100	Clmb Chase	4¼	4¼	4¼	− [illegible]
14000	Elc Missils	5	3¾	4¼	− [illegible]
400	Exolon Co	10½	10½	10½	
500	Nwprt Elec	14	14	14	+ [illegible]
900	Pegasus In	15⅝	14⅞	14⅞	− [illegible]

Total sales 180,000 shares.

Source: *The Wall Street Journal,* July 1, 1977, p. 13.

Imagine having bought 100 shares at the high and selling them at the low. Your loss, including commissions, would be almost 40 percent.

It is important to read the explanatory notes accompanying the NYSE transactions. This material provides facts about dividend payments and other pertinent information. The amount of the dividend is listed immediately after the name of the company. Notice that American Airlines had not as yet paid a dividend in 1977. The explanatory footnotes state in part: "Unless otherwise noted, rates of dividends in the foregoing table are annual disbursements based on the last quarterly or semiannual declaration."

There were 18,500 shares of American Airlines traded on June 29, 1977. The price-earnings (P-E) ratio was listed as 5. The low price for the day was 10½ ($10.50 per share) and the highest price per share was $10.75. The closing transaction was at $10.75. The stock had closed at 10½ on June 28; therefore, there was +⅛ net change from the previous day's close.

The financial page provides similar information on issues traded on the American Stock Exchange. It also lists selected transactions on other exchanges: Boston; Midwest; Pacific; Philadelphia; Montreal; and Toronto. Figure 21-4 indicates that the individual stock information presented for "Other Markets" is less than that offered for the two biggest exchanges. "Other Markets" furnishes only sales, high, low, close and change. Furthermore, stocks that are also listed on other exchanges do not appear in this compilation—a number of corporations list their stock on several exchanges.

Of all the markets, the over-the-counter market carries the largest number of corporate issues. *The Wall Street Journal* lists daily transactions of the more active companies (see Figure 21-4). The ten most active stocks are reported along with a market diary. The *Journal* also provides dividend information and volume as well as bid and asked prices. Notice that shares in banks and insurance companies, including the financial giants in these fields, are ordinarily sold over the counter. Each day the *Journal* also lists over-the-counter transactions of the less active issues. However, only bid and asked prices are reported.

Information on select foreign securities may be found daily in the *Journal*.

INVESTMENT LITERATURE

John Stillman, founder of a department-store chain, and an eminently successful financier, has said, "Hard work is the price of stock-market success; few are willing to pay the price." Hard work, in the form of the careful study of investment literature over a reasonable period of time, is a helpful tool in improving your monetary position. There are many financial periodicals and books currently in print designed to meet the needs of people who have funds available for investment purposes.

Since securities should not be bought without adequate background and understanding of the problems confronting the investor, time spent in reading pertinent literature should result in a more favorable financial return on hard-saved dollars. Much of this data is available in public libraries, as well as in brokerage houses. Some investment firms have a reading room for perusal of current financial literature. Check to be sure that sources are up-to-date as changes occur rapidly, and outmoded writings can be detrimental. Keep abreast of political, economic, social and military events that have an impact on the stock market. A list of financial literature is provided at the end of this book.

CHOOSING A BROKERAGE FIRM

Once you have acquired an adequate background on securities and have accumulated the necessary funds, you must decide where to buy your bonds and stocks. There are many brokerage houses available for this purpose. It is desirable to select a well-established firm, conveniently located, large enough to provide a variety of services and known for its integrity, profitability, good service and growth (unscrupulous brokers have been caught "churning" securities—that is, buying and selling solely to maximize commissions). Before making a choice, I recommend visiting several establishments and finding out what each has to offer. The Yellow Pages in your telephone book will indicate the brokers available in your community. Select the institution that best meets your requirements.

I am frequently asked, "Do brokers really want my business? After all, I have very limited funds to invest." Although some firms are as helpful to the client with little money as to those with sizable funds, it is true that others, at least in recent years, have tended to neglect the little guy. The better firms, however, not only welcome the small investor but stress the need for an emergency cash reserve and insurance before buying stocks. They recognize that small investors may one day be large ones. Select your broker with care. Brokers within the same firm vary to a marked degree in age and temperament. Look for the person with whom you feel you can communicate well, and don't hesitate to change brokers if you are dissatisfied. Should you encounter real trouble, inform the home office and the local manager. A letter to the local BBB, consumer-affairs office or the SEC might also be desirable.

Dealing with a large international firm can be advantageous if you travel extensively. Merrill Lynch, Pierce, Fenner & Smith (MLPFS), Inc., for example, the world's largest securities firm, has 250 offices located in the United States, Canada, the Middle East, Australia, Europe, South America, the Philippines, the Republic of China and Japan. MLPFS deals in stocks, bonds, commodities, the money market, mutual funds, real-estate financing and investment-advisory services. A well-managed organization, it succeeded in making a profit and even expanding in the dismal 1969–1970 period, when a number of securities firms failed.[7] According to a *Wall Street Journal* report:

> Observers say Merrill Lynch owes its continued success at a time when other firms are losing money, laying off workers and even closing their doors, to its long-standing adherence to well-worn precepts of professional management that are often lacking in the clubby traditions of Wall Street. It handles its assets conservatively; it believes in teamwork, training, advance planning and diversification.[8]

Going on to point out other well-managed firms, the article stated:

> And, of course, despite the relentless flow of bad news in the securities business, many firms still are operating efficiently and profitably. Among the more successful often cited are such firms as Reynolds & Co., Paine, Webber, Jackson & Curtis, Shields & Co., and Salomon Brothers & Hutzler.[9]

A variety of free services are obtainable from various brokerage firms. It pays to know what these are. Many companies have extensive research facilities and can obtain detailed recommendations to fit your needs from their home offices. As noted above, a library stocked with excellent financial publications is frequently available. Surveys on individual corporations, particular industries, or of a general nature, can often be secured. In certain cases, informative pamphlets dealing with financial statements and stock-market terminology may be provided.

In most instances, your securities can be held by the brokerage house, and it will send you the dividends or let them accumulate as desired. Recent university graduates who are employed by large corporations and subject to frequent transfers may welcome the privilege of leaving securities with their brokers. After all, the collection of bond interest, stock dividends, transfers, redemptions, purchases and sales involves tedious detail work. If funds are left sitting with certain companies for reinvestment, minimal interest may be paid—except in states where this is prohibited.

---

[7]For a good insight into MLPFS, read the Prospectus (4,000,000-shares offering) dated April 23, 1971.
[8]Charles N. Stabler. "Firm of the Future." *The Wall Street Journal,* July 23, 1970, p. 1.
[9]Ibid., p. 6.

If you leave your funds and securities with a brokerage firm, however, I suggest that you have them forward all interest and dividends received directly to you. Why let the broker use your money for free, when he would have to pay 10 to 15 percent elsewhere? And be sure that all securities are registered in your name. A number of firms have failed in recent years. Some clients have lost their money and had great difficulty obtaining their securities. Such losses occurred in spite of a federal statute in 1970 creating a Securities Investor Protection Corporation (SIPC) that protects investors' holdings up to $50,000.[10] You may wish to heed *Forbes'* advice and keep all securities in your safe-deposit box.

Your brokerage house is there to help you, but as an investor you will be interested in active participation in the search for appropriate securities for your portfolio.

AVERAGES AND INDEXES

Averages and indexes are extremely useful tools in determining the health of the stock market. The answer to that often-asked question "How is the market doing?" depends on the statistical information consulted. The stock market in the broadest sense is composed of the thousands of companies which have made their stock available to the public. A complete listing of these would include dealings on the New York Stock Exchange, American Stock Exchange, Philadelphia Exchange, Boston Exchange, Midwest Exchange, Pacific Exchange, various foreign exchanges and the many unlisted equities bought and sold in over-the-counter transactions. It would be extremely difficult to use *all* corporate stocks in determining what happens in the marketplace as a result of the multitude of daily purchases and sales. Therefore, trading in limited numbers of shares is drawn upon for purposes of evaluation.

Numerous concerns offer statistical compilations reflecting the state of the market. The advent of the computer age, for example, has made it possible to compute daily the average price of all stocks listed on the New York Stock Exchange. Other well-known averages are those of Dow Jones, Standard & Poor's, and the American Stock Exchange index. There is also an indicator for over-the-counter issues, prepared by the National Association of Security Dealers. My last class, with the assistance of the university computer, developed an index for over-the-counter issues in the New Orleans area.

---

[10]Some brokerage firms provide additional surety-insurance-policy protection for each investor's securities and have a special policy against robbery, fire or natural disaster.

Dow Jones

The Dow Jones Averages (DJA) are the best-known of the market computations. The composite average consists of three categories—industrials, transportation and utilities—each comprising large and well-established companies. Sixty-five "blue-chip" giants of American industry currently comprise the DJA. The most popular of the four averages is the industrial category, whose origin may be traced back to 1896.

The daily Dow Jones Industrial Average (DJIA) was at first computed by adding up the current market prices of the stocks and dividing the aggregate by the number of corporations. Let us assume that at the close of business on a particular day in 1897, the share values totaled $600. This figure would have been divided by 12 (the number of companies in the Dow Jones Industrial Average at that time), for an average market price of $50. If this figure had been $49 the day before, it could be said the market was up for the day.

Over the years, the number of corporations comprising the Industrial Average was increased to its present total of thirty. To permit appropriate comparisons, it has been essential to make frequent adjustments in the divisor to provide for various actions, such as stock splits and increased capitalization. The divisor now stands at 1.443.[11]

The Dow Jones Industrial Average reached 1,052 in early 1973, establishing an all-time peak. In 1929, it peaked at 381 and then followed with a low of 41 in 1932. In 1977 the thirty industrials were nearly twenty-three times above their depression bottom of 1932, and have risen over 350 points since their low in 1974. However, the investor who bought the DJI stocks at 1,052 in 1973 would have lost money if he sold after that date. For example, in 1974 the DJI slumped to 578 and has never risen above 1,015. Since 1965 the DJI has had a lateral movement, with considerable variation in price. These marked fluctuations show that timing is important in the purchase and sale of securities.

But regardless of how the averages move, there are extensive disparities in the progress of individual issues. Although there have been substitutions made over the years in the composition of the Dow Jones Industrial Average, it is possible to make comparisons among those in the group today. Some have had limited advances since 1932, while others have shown significant increases. Such differences in corporate issues are evident in good times and bad. For example, in 1977, International Harvester ranged from 26 to 37⅞, and General Motors fluctuated between 62 and 78½.

Since the Dow Jones Industrial Average is composed of the so-called

---

[11]*The Wall Street Journal,* March 16, 1978, p. 31.

corporate giants, it may show a somewhat divergent picture from other averages which embrace larger numbers of stocks and smaller companies. The DJIA, however, continues as the most popular index and the one found most frequently in various publications. It helps give the investor a general picture of how the market is doing.

Although the market varies from average to average, the secular trend is one of rising prices with intermittent ups and downs. What particularly interests the investor is the vast difference in what happens to particular corporations. The market in general may decline over a period of time while individual securities are experiencing a remarkable advance.

As a potential investor, you are interested in finding the appropriate securities for your portfolio. In the next chapter, we will look at methods of selecting stocks and developing an investment program.

22

STOCK ANALYSIS & YOUR INVESTMENT PROGRAM

IMPORTANCE OF SECURITY ANALYSIS

The Penn Central's problem was "not one of mismanagement but one of unmanageability." These pearls of wisdom came from the former chairman of the Penn Central Transportation Company, Stuart T. Saunders, speaking before a congressional subcommittee in July 1970. A few weeks earlier, Penn Central had filed a petition under the Bankruptcy Act because it lacked the funds to pay its current debts and was unable to obtain further loans. The stock of the parent company plummeted from $71.75 per share in 1969 to $5.62 on announcement of bankruptcy proceedings. Since 1969, the Penn Central has continued to face serious financial and managerial problems. These difficulties have been reflected in the small price people are willing to pay for the stock. At this writing, it is selling for $1.25 per share, and in the past seven years has never sold higher than 7⅞.

The importance of selecting a company with first-rate management is apparent from the Penn Central example. Also apparent is the advantage of doing your own stock analysis prior to investing your hard-earned money, since a number of so-called experts in security analysis were left red-faced and in the red. Equity Research Associates, a respected research concern located in New York City, issued a report in January 1969 advising its customers to buy Penn Central and forecasting a "considerable turnaround by the railroad." The author of the Equity report regretted only that he was not permitted to see current cash-flow statements.[1]

It is also interesting to note that fifteen key executives in Penn Central were in the process of selling their shares just before the bankruptcy announcement, at prices ranging from forty to seventy dollars per share. They claimed no inside knowledge, however, and reported their sales to the Securities and Exchange Commission (SEC).[2] Transactions of key executives can be obtained from the SEC and appear in *The Wall Street Journal.*

Unforeseen developments like the energy crisis and Watergate can also have a significant impact on prices of quality stocks. For example, between January 1, 1973, and December 31, 1974, certain key securities declined as shown in Table 22-1:

TABLE 22-1   Decline in Key Securities, 1973–74

	High 1973	Low 1974	Current June 30, 1977
Chrysler Corp.	44¼	7	16½
Disney (Walt) Prod.	119⅛	16⅝	36⅞
Goodyear	31⅞	11¾	20⅛
Howard Johnson	34⅞	4	11
McDonald's Corp.	76⅞	21¼	46
Winnebago Industries	27½	3	3⅞

[1]"Investing Firms Were Slow to Sour on Penn Central." *The Wall Street Journal,* July 14, 1970, p. 8.

[2]Fred L. Zimmerman. "Bailing Out, Officials Sold Stock as Carrier Was Nearing Disaster." *The Wall Street Journal,* July 14, 1970, p. 1.

Prior to the energy crisis, these issues had been highly recommended as splendid investments by a number of respected advisory firms. Although a healthy recovery has been made in most issues, it is apparent that many people who bought at the 1973 peak still show losses.

The Penn Central story and the energy example support the facts that stock selection is not an exact science and that no one has all the answers. Nor does the exchange process operate in a vacuum. Therefore, the stockholder must be constantly on the alert to protect his investments and oversee his investment program. Consult with the experts when necessary, but remember that no one knows your requirements as well as you do.

The following dialogue between a bartender (Pete) and a customer (Ed) amusingly points up the unpredictability of the stock market:

> *Pete:* "How'd the market do today?"
> *Ed:* "Down a little."
> *Pete:* "Well, as old J. P. Barnum said, it'll fluctuate."
> *Ed:* "You mean J. P. Morgan, don't you?"
> *Pete:* "Ah, hell, I don't know. One was with the stock market and the other one was with the circus, and there ain't too much difference."[3]

ROLE OF THE INVESTMENT MODEL IN STOCK ANALYSIS

In Chapter 21, we discussed the importance of keeping abreast of current financial literature. I also stressed the need to select a well-established brokerage firm suited to your needs. This chapter will deal with ways of gathering and analyzing data about the stock of your choice. The three approaches to stock analysis depicted in my Investment Model (Figure 22-1) require time and effort, particularly at first, but once you have chosen your format, adapted it to your needs and gone through the initial steps, it becomes relatively simple to proceed. In the long run, if you follow a logical program you will spend less time on money matters than your peers do. And speaking of time-saving, don't let yourself be rushed into making a stock transaction. Give it the same careful attention you accord to any significant expenditure, such as buying a car or home.

If, after careful consideration, you feel that you do not have the time or desire to handle your securities, you might want to put them into a first-rate investment company. We will discuss this alternative in Chapter 23.

---

[3]Adapted from "A Matching Pair," Ray Conway, *Redbook*, August 1970, p. 120.

Figure 22-1 A graphic overview of an approach to investment analysis.

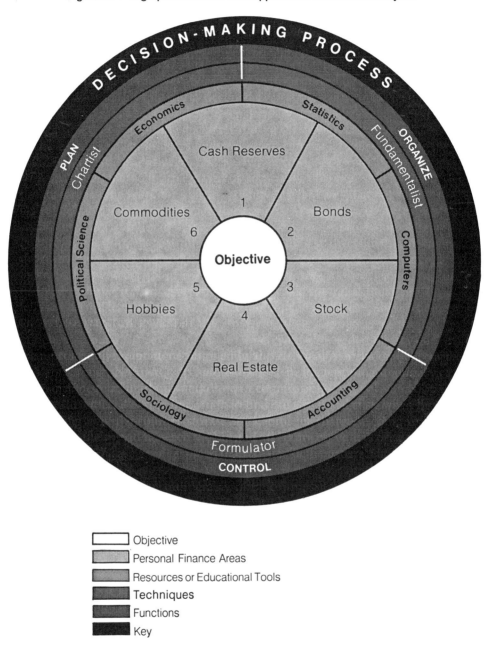

☐ Objective
▨ Personal Finance Areas
▨ Resources or Educational Tools
▨ Techniques
▨ Functions
■ Key

ESTABLISHING YOUR OBJECTIVE

Stocks provide an opportunity to meet a growth objective such as that presented in Chapter 1. If you are interested in taking the millionare route, it is important to select corporate securities that may provide a 10- to 15-percent return. Table 1-2 assumes a 10-percent return compounded annually over a 43-year period. However, if you begin your program later, you can achieve the same million-dollar goal before age sixty-five if you can obtain a higher annual return.

Two professors at the University of Chicago analyzed the results of *all* stocks traded on the New York Stock Exchange during a thirty-nine-year period (1926–65). Assuming the reinvestment of dividends while deducting all brokerage commissions and other fees, the study revealed the rate of return to be a surprising 9.3 percent. An examination of the Dow Jones Industrial Average between 1900 and 1977 also reflects a rate of return exceeding 9 percent!

The failure of these studies to calculate the impact of stock ownership on income-tax obligations is an important omission, since tax payments must be considered in planning investment programs. However, if you buy and hold your stocks, your only concern is the tax on the dividends. This can be a relatively small amount initially, if you purchase companies that plow most of their profits into expansion plans rather than dividends.

LOCATING GROWTH ISSUES

"Professor, it's fine to talk classroom theory about growth stocks in achieving our objective. But how do we go about finding them?" My response to this frequently asked question is that you should make use of the research that has been undertaken in this field. A number of splendid publications are available. Merrill Lynch publishes its *Review* bimonthly. It includes industries considered attractive for current purchase for appreciation.

Also available for consultation is Standard and Poor's monthly master list of recommended stocks. Seventeen were considered "aggressive" in regard to potential price appreciation, as reported in the May 1977 issue, including such diverse companies as American Standard, Continental Oil, PPG Industries and Weyerhaeuser.

Forbes magazine has several excellent columns in each issue pointing out appreciation situations, and a number of brokerage firms prepare lists of growth stocks.

Another approach to finding growth issues is to look at a number of corporate stocks in a specific industry. Merrill Lynch's pamphlets, published under the general title *Industry Report,* provide a ready list. The machinery pamphlet, for example, included ten issues for potential appreciation, as well as comments about the outlook for the machinery industry.

These sources can help you obtain a good idea of what securities may meet your requirements. Discussion with the head of the trust department at your family bank can also be helpful. Furthermore, your own work experience and observations in your community may lead you to good examples of fine growth stocks that suit your needs. It also pays to gather statistical data on the companies you think might be worthy of investment. Obtain their annual reports and quarterly statements. Note the growth in revenue, net income, dividends, retained earnings and the amount spent on research and development. Also secure from a broker Standard & Poor's *Stock Reports* on issues of interest to you. They provide valuable information for analysis purposes. All this data can be helpful in arriving at your decision to buy, sell or hold a stock—but again let me stress the importance of *doing your own research.*

TYPES OF STATISTICAL ANALYSIS

FUNDAMENTALIST APPROACH

Once you have acquired the necessary statistical data, what other kinds of information can help you to determine the issues to buy? The investment model in Figure 22-2 shows three approaches to stock evaluation: fundamentalist, chartist and formulator. Let us begin with the fundamentalist approach.

The fundamentalist takes a hard look at statistical data and other relevant factors in analyzing the investment merits of corporations. The following areas may be considered of importance in deciding on which growth securities to select.

Earnings

In order to survive and expand in our economic system, a corporation must make a profit. Ideally, from an investor's viewpoint, these earnings should increase yearly and at a faster rate than the Dow Jones Industrial Average, thus permitting the growth-minded company to plow back much of its profits for such undertakings as plant expansion, research and development and long-range planning. Such reinvestment should result in greater profits in the long run. Standard & Poor's *Stock Reports* permit you to compare earnings for up to a ten-year period. It is also helpful, where appropriate, to see what happened to a company in a period of real economic adversity, such as the depression thirties. This data can be obtained from *Moody's Industrial Manual,* which may be available in your community library. Establish, as well, how the company's earnings survived the recent deep recession, perhaps plotting the earnings on graph paper to better visualize the trend.

Dividends

As a potential stockholder, you should be concerned with a company's dividend payments. As we have noted, growth companies normally pay out little in the way of cash dividends. However, in the long run, dividend payments may be larger, in terms of original investment, than if you had placed your money in income-producing issues. This is apparent from consulting Figure 22-2. Note that a purchase of Coca-Cola shares in 1958 would have provided a 12.15-percent dividend ten years later, in contrast to, say, a 6-percent yield on an income-producing stock that was still paying that rate. IBM returned 6.34 percent by 1968, in contrast to, say, a twenty-year bond that was purchased in 1958 at 4 percent. In effect, common-stock ownership in growth companies can mean having your cake and eating it too. The stocks cited above provided the 1958 purchaser with both splendid growth and, eventually, a healthy dividend. The secret is to find these stocks—past performances is a good indication but not always the answer.

Figure 22-2 Growth, principal, and income of selected issues during the period 1958–68.

	1958			1968			
Stock	Market Price* 6/30	Dividend for Year	Income Yield	Market Price 6/30	Dividend for Year	President Income Yield on 1958 Price	Gain in Principal Value Since 1958
Polaroid	$ 7¼	$ .02	0.34%	$113¾	$ .32	4.41%	+1,469%
Coca-Cola	9⅞	.42	4.23%	73½	1.20	12.15%	+ 644%
Avon Products	9⅞	.15	1.55%	138¾	1.60	16.20%	+1,305%
Texaco	32⅜	1.08	3.34%	76¾	2.80	8.65%	+ 137%
Eastman Kodak	13⅜	.33	2.50%	79¼	.88	6.58%	+ 493%
IBM	41	.29	0.72%	353¾	2.60	6.34%	+ 763%
McDonnell-Douglas	2⅝	.07	2.67%	53⅝	.40	15.24%	+1,942%
Merck & Co.	18½	.47	2.52%	88	1.60	8.65%	+ 376%
Am. Home Products	16¼	.58	3.58%	64¼	1.30	8.00%	+ 295%
ITT	9⅞	.45	4.56%	55⅜	.85	8.61%	+ 461%

*Adjusted for stock splits and stock dividends

Source: ***Growth Stocks,*** Merrill Lynch, Pierce, Fenner & Smith, Inc., VS-11-68, pp. 4, 5.

Prices

The primary purpose of investing in growth issues is the capital-gains potential—that is, the expectation that the worth of the issue will appreciate at a faster rate than the stock market averages. There were remarkable price rises in selected issues for the ten-year period ending in 1968. McDonnell-Douglas, for example, advanced 1,942 percent. Stocks in this growth group certainly exceeded the 15-percent annual rise involved in becoming a millionare that we saw in Figure 1-3. However, the 1958–68 period was one of generally rising stock prices, during which the DJIA moved from approximately 479 to 918. In contrast, the period from June 30, 1968, to June 30, 1970, saw a downward movement in the market, with the average declining from approximately 918 to 690, and some of the growth issues falling even further than the DJIA: McDonnell-Douglas, 53⅜ to 13¼; Polaroid, 113¾ to 53; Avon, 138¾ to 70⅛. Likewise, between January 1973 and November 1974, the DJIA declined from 1052 to 578, while stocks like Disney fell even more precipitously from 119⅛ to 16⅝. The importance of timing stock sales and purchases is clear when we look at the 1973–1974 era. In contrast to the 45-percent loss in the DJI, certain "growth" issues declined 80 to 90 percent. It can take a long time to recover from a purchase made at a peak price.

In my view, growth stocks should be bought for the long pull. Market declines provide good purchase opportunities. Look what happened to individuals who put $1,000 into any of the following DJI issues during the gloomy days of World War II and held them for thirty years (Table 22-2):

TABLE 22-2 Rise in DJI Issues, 1943–73

	12/31/43	12/31/73	$ Gain	% Gain
Eastman Kodak	$1,000	$46,600	$45,600	4,560
Sears Roebuck	1,000	22,100	21,100	2,100
Procter & Gamble	1,000	19,500	18,500	1,850
Standard Oil of California	1,000	11,700	10,700	1,070
Goodyear	1,000	11,600	10,600	1,060
Texaco	1,000	11,100	10,100	1,010
Exxon	1,000	11,000	10,000	1,000

Other Quantitative Data

In order to make valid comparisons, it helps to look at important ratios (see Glossary for definitions) including liquidity ratios that reflect on a corporation's ability to meet its short-term obligations. Two of these are the current ratio and the acid-test ratio. Stock ratios of interest are price/earnings, earnings per share and yield. Profitability ratios indicate earnings in relation to sources that generate them, such as profit margin to total sales, net profit to total assets and net worth to net profit. It is also desirable to look at the cash flow, because without adequate money to meet its expansion and debt needs, a company can be in deep trouble. Other useful information may be book value, long-term debt and capital expenditures. This information can be obtained from the annual reports or from Standard & Poor's *Stock Reports* and *Stock Guide,* and *Moody's Industrial Manual.*

Recently, there has been considerable interest in a quantitative approach that measures stock volatility. This concept recognizes that in varying economic situations stocks will respond differently. For example, the Dow Jones Industrial Average reached 1,052 in 1973 and has been below that peak for the past four years. Yet some stocks have reached new highs since 1973. One way to find out the impact of the economy on individual common stocks is to use beta valuation to determine the volatility of one company in relation to a market index like Standard & Poor's or DJIA. Beta valuation is a recent statistical technique to measure a stock's performance against a market average. Stocks, based on their beta values, may be classified as aggressive or defensive. If one, for example, is the norm, then stocks with values less than one would be defensive—rise more slowly than the market average. But these stocks would also tend to fall less rapidly in a declining market. Contrariwise, stocks with beta values higher than one would be classified aggressive—rise more rapidly than the average. However, they would also tend to fall at a faster rate in a bear market.

Some brokerage firms now provide computer printouts analyzing portfolios that may include yield, price earnings, ratio, dollar income and volatility measured by beta values. You should take advantage of such a service when there is no charge for it. But keep in mind that it is based on past performance. It should serve as only one more piece of fundamentalist information to help you arrive at a sound investment decision.

Management

An admission of "unmanageability" by a corporation chairman such as Penn Central's indicates the type of company in which you should not place your funds for investment purposes. First-class leadership has a favorable influence on the success of any organization. Make every effort, prior to investment, to get information about the top managers. Companies with a rapid turnover of senior officers, for example, should be regarded with suspicion.

At the Ford Motor Company, a new president was hired in 1968 and fired in 1969.[4] This would have been a negative factor against Ford in comparing it with General Motors in the last quarter of 1969. Likewise, the short-sighted attitude of Avery Sewell, the aged and ultraconservative head of Montgomery Ward during the World War II era, resulted in the company's

---

[4]*The Wall Street Journal,* September 17, 1969, p. 1.

failure to expand its operations and its being outdistanced by its major competitor, Sears.

In contrast to the above failures, the able direction provided by the Watson family (IBM) and Joseph C. Wilson (Xerox) have been significant influences in the success of these corporations. Harvard Business School had this to say about Wilson:

> Upon graduation from the business School you joined your family's firm, which you saw not as the scene of security and business-as-usual, but as opportunity. You led the firm's spectacular commercial development of an interesting scientific novelty called xerography. The Haloid Company became the Xerox Corporation: invention became a revolution in the ways that offices, businesses, schools, and libraries are conducted; and your native Rochester became the fountainhead of its second world-leading industry. Though your work carried you about the globe often, you never lost sight of your own city and of the importance of its educational, governmental, and social services.
>
> Your lifelong dedication to company and community stands as a pattern for all businessmen to try to copy.[5]

Much information on management practices can be gleaned from reading a company's "Notice of Annual Meeting and Proxy Statement." This reveals, among other things, the remuneration of the top executives, including benefits, stock-option plan, savings-stock program and shares of common stock owned. From these data you can find out if management has a healthy stock investment in the company, or if the executives are milking the company for retirement benefits and other advantages beyond the norm for the industry.

In this era of social awareness, it is also important for the company leadership to be in the hands of people who demonstrate a sense of responsibility concerning the key issues of our time. There is much that industry can do in seeking solutions to such problems as hard-core unemployment, pollution, poor race relations, inadequate education, ecological imbalance, overpopulation, urban decay, alienation of youth, drug addiction, physical flabbiness, mental illness and improper allocation of resources. The following quote from a *Saturday Review* article points up the need for corporate responsibility:

> The social ferment, the changing structure of society, the overwhelming domestic problems afflicting the nation—each has had its impact on the American corporation. The public's demand that the large industrial organizations provide some leadership in solving the ills of the cities has wrought changes in the role of the corporation. No longer can a corporation tend to its profit-making alone, while by-passing issues once considered beyond the concern of business managers. . . . Business is

---

[5]*Harvard Business School Bulletin,* July–August 1970, p. 34.

now compelled to perform a new role. The public demands it, and wise managers know that to ignore that demand is to court disaster. Acceptance of public responsibilities, far beyond the basic one of making a profit, is now a must for those corporate heads who believe that what remains of the private sector is worth preserving.[6]

Personal Observation and Evaluation

Annual reports and earnings published by corporations must be studied carefully. Yearly statements are geared to permit companies to put their best foot forward; therefore, this information should be taken with a grain of salt. A more objective viewpoint can be obtained from relevant news articles in such publications as *Fortune, Forbes, The Wall Street Journal, The New York Times,* and *Barron's.* It also pays to read the daily paper for events that may have a direct impact on the company. Good journalism tries to "tell it like it is."

In evaluating an earnings report, remember that if it is a consolidated report you have no way of determining what the subsidiaries are doing. Several may be operating at whopping losses. Also, the asset of goodwill (see Glossary) may be stated out of proportion to its true worth—normally on the inflated side, but occasionally too low. Nonrecurring earnings may not be clearly indicated and may give a misleading picture.

Remember, as well, that accounting practices are not completely uniform. The depth of each firm's scrutiny in preparation of the accounting statements may be dependent upon funds received for this purpose and local ground rules. And make a point of reading the footnotes accompanying annual reports. They can be most revealing.

There is no substitute for personal observation wherever possible. Over-the-counter firms located in your community can be readily observed. A branch store or plant of a large corporation can also furnish information. Talk to the executives and workers; look over the facilities; examine the quality of the products or services. How do these products compare with those of their competitors? Are they wll received? Do they hold up over a reasonable period? Is the service satisfactory?

Historical Context

The movement of corporate securities is influenced by political, social, economic and military factors. The political decision, for example, to pull out of Vietnam had a decided impact on companies providing materials for use in that war. A military decision to produce a new rifle or airplane affects the industries that gain the contracts. A severe economic recession in a particular locality has a drastic effect on retailers in that region. The social implications of race riots,

---

[6]"Profit Alone Is Not Enough." *Saturday Review,* August 8, 1970, p. 55.

campus unrest and low-income housing have a definite influence on the profits of any corporation involved. Therefore, it is important to keep informed about the news, and in particular, about the impact current events may have on securities you may wish to buy.

Human Intangibles

Psychological and emotional factors must also be considered in stock evaluation. What makes a person buy or sell? What role does intuition play? Two enlightened investors can arrive at opposite decisions with respect to a particular stock. And sometimes the market itself is influenced by unexpected psychological factors. Both President Kennedy's death and President Eisenhower's heart attack caused sharp declines in the market, although neither event entailed changes in the general economy or corporate leadership and its profit potential. Nevertheless, key stocks sank briefly from 5 to 10 percent due to emotional decisions to sell. Another intangible phenomenon is the tendency toward undue pessimism in times of recession and overoptimism in periods of a bull market.

CHARTIST APPROACH

This approach to stock evaluation relies on the use of charts. By plotting daily price fluctuations chartists discern patterns in the movement of their issues. These trends determine whether to buy, sell or hold a particular stock. Such record keeping involves time and work, but there are firms that will provide this service for a fee.

Chart interpretation varies with the individual. It is generally agreed, however, that when a chart breaks out of a range, this is an indication to buy or sell. Let us assume, for example, that stock X has been operating in a range of 28 to 38 for seven months and suddenly moves above 38 on volume. This could indicate a strong buy signal.

Chartists rely upon a variety of chart formations, such as head and shoulders, rectangles, flags and triangles. The buy, sell and hold indicators vary among chartists, for this is far from an exact science and involves guesswork. For a detailed discussion of charts, you may wish to read *How Charts Can Help You in the Stock Market,* by William L. Jiler. Another helpful guide is *Daily Basis Stock Charts* prepared by Trendline, 345 Hudson Street, New York, New York 10014, in which individual charts present daily high, low and closing prices for each of 744 listed stocks. This excellent weekly publication also provides fourteen charts of technical indicators and indexes on such areas as short-interest ratio, odd-lot index, upside-downside volume and odd-lot short sales.

Trendline's weekly publications also provide important fundamentalist material, including yearly price movements over a period of ten years, monthly volume, capitalization information and current statistical data on earnings, dividends, cash flow, profit margin and yields.

In theory, charting permits you to cut your losses and let your profits continue to grow. This same theory holds true in the field of commodities, which will be discussed in Chapter 26. For example, if stock X moves above 38 by two points and then falls back below 35, the chart might inform you that you should liquidate your holdings. The fundamentalist, in contrast, has no cutoff point for a decision to buy or sell.

FORMULATOR APPROACH

Practitioners of this approach handle their stocks according to formulas. This approach can be combined with the fundamentalist view to trigger certain buy or sell actions. For example, you may wish to keep a balance in your portfolio of 80 percent stock and 20 percent bonds. In a market advance, your formula may call for a portfolio to double before you would sell stock and buy bonds to keep the same ratio. Suppose you initially had $2,000 in bonds and $8,000 in stocks. If the value of your stock moved from $8,000 to $18,000, you would sell $2,000 in securities and increase bonds by the same amount.

Another formula approach is based on the Dow Jones Industrial Average. The higher it goes, the more stock you would sell, converting the proceeds into bonds. Conversely, when the average goes down, you increase stock and sell bonds. The problem with this formula is the difficulty in determining at what levels to buy and sell. You do not want to sell out stocks too soon in a long-lasting bull (rising) market. For example, if you had planned in 1952 to be 100 percent in stocks when the DJIA stood at 250 and to sell out completely at 400, you would be sitting a long time (since 1955) in bonds while the DJIA moved to 1,052. (As we have seen, it has not been lower than 420 since.)

Dollar Averaging

In a sense, dollar averaging can be considered a formula approach. This is a systematic stock-purchase plan that involves investing the same number of dollars each month, or in whatever period you may select, in order to purchase shares of a corporation, thus buying the most shares in periods of lower prices. In the long run, this dollar averaging would normally cost you less than if you bought the same number of shares periodically. The secret, of course, is to find a stock that has a healthy growth in spite of fluctuations. If your stock should have a marked decline over a period of years, dollar averaging or not, you will lose money.

Dollar Availability

Although dollar averaging looks fine on paper, the investor may not have the same amount of money available at regular intervals. Therefore, I believe it is sounder to invest on a dollar-availability basis. This allows you to put the increased dollars to work at once if a raise or bonus comes your way. Within the dollar-availability concept, it is possible to use a portion for dollar-averaging purposes and yet keep *all* your funds working. If the market appears over-priced at the time you receive a healthy bonus, these supplemental funds can be temporarily placed in a cash-reserve investment.

OTHER INVESTMENT CONSIDERATIONS

After you have acquired stock-market experience, you may wish to consider the areas of undervalued issues, short selling and options. Let me stress, however, that operating in these areas requires considerable knowledge of market pro-cedures. Let us examine each of these areas in turn.

UNDERVALUED ISSUES

Although I have stressed my belief that the average investor should stick with quality stocks, there are occasional opportunities to purchase issues with high book values that are decidedly underpriced.

This ability to find undervalued securities, however, is normally limited to professionals. A good example of a bargain buy is one made by the securities firm of Allen & Co., which today has a net worth of about $80 million. According to *The Wall Street Journal,* "One of the firm's more notable invest-ments took place in 1938, when Allen & Co. was worth less than $1 million. It bought Missouri Pacific Railroad preferred stock at 20¢ a share when the line was bankrupt. Several years later, when the railroad was back on its feet, the stock was sold for more than $10 a share."[7]

SHORT SELLING

A look at the DJIA for the past fifty-seven years shows a great deal of upward and downward movement. It is apparent that the movement down is more rapid than up. The sophisticated investor capitalizes on the down side (bear market) as well as the up side (bull market). People like Joseph Kennedy made a fortune by short selling in the market crash beginning in October 1929. A short

---

[7]*The Wall Street Journal,* August 4, 1970, p. 1.

sale, in contrast to the usual buying long, is selling shares you don't own,[8] with the expectation of buying them back later at a lower price. For instance, a person who sold short 100 shares of Disney (Walt) Prod. at 119, in 1973, and bought it back at 17, in 1974, made a profit—less commissions—of $10,200. But short selling is a sophisticated technique, and I do not recommend it for the novice. A stock can go down only as far as zero, but on the up side there is no limit. Thus, if you make a whopper of a mistake, you can lose a tremendous amount unless you cover your loss quickly. Keep in mind that you must cover a short sale at some point—that is, buy the stock you are short. In the meantime, you also have to pay dividends to the party who lends you his stock during the period you are short.

PUT AND CALL OPTIONS

A *call* may be defined as "the right to buy shares of a certain stock, if desired, at a set price within a given period of time as specified in the contract." A *put* is the opposite of a call and thus is "the right to sell shares of a certain stock, if desired, at a set price within a given period of time."

Call options have become big business since April 1973, the date of the opening of the Chicago Board Options Exchange (CBOE). This mechanism is the first to act as a central marketplace where call options can be bought or sold. The CBOE is a registered national securities exchange with all the regulatory and price-dissemination capabilities associated with exchange trading. All CBOE options are registered securities. Prior to 1973, firms specializing in puts and calls did very limited volume in the over-the-counter markets. In view of the CBOE success the American, Philadelphia, Midwest and Pacific Exchanges have established similar central marketplaces for dealing in options.

The CBOE dealt only in call options between 1973 and 1976. In 1977, it also began dealing in put options.[9] The growth of the option business has been remarkable. In mid-1974 there were thirty-two companies whose common stock had been approved as underlying stock for option transactions on the CBOE. Now there are nearly seven hundred on five different exchanges. The closing prices of various put and call options appear daily in *The Wall Street Journal*.

---

[8]How do you sell shares you don't own in the first place? The seller's broker may obtain the shares for delivery to the buyer from one of several sources: The company's on hand inventory; another brokerage firm; a client who agrees to lend his stock for this purpose. Repayment of the borrowed shares is made from those obtained when the later purchase order is made.

[9]Put-option trading on five exchanges began June 3, 1977. There were only twenty-four companies whose common stock had been approved as underlying stock for put-option transactions. The owner of a put option has the right to sell one hundred shares of an underlying stock at a specified price (the striking or exercise price) at any time prior to the expiration of the option.

The primary attractions for a purchaser of call options are (1) the opportunity to make a large amount of money with a small investment and (2) predetermined risk. As pointed out in the definition, a call is the *right* to buy shares. However, an option costs only a small portion of what it would take to buy one hundred shares of the stock itself, and the investor's risk exposure is limited to the price paid for the option. This cost usually ranges from 5 to 20 percent of the stock price, with the length of the option varying from one to nine months. This leverage feature permits a large profit, but it also has a major risk factor that can easily result in the loss of the investment.

The risk is apparent from the example in the prospectus issued by the CBOE:

> This risk of Options may be illustrated by comparing Investor A, who for a total investment of $5,000 (plus a $71.50 commission, prescribed by the New York Stock Exchange) buys 100 shares of XYZ stock at $50 per share, with Investor B, who invests $5,000 (plus a $127 minimum commission prescribed by the Exchange) in Options covering 1,000 shares of XYZ at an exercise price of $50 per share.[10] Both A and B anticipate a rise in the market price of XYZ, but should their expectations not be realized and XYZ fall in market price, A's loss would be quite different from B's. If by the expiration of the Option XYZ stock has fallen to $45 per share (and assuming XYZ has paid no dividends), A will have suffered a paper loss of $500 (plus being out-of-pocket the $71.50 commission), and his investment will be worth $4,500. He will not be required to realize this loss, and may recover it should XYZ later rise in price while he still owns the 100 shares. Investor B, on the other hand, will have suffered the loss of his entire $5,000 (plus the $127 commission) with no possibility for recovery. Indeed, in the above example Investor A would have had no gain or loss (other than commission paid) if the market price of XYZ had remained at $50, but Investor B would have lost his entire investment. Moreover, if XYZ had paid dividends, they would have been received by A as a stockholder, but not by B as the holder of an Option.[11]

If you desire further information on options I suggest that you read a recent book titled *Buying Options.* It covers the subject well.[12]

Again, my recommendation is to stay away from short selling, puts and calls and other intricate transactions until you have had considerable market

[10]This example, as well as all other examples in this prospectus, is based upon hypothetical values that are not necessarily indicative of the values in any actual transaction.

[11]"Certain Risk Factors." *Prospectus,* Chicago Board Options Exchange Clearing Corporation, April 26, 1974, pp. 4, 5.

[12]A. Rodolakis and N. Tetrick, *Buying Options: Wall Street on a Shoestring.* Reston, Va.: Reston Publishing Co., Inc., 1976.

experience and can devote ample time to investments. Until then, buy quality growth issues and hold them for the long pull. No one can predict frequent stock fluctuations, but history has proved that over the years our economy has risen and the stock market with it. There is every indication that this trend will continue in the foreseeable future.

STOCKHOLDER PROTECTION

Management tends to disregard the views of its minority stockholders, as those who attend annual stockholders' meetings well know. Many corporate directors consider such meetings a necessary evil, especially when the shareholder-management relationship is strained.

It is those with the power who are heard and who achieve their goals. Look at union accomplishments at the bargaining table with corporate executives. Ponder the financial benefits accruing to football players since they have banded together and demanded a greater share of the profits from the owners. Why shouldn't stockholders with limited holdings unite and make their influence felt? By demanding representation on the board of directors they could influence policy and protect their interests.

One example of stockholders organizing for action took place when minority stockholders of Penn Central who were living in the Miami, Florida, area met on July 27, 1970, and took the following steps:

Agreed on the text of a petition to Florida congressmen and senators, urging their support and action;
Gave themselves an organizational name;
Named finance, legal, correspondence and publicity committees;
Elected a chairman . . . and directors;
Assessed themselves two cents per share for working capital;
Decided to record their views in a letter to U.S. District Court Judge John P. Fullam, who is handling the railroad's bankruptcy case;
Planned to send members to other Florida cities in an effort to expand the movement within the state.
Included in the petition to legislators and the letter to Fullam are recommendations that they do all they can to:
Conserve the remaining assets of the company;
Reduce "featherbedding" among union member employees;
Allow the railroad to cut out passenger traffic;
Place a minority stockholder on the P-C board of directors;
Cut off the pensions of deposed directors of the railroad.[13]

[13]"Pennsy Shareholders Rally for Action." Miami *Herald,* July 24, 1970, p. 3.

TABLE 22-3 Format for a hundred-thousand-dollar Growth Portfolio

Name of Company	Ticker Symbol	Institutional Holdings[1]		Common Shares Outstanding[1] (000)	Total Dividends or Interest	Yield	High-Low Between 1960–72	Earnings Per Share 1973[1]	High-Low 1973–74	Price Earnings Ratio 1973[1]
		Number of Companies	Number of Shares (000)							
American Airlines, Inc.	AMR	111	5,643	28,486	$0	0	49⅛–7⅝	$ 1.40d[3]	25⅜–7⅝	Deficit
American Metal Climax, Inc.	AMX	106	3,083	23,743	495.00	3.6%	43½–13½	2.43	52⅞–29	11
International Business Machines	IBM	1,150	14,593	146,713	512.00	1.3%	341⅜–58	10.79	365¼–218¾	22
Lone Star Industries, Inc.	LCE	34	1,866	10,785	600.00	6.3%	33¾–14⅛	2.57	25¾–15	7
Schering-Plough Corporation	SGP	187	5,647	52,574	480.00	1.1%	70⅛–3⅞	1.97	87⅝–61¾	36
Warner & Swasey Company	WS	26	198	3,503	480.00	3.9%	57⅞–7⅝	3.52	43¼–22	9
Xerox Corporation	XRX	602	9,881	79,144	100.00	.9%	171⅞–17⅛	3.80	170–104¾	30
Local Bank Savings Account at 5%					98.38	5.0%				
Total Investment					$2,765.38	2.77%				

Name of Company	Number of Shares Bought	Date Purchased	Price Per Share[2]	Broker's Commission	Total Cost	Dividends Per Share[2]	Total Dividends or Interest
American Airlines, Inc.	800	5/9/74	10¼	$165.37	$8,365.37	$0	$0
American Metal Climax, Inc.	300	5/9/74	46	188.83	13,988.83	1.65	495.00
International Business Machines	100	5/9/74	226	74.75	22,674.75	5.12	512.00
Lone Star Industries, Inc.	600	5/9/74	15⅝	163.74	9,538.74	1.00	600.00
Schering-Plough Corporation	300	5/9/74	70½	224.25	22,874.25	.80	480.00
Warner & Swasey Company	400	5/9/74	30½	140.70	9,290.70	1.20	480.00
Xerox Corporation	100	5/9/74	112¼	74.75	11,299.75	1.00	100.00
Local Bank Savings Account at 5%		5/9/74			1,967.61		98.38
Total Investment					$100,000.00		$2,765.38

Standard & Poor's Stock Guide, April 1974.

BUILDING A MODEL PORTFOLIO

A splendid way to gain experience, free of cost, is to simulate the purchase and sale of securities for, perhaps, a one-year period, or until you actually have the funds, knowledge and confidence to invest wisely. Those who already own securities may also wish to participate in such simulation. A radio listener wrote me as follows: "I have been buying stocks helter-skelter for years. Your suggestion to compare, over a one-year period, my own issues with those I carefully selected on a simulated basis proved most helpful. I now buy based on sound analysis and have increased the value of my portfolio substantially."

Assume that you have received $100,000. How would you go about investing it in growth issues? You may wish to use one of the three approaches explained in this chapter. Keep a record of your "transactions" by using a format like that presented in Table 22-3. You may find that over a one-year period, it is the broker who makes the largest profit. It is better to practice with play money, and lose, than to get burned with your own funds.

Most important to you as a potential investor is what happens to the companies selected in your hypothetical portfolio. Let me again stress that the market in general may decline over a period of time while individual securities are experiencing remarkable advances. An effective way to visualize the variation in stocks is to visit a local brokerage firm and personally observe fluctuations in selected issues. It is quite an experience to watch the ticker tape and note price movements on shares traded on the New York and American exchanges. Ticker symbols are easily memorized and can be found in numerous helpful publications, such as Standard & Poor's *Stock Guide,* often obtainable free of charge from a broker.

23

INVESTMENT COMPANIES: MUTUAL & CLOSED-END FUNDS

Investment companies may be defined as commercial enterprises that obtain money from institutions and individuals for the primary purpose of investing these funds in short-term debt,[1] bonds and/or stocks in order to achieve such objectives as safety, growth and income.

TYPES OF INVESTMENT COMPANIES

There are two major categories of investment companies—closed-end and open-end. The open-end companies are frequently referred to as mutual funds. Shares of mutuals are sold at net asset value (see below) plus a loading charge, in the vast majority of cases. These "leading" or sales charges vary and some companies do not have them at all. First organized in 1929, open-end companies showed remarkable growth until 1970, when they were affected by the stock-market decline.

The second category of investment enterprise, the closed-end, has not shared in the amazing growth of the mutuals, for reasons which we will examine later in the chapter. Closed-ends are purchased and sold like regular corporate issues through stock-brokerage firms. Alone in the field until 1929, they suffered badly in that year's market crash.

A BIT OF HISTORY

The first investment company can be traced back more than 155 years to Belgium. From there the concept moved to Great Britain, where it developed rapidly. The objective of the early English companies was to provide financial-management guidance for money collected from a variety of private and business sources. These funds were invested initially throughout the British Empire and later worldwide.

The Scotch-English investment philosophy was conservative by nature and portfolios flourished. This European success prompted several American financiers to organize similar closed-end companies shortly before the end of the nineteenth century. These, too, prospered, but the bull-market twenties saw a changing philosophy. Certain investment-company managers placed reckless emphasis on fast-moving issues until the bubble burst in late 1929, causing many firms to fail. This resulted in a loss of public confidence in closed-end investment and fostered the establishment of federal requirements as prescribed in the Securities and Exchange Act (1933) and the Investment Company Act (1940).

---

[1]Short-term debt normally matures in one year or less.

Restoration of public confidence was slow to come; it is only since the nineteen fifties that investors in the United States have looked upon mutuals favorably. Table 23-1 indicates that in 1940 mutuals had net assets of less than .5 billion, as compared with 2.5 billion a decade later. But note that between 1960 and 1969 net assets increased by 31.3 billion. The rapid growth of the number of shareholders in recent years is also readily apparent; by 1969, the figure exceeded 10 million, as contrasted to less than 5 million in 1960.

TABLE 23-1   Growth of Mutual Funds

Year	Assets	Shareholder Accounts
1940	447,959,000	296,056
1945	1,284,185,000	497,875
1950	2,530,563,000	938,651
1955	7,837,524,000	2,085,325
1960	17,025,684,000	4,897,600
1965	35,220,243,000	6,709,343
1969	48,290,733,000	10,391,534
1973	46,518,535,000	10,330,862
1976	50,941,923,000*	9,055,271**

*Includes $3,404,437 in money market assets
**Includes 175,858 money market shareholder accounts

Source: Investment Company Institute, Washington, D.C.

Between 1969 and 1973, however, mutuals found a less receptive public. This was reflected in a small-percentage reduction in assets and stockholders. Assets were reduced by 1.8 billion (.4 percent), and the shareholders declined by 10,672 (.6 percent). During much of this period the market did poorly, and some investors looked to other outlets for their funds. Clearly, assets of mutuals would have declined even further if a number of companies had not introduced new types of funds specializing in money-market instruments. These new funds will be discussed later in the chapter. A look at the 1980 estimate indicates a further small decline. In my view, lower interest rates, competition from options and other investment areas will preclude growth.

The primary reason for the growth of mutual funds in the United States has been their aggressive marketing methods. The profit potential in the mutual field has resulted in increased competition. Everyone wants to get into the act—insurance companies, banks, brokerage firms and retail outlets. For years, Merrill Lynch, Pierce, Fenner & Smith kept out of mutuals. Several members of its staff assured me, "There are better ways to invest your money." However, 1969 saw MLPFS establish its first mutual-fund department and it now has three funds of its own. Sears entered the mutual-fund field in 1970, drawing upon the vast resources of its Allstate Insurance subsidiary.

Just as closed-end funds came here from Europe, a group of American businessmen decided to introduce the open-end concept abroad. Financier Bernard Cornfeld coined the term "people's capitalism" and twenty-five years ago began marketing his operations worldwide.[2] By 1970 he controlled twenty mutual funds offering a variety of programs and sold by several thousand salesmen. His Geneva-based empire crumbled in the spring of 1970, when the Dow Jones Industrials declined 36 percent and his organization faced a cash-shortage crisis. Cornfeld resigned as chairman of the parent company (I.O.S. Ltd.), and efforts to keep the organization intact failed. During the early seventies, many unhappy foreign investors spoke bitterly of "Cornfeld's" rather than of "people's" capitalism.

Although no major American mutual fund has been in serious trouble since 1970, a number have reported that redemption of shares is exceeding sales by a considerable margin. Many small investors became disenchanted with mutuals as they watched the value of their holdings drop. Where, they wondered, was that glowing potential described by the mutual-fund salesman? Between 1968 and 1973, for example, the Dreyfus Fund's net-asset value depreciated by over 30 percent, in contrast to only 2.5 percent for the Dow Jones Industrial Average. During the period from January 1972 to June 1973, the Dreyfus Fund had sales of only $190 million, against $550 million in redemptions.

The bear-market bash of 1970 proved a rude awakening for aggressive young fund managers of the high-flying sixties who had sacrificed safety to trade in "go-go" companies and letter stocks.[3] Some learned their lesson the hard way by losing their jobs. Others were eliminated in 1974 when the Dow Jones Industrials hit 578.

During the past seven years, most fund managers have returned to a more conservative approach. This attitude was made apparent at a meeting in Italy on June 1, 1970, conducted by a London brokerage firm. In attendance were several hundred fund managers, bankers and financiers from the United States and Europe. The leading discussion topics included "Tighter regulation of mutual funds in most European countries; the demise of the 'star system'[4] of portfolio management in both the U.S. and Europe; and a general retrench-

[2]The SEC prohibited the sale of Cornfeld's funds in the United States.

[3]Letter stocks are unregistered or restricted issues. According to the federal securities law, they cannot be traded publicly but can be sold only in certain private transactions that are exempt from SEC regulations. Such securities are called "letter stocks" because buyers normally sign letters stating that they are purchasing such securities for investment reasons and not for public sales in the foreseeable future.

[4]An investment-management concept stating that one bright individual can manage a portfolio better than a group can. The "star" often bought speculative issues (referred to as a "go-go" philosophy), because his income depended on results.

ment from a speculative to a conservative investment approach with strong stress on corporate earnings."[5] The importance of company earnings and the price-earnings ratio was pointed up by the treasurer of the Ford Foundation, which has a $2.5 billion investment portfolio: "We do not only want to know what a company's earning, but how these earnings are generated."[6]

HOW OPEN-END COMPANIES WORK

Let us now examine the mutual fund more closely in terms of its capital structure, cost of purchase, objectives, income and capital gains, and annual charges.

CAPITAL STRUCTURE

The balance sheet of the average mutual fund will usually show that its capitalization is made up entirely of common stock. A day-to-day check as to the number of shares outstanding would reflect variations. As new sales are consummated, the number of shares increases. Decreases occur when shareholders redeem their stock for cash. It should be noted that mutual-fund stockholders pay for the expense of constant sales and redemptions, which may involve as little as one share. However, there is normally a minimum dollar-purchase requirement.

PURCHASE COSTS

As noted above, shares are generally sold at net-asset value plus a loading charge. The net-asset value can be computed by subtracting liabilities from assets and dividing by the number of shares outstanding. Assume, for example, that X Mutual Fund, as of today, has assets of $110 million, $10 million in liabilities, and ten million shares of common stock outstanding. The sales charge is 9 percent. Accordingly, the per-share net-asset value is $10,000 and the cost to the buyer is $10.90. Normally, there is no charge for redeeming shares for cash. Nevertheless, with a 9-percent sales charge, if there should be no change in net-asset value, it may take three years to recoup this initial outlay in dividend payments.

There are wide variations in "loading charges" imposed by open-end companies. (Those with no sales charge are referred to as "no-load com-

---

[5]Ray Vickers. "Prolonged Bear Market Leads to Change in Money Management in Europe, U.S." *The Wall Street Journal,* June 22, 1970, p. 7.
[6]Ibid.

panies.") I like to compare the load versus no-load situation to a track meet among top performers. Nine yards is difficult to make up, and in a short race it's a virtual impossibility.

In striking contrast to the no-load is a first-year charge of 55 percent that is imposed if a twelve-and-a-half-year plan (front-end load) is terminated within the first twelve-month period. This heavy initial cost is similar to the insurance-company approach in which the salesman, as a powerful inducement to have him sell long-term endowment plans, gets a commission of 50 percent of the first year's payment. In a front-end-load plan calling for $1,000 annually, the company pockets $550 and the person making the sale earns $275! The main argument for buying the long-term contract is that, like insurance, it forces a systematic payment. However, a good number of those who do not complete the required years take a sizable loss. In the event that 150 monthly deposits are made over the twelve and a half years, the load could be 10 to 11 percent (including the insurance rider). The average charge on mutual funds for the small investor ranges from 7 to 9 percent, but many companies scale down this cost with increasing dollar investments.

The amount of the "load" may be a significant factor to you as a prospective purchaser. These charges can be determined by consulting daily listings in *The Wall Street Journal* (Figure 23-1). The load should be computed on both the net-asset value (NAV) and the selling price (offer). As an illustration, let us take the Lexington Research Fund, with an NAV price of $14.85 and an offer price of $16.23. The spread is $1.38. The load percentage is obtained by dividing the $1.38 spread by the NAV price of $14.85, which approximates 9.3 percent. However, based upon the offer price of $16.23, the sales charge is lowered to 8.5 percent.

Figure 23-1 The price ranges of mutual funds.

Mutual Funds

Wednesday, June 29, 1977

Price ranges for investment companies, as quoted by the National Association of Securities Dealers. NAV stands for net asset value per share; the offering includes net asset value plus maximum sales charge, if any.

	NAV	Offer Price	NAV Chg.
Acorn Fnd	16.13	N.L.	+ .02
Adv Invest	9.88	N.L.	+ .01
Aetna Fnd	7.41	8.10	− .01
Aetna InSh	13.09	14.30	− .03
Afuture Fd	9.32	N.L.	+ .04
AGE Fund	6.00	6.12	...
Allstate	8.56	N.L.	+ .02
Alpha Fnd	10.81	N.L.	...
Am Birthrt	9.97	10.90	− .01
Am Equity	5.18	5.66	+ .01
American Funds Group:			
Am Bal	8.13	8.89	...
Amcap F	5.68	6.21	...
Am Mutl	9.99	10.92	− .01
Bnd FdA	15.07	16.47	− .01
Cap FdA	6.37	6.96	...
Polaris	3.37	3.69	− .01
Lexington Group:			
Cp Ledrs	13.48	14.84	− .12
Growth	9.35	10.22	+ .03
Income	10.63	11.62	...
Resrch	14.85	16.23	− .01
Lifeins Inv	7.50	8.19	...
Lincoln National Funds:			
Selct Am	7.21	N.L.	− .01
Selct Spl	12.57	N.L.	− .02
Loomis Sayles Funds:			
Cap Dev	10.78	N.L.	+ .01
Mutual	13.12	N.L.	− .01
Lord Abbett:			
Affilatd	8.19	8.83	− .02
Bnd Deb	11.68	12.77	...

Source: *The Wall Street Journal*, June 30, 1977, p. 24.

As a contrast to computing the load, it may also be of interest to look at the no-loads. They can be found in Figure 23-1 with "N.L." in the Offer Price column after their names. Since the no-load funds have no special group of people actively selling their shares, this eliminates the need for a sales charge.[7] However, both the no-load and load funds charge on annual fee for their management services.

OBJECTIVES

The objectives of investment companies vary markedly. Some funds concentrate on safety and income; others are more concerned with growth. I spoke earlier of the wave of speculative buying that occurred in the sixties. Certain companies today, known as *hedge funds* (see Glossary) purchase securities with borrowed dollars to obtain leverage and make short sales (see Chapter 22). Borrowing and short selling can produce large profits but can also lead to disastrous losses should the market decline.

In contrast, investment companies specializing in short-term debt have done well in this era of high inflation. These companies were organized, beginning in 1972, to provide small investors an opportunity to invest in funds specializing in such holdings as U.S. Treasury bills, commercial paper and certificates of deposit. Investing exclusively in these money-market instruments enabled shareholders to receive up to 8 or 9 percent in 1974 and 1975. Somewhat reduced short-term interest rates in 1976 and 1977 resulted in the decline of shareholder holdings and the reduction of interest payments to the 6 to 7-percent level.

In order to achieve different objectives, various funds follow different courses of action. This is reflected in their portfolio holdings. For instance, a conservative fund emphasizing protection of capital with a relatively stable income may concentrate its investments primarily in highest-quality bonds with short to medium maturities. In contrast, certain mutual funds invest principally in speculative common stocks, giving primary emphasis to growth that they hope will outpace the Dow Jones Industrials, with income a secondary consideration. A mix of both income and growth can be found in balanced funds.

INCOME AND CAPITAL GAINS

We have determined that there are differences in mutual funds with regard to the loading charge, other costs and objectives. Now let us consider income and capital gains paid to shareholders.

[7]For two reports on the increasing popularity of no-load funds, refer to: "Bought, Not Sold." *Barron's,* May 24, 1971, p. 3; and "Funds Keep Growing." *Changing Times,* October 1973, p. 6.

I have heard friends of mine comment on the high return paid by certain mutual funds they own, but a careful check has often indicated that in arriving at the yield, they included both income and capital gains. The former is paid by virtue of interest and dividends from bonds and stocks held by investment companies. The latter is obtained by profitable sales on securities held in one's portfolio. It is important to realize that a capital gain is a return of principal. As an illustration, if X Mutual Fund purchased 10,000 shares of General Motors for $600,000 and made a sale at $660,000, it would have a realized capital gain of $60,000 (less brokerage charges) that would be available for distribution to shareholders. This is in fact giving the investor back a portion of his equity, and should not be construed as income.

ANNUAL CHARGES

The managers of investment companies are responsible for the administration of their funds. The annual fee for this supervision is normally half of 1 percent

TABLE 23-2 Statement of Income and Expenses, Loomis-Sayles Mutual Fund, for the Year Ended December 31, 1976

Investment income

Income	
Dividends	$2,527,605
Interest	2,579,488
	5,107,093
Expenses	
Management fee	588,037
Directors' fees and expenses	13,513
Custodian	753
Transfer agent	101,349
Audit	16,050
Legal	4,740
Printing	30,383
State excise tax	34,800
Miscellaneous	334
	789,959
Net investment income	$4,317,134

The total of the management fee and other expenses is 15.55 percent of the total investment income.

Source: Loomis-Sayles Mutual Fund, 47th Annual Report, 1976, p. 23.

of average net assets.[8] This and other administrative and operating costs are deducted from the sum available for income payments.

Costs incurred by the Loomis-Sayles Mutual Fund are shown in Table 23-2. For the year 1976, these expenses approximated 15½ percent of the Fund's total income. You should anticipate annual costs in the 16-percent area in making any projections on net income. Accordingly, if Z Mutual Fund has a portfolio consisting of the Dow Jones Industrials that are expected to pay out 4 percent for the current year, you can anticipate that Z Fund will give its shareholders about 3.4 percent. The latest annual-income and capital-gains data on mutuals can be found weekly in *Barron's*. More detailed information on mutuals is available in *Barron's* on a quarterly basis.

HOW CLOSED-END COMPANIES WORK

Closed-end investment firms show a decided contrast to the amazing expansion of mutuals. The number of shareholders actually declined from 310,000 in 1948 to approximately 249,000 in 1957, but by 1976 had risen to approximately 400,000. The financial worth of these companies increased from about $750 million in 1948 to $1.5 billion in 1957, and eighteen years later stood at $4.5 billion.

REASONS FOR POOR GROWTH

The disparity in growth between the two major categories of investment companies may be accounted for in some degree by the fact that while mutuals are aggressively sold by a hard-working sales force, closed-ends are purchased and sold like regular corporate issues, through stockbrokerage firms. In addition to this lack of a specialized group to market their product, closed-ends have never really recovered from the blow they suffered in the 1929 market crash. Finally, the very makeup of closed-end companies hinders rapid growth, since their form of capitalization is relatively fixed. For example, if Y Closed-End Company has 10 million shares of common stock outstanding, this number will not vary through daily sales and purchases. As a prospective purchaser of 100 shares, you would have to buy this amount out of the 10 million currently held by various stockholders. Thus, the price of each closed-end sale is determined in the same way as that of other marketable corporate securities.

[8]In the larger funds, this may apply to only the first $100 million, with three-eighths of 1 percent charged on amounts above this figure.

PURCHASING PROCESS

Closed-ends are usually listed on organized exchanges, such as the New York Stock Exchange and the American Stock Exchange. Each transaction is based upon supply and demand for the particular closed-end-company shares operating in a free economy, and is not related to the net-asset value. As an illustration, the Y Company may have a per-share net-asset value of ten dollars and be currently selling at twelve dollars. At other periods, the stock may be purchased at a discount.

Note the advantage to be gained from a yield standpoint by making a purchase at a sizable discount from net-asset value. If Y Company shares can be bought at a 50-percent discount and are earning 3 percent (after all expenses) on current holdings, it means that shareholders buying at this time could receive a yield of 6 percent. In periods of prosperity, closed-end companies normally sell for close to net-asset value or, in some instances, at premiums. However, there is variation among firms, and you should get this information about the company you are interested in before purchasing.

LEVERAGE

Many closed-end companies have a capitalization composed entirely of common stock, while others have various degrees of leverage. Leverage is a two-edged sword. It can work to the advantage of a holder of common stock in periods of good earnings and be detrimental in times of limited company income. Let us take the hypothetical Z Leverage Investment Company, which is capitalized as follows: four million dollars in bonds paying 3-percent annual interest; four million dollars in preferred stock providing a 5-percent dividend; and two million dollars in common stock. The common is eligible for those earnings remaining after payment is made to bondholders and preferred stockholders.

Assuming that in 1977, Z Leverage Investment Company had a net income of $600,000 on its capitalization, it would then have $280,000 available for the common shareholders. If the entire amount were paid out, it would give this group a 14-percent return. In contrast, if Z's net earnings were only $320,000 in 1978, the common stockholders would receive no return on their investment.

Shares of a closed-end fund with leverage (other factors being relatively equal) may be expected to fluctuate more than those of a company with a single type of capitalization. The potential investor must examine the capital structure and other significant factors prior to purchase. Examples of closed-end companies that have leverage are Tri-Continental and General American Investors.

COSTS

Normal brokerage charges constitute the cost of buying and selling shares in closed-end companies. For example, Tri-Continental closed at 21⅛ per share in its final round-lot trade on the New York Stock Exchange on July 1, 1977. The brokerage fee to purchase 100 shares would approximate $47.50, for a total purchase price of $2160.00. If the shares are sold seven months later at the same price, the round-trip transaction (including New York state tax[9] and SEC fee) could be consummated at an approximate cost of $100, or 4.6 percent. However, if any ten shares were bought and sold in the same seven-month period, it would cost 17 percent. Here again, the odd-lot purchase may pay twelve and a half cents per share above the round-lot and sell at twelve and a half cents below the market price.[10]

EMERGENCE OF NEW FUNDS

New products stimulate sales, and investment-company managers are always looking for fresh approaches in obtaining additional business. The hottest new development in recent years has been the money-management fund, specializing in portfolios consisting of such short-term-debt items as Treasury bills, commercial paper and bankers' acceptances. Dual-purpose closed-end investment companies are another recent development. This concept permits one group of shareholders to receive all the income for a set period—perhaps twelve years. At the end of this time, all capital gains that may have accrued are given to the second category. This information appears in *The Wall Street Journal* every Monday. The daily price of both the income and capital-gains shares can be found in newspapers reporting complete stock-exchange transactions. For example, Scudder transactions on June 29, 1977, were as follows:

TABLE 23-3 Scudder Transactions

High	Low	Stocks Div	Sales in 100's	High	Low	Close	Net Chg.
8	6½	Scud DuoVst	40	7⅜	7⅛	7¼	...
9½	8⅞	Scudder pf .83c	40	9	9	9	+⅛

Source: *The Wall Street Journal,* June 30, 1977, p. 25.

[9]Assuming sale by an out-of-state resident not employed in New York. See Figure 21-4 for commission rates of one firm.

[10]MLPFS eliminated the odd-lot differential on all its transactions beginning January 1976. Their own computer capabilities no longer required the need of a middleman to handle odd lots.

Dual-purpose closed-ends, according to one salesman, offer the best of both worlds—good income for the income-oriented and good capital-gains potential for the growth-minded. Unfortunately, the reverse can also apply—particularly in the periods of low income (in contrast to bonds) and when capital gains may end up at maturity as capital losses.

A third recent development has been increased fund activity in bonds with tax-exempt features, because of higher interest now being paid by states and municipalities and because the affluent society finds more people in the higher tax brackets looking for ways to increase their after-tax income. Money managers have capitalized on this situation by providing tax-exempt-bond funds. Brokerage firms frequently sponsor Municipal Investment Trust Funds. A prospectus is issued on each trust indicating the number of units and the principal amount of bonds in the fund at initial offering to the public. The objectives, composition, distribution of principal and interest, current return and sales charges are shown in the prospectus. It also contains much information about each of the bond issues purchased and should be studied with care prior to the purchase of any investment-company or corporate offering. If you are interested in bond funds, be sure to take a hard look at the bond ratings (see Chapter 20) to determine their quality. Maturity costs and interest income should also be considered.

This Municipal Investment Trust Fund offers the small investor an opportunity to receive a mix of tax-exempt bonds and permits taking advantage of the current high interest. However, small investors can purchase municipals directly with a minimum of $1,000, selecting only the best-rated issues, rather than investing in the medium- and upper-medium-grade issues included in a number of trust portfolios. More important, the tax exemptions are more advantageous to those in higher income brackets.

A fourth new type of fund moved into the fast-expanding option market in 1977. The objective of such open-end investment companies is to obtain high current income by investing in those dividend-paying common stocks in which call options are traded on the five exchanges. The funds write covered call options on these securities. Thus, fund income available to shareholders comes primarily from dividends and premiums from expired call options. It will be interesting to observe in the years ahead if these option-income funds can generate higher returns to shareholders than income-oriented investment companies which do not have options in their portfolios.

Other specialized funds include: 1) funds consisting of U.S. Government issues; 2) funds with a mix of commodities and securities; 3) funds comprising commodities exclusively comparable to averages like Standard & Poor's and Dow Jones; 4) funds with portfolios that provide results and 5) tax-exchange funds that permit a person to exchange his own securities for fund shares without paying a federal capital-gains tax.

COMMODITY FUNDS

A major drawback to the commodity fund is its higher cost of doing business. The normal investment company does not pay a federal corporate tax if it is registered with the SEC in accordance with the Investment Company Act of 1940. This act permits such exemption if the fund pays out at least 90 percent of income and capital gains annually to shareholders and if a maximum of 70 percent of the capital gains are held for more than six months. A commodity fund seldom has an opportunity to make long-term capital gains, and would therefore be subject to the corporate tax rate. It is also ineligible for the tax break given other funds in accordance with the 1940 act, because it deals in commodities exclusively. Further information on commodities can be found in Chapter 26.

OPEN-END VS. CLOSED-END

I am frequently asked, "Which do you prefer, open- or closed-end companies?" As with all forms of investment, each group has its desirable and undesirable features. The advantages offered by open-ends include the spreading of risk through diversified holdings; management supervision; no redemption fee; a wide variety of types of funds from which to select in order to meet one's objectives; and the privilege of turning in shares for cash at the net-asset value.

On the negative side are the high business costs. As we have seen, the initial charge made by the majority of funds is in many instances 7 to 9 percent for small purchases. The annual management fee plus other expenses may reach 15 to 20 percent of annual earnings from dividends and interest, particularly since mutuals have a great deal of turnover resulting from share redemptions and sales. There is also the specter of what might happen in the event of a heavy and persistent sell-off in the market if the funds endeavored to unload to meet the demands for cash at the net-asset value—a fear that was highlighted when Cornfeld's overseas empire collapsed.

Closed-ends, like open-ends, offer their shareholders diversification and management supervision. Added to this is the opportunity to buy at below net-asset value and profit from purchase and sale costs comparable to other corporate issues listed on the organized exchanges. Disadvantages relate to management expenses, occasional disparity on the premium side between selling price and net-asset value and the heavy expenses involved in round-trip transactions on small odd lots.

If you wish to go the investment-company route, it may be desirable to hedge by splitting your savings between a suitable open-end (preferably no-load) and a closed-end company. The significant point is to select the right funds to meet your objectives. Let us look at factors to consider in determining what companies are best suited to your particular investment program.

HOW TO SELECT AN INVESTMENT COMPANY

A number of techniques have been proposed by experts for evaluating investment companies. Although no general solution can satisfy each individual need, there are certain factors that may aid readers who accept my concept of the composition of a securities portfolio:

1. Allow ample time for appropriate study prior to purchase; do not let a salesman convince you that the deal must be closed immediately. Before buying, obtain pertinent literature. In the case of an open-end fund, read the prospectus. It provides useful data, including a history of the company, policies and objectives, sales commissions, management fees, asset-value determination, purchase and withdrawal plans, retirement plan for self-employed, financial statements that reflect holdings and capital structure, costs involved in running the business, past earnings, income and capital gains payments, affiliations of officers and directors, audits and reports to shareholders. Next, read the latest annual report, to determine results for the past year. A current quarterly report, which can usually be obtained from the company, permits an up-to-date portfolio examination.

2. Select a company that meets your objective. Stress has been placed in previous chapters upon having a diversified portfolio in order to achieve the goals of safety, income and growth. Prior to investment in stocks, I have recommended placing your money in an insurance program, bank account and U.S. government bonds. This type of coverage provides safety and income. In accordance with this approach, you should select an investment company which has the bulk of its money in growth-type common stocks.

As we have seen, different funds invest their holdings differently—that is, in bonds primarily, in bonds and stocks or in stocks primarily. If you have the necessary cash reserve, all that is lacking to achieve adequate diversification is appropriate common stock. To attain the growth objective, you should complete your portfolio by purchasing ownership equities with this attribute. A list of investment companies indicating the type of holdings of each, can be found in the current edition of Wiesenberger's *Investment Companies*. [11]

---

[11] Arthur Wiesenberger. *Investment Companies.* New York: Wiesenberger Service, Inc., current edition.

3. Determine the loading charges of the companies under consideration. As noted earlier, these can vary greatly. If your money is invested for relatively short periods, with other factors generally comparable, it is particularly advantageous to select a no-load fund.

4. Establish the relationship of the management fee and other expenses to income. How much must you pay for the privilege of having a group of people invest your money for you? Look into this charge, as well as into the additional costs in running the business, such as custodian's fee, auditing, registration, legal expenses, printing and taxes. The management fee will vary. In some cases it is ½ to 1 percent of the net assets, payable quarterly in amounts equal to ⅛ of 1 percent of the average value of the fund in the preceding quarter. Add all other expenses to the annual management charge and divide this total by the income of the same period. The result is the ratio of operating and management expenses to total investment income.

5. Look into the history of the company and the background of its present officers and directors. Give consideration to the size of the company, the length of time it has been in business and its ability to weather economic adversity. Do the managers have the necessary experience? Has the organization expanded steadily and increased its number of shareholders?

6. Examine the company's income and growth over the years. Give special attention to potential income and capital gains. It takes good earnings and corporate growth to provide shareholder profits. Capital gains are achieved as a result of rising prices in the stocks held by the investment company. The growth aspect comprises two categories: realized gains that are returned to the shareholders as the result of profitable sales, and unrealized gains that are retained in the fund's portfolio. The second type of growth can be achieved by the investor if he wishes to sell his shares, as they are normally redeemable at net-asset value. Investment companies usually sell some of the securities on which they have made yearly profits in order to distribute capital gains to stockholders. This may or may not be a sound investment decision, but it is certainly a good talking point for the sales force. Keep in mind, however, that sales and purchases cost the investment company money.[12]

Although past accomplishments do not ensure future performance, they merit serious consideration. As a basis for comparing earnings over a reasonable period of time, determine the average yield for the past ten years. This is done by adding up the per-share net income for each year and dividing the result by the total per-share net-asset value for the same period. It is essential to use net income only, because realized gains are a return of principal.

To determine the growth of each investment company under consider-

---

[12]By buying stocks yourself, you can select your own time to sell, which works to your advantage from an income-tax standpoint.

ation, use the figures for the per-share net-asset value at the beginning and end of the ten years, and the per-share realized appreciation for the same period. (These figures can be obtained from either Wiesenberger or the individual prospectus.) Subtract the beginning net-asset value from the figure ten years later—this provides the unrealized capital gains. Add to this total the realized gain distributed to shareholders for the ten-year period. Next, divide the overall capital gain (realized and unrealized) by the beginning net-asset value to obtain a comparative measure of growth for each investment company.

Let us take a hypothetical case. Assume that as of December 31, 1967, the per-share net-asset value of company X was $50 and that ten years later it stood at $100. The unrealized capital gain is $50. The realized gains paid to shareholders over the ten-year period amounted to $25. By adding the two gains—obtaining a total of $75—and dividing by the December 31, 1967, per-share net-asset value of $50, we arrive at a growth factor of +1.5. This permits ready comparison of various funds.

7. Employ a rating factor. Let us assume that you have selected five companies that meet your objective. The next step is to give each of these companies a numerical rating from 1 to 10 in each of the following five areas: loading charge; management fee and other expenses in relation to income; income; growth, including both realized and unrealized capital gains; and history of the company and background of the present officers and directors.

Under this rating system, the best of the five companies could receive a maximum of fifty points, and the poorest a minimum of five. In four of the five areas, you will have quantitative data to help you arrive at your rating; placing a rating on history and background will require qualitative analysis. This system can be used to evaluate both mutual and closed-end funds. In the latter case, however, it is necessary to delete the loading-charge factor and substitute selling price in relation to the net-asset value. It is frequently possible to buy closed-end funds at a price much below the market value of their holdings.

Do-it-yourself rating takes time and effort, but the reward can be king-sized in terms of income and growth. As with stock analysis, I recommend that you make your own evaluation if possible. As an alternative, consult a respected investment advisor, a financial magazine that rates investment companies, and/or brokers and salesmen.

24
REAL ESTATE

"Iowa farmland nearly triples in price since 1972"; "New home costs double between 1970 and 1977"; "Californians wait in line 48 hours to be eligible to sign up for houses under construction"; "Sale of houses increases twofold in localities in Arizona, Florida and Colorado." These recent headlines reflect the real-estate boom in certain areas in the United States. But this chapter offers a word of caution because paying a peak price is not usually a sound investment. According to Webster, real estate is "land and its . . . buildings . . . its improvements and its natural assets (as minerals, crops, waters) and with the inclusion of . . . rights that follow ownership of the land. . . ." Once your portfolio contains cash reserves, bonds and stocks, it is time to give serious consideration to this form of investment.

There are three ways you can place your money in real estate. These include the purchase of raw land, the purchase of property and the acquiring of indirect interest through trusts and companies specializing in realty ventures. In this chapter we will examine all three of these areas in an attempt to determine which fits in best with your personal-finance program.

When dealing in real estate, it is important to realize that greater patience is needed to maximize profits than with other forms of investment. If you are forced sell real estate at the wrong time, it can mean financial disaster. The recession of 1974–1975 found a number of individuals and companies unable to meet their mortgage payments. Many suffered huge losses. It is essential, in my view, not to overextend yourself and to have created adequate reserves to meet emergencies before launching into real-estate ventures.

Another important consideration in the real-estate world is the time factor, which plays a major role in buying and selling property. Time is obviously on the side of the young, as is pointed out poignantly below:

I know Southern California land is skyrocketing in value, but:

Age 25: "Not now, I'm young and there's plenty of time. When I'm making a little more. . . ."

Age 35: "I've a growing family to support. It takes all I make just to keep us going."

Age 45: "With two kids in college, I just can't afford it. Wait until they are out on their own, and then. . . ."

Age 55: "I know I should, but things aren't easy at my age. Maybe something will break in a year or two. . . ."

Age 65: "If only I had invested a little each month—I could retire comfortably without these money worries. If only I'd looked ahead. . . ."[1]

---

[1]Document by Land Consultants of America, Inc., Los Angeles, California.

INVESTING IN LAND

Land is a precious commodity, and the continuing rise in world population will make it even dearer in years to come. With ever-greater numbers of people occupying a relatively[2] constant supply of land, habitable terrain will obviously become increasingly scarce.

California, for instance, currently has a population of twenty million, a figure that is expected to double in the next thirty years. In Hawaii, it is very difficult to obtain ownership of a piece of land; terrain is normally available only on a lease basis. A number of foreign countries have also adopted this policy.

Land prices in the United States over the past fifty-three years reflect the marked increase in the value of terrain. In 1922, land in this country was valued at $93 billion, a figure which had zoomed to over $1,285 trillion in 1975.

This is not the whole story, however. Although we have all heard tales of remarkable profits being made by buying land at a bargain and selling it for many times the original cost, there is another side to the coin. Like the stock market, land values fluctuate in accordance with many other factors. Although in some areas they are now as much as four hundred times what they were twenty years ago, many people who made land investments near military bases and now-defunct NASA facilities have lost money (in Chapter 10 I speak of the opposite side of the coin—the bargain purchases available in these areas). Such disasters as earthquakes, floods and landslides can also result in bankruptcy in heavily financed land. The current energy recession has caused land values to decline sharply in certain localities. Then, too, there is always the danger of getting involved in unsavory deals. In 1975, for example, scandals in Arizona land sales caused some people to lose 100 percent of their original investment.

RISK OF EXPLOITATION

Unfair practices in the sale of land were highlighted in a *Wall Street Journal* article. The *Journal* stated that two major land companies—Horizon Corporation and Amrep Corporation—had been accused by the Federal Trade Commission of using "unfair and deceptive practices" to sell lots from large tracts they own in five states.[3]

---

[2]"Relatively" because there are means of increasing land utilization by taking arid or swampy areas and making them habitable; fill can make shallow waters usable; buildings can be made taller to accommodate more people.

[3]"Horizon Corp., Amrep Accused by FTC of 'Unfair' Practices in Sale of Land." *The Wall Street Journal,* March 18, 1975, p. 10.

SCOUTING FOR TERRAIN

One way to make money in land is to buy it on the outskirts of a dynamic growth area before the general public realizes what is taking place. Such an approach adopts the adage, "Buy it by the acre and sell it by the lot," and requires much hard work in the way of market research. Consideration must be given to the potential movement of city dwellers to suburban areas, the direction in which the city will grow and what new industries or other developments will make the land appreciate. For example, a new university attracting thousands of students could have a decidedly favorable effect on land values in the vicinity.

As with love and war, it would appear that all is fair in seeking out information on actions that will have an impact on land prices. If forewarned, the astute buyer can act quickly before prices rise. You may know that a state's population will double by the year 2000—but the trick is to find out where in the state the primary growth will occur. Some cities may triple in size and others decline. Then, too, you must pinpoint that section of the community where the big boom will take place.

Industry, however, is clever in disguising its moves. According to a *Wall Street Journal* report: "It's a real problem for some corporations. They say as soon as word gets around that they are looking for land, the landowners try to fleece them, asking several times what they would ask from an individual. But many corporations have found a solution: They cover their tracks."[4]

Indeed, large corporations preparing to buy land go to unusual lengths to hide their identities. They employ intermediaries to do their purchasing over a period of time, and the negotiations often take on aspects of a CIA operation, cloaked in mystery. For example, the boss of ". . . General Motors Corp.'s Argonaut Realty division says he sometimes gives the desk clerk an alias when he checks into a small-town hotel. He and his men carry cash or blank money orders to buy options, instead of using traceable checks."[5]

Nevertheless, as with the CIA, leaks do occur: "The representative of a large Midwest company, stopped for speeding, not only disclosed his name and company to the policeman, but also confided the company was going to build a plant nearby and suggested maybe the officer would like a new job."[6]

We have already noted the growth potential in the state of California. Allen & Co., a securities firm with an $80-million net worth, invested its own capital in this area. A *Journal* article stated, "Among other things, the Allens have bought tracts in Palo Alto and San Jose, California, which it hopes will eventually be turned into commercial developments.[7]

[4]"Land-Seeking Firms Use Ruses to Keep from Getting Stung." *The Wall Street Journal,* April 14, 1967, p. 1.

[5]Ibid.

[6]Ibid.

[7]"Little Known Financier, Astute but Unorthodox, Builds a Huge Fortune." *The Wall Street Journal,* August 15, 1970, p. 1.

TIPS FOR THE LAND BUYER

When you are in the market for a piece of land in a certain location, learn as much as you can about the future of that area. Read the newspaper ads to check out prices. Take a hard look at the available sites. Ask brokers about the terrain you are interested in buying. A check at the county seat can also be advantageous. The county clerk can furnish information regarding the ownership of the property that you wish to purchase. This will permit direct contacts and avoid brokers' commissions. You may also uncover people who can't meet their taxes and might be willing to sell at a reasonable figure. When it comes to closing the deal, be a tough bargainer. You can expect the seller to be equally astute in seeking a fair price.

The purchase of land is made on a different basis from that of property. You can't obtain long-term loans from mortgage companies. The seller may, however, agree to take a mortgage. The land contract is another means of financing the transaction. It is comparable to buying furniture or a car on time. The seller retains title until payment has been completed.

FINANCING LAND PURCHASES

Borrowing money can be expensive and there are other financial considerations involved in land purchasing that should be considered as well. In determining if a site is a good buy, it is important that you compute all costs. Let us take an example of a piece of land purchased for $10,000, held for five years and sold for $20,000.

TABLE 24-1 Sample Costs of Land Ownership

Cost	
Initial land cost	$10,000*
Mortgage interest at 9%	4,500
Taxes	1,500
Maintenance (grass cutting)	200
Sales commission, 10%	2,000
Total cost after 5 years	$18,200

Profit	
Land sale price	$20,000
Total costs	18,200
Net profit before taxes	$ 1,800

*The assumption is made that the principal is not repaid until after the land is sold.

The average yearly profit amounts to $360, or 3.6 percent on the original investment; however, by the end of five years, the cost has increased to $18,200, and therefore the return is actually less than 2 percent per year on the *total* investment. In contrast, if you put the $10,000 to work in a safe investment like U.S. Treasury notes, you could earn from $600 to $800 a year. And this annual return would increase with each passing year if you invested that additional $8,200 over a five-year period.

It is apparent that making a profit on land requires a sizable appreciation over the years. Tax costs, maintenance and interest expense must be checked with care prior to purchase, and it also helps to eliminate the sales commission. The rate at which you can borrow money is a key determinant of whether such an investment will be worthy of your money and time. In periods of high interest, investing in land won't pay unless you are able to obtain a 20- to 25-percent annual appreciation in the terrain.

INVESTING IN PROPERTY

In Chapters 10 and 11, we spoke of housing from the viewpoint of a dwelling place. We will now consider property as a source of income or capital gains. (A review of Part Three should prove helpful since the basic methods of selection it discusses also apply to choosing housing for investment purposes.) Such factors as location, construction, loan rate and market conditions must be considered, and the question of whether to buy or build must be resolved. It would appear that you can normally do better, from an investment standpoint, by building a house or small apartment unit yourself.[8]

LEASING A HOME

Buying for rental purposes is a common form of property investment. Before doing so, however, you must determine what return you will receive in contrast to placing your money elsewhere. (This should not be the sole criterion, of course, because there is an advantage to diversifying your investments. Property is one more bastion in your financial fortification.)

What can you expect to earn on your property? A normal monthly income should approximate 1 percent of the property cost—somewhat more if you build the house yourself—but it is wise to provide a 25-percent margin in your computations. Thus, on a $40,000 house, the income should approximate $400 a month; but in some situations you might receive $300, and in other cases $500.

Take the case of Mr. Hanover Hamllits of Washington, D.C., an imaginary builder who, like flesh-and-blood Capitolites, rents to foreign

---

[8]Larger commercial properties should not be considered until you have experience in smaller real-estate ventures.

dignitaries working in local legations. He receives approximately 20 percent above the going rate from this clientele. They take fine care of his properties, and as a result he has moved from selling his homes on completion to renting to members of the diplomatic corps. He also finds that the rate of return on the original investment increases each year that he holds the property, because he raises rents periodically and at a faster rate than the increase in maintenance costs and taxes. At the end of eight years, or sooner if the market is favorable, he sells each house.

Tax Breaks and the Rental Home

A prime advantage to owning property for rental purposes is the tax break in regard to depreciation. This can be clearly illustrated by the following breakdown of Mr. Hamllits' annual income and expenses seen from a federal income-tax perspective.

His fourth house cost him $40,000 to build in 1975. He paid $5,000 for the land and borrowed the remainder at 9 percent, making a five-year loan with principal to be paid at the end of the fifth year. It was apparent that the high interest rate in 1975 would be a major part of expenses, amounting to $3,150 annually.

Hamllits finished the house in December 1975, and leased it to a consul general on January 1, 1976. The going rental rate was $400 a month, but he obtained $480. His annual property tax was $400 and he expected this to increase the next year. Insurance was currently $160, but this also was due to rise. Labor costs forced him to do much of the maintenance himself, but he still spent $280. Depreciation was initially written off at 5 percent. Rent collection and other supervision would have cost him $288 a year but, as with the maintenance, he decided to handle this himself.

TABLE 24-2 Income and Expenses, Hamllits' House #4
January 1 to December 31, 1977

Income:		$5,760
Expenses:		
Interest (9%)	$3,150	
Property taxes	400	
Insurance	160	
Maintenance	280	
Depreciation	1,750	
Supervision	0	5,740
Net profit before taxes		$ 20
Federal taxes (50% bracket)		10
Net profit after taxes		$ 10

Hamllits' House #4 reported a profit before taxes of $20. However, actual outlay of funds in relation to income presents a different picture. No payout is made for the $1,750 in depreciation; so from a funds-flow standpoint, Mr. Hamllits spent $3,990 and thus had a cash balance of $1,770. This gave him a return of over 35 percent on his $5,000 investment. (Even if he had rented the property at $400 per month, his return would have approximated 16 percent.) Thanks to his depreciation write-off, he paid only $10 in federal income tax (Table 24-2). Furthermore, by building a quality home, he can anticipate a yearly appreciation on his investment and a healthy profit at sale time.

FUNCTION OF LEVERAGE

The subject of leverage was discussed in relation to the stock market in Chapters 22 and 23. In the area of real estate, the leverage factor permits the investor to utilize a small initial equity. In Hamllits' case he used $5,000 of his own money to buy the land and borrowed $35,000. Some people borrow 95 to 100 percent of the property cost. Mr. Hamllits obtained a five-year loan, but it is possible to secure twenty-five- to thirty-year mortgages. A loan that can be assumed for a long period may be highly advantageous in view of the long-term inflationary trend, because it permits repayment of principal in lower-cost dollars.

The significance of leverage is more pronounced on property than on securities, because of increasing realty values. This can be illustrated as follows:

1. A $1,500 investment may obtain the use of $30,000 in property. Thus, a 5-percent equity has 95-percent leverage.
2. The rent is determined by the property valuation. In this case, normal return would be $300 per month.
3. Depreciation is allowed on the total cost of the building.
4. All increases in rent and appreciation accrue to the owner.

Leverage, however, is a two-edged sword. If rents are not forthcoming and no other source of income is available, it can result in a forced sale or bankruptcy.

NEED FOR DIVERSIFICATION

The higher the leverage, the larger the risk. This is great if you have bet on a winner, but can wipe you out if you don't have adequate resources behind you in case you lose. An investment program that includes several properties in various localities reduces risk. If a person has only one rental property and it becomes vacant, there is a total loss of income. Payments on principal, upkeep, taxes and insurance must be met from other sources. As the number of sound rentals increases, the chance of total income loss is reduced. Furthermore, each additional lease contributes to greater income for meeting expenditures. This

437

permits flexibility in securing cash to pay fixed expenses on vacancies. In the event of a recession, the buildup of equity also offers an owner greater opportunity to refinance his mortgages at a reduction in fixed monthly payments.

From a diversification viewpoint, there is also a distinct advantage to owning a modest four-unit apartment house rather than an expensive home. The chances of all apartments in a well-situated building being unoccupied are remote, whereas a high-priced home can remain vacant indefinitely unless bargain rentals are provided.

IMPORTANCE OF APPRAISALS

Before purchasing any type of real estate, it is essential to have it appraised in order to get an estimate of its current value. You can consult a professional appraiser for this purpose and confer with local real-estate brokers. It will save you time and mistakes to consider the following points in determining property values:

1. *Location.* Rentals should be looked at in regard to proximity to schools, churches, shopping and adequate transportation. Consider the adequacy of police and fire protection, as well as the relationship to other properties in that locality. To make a valid comparison requires weighing each factor equitably. No two buildings will be exactly alike, and this is what makes a decision difficult.
2. *Condition.* Age and physical condition should be studied with care. It would be unfair to compare a poorly maintained building with well-kept property. Normally, the newer building will enjoy higher rents and lower operating costs.
3. *Allowances.* On income property, allowance must be made for income lost as a result of vacancies and periodic turnover. Repairs, redecorating and other renovation may be required before property is acceptable to new tenants. There are also losses due to occupants who may be willfully destructive or present bad checks, and cost you plenty in legal expenses and other headaches. These losses will be reduced with experience. But it always pays to make a thorough appraisal— including an investigation of a potential lessee.

PROPERTIES AS INCOME SOURCES

Properties create profits from two sources: rentals and appreciation. Income may be estimated based upon returns from comparable housing in the area, but judging property appreciation is more difficult. Income accrues from current monthly cash payments and reduction in principal. In contrast, a capital gains is not obtained until the unit is sold.

As noted above, depreciation is deductible yearly for federal income-tax purposes. From a tax standpoint, it is considered a partial return on the basic cost of the housing. In reality, it is income, because property increases in value faster than the deterioration of the structure.[9] The fact that depreciation is tax-deductible makes it especially attractive to people in higher tax brackets. On a profitable sale of property, the maximum tax is 25 percent of the capital gain.

IMPACT OF THE ENERGY SHORTAGE

The formal announcement of the energy crisis, in late 1973, ushered in a whole new ballgame in real estate. Values have declined in a number of suburban locations, while urban property has risen in price. It is imperative that any property investments be analyzed with respect to the energy shortage. One real-estate authority expressed his views as follows:

> The impact of a sustained energy crisis on the continuing need for new housing will inevitably bring about basic changes in the type and location of residential construction. For the ailing central cities, it could mean a revival of construction with both families and businesses returning to a more central location where utilities are in some cases now underutilized as a result of earlier urban erosion and where the facilities for common carrier transportation exist.
>
> It is new housing, especially single-family units, that will experience major changes if the current energy crisis becomes a long-term fact of life.
>
> Regional coordination of all construction, so often praised in theory, will become a necessity to balance the demand for space against the available supply of fuel, gas, and electricity. Moreover, the new housing that is built on land closer to the central city will cost more because of the increase in the cost of land.
>
> Under these circumstances, single-family homes on individual plots may simply become impractical, since the additional cost of materials and labor would tend to price such housing out of its market. This could lead to a wide-scale revival of duplex and row housing, which was the solution to urban housing needs as early as a century ago. Indeed, the construction of townhouse condominiums in many parts of the country in recent years may well portend this trend.[10]

---

[9]From a technical standpoint, depreciation cannot be considered a partial return on the basic cost of housing. If the value of the property increases and the depreciation schedule is not adjusted accordingly, the property owner is erroneously overstating his wealth.

[10]Emanuel M. Brotman (chairman of the board and president of J. I. Kislak Mortgage Co.), "Housing Changes to Come." New Orleans *Times Picayune*, December 16, 1973, Sec. V, p. 15.

FIRMS SPECIALIZING IN REAL ESTATE

The remarkable growth, up to 1974, of companies specializing in real estate may be attributed to a recognition by astute financiers of the profit potential in this area. There have been three choices available to investors in recent years: trusts, companies and syndicates.

REAL ESTATE TRUSTS

Real Estate Investment Trusts (REITs) are similar in concept to the closed-end investment companies discussed in Chapter 23. REITs began to gain popularity about fifteen years ago, when they were permitted to qualify as real estate investment trusts in accordance with the Internal Revenue Code. In order to qualify as business trusts, they must pay out to the shareholders annually at least 90 percent of their taxable income, thus avoiding federal income tax. This 90-percent-or-greater distribution does not include capital gains, which may be dispensed at the pleasure of the management (trustees).

The purpose of these trusts is to provide individuals with an opportunity to invest in various real estate holdings. However, they do not always make astute investments. Hubbard Real Estate Investments, for example, was formed in 1969. A Standard and Poor's report stated:

> This real estate investment trust invests primarily in operating property leased to major corporations. In October 1975, the Hubbard's largest tenant, W. T. Grant, filed for protection under Chapter IX of the Federal Bankruptcy Act. The establishment of a $6.5 million reserve for carrying costs and possible losses on the Grant properties in the October 1975 quarter resulted in a small loss for fiscal 1975. The absence of such charges has permitted a restoration of profitable operations in 1976.[11]

Note that Hubbard is listed on the New York Stock Exchange. It has over four million shares outstanding, with assets of over ninety million dollars. Its stockholders number 22,200. Hubbard can also distribute to shareholders funds paid out of appreciation; these are tax-free.

A drawback to dealing with REITs is the sizable counseling charge involved. According to Standard & Poor's report, Hubbard's "advisor received an annual fee based on a percentage of the trust's gross income."[12] In the past this fee has been equal to 4 percent of the gross income of the trust, reduced to the extent the advisor receives fees or additional compensation from others in connection with the sale of properties to the trust. You will have to determine

[11]Standard & Poor's *Standard NYSE Stock Reports,* vol. 43, No. 114, June 14, 1976, p. 1168.
[12]Ibid.

for yourself if you can do a better job by direct investment in property. With a 4-percent gross-income advantage (plus other costs), I believe that you can beat the trusts. Another drawback to REITs is the potential sharp loss in price when property values decline in a recession and interest rates climb markedly.

Recent trusts have been adding a sweetener in the form of warrants. The prospectus of Citizens and Southern Realty investors, for example, indicated a plan to issue 2,500,000 shares at twenty dollars per unit, for a total of $50 million. Each share carried a warrant to purchase an additional one-half share of the trust. Citizens and Southern intended to invest most of its proceeds in construction loans. Keep in mind that in such ventures, underwriters as well as trust advisors make money. A middleman's take of this kind should be avoided by the astute investor whenever possible.

In 1974, REITs and real estate companies experienced hard times. Several REITs went bankrupt. Others found that the prices of their stock had declined sharply. Hubbard, for example, ranged from 9⅛ to 19⅝ in 1974, as compared with 20 to 25½ in 1971. Kaufman and Broad went from the 38¼–52¼ spread in 1972 to 2¼–14¾ in 1974.

The Wall Street Journal commented on the remarkable price fluctuations in REITs as follows:

> For those investing in the stock of the so-called REITs, the roller-coaster ride has been dizzying. When they were formed at the turn of the decade, the trusts were an immediate hit because they allowed small investors to participate in the real estate boom.
>
> The trusts made tidy profits by lending to developers at rates several percentage points above the rates on money they borrowed, and the profits were tax-free as long as they passed 90% along to shareholders in dividends.
>
> So investors got handsome yields and—for a while—capital gains as well. But when the balloon burst a year ago, many REITs began a seemingly endless descent. Shares of the biggest REIT, Chase Manhattan Mortgage & Realty Trust, for example, had climbed from the original $25 in mid-1970 to $70 in 1973, but now have sunk to less than $7 on the New York Stock Exchange.
>
> A smaller institution, First Wisconsin Mortgage Trust, originally offered in December 1971 at $25, soared to almost $45 in 1973 before plunging to about $9 last April, when its trading was halted by the Big Board.[13]

Why the sharp decline in 1974? The high cost of borrowing money, the housing recession and defaults by some lessees were surely contributing factors. But by

[13]David Gumpert and Mark Starr. "How Two Realty Trusts Gave Backers Big Gains—And Then Big Losses." *The Wall Street Journal,* March 14, 1975, p. 1.

April 1975, things were on the mend for a number of REITs. By March 1977, Hubbard had recovered from a low of 9⅛ to 17⅝. Kaufman and Broad was selling at 6¼—three times its earlier low. Cheaper money and the real estate boom have been prime factors.

REAL ESTATE COMPANIES

A number of corporations have been organized to deal primarily in real estate. They are listed on various exchanges and their assets are sizable. Take the example of Transnation Development Corporation, formed in June 1969, with $62 million in assets. According to its board chairman, "Transnation's business is to acquire, service and develop commercial, residential and recreational properties both in the U.S. and abroad."[14]

Transnation's real estate holdings were spelled out as follows:

> The ownership and operation, through CTE, of two race tracks near Chicago—Arlington Park and Washington Park—and the new, 430-room Arlington Park Towers hotel located on the grounds at the Arlington Park race track. CTE also holds approximately 450 acres of undeveloped land in the area of the race tracks which are suitable for future residential, industrial and commercial development.
>
> An 80% interest in a partnership to construct and operate an 88-acre World Trade and Cultural Center—Pacific World—which will serve as a unique shopping center-showcase for the wares of countries in the Pacific Basin. Ground has already been broken for the initial phase of the development.
>
> Architectural planning for construction of a 1,000-room hotel at Chicago's O'Hare International Airport, the world's busiest. Transnation has entered into a twenty-year lease with the city of Chicago giving it exclusive hotel rights on the present airport grounds.
>
> Construction of a sophisticated metallurgical laboratory for Taylor Forge at its Gary, Indiana, plant and participation in the construction of a new Taylor Forge facility in Memphis, Tennessee.[15]

Transnation was listed on the Pacific Stock Exchange. There were three million shares outstanding. Its consolidated balance sheet reflected land, buildings and equipment of over $63 million, with nearly $20 million depreciation allowance.[16]

Various realty investment companies specialize in various aspects of real estate. These include diversified companies, construction firms and local devel-

---

[14]*1969 Annual Report to Shareholders,* signed by Philip J. Levin, chairman of the board and president, June 18, 1970, p. 11.

[15]Ibid.

[16]Transnation Development Corporation was acquired by the Madison Square Garden Corporation in a transaction completed in March 1971.

opment organizations. The above-mentioned Kaufman and Broad, organized in 1965, is the largest independent builder of homes in the United States. By using mass-production techniques, it has supplied homes to the large middle-income market and now has housing developments in Chicago, Detroit, Los Angeles, New York, San Francisco and Paris, France.

From an investor's viewpoint, investment in a real estate company normally permits excellent marketability. The sizable holdings of such companies also provide safety through diversification. In analyzing a firm's income and expense statements, it is essential to look at the cash flow. Transnation, for example, listed $1,927,421 in depreciation. If this amount were added to their income, before federal income taxes, it would reflect an increase of 68 percent.

There is a prime distinction, from an investor's perspective, between a trust and a realty company. The former pays out its yearly income to shareholders and avoids taxes. This normally provides recipients with a favorable yield. A realty company is taxed on its income but may plow back a majority of the after-tax earnings for further growth. Therefore, its yield may be lower than that of the trust, but the potential rise in its stock price may be greater.

REAL ESTATE SYNDICATES

Another approach to indirect investment in property has been through syndicates. This medium was in vogue during the Eisenhower era. Much like the trust, it permitted the individual with limited capital to obtain an equity in real-estate holdings. However, in the syndicate he became a limited partner in a specialized real-estate project. The managers were supposedly individuals with professional real-estate experience who pooled funds for investment in income-producing property. The rewards to individual investors came from high tax-free return.

The syndicate would write off depreciation rapidly, and yields reached as high as 10 percent in the early years. However, unsound property investments resulted in certain syndicates' paying low yields. The investor was further pinched by the exorbitant fees charged by certain firms for their professional management guidance. The lack of any plan to buy back investments of limited partners and few regulatory checks further militated against this type of investment. The Securities and Exchange Commission had no control over the activities of these syndicates because they were exclusively intrastate operations. Syndicates had their day but no longer exist.

INVESTING IN LOW-INCOME PROPERTY

The Black Panther Party in New Orleans made national headlines in September 1970. Fourteen members had barricaded themselves in a house when the

443

police made an early-morning raid. In the ensuing shoot-out, a number of people were wounded. All fourteen people were arrested and bond was set at $100,000 for each. The members were to appear before a local judge, but he asked to be excused. It was stated that he owned the house the Panthers were renting—and also that he owned other sites in that low-income area. During an inspection of his property the next day, the judge had his car stoned.

The profits are large for those renting property to low-income families. Some of the wealthiest families and institutions in America have made their fortunes by this means. Maintenance is minimal and slum dwellers seldom know how to initiate complaints. Slum landlords make money by deferring maintenance. They are in fact taking income from tenants in the form of capital accretion.

One of my students made a pilot study of slum ownership in New Orleans. He called holdings of this kind "a classic confrontation between economic self-interest and the moral code of the individual."[17] The report indicated that owners in one slum area included a theological seminary, a church and some prominent citizens. The largest single landowner, however, was a professional slum speculator who was prominent in civic affairs. A one-time member of the Citzens' Committee for Better Housing, he had been forced to resign when a fire destroyed one of his tenements. "The Fire Department investigation found the structure was in flagrant violation of the city fire, electrical, and housing ordinances."[18]

There are clearly more desirable ways to make a fair return on your money than by exploiting the poor. Furthermore, today's slum dweller is less passive than in years gone by. A social consciousness is awakening in America, and the risks for the slumlord are on the rise—not only in the form of demands for property improvement but also in the form of threats against life and limb.

[17]Taylor E. Clear. "Private Property and Public Responsibility." unpublished term paper at LSUNO, p. 16.
[18]Ibid.

25

PROFITABLE HOBBIES: HIGHLIGHTING NUMISMATICS & GOLD

Americans confidently expect that in the years to come, the workweek will diminish and more leisure time will be available for the enjoyment of hobbies. Leisure-time pursuits based on collecting can offer particularly rich rewards.

True collectors of art, antiques,[1] stamps or coins receive much pleasure from the beauty of their collections. And there are other rewards as well. The serious collector can realize financial gains from his investment.

Hobby possibilities are as broad as your imagination, but we will focus here on two hobbies that offer good profit potential. Numismatics (coin collecting), the first hobby to be examined, can be embarked upon with very limited funds. In contrast, investing in gold requires a sizable investment to be profitable.

THREE SUCCESS STORIES

The mobility of our society can be expected to increase in the years ahead, particularly for the young and those seeking fresh challenges. As noted in Chapter 10, it is important to keep yourself mobile if you wish to capitalize on new opportunities. Potential hobbies frequently present themselves as a result of business transfers, so it is worthwhile to check into hobby possibilities wherever you may live. The following three cases illustrate how people can build sizable nest eggs by capitalizing on their leisure time.

The energetic wife of a foreign-service-officer friend took an interest in shell collecting while living in Okinawa. She haunted the library to obtain every available article on the subject and interviewed the local conchologists while attending Ryukyu University. The islands offered a fine opportunity to build up a collection: plenty of easy-to-acquire shells, cheap labor, a ready market. Initially she sold her merchandise locally, but soon she began exporting it to the United States. By the time of her departure four years later, her income exceeded her husband's take-home pay.

Another acquaintance, a manager with a large oil company, turned to the art field on assignment in Paris. First he went to school at the Sorbonne and acquired a fine background. He traveled throughout Europe looking for good buys, but devoted most of his efforts to scouring the French capital. In one purchase and sale, he netted five thousand dollars after taxes. His philosophy: "Spend as much time as possible learning about the subject—read, read, read, then shop, shop, shop. It is a tricky business, but I gained great satisfaction from bargaining with Parisians and making money on it."

[1]A *Barron's* article, "Spirited Bidding," February 1, 1971, p. 9, points out that antique collectors look for "beauty and rarity, not for bargains." However, the profit opportunities are also mentioned.

The third success story relates to a hobby of my elder son's—coin collecting. This field seems to offer the greatest growth opportunity with the least degree of risk, *if* the collector follows some basic rules. Here's how one young man's experience began.

"Dad, I've found an uncirculated 1909-S VDB! Believe it or not, this Lincoln penny is worth seventy bucks!"[2] Our son had struck a miniature gold mine while searching through a roll of fifty pennies obtained at the local bank. Since the day he was introduced to coin collecting while completing his Eagle Scout merit-badge requirements, the whole family has found this hobby to be a fascinating adventure. My stint in the service proved to be a great advantage in building up a collection; in each area of the United States and overseas, we found specialized opportunities for obtaining unusual coins and participating in community activities with others having similar interests.

Today there are over eleven million coin collectors (called numismatists) in the United States who enjoy the fun and profits of this popular hobby. Our family had heard of get-rich-quick schemes before, and all of them had proved to be empty promises. But as numismatists, we have discovered potential profits in our pockets—all on a no-risk basis. An authority on coin collecting, Mr. S. Ruddel of Ormond Beach, Florida, put it this way:

> "Fifty years ago, one could have taken this sound advice: Take all Indian-head cents and Liberty-head nickels out of circulation that you can afford and you will provide yourself with a retirement nest egg. Thirty years ago, one would say, Save all the Buffalo nickels and zinc cents (1943) and all Lincoln cents dated before 1935, and you had it made. Ten years ago, would-be coin collectors were advised to save silver dollars, "S" minted coins, proofs, uncirculated cents, buffalo nickels and mercury dimes. Five years ago, gold coins could have been bought at reasonable prices. Today, the wise numismatist is saving all silver coins prior to 1965, Canadian silver dollars, crown size and ½ crown size silver coins of foreign countries, proofs, mint sets, uncirculated items, including copper pennies and Bicentennial dual-dated (1776–1976) quarters, halfs and dollars."

Now let us examine the world of the coin collector more closely, in terms of making money from money and other pleasurable rewards.

---

[2] 1909 is the issue date of the coin. "S" indicates that it was minted in San Francisco. "VDB" stands for Victor D. Brenner, the designer of the Lincoln penny. The first such coin appeared in 1909 to honor the memory of President Lincoln on the hundredth anniversary of his birth. For a short time, Mr. Brenner's initials appeared on the 1909 penny and, because of its limited supply, this is a rare item—a wonderful find for any numismatist.

NUMISMATICS

REAPING A CASH HARVEST

Coin hunting can provide a real addition to the household income. We have friends in Washington, D.C., who acquire coins of small denominations that are currently in circulation. The search is continuous, family members scanning all loose change from grocery money and earnings. As a result of this constant scrutiny, our friends have sold several collections at more than a thousand times their original cost.

Another of our acquaintances, an anthropology professor, has devoted many years to buying and selling coins on a large scale. He specializes in new coins of small denominations (pennies, nickels, dimes) and proof sets. Buying in huge quantities and unloading on a systematic basis has netted him the additional income to meet college tuition costs for his two sons.

An American businessman friend working in Europe discovered that there was a bonanza of U.S. coins with good dates available oversees. He contacted a number of French and German families interested in numismatics and came up with a superb Indian-head collection valued at eight hundred dollars; his cost was twenty-four. He also found it profitable to visit foreign banks and U.S. facilities such as American Express in order to obtain rolls of new coins, which resulted in additional good finds.

A down-to-earth expression of the rewards of coin hunting was pointed up in an article that my son Richard wrote for *The Numismatist,* a publication for collectors:

> I am presently a sophomore in high school and took in this project [of looking for Lincoln pennies] during my summer vacation. It required a portion of fifty working days, with an average of two thousand coins scrutinized at each sitting. Initially, I spent four hours daily checking this number, but by practice I cut the time to two hours per 2,000, or one coin every 3.6 second—including unwrapping, sorting, and rerolling. My total time expended in this venture came to 160 hours. This considered trips to the local bank, preparation of filing data, and other directly related chores.
>
> My collection has been appraised at one hundred and sixty-four dollars—an hourly rate slightly in excess of a dollar per hour.[3]

Collecting was to reward my son more handsomely than this. The Lincoln penny he found is now worth two hundred dollars—twenty thousand times its face value—and helped to finance his college education.

[3]*The Numismatist,* January 1959, p. 41.

NONMONETARY REWARDS OF NUMISMATICS

There is more to coin collection than the profit motive. Coins have been issued in our country since the seventeenth century. Each has an interesting background that can contribute to an appreciation of the history of the United States. And, as noted earlier, coin collecting is a good family project. Every school-age member can join in looking for rare material, while preschoolers can help by opening their piggy banks. A "coin day" can be set aside once a month, with the whole family attending a coin-club meeting or visiting the neighborhood numismatic dealer. Vary the fun by collecting birth sets (a penny, nickel, dime, quarter and half-dollar dated the year of the person's birth). Our neighbor finds this hobby ideal for his aged, bedridden mother, who now **spends** many happy hours competing with her grandson for the best family collection.

Unlike stamps, U.S. coins can always be redeemed at face value. Cash is cash; circulated stamps are "finis," but circulated cash keeps circulating. Thus, the collector is assured that his collection can always be spent. But despite its durability, hard currency requires care in handling and storing in order to maximize its value. Therefore, as your collection takes on value, it is important to protect it with insurance coverage. Collectors often keep their valuable pieces in a vault, and all professionals are careful in properly protecting their finds. The importance of adequate protection, and a testimony to the durability of coins, is apparent from a newspaper article:

> Fire Chief Dallas W. Greene, Jr., said firefighters found a wooden chest in the surgeon's attic containing more than $10,000 in silver dollars and some $20 gold pieces. The chest was damaged by the fire and the coin collection, which weighed over 600 pounds, filled two garbage cans in which the money was placed for safe-keeping.[4]

IMPORTANCE OF SELECTIVITY

Many novice numismatists start out with the mistaken idea that they would collect everything. In spite of their good intentions, they soon give up with little to show for their efforts but a pile of junk. Observing the following rules will help you collect with maximum effectiveness:

Rule One: Limit your area of concentration. For example, you might want to obtain U.S. pennies from 1856 to the present time, which involves only two groups: Indianheads (1856–1909) and Lincolns (1909 to date).

Rule Two: Secure desired items at reasonable cost and effort. It is difficult to collect items out of circulation, such as early American coins. There-

---

[4]New Orleans *Times Picayune,* March 21, 1968, Sec. 1, p. 8.

fore, narrow your field to U.S. lower-face-value coins minted within the past sixty-eight years—Lincoln cents, 1909 to date; buffalo nickels, 1913–1938; Jefferson nickels, 1938 to date; mercury dimes, 1916–1945; and Roosevelt dimes, 1946 to date. These sets can be acquired from coins in circulation with the expenditure of limited funds. In view of their fast-growing popularity, a person who holds on to full sets may reap relatively rich profits. Another approach is to concentrate on all silver coins (dimes, quarters and half-dollars) prior to 1965. In addition, Kennedy half-dollars with dates from 1965 through 1970 contain 40 percent silver and may appreciate. Uncirculated copper pennies also offer good growth possibilities.

IMPORTANCE OF QUALITY

There are three factors that determine the value of a coin: the number made, the demand and the quality. Of the three, quality is the most important. For instance, a 1931 Lincoln penny (manufactured at the Denver mint, with total production of 4,480,000) in poor condition is worth little more than its face value. In contrast, the same penny in new or uncirculated condition may be valued in today's retail market at forty dollars.

Why is there such a big difference in price just because a coin looks new or old? When I asked a well-known collector this question, he replied: "Most folks consider a penny just a penny, or a nickel just a nickel. However, numismatists want beauty in a coin, in much the same way most people prefer a new car to an old jalopy."

Since numismatists are finicky about quality, a successful collector should be familiar with the following collector's terms:

Mint Marks

Coins are currently minted at Philadelphia, Denver and San Francisco. The coins from Denver have a "D"; San Francisco an "S"; and no mint mark is on those produced in Philadelphia.[5] The U.S. Government has designated Philadelphia as the main mint. Denver is the only branch mint in operation today. However, the San Francisco Assay Office currently produces proof sets and some regular coins. Branch mints were at one time in operation at New Orleans (O), Carson City, Nevada (CC), Charlotte, North Carolina (C), Dahlonega, Georgia (D), and San Francisco (S).

The Coinage Act of 1965 stated that no mint marks would be utilized for five years. Congress, however, reduced this period and mint marks reappeared on coins in 1968.

---

[5]There was an exception: Five-cent pieces that were struck in Philadelphia from 1942 to 1945 have a "P".

Proof Coin Set

This is a set of six coins—a penny, nickel, dime, quarter, half-dollar and dollar. Each coin is given special treatment to produce a bright luster and well-struck appearance. The pieces are prepared from special blanks, and each coin is struck twice on a special press. Current sets are obtained from the San Francisco Mint and neatly packaged in a newly designed precast plastic container. The current year may be purchased for $7.00 per set by writing to the San Francisco Assay Office, 55 Mint Street, San Francisco, California 94175. There is a limit of five sets per order. The 1964 set (3,950,762 produced) was quickly oversubscribed. Because John F. Kennedy appeared on the half-dollar for the first time, it was already quoted at a premium before distribution. The mint later reopened purchases but reduced quantities from 100 to 2 per person. The Kennedy 1964 set, currently retailing at $5.00, cost only $2.10 when purchased from San Francisco in 1964.

Special Mint Set

This is a set composed of five uncirculated coins—a penny, nickel, dime, quarter and half-dollar. Sets were obtainable from San Francisco for a three-year period (1965–1967). They were made from specially prepared and polished dies. Proof coin sets were not made during the period 1965–1967 owing to the coin shortage, and these special mint sets served as a substitute. The 1965–1966 issues used a protective cellophane wrapping similar to that of precious proof sets. In 1967, the special mint sets came in an attractive plastic container.

Uncirculated Coin Set (Mint Set)

This is a set of coins minted on high-speed presses for general circulation from the Philadelphia, Denver and San Francisco mints. The 1976 set sold for six dollars and included thirteen coins as follows: three pennies (San Francisco, Denver, Philadelphia), two each of nickels, dimes, quarters, halves and Eisenhower dollars from Philadelphia and Denver. The set currently sells at retail for a small premium.

Uncirculated. These coins look new in every respect—with no evidence of wear or loss of original brilliance in the newer pieces.

Almost Uncirculated. Similar to uncirculated, except showing some loss of luster and the slightest indication of use.

Very Fine. Exhibiting small indication of circulation. Minor erosion on key points, such as word "Liberty" on the Indian-head penny.

Fine. The design is clear but examination reveals some wear, such as high points on face of the Lincoln penny.

Very Good. Shows its age but permits easy recognition of the date and all other key points.

Good. The prime features are recognizable. However, much wear is obvious.

Fair. Examination points up heavy usage that makes it difficult to read such items as the motto, date and design.

Poor. Damaged in some major manner—bent, notched, drilled or having some other significant fault. Spurned by collectors and in the vast majority of cases has no extra value.

Remember, however, that the above categories (except for proof and mint sets) are guides only; each collector must interpret the ratings for his particular coins. To complicate matters further, various additional gradations are utilized. Some numismatists, for example, use the terms "extra fine" and "brilliant uncirculated." Because of this lack of an established standard, one expert lamented, "Describing a coin's condition is about as hard as explaining the taste of a five-course dinner."

Always try to upgrade the quality of your coins. In the long run, this policy will greatly enhance their value. Shoot for an uncirculated collection.

IMPORTANCE OF QUANTITY AND DEMAND

Quantity and demand, along with quality, help determine price. Only 484,000 of the valuable 1909-S VDB were minted. Contrast this figure with that of the 1909 Philadelphia-struck Lincoln penny, whose quantity totaled 72,702,618. The former may retail at forty times the latter.

A good way to keep in touch with current mintage is to check the reports published by the Treasury Department. The 1977 total (through March, for example, was 36,907 Bicentennial 40-percent silver proof sets minted, in contrast to 1,111,265,980 pennies.

What part does demand play in price? Let's compare the 1909-S VDB (484,000 minted) with the 1857 large cent (333,456 minted). Each has low mintage, and yet there is considerable variance in price for these two coins in good condition; in view of the Lincoln's popularity, the 1909-S VDB is currently worth five 1857s.

HOW TO JOIN THE COIN HUNT

Many people have the idea that collecting coins is a rich man's hobby. They are surprised to learn that success requires little expense but lots of time and effort. It is helpful to have the following equipment: an inexpensive magnifying glass, a good display folder and an authoritative publication such as *A Guide Book of*

United States Coins (latest edition) by R. S. Yeoman.[6] These items may be purchased from any coin dealer for from five to ten dollars, depending on the type of coin album purchased. A number of department stores and specialty shops also carry coin equipment, and it pays to shop around to obtain the best price. Whitman coin folders can be purchased at this writing for seventy-five cents, in contrast to five dollars and up for various albums prepared by the Coin and Currency Institute, Inc. However, the latter are handsome volumes that are a must for the advanced collector.

It would also be helpful to join the American Numismatic Association, an educational and nonprofit organization. The association was founded in 1891 and has about thirty thousand members from every state and many foreign countries. A splendid monthly publication, *The Numismatist,* is sent to members and provides information on latest developments in the field as well as historical background. The organization welcomes to membership anyone eleven years of age or over who has a sincere interest in numismatics. Admittance fee and first-year dues cost twenty dollars; succeeding annual dues are fifteen dollars. If you desire to join, or wish further information, write to the Executive Director, P. O. Box 2366, Colorado Springs, Colorado 80901.

The least expensive way to start a collection is to concentrate on U.S. coins minted within the last sixty-eight years and obtaining them by the do-it-yourself method. Let us assume that you have decided on Lincoln-heads. Go to the bank and make a five- or ten-dollar purchase of pennies (unless you have a good account at the bank, however, this may not be possible because of the penny shortage. If you are turned down, contact a coin club and obtain your cents from other members).

Upon returning home, select a suitable work area. Be sure to sit at a table with good light. Have Yeoman's coin book at your side as a ready reference. In this manner you can find out which Lincolns are valuable. Remember that quality, demand and the number minted determine the price. It is also wise to keep extras of hard-to-get cents because they are valuable as trading material.

Make a habit of extending your search to every bank with which your family deals. Why? First, to avoid being a nuisance; second, to prevent having to sort through coins you've already seen. One more tip, and an important one: Be nice to the tellers!

I can state from experience that an entire Lincoln-head collection can be found by the do-it-yourself method. However, it requires a great deal of time, coupled with luck, to find some of the rarest. If you decide to collect a complete set of Lincoln pennies, it will be necessary to obtain 143 different coins. Although the design spans only seventy years (1909 to date), coins bearing the

---

[6]This book lists the retail prices of coins. Yeoman also publishes *Handbook of United States Coins,* which provides dealer prices.

same dates have been minted in three localities (Philadelphia, Denver and San Francisco). At present they are manufactured in Philadelphia and Denver. The "D" or "S" marking appears just below the date on cents from Denver and San Francisco.[7]

Coins circulate in greatest abundance within their respective areas. The numismatist in Philadelphia finds it more difficult to obtain "S" coins than does the person living in San Francisco. Therefore, it is wise to obtain the help of your friends and relatives in other parts of the country, and on vacations to stock up on coins of the area you visit.

A "coin hound" exploits all sources in his never-ending search for that little disk of metal. He probes attics, locked boxes and piggy banks. Some of the richest coin finds have been turned up in this manner. My son's collection began when he stumbled on sixty Indian-head pennies my wife had saved as a girl and stored away in an old trunk. Incidentally, noncollectors who have old coins should realize that they are the perfect Christmas or birthday gift for the numismatist.

COIN CLUBS

In order to complete a set within a reasonable period, it is helpful to join a local numismatic society where you will meet experienced collectors. Fellow numismatists are always ready and willing to lend a helping hand. Most clubs are extremely active, sponsoring coin swapping, auctions, informative talks, unusual displays and parties. You will derive even more fun and enjoyment from your hobby by joining the local club.

A number of business and government organizations have their own clubs. The Office of the Secretary of Defense, for example, has an energetic group that meets monthly. A recent session included a coin auction, the sale of numismatic supplies below cost, refreshments and door prizes. Each youngster attending was given a souvenir medal.

DEALING WITH DEALERS

At some point during your collecting career, you will desire to contact a coin dealer. To find the names and addresses of those in your area, consult the Yellow Pages of the telephone book.

The coin dealer is like any other businessman—he must make a profit to stay in business. If he sells you a 1931-S Lincoln head in fine condition for $30, it *may* be possible to sell it back for half that price. I say "may," because if he is

---

[7]The Coinage Act of 1965 stated that no mint marks would be utilized for five years. Congress, however, reduced this period, and mint marks reappeared on coins in 1968.

heavily stocked in coins of that year, or is low in cash, he might not buy it. Normally, it is wise for the beginner to obtain his merchandise through general circulation or coin clubs rather than needlessly improving the dealer's financial position.

However, to obtain certain rarities a collector may be required to buy from the dealer. As in any profession, you will find people who are fair and honest and those who are not-so-fair and not-so-honest. Before you lay out any hard-earned dollars, it will therefore pay you to check on the approximate going price of the desired coin and the reputation of the dealer. Make it a hard-and-fast rule that the dealer should be your first stop for information and equipment and the last stop for coins.

A visit to a leading coin dealer can be a delightful experience. He will have exciting material on display. Up-to-the-minute coin quotations are available—a service similar to that found in stock-brokerage offices. It is also interesting to note the protective measures taken today, perhaps including a uniformed guard, closed-circuit TV, camera equipment, special locks on doors, a burglar-alarm system connected to fire and police headquarters, hot-line phone to the FBI and a guard dog on night duty when the shop is closed.

Here in New Orleans, Mardi Gras dominates the area. Many coin dealers specialize in doubloons—metallic coins in a wide variety that are given away during the carnival season. Almost every family in the Crescent City has some type of doubloon collection. These range in value from zero to thousands of dollars. During Mardi Gras, enterprising youngsters can be observed catching doubloons tossed from passing floats and promptly selling them to tourists for the best price they can obtain.

CARE AND DISPLAY OF COINS

Treat your coins as if they were delicate china. Remember, condition is a prime determinant of price. Always hold a new coin at the edge, for even the slightest perforation or discoloration lowers its value. Be sure that you have proper coin folders in which to keep your collection and a safe, clean place for storing extras. Cardboard and plastic coin cases are available for exhibiting and protecting your collection. Display your coins with pride.

There is some controversy at the present time as to whether coins should be cleaned. There are numerous solutions and mixtures on the market that give old coins a shiny appearance. My recommendation is to leave the coin alone unless dirt covers a vital area like the date or mint mark. In such a case, clean the coin carefully by immersing it in hot soapy water and drying it with a soft cloth. Most dealers and experienced numismatists do not place as high a value on polished coins.

SUPPLEMENTARY READING MATERIAL

I have only touched on the complex and fascinating hobby of numismatics here. If you want to become a successful collector, I heartily recommend that you bone up on the subject before investing your time, effort and money. In addition to reading Yeoman's book, visit your local library and obtain current relevant magazines, including *The Numismatist* and *The Numismatist Scrapbook*. See the Bibliography at the end of this book for additional reference.

I wish you good coin collecting! And now let us turn to the subject of gold as a potential money-making hobby.

GOLD AS A HOBBY

THE NEW GOLD RUSH

In contrast to collecting pennies or other coins in circulation, dealing in gold requires a sizable investment to be profitable. Gold became the hottest topic in town beginning December 31, 1974, when it became legal for American citizens to buy gold bullion. A major reason for the big publicity splash was that many businesses felt that trading in gold would bring in real profits. Banks, advisory services, brokerage firms, department stores, coin dealers and futures markets advertised prominently in such papers as *The Wall Street Journal* and *The New York Times*. Their captions read:

"Merrill Lynch answers your questions about gold."

"Color it gold. Dec. 31, the New York 'merc' [Mercantile Exchange] begins to trade GOLD FUTURES. One kilo contract"

"Before you buy your first bar of gold Englehard suggests you read this."

"GOLD FUTURES. The World's Largest Metals Exchange is trading a 100-troy ounce contract"

"Don't buy gold until you read our free booklet 'Gold: The Three Alternatives' "

" 'We store more than Gold.' First National City Bank"

"The people who brought you Deutche marks, Francs, Pounds, Dollars, Pesos, Guilders, and Yen, now bring you the world's most active Gold Futures contract!"

Newspapers, magazines, radio and TV drenched the American people with information on the forthcoming opportunity to own gold. A *Newsweek* feature story titled "The New Gold Rush" presented its view of the gold fever:

> Not since the great rush west of 1849 has the American psyche been so passionately infected by gold fever. Come Dec. 31, Americans will once again be allowed to own gold at home—something they haven't been

permitted to do for more than 41 years. In a time of pervasive economic uncertainty, that prospect is a heady one, and the nation has been swept up in a gold frenzy whose intensity defies logic and whose potential depth and duration have the government worried.

Millions of Americans—their savings and investments gutted by inflation, their morale shattered by recession, their confidence in the future shaky—suddenly find themselves transfixed by the beguiling glitter of gold. In an unsteady world, its timeless lure as the eternal and ultimate measure of wealth has become overwhelmingly attractive. Experts estimate that in the first binge of buying next month, Americans may snap up 10 million ounces of the stuff—at a cost of $1.8 billion. By the end of next year, some predict, private citizens may have handed over as much as $5 billion in exchange for reassuringly tangible gold.[8]

The gold bonanza for world speculators seemed enormous. After all, foreign governments for many years had been able to buy gold from the United States at thirty-five to forty-two dollars a troy ounce.[9] Furthermore, citizens living in other countries could buy gold on the open market at from thirty-five to forty-five dollars until 1972. These purchasers saw a huge profit potential in the U.S. market. As a result, gold climbed to about two hundred dollars an ounce on the European exchanges shortly before Americans became eligible to buy bullion at the end of 1974. The viewpoint of one foreign speculator was summed up recently by a French finance official with whom I served for three years in NATO. "Your government made gold available to other countries at thirty-five dollars an ounce and your reserves declined from thirty-seven billion ounces to eleven billion ounces. Your government halted sales much too late and now realizes the psychological value of an adequate stockpile. And now the American people will want gold so badly, you will soon pay three hundred to five hundred dollars an ounce for it. Sure we will sell it back. Some of us bought bullion for forty dollars an ounce and at four hundred dollars we'll net a nice thousand-percent profit. Even if we pay the current rate of two hundred dollars we can make a fifty-percent gain in a few months. Then when the price goes down again we can buy it back from you."

U.S. officials became so concerned about a mass rush by Americans to buy gold that they issued warnings about the adverse impact it could have on the economy. Virginia Knauer, President Ford's Special Assistant for Consumer Affairs, warned that "Consumers may find that the purchase of gold is more of a minefield than a gold mine unless they are familiar with the risks." Arthur Burns, Chairman of the Federal Reserve Board, told a congressional sub-committee that a major diversion of funds from financial institutions could

---

[8]"The New Gold Rush." *Newsweek,* December 16, 1974, p. 78.

[9]An ounce containing twenty pennyweights or 480 grams.

endanger recovery from the recession. There was deep concern that Americans would withdraw massive amounts from savings banks, savings and loan associations, credit unions and the money market.

The U.S. Treasury decided to try to curb the flow of dollars overseas for gold. On December 3, 1974, Treasury Secretary William Simon announced that the U.S. Government would hold a public auction on January 6, 1975, for up to 2 million ounces of its 276-million-ounce gold supply. Mr. Simon said that the Administration had decided to sell some of its gold reserves since otherwise lifting the gold ownership ban would have "an adverse effect on our efforts to bring inflation under control." His reasoning was that without this auction the price of gold would rise and tend to lower the value of the dollar in international trade. The end result would be to worsen our balance-of-payment deficit.

The auctioned U.S. gold was to be available in four-hundred-ounce bars to both U.S. and foreign investors. The sale was to be a responsibility of the General Services Administration (GSA). The large lots (a four-hundred-ounce bar was equivalent, on January 6, 1975, to about $70,000) simplified the government's selling job but eliminated most individuals because of the sizable purchase cost.

Money obtained from the gold sale (an estimated $325 to $350 million) would permit the Treasury to reduce its borrowing in the form of bills, notes and bonds. Thus, the government reasoned, institutional buyers such as banks would reduce their purchases of Treasury issues and have more money to supply client needs.

December 31, 1974, arrived with the anticipation of huge profits by foreign speculators, gold dealers and many institutions. But to the everlasting credit of the American consumer, the gold rush turned into a gold bust. Gold, as stated previously, reached $200 an ounce in some foreign markets but had declined to $173 an ounce by the time the U.S. Government held its auction on January 6, 1975.

The General Services Administration received offers for less than half the bullion being auctioned, selling 753,000 ounces at an average price of $165.65 for a total sale of $124,800,000.

According to Thomas W. Wolfe, director of the Treasury Department's Office of Domestic and Silver Operations: "The experience of the first week of gold ownership shows that expectations by foreign speculators that Americans would flock to gold markets has failed to materialize."

My own negative view on buying gold, in 1974, is evidenced by the following statement that appeared in a textbook of mine that was published in January 1975: "Individuals who invested in gold coins, in 1972, made substantial profits. But today the price is much higher and the risk of losing money through such investments is greater. In my view, gold coins should only be bought on sharp declines."[10] This same recommendation holds today. Although U.S. $20 gold pieces have dropped in price from $380 to $240 since I made the above statement, there are still better places to invest money than gold. But given a further decline, dealing in gold could become a profitable hobby. Should this time come, let's look at how you can invest in gold for fun and profit.

METHODS OF INVESTING IN GOLD

An investment in gold may be made in a number of ways. We will consider six possibilities here. The first two options have been open to U.S. citizens since December 31, 1974. The remaining four options were available prior to that date.

BULLION. Gold bullion is noncoined metal in bar or ingot form.[11] Direct transactions in gold bullion may be made through such sources as coin and bullion dealers, individuals, clubs, department stores and banks (and there is always the possibility that the U.S. Government might have another public auction). The size in which gold bullion may be bought varies from tiny wafers of an ounce or less to four-hundred-ounce bars.

Keep in mind, however, that transactions in gold bullion can be expensive. Possible costs could include the following:

a. Commission charged on each purchase. Normally, the larger the dollar amount bought, the smaller the fee. Prior to purchase, it is desirable to check the spot price of gold quoted in *The Wall Street Journal*;
b. Delivery charge;
c. Assay test. This may be necessary to determine if your bullion has the gold content you paid for;
d. State and local sales tax;
e. Transaction fees;
f. Storage expense;
g. Insurance;
h. Commission on selling plus possible shipping, insuring, taxes and assay expenses;
i. Loss of interest on money that could be invested elsewhere. For example, if you can earn 6 percent a year in tax-free municipals, and are in the 50-percent tax bracket, your gold would have to appreciate at least 8 percent annually (assuming 25 percent capital-gains tax). And this 8 percent would have to be free and clear after deducting all costs, which could reach 15 to 20 percent of the initial investment.

[10]*Guide to Personal Finance.* Englewood Cliffs, N.J.: Prentice-Hall, Inc., 1975, p. 370.
[11]A mold into which metal is cast.

If you are considering the gold bullion route as an investment, Engelhard Minerals and Chemicals Corporation has issued helpful information. Its ad, the headline of which was quoted earlier, went on to point out the fact "that transactions in gold bars differ from most transactions you may be familiar with such as buying and selling stocks, bonds, and real estate." Engelhard suggests that you do the following before buying your first bar of gold:

1. Decide for yourself why you want to buy gold. For centuries many people have considered gold to be the ultimate store of value. Some people believe that gold today represents a hedge against inflation, tending to increase in value over the years as inflation reduces the purchasing power of money. Still others think that history supports the role of gold being most valuable in periods of deflation.

You may want to buy gold for these or other reasons, both for yourself and your family or as a gift. This is for you to decide.

2. Consider what size or combination of sizes you want to own. Engelhard will have gold bars available in a variety of sizes for sale through financial institutions. The sizes are expected to range from ½ to 100 troy ounces, as follows: ½, 1, 5, 10, 16.075 (½ kilo), 25, 32.150 (1 kilo), 50 and 100 ounce bars.

The prices of these bars to you will reflect the cost of the gold itself plus the costs of manufacturing, insurance and shipping, applicable taxes and transaction fees. By buying larger sizes, rather than smaller ones, you will get more gold for your money. For example, the cost of a single 10-ounce bar at any given time will normally be less than the total cost of 10 individual one-ounce bars.

3. Decide where you want to keep your gold. You can keep your gold yourself or have it stored for you. This is an important decision.

If you take possession of the gold, you then will be concerned with how to store it safely because of its value. In addition, if you want to sell your gold at some future time after you have physically received it, each bar may have to be assayed to determine to the satisfaction of the buyer that it is still authentic and has not been altered. An assay is a complicated chemical analysis of gold.

On the other hand, if you leave your gold in the custody of recognized financial institutions—without your ever having taken physical possession—you can avoid charges and delays due to the necessity of an assay on resale. You should consult your financial institution about the services it plans to offer in this connection.

4. Know what's involved if you want to sell your gold. Many financial institutions which sell gold will probably also repurchase gold from you. The buying prices at any given time will be determined by each financial institution. However, you can expect that the buying price (the "bid" price) will be lower than the then current selling price (the "asked" price).

Remember, too, that changes in the price of gold are continuous—gold prices can vary markedly even in the course of a single day. Buying and selling gold at short intervals in the hope of making speculative profits can be full of dangers.

5. Be certain the gold you buy is of unquestionable authenticity. Your best protection against possible counterfeiting or fraud is the mark, stamped on the gold bar itself, of a recognized refiner—plus the integrity of the seller from whom you bought it. . . . It must be recognized that gold (and any gold refiner's stamp) is subject to the danger of counterfeiting. This is particularly true once gold has left the physical possession of the financial institutions. For our part, we will distribute our gold bars directly to leading financial institutions. If there is no break in the chain of physical possession between a financial institution and yourself, this will be strong additional assurance against the risk of counterfeiting.[12]

GOLD FUTURES. Since December 31, 1974, it has been legal to trade in gold futures in certain North American markets. A basic explanation of commodity futures markets, to include gold, is presented in Chapter 26.

COINS. In 1933, the U.S. Government made it illegal for a U.S. citizen to own gold. A major exception was made for numismatists, who could collect gold coins. Banks and other parties, however, had to turn in their holdings.

Collecting gold coins used to be a hobby primarily for wealthy individuals who desired to acquire rare items and obtain an extensive variety of pieces. But accompanying the gold-buying craze that affected most income brackets prior to the legalization of gold-bullion ownership in the U.S. came a major rise in the price of gold coins. For example, in 1972 it was possible to buy an uncirculated common-date U.S. $20 gold piece (double eagle) for $70. This same coin sold for $380 in 1974.

The first U.S. gold coins were five-dollar pieces (half eagles) minted in 1795. Between 1795 and 1933 the following denominations were struck (Table 25-1):

TABLE 25-1 Denominations of U.S. Gold Pieces, 1795–1933

Denomination	Title	Years Minted
$1.00	Gold Dollar	1849–1889
2.50	Quarter Eagle	1796–1907*
3.00	Three-Dollar Gold Piece	1854–1889
4.00	Four-Dollar ("Stella")	1879–1880
5.00	Half Eagle	1795–1929*
10.00	Eagle	1795–1933*
20.00	Double Eagle	1849–1933

*Dates not inclusive

---

[12]"Before You Buy Your First Bar of Gold, Engelhard Suggests You Read This," ad appearing in *Newsweek,* December 16, 1974, pp. 30–31.

461

The $20 gold piece was authorized by the Act of March 3, 1849, and accounted for by far the largest number of gold coins minted. It weighs 516 grains, .900 fine and is currently the most popular U.S. gold coin being purchased. The double eagle is equivalent to almost an ounce of pure gold bullion.[13] In 1974, when gold bullion was selling for $180 an ounce, the double eagles brought a premium of 110 percent (see above). This was due in part to its numismatic value and in part to the pervading gold fever.

Since gold in coin form could be legally sold in the United States, the marked increase in the price of gold, beginning in 1972, resulted in three foreign governments—Austria, South Africa and Mexico—striking gold coins. Austria issued the 100 Coronas, 4 ducat and 1 ducat piece; South Africa struck the Krugerrand; and Mexico, the 50 Peso. These newly struck gold coins sold for slightly above the price of their gold content, in contrast to coins like the U.S. $20 double eagle, which at this writing has numismatic value in addition to its gold content. The price differential is apparent from the following quotes:

TABLE 25-2   Gold Coin Quotes—February 3, 1978

		Bid	Asked
Mexican 50 Peso	(1.2 troy ounces)	$221.50	$223.00
South African Krugerrand	(1 troy ounce)	181.00	182.25
Austrian 100 Corona	(.98 troy ounce)	178.50	180.00
U.S. $20 Gold Piece	(.97 troy ounce)	261.50	266.50

STOCKS. There are several publicly held corporations that are in the gold-mining business. Some specialize in gold ore, while for others gold is only a by-product. Once again, as stressed in Chapters 21 and 22, you should only buy stock in companies with fine track records. Gold stocks reached their peak in 1973–1974. At this writing, selected gold stocks are selling in the over-the-counter market as follows:

	July 5, 1977	1973–74 high
Anglo American Gold Investors	15½	77¼
President Branch Gold Mining	10⅛	44⅛
Vaal Reefs Exploration	12¾	65⅞

People who bought sound gold stock in 1972 or earlier show a solid profit and have received dividends. But those who bought at the 1974 peak show a sizable loss today. Thus, timing is very important. In relation to past prices gold is still high. Of course, it is possible to sell gold stock shares short (see Chapter 22) if

[13]There are 480 grains in one troy ounce of gold bullion, whereas a double eagle has only 464.4 grains of pure gold.

you think the price will decline. But selling short involves considerable speculation. My advice is that if gold stocks should decline markedly, their purchase would be a sound investment for the long term both from satisfactory income and possible appreciation. A word of caution about South African gold securities, however: You must consider the political as well as economic factors in arriving at a decision of whether to buy, sell or hold their mining stocks.

MUTUAL FUNDS AND CLOSED-END INVESTMENT COMPANIES. There are several closed-end investment companies and a mutual fund specializing in gold stocks. These include International Investors (mutual fund), ASA Limited (NYSE) and Precious Metals Holding (over-the-counter). Remember that if you buy a mutual fund, the investment company deducts an annual fee for managing the fund. In most cases you also must pay a sizable sales commission on the initial purchase. I suggest that you read Chapter 23 on Investment Companies before going the mutual route.

JEWELRY. Gold may be found in a variety of items sold in jewelry stores and other commercial outlets. Rings, watches, bracelets and such, containing varying amounts of gold, are available for purchase. These range from "gold-filled" items that have virtually no gold content to gold jewelry with a content of "14 karats."[14] Fourteen-karat items, American favorites, contain 14/24th of gold with other elements making up the remaining 10/14th. Pure gold would be of insufficient hardness to provide the necessary durability. However, in many overseas markets you will find "18 karat" gold items. For example, Rolex and other fine watches are normally available in Europe in 18-karat gold. In the U.S., Rolex and its competitors can be bought with either 14 karats or 18 karats. From an investment standpoint you obtain 1/6th more gold in the 18-karat purchase.

In my view, with few exceptions, jewelry containing gold is *not* a good investment. There is too big a markup for the wholesaler and retailer. I recall a Rolex distributor displaying his $1,000, 18-karat watches at West Point. He sold them to the military for $500 and still made a nice profit. There was also a healthy cut remaining for the Swiss manufacturer. The gold made up only a small part of the retail price. However, if you should receive a gold heirloom made by a master craftsman, this could have considerable value—not for its gold content but for the workmanship. Be sure to have such items appraised by a reputable firm.

WHICH METHOD OF GOLD INVESTMENT IS BEST?

Although gold transactions may be successfully accomplished in all of the ways described above, *I believe the soundest approach is to deal in this metal through U.S. coins and stock.*

---

[14]A karat is a unit of weight for precious metals. A unit of fineness for gold is equal to one twenty-fourth part of pure gold in an alloy.

A WORD OF CAUTION

The fact that gold is an expensive investment means that its purchase should be approached with caution. President Ford's Office of Consumer Affairs provided the following splendid advice that should be read carefully by all prospective buyers:

1. Be wary of unsolicited correspondence or calls from strangers offering to sell you gold or gold investments.
2. Be skeptical of promises of spectacular profits. Ask yourself: Why am I being offered this golden opportunity?
3. Resist pressures to make hurried, uninformed investment decisions.
4. Be suspicious of claims of new, secret or exotic processes to extract gold.
5. Seek independent advice from a person you trust and who is knowledgeable.
6. Consider the risks in relation to your own financial position and needs.
7. Find out if the company has registered with the Securities and Exchange Commission or state securities agency.
8. Attempt to determine the seller's markup, or how much it cost the seller to purchase the gold.
9. Ascertain what costs, in addition to the quoted price of gold, are involved. For example, you may be required to pay a refining charge, assay fees, commissions, shipping and storage fees, insurance costs and sales tax.
10. Demand a written guarantee concerning weight and fineness, or pureness. Some gold bears a refiner's mark assaying its weight and fineness; however, there aren't any federal standards.
11. Attempt to make your purchases through local, reputable firms. (Firms including the term "exchange" in their name shouldn't be assumed to constitute an association or group of firms that provide a public market for buyers and sellers.)
12. Obtain in writing the terms of your purchase—for example, when and how the gold will be delivered and stored, including what security precautions will be taken to ensure that your gold isn't shaved or that counterfeit gold isn't substituted.
13. Ask whether the gold will be segregated and stored in your name (not the seller's or supplier's). Make sure you receive a written receipt showing that the requisite amount of gold is being stored for your account by a reputable concern.
14. Ask whether there will be a ready market for the gold in the form being offered to you. You may have to pay to have your gold reassayed, recast into a different shape, size and/or transported to a distant market before you can sell it.[15]

[15]Release issued by the White House Office of Consumer Affairs, December 9, 1974.

GOLD AND YOUR PORTFOLIO

As I have already acknowledged, gold bullion proved to be a fine investment for people who were eligible to buy it in 1972 or earlier. Likewise, Americans who purchased gold coins or gold stocks in 1972 or before showed fine profits two years later. But those who made purchases at the gold peak, in late 1974, currently show losses. But in my view, there are presently better investments in such areas as growth stocks in major U.S. corporations and choice real estate. If there is a further decline in the price of gold, it could become a good buy again. However, I would not invest more than 5 percent of a portfolio in gold.

26

COMMODITIES

The commodity futures market is designed for the venturesome. "Teddy Roosevelt Would Have Made a Great Commodity Trader" proclaimed one advertisement, going on to state, "It takes a certain personality to be a successful trader and Teddy had it. An analytical mind. Cool. Decisive. Patient. Courageous. Disciplined."[1] Given those requirements, it is little wonder so few make money in this field.

Success in the futures market depends on more than personality, however. A detailed study of the commodity in question, including factors that affect its supply and demand, is essential. Once in the market, you must act quickly on news relating to your product, adjusting to "acts of God" and being able to assess the impact of current events on trading. A bit of clairvoyance also helps, for you must try to foresee what the effect of U.S. Government actions will be. Indeed, trading in futures, unlike long-term investments, requires close and constant attention.

DEVELOPMENT OF THE FUTURES MARKET

Commodity futures markets developed in this country as our nation moved from an agrarian to a manufacturing economy. In the beginning, the farmer who wanted bread on the table grew wheat and ground it himself. His wife used the flour to bake the edible bread. The process of transforming a commodity into a consumable was accomplished at home.

As our population expanded, people became more dependent upon others to do the processing for them. As the demand for the farmer's products increased, so did the number and size of the processors, and the complexity of the processing system resulted in a greater time lapse from the planting of a crop until its availability for the consumer. For this reason, a farmer preparing plantings to yield twenty thousand bushels of corn could face bankruptcy if the price declined a few cents a bushel before his crop was ready for sale. And in the same way, a wheat processor might be in financial trouble if the price of wheat fell sharply during the time he held it.

The avoid the risk of future price changes, farmers, manufacturers, processors, warehouse operators and other businessmen sought out people willing to assume that risk for them. The outgrowth of their search was the development of the commodity futures markets.

---

[1]*The Wall Street Journal,* December 29, 1970, p. 19. (Advertiser: Chicago Mercantile Exchange, 440 West Jackson Boulevard, Chicago, Illinois.)

ESTABLISHING COMMODITY EXCHANGES

Interested parties discovered that it took the following conditions to induce speculators to accept the risks involved in playing the futures game:

1. The opportunity to make a healthy profit with limited money;
2. The trading of commodity units of a similar quality and quantity;
3. Uniform terms of payment;
4. Public recording of the prices of all transactions;
5. Reliable buyers and sellers;
6. A ready market for the sale of commodities to obviate taking delivery;
7. A marketplace with high standards.

These conditions have been met since Civil War days, and today individuals can buy or sell any of the more than seventy items traded in the various futures markets. The importance of these markets was recognized by President Nixon on the occasion of the fiftieth anniversary of the Chicago Mercantile Exchange. The President wrote, "By fostering sound practices in futures trading and by encouraging active trade in an increasing number of commodities, you continue to contribute meaningfully to the growth and well-being of American private enterprise and of the national economy."

These "sound practices" are unfortunately not universally observed; thus, it is essential to limit all business to commodity exchanges known to foster fair trading. A *Wall Street Journal* article titled "Questions Are Raised Over Commodity Deals on West Coast Market" said in part:

> The flamboyant West Coast Commodities Exchange proudly bills itself as the world's largest privately owned commodities exchange and says that it is run for the public benefit under "fair principles of trade." There's little doubt about the first claim, since other commodities exchanges are owned by their member firms, not individuals. But there is mounting doubt about the second.
>
> There is considerable evidence that the West Coast Commodities Exchange has been systematically used by its controlling stockholders for their own benefit.[2]

HOW THE COMMODITY MARKET WORKS

What is actually traded in futures markets is not silver, plywood, platinum, orange juice, soybeans or other products. The participants are in fact trading "futures contracts." Each contract is a guarantee that the seller will deliver a

[2]*The Wall Street Journal,* December 6, 1973, p. 1.

specified amount of a stated grade of a certain commodity at a designated future time. This commitment must be met, regardless of the price of that commodity or of any other conditions that might occur prior to that future date. Conversely, the buyer has an obligation to accept delivery at that designated future date. For example, the person who in August buys a March futures contract of silver must either accept delivery seven months later or sell his contract before that date.

HEDGING

There are two categories of people in the commodites markets. One group, wishing to avoid the risks of price fluctuations, hedges (see below) to accomplish this objective. The second group, the speculators, seeks to assume this very risk, because of the profit potential. The speculators may assume this risk by purchasing the hedgers' contracts. The speculators in fact provide an active market that enables the hedgers to avoid risks.

Hedging is a protective measure designed to reduce the risk of loss due to price changes while a raw product is in the processing stage. It minimizes risk by taking advantage of the parallel movements of the prices of a given commodity in the current market[3] and the prices of futures contracts in that commodity. You hedge by taking a position in the futures market that is opposed to your current position, a kind of betting against yourself. The hedge works because of the fact that futures prices tend to move up and down in harmony with cash prices.

An Example of Hedging[4]

On January 15, a feedlot operator buys 100 feeders, weighing an average of 600 pounds, at $60 per hundredweight (cwt.) for a total cost of $36,000. He hopes to market them as steers at 1,000 pounds. Based on his best cost estimate, he calculates his cost of weight gain, including labor, at $45 per hundredweight, for a feeding cost of $18,000 to bring his cattle to marketing weight. His total cost in preparing the herd for market is $54,000. Therefore, he must sell his cattle at $54 per hundredweight merely to recover his investment. Since the cattle will be ready for market in August, the feedlot operator looks at the August cattle-futures price on the Chicago Mercantile Exchange and notes that the price quoted on January 15 is $56.90. Although the August future is $2.90

---

[3]This is also referred to as the "cash" or "spot" market. It is the price you can receive for your commodity today.

[4]This example was taken from "Price and Loan Protection through Hedging," Chicago Mercantile Exchange, pp. 9-10.

per hundredweight above the feeder's calculated break-even point, the local market price to be received by the feeder must be adjusted to the Chicago equivalent to compute the estimated profit (Table 26-1):

TABLE 26-1 Estimating Costs of Feedlot Operation by Hedging

		Per Cwt.
Cost of shipping cattle to Omaha* and allowance for additional shrinkage (known as **basis**)		$1.00
Futures commission brokerage		.10
Margin costs on futures contracts (interest)		.08
Quality adjustments for low choice steers†		.22
		$1.40
Total adjustment for local area:		
Chicago futures prices	$56.90	
Less localizing costs	−1.40	
Chicago cash equivalent	$55.50	
Localized futures price	$55.50	
Feedlot operator's cost	−54.00	
Net profit	$1.50 per cwt.	

*The four delivery points are Omaha, Nebraska; Guymon, Oklahoma; Peoria, Illinois and Sioux City, Iowa.
† Most futures contracts call for delivering certain percentages of the total lot at grades above or below what is called for in the contract, with proper allowance or adjustment required.

As Table 26-1 shows, the feedlot operator can expect a profit of $1.50 per hundredweight if he hedges properly. After reviewing various market forecasts, the feedlot operator expects a decline in the cash market and calls his broker to sell two August contracts, each covering forty thousand or more pounds of choice steer. He has now effectively protected 80 percent of his total expected beef production against a price decline.

Assume first that cash prices decline during the January–August period, reaching $53.80 by August. This would leave the feeder with a loss of 20 cents per hundredweight were he forced to sell in the cash market at the time. As we have seen, futures prices generally move along the same pattern as cash, so that futures would have declined proportionally. In the following example (Table 26-2), we will assume that the feedlot operator bought back his August futures contract at $55.20 per hundredweight and simultaneously sold his cattle at $53.80 per hundredweight in the local market:

TABLE 26-2 Feedlot Operator's Profit on
Futures-Contract Gain

Gain on the futures contract	$1.70
Loss on the cash market	−.20
Net profit	$1.50 per cwt.

Now, suppose that the cash prices rise between January and August. Should they reach $57.80, the feedlot operator would realize a profit of $3.80 per hundredweight on the sale of his cattle in his normal marketing channel. In this instance (Table 26-3), futures would have risen perhaps to $59.20, or a $2.30-per-hundredweight loss on his futures contract.

TABLE 26-3 Feedlot Operator's Profit on
Cash-Market Gain

Gain on the cash market	$3.80
Loss on the futures contract	-2.30
Net profit	$1.50 per cwt.

In a rising market, the feedlot operator would have made more profit had he not hedged, but he calculated that the hedge would assure him of a *reasonable* return.

In this example, the feedlot operator has been protected from the risks of fluctuating prices. In contrast to the hedger, the speculator profits or loses through changes in either the cash or the futures markets.

FACTORS INFLUENCING COMMODITY PRICES

The demand for a given commodity is influenced in part by general business conditions and international events. In good times, for instance, there will be more sales of quality beef and of items using silver and platinum. If news reports indicate the possibility of a war between China and Russia, it may mean the loss of export markets, which could result in a decreased demand and decline in the prices for some commodities. Labor problems that result in a protracted auto strike often hurt production and lead to the stockpiling of raw materials (commodities).

Weather and farm conditions also influence commodity prices. A recent corn blight had an impact on the future availability of that crop. But the U.S. Government is perhaps the most important factor to be considered in commodity trading, since it exerts controls over acreage allotments, subsidies, farm loans, market quotas, storage measures and emergency food donations. Such actions can greatly influence the supply or demand of commodities.

SOURCES OF COMMODITY INFORMATION

There is an abundance of reference material available to help you become a proficient student of the commodity market.

The Wall Street Journal

The *Journal* devotes at least half a page of each edition to pertinent information on commodities. Qualitative data include a column that presents current events with headlines like these:

"Platinum Futures Prices Climb; Several Factors Fuel Speculation"

"Wheat Futures Prices Fall Sharply on Rumors Disputed by Exporters of Japan Cancellations"

"Silver Futures Fall, Then Regain Most of Drop as Short Sellers Have Difficulty Covering"

"Some Stores Are Using Eggs as Loss Leaders Due to Drop in Demand as Holidays Approach"

"Trading in Interest Rate Futures Top Expectations, Analysts say"

"Some Soybean Oil Contracts Fall the Limit on Report of Low Brazil Price, Quiet Exports"

Key *Journal* articles go on to highlight news that may be helpful to the commodities trader. One such story ran the lead "Short Sellers in Maine Potatoes Miss Deadline; Default is Biggest Ever" and continued:

Short sellers failed to meet the 3 p.m. deadline yesterday for delivering nearly 50 million pounds of potatoes to fulfill the remaining open positions in the expired May 1976 Maine potato future contract on the New York Mercantile Exchange. It was the most massive default to occur against any futures contract in the history of U.S. commodity trading, traders said.

Of the 1,911 contracts of 50,000 pounds each that were left open when the May 1976 contract expired May 7, a total of 914 contracts were settled either by the sellers delivering Maine potatoes to the buyers or by some other arrangement made between the sellers and buyers permitted under rules of the New York exchange.

Brokerage houses, which are clearing-house members of the exchange and represent the short sellers, will be held liable for the price difference if the potatoes have to be bought by the exchange at a higher price than that at which the traders sold the contracts short. Also, the clearing-house members representing the short sellers may be liable to fines imposed by the exchange because of the delivery default. The clearing-house members, in turn, they can pass along the damages to their customers who have defaulted on the contracts.[5]

In addition to articles, the *Journal* supplies ample statistical information on commodities. The price of silver futures, for example, is quoted in both Chicago (Chicago Board of Trade) and New York (Commodity Exchange, Inc.). Although both Chicago and New York provide trading facilities for silver, there are more silver contracts being consummated in New York at the present time. The September 1978 silver futures opened in New York on July 5, 1977, at $471.50 and closed at $475.00. It was up forty cents, or forty points, from the close of the previous day. Its high and low for the season ranged from $521.50 to $468.30. Estimated sales for the day totaled 12,000 contracts, a figure that included all transactions in each of the thirteen future months.

If you had purchased one silver contract (five thousand ounces) at the season's low and sold at the high, your profit would have been $2,660 (less commission). Conversely, your loss would have been in the same amount, if you had bought at the peak and sold at the bottom.

The *Journal* also provides spot or cash prices on seventy-three commodities that have been listed under seven headings: foods; grains and feeds; fats and oils; textiles and fibers; metals; precious metals; and miscellaneous.

A comparison with the futures prices of silver for the month of this writing (July) reflects a close relationship. The price differentials for various months are based, in the case of silver, on interest and storage charges. For example, if you bought one spot silver contract (five thousand troy ounces) for $24,700 (plus commission), you would normally have to pay storage charges for safekeeping. Meanwhile, you would be losing interest on the $24,700 if it was your money, or paying out interest if you had borrowed to make the purchase. This incremental difference is apparent from the progressive monthly increases in silver futures as reflected in Figure 26-3. A July 1977 contract on the Commodity Exchange, Inc., New York, would have cost $21,970 (plus commission) in contrast to $23,750 (plus commission) for September 1978.

Volume and open interest are of concern to both the hedger and the speculator. This information appears daily in *The Wall Street Journal*. Silver, for example, one day in 1977, showed total open contracts of 156,085, down 2,495.[6] Monthly contracts are also listed. An active market is important to the trader, as it permits him to buy or sell easily.

---

[5]Shirley Jackewicz. *The Wall Street Journal,* May 26, 1976, p. 26.

[6]An open contract is one which has been purchased or sold without the transaction having been completed by subsequent sale or repurchase, or actual delivery or receipt of the commodity.

Finally, the *Journal* publishes commodity indexes. Like the stock-market averages, they give you an indication of trends—both spot and futures. They are compiled from the daily quotations on the cash and futures markets. In addition to the Dow Indexes, there are also other indexes which indicate the direction of the general commodity price level. The most popular spot index is prepared by the U.S. Bureau of Labor Statistics and consists of twenty-two commodities. Its purpose is to measure the trend of those commodities that, as a result of a healthy volume of daily trading, are sensitive to forces affecting cash markets and traders' estimates of current and future economic conditions. The commodities included are either raw materials or commodities very near initial production.

The Reuter's Daily Index

This index reflects prices of European commodities and other markets. In addition to such items as wheat, cotton, sugar and rubber, it includes certain commodities not traded on U.S. exchanges, including copra, hemp and shellac.

Government Publications

The federal government publishes a number of valuable documents. The departments of Agriculture and Commerce can be contacted to secure these data. The Commodities Futures Trading Commission (CFTC)[7] for instance, provides weekly, monthly and annual reports on various commodities, including information on large traders.

Additional Sources

Commodities firms issue a variety of factual literature, including weekly market letters, special studies and informative pamphlets. Commodities exchanges prepare helpful documents, and there are also companies specializing in the preparation of numerous studies pertaining to commodities. If you have found a first-class stock-brokerage firm, it may well have an excellent commodities department. Check to see if the firm has a good library and can provide you with appropriate material.

A sample list of material available in one field—silver—includes 1) "What You Should Know About Silver Futures," a pamphlet prepared by the Chicago Board of Trade; 2) "Quarterly Metals Situation" and "Silver in the 70's," by the Commodity Research Department, Bache & Co.; 3) "Understand

---

[7]Since April 1975, all commodity futures trading has been regulated by this independent government agency. The address of the CFTC is: 1120 Connecticut Avenue, N.W., Washington, D.C. 20036.

the Silver Futures Market," *Commodity Yearbook,* current edition, Commodity Research Bureau, New York; and 4) "Silver Situation Report," Merrill Lynch, Pierce, Fenner & Smith, Inc. Selected available material on other commodities can be found in the Bibliography at the end of this book.

COMMODITY EXCHANGES

In addition to having a knowledge of information sources, the futures trader should be familiar with which commodities are traded on the twelve exchanges in the United States and Canada, and on what terms. Silver, for example, is traded on the Commodity Exchange, Inc., New York. Trading hours are 10:00 A.M. to 2:15 P.M. (New York time), Monday through Friday. A single contract is five thousand troy ounces. The minimum fluctuation is one-tenth of a cent per ounce, or five dollars per contract. Silver futures are also traded on the Chicago Board of Trade. Trading hours are 10:00 A.M. to 2:25 P.M. The size of one contract and minimum fluctuation is the same as New York. Shop around to compare commission costs among various brokers. There are no longer fixed rates, so it can save you money to compare with care.

Exchanges have established rules fixing daily trading limits, for the purpose of precluding drastic price movements caused by major catastrophes such as war threats or other significant happenings. For example, a recent corn-blight announcement might have resulted in a much sharper reaction were it not for the established ceiling. Silver, for instance, has a limit of 40 cents per ounce as its permitted range between the day's high and low. There is a 20-cent limit above or below the previous close. Thus, if you have purchased one contract at $5.00 per ounce at the close, it could go down no further than $4.80 and up no more than $5.20 the next day. However, if you bought at the day's low, $5.00, the price could not go above $5.40 for that day.

Each exchange posts minimum margin requirements. The minimum silver margin varies according to the per-ounce price of a contract. A straddle[8] calls for a five-hundred-dollar minimum regardless of price. Keep in mind that each exchange sets minimums for its members, but the commodities firms can ask their traders for additional amounts.

A SILVER FUTURES TRANSACTION

Armed with our background information, let us take a look at a hypothetical silver futures transaction.

[8]Buying a futures contract in one market and concurrently selling the same commodity in another market.

1. On July 6, 1977, Dr. Arco Amllits checks *The Wall Street Journal* and notes that the previous day's closing price of silver for September 1978 delivery on the New York market is 475.00. He also notes that September is an active month, with 13,569 open contracts. (Figure 26-3). Arco has followed the silver market with interest for the past ten years. His medical practice takes most of his waking hours, but he has also found time to keep a chart reflecting the general pattern of silver-price movements. As a numismatist, Arco has read much about silver conditions. In April 1970, he predicted that when the U.S. Government stopped selling silver in November of that year, futures would react with a good upswing. He was right and made a sizable profit. As a successful physician, he can afford the speculative challenge of futures and enjoys the challenge.

2. Arco calls his friend Bo Broker to determine the price of September silver. "Four hundred and eighty. It picked up a hundred points since the open," Bo tells him. Arco makes his decision: "Buy me one contract for September 1978 delivery. I'd like to buy several contracts and pyramid it if silver moves up, but I don't have the nerve."

3. Bo Broker writes and time-stamps an order form. It is immediately transmitted to the floor of the Commodity Exchange in New York, where it is executed by a floor broker.

4. A few minutes later, Bo calls his friend Arco, confirming the transaction. "Thanks, Bo, put in a stop-loss order[9] at four hundred and fifty-five just in case I'm wrong. I'll drop by this afternoon to give you the necessary eight-thousand-dollar margin requirement. But I don't see why you require five hundred dollars above the exchange minimum!" "It's like doctors' fee—since when are *they* standardized?" Bo retorts.

SPOT TRADING

In contrast to the futures markets, where delivery is rarely taken, commodities are also sold through spot trading. The cash or spot trade may involve the physical transfer of merchandise. It is a current transaction as opposed to a futures contract. This is how the spot silver-coin market operates.

In 1964, many people stood in line for hours in order to purchase one thousand silver-dollar lots from the Treasury Department at face value.[10] These

---

[9]Instructions to a broker to sell (or buy) at a definite limit above or below the prevailing price. Its purpose is to limit losses. This sounds good in theory, but there may not be a buyer or seller available.

[10]The Treasury sold the 1,000 silver dollars loose in a single canvas money bag of the type used by the U.S. Mint. Each bag of coins weighs approximately sixty pounds.

dollars immediately disappeared from public circulation and quickly sold at a premium. Until recently, thousand-dollar bags of silver dollars were traded in the spot market.[11] However, trading in this commodity proved to be limited and was discontinued. In contrast, thousand-dollar bags of circulated silver coins became popular as a hedge against inflation and began trading in the spot market.

How would you go about trading in the silver-coin spot market? You would begin by contacting your local broker. Assuming that you thought the price would rise on the coins during the year, you would direct a "buy" of one contract of circulated spot silver coins.[12] Your broker would contact the New York Mercantile Exchange, which provides the facilities for trading. Once the transaction was complete, New York would notify your broker, and you would have purchased $10,000 in circulated silver coins for, say, $35,700 plus a $33 commission and a $2 service charge. You could either leave the coins in New York and pay storage charges or have them shipped. The costs, including commission, would run from $150 to $200, depending upon distance.

A local broker tells me that the spot market is only moderately active and is not a good place to speculate. He suggests that those desiring silver coins go to a coin dealer. My own investigation confirmed that several coin dealers were asking less than the price in the spot market. In contrast to a $35,700 charge through an exchange, dealers were asking $34,000 to $35,600, exclusive of shipping costs. Furthermore, coin dealers would sell a thousand-dollar bag at their quoted price, whereas a purchase on the New York Mercantile Exchange required a ten-bag investment.

My own view is that if you want silver coins of any domination, you should obtain them from a fellow collector instead of going through middle-men such as exchanges or coin dealers.

RISKS AND REWARDS OF COMMODITY TRADING

"The Commodity Markets These Days Are Where the Action Is!" The article that followed this headline in *Barron's* a few years ago was about "the increased interest in futures trading." The writer supported his statement by showing the marked growth in the number of commodities being traded. According to one

---

[11]There were trades in circulated ("used") silver dollars as well as transactions in uncirculated ("new") Morgan and Peace dollars. All had different quotes, but the contract unit was the same—1,000 silver dollars.

[12]One contract is $10,000 in circulated silver coins. These coins are placed in ten canvas bags, with each bag containing $1,000.

estimate, there are a million and a half people active in the commodities market, a number that is expected to double in five years. Of the total participants, 85 to 90 percent are speculators.

Barron's went on to report this chilling statistic:

> Seventy-five to eighty percent of the time, speculators lose. For this reason, many commodities houses and commodities departments of the large brokerage firms stress the criterion of suitability in taking on clients. A strong financial position often isn't enough. Says William Clayton, a partner in E. F. Hutton: "You have to be able to control your emotions—fear and greed, primarily—and you have to be trained to take losses quickly. The client must have emotional stability."[13]

More than eight years later, the commodity markets are still "where the action is." Trading volume continues to increase, and there have been remarkable price fluctuations in many commodities. For example, coffee fluctuated between $1.15 and $3.39 per pound. A silver futures contract sold for as low as $4.25 an ounce last year, in contrast to a recent high of $5.43. Kansas City wheat varied from $2.27 a bushel to $4.13. Hogs ranged from $32.60 to $49.00 per hundredweight. A thousand-dollar bag of circulated silver coins moved from a bottom of $29.86 to a high of $38.24 in the futures markets. And let's not forget that a futures contract in sugar varied between eight cents and sixty-three cents. At this writing, a September 1978 contract was being traded at a modest nine cents per pound. There is money to be made in the commodities market so long as there are healthy fluctuations, either up or down—and so long as you are qualified to make the correct decisions.

One reason for the action in commodities had been the potential for beating the rapid rise in the cost of living. A *Time* magazine cover story pointed out that commodities were among the "winners from inflation":

> COMMODITIES. Last year the hottest items were soybeans and wheat; this year the fastest action is in sugar and metals. On the Chicago Board of Trade, Dealer Larry Blum says, "Silver was going up in a day as much as it ordinarily does in a year." The biggest silver speculator is Dallas centimillionare Nelson Bunker Hunt, who has used his petrowealth to buy millions of dollars worth of futures contracts for silver. Unlike most commodities gamblers, Hunt has accepted delivery on some of the metal, which he apparently intends to hoard until the price goes higher.[14]

The thought of beating inflation is tempting indeed, but a broker friend of mine stresses the fact that no one should enter the commodities market who does not

---

[13]"Exciting Futures." *Barron's,* December 1, 1969, p. 3.
[14]"Inflation—Seeking Antidotes to a Global Plague." *Time,* April 8, 1974, p. 76.

have sufficient funds available to meet emergencies. He pointed out as well that one firm requires a person to have a net worth of $50,000 in liquid assets before it will open a commodity account for him.

The risk involved in trading in commodities is neatly summed up as follows:

> Commodity speculation . . . is a high-risk business and suitable only for a relatively small group of people. In order to be successful, indeed in order to survive at all, the speculator must be astute, a proficient student of the commodity, and have considerable nerve and money and a great deal of pure luck! What the wise speculator has going for him, however, is that he can play known odds, which are fundamentally in his favor.[15]

But commodity trading has its rewards as well as its perils, and they may be king-sized for a small investment, especially if the trader uses "money leverage." For example, a contract for New York silver futures may require a minimum margin of $5,000.[16] Such a contract represents ten thousand troy ounces. Therefore, if silver is selling for $4.75 an ounce, the $5,000 is controlling $47,500. (There are other commodities in which even less margin[17] is required to control greater amounts.) Furthermore, a change in price of even twenty cents an ounce represents a profit or loss of $2,000. Thus, you stand a chance of making a 40-percent profit in one day. It is important to keep in mind, however, that a similar decline results in a comparable loss.

In spite of the rewards, then, there is no question but that speculators are engaging in a very risky business. Yet, in the chapters on securities, we have seen that there is also great risk for those who buy certain stocks at high prices. Bondholders suffered when, after they had made purchases during periods of low interest rates, they sold in recent years. People who keep cash in the mattress are losing out to inflation, as well as taking the risk of fire or theft. Nevertheless, commodity speculation is the riskiest area of all. Accordingly, in terms of your overall investment program, I would advise putting funds in commodities only after developing the basic investment portfolio described in Chapters 19–25.

GUIDELINES FOR THE SPECULATOR

To keep you from becoming one of the 75 to 80 percent of speculators that lose, the Chicago Mercantile Exchange stresses the importance of studying

---

[15] New York Coffee and Sugar Exchange, Inc. *How Businessmen Use Commodity Futures Trading*, pp. 10-11.

[16] The minimum margin for silver futures (as established by the Commodity Exchange, Inc., New York) varies based upon the per-ounce price of a contract.

[17] Margin is cash, or equivalent, deposited with a broker as a guarantee of fulfilling a futures contract.

various items of statistical information, and goes on to list "other guides relating to futures trading which veterans in the business follow":

> a. Limit losses. When the market goes against the speculator's judgment, he should terminate his contract. On the other hand, when profits are rising, he might consider letting them accumulate. Too often, traders accept small profits (before the trend even approaches the peak) but stay with an adverse price movement hoping the trend will reverse. The speculator should cut these losses short and wait for a more favorable climate in the market. In the course of a year, a trader will take 20 small losses and only 10 profits, but may well be on the profitable side for the year.
>
> b. Use stop orders. Because commodity prices fluctuate so rapidly, stop orders can be effective in protecting profits or limiting losses to minimum amounts.
>
> c. Set a price objective before initiating a position in the market. Determine how far the market would have to move against the position before you had to admit a wrong position had been taken. Use of stop orders can be very effective here. Otherwise, in most cases, let the prices rise to the predetermined price objective.
>
> d. Use a pyramiding technique. That is, add to the initial position only when there is a profit on the initial position and then add in successively smaller amounts.
>
> e. Don't overspeculate in any one contract. Use only a portion of your risk capital in any one contract.[18]

You may also want to ask yourself if you are the speculator type. We have already seen William Clayton's definition of a successful dealer in commodities. Here is what the Chicago Mercantile Exchange has to say: "First of all, he's rather young, rather affluent and quite well educated. These things we know from a survey we did recently. But a successful commodity trader is a good deal more than that. He's something like a good general—able to evaluate information, create a strategy and follow it through. And, like a good general, he knows when to conserve his forces and, yes, even when to retreat. A good commodity trader, you see, can lose a lot of skirmishes and still win the war."[19]

Keep in mind, however, that to lose numerous skirmishes in order to win the war requires considerable financial resources. Before you enter the commodities market, I suggest that you ask yourself: Do I have the funds with which to lose before I *may* begin to win?

---

[18]Chicago Mercantile Exchange. *Trading in Tomorrows,* pp. 6–7.
[19]*The Wall Street Journal,* April 10, 1975, p. 21. (Advertiser: Chicago Mercantile Exchange, 440 West Jackson Boulevard, Chicago, Illinois.)

Part Seven

TAXES, RETIREMENT & ESTATE PLANNING

Although taxes are a major expenditure, I have deliberately reserved discussion of this topic for the closing section of this book. That is because in order to prepare your income taxes to your best advantage, within the limits of the law, it is helpful to be familiar with the background material presented in my earlier chapters on budgeting, insurance, stocks, bonds, savings institutions, commodities, real estate, housing and hobbies.

In Chapter 2, we discussed the importance of the budget process. You may find that a larger percentage of your budget is going for taxes than you realize. The higher your income, the more important it becomes to consider tax costs. After all, it's your net income that counts—the amount available *after* deducting tax expenditures. Whatever your income, however, you should find a careful study of Chapter 27 helpful in minimizing your tax outlay.

The way you handle your tax matters has a direct effect on the subject of Chapter 28: Retirement. If you have done a good job in managing your money throughout your lifetime, you should encounter no major financial problems in retirement or estate planning.

Chapter 28, therefore, stresses the importance of using a good budgetary approach in arriving at your retirement needs. During my research visits to retirement areas in Florida, I have been repeatedly struck by the tragic financial plight of many elderly. Sound money management *prior* to leaving the active work force can alleviate this problem.

27

TAXES: HIGHLIGHTING INCOME TAXES

A major barrier to acquiring a fortune today is the sizable tax bite taken out of each dollar—and it is safe to assume that taxes will increase during your lifetime. The social and environmental problems facing our nation are enormous. Pollution, decay of inner cities, inadequate educational facilities, the energy shortage and racial discrimination are only a few of the areas in which citizens are demanding that the government take action. The solution of these problems requires a great deal of money.

Revenue to meet these needs comes primarily from a multitude of taxes. They may be included in the price of food, clothing and other items, in the form of a sales tax; they may be "hidden," as is the case with liquor and cigarettes; or they may be raised through direct assessment on property. The major source of revenue, however, is the federal income tax. A number of states and some cities levy their own additional taxes on income but take a much smaller bite of your dollar.

This chapter will look at the variety of taxes that an individual must pay. However, primary attention will be devoted to the federal income tax because this normally is the heaviest tax burden that U.S. citizens must assume.

FEDERAL INCOME TAX: TO BE AVOIDED, NOT EVADED

Today's heavy tax load makes it essential that you avoid taxes wherever possible. This is a very different thing, however, from tax evasion.

Your goal should be to pay what is due and legal—but not a penny more. This will help immeasurably in achieving your monetary objective, whatever it may be. Randolph W. Thrower, former Commissioner of Internal Revenue, made this statement in a special message to taxpayers: "It is our hope that the new federal income tax forms will . . . encourage you to take full advantage of the tax benefits the law provides."[1]

President Carter took full advantage of the tax benefits the law provides in filing his 1975 returns. The White House confirmed in June 1977 that the Internal Revenue Service was checking the tax returns of the President (filed jointly with his wife). His income, in 1975, totaled $136,138.92 and he paid $17,484.14, or approximately 13 percent. The reason for this very low percentage is that Mr. Carter claimed a $41,702 investment credit for his portion of a peanut shelter purchased for his Plains, Georgia, company. He also reduced his taxes by averaging his income with the previous four years.

Another example of avoiding income taxes was pointed up, in 1973, by

---

[1] *Federal Income Tax Forms,* Internal Revenue Service, Department of the Treasury, 1969, p. 1.

the disclosure of payments by President Nixon. As indicated in Table 27-1, his yearly tax payments between 1969 and 1972 varied from a high of $72,682.09 in 1969 to a low of $792.81 in 1970.

TABLE 27-1 President Nixon's Income-Tax Payments, 1969–72

	1969	1970	1971	1972
Total income	$328,161.52	$262,942.56	$262,384.75	$268,777.54
Deductions	178,535.10	307,181.92	255,676.69	247,569.77
Exemptions	1,800.00	none	1,350.00	1,500.00
Taxable income	147,826.42	none	5,358.06	19,707.77
Total tax paid	72,682.09	792.81	878.03	4,298.17

There were three major areas in which President Nixon endeavored to avoid taxes. First, he took $482,018 in deductions between 1969 and 1972 for donation of his vice-presidential papers to the government; second, he paid no capital-gains tax on the sale of either a portion of his San Clemente, California, property or his New York apartment; and third, certain improvements made to his San Clemente and Key Biscayne real estate were not reported as taxable income. The White House indicated that in all three instances the President had acted upon information received from certain lawyers and accountants who prepared his income-tax returns. President Nixon may, in fact, have tried to avoid more than the law allows.[2] Surprisingly, the Internal Revenue Service (IRS) did not challenge his figures at the time his returns were submitted. However, when the low amount of the tax payments made by the President in 1970–1972 was revealed in the fall of 1973, the President asked the congressional Joint Committee on Internal Revenue Taxation to review his returns, saying that if the committee decided against him, he would pay the back taxes. The congressional staff report, released April 3, 1974, recommended that the President pay an additional $476,431. The entire deduction for the vice-presidential papers was disallowed, and it was suggested that he pay additional taxes for the profit made on the San Clemente land deal and the sale of his New York condominium. The IRS also reviewed President Nixon's returns and on April 2, 1974, ruled that he owed $432,787 plus interest, amounting to a total of approximately $465,000. The President agreed to pay the IRS figure because the Joint Committee staff report indicated that the proper amount to be paid must be determined by the IRS. The White House statement pointed out:

[2]The word "may" is used because the President did not take the decision to the courts. Senator Carl T. Curtis, Republican from Nebraska, commented on the President's motives as follows: "I think the President has paid his taxes because he gave his word he would pay what was found due. I still think he would have a very good chance of winning if the case was disputed."

Any errors which may have been made in the preparation of the President's returns were made by those to whom he delegated the responsibility for preparing his returns and were made without his knowledge and without his approval. The Internal Revenue Service had told the President that $140,080.97 of back taxes were for 1969, and did not have to be paid because the statute of limitations for that year had expired.

It is apparent from the Nixon case that it is wise to avoid only those taxes that are truly avoidable. Otherwise, you'll be faced with a lot of headaches and the payment of additional interest. Moreover, the penalty for tax evasion can be high indeed. Spiro Agnew lost his vice-presidency because he failed to report earnings on his federal income-tax returns. So, when it comes to tax payments, familiarize yourself with the income-tax laws, then follow Mr. Thrower's advice and stick to "the tax benefits the law allows." If you have any questions about what is allowable, call the IRS while preparing your return. Their representatives can be most helpful. Later in this chapter we will list income which the IRS specifically exempts from taxation.

A review of income-tax laws over the past sixty-five years indicates that changes have been frequent. You can be sure there will be continuing modifications in the future. Therefore, it is important to read with care the instructions accompanying the annual Federal Income Tax Forms. For example, in 1976 a letter from the Commissioner of Internal Revenue accompanying these forms pointed up major changes that occurred as a result of a 1976 law. The Commissioner's letter said in part:

> The 1976 Tax Reform Act may affect your taxes substantially. An expanded and simplified credit for the elderly has replaced the old retirement income credit. A credit for child care expenses is available to all eligible taxpayers, whether or not they itemize deductions. On the other hand, the former exclusion for sick pay has been replaced by a more restrictive disability income exclusion.
>
> Completing your return this year could be more difficult. This year all taxpayers, whether or not they itemize their deductions and regardless of the size of their income, will need to compute taxable income. . . . Also, last year's simple credit for personal exemptions has been replaced by a larger, but more complex, general tax credit.[3]

Six important provisions of the Tax Reform Act became effective after 1976:

1. *Capital gains and losses.* In 1977 property had to be held for more than nine months to receive long-term capital-gain or loss treatment. The holding period went to twelve months in 1978.

[3] *1977 Federal Income Tax Forms,* Internal Revenue Service, Department of the Treasury, 1978, p. 1.

486

2. *Capital losses.* The net capital loss that may reduce ordinary income was increased from $1,000 to $2,000 in 1977, and to $3,000 in 1978.

3. *Moving expenses.* For 1977 the minimum distance requirement for business-related moves was reduced from fifty to thirty-five miles. The maximum deduction for house-hunting trips, temporary quarters, selling and purchasing expenses and so on, increased from $2,500 to $3,000.

4. *Sale of residence by the elderly.* The base amount to be considered in the election to exclude gain on the sale of a residence by an individual aged sixty-five or older increased from $20,000 to $35,000 in 1977.

5. *Alimony.* For 1977 alimony was an adjustment to gross income rather than an itemized deduction. Thus, a person may claim the standard deduction in addition to deducting alimony.

6. *Dependency exemption for divorced parents.* For 1977 the rule allowing a dependency exemption to a noncustodial parent who provides $1,200 or more support for the child (or children) was changed to require $1,200 support for each child.

President Carter hopes to simplify our federal income-tax forms. As part of his tax-reform package he proposes to provide direct tax credits in lieu of personal exemptions. But Congress can expect to make numerous changes prior to passage of that act.

In the meantime, it is important to be familiar with the current forms.

A BIT OF HISTORY

The roots of the United States federal income tax reach back to pre-World War 1. The Sixteenth Amendment to the Constitution, passed in 1913, authorized the U.S. government to "... lay and collect taxes on incomes, from whatever source desired." The first permanent individual income tax in the United States became effective on March 1, 1913. The initial rates were modest, but this is far from the case today! Table 27-2 shows the difference in after-tax income for a single person at various times between 1912 and 1976.

TABLE 27-2 Sample After-Tax Incomes for Single Americans

Year	Taxable Income	Remaining after Taxes
1912	$10,000	$10,000
1915	10,000	9,930
1929	10,000	9,910
1942	10,000	8,412
1952	10,000	7,044
1962	10,000	7,360
1977	10,000	7,916

In 1913, less than 1 percent of the people of the United States paid an income tax. The rate was graduated from 1 percent on the first $20,000 of taxable income to 7 percent on the excess over $500,000. Today, a single person's rate ranges from approximately 26 percent on the first $20,000 to 70 percent above $100,000, and 75 percent of all income earners pay an income tax. Of the eighty-one million taxpayers, the majority are eligible to file on either a simple half-page form (1040A) or the first two pages of Form 1040.

WHO MUST FILE A RETURN?

Every citizen of the United States and every resident alien, adult or minor, who receives more than a specified amount of income in one year (see below) must file an individual income-tax return (Short Form 1040A or Form 1040). You must file a return if you are in one of the following categories with income as indicated on Table 27-3:

Table 27-3 Who Must File a Return

File a return if you are:	And your gross income is at least:
Single (legally separated, divorced, or married living apart from your spouse for the entire year with dependent child) and:	
—You are under 65	$2,950
—You are 65 or older	3,700
A person who can be claimed as a dependent on your parent's return, and have taxable dividends, interest, or other unearned income of $750 or more	750
A qualifying widow(er) with dependent child and:	
—You are under 65	3,950
—You are 65 or older	4,700
Married filing jointly, living with your spouse at the end of 1977 (or at date of death of spouse), and:	
—Both of you are under 65	4,700
—One of you is 65 or older	5,450
—Both of you are 65 or older	6,200
Married filing separately or married but not living with your spouse at the end of 1977	750
A person entitled to exclude income from sources within U.S. possessions	750
Self-employed and your net earnings from self-employment were at least	400

Source: 1977 Instructions for Form 1040, IRS pamphlet, p. 4.

TYPES OF FORMS AND WHERE TO GET THEM

The IRS mails forms and schedules, whenever practicable, to taxpayers based upon the returns they filed the preceding year. The IRS prepared two forms in 1976 for the submission of income tax information.

Short Form 1040A may be used if all your income was from wages, salaries, tips, other employee compensation, dividends, and not more than four hundred dollars in interest, and you do not itemize deductions.[4] See Figure 27-1 for a copy of 1040A. As you can see, the Short Form is not difficult to complete. All wages, salaries, tips and other employee compensation must be listed on line 9. Dividends and interest income should be included on lines 10 and 11. Then add lines 9, 10c and 11 and place the total on line 12. From this point on, you can take advantage of the IRS's generosity if you like and let it figure your taxes due. Should you so decide, you need only complete lines 20a, b, c and d, and 21. Sign your return and, if appropriate, attach copy B of Form W-2.[5]

Now let us turn to the more complex Form 1040, which may include a number of attached schedules in addition to the main form. Taxpayers receiving a Form 1040 package may find that it includes not only Form 1040— U.S. Individual Income Tax Return—but also a number of the following: Schedules A and B for itemized deductions and dividend and interest income; Schedule C, for profit (or loss) from a business or a profession (sole proprietorship); Schedule D, for capital gains and losses; Schedules E and R, for supplemental-income and retirement-income credit computation; Schedule F, for income from farming; Schedule G, for income averaging;[6] and Schedule SE, for reporting net earnings from self-employment. If you wish to correct your income-tax return you should obtain Form 1040X (Amended U.S. Individual

---

[4]Each taxpayer must decide for himself whether or not he wishes to itemize deductions. Work out the results for itemization as against the standard deduction. If you are single and earn over $15,000, you may have a smaller taxable income if you itemize your deductions, because of the $2,200 limit on the standard deduction. If you itemize deductions, it is most important that you keep detailed records. *The Internal Revenue Service will not accept approximations.* Some people find that it is possible to save by using the standard deduction one year and itemizing the next. In the year they are using the standard deduction, they wait to pay their charitable contributions, medical costs and so on until the first of the following year.

[5]Wage and Tax Statement provided by your employer. Only your employer can issue your W-2 form or correct it. If you are unable to secure Form W-2, contact an Internal Revenue Service office.

[6]The Internal Revenue Service office income-averaging method of computing taxes may be to your advantage if your income has increased substantially this year. In arriving at your taxable income, you use the current year's income and that of the four preceding years. Read the General Instructions accompanying Schedule G for further information.

Figure 27-1   Short Form 1040A can generally be utilized if your income is $40,000 or less if you are married and filing a joint return, and $20,000 otherwise, and all your income is from wages, salaries, tips, other employee compensation, and not more than $400 in dividends, or more than $400 in interest and you do not itemize your deductions.

Form 1040A
Department of the Treasury—Internal Revenue Service
U.S. Individual Income Tax Return **1977**

Use IRS label. Otherwise, print or type.		
First name and initial (if joint return, give first names and initials of both)	Last name	Your social security number
Present home address (Number and street, including apartment number, or rural route)	For Privacy Act Notice, see page 9 of Instructions.	Spouse's social security no.
City, town or post office, State and ZIP code	Occu-pation Yours ▶ Spouse's ▶	

Presidential Election Campaign Fund
Do you want $1 to go to this fund?. . . . .   Yes / No
If joint return, does your spouse want $1 to go to this fund?   Yes / No
Note: Checking "Yes" will not increase your tax or reduce your refund.

Filing Status
Check Only One Box

1 ☐ Single
2 ☐ Married filing joint return (even if only one had income)
3 ☐ Married filing separately. If spouse is also filing, give spouse's social security number in the space above and enter full name here ▶.................
4 ☐ Unmarried Head of Household. Enter qualifying name ▶   See page 6 of Instructions.

Exemptions
Always check the "Yourself" box. Check other boxes if they apply.

5a ☐ Yourself   ☐ 65 or over   ☐ Blind
b ☐ Spouse   ☐ 65 or over   ☐ Blind
Enter number of boxes checked on 5a and b ▶ ☐

c First names of your dependent children who lived with you ▶.............................
Enter number of children listed ▶ ☐

d Other dependents: (1) Name	(2) Relationship	(3) Number of months lived in your home.	(4) Did dependent have income of $750 or more?	(5) Did you provide more than one-half of dependent's support?

Enter number of other dependents ▶ ☐

Add numbers entered in boxes above ▶ ☐

6 Total number of exemptions claimed . . . .

7 Wages, salaries, tips, and other employee compensation. (Attach Forms W–2. If unavailable, see page 11 of Instructions) . . . . | 7 |

8 Interest income (see page 4 of Instructions). . . . . | 8 |

9a Dividends............................ | 9b Less exclusion .... | Balance ▶ | 9c |
(See pages 4 and 11 of Instructions)

10 Adjusted gross income (add lines 7, 8, and 9c). If under $8,000, see page 2 of Instructions on "Earned Income Credit." If eligible, enter child's name ▶ | 10 |

11a Credit for contributions to candidates for public office. Enter one-half of amount paid but do not enter more than $25 ($50 if joint return) . . . . | 11a |

IF YOU WANT IRS TO FIGURE YOUR TAX, PLEASE STOP HERE AND SIGN BELOW.

b Total Federal income tax withheld (if line 7 is larger than $16,500, see page 12 of Instructions) . . . . | 11b |

c Earned income credit (from page 2 of Instructions) . . . . . . | 11c |

12 Total (add lines 11a, b, and c) . . . . | 12 |

13 Tax on the amount on line 10. (See Instructions for line 13 on page 12, then find your tax in Tax Tables on pages 14–25.) . . . . | 13 |

14 If line 12 is larger than line 13, enter amount to be **REFUNDED TO YOU** . . . . ▶ | 14 |

15 If line 13 is larger than line 12, enter **BALANCE DUE.** Attach check or money order for full amount payable to "Internal Revenue Service." Write social security number on check or money order . . ▶ | 15 |

Under penalties of perjury, I declare that I have examined this return, including accompanying schedules and statements, and to the best of my knowledge and belief, it is true, correct, and complete. Declaration of preparer (other than taxpayer) is based on all information of which preparer has any knowledge.

Please Sign

Your signature   Date

Spouse's signature (if filing jointly, BOTH must sign even if only one had income)

Paid preparer's signature and identifying number (see Instructions)

Paid preparer's address (or employer's name, address, and identifying number)

Please Attach Copy B of Forms W–2 Here
Please Attach Check or Money Order Here

Source: Internal Revenue Service, Department of the Treasury.

Income Tax Return). In addition, Form 1040-ES, for making estimated tax payments is mailed separately to those who require it. Any required form or schedule that you do not receive can be obtained from an IRS office or many banks and post offices. Forms can also be obtained by filling out an order form provided by the IRS. Once a person is on record for paying his taxes, the IRS will send him the necessary forms each year.

Certain specialized forms are available only at Internal Revenue Service offices. These include the following: Form 1310, Statement of Claimant to Refund Due Deceased Taxpayer; Form 2106, Employee Business Expenses; Form 2120, Multiple Support Declaration; Form 2210, Underpayment of Estimated Tax by individuals; Form 2440, Sick-Pay Exclusion; Form 3468, Computation of Investment Credit; Form 3903, Moving Expense Adjustment; Form 4136, Computation of Credit for Federal Tax Gasoline, Special Fuels, and Lubricating Oil; Form 4562, for optional use by individuals, etc., claiming depreciation; Form 4683, U.S. Information Return on Foreign Banks, Securities, and Other Financial Accounts; Form 4684 for reporting gains and losses resulting from casualties and thefts; Form 4797, Supplemental Schedule of Gains and Losses; Form 4798, for computing a capital loss carryover from the current year to a succeeding taxable year; Form 4831, for reporting rental income; Form 4832, Asset Depreciation Range (for determining a reasonable allowance for depreciation of designated classes of assets); and Form 4835, for reporting farm rental income and expenses.

If you are in a locality which has no IRS office, you can write to the district director responsible for your state (see Figure 27-2). If there is more than one district office in your state, send the order to the office nearest you.

IRS PUBLICATIONS

The IRS provides the following free publications that you may find useful: 17, *Your Federal Income Tax*; 54, *Tax Guide For U.S. Citizens Abroad*; 334, *Tax Guide For Small Business*; 501, *Exemptions and Dependents*; 502, *Medical Expenses*; 503, *Child Care and Disabled Dependent Care*; 506, *Computing Your Tax Under the Income Averaging Method*; 521, *Moving Expenses*; 522, *Sick Pay*; 523, *Selling Your Home*; 524, *Retirement Income Credit*; 526, *Contributions*; 529, *Miscellaneous Deductions*; 530, *Homeowner's Deductions*; 532, *Students and Parents*; 545, *Interest Expense*; and 552, *Recordkeeping Requirements*. These pamphlets are available at the addresses shown in Figure 27-2.

Be sure to read with care the information furnished each year with your federal income-tax forms. Some modifications are made annually, either in the forms themselves or in specific provisions that affect the amount of payment due.

The completed tax return should be mailed to the appropriate Internal Revenue Service Center.

Figure 27-2   Addresses of Internal Revenue offices supplying free forms and publications.

Alabama—Birmingham, Ala.   35203
Alaska—Anchorage, Alaska   99510
Arizona—Phoenix, Ariz.   85025
Arkansas—Little Rock, Ark.   72203
California—P.O. Box 12626, Fresno, Calif.   93778
Colorado—Denver, Colo.   80202
Connecticut—Hartford, Conn.   06103
Delaware—Wilmington, Del.   19801
District of Columbia—Baltimore, Md.   21201
Florida—Jacksonville, Fla.   32202
Georgia—Atlanta, Ga.   30303
Guam—Agana, Guam   96910
Hawaii—Honolulu, Hawaii   96813
Idaho—Boise, Idaho   83724
Illinois—Chicago, Ill.   60602
   Springfield, Ill.   62704
Indiana—Box 44026, Indianapolis, Ind.   46244
Iowa—Des Moines, Iowa   50309
Kansas—Wichita, Kans.   67202
Kentucky—Box 1735, Louisville, Ky.   40201
Louisiana—New Orleans, La.   70130
Maine—Augusta, Maine   04330
Maryland—Baltimore, Md.   21201
Massachusetts—Boston, Mass.   02203
Michigan—Detroit, Mich.   48226
Minnesota—St. Paul, Minn.   55101
Mississippi—Jackson, Miss.   39202
Missouri—St. Louis, Mo.   63101
Montana—Helena, Mont.   59601
Nebraska—Omaha, Nebr.   68102
Nevada—Reno, Nev.   89502
New Hampshire—Portsmouth, N.H.   03801
New Jersey—Newark, N.J.   07102
New Mexico—Albuquerque, N. Mex.   87101
New York—Albany, N.Y.   12207
   Buffalo, N.Y.   14202
   New York City, Box 1040, Brooklyn, N.Y.   11232
North Carolina—Greensboro, N.C.   27401
North Dakota—Fargo, N. Dak.   58102

Ohio—Cleveland, Ohio   44199
   Cincinnati, Ohio   45202
Oklahoma—Oklahoma City, Okla.   73102.
Oregon—Portland, Oreg.   97204
Panama Canal Zone—Director, Office of International Operations, Internal Revenue Service, Washington, D.C.   20225
Pennsylvania—Philadelphia, Pa.   19108
   Pittsburgh, Pa.   15222
Puerto Rico—Director's Representative, U.S. Internal Revenue Service, 255 Ponce de Leon Avenue, Hato Rey, Puerto Rico   00917
Rhode Island—Providence, R.I.   02903
South Carolina—Columbia, S.C.   29201
South Dakota—Aberdeen, S. Dak.   57401
Tennessee—Nashville, Tenn.   37203
Texas—Box 2929, Austin, Tex.   78767
   Dallas, Tex.   75202
Utah—Salt Lake City, Utah   84101
Vermont—Burlington, Vt.   05401
Virginia—Richmond, Va.   23240
Virgin Islands—Department of Finance, Tax Division, Charlotte Amalie, St. Thomas, Virgin Islands   00801
Washington—Seattle, Wash.   98121
West Virginia—Parkersburg, W. Va.   26101
Wisconsin—Milwaukee, Wis.   53202
Wyoming—Cheyenne, Wyo.   82001

Foreign Addresses—Taxpayers with legal residence in foreign countries: If European APO, send order blank to: IRS, Box 1040, Brooklyn, N.Y. 11232. If Pacific APO, send order blank to: IRS, San Francisco, Calif. 94102. Send letter requests for other forms and publications to: Director, Office of International Operations, Internal Revenue Service, Washington, D.C. 20225.

Source: Internal Revenue Service, Department of the Treasury.

PREPARING YOUR RETURN

People tend to gripe about how difficult it is to make out a tax return, particularly since the recent revisions in the tax forms. Although some complaint is justified, I believe that most people can file their own returns and strongly advise that they do so. A majority of the eighty-one million taxpayers are eligible to use either the 1040A Short Form or the first two pages of the standard 1040 Form. And if you prepare your own form from the start, it becomes relatively easy to continue doing so through the years as the task becomes more complex. Furthermore, as noted above, many taxpayers can have the IRS compute their tax for them, after they themselves have filled in certain information.

You can, of course, pay to have your tax returns prepared by "experts." In our community alone, listings of companies offering this service take up half a page in the telephone directory. But why pay someone else to do a job that anyone with a reasonable amount of intelligence, fairly uncomplicated sources of income and up-to-date records of income and expenditures should be able to do for himself? Besides, no one is as familiar with your financial affairs as you are. If you have a problem, write, call or visit the IRS and they will give you the answer free. This IRS service was highlighted by the current commissioner of Internal Revenue, Donald C. Alexander. He wrote: "Call us toll-free for answers to your Federal tax questions. . . . To help us provide courteous responses and accurate information, IRS supervisors occasionally monitor calls. No record is made of the taxpayer's name, address or Social Security number except when, at taxpayer request, a follow-up telephone call must be made." Mr. Alexander also made this important point: "If you decide to have someone else help you, be sure to select a qualified person."[7]

One last tip: Begin your tabulations early—in February, if possible—so that you don't get caught in a last-minute rush.

How to Prepare a Return: A Sample Case

Tom and Tricia Tee Tamllits, out of school just a year, believed that by working together on their income tax they could save time and money. They had been working in New Orleans since January 1977. Early in February 1978 they went to their bank to pick up the 1977 federal income-tax forms.

After reading the IRS material carefully, they assembled the necessary records to complete Form 1040 and the appropriate schedules. Tom and Tricia were glad to see that the IRS provides an extra copy of each form, permitting them to make a duplicate (file) copy of everything submitted. They tackled Form 1040 (Figure 27-3) by first filling out their names, address, Social Security numbers[8] and occupations. Tricia and her husband decided not to designate one dollar each of their taxes for the Presidential Election Campaign Fund; therefore, they checked the "No" boxes. They next checked their filing status as married, filing a joint return. This entitled them to two exemptions (6a, 6).

---

[7]Source: IRS Instructions for Form 1040.

[8]If you don't have a number, file Application Form SS-5 with the local office of the Social Security Administration. If you don't receive your number prior to filing your return, enter "Applied For" in the space provided for the number.

Figure 27-3   The Tamllits' Income Tax return for 1977 (Form 1040).

Form **1040** Department of the Treasury—Internal Revenue Service
U.S. Individual Income Tax Return 1977

For the year January 1–December 31, 1977, or other taxable year beginning _____ , 1977 ending _____ , 19 ___

| First name and initial (if joint return, give first names and initials of both) | Last name | Your social security numb |
| Tom T. and Tricia T. | Tamllits | 0 00 00 000 |

Present home address (Number and street, including apartment number, or rural route)   121 Richton Avenue   For Privacy Act Notice, see page 3 of Instructions.   Spouse's social security no   000 00 0000

City, town or post office, State and ZIP code   New Orleans, La 70122

Occu-pation   Yours ▶ Accountant   Spouse's ▶ Manager-store

Presidential Election Campaign Fund
Do you want $1 to go to this fund? . . . . Yes ☐ No ✔
If joint return, does your spouse want $1 to go to this fund? . Yes ☐ No ✔
Note: Checking "Yes" w not increase your tax or duce your refund.

Filing Status
Check Only One Box
1 ☐ Single
2 ✔ Married filing joint return (even if only one had income)
3 ☐ Married filing separately. If spouse is also filing, give spouse's social security number in the space abo and enter full name here ▶ ....
4 ☐ Unmarried Head of Household. Enter qualifying name ▶ .... See page 7 of Instructio
5 ☐ Qualifying widow(er) with dependent child (Year spouse died ▶ 19 ___). See page 7 of Instructio

Exemptions
Always check the "Yourself" box. Check other boxes if they apply.
6a ✔ Yourself   ☐ 65 or over   ☐ Blind   Enter number of boxes checked on 6a and b ▶
b ✔ Spouse   ☐ 65 or over   ☐ Blind
c First names of your dependent children who lived with you ▶ ....   Enter number of children listed ▶

d Other dependents:

| (1) Name | (2) Relationship | (3) Number of months lived in your home. | (4) Did dependent have income of $750 or more? | (5) Did you provide more than one-half of dependent's support? |
| | | | | |

Enter number of other dependents ▶

7 Total number of exemptions claimed . . . .   Add numbers entered in boxes above ▶

Income
8	Wages, salaries, tips, and other employee compensation. (Attach Forms W-2. If unavailable, see page 5 of Instructions.)	8	22,000
9	Interest income. (If over $400, attach Schedule B.)	9	2,235
10a	Dividends (If over $400, attach Schedule B) .... 325.00, 10b less exclusion 100.00, Balance ▶	10c	225

(See pages 9 and 17 of Instructions)
(If you have no other income, skip lines 11 through 20 and go to line 21.)

11	State and local income tax refunds (does not apply if refund is for year you took standard deduction) . . .	11	
12	Alimony received	12	
13	Business income or (loss) (attach Schedule C)	13	
14	Capital gain or (loss) (attach Schedule D)	14	236
15	50% of capital gain distributions not reported on Schedule D	15	
16	Net gain or (loss) from Supplemental Schedule of Gains and Losses (attach Form 4797) . .	16	
17	Fully taxable pensions and annuities not reported on Schedule E	17	
18	Pensions, annuities, rents, royalties, partnerships, estates or trusts, etc. (attach Schedule E) . .	18	
19	Farm income or (loss) (attach Schedule F)	19	
20	Other (state nature and source—see page 9 of Instructions) ▶	20	
21	Total income. Add lines 8, 9, and 10c through 20 . . . . ▶	21	24,696

Adjustments to Income   *(If none, skip lines 22 through 27 and enter zero on line 28.)*

22	Moving expense (attach Form 3903)	22	
23	Employee business expenses (attach Form 2106)	23	
24	Payments to an individual retirement arrangement (from attached Form 5329, Part III)	24	
25	Payments to a Keogh (H.R. 10) retirement plan	25	
26	Forfeited interest penalty for premature withdrawal	26	
27	Alimony paid (see page 11 of Instructions)	27	
28	Total adjustments. Add lines 22 through 27 . . . . ▶	28	-0-
29	Subtract line 28 from line 21	29	24,696
30	Disability income exclusion (sick pay) (attach Form 2440)	30	
31	Adjusted gross income. Subtract line 30 from line 29. Enter here and on line 32. If you want IRS to figure your tax for you, see page 4 of the Instructions . . . . ▶	31	24,696

32 Amount from line 31	**32**	24,696 00
33 If you itemize deductions, enter excess itemized deductions from Schedule A, line 41 . . . . ⎱		
If you do NOT itemize deductions, enter zero. . . . . ⎰	**33**	-0-
Caution: *If you have unearned income and can be claimed as a dependent on your parent's return, check here ▶ ☐ and see page 11 of the Instructions. Also see page 11 of the Instructions if:*		

● You are married filing a separate return and your spouse itemizes deductions, OR
● You file Form 4563, OR
● You are a dual-status alien.

34 Tax Table Income. Subtract line 33 from line 32	**34**	24,696 00

Note: See Instructions for line 35 on page 11. Then find your tax on the amount on line 34 in the Tax Tables. Enter the tax on line 35. However, if line 34 is more than $20,000 ($40,000 if you checked box 2 or 5) or you have more exemptions than those covered in the Tax Tables for your filing status, use Part I of Schedule TC (Form 1040) to figure your tax. You must also use Schedule TC if you file Schedule G (Form 1040), Income Averaging.

35 Tax. Check if from ☑ Tax Tables or ☐ Schedule TC	**35**	4,193 00
36 Additional taxes. (See page 12 of Instructions.) Check if from ☐ Form 4970, ☐ Form 4972, ☐ Form 5544, ☐ Form 5405, or ☐ Section 72(m)(5) penalty tax	**36**	
37 **Total.** Add lines 35 and 36 . . . . ▶	**37**	4,193 00

38 Credit for contributions to candidates for public office	**38**		
39 Credit for the elderly (attach Schedules R&RP)	**39**		
40 Credit for child and dependent care expenses (attach Form 2441) .	**40**		
41 Investment credit (attach Form 3468)	**41**		
42 Foreign tax credit (attach Form 1116)	**42**		
43 Work Incentive (WIN) Credit (attach Form 4874)	**43**		
44 New jobs credit (attach Form 5884)	**44**		
45 See page 12 of Instructions	**45**		
46 Total credits. Add lines 38 through 45	**46**		
47 **Balance.** Subtract line 46 from line 37 and enter difference (but not less than zero) . . . . ▶	**47**	4,193 00

48 Self-employment tax (attach Schedule SE)	**48**	
49 Minimum tax. Check here ▶ ☐ and attach Form 4625	**49**	
50 Tax from recomputing prior-year investment credit (attach Form 4255)	**50**	
51 Social security tax on tip income not reported to employer (attach Form 4137)	**51**	
52 Uncollected employee social security tax on tips (from Form W–2)	**52**	
53 Tax on an individual retirement arrangement (attach Form 5329)	**53**	
54 **Total tax.** Add lines 47 through 53 . . . . ▶	**54**	4,193 00

55 Total Federal income tax withheld (attach Forms W–2, W–2G, and W–2P to front)	**55**	2,998 28	
56 1977 estimated tax payments (include amount allowed as credit from 1976 return)	**56**		
57 Earned income credit. If line 31 is under $8,000, see page 2 of Instructions. If eligible, enter child's name ▶..................	**57**		
58 Amount paid with Form 4868	**58**		
59 Excess FICA and RRTA tax withheld (two or more employers) . . .	**59**		
60 Credit for Federal tax on special fuels, etc. (attach Form 4136) . .	**60**		
61 Credit from a Regulated Investment Company (attach Form 2439)	**61**		
61a See page 13 of Instructions	**61a**		
62 **Total.** Add lines 55 through 61a . . . . ▶	**62**	2,998 28	

63 If line 62 is larger than line 54, enter amount **OVERPAID** . . . . ▶	**63**	
64 Amount of line 63 to be **REFUNDED TO YOU** . . . . ▶	**64**	
65 Amount of line 63 to be credited on 1978 estimated tax . . . . ▶ | **65** |		
66 If line 54 is larger than line 62, enter **BALANCE DUE.** Attach check or money order for full amount payable to "Internal Revenue Service." Write social security number on check or money order . . . ▶ (Check ▶ ☐ if Form 2210 (2210F) is attached. See page 14 of Instructions.)	**66**	1,194 72

Under penalties of perjury, I declare that I have examined this return, including accompanying schedules and statements, and to the best of my knowledge and belief, it is true, correct, and complete. Declaration of preparer (other than taxpayer) is based on all information of which preparer has any knowledge.

▶ *Tom T. Tomelits*   4/15/78 ▶
Your signature   Date   Paid preparer's signature and identifying number (see Instructions)

▶ *Tricia P. Tomlitts*   ---
Spouse's signature (if filing jointly, BOTH must
sign even if only one had income)   ▶ Paid preparer's address (or employer's name, address, and identifying number)

Reporting Salary / The Tamllits' first dollar figure was entered on line 8 of their 1040 Form. Tom and Tricia reported an income from "Wages, salaries, tips, and other employee compensation" of $22,000. Their only source of funds in this category was their 1977 salaries from the ABC and XYZ corporations. In view of the fact that they had been placed on their companies' payrolls as of January 1, 1977, they reported their compensation for the entire year. Tom and Tricia's employers had provided them with W-2 Forms in January 1978. These indicated that Tricia and Tom had wages paid subject to withholding in 1977 for a combined total of $22,000; federal income-tax withheld: ($3,132.00; and Social Security[9] tax withheld: $1,287.00. In addition, Tom and Tricia worked in a state with its own income tax, which had also been deducted from their monthly salaries. The W-2 Forms were furnished in triplicate—the originals to be attached to Form 1040; the second copies to be used for filing state income tax returns; and the third to be retained for their own records.

Reporting Other Income / Now came the more difficult part: reporting their other income. Tom and Tricia realized that it is obligatory to report all sources of income except those specifically exempted. Income that must be reported includes the following:

wages, salaries, bonuses, commissions, fees and tips;
dividends;
earned income from sources outside U.S.;
earnings (interest) from savings and loan associations, mutual savings banks, credit unions and so on;
interest on tax refunds;
interest on bank deposits, bonds, notes;
interest on U.S. savings bonds;
interest on arbitrage bonds issued after October 9, 1969, by state and local governments;
profits from businesses and professions;
the taxpayer's share of profits from partnerships and small business corporations;
pensions, annuities, endowments, including lump-sum distributions;
supplemental annuities under Railroad Retirement Act (but not regular Railroad Retirement Act benefits);
profits from the sale or exchange of real estate, securities or other property;
sale of personal residence;
rents and royalties;
the taxpayer's share of estate or trust income, including accumulation;
employer supplemental unemployment benefits;
distribution from trusts;

[9]The correct term is F.I.C.A., which stands for Federal Insurance Contributions Act.

alimony, separate maintenance or support payments received from and deductible by the taxpayer's spouse or former spouse;

prizes and awards (contests, raffles or such);

refunds of state and local taxes (principal amounts) if they were deducted in a prior year and resulted in tax benefits;

fees received for jury duty and precinct election-board duty;

fees received by an executor, administrator or director;

embezzled or other illegal income.

Nontaxable Income / Tricia and Tom also checked with care to see what income was specifically tax-exempt. Examples of income that should not be reported include:

disability retirement payments and other benefits paid by the Veterans Administration;

dividends on veterans' insurance;

life-insurance sums received at a person's death;

workmen's compensation, insurance, damages and so on for injury or sickness;

interest on certain state and municipal bonds;[10]

federal Social Security benefits;

gifts, money or other property inherited by, or willed to, the taxpayer;

insurance repayments that were more than the cost of the taxpayer's normal living expenses should he lose the use of his home because of fire or other casualty. Repayment of the amount spent by the taxpayer for normal living expenses must be reported as income.

Reporting Dividends and Interest / Only Tom was fortunate enough to have received outside income early in life. His parents had set aside IBM stock for his college education, but he had decided to live at home and attend the University of Southern California. When he graduated, his father gave him $35,000 that had not been required for his schooling. Tom had taken a course in personal finance and proceeded to invest his nest egg in high-yield U.S. Treasury notes, stocks and cash reserve. Tricia had done it the hard way, working her way through school, and considered herself fortunate to be out of debt. She had no outside income.

The fact that Tom and Tricia had kept good records helped in posting the information on line 10a of Form 1040. Table 27-4 presents the format the Tamllits used to record their dividends and interest. As you will note, Tom had stock in four corporations plus a no-load mutual fund. He correctly did not include the $10 capital-gain distribution as a dividend. Therefore, he entered

[10]As you move into the higher tax brackets, take advantage of tax-exempt investments.

TABLE 27-4 Worksheet Tom Tamllits Used to Record His Yearly Dividends and Interest

| | Dividends Received in 1977 | | | | | |
	1977 Estimate (as of 1/1/77)	1/1-3/31	4/1-6/30	7/1-9/30	10/1-12/31	Total
Stock						
ABC Co.	$ 80.00	$20.00	$ 20.00	$20.00	$ 20.00	$ 80.00
DEF Co.	100.00	25.00	25.00	25.00	35.00	110.00
GHI Co.	40.00	10.00	10.00	10.00		30.00
LKM Co.	80.00	22.50	22.50	22.50	22.50	90.00
NOP Fund (no-load)	15.00	3.50	3.50	3.50	4.50	15.00
Total	$ 315.00	$81,00	$ 81.00	$81.00	$ 82.00	$ 325.00
NOP Fund (cap. gain)	8.00				10.00	$ 10.00
	Interest Received in 1977					
CR Credit Union	$ 48.00	$12.00	$ 12.00	$15.50	$ 15.50	$ 55.00
ST Savings & Loan Assn.	50.00	12.50	12.50	12.50	12.50	50.00
8% U.S. Treasury note	2080.00		1040.00		1040.00	2080.00
UV National Bank	50.00	12.50	12.50	12.50	12.50	50.00
	$2228.00	$37.00	$1077.00	$40.50	$1080.50	$2235.00

the figure of $325 on Form 1040, line 10a.[11] Next, on line 10b, Tom took advantage of the $100 dividend exclusion on his stock that the law authorizes.[12] Thus, on line 10c, he wrote $225. He and Tricia also decided to fill out Part I of schedule B (Figure 27-4), although the IRS only required the submission of this part if the taxpayer received more than four hundred dollars in gross dividends.

Tom's interest income came from four sources, as recorded in Table 27-4:

1. Earnings from the QR Credit Union (5½ percent on $1,000)
2. ST Savings and Loan Association ($1,000 at 5 percent)
3. 8 percent U.S. Treasury note ($26,000)[13]
4. UV National Bank savings account ($1,000 at 5 percent)

[11]The Tamllits decided to round off all computations to whole dollars, which they were permitted to do in accordance with the IRS instructions. The eliminated amounts less than fifty cents and increased any amounts from fifty through nine-nine cents to the next higher dollar.

[12]If you file a joint return, the law allows you and your spouse to exclude up to $200. However, neither can use any part of the $100 exclusion not used by the other. Tom planned to put the stock in joint ownership so next year they could take the $200 deduction.

[13]As noted in Chapter 20, if Tom had purchased Series E United States savings bonds, he could have reported the interest in one of two ways: He could have either deferred reporting the interest until the year the bonds were cashed, or listed the interest each year.

Figure 27-4 The Tamllits' dividend and interest income for 1977 (Schedule B, Form 1040).

Name(s) as shown on Form 1040 (Do not enter name and social security number if shown on other side)	Your social security number
Tom and Tricia T. Tamllits	000 : 00 : 0000

Part I Interest Income

If you received more than $400 in interest, complete Part I. Interest includes earnings from savings and loan associations, mutual savings banks, cooperative banks, and credit unions as well as interest on bank deposits, bonds, tax refunds, etc. Interest also includes original issue discount on bonds and other evidences of indebtedness (see page 17 of Instructions). (List payers and amounts.)

QR Credit Union	55	00
ST Savings-Loan Assn	50	00
8% US Treasury note	2080	00
UV National Bank	50	00

Part II Dividend Income

3 If you received more than $400 in gross dividends (including capital gain distributions) and other distributions on stock, complete Part II (see Note below and page 17 of instructions). (List payers and amounts—write (H), (W), (J), for stock held by husband, wife, or jointly.)

ABC Co. (H)	80	00
DEF Co (H)	110	00
GHI Co (H)	30	00
KLM Co (H)	90	00
NOP Fund - Div (H)	15	00
NOP Fund - Cap. Gain (H)	10	00

4 Total of line 3	335	00
5 Capital gain distributions (see page 18 of Instructions. Enter here and on Schedule D, line 7). See Note below	10	00
6 Nontaxable distributions (see page 18 of instructions) . . .		
7 Total (add lines 5 and 6)	10	00
8 Dividends before exclusion (subtract line 7 from line 4). Enter here and on Form 1040, line 10a	325	00

otal interest income. Enter here and n Form 1040, line 9 . . . . **2235 00**

e: If you received capital gain distributions and do not need Schedule D to report any other gains or losses or to compute the alternative tax, do not file that schedule. Instead, enter 50 percent of capital gain distributions on Form 1040, line 15.

B

Part III Foreign Accounts and Foreign Trusts

If you are required to list interest in Part I or dividends in Part II, **OR** if you had a foreign account or were a grantor of, or a transferor to, a foreign trust, you must answer both questions in Part III. (See page 18 of Instructions.)

d you, at any time during the taxable year, have any interest in or signature or other authority over a bank, curities, or other financial account in a foreign country (except in a U.S. military banking facility operated by a S. financial institution)? . . . . ☐ **Yes** ☐ **No**

"Yes," see page 3 of instructions.

ere you the grantor of, or transferor to, a foreign trust during any taxable year, which foreign trust was in ing during the current taxable year, whether or not you have any beneficial interest in such trust? . . . ☐ **Yes** ☐ **No**

"Yes," you may be required to file Forms 3520, 3520-A, or 926.

Thus, his total interest income came to $2,235. He posted the information from Table 27-4 on Schedule B, Part I, and the total of $2,235 he entered on Form 1040, line 9. As you note, line 9 states: "If over $400, attach Schedule B."

Reporting Sales or Exchange of Property / Tom reported a profit on his first round-trip stock transaction. He had bought 100 shares of his WX Corporation at 18⅜ and sold it at 23⅛. The fact that it was held in his portfolio for more than nine months permitted him to report it as long-term capital gain in Schedule D, line 6 (Figure 27-5). This meant that his tax on the profit would be no more than half what it would have been if he had held it nine months or less.[14]

The capital gain of ten dollars from his 100 shares of the NOP Fund is listed in line 7, Figure 27-4. The capital gains of such regulated investment companies are all long-term, regardless of how long the recipient may have owned stock in the fund.

Tom's total net gain (line 13) amounted to $472, as indicated in Part II, Schedule D. He posted this total to Part III, line 14. He then entered 50 percent of line 14 on line 15a. Next, Tom subtracted line 15a from 14 and entered the amount of $236 on line 15b and line 30, Form 1040. As the $236 was the only income he received (other than wages, dividends and interest), this was the amount he entered on line 14, Form 1040. Then Tom and Tricia computed their adjusted gross income (line 31), which added up to $24,696.

Itemizing Deductions / Tricia and Tom knew that their itemized deductions would not equal the standard deduction—(zero bracket amount)—$3,200. They had some subtractions but could not take advantage of the two areas that provided the largest potential: interest on mortgage payments and taxes on real estate. And as they had no car, there were no deductions for gasoline taxes or interest paid on an auto loan. However, they considered it good practice to fill out the appropriate form, for in later years this could mean a sizable saving.

Their computations on itemized expenses were listed in Schedule A (Figure 27-6). The total figure amounted to $1,506 (line 40, Schedule A), in contrast to the $3,200 standard deduction.

Computing Taxes Due / The Tamllits were now ready to determine the sum due the U.S. Government by April 17, 1978. They used the reverse side of Form 1040 to compute their taxes. First they listed their adjusted gross income from line 31, Form 1040. They did not itemize their deductions so this left them with a

---

[14]When your income exceeds twenty thousand dollars you should begin seeking out long-term capital gains, since money received from this source is taxed at a maximum rate of 25 percent. Beginning in 1978, property must be held for more than twelve months in order to be eligible for the long term capital gains tax.

Figure 27-5   The Tamllits' capital gains, 1977 (Schedule D, Form 1040).

SCHEDULE D (Form 1040) Department of the Treasury Internal Revenue Service	**Capital Gains and Losses** (Examples of property to be reported on this Schedule are gains and losses on stocks, bonds, and similar investments, and gains (but not losses) on personal assets such as a home or jewelry.) ► Attach to Form 1040. ► See Instructions for Schedule D (Form 1040).	**1977**

Name(s) as shown on Form 1040	Social security number
Tom T. and Tricia T. Tamllits	000 : 00 : 0000

Part I   Short-term Capital Gains and Losses—Assets Held Not More Than 9 Months   **D**

a. Kind of property and description (Example, 100 shares of "Z" Co.)	b. Date acquired (Mo., day, yr.)	c. Date sold (Mo., day, yr.)	d. Gross sales price	e. Cost or other basis, as adjusted (see Instruction F) and expense of sale	f. Gain or (loss) (d less e)

2 Enter your share of net short-term gain or (loss) from partnerships and fiduciaries	**2**		
3 Enter net gain or (loss), combine lines 1 and 2	**3**		
4 Short-term capital loss carryover attributable to years beginning after 1969 (see Instruction I)	**4**	(	)
5 Net short-term gain or (loss), combine lines 3 and 4	**5**		

Part II   Long-term Capital Gains and Losses—Assets Held More Than 9 Months

a. Kind of property and description	b. Date acquired	c. Date sold	d. Gross sales price	e. Cost or other basis	f. Gain or (loss)
Security—100 sh WV Corp	Feb 20, 1977	Dec 21, 1977	2,350.00	1,888.00	462 00

7 Capital gain distributions	**7**	10	00
8 Enter gain, if applicable, from Form 4797, line 4(a)(1) (see Instruction A)	**8**		
9 Enter your share of net long-term gain or (loss) from partnerships and fiduciaries	**9**		
10 Enter your share of net long-term gain from small business corporations (Subchapter S)	**10**		
11 Net gain or (loss), combine lines 6 through 10	**11**	472	00
12 Long-term capital loss carryover attributable to years beginning after 1969 (see Instruction I)	**12**	(	)
13 Net long-term gain or (loss), combine lines 11 and 12	**13**	472	00

Part III   Summary of Parts I and II (If You Have Capital Loss Carryovers From Years Beginning Before 1970, Do Not Complete This Part. See Form 4798 Instead.)

14 Combine lines 5 and 13, and enter the net gain or (loss) here	**14**	472	00
15 If line 14 shows a gain—			
a Enter 50% of line 13 or 50% of line 14, whichever is smaller (see Part IV for computation of alternative tax). Enter zero if there is a loss or no entry on line 13	**15a**	236	00
Note: If the amount you enter on line 15a is other than zero, you may be liable for minimum tax. See Form 4625 and instructions.			
b Subtract line 15a from line 14. Enter here and on Form 1040, line 14	**15b**	236	00
16 If line 14 shows a loss—			
a Enter one of the following amounts: (i) If line 5 is zero or a net gain, enter 50% of line 14; (ii) If line 13 is zero or a net gain, enter line 14; or, (iii) If line 5 and line 13 are net losses, enter amount on line 5 added to 50% of amount on line 13	**16a**		
b Enter here and enter as a (loss) on Form 1040, line 14, the smallest of: (i) The amount on line 16a; (ii) $2,000 ($1,000 if married and filing a separate return); or, (iii) Taxable income, as adjusted (see Instruction J)	**16b**	(	)
Note: If the amount on line 16a is larger than the loss shown on line 16b, complete Part V to determine Post-1969 Capital Loss Carryovers from 1977 to 1978.			

Figure 27-6 The Tamllits' itemized deductions, 1977 (Schedule A, Form 1040).

Schedules A&B—Itemized Deductions AND Interest and Dividend Income

(Form 1040)
Department of the Treasury
Internal Revenue Service

▶ Attach to Form 1040. ▶ See Instructions for Schedules A and B (Form 1040).

1977

Name(s) as shown on Form 1040

Tom T. and Tricia T. Tomllits

Your social security number

000 : 00 : 0000

Schedule A Itemized Deductions (Schedule B is on back)

Medical and Dental Expenses (not compensated by insurance or otherwise) (See page 14 of Instructions.)

1 One-half (but not more than $150) of insurance premiums for medical care. (Be sure to include in line 10 below) . . .	120	00
2 Medicine and drugs	39	00
3 Enter 1% of line 31, Form 1040 . . .	246	96
4 Subtract line 3 from line 2. Enter difference (if less than zero, enter zero) . .	-0-	
5 Enter balance of insurance premiums for medical care not entered on line 1 . .	120	00
6 Enter other medical and dental expenses:		
a Doctors, dentists, nurses, etc.	161	00
b Hospitals		
c Other (itemize—include hearing aids, dentures, eyeglasses, transportation, etc.) ▶ *Eyeglasses*	47	00
7 Total (add lines 4 through 6c) . . .	328	00
8 Enter 3% of line 31, Form 1040 . . .	740	88
9 Subtract line 8 from line 7 (if less than zero, enter zero)	-0-	
10 Total (add lines 1 and 9). Enter here and on line 33 . . . . . . ▶	120	00

Taxes (See page 14 of Instructions.)

11 State and local income	362	00
12 Real estate		
13 State and local gasoline (see gas tax tables)		
14 General sales (see sales tax tables) . .	324	00
15 Personal property		
16 Other (itemize) ▶		
17 Total (add lines 11 through 16). Enter here and on line 34 . . . . . ▶	686	00

Interest Expense (See page 16 of Instructions.)

18 Home mortgage		
19 Other (itemize) ▶		
20 Total (add lines 18 and 19). Enter here and on line 35 . . . . ▶		

Contributions (See page 16 of Instructions for examples.)

21 a Cash contributions for which you have receipts, cancelled checks or other written evidence	700	0
b Other cash contributions. List donees and amounts. ▶		
22 Other than cash (see page 16 of instructions for required statement)		
23 Carryover from prior years		
24 Total contributions (add lines 21a through 23). Enter here and on line 36 . . ▶	700	0

Casualty or Theft Loss(es) (See page 16 of Instructions.)

25 Loss before insurance reimbursement . .		
26 Insurance reimbursement		
27 Subtract line 26 from line 25. Enter difference (if less than zero, enter zero) .		
28 Enter $100 or amount on line 27, whichever is smaller		
29 Casualty or theft loss (subtract line 28 from line 27). Enter here and on line 37 . ▶		

Miscellaneous Deductions (See page 16 of Instructions.)

30 Union dues		
31 Other (itemize) ▶		
32 Total (add lines 30 and 31). Enter here and on line 38 . . . . . . ▶		

Summary of Itemized Deductions (See page 17 of Instructions.) **A**

33 Total medical and dental—line 10 . .	120	0
34 Total taxes—line 17	686	0
35 Total interest—line 20		
36 Total contributions—line 24	700	0
37 Casualty or theft loss(es)—line 29 . .		
38 Total miscellaneous—line 32		
39 Total deductions (add lines 33 through 38). ▶	1506	0
40 If you checked Form 1040, box: 2 or 5, enter $3,200 1 or 4, enter $2,200 3, enter $1,600	3200	0
41 Excess itemized deductions (subtract line 40 from line 39). Enter here and on Form 1040, line 33. (If line 40 is more than line 39 see "Who MUST Itemize Deductions" on page 11 of the Instructions.) . . ▶		

Source: Internal Revenue Service, Department of the Treasury.

Figure 27-7 The Tamllits' 1978 estimated tax worksheet and declaration (Voucher 1).

1978 Estimated Tax Worksheet (Keep for your records—Do Not File)

Name	Social Security Number
Tom T. and Tricia T. Tamllits	000 00 0000

1 Enter amount of Adjusted Gross Income expected in taxable year		25,796.00
2 a If you expect to itemize deductions, enter the estimated total of those deductions. If you do not expect to itemize deductions, omit lines 2a and b, and enter zero on line 2c. (See Caution in Instruction 12.) .		
b Enter { $3,200 if married filing a joint return (or qualifying widow(er)) / $2,200 if single (or head of household) / $1,600 if married filing a separate return }		
c Subtract line 2b from line 2a (if zero or less, enter zero)		-0-
3 Subtract line 2c from line 1. (See Instruction 12)		25,796.00
4 Exemptions ($750 for each, including additional exemptions for age and blindness)		1,500.00
5 Subtract line 4 from line 3. This is your estimated taxable income		24,296.00
6 Tax. (All filers compute tax on the amount on line 5 by using Tax Rate Schedule X, Y or Z from the 1977 Form 1040 instructions.)		4,730.72
7 General tax credit (see Instruction 13)		180.00
8 Subtract line 7 from line 6. Add to this amount any additional taxes from Instruction 14		4,550.72
9 Credits (credit for the elderly, credit for child care expenses, investment credit, etc.)		
10 Subtract line 9 from line 8		4,550.72
11 Tax from recomputing a prior year investment credit and work incentive (WIN) credit		
12 Estimate of 1978 self-employment income $.................................; if $17,700 or more, enter $1,433.70, if less, multiply the amount by .081. If joint declaration and both have self-employment income, make separate computations . .		
13 Tax on premature distributions from a self-employed retirement plan or an individual retirement arrangement		
14 Add lines 10 through 13		4,550.72
15 (a) Earned income credit (see Instruction 15)		
(b) Estimated income tax withheld and to be withheld during 1978	3,332.00	
(c) Credit for Federal tax on gasoline, special fuels, and lubricating oil (see Form 4136)		
Total (add lines 15(a), (b) and (c))		3,332.00
16 Estimated tax (subtract line 16 from line 14). Enter here and in Block A on declaration-voucher. If $100 or more, file the declaration-voucher, if less, no declaration is required		1,218.72
Computation of installments— If declaration is due to be filed on: { April 17, 1978, enter ¼ . . . . of line 17 here and / June 15, 1978, enter ⅓ . . . on line 1 of original / September 15, 1978, enter ½ . . and subsequent / January 15, 1979, enter amount . . declaration-vouchers }		304.68

Note: *If your estimated tax should change during the year, you may use the amended computation on page 1 to determine amended amounts to enter on your declaration-voucher.*

2

Detach here

1040-ES
Department of the Treasury
Internal Revenue Service

Estimated Tax Declaration–Voucher for Individuals—1978
(To be used for making declaration and payment)

Voucher **1**
(Calendar Year—Due April 17, 1978)

	B. Overpayment from last year credited to estimated tax for this year	If fiscal year taxpayer, see Instruction 11.
Estimated tax for the year ending **Dec. 19 78** (month and year)		• Do not file this declaration–voucher if your total estimated tax for the year is less than $100.00.
1,218.72	$	Return this voucher with check or money order payable to the Internal Revenue Service. For where to file your declaration–voucher, see Instruction 4.
amount of this installment . . . ▶	$304.68	
amount of overpayment credit from last year (all or part) applied to this installment (see Instruction 9) . . ▶		
amount of this installment payment subtract line 2 from line 1) . . . . ▶	$ 304.68	
e this original declaration–voucher even if line 3 is o.		

Your social security number	Spouse's number, if joint declaration
000 00 0000	000 00 0000
First name and middle initial (of both spouses if joint declaration)	Last name
Tom T. and Tricia T.	Tam llits

gn ▶ *Tom T. Tamllits*
Your Signature

ere ▶ *Tricia T. Tamllits*
Spouse's signature (if joint declaration)

Address (Number and street)
121 Richton Ave.

City, State, and ZIP code
New Orleans, La. 70122

Please type or print

urce: Internal Revenue Service, Department of the Treasury.

tax table income of $24,696. Next they turned to Tax Table B. Tom and Tricia used column 2 of this table which applied to "Married Filing Jointly and Qualifying Widow(er)s." Their tax came to $4,193, which they entered on lines 35 and 37. As they had no credits or other taxes they posted the $4,193 on lines 47 and 54. Their federal income tax for the year 1977 amounted to 17 percent of their gross income! From this $4,193 they deducted the amount withheld by their employers (line 55). They found that their balance due was $1,194.72; this payment was required by April 17, 1978. Tricia and Tom had one more form to complete.

Determining Estimated Tax / Tom and Tricia learned from the instructions on the tax form that they must file a "Declaration of Estimated Tax for Individuals" (Form 1040-ES). The purpose of this filing was to ensure their paying taxes on income other than their salary, on which the taxes were withheld by their employer. This declaration, they read, is required of every citizen of the United States if the total estimated tax (line 17 of the worksheet) is $100 or more and the person:[15]

1. Can reasonably expect to receive more than $500 from sources other than wages subject to withholding; or,
2. Can reasonably expect gross income to exceed—
   a. $20,000 for a single individual, a head of a household or a qualifying widow or widower;
   b. $20,000 for married individual entitled to file a joint declaration with spouse, but only if the spouse has not received wages for the taxable year;
   c. $10,000 for a married individual entitled to file a joint declaration with his spouse, but only if both spouses received wages for the taxable year; or,
   d. $5,000 for a married individual not entitled to file a joint declaration with his spouse.

Tom and Tricia first filled out the estimated-tax worksheet (Figure 27-7). Tricia's employer had given her a $1,000 raise, so their combined salary would be $25,796 in 1978. They expected their additional investments in 1978 to increase their other income by $100. After taking their exemptions and deciding not to itemize their deductions, they listed their taxable income as $24,296. Next, they found their tax ($4,730.72) prior to the $180 tax credit and checked their records to find the amount their employers would be withholding ($3,332.00).

[15]Also every resident of the United States, Puerto Rico, Virgin Islands, Guam and American Samoa.

Tom and Tricia knew that they must file their estimated-tax declaration on or before April 17, 1978. Their estimated tax could be paid in full with the declaration or in equal installments on or before April 17, 1978; June 15, 1978; September 15, 1978; and January 15, 1979. They decided to pay their estimated tax quarterly. "Why not keep our money working by drawing interest or dividends instead of paying in advance? We'll wait until the due date in each instance," they said. The couple made their check for $304.68 payable to "Internal Revenue Service" and posted the amount on Voucher 1, Form 1040-ES (Figure 27-7). They put their first installment in the mail on April 17, 1978.

Tom and Tricia realized that there may be a penalty for failure to make estimated payments on time. By checking Form 1040-ES they found:

> A penalty may be imposed by law for underpayment of estimated tax installments. the penalty does not apply if each installment is paid when due and (a) is at least 80% (66⅔% for farmers and fishermen) of the amount due (exclusive of minimum tax on items of tax preference) on the basis of the tax shown on the return for the taxable year, (b) is at least as much as would have been paid if based upon the tax (including self-employment tax) shown on your 1977 return, or (c) is based on a tax computed at 1977 rates, using the personal exemptions allowed for 1978, but otherwise on the basis of the facts shown on your 1977 income tax return and the law applicable for 1977. For additional exceptions in unusual cases see Form 2210. Farmers and fishermen see Form 2210F.

Tom and Tricia were now finished computing their tax returns. They agreed that it had not been as difficult as they had anticipated but realized that they had been greatly aided by their good record keeping. They vowed to keep their records up-to-date so that they would be able to file as rapidly next year.

OTHER FEDERAL INCOME TAX CONSIDERATIONS

Now let us look at other aspects of the federal income tax that we have not yet discussed.

Returns for Married Couples

As we have seen, married couples have a choice in filing their returns. One method, used by the Tamllits, is to file a joint return, in which husband and wife combine their incomes and deductions. To file a joint return you must be married, citizens of the United States and both using the same accounting period. Marriage status is determined as of the last day of the year, so there may be a tax advantage to marrying in December.

505

The joint return has a lower tax rate, which usually results in a tax saving. However, for married taxpayers who are domiciled in a community-property state,[16] there may be a tax saving if they file separate returns. In order to determine which alternative is most advantageous for you, compute your tax on both a joint and a separate basis. The IRS has prepared a worksheet that provides a *comprehensive example*[17] in which, by filing separate returns, a married couple saves $25.40.

Separate returns can often be advantageous in common-law states, under circumstances similar to those described for married taxpayers in community-property states. In either case, the primary savings is made in the medical-expense deduction.

On separate returns, the method of claiming deductions must be the same. Therefore, if one of the two persons claims the standard deduction, the other must also use the standard deduction.

Joint Return for a Widow or Widower with a Dependent Child

A widow or widower may file a joint return under the following circumstances:

1. her (his) husband (wife) must have died within the two preceding tax years;
2. she (he) must have been entitled to file a joint return with her (his) husband (wife) the year of his (her) death;
3. she (he) must have not remarried;
4. she (he) must have a child or stepchild who qualifies as a dependent;
5. she (he) must make her (his) home the principal abode of the dependent child, except for temporary absenses for vacation and school.

Unmarried Head of Household

There are special tax rates for a person who can meet the tests for being an "unmarried head of household." To use these tax rates, you must, on December 31, be single or legally separated, and qualify for category 1 or 2 below:

1. You have paid more than half the cost of keeping up a home which was the main home of your father or mother, whom you can claim as a dependent (you do not have to live with that parent).
2. You have paid more than half the cost of keeping up your home which, except for temporary absences for vacation, school or such, was lived in all year by one of the following:
   a. Your unmarried child, grandchild, foster child or stepchild. This person did not have to be your dependent;

---

[16]Arizona, California, Idaho, Louisiana, Nevada, New Mexico, Texas and Washington.
[17]*Community Property and the Federal Income Tax,* Publication 555 (10-73), p. 7.

b. Any other relative you can claim as a dependent (check with the IRS to determine eligibility), provided he or she is not your dependent under a multiple-support agreement (a situation in which two or more taxpayers support the relative, with no one party providing more than half the support).

Rental Income

If you should own a home or any other property and decide to rent it, the income must be reported in Schedule E (income from pensions, annuities, rents, royalties, partnerships, estates, trusts, and so on), Form 1040. Any expenses incurred from rental property can be deducted in the schedule in determining adjusted gross income, even if you use the standard deduction. The expenses that are deductible from gross rents are divided into two groups: depreciation, and other expenses (repairs and such).

The Depreciation Factor / Depreciation is allowed only on property you use for income purposes. You cannot depreciate your own home if you do not rent out some portion of it. The total depreciation on a property may not exceed the cost of the property. Let us look at several methods of determining depreciation.

The most frequently used method is called straight-line depreciation. The useful life of the property to be depreciated must be determined, and this amount of time is divided into the cost of the property less salvage value. This gives you the cost per unit of time, usually a year, and this cost is deductible from income each year until the cost is recovered.

Another method of determining depreciation is known as declining balance. A uniform rate is applied each year to the remaining cost of the property as determined at the beginning of each year. But depreciation must end when the unrecovered cost is reduced to salvage value. This depreciation is subtracted from the cost of the property before figuring the next year's depreciation.

Taking the sum of the year's digits is a third common method of depreciation. The deduction for each year is computed by multiplying the cost or other basis of the property (reduced by the estimated salvage value) by the number of years of useful life remaining, and dividing the product by the sum of all digits corresponding to the years of the useful life of the property. In the case of a four-year life, this sum would be $10(4+3+2+1)$. For the first year, four-tenths of the cost reduced by the estimated salvage value would be permitted; for the second year, three-tenths; for the third, two-tenths; and for the final year, one-tenth.

There are other depreciation methods, and you may use any consistent technique that does not result at the end of the year in accumulated allowances greater than the total of those that would have resulted from the use of the declining-balance method. This limitation applies only during the first two-thirds of the property's useful life.

NONFEDERAL TAXES

Although the federal income tax normally is the heaviest tax imposed upon an individual, there are other taxes that reduce the dollars available to you for savings and expenditures. You should be familiar with these taxes in order to arrive at sound money-management decisions.

Recently an executive with a major oil company had an opportunity to move to New York City at a 25-percent increase in salary. He decided against the move, however, after weighing all financial costs including taxes. "In my present place of residence," he noted, "I pay no state or city tax. My property tax is minimal and we have only a small sales tax on nonfood and clothing items. I would actually be losing money—about 10 percent—if I relocated."

Let us examine each of the taxes cited by the canny executive, beginning with state and local income tax.[18]

STATE AND LOCAL INCOME TAX

Each state independently determines the tax load it will place on its residents. Some states have no state income tax at all, while others impose a heavy burden on the wealthy. State taxes, like federal, are progressive—that is, the higher your salary, the larger the tax. Table 27-5 gives the rate charged a single person in one state (Louisiana) based on net income.

TABLE 27-5 Various Rates Charged a Single Person in One State Based on the Adjusted Gross Income*

Income	Rate for Single Person
	Amount of Tax
$10,000	$ 703
20,000	1,033
30,000	1,271
40,000	1,484
50,000	1,668
58,000 and above	1,785 plus 2.64% of Federal Income Tax in Excess of $57,000

*The present tax rate imposed by the state of Louisiana is determined by the amount reported on the Federal Income Tax return.

In addition to the state tax, some taxpayers must also pay an income tax to their municipalities. or the state may have no tax but the community might. This is the case in Ohio, where towns like Athens have an income tax. Athens imposes

[18]The do-it-yourself approach and other general concepts recommended for preparing your federal tax returns apply to state and local income taxes as well.

an income tax of 1 percent on all salaries, wages, commissions and other compensation earned or accrued each year. This tax applies to all residents of the city, and to nonresidents who received income from organizations in Athens. The purpose of the Athens tax is to provide funds for general municipal operations, maintenance of equipment, purchase of new equipment, extension, enlargement and improvement of municipal services and facilities, and capital improvements.

New York is an example of a state where taxpayers residing in certain cities must pay both state and local taxes.

PROPERTY TAX

Depending on the area, this tax may be imposed on real property only; on real and personal property; or on personal property only. The most popular local tax is that levied on real property—your home. The amount of tax depends on the value placed on your property and the assessment rate. This may vary from community to community in a state. In the city of New Orleans, for example, the valuation placed on property may approximate 10 percent. Thus, a $100,000 home may be assessed at $10,000. I say "may" because people have been known to "confer" with their assessor and have the valuation reduced. There is also a $2,000 homestead exemption for nonveterans and a $5,000 exemption for veterans. The assessment rate applied to the valuation is $43.70 per thousand.

A community adjacent to New Orleans, however, has a much lower assessment. In fact, most of the people in that area pay virtually no property tax on their homes.

In addition to, or in lieu of, the real-estate property tax there may be taxes imposed on other possessions such as your car and household furniture. Some states tax intangibles like stocks and bonds.

SALES TAX

Sales-tax revenue may be shared by your state and local community. For instance, the state may charge 3 percent and the city 2 percent; an adjacent community may impose only 1 percent. This is called a regressive tax because the same rate is charged to everyone, regardless of income. Some states impose the tax on all items, while others may exempt certain items like food and medicine.

OTHER TAXES

Another category of taxes imposed by federal and/or state governments, the aforementioned "hidden taxes," are included in the price you pay for items such as gasoline, liquor and cigarettes. You will also be asked to pay import taxes on merchandise you bring in from foreign countries.

28
RETIREMENT, WILLS & TRUSTS

RETIREMENT

Retirement may be defined as withdrawal from the active work force, normally owing to advancing years. The decision to retire is a complex one, involving many factors. In keeping with the scope of this book, however, we will limit our discussion here to the financial aspects of retirement. For further information on retirement matters, I recommend that you visit your local library or bookstore.

Ideally, you should begin to plan the financial aspects of your retirement prior to accepting your first job. From the beginning, thought should be given to when you wish to retire and whether the company you select has a pension program that corresponds with your desires. Coupled with this is the necessity to begin a sound investment program early in life which can provide both the additional income needed at retirement and a healthy estate. If you have given adequate long-range attention to the development and maintenance of a lifetime personal-finance program, you should be able to answer the question "Will I have sufficient yearly income to support my family once I stop working?" with a confident "Yes." As stressed throughout this book, retirement considerations are an important part of the total responsibility of a successful money manager.

SOURCES OF RETIREMENT INCOME

Income From Pensions

Retirement may be forty to forty-five years away for the current college graduate. However, some organizations provide pensions after twenty years of service. For example, the army has a program has a program that could give a newly commissioned second lieutenant the promise of retirement at age forty-one, assuming that he entered the service upon graduation. His pension would be 50 percent of his base pay. If he remained another ten years, the pension would rise to 75 percent.

In contrast to the military, there are firms that require people to remain at work until age fifty-five or sixty prior to receiving payments, and maximum benefits may not accrue until age sixty-five or seventy. Payments may vary markedly from 10 to 80 percent of an employee's salary in the year prior to retirement. Factors that may be considered in determining the dollar amount include length of service, age and average annual pay. Other things being equal, the higher the salary, the higher the retirement payment.

Many organizations have based their maximum benefits upon retirement at age of sixty-five. This means that the retiree would be simultaneously eligible for the maximum Social Security payments. If you retire in your forties or fifties, however, you must wait to receive Social Security benefits until age sixty-two.[1] A number of corporate and government pensions like Social Security (see Chapter 17) work on an inflation-proof system—that is, the payments increase to recipients in consonance with a rise in the Consumer Price Index (CPI). In years ahead, it can be expected that this will be increasingly the case. Furthermore, the amount of the pension (combined with Social Security) should provide an adequate standard of living in some cases. A *Barron's* article stated:

> The United Steel Workers recently won retirement benefits for some members which rival the pie-in-the-sky dreams of old-time labor leaders. Welcome as they are to retiring workers, trying to cope with inflation, they also foreshadow sharp boosts in pension costs for much of U.S. business. Thanks to the first cost-of-living clause negotiated in a major industrial contract, USW's can and aluminum members will receive annual pension hikes amounting to 65% of any rise in the Consumer Price Index. Including Social Security benefits, they will be guaranteed 85% of their on-the-job pay. . . .
>
> Although can and aluminum workers account for only 100,000 of USW's 1.4-million membership, President I. W. Abel indicates that similar demands will be made in other contracts, notably for the 520,000 steel workers. In fact, cost-of-living pensions boosts will be key talking-points in labor negotiations this year involving seven million union members. . . .
>
> Not only does President Abel expect the settlement to become standard throughout the industry, but John Tomakyo, director of the union's pension operations, also calls the 65% cost-of-living escalator merely "a foot in the door. We'll be back in three years trying to improve that coverage."[2]

Rising inflation has been the primary impetus behind the increasing demand for annual raises in retirement benefits. The move from a 2.3 percent inflation rate in the sixties to a peak of 11 percent in 1974 caused considerable hardship for many of those with fixed incomes.

Income From Fixed and Growth Investments

In addition to certain pensions, and all Social Security payments, there are other sources of income capable of keeping pace with rising costs. These sources include good real estate, profitable hobbies, quality common stock and

[1]The Social Security payments are 20% less if taken at age 62 than the full benefits would be if one waited until age 65.
[2]Dana L. Thomas. "Escalating Pensions," *Barron's,* March 18, 1974.

home ownership. The importance of acquiring growth investments during your working years has been stressed throughout this book. However, in accordance with my concept of diversification, your preretirement portfolio should also include prime-quality fixed-income holdings, such as U.S. Treasury notes and bank savings accounts. In the event of a depression or major recession, these investments would continue paying their annual return, and the principal would remain intact. In contrast, the growth holdings may decline markedly and income therefore shrink drastically.

Another advantage to building up substantial savings while you work is that you may be forced to retire prior to the time you anticipated. A chilling CBS-TV program pointed out that the decision as to date of retirement may not always rest with the employee.[3] To illustrate this point, Mike Wallace presented the case of a man who had wanted to retire at age sixty-five but whose corporation decided to provide his pension five years earlier. The result: Instead of his anticipated $800-a-month check, he received only $125. On top of this, his profit-sharing program paid him $10,000 instead of the approximately $75,000 he had expected at sixty-five. The lack of Social Security payments, coupled with low income, forced him to re-enter the job market, but his age precluded finding a position. With only his unemployment compensation, meager pension and minimum savings to keep him afloat, life was very difficult from a financial standpoint.

Unfortunately, similar cases can be expected to occur in the future. Some companies retire people early in order to survive financially. Others have no pension program. A number of workers encounter health problems and are forced to quit before they are entitled to receive retirement benefits. Such situations point up the importance of having a sound personal-finance program that offers a variety of protective measures, including adequate insurance (health, accident, life and so on), appropriate savings accounts and growth investments.

RETIREMENT PLANS

In addition to the sources of income cited above, you may be eligible to profit from either the Individual Retirement Account (IRA) or the Keogh plan.

Individual Retirement Account

On September 2, 1974, President Ford signed into law the Employee Retirement Income Security Act of 1974. Included within this law was a provision establishing an Individual Retirement Account. The IRA passage enables taxpayers not covered by retirement plans provided by employers to establish their own tax-sheltered individual plan by deducting contributions on their

---

[3]CBS, "60 Minutes," with Mike Wallace and Morley Safer, March 24, 1974.

federal income-tax returns of 15 percent of compensation up to $1,500. The tax-sheltered advantage of IRA was pointed out in a *Barron's* article:[4]

> At the heart of IRA—on this score it differs not at all from other qualified pension programs—is the ability to put away pre-tax dollars and have them accumulate interest or appreciate during one's working years. The advantages can be demonstrated easily. To put aside the top $1,500 allowed under IRA (or 15% of earned income, whichever is less) on an after-tax basis for someone, say, in the 25% bracket, would require $2,000. But let's assume in both cases—using pre- and after-taxes—that one starts with $1,500. Under IRA, the full amount could be invested. The individual not establishing such an account, contrariwise, would have only $1,125 a year to set aside.
>
> ### Softening the Bite
>
> Hence, the person using after-tax dollars in 15 years would have accumulated a total of only $16,875. The IRA program, by contrast, over the same time span would have allowed some $22,500 to be paid into the fund. That's a gain of 33%. Moreover, it makes no allowance for the possibility that the money put aside under IRA, which is tax-deductible regardless of whether an individual itemizes his deductions or takes the standard deduction, may lower his tax bracket a notch or so. At the end of 25 years, the differences between the two methods of contributing are even more striking—$28,125 accumulated on the after-tax basis, and $9,375 more under IRA.
>
> But even that doesn't tell the full story, for it neglects the tax-sheltered aspect of IRA. Thus, if one factors in an 8% growth over 25 years, but also considers that dividend and interest would be subject to yearly taxes under a non-IRA program, the total worth of the account at the end of this period would be $66,780. Under IRA, the account accumulated at the same rate of gain, but because of the tax-shelter, would be worth $123,000 or $56,220 more.

In contrast to setting aside up to $1,500 annually, there is another provision of the Act that permits individuals who receive a lump sum from a company retirement program to reinvest the entire amount in an Individual Retirement Account. This sum remains tax-sheltered until distribution—which cannot begin until age fifty-nine and a half and must begin at age seventy and a half. At that time distributions are taxed at ordinary income rates.

Keogh Pension Program

The Employee Retirement Income Security Act of 1974 also authorized self-

---

[4]Anreder, Steven S. "Up the IRA," *Barron's*, March 17, 1975, p. 5.

employed individuals (lawyers, doctors, writers, composers, independent businessmen and such) to increase their deductible contributions from the lesser of $2,500, or 10 percent of earned net income, to the lesser of $7,500, or 15 percent of earned net income.

The beauty of the Keogh plan is the tax-shelter feature and the fact that you may be able to set aside up to $7,500. This tax-shelter feature means that the money saved annually, as well as future earnings or gains, are not subject to taxation until retirement. At that date, most people should be in a lower tax bracket.

A Cautionary Note / In my view both the IRA and Keogh plans can be advantageous to individuals who do not have other adequate retirement plans. However, keep in mind that you may want the latitude to invest money today with the freedom to change it tomorrow. IRA and Keogh preclude this flexibility.

CAN I AFFORD TO RETIRE?

In order to determine whether you are in an adequate financial position to retire, utilize the budgetary process presented in Chapter 2. First, prepare a balance sheet in a format similar to Table 28-1. Next, make up an income-and-

TABLE 28-1 Where I Will Stand at Retirement—December 31, 1983 (Age 55)

My worldly possessions:		
Cash on hand	$ 200	
Cash in checking account	2,000	
Cash in bank	10,000	
Cash in S&L association	10,000	
U.S. Treasury note	30,000	
Corporate stocks:		
Shares, ABC Co.	6,000	
Shares, DEF Co.	7,000	
Shares, GHI Co.	8,000	
Shares, JKL Co.	9,000	
Shares, PQR Co.	10,000	
Car	3,000	
Furniture	10,000	
Clothing	5,000	
Home	40,000	
		$150,200
My debts:		
Notes payable	$ 5,000	
Car payments	1,000	
Furniture payments	2,000	
Home mortgage	12,000	
		20,000
My true worth		$130,200

expense statement (Table 28-2). In my opinion, the time to prepare this detailed information is five years prior to your earliest planned retirement date. This will give you adequate time to be ready financially for the new challenges facing the retiree. If you try to draw up such a detailed statement much earlier, there may be too many unforeseen changes in your retirement plans to make it a valid working tool.

TABLE 28-2 My Estimated Income and Expenses in
First Year of Retirement—
January 1–December 31, 1984

Income:		
Pension	$10,000	
Social Security		
Veterans Administration benefits	600	
Earnings (part-time work)	1,000	
Annuity	600	
Interest	2,400	
Dividends	1,800	
Profitable hobby	500	
Real estate	2,400	
Total income, 1st year retirement		$19,300
Expenses:		
Home	$ 4,000	
Food	3,000	
Car	1,000	
College expenses	4,000	
Clothing	800	
Vacation and recreation	1,000	
Medical	1,200	
Taxes	4,000	
Total expenses, 1st year retirement		19,000
Savings		$ 300

Once the above two statements have been prepared, you can proceed to analyze them. Table 28-1 points out that "I" should be in satisfactory shape financially on retirement. He has $150,200 in worldly possessions and only $20,000 in debts. Thus, his true worth amounts to $130,200. A review of estimated income and expenses in the first year of retirement (Table 28-2) indicates that savings of $300 are anticipated. "I" has been generous in his estimate of expenses and allowed for a 7-percent annual rate of inflation in the five-year period prior to retirement. His budgeted expenses provide for his youngest son to enter the state university in 1984. Cost projections indicate that $4,000 should be adequate for the freshman year. His two other children are married and require no financial assistance.

The pension that "I" will receive is from a major corporation that has an excellent funded program. It is also protected by a sound insurance policy, and payments will rise in accordance with the CPI. Both his growth and fixed-

TABLE 28-3 My Long-Range Financial Retirement Program
(As of December 31, each year)

	1st year (55)	2nd year (56)	5th year (60)	10th year (65)	15th year (70)	20th year (75)	25th year (80)
My worldly possessions:							
Cash on hand	$ 200	$ 200	$ 200	$ 200	$ 200	$ 200	$ 200
Cash in checking account	2,000	2,000	2,000	2,000	2,000	2,000	2,000
Cash in bank	10,000	10,000	10,000	10,000	10,000	10,000	10,000
Cash in S&L association	10,000	10,000	10,000	10,000	10,000	10,000	10,000
U.S. Treasury notes	30,000	30,000	30,000	30,000	30,000	30,000	30,000
Corporate stocks:							
Shares, ABC Co.	6,000	6,300	7,296	9,306	11,880	15,162	19,320
Shares, DEF Co.	7,000	7,350	8,512	10,851	13,860	17,689	22,540
Shares, GHI Co.	8,000	8,400	9,728	12,408	15,840	20,202	25,760
Shares, JKL Co.	9,000	9,450	10,944	13,959	17,820	22,743	28,980
Shares, PQR Co.	10,000	10,500	12,160	15,510	19,800	25,270	32,200
Shares, STU Co.							8,853
Car	3,000	3,000	3,000	3,000	3,000	3,000	3,000
Furniture	10,000	10,000	10,000	10,000	10,000	10,000	10,000
Clothing	5,000	5,000	5,000	5,000	5,000	5,000	5,000
Home	40,000	40,000	40,000	40,000	40,000	40,000	40,000
Total	$150,200	$152,200	$158,840	$172,234	$189,400	$211,266	$247,853
My debts:							
Notes payable	5,000	5,000	5,000	5,000			
Car payments	1,000	700	700	700			
Furniture payments	2,000	2,000	2,000	2,000			
Home mortgage	12,000	12,000	12,000	12,000	10,760	1,397	
Total	$ 20,000	$ 19,700	$ 19,700	$ 19,700	$ 10,760	$ 1,397	0
My true worth	$130,200	$132,500	$139,140	$152,534	$178,640	$209,869	$247,853

TABLE 28-3 (Cont'd.)

	1st year (55)	2nd year (56)	5th year (60)	10th year (65)	15th year (70)	20th year (75)	25th year (80)
My estate:							
Insurance	$ 30,000	$ 30,000	$ 30,000	$ 30,000	$ 30,000	$ 30,000	$ 30,000
Total estate	$160,200	$162,500	$169,140	$182,534	$208,640	$239,869	$277,853
My income:							
Pensions	$ 10,000	$ 10,500	$ 12,160	$ 15,510	$ 19,800	$ 25,270	$ 32,200
Social Security				8,000	9,728	12,408	15,840
Veterans Administration benefits	600	630	730	931	1,188	1,516	1,932
Earnings (part-time work)	1,000	1,000	1,000	1,000	1,000	1,000	1,000
Annuity	600	600	600	600	600	600	600
Interest	2,400	2,400	2,400	2,400	2,400	2,400	2,400
Dividends	1,800	1,890	2,189	2,792	3,564	4,549	5,796
Profitable hobby	500	500	500	500	500	500	500
Real estate	2,400	2,400	2,400	2,400	2,400	2,400	2,400
Total	$ 19,300	$ 19,920	$ 21,979	$ 34,133	$ 41,180	$ 50,643	$ 62,668
My expenses:							
Home	4,000	4,200	4,864	6,204	7,920	10,108	12,880
Food	3,000	3,150	3,648	4,653	5,940	7,581	9,660
Car	1,000	1,050	1,216	1,551	1,980	2,527	3,220
College expenses	4,000	4,200	4,864				
Clothing	800	840	973	1,241	1,584	2,022	2,576
Vacation and recreation	1,000	1,050	1,216	1,551	1,980	2,527	3,220
Medical	1,200	1,260	1,459	1,861	2,376	3,032	3,864
Taxes	4,000	4,186	4,659	8,132	10,037	12,596	15,810
Total	$ 19,000	$ 19,936	$ 22,899	$ 25,193	$ 31,817	$ 40,393	$ 51,230
My savings	$ 300	$ 16	$ 920	$ 8,940	$ 9,363	$ 10,250	$ 11,438

income securities are of prime quality. Accordingly, the yearly income can be depended upon unless a major disaster occurs.

Once "I" has determined that he will have sufficient financial resources to meet retirement expenses the first year, he can proceed to develop his long-range retirement plan (Table 28-3—the third step in the budget process. Let us look at how "I" went about it. He decided to play it safe and go beyond the normal life expectancy for himself and his wife. His primary concern was whether sufficient funds would be available for them to maintain an adequate living standard for the next twenty-five years. An analysis of Table 28-3 indicates that not only can "I" meet all expenses each year from estimated income, but throughout the twenty-five-year-projection his net worth will increase. Thus, the estate for his heirs and for charity will rise with each passing year. Likewise, if he and/or his wife live well beyond the projected period, they should have no financial problems.

Estimating Relocation Costs

In preparing your retirement financial statements, adequate funds should be provided in the event that you decide to relocate. Allow for moving expenses, new furnishings and perhaps investment in land on which to build a home. Be sure to check with care any land purchase. *Never buy without seeing the real estate in question first.* People in cold climates often plan to settle one day in a distant locality like sunny Florida or Arizona. Some buy land from advertisements or from salesmen in their own area without visiting the property or having any idea of its true value. The following story points out the importance of a personal look:

> The Federal Trade Commission tentatively adopted a consent order barring GAC Corp. from continuing what the FTC alleges are deceptive means to sell worthless land to unsuspecting buyers in Florida and Arizona.
>
> The agreed-to-order would force GAC, one of the nation's biggest land developers, to refund money to some customers and to give others a chance to exchange what the FTC considers useless land for better GAC property. Overall, the FTC said, the arrangement could cost GAC more than $17 million.
>
> The regulatory agency said in Washington the settlement is part of the FTC's nationwide investigation into deceptive land sales. J. Thomas Rosch, director of the FTC's Bureau of Consumer Protection, said about 30 other companies are under scrutiny.
>
> Mr. Rosch said many persons bought GAC land sight unseen, and FTC investigation later found much of the land was under water. . . .
>
> The consent order says GAC must warn customers of such hazards as the "uncertainty of the future value of the land" and the "difficulty of reselling it." Sales contracts would have to suggest that the prospective buyer consult a real estate professional, the FTC said.

It said much of the land sold isn't "an excellent investment involving little or no financial risk to purchasers," as claimed. Furthermore, the agency said, GAC salesmen frequently would "unfairly solicit the signing of contracts at dinner parties and other sales gatherings" where purchasers "won't read or understand completely" the terms of the contracts.[5]

Computing Retirement Housing Costs

It is extremely important to estimate your total housing costs upon retirement. This is particularly true if you plan to move to another area. Here is a tale of woe involving one retired couple, who contacted me after my recent appearance on a Miami radio program[6] and related the following story:

"We sold our business in Chicago, in 1975, and decided to move to Florida. Our total proceeds of $200,000 were invested in U.S. Treasury bonds. Our income from bonds, social security and a small annuity amounted to $20,000. We thought this would permit us to live well in the Palm Beach-Miami area. We selected an apartment that advertised: 'Come to Florida's gold coast and live in our one-bedroom apartment for $399.' This price seemed perfect for our pocketbook. Innocents that we were, we drove to our dream home in Florida. The brochure spoke of an Olympic-size swimming pool, cabanas, tennis courts, shuffleboard courts, putting green, massage, sauna and exercise room, entertainment, dining room, valet service, enclosed garage. We signed a three-year lease on arrival. The apartment building was attractive. But instead of $399 a month, or $4,788 annually, here is what we paid.

Monthly cost.
$449.00 Rent for our one-bedroom apartment. The $399 unit turned out to be on the second floor, with an unattractive view, and too much noise. Each floor above the second cost an extra $5.
25.00 Electricity
18.00 Phone (local)
25.00 Garage
20.00 Valet to deliver and return car to the garage. It was difficult to park the car ourselves—sharp turns, dark and dangerous.
5.00 Tips for Valet
17.00 Cleaning car
5.60 Washer (35¢) and dryer (35¢). There was a 40-percent increase the first month we arrived—from 25¢ to 35¢.
104.00 Cabana
25.00 Tips for cabana boys
$693.60

[5]"GAC Agrees to Make Land-Sales Refunds and to Swap Some Lots Under FTC Order," *The Wall Street Journal*, March 27, 1974, p. 14.
[6]Guest on the "Money Man" talk show between 7:15 and 9:00 P.M., March 30, 1975, WKAT, Miami, Florida.

"We had the following housing-related expenses the first year:

```
$  8,323.20   For our apartment
      898.00   Two months' deposit in advance to cover "possible
               damage." In three instances, when neighbors left they
               received no money back. The landlord charged for all
               tack marks, linoleum scratches, wallpaper removal.
      140.00   Christmas tips to employees
       97.00   Long-distance calls to family in Chicago
    3,976.00   Moving costs
    1,829.00   Drapes and other items required for the apartment
  $15,263.20
```

"Our three-year lease stated that the rent would be raised 5 percent each year for the next two years. Also, the fine print in the agreement required that if local real-estate taxes increased, the tenants must pay their proportionate share of such additional assessment.

"What a jolt when we added up our total expenses at the end of the year and arrived at a figure of over $30,000:

```
$15,263.20   Housing-related
  3,660.00   Food
  1,135.00   Dining out and entertainment
    841.00   Upkeep
  2,749.00   Insurance: health, property, car, life
  4,142.00   Taxes
  1,973.00   Clothing
    649.00   Miscellaneous
$30,412.20
```

"We had to dip into savings and sell several of our Treasury bonds to make ends meet. But some of our neighbors had it even worse. One friend had to move before his lease expired because he couldn't afford to stay. The landlord, however, required that he pay the last three months of rent. Another retiree paid $1,530 in advance (two months' deposit and one month's rent in advance). His wife died a week prior to their moving in. The landlord refused any refund and even threatened to make him pay the entire three-year lease.

"We plan to stick/it out for the three years but have made drastic cuts—eliminated the cabana, sold the car, write instead of calling long-distance. Our new monthly budget looks like this:

```
$   449.00   Rent
     25.00   Electricity
     18.00   Phone
      5.60   Washer and Dryer
     21.00   Bus and taxi
    350.00   Food and entertainment
    100.00   Insurance
    100.00   Clothing
     50.00   Miscellaneous
    170.00   Taxes
$1,288.60
```

$1,188.60 × 12 = $15,463.00 annually.

521

"After selling several bonds and withdrawing savings, our estimated income is $19,300. Although we have a nearly $4,000 margin of safety, we somehow hope to build back our $200,000 nest egg.

"We had high expectations for a carefree life in our retirement years. Instead, we are economizing as we did in the first years of our marriage. We are forced to take the bus most of the time for our shopping. This means carrying heavy bundles. The nearest grocery store is four miles away. How foolish of us not to have considered the availability of shops in selecting our apartment. Items and service in this area are far more costly than we had anticipated. For example, one of us needed to have some extensive dental work done. The dentist at home gave us a figure of $1,700. Here the lowest estimate we received was $2,900. It is apparent that we would have been much better off if we had stayed at home."

WILLS AND TRUSTS

Nobody likes to think about dying. Yet, in spite of the fact that death seems a million years away to young people, come it must. Although life expectancy today averages sixty-eight years for males and over seventy-five for females, car accidents alone caused over 43,000 fatalities in 1976.

The preceding chapters have discussed means of accumulating worldly possessions, and most of us work hard to achieve this goal; but no one has found a way to take his earnings with him. There are, however, means of specifying how you would like your wealth distributed after your death. A number of people fail to take advantage of this machinery, thus placing an unnecessary financial and mental burden on their families.

This section of the chapter will discuss the important matter of wills and trusts—including living trusts—and conclude with a brief look at probate costs, company benefits and estate taxes. In order for your assets to be distributed after your departure in accordance with your wishes, appropriate estate planning is required. Wills and trusts are vehicles for achieving this distribution. This is an area in which you will want to exercise the managerial function of planning to its fullest. After all, you probably won't be coming back to make any necessary changes.

WILLS

A will is a legal document that stipulates the way in which your worldly possessions will be distributed when you die. Each state has established its own laws with respect to what standards a will must meet. You may make a will from eighteen on, disposing of your real and personal property.

A lawyer recently told me, "I have been involved in wills for twenty-two years but can't get around to drawing up my own. Like many others, I keep thinking all men are mortal with one exception."

This refusal to contemplate death often hinders otherwise rational people from undertaking the important responsibility of making a will and doing appropriate estate planning. It is an ideal area for procrastination because they are no timetables to meet—or so we like to believe. Or perhaps you share the attitude of a feisty financier: "Hell, let them squabble over it!" Squabble they must, because the various states have no provisions for the efficient transfer of property from the deceased to their heirs. Thus, there are several valid reasons for drawing up your will.

Your worldly possessions, regardless of size, represent a lifetime of work; and most of us have a pretty good idea of whom we would like to enjoy the fruits of our efforts. Unfortunately, the laws of the state may not be in agreement with the decedent's wishes *if he has not expressed them in writing.* If there is no will, the property must pass to the heirs in accordance with state formulas. These vary markedly from state to state. And since each state is jealous of its right to taxes on a deceased person's estate, you should also be clear as to the location of your domicile, so that your fortune is not involved in a long court action concerning where your true residence is.

Also, if you leave no will, the administration of your estate will be subject to frequent examination by the courts. This is a costly venture, paid for by the estate; in the case of a small estate this can be virtually ruinous. Most lawyers' fees, court expenses, executors' fees, administrators' charges and other costs can be greatly reduced through preparation of a will. The provisions of the will can also produce sizable tax savings.

WILL FORMAT

An example of a will and its format is presented in Figure 28-1. This will would be appropriate where there is no heir to be considered except the wife, and when the estate is to be divided according to law if the wife dies first. *It is a sample format only and should not be utilized without consulting an attorney.*

Note that the will specifies who is to receive the testator's[7] property. In this case, it is Mrs. Lamllits who receives "all the property . . . of whatever nature, real, personal or mixed to be hers absolutely and in fee simple."[8]

---

[7]The person who has made the will. A testatrix is a female testator.
[8]*Fee simple* is giving the ownership of the property with unrestricted rights to dispose of it.

Figure 28-1 Format of a last will and testament.

LAST WILL AND TESTAMENT

OF

LARCO LABERTO LAMLLITS

Know all men by these presents that I, Larco Laberto Lamllits, a legal resident of the state of Michigan, being of full legal age and sound and disposing mind and memory, do hereby make, publish, and declare this instrument as my last Will and Testament.

1. I hereby revoke all wills or parts of will heretofore made by me.

2. I direct that my just debts and funeral expenses be paid.

3. I give, devise, and bequeath to my wife, Lora Lazellia Lamllits and her heirs, all the property of which I may die possessed, of whatsoever nature, real, personal or mixed to be hers absolutely and in fee simple.

4. I hereby appoint my wife, Lora Lazellia Lamllits, as my Executrix, and I direct that she be permitted to serve without bond and that no proceedings be had with reference to my estate except such as may be legally essential.

5. I authorize and empower my Executrix, if and whenever in the settlement of my estate she shall deem such action advisable, to sell at private or public sale, at such price as she shall consider proper, the whole of any part of my real or personal estate, or both, and to execute good and sufficient deeds and other instruments necessary or proper to convey and transfer the same to the purchaser or purchasers thereof, and such purchaser or purchasers shall not be bound to see to the application of the purchase money.

In testimony whereof, witness my hand at Pine Lake, Michigan, this First day of January, 1978.

_____

Signature of Testator

The foregoing instrument was signed, published, and declared by the testator therein named, Larco Laberto Lamllits, as and for his Last Will and Testament, in our presence, and we, in his presence, and in the presence of each other, and at his request, have hereunto subscribed our names as attesting witnesses at Pine Lake, Michigan, this First day of January, 1978.

Signature of Witnesses   Address   Phone

_____   _____

_____   _____

_____   _____

The will also provides that "just debts and funeral expenses be paid." It is wise to keep in mind that burial costs can be unduly high. (There is an interesting book on this subject by Ruth Mulvey Harmer, titled *The High Cost of Dying*.[9] Do not let emotions dominate your thinking if you have the responsibility for funeral arrangements. Try to remain practical. Some people are specific in their wills as to the type of casket and other arrangements they desire, and may even state approximate costs.

[9]Published by Crowell, Collier and Macmillan, Inc., New York, 1963.

The will should also name an executor[10] or executors. (If it has not, the court will make the selection.) It could appoint an individual, a bank or a trust company. In our sample will, Mrs. Lamllits was appointed the executrix, with explicit authority ". . . to sell at private or public sale, at such price as she shall consider proper, the whole or any part of my real or personal estate, or both, and to execute good and sufficient deeds and other instruments necessary or proper to convey and transfer the same to the purchasers thereof. . . ."

Had he so chosen, Mr. Lamllits could also have made a provision in his will for money to be left to charity, to institutions such as universities, or to other individuals. Instead of leaving all his possessions outright, the testator can leave some or all in trust, in which case he would designate a company or individual to perform this function.

No mention was made of life insurance in the sample will. This is because insurance proceeds are usually paid directly to the person designated as beneficiary in the policy, either in a lump sum or over a period of time, saving both administrative and tax expenses. If the benefits from an insurance policy are payable to an estate, the funds become part of the net worth, to be distributed with the other possessions in the will.

Three witnesses may be required but some states accept only two. It is desirable to have youthful persons as witnesses; they are more likely to be around at the time the will is probated.[11] Changes in witnesses' addresses should be kept readily available with other important documents.

If Mr. Lamllits later desired to make a minor change in his will, he could make a codicil—an addition or alteration. It could elaborate on current provisions or add new ones. In the event that important changes are necessary, it is best to write a new will.

Although the Lamllits will called for no unusual provisions, some people do include interesting stipulations. Heinrich Heine, the German poet, left a will giving his property to his wife on one condition—that she remarry. "Because," Heine stated, "then there will be at least one man to regret my death."[12] John D. Morgan bequeathed $2 million to his two daughters but required that a test be made to determine if they ". . . understand the principles of sound investments."[13]

---

[10]A person designated to carry out the provisions of a will. An executrix is a female executor.

[11]Probate is the action or process of proving before a competent judicial authority that a document offered for official recognition and registration as the last will and testament of a deceased person is genuine.

[12]Robert S. Menchin. *The Last Caprice,* New York: Simon & Schuster, Inc., 1963.

[13]Ibid., p. 71.

AUXILIARY DOCUMENTS

In addition to your will, there are other papers and documents that should be available to your survivors. Some of the following may be essential in order for them to obtain the benefits to which they are entitled:

1. Birth certificate for yourself and each dependent in your family;
2. Your Marriage Certificate;
3. Your Social Security number;
4. Titles, deeds and mortgage documents on your home, car and other property;
5. Your insurance policies—health, life, accident, property and any others;
6. Appropriate proof of your military service;
7. Your financial records, including a list of company benefits.

EXECUTOR/ADMINISTRATOR

In your will you may name a trust company or bank, instead of an individual, as your executor. Upon your death, the bank would have the will admitted to probate, collect and inventory all assets, pay the debts, manage the property, submit a final account to the court and effect the distribution.

Of course, a bank does not always have a personal interest in conserving your money, and might give limited care to maximizing assets. Also remember that there is a cost involved for this service. The charge for the executor function, in one state, is 2½ percent of the value of the inventory.[14]

You may reduce this fee in your estate by naming your wife, as Lamllits did, or a relative or friend to perform this function. You may also exempt your executor from posting a surety bond,[15] which will otherwise be required.

If you die without a will, or if the executor you have named is unwilling to act, a bank may be named administrator by the probate court upon the request of one of the relatives or beneficiaries. The duties and functions are the same as for an executor.

TRUSTS

THE LIVING TRUST

Once you have acquired a sizable nest egg, you may wish to consider an area that has received increased attention in recent years. It is referred to as the living

---

[14]Established by Article 3351 of the Louisiana Code of Civil Procedure.
[15]A bond guaranteeing performance of a contract or obligation.

trust and is created during a person's lifetime, in contrast to the testamentary trust, which is created by his will and becomes operative only after death. The living trust is designed to provide investment income to a person while he is alive and then offer an economical means of passing property on to those who are to receive it ultimately. Under a living trust, a bank or trust company assumes the administrative functions, and the owner may retain any amount of control over the investments that he desires.

A living trust may be either revocable or irrevocable; it is up to you to make the decision. The irrevocable trust is committed irrevocably and offers income- and estate-tax advantages. The drawback is that once you have made the commitment, you cannot, of your own will, recover the trust property. The revocable trust leaves you with the latitude to change or cancel it if you so desire.

You may wish to establish a living trust for either your own or another's benefit. Perhaps you have acquired property, the management of which is too time-consuming. Through the living trust, the constant record keeping, estimating of taxes and other responsibilities can be shifted to a trustee. By means of a living trust, you can receive current benefits and also provide appropriate protection for your beneficiaries after your death. A prime advantage of the revocable living trust is that you have a firsthand opportunity to observe the trustee. This enables you to evaluate his investment-management talents, and if he doesn't perform to your satisfaction, you can seek a replacement promptly.

Let us assume that you acquire a financial fortune early in life. Thanks to a generous grandparent and a good job, you accumulate $100,000 by age twenty-nine. Your work keeps you traveling, and you don't have time to give this money appropriate attention. Accordingly, you decide to establish a revocable living trust, making yourself the beneficiary. As an eligible bachelor with no serious intentions, you decide to make your widowed mother, age forty-nine, the recipient of this trust in case of your demise. You also specify that your younger sister, age eighteen, should be the beneficiary on the passing of your mother. The trust must be terminated at a set date in the future, with the principal distributed in accordance with your wishes. In your trust agreement, you may direct the trustee to manage your securities for you—invest principal, reinvest capital gains and income and provide protection and custody of the securities. The trustee takes care of such duties as cashing in matured bonds, exercising stock rights, collecting income and completing purchases and sales of bonds, stocks and money-market instruments.

THE TESTAMENTARY TRUST

An alternative to the living trust is the traditional trust arrangement for after death. A trustee is appointed in a will to manage assets for the decedent's family or others. This so-called testamentary trust may involve the bank or trust company in many of the same functions performed for the living trust. It could also involve such trust services as probating the will, collecting and safeguarding assets, settling debts and minimizing taxes.

Here is how the estate of the late President Eisenhower, a resident of Cumberland Township in Pennsylvania, was settled. Upon his death in 1969, the President had an estate of approximately $2,870,000. Debts and administrative costs resulted in a residue of about $2,730,000 according to a Pennsylvania state inheritance-tax return. He left the bulk of his estate in trust for his wife and son. A *Wall Street Journal* article stated:

> The return listed $1,547,809 in assets held in trust by Mercantile Safe Deposit & Trust Co., Baltimore, Md., and his son, John S. D. Eisenhower, currently U.S. Ambassador to Belgium.
>
> Royalties earned on publications with Doubleday & Co. accounted for $519,434. Intangible personal property totaled $261,793, largely in bank accounts, securities and notes.
>
> Tangible property was $211,894, consisting largely of cattle, farm equipment, home and office furniture. These were left to his widow, Mamie. The remainder of the estate will go into trust for her and their son.[16]

THE ROLE OF GUARDIAN/CONSERVATOR

Another function a bank or trust company may perform is to act as guardian for the estate of a minor or the conservator of the estate of a person adjudged to be mentally or physically incompetent. The bank's duty is to manage, under court supervision, the person's property as it would under any trust agreement.

The success of such an arrangement is dependent, as in other trust functions, upon the quality of the trustee. I know of a bank that put the bulk of a man's estate assets into real estate. The property was a bad investment, and income to the widow and her young son stopped. It took a court action to force the bank to return the money to the estate.

The fee for such administration may be a percentage of income received, and in such a case there may be an incentive to earn higher yields with possible risk to principal.

If you have minor children, it is important to designate a guardian in your will. This permits you to select the person you would like to act in this capacity in the event you and your spouse die together.

[16]*The Wall Street Journal,* October 19, 1970, p. 21.

THE INSURANCE TRUST

Insurance trusts are created by life-insurance policies payable to a designated trustee. Upon the death of the owner, the policies form the bulk of the trust, to which other assets may be added. Life-insurance trusts are a popular estate-planning device today. This type of trust has the advantage of concentrating an estate and managing its principal with discretion when life insurance forms a large part of the total assets. Insurance trusts escape probate costs and federal estate taxes and, like trusts and wills, are an essential element in estate planning. In order for insurance policies to escape estate taxes, the insured must have no control over the policy, according to a recent ruling:

Avoiding taxation when a policy pays off is tricky. The law says the proceeds are to be included in the taxable estate if the insured person had any control over the policy. Did he personally own it? Could he change the beneficiary or cancel the policy? Could he pledge it for a loan? If the answer to any such question is yes, the proceeds are taxable. So the idea is to transfer all such controls to someone else before you die.

When James H. Lumpkin, Jr., died, he was participating in a group insurance plan at the company where he worked. Lumpkin had none of the normal controls over the policy. But he could vary the pace at which its proceeds would be paid out. The Tax Court earlier said that one control wasn't significant enough to make the proceeds part of the estate. But a U.S. appeals court disagrees. And it adds that Lumpkin could have avoided the problem if he had given the payout control to someone else.[17]

TRUST-MANAGEMENT COSTS

Annual charges for trust management vary, so it is a good idea to shop around before you settle on a bank or trust organization. A check with four institutions found the average charges shown in Table 28-4:

TABLE 28-4 Selected Annual Charges for Trust Management

Principal charge	
First $100,000	$3.00 per $1,000
Next $200,000	$2.00 per $1,000
Next $200,000	$1.00 per $1,000
Over $500,000	$ .50 per $1,000
Income charge:	
5% of the first $25,000	
3% above $25,000	
Minimum fee $150.00	

[17]*The Wall Street Journal,* March 28, 1973, p. 1.

In addition to the annual charges listed in Table 28-5 these institutions had the following fees for services rendered in the initial probate of an estate:

3% of the first $500,000
2% of the next $2,000,0000
1½% of the balance
Minimum Fee—$2,000

All of the banks pointed out that additional charges would be made for such items as complex tax settlements, large real-estate holdings and prolonged legal battles.

It is apparent that the larger the estate, the smaller the overall percentage of charges for its probate work and administration. Of course, management costs should be only one factor in arriving at your decision; most important is that the firm has acquired a good reputation over many years of successful trustee management.

GUIDELINES AND SUMMARY

Given the importance of wills and trusts, I will risk repetiton by concluding this section with a list of guidelines to help you ensure the well-being of those you leave behind:

1. Make a will early in life. If you die without one, your property will be divided according to the law of your state, and this may not be in your best interest.
2. Use an able lawyer to draw up your will. If you don't, it is possible that the necessary legal requirement will not be met, and the will could be invalidated.
3. Update your will as circumstances change, in order to meet your current wishes.
4. If you decide on going for the million-dollar objective, or some other goal you deem appropriate, you should give its distribution serious thought. In addition to providing for your family, you can do much good with your money through contributions to worthy causes. Perhaps your own community may be in need of assistance.
5. Provide for flexibility in your will and trust arrangements. Be sure to select a competent lawyer for your legal matters, and if you go the trust route, select a company with a distinguished record. Over the years, institutions have failed and beautifully drawn trusts gone for naught because of inefficient estate management.
6. The purpose of estate planning is to see that the maximum amount of your assets will be transferred from you to the individuals and/or organizations you desire as recipients. This can best be accomplished

by letting as few people as possible get a cut of the estate melon. Keep your administrative costs within reason and exploit every tax-savings aspect.

PROBATE COSTS

The estate may pay the costs of probate, and this can be a sizable figure. For example, one Ohio court lists several attorney's fees as follows:

1. Four percent on all probate property. This is based upon total valuation of probate property, without distinction as to real or personal property.
2. Two percent on decedent's interest in all nonprobate assets listed either in Ohio inheritance and/or the federal estate-tax petitions.
3. Minimum fee for legal services rendered the fiduciary in the administration of an estate is two hundred dollars.[18]

There has been discussion in recent years about avoiding probate. Stocks held jointly with right of survivorship, irrevocable living trusts and life insurance are means of escaping probate costs. A few years ago, Norman F. Dacey wrote a popular book on the subject, *How to Avoid Probate.*[19] The book raises interesting issues and I recommend it for your reading.

In 1973, Wisconsin became the first state to pass a do-it-yourself probate law. Since its passage, many Wisconsin residents have done their own probate work at considerable savings in money and time. At present eleven states have adopted the Uniform Probate Code, which makes it easier for individuals with no legal background to probate estates. However, in complex probate situations, it normally pays to consult a first-rate attorney who specializes in such matters.

A friend of mine tells the following story about the problems he encountered in settling his father's small estate:

"Dad did not place his only piece of property in joint ownership, and as a result, it had to be probated at an estimated cost of eight hundred dollars. It took me two weeks' vacation to run down Dad's records—they were scattered throughout his house, office and even the garage. I never did find them all. I sure intend to put my own affairs in order and to avoid probate wherever possible."

COMPANY BENEFITS

We spoke earlier of having documents available for your survivors, including a

[18]Source: Probate court, Athens County, Ohio.
[19]Crown Publications, New York, 1965.

list of company benefits. Any such benefits, which can amount to a sizable sum, are not required to pass through probate.

If you work in civil service for the federal government, the benefits available to your heirs may include Federal Employees' Group Life Insurance, lump-sum retirement benefit, unpaid compensation for salary, balance of deductions for purchase of savings bonds, lump-sum payment for leave, travel expense, cash awards and allowance. In addition, if your job is with the federal government, your estate will automatically go to the following persons and in this order:

1. To your widow (or widower);
2. If neither of the above, to your child or children in equal shares, with the share of any deceased child distributed among the descendants of that child;
3. If none of the above, to your parents in equal shares, or the entire amount to the surviving parent;
4. If none of the above, to the executor or administator of your estate;
5. If none of the above, to the persons or persons determined to be entitled under the laws of the state in which you were domiciled.

However, if you wish to name some person or persons not included in the above list, or if you wish to name these persons but in a different order, you need only state this in your will.

ESTATE TAXES

I have indicated that some probate costs can be avoided. However, in computation of the taxes due Uncle Sam, all your property must be listed, including such items as life-insurance policies, real estate, gifts in contemplation of death, mortgages, notes and cash, stock and bonds, annuities, property in joint ownership and revocable trusts.

This gross amount may be reduced by the cost of burial, lawyers' fees, debts, mortgages and liens, losses during administration and, most important, a marital deduction.

The Tax Reform Act of 1976 made important changes in regard to estate taxes beginning in 1977. The smaller estates benefited from the new law, with some larger estates paying more taxes. The previous law allowed half of an estate to go to the surviving spouse tax-free. The 1976 Act permits the greater of $250,000 or 50 percent of the decedent's adjusted gross estate. The $60,000 filing requirement for estates of decedents who are U.S. residents and citizens was modified as follows:

TABLE 28-5   Estate Taxes

The individual dies in:	And the gross estate exceeds:
1978	$134,000*
1979	$147,000*
1980	161,000*

For individual dying after 1980, an estate tax return must be filed if the gross estate exceeds $175,000.*

*These amounts are reduced by taxable gifts made after 1976, the amount allowed under the specific exemption for gifts made after September 6, 1976, and certain other lifetime transfers.

Other changes related to gifts; orphan's exclusions; certain valuation of real property; farms or closely held businesses; generation-skipping transfers; IRA and Keogh plans; carryover basis of property.

Let us now turn to the importance of the marital deduction. Assume that a couple reach the million-dollar objective discussed in Chapter 2. Table 28-6 shows how the federal estate tax would be computed if the husband, in 1977, left his widow half his adjusted gross estate:

TABLE 28-6   The Estate of Husband With Marital Deduction

Gross estate	$1,000,000	
Less: Burial, claims, legal costs, other debts and expenses	50,000	
Adjusted gross estate		$950,000
Maximum marital deduction	475,000	
University bequest	20,000	
Taxable estate		$275,000
Estate tax before credit		$ 79,300
Unified credit (1977)*		30,000
Federal estate tax		$ 49,300

Table 28-7 shows the tax if the marital deduction is not used:

TABLE 28-7   The Estate of Husband Without Marital Deduction

Gross estate	$1,000,000	
Less: Burial, claims, legal costs, other debts and expenses	50,000	
Adjusted gross estate		$950,000
University bequest	20,000	200,000
Taxable estate		$750,000
Estate tax before credits		$248,300
Unified credit (1977)*		30,000
Federal estate tax		$218,300

*By 1981 this will increase to $47,000.

533

By using this deduction, the husband saved $169,000—and the dollar benefits increase with the size of the estate. However, the marital deduction may not be the best decision in every case. Keep in mind that the *excluded interest must be included in the estate of the surviving spouse* if she retains ownership until her death. The IRS puts it well:

> The desire to save taxes by maximum use of the marital deduction may conflict with particular needs in a given situation. For example, a widower remarrying might want to provide for his second wife's support and maintenance after his death but at the same time be certain that ultimately the property would go to his children and grandchildren. He could not assure himself of this second goal and still qualify the property for the marital deduction. The potential loss to his children could outweigh the tax benefit derived from the marital deduction.[20]

In addition to the federal government, your state can be expected to take a piece of your fortune. However, it will be a much smaller portion than the amount taken by the U.S. Government. The state may impose its own estate or inheritance tax. The latter is a tax levied on the property received by the beneficiary.

CONCLUSION

In concluding our discussion of retirement, wills and trusts, let us see how these topics fit into your overall financial picture. Effective estate planning and determination of the financial aspects of retirement are much easier if you have included them from the beginning as two aspects of a sound personal-finance program. In Chapter 1, retirement and estate planning, along with taxes, was cited as one of the seven general areas to be considered in the development of a successful financial portfolio. In all seven areas, the managerial functions of planning, organizing and controlling serve to assist you in arriving at sound financial decisions.

By following my management approach to personal finance, you should achieve financial health at an early date. You can then move on to the next phase of your plan, the building up of an investment program that contains cash reserves, bonds, stock and perhaps other ventures such as real estate, hobbies and commodities. Concurrently, you will satisfy your insurance and housing requirements, and over the years make every effort to minimize tax payments in accordance with existing state and federal laws.

---

[20]Internal Revenue Service. *Tax Coordinator.* Department of the Treasury, March 10, 1977, pp. 46, 306.

From the start, you will maintain orderly financial records, as illustrated in Chapter 2. These computations will include your yearly net worth as well as the value of your estate—material that you will find most helpful in your retirement and estate planning. And the utilization of management functions (Figure 1-2) will help you to have your affairs in order when you die.

The planning aspect is particularly vital in successfully passing on your worldly possessions in the manner you desire. You may not achieve immortality—at least in the flesh—but you can, to a degree, make your financial influence felt by your descendants. However, effective financial management requires your efforts while alive in order to make an impact in the future. Likewise, sound planning is essential if you are to make the correct decisions with respect to retirement.

We have come a long way together through the highways and byways of personal finance. Let me leave you with the following advice, which sums up all that we have discussed along the way: Manage your personal finances so that they are a source of enjoyment in life and a source of benefit when you are gone.

APPENDICES

I. FINANCIAL PERIODICALS AND SERVICES

The publications listed here will be of interest to those readers who may desire additional information about the various areas of personal finance discussed in this book. Many of the periodicals and services can be found in libraries.

Periodicals

Periodical	Frequency of Publication	Yearly Subscription Rate	Publisher	Type of Information
Agriculture Letter	Weekly	Free	Federal Reserve Bank, Chicago, Ill.	Agricultural conditions
American Stock Exchange Quarterly Report	Quarterly	Free	American Stock Exchange, New York, N.Y.	Summation of exchange activity on quarterly basis
Bank and Quotation Record	Monthly	$75.00	National News Service, New York, N.Y.	Quotations on extensive range of listed and unlisted securities
Bankers Monthly	Monthly	$12.00	Bankers Monthly, Inc., Northbrook, Ill.	National magazine of banking and investments, financial news and investment analyses
*Barron's	Weekly	$32.00	Dow Jones & Co., Inc., New York, N.Y.	General business and financial newspaper with market quotations
Business in Brief	Bimonthly	Free	Chase Manhattan Bank, New York, N.Y.	Report on current business and economic conditions in U.S.
*Business Week	Weekly	$21.50	McGraw-Hill, Inc., New York, N.Y.	Business publication covering many economic areas
*Changing Times	Monthly	$9.00	The Kiplinger Washington Editors, Inc., Washington, D.C.	Articles of consumer interest
Commercial and Financial Chronicle	Semiweekly	$95.00	National News Service, Inc., New York, N.Y.	Primary statistics of listed exchanges (Monday edition); general commercial and financial news (Thursday edition)
Commodity Research Report	Weekly	Free	E. F. Hutton & Co. Inc., 1 Chase Manhattan Plaza, New York, N.Y.	Commodities review and outlook

*An asterisk designates those found to be of most help.

Periodical	Frequency of Publication	Yearly Subscription Rate	Publisher	Type of Information
*Consumer Reports	Monthly	$11.00	Consumers Union of U.S., Inc., Mount Vernon, N.Y.	Informative articles on consumer goods and services
Dun's	Monthly	$7.00	Dun & Bradstreet Publications, New York, N.Y.	Business graphs and essays on finance and management
Federal Reserve Bulletin	Monthly	$6.00	Board of Governors of FRB, Washington, D.C.	Current economic developments, including statistical material
Federal Reserve Bank of New York Monthly Review	Monthly	Free	Federal Reserve Bank of New York, New York, N.Y.	Comprehensive review of the preceding month's business situations and money and bond market
Financial Analysis Journal	Bimonthly	$24.00	Financial Analysts Federation, New York, N.Y.	Articles and transcripts of speeches of interest to securities analysts
Financial & Business Review	Monthly	Free	Thompson & McKinnon, 2 Broadway, New York, N.Y.	Covers the broader aspects of the national financial and business picture
Financial Executive	Monthly	$15.00	Financial Executive Institute, Inc., New York, N.Y.	Articles on finance and investment
Financial World	Semimonthly	$27.00	Marco Publishing Corp., New York, N.Y.	General financial interest
*Forbes	Semimonthly	$15.00	Forbes Inc., New York, N.Y.	Articles concerning companies and industries as investments
*Fortune	Monthly	$17.00	Time, Inc., New York, N.Y.	Various comprehensive business articles
*Harvard Business Review	Bimonthly	$18.00	Harvard Graduate School of Business Administration, Boston, Mass.	General business articles; some articles on investments
The Journal of Business	Quarterly	$12.00	University of Chicago Press, Chicago, Ill.	Sophisticated academic articles on business and investments
The Journal of Finance	5 times a year	$25.50	American Finance Assn., New York, N.Y.	Academic articles on finance, including investments

Periodical	Frequency of Publication	Yearly Subscription Rate	Publisher	Type of Information
*Money	Monthly	$14.95	Time Inc., Chicago, Ill.	Timely articles on a variety of personal finance subjects
Monthly Economic Letter	Monthly	Free	First National City Bank of New York, N.Y.	Letter on economic conditions and government finance
Nation's Business	Monthly	$39.75 for 3 years	Chamber of Commerce of the U.S., Washington, D.C.	General business magazine, consumer-oriented
Review of Economics and Statistics	Quarterly	$15.00	Harvard U. Press, Cambridge, Mass.	Academic articles on economic subjects; some on investments
Summary of Business Forecasts	Annually	Free	Federal Reserve Bank of Richmond, Richmond, Va.	Opinions about expected business activity in the upcoming year
Survey of Current Business	Monthly	$20.00	U.S. Dept. of Commerce, Washington, D.C.	Business and financial survey; includes statistical tables
Thompson & McKinnon Commodity Letter	Weekly	Free	Thompson & McKinnon 2 Broadway, New York, N.Y.	Review of most active commodities with short- and long-term projections
*The Wall Street Journal	Daily, Monday through Friday	$45.00	Dow Jones & Co., Inc., New York, N.Y.	General business and finance newspaper with market quotations
*Weekly Commodity Digest	Weekly	Free	Bache & Co., Inc., New York, N.Y.	Commodity review
Weekly Grain Letter	Weekly	Free	The Siegel Trading Co., Inc., 100 N. Lasalle St., Chicago, Ill.	Review of grain commodities of the past week
Weekly Mercantile Letter	Weekly	Free	The Siegel Trading Co., Inc., 100 N. Lasalle St., Chicago, Ill.	Review of the mercantile trading commodities
World Business	Quarterly	Free	Chase Manhattan Bank, Inc., New York, N.Y.	Survey of current business conditions throughout the world

Services

Service	Frequency of Publication	Publisher	Type of Information
Babson's Reports	Weekly	Babson's Reports, Inc. Wellesley Hills, Mass.	Views on the stock market to include recommendations
Daily Graphs	Weekly	William O'Neil & Co., Inc., P. O. Box 24933, Los Angeles, Calif.	Comprehensive chart service on the stock market
Dines Letter	Semimonthly	Dines Letter, P.O. Box 22, Belvedere, Calif.	Combines important technical, psychological and business indicators concerning market; highlights on gold
Dow Theory Le Hers Inc.	36 times a year	Dow Theory LeHers, Inc., La Jolla, Calif.	Forecasts of stock market based on Dow Theory
Edison Gould's Findings & Forecasts	24 times a year	30 Rockefeller Plaza, New York, N.Y.	Forecast of stock market trends supported by technical material
Futures Market Service	Weekly	Commodity Research Bureau, Inc., 1 Liberty Plaza, New York, N.Y.	Eight-page report covering commodity market analysis and fundamental data
Holt Trading Advisory	Weekly	The Holt Trading Advisory, 277 Park Ave., New York, N.Y.	Provides specific guidelines in regard to the stock and options market
Investors Intelligence	24 times a year	Investors Intelligence Inc., 2 East Ave., Larchmont, N.Y.	What leading investment services think about the market

*Moody's Investors Service, New York, N.Y.:

Service	Frequency of Publication	Publisher	Type of Information
Moody's Bank and Finance Manual	Yearly (supplemented twice weekly)		Facts and figures on financial enterprises
Moody's Industrial Manual	Yearly (supplemented twice weekly		Information on industrial stocks, history, management, financial data
Moody's Municipal and Governments Manual	Yearly (supplemented twice weekly)		Information and ratings on governments, municipals, foreign bonds
Moody's Public Utility Manual	Yearly (supplemented twice weekly)		Information on public utilities, plus special studies on market areas
Moody's Transportation Manual	Yearly (supplemented twice weekly)		Information on transportation companies such as air, rail, bus, oil pipelines, tunnel and bridge companies, trucking
Computer Industry Survey	Periodical supplements		Report explores significant developments in the industry

Service	Frequency of Publication	Publisher	Type of Information
Creative Analysis	Yearly		Numerous companies covered: data compiled by computers; comparison with other companies and industries
Dividend Record	Twice-weekly and annual issue at year end		Dividend information on various issues
Bond Record	Monthly		Issues, current prices, call prices, ratings and other statistics on numerous bonds
Handbook of Common Stocks	Quarterly		Statistics and background on common stocks
Stock Survey	Weekly		Investment advice on a wide variety of stocks, analyses of individual stocks and groups
Bond Survey	Weekly		Comments and recommendations on issues in various bond categories
Insurance and Financial Stocks	Biweekly		Discusses equities of life, fire and casualty insurance companies, banks, etc., with buy, sell, hold recommendations
The Morgan Guaranty Survey	Monthly	Morgan Guaranty Trust Company, 23 Wall Street, New York, N.Y.	Devoted to business and financial conditions and topics of general interest
Spear & Staff, Inc., Babson Park, Mass.:			
Com-stat	Weekly		Computer-based advisory service
Spear Market Letter	Weekly		Market policy and recommendations
Special Situation Reports	Periodically		Special developments affecting stocks
Science Investment Reports	Biweekly		Stock investment advice in area of science
Oil Statistic Bulletin and Canadian Oil Reports	Biweekly		Covers oil and gas industries
*Standard & Poor's Corporation, New York, N.Y.:			
The Outlook	Weekly		Specific advice on individual stock; analyzes and projects business trends

Service	Frequency of Publication	Publisher	Type of Information
Poor's Investment Advisory Survey	Weekly		Portfolio advice—follows specific stocks until sold; also recommends bonds
Daily Basis Stock Charts	Weekly		Numerous stocks plotted on a daily basis
Current Market Perspectives	Monthly		Book of charts on 100 issues shows Hi-Lo-Close for five years
OTC Chart Manual	Bimonthly		Charts the most active over-the-counter stocks
Stock Guide	Monthly		Data on numerous common and preferred issues
Bond Guide	Monthly		Descriptive and statistical data on 3,000 corporate bonds
Stock Summary	Monthly		Condensed information on widely traded stocks
Foreign Securities Survey	Monthly		Analysis opinions on foreign stocks and bonds
Dividend Record	Daily, weekly, quarterly		Authority on dividend details
Fact and Forecasts	Daily		Data on immediate market situations, brokers' opinions, comments on mutual funds, etc.
Corporation Records	Daily revisions		Comprehensive data on corporations in 6 looseleaf binders
Industry Surveys	Yearly, with 3 or 4 supplements		Surveys various industries
Listed Stock Reports	Periodically revised		Data on numerous issues, including financial data, latest developments, etc.
American Exchange Stock Reports	Periodically revised		Data on American Exchange issues, financial aspects, current items, etc.
Unlisted Stock Reports	Periodically revised		Regional and over-the-counter stocks surveyed
Bond Outlook	Weekly		Surveys bond market, makes buy and sell recommendations
Municipal Bond Selector	Bimonthly		Rates municipals
Convertible Bond Reports	Weekly		Information on convertible bonds, ratings, etc.

544

Service	Frequency of Publication	Publisher	Type of Information
Status of Bonds	Yearly, with 5 annual supplements		Covers all corporate and most important municipal bonds, call status, defaulted issues, etc.
Called Bond Record	Semiweekly		Reports calls and tenders, sinking-fund proposals, defaulted issues, forthcoming redemptions, etc.
New Issues Service	Weekly		Information on new issues to be sold, with follow-up after issue
Transportation Service	Periodically		Includes several publications: *Weekly Transportation Outlook, Railroad Operations Results,* etc.
Trendline	Weekly		Daily-basis stock charts of numerous stocks and key indicators
Register of Corporate Directors and Executives	Yearly, with 3 supplements		Directory of executive personnel
Analysts Handbook	Monthly		Per-share data on various industries and S&P's 425 Industrials
Stock Market Encyclopedia	Yearly		Data on many stocks; S&P's opinion of investment merit, charts
Stock Chart Service	Weekly	R. W. Mansfield Co., Jersey City, N.Y.	Charts on numerous stocks
Stock Trend Service	Tuesdays and Fridays	Stock Trend Service Inc., 97 Dwight St., Springfield, Mass.	Evaluation of technical statistical data with buy, sell, hold recommendations
United Business Investment Report	Weekly	United Business Service Co., 210 Newbury St., Boston, Mass.	Weekly forecast of stock and commodity price movements
Value Line Investment Survey	Weekly	Arnold Bernhard & Co., Inc., 5 E. 44th St., New York, N.Y.	Continuous analysis and review of numerous stocks; also special situations in various industries
Weekly Financial Digest	Weekly	Manufacturers Hanover Trust Co., 350 Park Ave., New York, N.Y.	Selected Federal Reserve data, bank-loan figures, business indicators, securities market, New York and international money markets, etc.
Zweig Forecast	18 times a year	Zweig Forecast, 747 Third Ave., New York, N.Y.	Emphasizes the importance of timing based on technical indicators. Martin Zweig appears as a guest on the TV program titled Wall Street Week

II. GLOSSARY

Chapter 1 / Successful Money Management

Consumer Price Index (CPI) A monthly index prepared by the Department of Labor that can be helpful in keeping track of inflation. It is a statistical measure of changes in prices of five major categories of goods and services bought by urban wage earners and clerical workers.

Decision-making process The factors a manager can utilize to arrive at a course of action. These factors include: the objective; areas of responsibility; resources and functions.

Financial health The elimination of money worries by having income exceed expenditures and assets in excess of liabilities. It includes establishing and maintaining a sound lifetime money-management program.

Inflation A marked increase in prices caused by a rising amount of money in relation to available goods and services.

Investment portfolio Stocks, bonds, money-market instruments and other securities held by an individual.

Management functions The duties that must be performed by a person in order to manage his money wisely. There are three major management functions: planning, doing, checking.

Money management The development and implementation of a sound personal-finance program to best meet your objectives. Achievement of these objectives requires an understanding of all investment sources and their interrelationship. It also requires knowledge of a sound spending program.

Objective The primary financial goal. The objective should provide answers to the questions of what, when, where, how and why.

Personal-finance model A graphic portrayal that presents an overview of the book (Figure 1-1). The model consists of five components: objective; personal-finance areas; resources or educational tools; functions to be performed; the decision-making process.

Chapter 2 / Budgeting

Assets What an individual or organization owns plus what is owed to it. Assets may be tangible, like a home, or intangible, like a stock certificate.

Budget A financial statement of an individual or organization that may present estimated income and expenses for a set period of time.

Budget process A financial concept divisible into five phases: 1) Determine net worth; 2) Estimate income and expenses for the current year; 3) Develop a long-range plan based upon the primary objective and intermediate goals; 4) Maintain records indicating actual income and expenses; 5) Compare the plan with actuality and modify the estimates where appropriate.

Capital Worldly possessions that include such items as cash, savings accounts, bonds, stock, personal property, household furnishings and real estate.

Cash The official medium of exchange of a country. In the United States, dollars and cents are the legal tender. For example, on each Federal Reserve Note paper dollar (and all other denominations) it states: "This note is legal tender for all debts, public and private." Prior to 1967, paper-dollar silver certificates were available that stated: "This certifies that there is on deposit in the Treasury of the United States of America one dollar in silver payable to the bearer on demand."

Cash flow The net income of an individual or company. For an individual this would include such items as salary, dividends, interest, rents and royalties. From this total would be deducted taxes and other expenses. However, included in the net-income figure would be any noncash charges for depreciation and depletion. In essence, cash flow indicates the net amount of dollars available. For example, annual depreciation on rental property might be deducted as an expense. However, no cash is spent until a replacement is acquired.

Cash items Cash, bank deposits, U.S. Government issues and other securities that are considered the same as cash.

Current assets Cash, cash items, inventories and notes and accounts receivable due within one year.

Current liabilities Accounts and notes payable, accrued taxes, interest, declared dividends and other claims that are payable within one year.

Debt Money, or other commodity or service, that an organization or individual owes to another organization or individual.

Depreciation A periodic charge against income to spread the cost of such items as equipment and buildings over their estimated useful life.

Disavings Expenditures in excess of disposable income.

Dividend The payment made by a corporation to its stockholders as a return on their investment.

Equity The net worth of a corporation that measures the interest of stockholders in a corporation. It can be determined by subtracting the total liabilities from the total assets. Equity may also be applied to an individual's net worth. (See the definition for net worth, below.)

Garnishee A legal action that enables a creditor to receive a debtor's salary up to the specified amount of the debt.

Income The inflow of money received by an individual or organization from such sources as salary, dividends and interest for a stated period of time.

Liabilities Amounts owed. This includes such short-term items as accounts and notes payable as well as long-term debts.

Net income The true profit of an individual or corporation after deducting all expenses, including taxes.

Net worth (Equity) What an individual (or organization) owns minus what he owes. The result indicates a net ownership of all tangible and intangible resources.

Outlay Expenditure.

Chapter 3 / Consumer Protection

Consumer A person who uses goods and services.

Consumer credit Credit provided to a person in order that he may purchase goods or services.

Consumer Credit Protection Act An act safeguarding the consumer in connection with the utilization of credit by requiring full disclosure of the extent and conditions of finance charges in credit transactions or in offers to extend credit; restricting the garnishment of wages; and creating the National Commission on Consumer Finance to study and make recommendations on the need for further regulation of the consumer-finance industry.

Consumer protection Laws, statutes and organizations that can help the individual receive fair treatment in the purchase of goods, services and credit.

Credit The right granted by a creditor to a debtor to defer payment of debt or to incur debt and defer its payment.

Credit sale Any sale with respect to which credit is extended or arranged by the seller.

Creditor An individual (or organization) who regularly extends or arranges for extension of credit for which a finance charge is required, whether in connection with loans, sales of property or other such services.

Chapter 4 / Consumer Credit

Cash credit Lending of money.

Charge account An individual's account with a creditor which enables him to buy goods (and/or services) and pay for it at a later date.

Charge-a-plate An embossed address plate issued by a company and utilized by an individual to purchase goods and/or services on credit.

Credit card A 2 x 3½-inch plastic card that permits the owner to buy goods and/or services on credit.

Installment One of the segments into which a debt is divided when payments are made at intervals.

Sales Credit Charge accounts and installment sales.

Chapter 5 / If It's Money You Must Borrow

Collateral Property provided by a borrower to a lender that is used as security to protect the lender's loan.

Debt Money owed by one person (or organization) to another.

Interest The cost charged for borrowing money.

Loan Money lent by one person (or organization to another, usually at interest.

Loan consolidation The combining of loans outstanding to various companies into one loan for the total amount.

Loan shark An individual who lends money at exorbitant rates, above what the law allows.

Pawnbroker A lender who loans money upon the security of valuable personal property (collateral) which is pledged by the borrower.

Pledge A piece of property held by the lender with title to the property remaining with the borrower, provided payment is made within a stated time.

Chapter 8 / Transportation

Annual auto depreciation Yearly loss in the dollar value of a car. Depreciation can be determined by finding out what your car is currently selling for in the marketplace, looking in the NADA manual for a car one year older and computing the difference. Normally the higher the initial purchase price, the greater the dollar depreciation.

Car loan Money borrowed for the purpose of buying a car. Funds may be obtained from a credit union, car dealer, bank, insurance company or loan company. It is desirable to check with several sources in order to obtain the best deal. A maximum down payment and paying off the loan in the shortest time is normally the best policy.

Maintenance The labor of keeping something in a state of repair. Good maintenance will cut costs, reduce need for repairs and keep a vehicle in satisfactory working condition.

Manufacturer's suggested list price (Sticker price) The price that is posted on a window of a car in the dealer's showroom. A car dealer normally buys a vehicle for 75 to 81 percent of the list price. Profit differential on accessories may run up to 40 to 50 percent.

Chapter 9 / Large Appliances

Compact system One of three main categories. It consists of a receiver (radio), turntable (record player), speakers and sometimes a tape player-recorder.

Component system One of three main stereo categories. All items, such as turntable, tape, deck, receiver and speakers, are bought separately, in contrast to a compact system, which is a one-package purchase.

Console system One of three main stereo categories. It is a self-contained unit that includes speakers, receiver, turntable and sometimes tape deck.

Service agreement A written contract, usually annual, offered by a company in which is stated what services it will provide in return for a specified fee.

Total System Budget (TSB) A determination of how much money a person will have to spend initially and for upkeep on stereo equipment.

Warranty A written guarantee of the integrity of a product and of the manufacturer's obligation to replace the unit or repair parts.

Chapter 10 / Should I Rent or Buy?

Condominium Apartment building in which title to each apartment rests with the purchaser. Ownership includes a pro-rata share of all land improvements. Owner need not have consent from other owners in order to sell his apartment.

Conventional home A standard detached residential building designed for family living. It is the most popular form of accommodation and the goal of the majority of families in this country. Choices available are dependent on financial resources. Virtually all homes are purchased with the assistance of some loan arrangement.

Cooperative apartment A dwelling constructed for a group of people who incorporate for the purpose of sharing ownership of the building and land. Their ownership is reflected in their shareholdings, which enable them to reside in their apartments. Maintenance and tax responsibility rest with the corporation. Each owner has voting rights and an individual owner cannot sell his apartment without the consent of the other members of the cooperation.

Federal Housing Administration loan A federal government loan program. It provides an opportunity to obtain a loan at less than the going rate to anyone who has good credit, steady work and the necessary cash down payment. An appraisal of the prospective dwelling is required.

GI loan Veterans Administration home-loan program that guarantees the lending-agency loan for qualifying veterans. Homes are subject to VA appraisal. No down payment is required and thirty-year loans may be obtained.

Mobile home A trailer-type dwelling used as a permanent residence. It is usually connected to utilities and is designed without a permanent foundation. A primary advantage is the lower initial cost. Conventional loans may be obtained on mobile homes.

Mobile park A facility providing land, conveniences and services for mobile homes. Parks range from luxurious sites with all the conveniences of quality apartment living to ugly eyesores that are noisy, dirty and offer poor service.

Motor home An automotive vehicle built on a truck or bus chassis and equipped as a self-contained traveling home. Used primarily for vacations, it permits the owner to stop in any locality.

Option to buy The opportunity to purchase a home or condominium that one is renting. This right gives the renter such advantages as being able to thoroughly check the house, raise down-payment money and decide if the community is right for him. The owner's prime advantage in granting the option may be that it is the only way to obtain a potential sale.

Recreational home Living accommodations (generally used only for recreational purposes) ranging from a tent camper to an elegant motor dwelling.

Chapter 11 / Subcontracting Your Home

Budget A schedule for estimating expenses for a given period. It can be used by management as both a planning and control document.

Critical path The sequence of events that indicates the minimum time required to complete a project.

Feedback The receipt of information by management obtained both from within and outside an organization. A primary means of effective feedback is through conversation with employees.

Floor joists Floor-framing lumber which extends from the outer foundation walls to interior beams.

Footings The concrete base of a foundation wall.

Foundation wall A masonry wall supporting the house.

Incentives Rewards utilized to motivate individuals in an organization.

Leader The "boss" manager, or head of any organization.

Maintenance Work required to keep equipment operating.

Management The art and science or supervising an organization. Also, the supervisory members of an organization.

Manpower The total output of labor in an activity to achieve an objective.

Millwork Doors, trim, shelving, windowsills and other finishing work.

PERT (Program Evaluation and Review Technique) A manager's tool for defining and coordinating what must be done to accomplish successfully the objectives of a project within an established time frame.

Sheathing The first covering of boards or waterproofing material on the outside wall of a frame house.

Speculation A home built for the purpose of selling it to anyone willing to pay the price. This is in contrast to a custom-built house that has been contracted for prior to construction.

Studs Horizontal lumber nailed to vertical lumber, which comprises the wall frame. The boards are usually sixteen inches apart.

Subfloor Wood sheeting nailed to floor joists.

Terrazzo A mosaic flooring made by embedding small pieces of marble or granite in marble and polishing.

Chapter 12 / Landscaping

Annual A plant that lasts one year or season.

Bermuda grass An attractive southern European grass.

County agents Located in every state, they work with a land-grant university and are paid in part from funds provided by the Department of Agriculture. They will furnish you with free publications and will test your yard soil to determine what may be needed to improve it.

Horticulture The science and art of growing fruits, vegetables, flowers and ornamental plants.

Landscape maintenance The upkeep of a yard that may be accomplished by a gardener, a lawn-care company or by doing it yourself.

Landscaping Changing the natural features of a plot of ground so as to make it more attractive, as by adding lawns, trees, bushes.

Lawn A ground cover that is important in keeping soil from washing away, as well as for aesthetic purposes. Lawns may be established in several ways. Lawn sod enables you to cover an entire area very quickly, but it is expensive. You may cover a portion of the area with sod and, if you distribute it well, the entire lawn will be covered in time. The least expensive method, requiring more time, is the planting of cuttings.

Lawn-care company A firm that treats your lawn a specified number of times a year. The charge is normally based on the square footage involved.

Perennial As applied to plants, present at all seasons of the year.

Professional landscaper One will prepare a landscape design for your house and give an estimate on what the entire job will cost.

St. Augustine grass A perennial creeping grass of the southern U.S. that is valuable as a sand binder and as a sod grass.

Zoysia Matrella Creeping perennial lawn grass having fine leaves and suitable especially for warm regions.

Chapter 13 / Protecting your Property

Bar lock A device that is installed in pairs, with one lock at the base and the other at the top of a door. Each lock has a metal protection that is inserted in either the ceiling or the floor.

Burglar-alarm system A warning-bell device that provides both psychological and physical protection from potential intruders by going off upon forced entry. This system may or may not be connected directly to police headquarters or the alarm company.

Dead lock A lock installed in the face of a door, obtainable with or without a key, that normally has a rectangular-shaped projectile which is inserted into the hole of the frame to lock the door.

Fire-alarm system Equipment that detects fire and sounds a warning. Such a system may also detect heat and smoke.

Motion-detection system A wireless radar device that can be purchased to alert a family of potential intruders. These devices can be placed in strategic locations such as by doors and windows. An alarm is sounded when a person passes within a certain distance.

Security Actions taken to make a residence safe from intruders, fire and smoke.

Systems approach to security A consideration of each security device in relation to total home-protective needs.

Vertical bolt An auxiliary lock which is screwed onto the door and frame. It prevents a burglar from jimmying the door because it has a pin which fits into a plate.

Wireless monitor system A system in which small radio transmitters are placed on windows and doors and a master control is installed. If an entry is made, the device sounds an alarm and alerts the alarm company's office, which in turn calls the police.

Chapter 14 / Maintenance, Repairs, Improvements

Bid An offer of a price on services to be rendered on home improvements. One should obtain several bids from reliable contractors. The best sources of information on reliability are the Better Business Bureau and references from previous customers.

Contract An agreement between two parties. It should be in writing and in sufficient detail to avoid misunderstandings.

Credit plans Home-improvement loans offered by firms with payments spread over thirty-six to sixty months.

Preventive maintenance Taking proper care of equipment prior to its breaking down. Advantages: longer life, reduced repair bills.

Chapter 15 / Swimming Pools

Algae A microscopic plant life that thrives and multiplies very rapidly, especially in warm, unchlorinated water. Algae cause slimy patches and stains to develop on the bottom and sides of the pool. There are many strains of algae, but the most common are the green, reddish brown or black.

Floater A device used on the surface of your pool water for dispensing dry chlorine in tablet form.

pH A numerical rating that indicates the acid or alkaline condition of water. A pH of 7 is neutral; a rating over 7 indicates alkalinity; and a rating of under 7 indicates acidity.

Skimmer A metal or plastic screen used to remove debris from pool water. It can be permanently built into the wall of an in-ground pool or it may be a simple device attached to the intake line of the filter of an above-ground pool. Some pool owners use a manual skimmer, which is a netlike device attached to the end of a pole.

Stabilizer (Conditioner) A special chemical agent (cyranuric acid) which, when applied to pool water in the recommended amount, slows the dissipation rate of the chlorine residual (especially useful in warmer climates).

Chapter 16 / Moving

Bill of lading A receipt for one's household possessions provided by the mover and indicating the tare weight of the van.

Estimator A moving-company representative who will make an estimate of the total charge for a move to include costs for transportation, valuation, pickup and delivery, storage, handling and special services.

Loss protection Protection for a family's household possessions in the event of damage.

Moving company This may be either an interstate carrier or a local firm specializing in short-haul moves of household possessions. A variety of services may be provided, such as packing, loading, storing and providing against loss or damage.

Net weight By subtracting the tare weight from the gross weight (tare weight + weight of possessions) one arrives at the net weight, or weight of possessions on which the moving charge is based.

Physical-inventory record The moving company's list of a family's household goods that indicates the condition of each item.

Tare weight The weight of a moving van prior to the placement of one's household possessions of it.

Temporary storage The period a carrier will store a family's household possessions in accordance with the terms and conditions of their contract (usually no more than 180 days). After this time, the goods go into permanent storage and warehouse rules apply.

Chapter 17 / Insurance (Life)

Definitions in this section are from the *Life Insurance Fact Book,* 1976 edition, published by the Institute of Life Insurance, 277 Park Avenue, New York, N.Y. 10017.

Accidental-death benefit A provision added to an insurance policy for payment of an additional benefit in case of death by accidental means. It is often referred to as "double indemnity."

Actuary A person professionally trained in the technical aspects of insurance and related fields, particularly in the mathematics of insurance, such as the calculation of premiums, reserves and other values.

Agent A sales and service representative of an insurance company. Life insurance agents may also be called underwriters.

Annuitant The person during whose life an annuity is payable, usually the person to receive the annuity.

Annuity A contract that provides an income for a specified period of time, such as a number of years or for life.

Annuity certain A contract that provides an income for a specified number of years, regardless of life or death.

Application A statement of information made by a person applying for life insurance. It is used by the insurance company to determine the acceptability of the risk and the basis of the policy contract.

Assignment The legal transfer of one person's interest in an insurance policy to another person.

Automatic premium loan A provision in a life insurance policy authorizing the company to pay automatically by means of a policy loan any premium not paid by the end of the grace period.

Beneficiary The person named in the policy to receive the insurance proceeds at the death of the insured.

Broker A sales and service representative who handles insurance for his clients, generally selling insurance of various kinds and for several companies.

Business life insurance Life insurance purchased by a business enterprise on the life of a member of the firm. It is often bought by partnerships to protect the surviving partners against loss caused by the death of a partner, or by a corporation to reimburse it for loss caused by the death of a key employee.

Cash-surrender value The amount available in cash upon voluntary termination of a policy before it becomes payable by death or maturity.

Claim Notification to an insurance company that payment of an amount is due under terms of a policy.

Convertible term insurance Term insurance that can be exchanged, at the option of the policyholder and without evidence of insurability, for another plan of insurance.

Credit life insurance Term life insurance issued through a lender or lending agency to cover payment of a loan, installment purchase or other obligation, in case of death.

Declination The rejection by a life insurance company of an application for life insurance, usually for reasons of the health or occupation of the applicant.

Deferred annuity An annuity providing for the income payments to begin at some future date, such as in a specified number of years or at a specified age.

Deferred group annuity A type of group annuity providing for the purchase each year of a paid-up deferred annuity for each member of the group, the total amount received by the member at retirement being the sum of these deferred annuities.

Deposit-administration group annuity A type of group annuity providing for the accumulation of contributions in an undivided fund out of which annuities are purchased as the individual members of the group retire.

Disability benefit A provision added to a life-insurance policy for waiver of premium, and sometimes payment of monthly income, if the insured becomes totally and permanently disabled.

Dividend addition An amount of paid-up insurance purchased with a policy dividend and added to the face amount of the policy.

Double indemnity An accidental-death benefit providing for additional payment of an amount equal to the face of the policy in case of death by accidental means.

Endowment insurance Insurance payable to the insured if he is living on the maturity date stated in the policy, or to a beneficiary if the insured dies prior to that date.

Expectation of life (life expectancy) The average number of years of life remaining for persons of a given age, according to a particular mortality table.

Extended-term insurance A form of insurance available as a nonforfeiture option. It provides the original amount of insurance for a limited perod of time.

Face amount The amount stated on the face of the policy that will be paid in case of death or at the maturity of the contract. It does not include dividend additions, or additional amounts payable under accidental death or other special provisions.

Family-income policy A life insurance policy, combining whole life and decreasing-term insurance, under which the beneficiary receives income payments to the end of a specified period if the insured dies prior to the end of the period, and the face amount of the policy either at the end of the period or at the death of the insured.

Family policy A life insurance policy providing insurance on all or several family members in one contract, generally whole-life insurance on the husband and smaller amounts of term insurance on the wife and children, including those born after the policy is issued.

Fraternal life insurance Life insurance provided by fraternal orders or societies to their members.

Grace period A period (usually thirty-one days) following the premium due date, during which an overdue premium may be paid without penalty. The policy remains in force throughout this period.

Group annuity A pension plan providing annuities at retirement to a group of persons under a single master contract, with the individual members of the group holding certificates stating their coverage. It is usually issued to an employer for the benefit of employees. The two basic types are deferred and deposit administration group annuities.

Group life insurance Life insurance issued, usually without medical examination, on a group of persons under a single master policy. it is usually issued to an employer for the benefit of employees. The individual members of the group hold certificates stating their coverage.

Individual-policy pension trust A type of pension plan, frequently used for small groups, administered by trustees who are authorized to purchase individual level-premium policies or annuity contracts for each member of the plan. The policies usually provide both life insurance and retirement benefits.

Industrial life insurance Life insurance issued in small amounts, usually not over $500, with premiums payable on a weekly or monthly basis. The premiums are generally collected at the home by an agent of the company.

Insurability Acceptability to the company of an applicant for insurance.

Insurance examiner The representative of a state insurance department assigned to participate in the official audit and examination of the affairs of an insurance company.

Insured The person on whose life an insurance policy is issued.

Lapsed policy A policy terminated for non-payment of premiums. The term is sometimes limited to a termination occurring before the policy has a cash or other surrender value.

Legal-reserve life insurance company A life insurance company operating under state insurance laws specifying the minimum basis for the reserves the company must maintain on its policies.

Level-premium insurance Insurance for which the cost is distributed evenly over the period during which premiums are paid. The premium remains the same from year to year, and is more than the actual cost of protection in the earlier years of the policy and less than the actual cost in the later years. The excess paid in the early years builds up the reserve.

Life annuity A contract that provides an income for life.

Life insurance in force The sum of the face amounts, plus dividend additions, of life insurance policies outstanding at a given time. Additional amounts payable under accidental death or other special provisions are not included.

Limited-payment life insurance Whole-life insurance on which premiums are payable for a specified number of years or until death if death occurs before the end of the specified period.

Mortality table A statistical table showing the death rate at each age, usually expressed as so many per thousand.

Mutual life insurance company A life insurance company without stockholders, whose management is directed by a board elected by the policyholders. Mutual companies, in general, issue participating insurance.

Nonforfeiture option One of the choices available to the policyholder if he discontinues the required premium payments. The policy value, if any, may be taken in cash, as extended term insurance or as reduced paid up insurance.

Nonparticipating insurance Insurance on which the premium is calculated to cover as closely as possible the anticipated cost of the insurance protection and on which no dividends are payable.

Ordinary life insurance Life insurance usually issued in amounts of $1,000 or more, with premiums payable on an annual, semiannual, quarterly or monthly basis. The term is also used to mean straight life insurance.

Paid-up insurance Insurance on which all required premiums have been paid. The term is frequently used to mean the reduced paid-up insurance available as a nonforfeiture option.

Participating insurance Insurance on which the policyholder is entitled to receive policy dividends reflecting the difference between the premium charged and actual experience. The premium is calculated to provide some margin over the anticipated cost of the insurance protection.

Permanent life insurance A phrase used to cover any form of life insurance except term; generally, insurance that accrues cash value, such as whole-life or endowment.

Policy The printed document stating the terms of the insurance contract that is issued to the policyholder by the company.

Policy dividend A refund of part of the premium on a participating life insurance policy, reflecting the difference between the premium charged and actual experience.

Policy loan A loan made by an insurance company to a policyholder on the security of the cash value of his policy.

Policy reserves The amount that an insurance company allocates specifically for the fulfillment of its policy obligations. Reserves are so calculated that, together with future premiums and interest earnings, they will enable the company to pay all future claims.

Preauthorized check plan A plan by which a policyholder arranges with his bank and insurance company to have his premium payments drawn, usually monthly, from his checking account.

Premium The payment, or one of the periodic payments, a policyholder agrees to make for an insurance policy.

Premium loan A policy loan made for the purpose of paying premiums.

Rated policy An insurance policy issued at a higher-than-standard premium rate to cover the extra risk involved in certain cases where the insured has impaired health or a hazardous occupation.

Reduced paid-up insurance A form of insurance available as a nonforfeiture option. It provides for continuation of the original insurance plan, but for a reduced amount.

Renewable term insurance Term insurance that can be renewed at the end of the term, at the option of the policyholder and without evidence of insurability, for a limited number of successive terms. The rates increase at each renewal as the age of the insured increases.

Revival The reinstatement of a lapsed policy by the company upon receipt of evidence of insurability and payment of past-due premiums with interest.

Separate account An asset account established by a life insurance company separate from other funds, used primarily for pension plans. This arrangement permits wider latitude in the choice of investments, particularly in equities.

Settlement option One of the ways, other than immediate payment in a lump sum, in which the policyholder or beneficiary may choose to have the policy proceeds paid.

Stock life insurance company A life insurance company owned by stockholders, who elect a board to direct the company's management. Stock companies, in general, issue nonparticipating insurance, but may also issue participating insurance.

Straight life insurance Whole-life insurance on which premiums are payable for life.

Supplementary contract An agreement between a life insurance company and a policyholder or beneficiary by which the company retains the cash sum payable under an insurance policy and makes payments in accordance with the settlement option chosen.

Term insurance Insurance payable to a beneficiary at the death of the insured provided death occurs within a specified period, such as five or ten years, or before a specified age.

Underwriting The process by which an insurance company determines whether or not and on what basis it will accept an application for insurance.

Variable annuity An annuity contract in which the amount of each periodic income payment fluctuates. The fluctuation may be related to security-market values, a cost-of-living index or some other variable factor.

Waiver of premium A provision that under certain conditions an insurance policy will be kept in full force by the company without further payment of premiums. It is used most often in the event of total and permanent disability.

Whole-life insurance Insurance payable to a beneficiary at the death of the insured whenever that occurs. Premiums may be payable for a specified number of years (limited-payment life) or for life (straight life).

Chapter 18 / Insurance (Other)

Boatowner's insurance An insurance package providing "all-risk" physical-loss protection, covering motors, equipment, accessories and boat trailers as well as furnishing watercraft liability for bodily injury, property damage and medical payments.

Comprehensive coverage Auto insurance which protects against loss caused by other than collision.

Comprehensive personal liability (CPL) Insurance coverage providing protection should one be held legally liable for actions resulting in accidental injuries to others or accidental damage to the property of others.

Farmowner's insurance Packaged policy that protects eligible farm buildings and farm personal property as well as farm dwelling against theft and CPL, and includes additional living-expense insurance.

Homeowner's insurance Insurance providing financial protection against fire, lightning, wind, hail and many other perils.

Liability protection Financial coverage against accident losses in which an individual has incurred a pecuniary obligation or responsibility.

Medicare A program of health insurance under Social Security aiding Americans aged sixty-five and older as well as many severely disabled people under sixty-five. The program provides hospital and medical insurance.

Mutual insurance company A type of auto-insurance company that belongs to the policy-holders and distributes its net earnings through rebates.

No-fault insurance Third-party auto insurance whereby the insurance company pays an initial sum in accident claims at once, regardless of which driver was at fault.

Personal-property insurance Coverage protecting against losses from fire, smoke, lightning, flood, earthquake, wind, explosion, certain transportation hazards and other related threats to personal property; and/or protection against losses from theft, burglary, robbery, larceny, riot, civil commotion, loss (cash to $100) and breakage of gemstones.

Stock insurance company One of the principal types of auto-insurance companies, owned by shareholders, who receive a portion of the profits annually in the form of cash dividends.

Chapter 19 / Banks, S&L Associations, Credit Unions and the Money Market

Bankers' acceptance A time draft that a bank has promised to honor at maturity. Bankers' acceptances are purchased on a discount basis and utilized in the import/export business.

Cash reserve Money saved that can be obtained immediately in the event one needs it.

Commercial paper Short-term negotiable promissory notes issued by large corporations for periods up to 270 days.

Credit union A federally chartered and supervised cooperative organization that is comprised of a group of people who pool their money to make loans to one another. Members receive interest from the union's short-duration, consumer-oriented loans.

Diversification Distribution of available funds into a variety of sound investments.

Money market Short-term securities, including federal government-agency issues, bankers' acceptances and commercial paper.

NOW account An interest-bearing checking account known as a Negotiable Order or Withdrawal account.

Proxy A document giving a power of attorney authorizing a specific person to vote your stock.

Savings and loan association A privately owned financial organization which is chartered under federal or state law. It is administered by a board of directors and provides loans for repair, construction, purchasing or financing of homes and other real estate.

Treasury bills Short-term bearer security issued on a discount basis and currently issued in denominations of $10,000, $50,000, $100,000, $500,000 and $1 million.

Chapter 20–23 / Bonds; Stocks; Investment Companies

The definitions in this and the other glossary sections relate only to the categories in which the terms occur. That is, a term here is given its financial definition; it may have others, secular or relating to other fields.

Accrued interest The interest that has accumulated on a bond between its issuance and a sale. This term describes the way bonds are priced. When a bond is purchased, the buyer pays the agreed price plus accrued interest.

Assets What an organization owns plus what is owed to it. Assets may be tangible, like a vehicle, or intangible, like a certificate of deposit.

At the market At prevailing prices. This is a term used in ordering the purchase or sale of securities.

Bear One who believes that the stock market will decline.

Bear market A market in which the price-trend is declining.

Bid and asked *Bid* is the price offered for a security by a purchaser. *Asked* is the price at which a security is offered for sale by a seller.

Big board A term often applied to the New York Stock Exchange.

Bond A formal evidence of a debt, in which the borrower agrees to pay the lender a specified amount, with interest at a fixed rate payable on specified dates.

Book value A computation arrived at by taking the assets of an organization at the balance-sheet values and subtracting all liabilities and the liquidation price of preferred stock, if any.

Bull One who believes that the stock market will rise.

Bull market A market in which the price trend is rising.

Call The right to buy shares of a certain stock, if desired, at a set price within a given period of time as specified in the contract.

Callable bonds Bonds that may be redeemed by the issuing corporation before the maturity date. Usually the company is required to pay a premium over their face value when they are called before maturity.

Capital structure or **Capitalization** The amount and type of securities authorized and issued by a corporation.

Cash flow The complete series of net proceeds and net outlays of cash related to a business activity.

Cash items Cash, bank deposits, U.S. government issues and other securities that are considered the same as cash.

Common stock Securities that have a right to dividends subordinate to all other stock of the corporation.

Consolidated financial statement An accounting report that gives an insight into the overall picture only. The parent company and its subsidiaries are treated as one organization.

Convertible bonds Bonds that may, at the option of the holder, be exchanged for a specified amount of other securities of the issuing firm.

Convertible preferred stock Preferred stock that may be converted at the option of the holder into common stock, on stated terms, within a specified period of time.

Cumulative preferred stock Preferred stock on which the dividends, if not paid in full, accumu-

late. The accumulations must be paid before any dividends can be paid on the corporation's common stock.

Current assets Cash, cash items, inventories and notes and accounts receivable due within one year.

Current liabilities Accounts and notes payable, accrued taxes, interest declared dividends and other claims that are payable within one year.

Day order An order given by a customer to his broker, good for one day only.

Debenture A long-term debt supported by the general credit of the issuing corporation.

Depreciation A periodic charge against income to spread the cost of such items as equipment and buildings over their estimated useful life.

Dividend The payment made by a corporation to its stockholders as a return on their investment.

Equity The net worth of a corporation that measures the interest of stockholders in a corporation. It can be determined by subtracting the total liabilities from the total assets.

Ex dividend Of a stock, without the dividend. The purchaser of the stock on or after the ex-dividend date will not receive payment of the dividend even though it is made at a later date.

First-mortgage bond A bond secured by a first mortgage on property of the issuing corporation.

Fixed charges Relatively constant expenses such as the interest on notes and property rental.

Funded debt Long-term debt normally maturing more than one year from date of issue.

Funds flow The complete series of proceeds and outlays of funds related to a business activity.

G.T.C. (open) order An order given by a customer to his broker that is good until canceled or executed.

Limited order A price set by the customer at which he will buy or sell. The broker is authorized to transact business "at or better than" the "limit" price.

Listed securities Corporation shares that have been approved for listing by a stock exchange.

Long Owning securities. It is the opposite of *short*.

Margin The value in a customer's account over the amount owed to the brokerage firm.

Municipal bond A bond issued by a political subdivision of a state, such as a county, city, town or district.

Net income The true corporate profit after deducting all expenses, including taxes.

Net working capital Current assets minus current liabilities.

Odd lot An amount of stock less than the established unit of trading.

Offer The price at which one is prepared to sell.

Over-the-counter Describes the market for securities not listed on an exchange.

Paper profit A profit resulting from the rise in price of a security that is still held in a portfolio. The security must be sold to change a paper profit into a realized profit.

Par The dollar amount assigned to shares by the corporation charter.

Participating bonds Bonds that are entitled to a stated rate of interest and may also share in the profits of the issuing corporation.

Participating preferred stock Stock that has an established rate of dividend and may be entitled to additional dividends.

Preferred stock A category of stock with priority over common stock in the distribution of dividends and assets.

Prior preferred stock A category of stock with priority as to distribution of dividends and assets over either preferred stock or common stock.

Prospectus A pamphlet that describes in detail a security offered for sale. It contains information about the corporation's business and its financial condition.

Proxy A written authority given by a shareholder to another person empowering the latter to vote stock owned by the stockholder.

Put The right to sell shares of a particular stock, if desired, within a given period of time at a specific price as fixed in the contract.

Refunding Refinancing a debt prior to maturity in order to secure better terms for the corporation.

Right A privilege granted to stockholders to buy new securities at a price generally below the prevailing market.

Round lot The unit of trading of an exchange, usually 100 shares.

Seat A membership on an exchange.

SEC Securities and Exchange Commission.

Short Having sold stock that is not owned, in anticipation of being able to buy it later at a lower price.

Stock dividend Additional shares of stock issued by a corporation to its stockholders.

Stock split The division of each present share into two or more shares.

Stop order An order instructing the broker to buy or sell at the market, if and when the price of the stock reaches a certain figure.

Street name Term applied to securities registered in the name of a recognized broker in lieu of the owner's name.

Switching The selling of one security and buying of another.

Tax-exempt bonds Securities issued by states or municipalities. The income derived therefrom is wholly or partially exempt from income taxes.

Warrant A certificate giving the right to purchase securities at a stipulated price within a specified time limit.

Chapter 23 / Investment Companies

Capital structure As applied to investment companies, this refers to the components of each company's capitalization, as found on its balance sheet.

Closed-end company An investment company from which shares are purchased and sold like regular corporate issues through stock-brokerage firms and in which capitalization is relatively fixed. The closed-ends are usually listed on organized exchanges. Recently closed-ends have been also called publicly traded funds.

Dual-purpose closed-end investment company A closed-end fund that permits one group of shareholders to receive all the income for a set period, after which period all capital gains that may have accrued are given to another group of shareholders.

557

Hedge fund An investment company that buys securities with borrowed dollars to obtain leverage and make short sales.

Investment company A commercial enterprise that obtains money from institutions and individuals for the primary purpose of investing these funds in short-term debt, bonds and/or stocks in order to achieve such objectives as safety, growth and income.

Letter stock Unregistered or restricted issues. Purchasers of these securities normally sign letters stating that they are purchasing such securities for investment reasons and not for public sales in the foreseeable future.

Loading (sales) charge A one-time fee imposed at time of purchase by many open-end companies (mutual funds). It normally varies from 7 to 9 percent.

Management fee An annual charge made by investment companies for the services they provide, including investing money made available to them by investors.

No-load company An open-end investment company that has no load (sales) charge.

Open-end company (mutual fund) An investment company whose capitalization is usually made up entirely of common stock. The number of its shareholders usually varies daily, depending upon the sales made as well as redemptions.

"People's capitalism" A term coined by Bernard Cornfeld and applied to the mutual-fund concept when he introduced it in foreign countries.

Chapter 24 / Real Estate

Appraisal A valuation of property by the estimate of an authorized person.

Land contract A contract between buyer and seller in which the seller retains title until payment has been completed.

Leverage Borrowing money at a given rate of interest and using it to obtain a higher return. The leverage factor in real estate permits the investor to utilize a small initial equity.

Property Something owned or possessed; specifically, a piece of real estate; something to which a person has a legal title.

Real estate From Webster's Dictionary: "Land and its . . . buildings . . . its improvements and its natural assets (as minerals, crops, waters) and with the inclusion of . . . rights that follow ownership of the land. . . ."

Real-estate company A corporation organized to deal primarily in real estate: such a company may be listed on the various exchanges.

Real-estate investment trust An organization specializing in real estate that obtains funds from stockholders for this purpose. In accordance with the Internal Revenue code it qualifies as a business trust by paying out to shareholders annually at least 90 percent of the trust's taxable income, thus avoiding federal income tax.

Real-estate syndicate An organization specializing in a particular real-estate project. Each individual participating in it becomes a limited partner.

Chapter 25 / Profitable Hobbies: Numismatics and Gold

Gold-filled Covered with a layer of gold.

Gold leaf A sheet of gold, varying from four- to five-millionths of an inch in thickness, that is used primarily for gilding.

Heirloom Something of special value handed down from one generation to another.

Numismatics The study and/or collection of money.

Numismatist A coin and/or paper-money collector and/or student of the subject.

Troy ounce An ounce containing 20 pennyweights, or 480 grains.

Troy weight A series of weights based on a pound of twelve ounces.

Chapter 26 / Commodities

Definitions in this section are adapted from Merrill Lynch, Pierce, Fenner & Smith, Inc., *How to Buy and Sell Commodities*, 1973, pp. 39–50.

Account sale statement A statement showing the net result of a purchase or a sale and its liquidation, with commission and all other charges included. Also called a *Purchase and sale,* or *P&S statement.*

Accumulation Buying by traders who expect to hold the contracts for a more or less extended period.

Afloat Of a commodity, on board ships en route to destinations indicated. *In transit* has the same meaning with regard to car shipments on land.

Arbitrage See *Spread.*

At the market Of orders to be executed, at the best possible price as soon as received in the trading ring or pit. Such orders are called *Market Orders.*

Basis Points difference over or under a designated future at which a cash commodity of a certain description is sold or quoted. A most important term for those who hedge.

Bear One who believes prices are heading lower. To *bear the market* is to press sales in a concentrated manner. A news item is considered *bearish* if it is expected to bring on lower prices.

Bid A price offered, subject, unless otherwise stated, to immediate acceptance for a specific amount of a commodity. For another definition of an entirely different type of bid, see *Privilege.*

Break A price decline, usually sharp.

Broker An agent entrusted with the execution of an order, the commission house that carries the account or a floor broker or pit broker who actually executes the order on the floor for the commission house. When reference is made to the last, it is best to call him a *Floor Broker.*

Bull One who believes prices are heading higher. To *bull the market* is to buy contracts steadily and vigorously. A certain item of news is considered *bullish* if it portends higher prices.

Buoyant Of a market, having prices that tend to rise easily, with a considerable show of strength.

Buy in To cover or liquidate a sale. *Shorts* are said to "cover" when they repurchase the contracts they sold originally.

Buy on close or **opening** To buy at the end or beginning of the session at a price within the closing or opening range.

Buyer's call See *Call sale.*

Cables Wire dispatches from foreign markets giving news and prices.

Call A designated buying-and-selling period resembling an auction, whereby trading on many exchanges is conducted in order to establish a price or price range for a particular time. It is important to note that during a call, trading is confined to one delivery month at a time.

Call cotton Cotton bought or sold on call. See *Call sale* and *Call purchase.*

Call purchase A purchase of a commodity of a specified quality under a contract providing for the fixing of the price in the future by the seller on the basis of a stipulated number of points above or below the price of a specified future on the day the contract price is fixed, which day is selected by the seller. Sometimes called *Seller's call;* generally applies to trading in cotton.

Call sale A sale of a commodity of a specified quality under a contract providing for the fixing of the price in the future by the purchaser on the basis of a stipulated number of points above or below the price of a specified future on the day the contract price is fixed, which day is selected by the buyer. Sometimes called *Buyer's call;* generally applies to trading in cotton.

Carrying broker The broker or commission house carrying the account of a client.

Carrying charges Those charges incurred in carrying the actual commodity for one or more days, weeks or months, generally including interest, insurance and storage, and sometimes including other pertinent items.

Cash commodity Same as *Spot commodity.* Originally a commodity on the spot, ready for delivery; now used to include also a commodity bought or sold to arrive or to be delivered at a later date.

Certified stocks The stocks of a commodity that have been certified as being deliverable on futures. They must be stored in warehouses designated and approved by the exchange concerned. (In grain, called *Stocks in deliverable position.*)

C.I.F. Price including the cost, insurance and freight to deliver a commodity to a specified location.

Clearances Volume of a commodity that has moved out of a particular port or ports on a particular date.

Clearing association or **house** A central agency (sometimes a separate corporation), set up by an exchange or authorized by it, through which transactions of members of the exchange are cleared and financial settlements effected. A *clearing member* is a member of an exchange who is also a member of the associated clearing association.

Clearing contracts The process of substituting principals to transactions through the operation of clearing associations in order to simplify the settlement of accounts.

Close The period at the end of the trading session during which all trades are officially declared as having been executed "at or on the close." On the New York Cotton Exchange, this period is the last half-minute of trading. The *closing range* is the range of actual sales during this period.

Commercial stocks Stocks of grain at all prominent grain centers, east and west, issued by the Department of Agriculture. See *Visible supply grain.*

Commission The fee charged by a broker for performance of a specific duty, such as the buying or selling of commodities.

Commission broker or **house** A firm that buys and sells for the account of customers. See also *Futures commission broker.*

Contract grades Grades that are deliverable on a futures contract. The basic contract grade is the one deliverable at par. There may be more than one basic grade.

Contract market Any board of trade or commodity exchange that has been designated by the Secretary of Agriculture to conduct a futures market.

Contracts of sale Agreements of sale or purchase, and agreements to sell or purchase.

Controlled account Any account for which trading is directed by a person other than the principal.

Cover Of a *Short,* to buy back the contract one has previously sold, thereby liquidating his position.

Current delivery See *Delivery month.*

Day orders Limited orders that are to be executed the day on which they are received and are automatically canceled at the close of the day if not executed meanwhile.

Deliverable stocks See *Certified stocks.* Said of grain where warehouse receipts are used to satisfy deliveries.

Delivery month The calendar month stipulated in a futures contract as the month of delivery. *Current delivery* is delivery during the present month. *Nearby delivery* is delivery in the nearest active month. *Distant delivery* is delivery in one of the months furthest off. See *Forward months.*

Delivery notice See *Notice of delivery.*

Delivery points Locations designated by futures exchanges to which the commodity covered by a futures contract may be delivered in fulfillment of such contract.

Delivery price The price fixed by the clearing house at which deliveries on futures are invoiced; also, the price at which the futures contract is settled when deliveries are made.

Differentials Usually (1) the premiums paid for the grades better than the basic grade, and (2) the discounts allowed for the grades lower than the basic grade. Sometimes these differentials are fixed by the contract terms, such as in the grains; at other times, as in cotton, commercial differentials apply.

Ease off To decline slowly, as prices.

Erratic Of a market, moving rapidly and irregularly.

Evening up Buying or selling to adjust an open market position.

Exchange of spot or cash commodity for futures The simultaneous exchange of a specified quantity of a cash commodity for the equivalent quantity in futures, usually because both parties carry opposite hedges in the same delivery month. Also known as *exchange for physical* or *against actuals.*

Farm prices The prices received by farmers for their products, as published by the U.S. Department of Agriculture as of the fifteenth of each month.

Fixation See *Call purchase* and *Call sale.*

Floor broker Any person who, in or around any pit, ring, post or other place provided by a contract market for the meeting of persons similarly engaged, engages in executing for others any order for the purchase or sale of any commodity for future delivery on or subject to the rules of any contract market, and who for such services receives or accepts a commission or other compensation.

Floor trader An exchange member who executes his own trades by being personally present in the pit or place provided for futures trading.

Forward months Futures contracts calling for a later or "distant" delivery.

Free supply Total stocks in general or specific locations, less what is owned or controlled by the government. Applies to those commodities that are in large surplus where the government owns sizable quantities of the surplus, or to medium-sized crops where surplus is almost wholly government-owned.

Futures Agreements to buy and receive or to sell and deliver a commodity at a future date, with these distinguishing characteristics: (1) All trades have the same unit of trading; e.g., the N.Y.C.E. contract is 100 bales; (2) the terms of all trades are identical; (3) a trade, therefore, may be offset later by a contra trade through the same broker; (4) all trades must be made by open outcry around a ring within the hours prescribed; (5) the contract has a basic grade but may have other grades deliverable; (6) delivery is made during a single calendar month (some markets outside the U.S.A. use a two-month delivery period); (7) the trades are cleared through a clearing house daily. (Traders in cash or spot goods usually refer to sales for shipment or delivery in the future as "deferred" or "forward" sales. Such sales, however, are not standardized as are futures contracts described above.)

Futures commission broker A firm or party engaged in soliciting or in accepting orders for the purchase or sale of any commodity for future delivery on or subject to the rules of any contract market, who, in or in connection with such solicitations or acceptances of orders, accepts any money, securities or property (or extends credit in lieu thereof) to margin any trades or contracts that result or may result therefrom. Futures commission brokers must be licensed under the Commodity Exchange Act when handling business in commodities covered thereby. (Called *Futures Commission Merchant* by Commodity Exchange Authority.)

Futures contract See *Futures.*

Futures exchange An association organized for the purpose of conducting trading in commodity futures. See *Contract market.*

Give-up A contract executed by one broker for the client of another broker, which the client orders given up to the latter broker. Generally speaking, the order is sent over the leased wires of the first broker, who collects a wire-toll from the other broker for the use of his wires.

Harden Of a market, to advance slowly.

Heavy Of a market, apparently having a number of selling orders overhanging the market without a corresponding number of buying orders.

Hedge In its simplest form, a sale of futures against a purchase of spots, or vice versa. It is a medium through which offsetting commitments are employed to eliminate or minimize the impact of an adverse price movement on inventories or other previous commitments.

In sight Having arrived, as an amount of a commodity, at a comprehensive group of terminal or central locations in or near producing areas.

In transit See *Afloat.*

Interest See *Long, Short,* and *Open interest.*

Inverted market A futures market in which distant-months contracts are selling below near-month contracts.

Job-lot contract A form of contract having a smaller unit of trading than the regular contract.

Life of delivery The period of time that has expired from the inception of trading in the delivery to the date of the last transaction.

Limit move The maximum fluctuation in price of a futures contract permitted during one trading session, as fixed by the rules of a contract market.

Limited order An order on which the client sets a limit on the price, as contrasted with a market order. (Orders may be limited in time as well as price; such orders are called *Time orders.*)

Liquidation Sale of a previously bought contract, otherwise known as *Long liquidation.* It may also be the repurchase of a previously sold contract, generally referred to as *Short covering.*

Loan price The price at which growers may obtain loans under government price-support programs; adding freight and handling gives *Terminal loan.*

Long Having bought more contracts than one has sold. (See *Short.*) *Long hedges* are purchases of futures made as a hedge against the sale of the cash commodity. *Long interest* is the sum total of all long contracts or the owners of such interest.

Long of the basis Having bought cash or spot goods and hedged them with sales of futures. One who is *long of the basis* has therefore bought at a certain basis on or off futures and expects to sell at a better basis for a profit.

Long pull Long run. One is said to buy for a long pull if he expects higher prices eventually, although declines may occur meanwhile.

Margin The amount deposited by a client with his broker to protect the broker against losses on contracts being carried or to be carried by the broker. A *Margin call* is a request either to deposit original margin or to maintain margin with added cash.

Market order See *At the market.*

Nearby delivery See *Delivery month.*

Net position The difference between the number of contracts long and the number short for account of an individual or firm.

Notice of delivery A notice given by the seller with details of delivery he will make of the actual commodity. *Notice day* is one the seller selects as the day on which he will issue a notice of delivery. Chicago Board of Trade notices are called *Intentions to deliver. Tenders* is the term in cotton. Some exchange notices are transferable; others are not. See *Transferable notice.*

Notice price See *Delivery price.*

Offer The price at which a seller offers to deliver a specific amount of a commodity, subject to immediate acceptance, unless otherwise stated.

Offset (1) The practice used by commission merchants of setting long against short commitments for the purpose of determining net positions; (2) the procedure by which an individual's long or short position is liquidated by an opposite transaction.

Omnibus account An account carried by one futures commission merchant with another, in which the transactions of two or more persons are combined rather than designated separately.

Open interest The number of unliquidated contracts. In any one delivery month, the short interest equals the long interest; that is, the total number of contracts sold equals the total number bought. Open interest is synonymous with *Open commitments* or *Open position.*

Option A term sometimes erroneously applied to a futures contract, because the seller has the option of fixing the day during the delivery month on which delivery may be made, the grade to be delivered, and the warehouse where delivery is to be made. Dealing in options—i.e., in puts and calls—is prohibited on all American commodity exchanges. See *Privilege.*

Original margin The initial deposit of margin with respect to a given commitment.

Overbought With heavy liquidation of weakly held long commitments appearing imminent.

Oversold With heavy covering of weakly held short commitments appearing imminent.

P&S Abbreviation of *Purchase and Sale.* See *Account sale* and *Purchase and sale statement.*

Paper profit The profit that would be realized if open contracts were liquidated as of a certain time or at a certain price.

Parity The calculated price that the producer needs to receive for his crop to cover his current costs to live and produce. It is computed monthly by the U.S. Department of Agriculture, and if received by farmers, would give relatively the same return the producer received in a ten-year base period. It also provides a yardstick of what farm income should be to equal current income in other parts of the economy. Its importance can be modified if price-support loans are set at lower percentages of parity. Other means of setting price supports are gaining favor.

Pit See *Ring.*

Point The minimum unit in which changes in a futures price may be expressed.

Position An interest in the market in the form of open or unliquidated commitments.

Position limit The maximum nonhedge position that may be held or controlled by one prson, in one commodity future or in all futures of one commodity combined, as fixed by the Commodity Exchange Authority. See *Reporting limit.*

Premium Generally, the excess of a cash-commodity price over a futures price or over another cash-commodity price, or the excess of one futures contract price over another.

Prices, clearing See *Settlement price.*

Primary markets Important centers at which

spot or cash commodities are originally accumulated for movement into commercial channels.

Private wires Telegraph or telephone wires leased for the exclusive use of the lessee.

Privilege A contract whereby the purchaser may, within a specified period, exercise the right of entering into a futures contract with the seller of the privilege contract at the price named. Privileges are also known as *Indemnities, Bid and Offers,* and *Puts and Calls.* Such contracts are illegal under the provisions of the Commodity Exchange Act in the commodities regulated by the act.

Professional One who devotes his time and activities to market operations.

Public elevators Elevators in which grain is stored in bulk for the public and in which grains of the same grade owned by different persons may be mixed together.

Purchase and sale statement A statement sent by a commission merchant to a customer when the latter's futures position has been reduced or closed out. It shows the amount involved, the prices at which the position was acquired and closed out, the gross profit or loss, the commission charged and the net profit or loss on the transaction. Frequently referred to as *P&S.*

Puts and calls See *Privilege.*

Pyramiding Margining additional trades through using accrued profits.

Rally A quick advance in prices following a decline.

Range The difference between the high and low prices of the futures during a given period.

Reaction A quick decline in prices following an advance.

Recovery An advance after a decline.

"Regular" warehouse A warehouse that has been officially approved by a grain contract market for the delivery therefrom of a commodity under a futures contract. In other commodities, such warehouses are usually called "licensed" warehouses.

Reporting limit An amount of a commodity set by the Secretary of Agriculture under the Commodity Exchange Act; the Commodity Exchange Authority considers all accounts that have positions at or above these amounts as "reportable status accounts."

Resting order If an order to buy, an order limited to a price below the market; if an order to sell, limited to a price above the market.

Ring A space on the trading floor of an exchange around which traders and brokers stand while executing futures transactions. In grain markets it is usually called a *pit.*

Round turn A purchase and its liquidating sale, or a sale and its liquidating purchase.

Sale buying or **Selling** Describing orders to buy or sell at regular price intervals up or down.

Seller's call See *Call purchase.*

Seller's option The right of a seller to select, within the limits prescribed by a contract, the quality of the commodity delivered and the time and place of delivery. The word *option,* however, should not be used to describe the contract itself. See *Option.*

Settlement price (1) The daily price at which the clearing house clears all the day's trades; (2) the price established by the exchange to settle contracts unliquidated because of *force majeure* or other causes.

Short One who has sold a futures contract that does not liquidate a previously bought contract for the same delivery month. In other words, he sells in expectation of buying back at a lower price. *Short* also describes his position. *Short hedges* are sales of futures made as hedges against holdings of the spot commodity or products thereof. *Short interest* is the sum total of all short contracts or the owners of such contracts.

Short of the basis Of a person or firm, having sold cash or spot goods and hedged them with purchases of futures. One who is *short of the basis* has therefore sold at a certain basis and expects to buy back at a better basis for a profit.

Sold-out market A market in which liquidation of weakly held contracts has largely been completed and offerings have become scarce.

Speculator A person entering into futures contracts for any purpose other than hedging. See *Hedge.*

Spot price The price at which the spot or cash commodity is selling. In grain trading, it is called the *cash price.*

Spread The difference between two delivery months in the same or different markets, or the sale of a contract in one against a simultaneous purchase of a contract in the other. Generally speaking, the same as a *Straddle*. Straddling between a foreign market and domestic market is often referred to as *Arbitrage*.

Stop-loss order An order placed at a definite limit above the prevailing market price (if a *buy stop*) or below the existing price level (if a *sell stop*) that will not become a market order and will not be executed until the stop price has been reached. When such an order is placed, an existing position will be liquidated only if there is a price movement adverse to the position. (One can also initiate a new position in this way, but it would be called simply a *Stop*.)

Straddle See *Spread*.

Surplus Supply of commodity above requirements.

Switch The sale of an already-existing long position and the simultaneous purchase of another position, or vice versa. It may be ordered done at the market or at a specified difference.

Technical position An attribute of a market believed to result from certain actions that have occurred. It might be partly demonstrated from known facts. In a sold-out market or in an oversold market, the technical position is said to be strong. On the other hand, in an overbought market, the technical position is said to be weak. The latter is due to the fact that heavy speculative buying has carried prices to a point where no further advance may be expected on the known news and a decline is probably imminent.

Tender price A term used in the cotton trade to designate a price of spot cotton that, if the expense incident to delivery be added thereto, equals the current price of the future. It may also mean the delivery-notice price.

Tenderable grades (and staples) Grades (and staples) that are designated as deliverable in settlement of a futures contract. Sometimes termed *Deliverable grades (and staples)*.

Terminal elevator An elevator located at a point of accumulation and distribution in the movement of agricultural products, generally grain.

Time order See *Limited order*.

Trading limit Prices above or below which trading is not allowed during any one day; also, under Commodity Exchange Act regulations,

the maximum amount of contracts any individual is allowed to hold at any time in the commodities covered by the act.

Transferable notice A written announcement issued by a seller signifying his intention of making delivery in fulfillment of a futures contract. The recipient of the notice may make a sale of the future and transfer the notice within a specified time to another party—on some exchanges directly, and on others through the clearing association. The last recipient takes delivery of the commodity tendered. See *Notice of delivery*.

Trend The direction prices are taking.

Variation margin Additional margin required during, or after the close of, the trading session by reason of price variations.

Visible supply grain Grain in terminal elevators at prominent grain centers east of the Rocky Mountains, including the quantities afloat on the Great Lakes and the Barge Canal. (See *Commercial stocks*.) The term may also be used in commodities other than grain but would apply to locations involved in those commodities.

Volume of trading The purchases and sales of a commodity future during a specified period. Since purchases equal sales, only one side is shown in published reports.

Warehouse receipt A document evidencing the receipt by a warehouseman (licensed under the United States Warehouse Act or under the laws of the state) of the commodity named in the receipt. Warehouse receipts are negotiable receipts covering commodities in warehouses recognized for delivery purposes by the exchange on which such futures contracts are traded.

Wash sale A fictitious transaction made usually for the purpose of creating apparent volume or price activity in the market; not permitted by the Commodity Exchange Act.

Chapter 27 / Taxes

Annuity An amount payable yearly or at other regular intervals.

Arbitrage Simultaneous purchase and sale of the same or equivalent security in order to profit from price discrepancies.

Bond An interest-bearing certificate of public or private indebtedness.

Capital-gains tax A tax placed upon persons who realize a profit from the sale of their securities.

Declining balance A uniform rate applied each year to the remaining cost or other basis of a property as determined at the beginning of each year.

Dividends A share in a pro-rata distribution of profits to stockholders.

Income tax A tax on the net income of an individual or business.

Income-tax return A form that must be filed by specified persons itemizing their net income and indicating the amount due the federal government, state or municipality.

Joint return A formal statement on a required legal form showing taxable income, allowable deductions and exemptions and computation of the tax due by married couples.

Negative income tax A concept that would result in the federal government's giving families monthly payments when their incomes were below a certain level.

Rental income Income that accrues to a person from renting his home.

Royalty Payment made to an individual such as a composer, writer or inventor for each copy of his work sold.

Stock Money or capital invested or available for investment or trading.

Straight-line depreciation The useful life of a property divided into the cost less salvage value.

Sum of the year's digits The result obtained by multiplying the cost or other basis of a property (reduced by estimated salvage value) by the number of years of useful life remaining, and dividing the product by the sum of all digits corresponding to the years of the useful life of the property.

Chapter 28 / Retirement, Wills and Trusts

Codicil A legal instrument made subsequently to a will and modifying it.

Conservator A person, official or institution designated to take over and protect the interests of an incompetent.

Executor The person appointed by a testator to execute his will.

Fee simple Giving the ownership of the property with unrestricted rights to dispose of it.

Guardian One who has the care of the person or property of another.

Living trust A fund providing investment income to a person during his lifetime and subsequently offering an economical means of passing on property to heirs.

Probate The action or process of proving before a competent judicial authority that a document offered for official recognition and registration as the last will and testament of a deceased person is genuine.

Testamentary trust A trust created by a person's will that becomes operative only after his death. Such a trust appoints a trustee to administer the deceased's property for the benefit of those specified in the will.

Testator A person who leaves a will or testament in force at his death.

Trustee A natural or legal person to whom property is legally committed to be administered for the benefit of a beneficiary.

Will A legal declaration of a person's mind as to the manner in which he would have his property or estate disposed of after his death; especially a written instrument legally executed by which a man makes disposition of his estate to take effect after his death.

BIBLIOGRAPHY

Adler, Joan. *Retirement Book: A Complete Early Planning Guide to Finances, New Activities and Where to Live.* New York: Morrow Publications, 1975.

Allentuck, Andrew D. and Gordon E. Bivens. *Consumer Choice.* New York: Harcourt Brace Jovanovich, Inc., 1977.

Bailard, Thomas E., David L. Biehl, and Ronald W. Kaiser. *Personal Money Management.* Chicago: SRA, 1977.

Beaton, William R. and Terry Robertson. *Real Estate Investment.* Englewood Cliffs, N.Y.: Prentice-Hall, Inc., 1977.

Best's Insurance Reports. Morristown, N.J.: A. M. Best Company, published annually.

Car Buying Made Easier. Dearborn, Michigan: Ford Motor Company, current edition.

Christy, George H. and John C. Clendenin. *Introduction to Investments.* New York: McGraw Hill Book Company, 1978.

Cohen, Jerome B., Edward D. Zinbarg and Arthur Zeikel. *Investment Analysis and Portfolio Management.* Homewood, Illinois: Richard D. Irwin, Inc., 1975.

Consumer Reports. *The Buying Guide Issue: The Facts You Need Before You Buy.* Mount Vernon, N.Y.: Consumer's Union, published annually.

Denenberg, Herbert. *The Insurance Trap—Unfair at Any Rate.* San Francisco, California: Russell Books, 1975.

De Salvo, Louis J. *Consumer Finance.* New York: John Wiley & Sons, 1977.

Epstein, David G. *Consumer Protection.* St. Paul, Minnesota: West Publishing Company, 1976.

Ficek, Edmund F., Thomas P. Henderson, and Ross H. Johnson. *Real Estate Principles and Practices.* Columbus, Ohio: Charles E. Merrill Publishing Company, 1976.

Fischer, Donald E. and Ronald J. Jordan. *Security Analysis and Portfolio Management.* Englewood Cliffs, N.J.: Prentice-Hall, Inc., 1975.

Galbraith, John K. *Money.* Boston: Houghton Mifflin Company, 1975.

Haft, Richard A. *Investing in Securities.* Englewood Cliffs, N.J.: Prentice-Hall, Inc., 1975.

Harper, Victor L. *Handbook of Investment Products and Services.* New York: New York Institute of Finance, 1975.

Hastings, Paul and Norbert Mietus. *Personal Finance.* New York: McGraw Hill Book Company, 1977.

Huebner, S. S. and Kenneth Black, Jr. *Life Insurance,* 9th edition. Englewood Cliffs, N.J.: Prentice-Hall, Inc., 1976.

Lang, Larry R. and Thomas H. Gillespie. *Strategy for Personal Finance.* New York: McGraw Hill Book Company, 1977.

Lasser, J. K. *Your Income Tax.* New York: Simon & Schuster, published annually.

Life Insurance Fact Book. American Council of Life Insurance, New York, published annually.

Meltzer, Yale L. *Putting Money to Work.* Englewood Cliffs, N.J.: Prentice-Hall, Inc., 1976.

Moody's Handbook of Common Stocks. Moody's Investors Service, Inc., New York, published quarterly.

Mutual Fund Fact Book. Investment Company Institute, Washington, D.C., published annually.

O'Donnell, Paul T. and Eugene L. Maleady. *Principles of Real Estate.* Philadelphia: W. B. Saunders Company, 1975.

Porter, Thomas W. and Durwood L. Alkire. *Wealth: How to Achieve It!* Reston, Virginia: Reston Publishing Co., Inc., 1976.

Prentice-Hall Federal Tax Course. Englewood Cliffs, N.J.: Prentice-Hall, Inc., published annually.

Riegel, Robert, Jerome S. Miller and C. Arthur Williams, Jr. *Insurance Principles and Practices: Property and Liability.* 6th edition. Englewood Cliffs, N.J.: Prentice-Hall, Inc., 1976.

Ring, Alfred and Nelson North. *Real Estate Principles and Practices.* Englewood Cliffs, N.J.: Prentice-Hall, Inc., 1976.

Rodolakis, Anthony and Nicholas Tetrick. *Buying Options.* Reston, Virginia: Reston Publishing Company, Inc., 1976.

Source Book of Health Insurance Data. Health Insurance Institute, New York, published annually.

Sprecher, C. Ronald. *Introduction to Investment Management.* Boston: Houghton Mifflin, 1975.

Stevenson, Richard and Edward Jennings. *Fundamentals of Investments.* St. Paul, Minnesota: West Publishing Company, 1976.

Stillman, Richard J. *Do It Yourself Contracting to Build Your Own Home: A Managerial Approach.* Radnor, Pennsylvania: Chilton Book Company, 1974.

Stillman, Richard J. *Personal Finance Guide and Workbook: A Managerial Approach to Successful Household Recordkeeping.* Gretna, Louisiana: Pelican Publishing Company, 1977.

Teweles, Richard J., Charles V. Harlow, and Herbert L. Stone. *The Commodity Futures Game—Who Wins? Who Loses? Why?* New York: McGraw Hill Book Company, 1974.

Trooboff, Benjamin M. and Fannie L. Boyd. *Personal Finance for Consumers.* Morristown, N.J.: General Learning Press, 1976.

Unger, Maurice L. *How to Invest in Real Estate.* New York: McGraw Hill, 1975.

Van Caspel, Venita. *Money Dynamics.* Reston, Virginia: Reston Publishing Company, Inc., 1975.

Wiesenberger, Arthur. *Investment Companies: Mutual Funds and Other Types.* New York: Wiesenberger Financial Services, Inc., published annually.

Yeoman, R. S. *A Guidebook of United States Coins.* New York: Western Publishing Company, Inc., published annually.

Your Federal Income Tax. Internal Revenue Service, Department of the Treasury, Washington, D.C., published annually.

Index